THE BLACK WORKER

VOL. 4

THE ERA OF THE AMERICAN FEDERATION OF LABOR
AND THE RAILWAY BROTHERHOODS

The Black Worker

A Documentary History from Colonial
Times to the Present

Volume IV

The Black Worker During the Era of the American Federation of Labor and the Railroad Brotherhoods

Edited by
Philip S. Foner and Ronald L. Lewis

Temple University Press, Philadelphia

Temple University Press, Philadelphia 19122
ⓒ by Temple University. All rights reserved
Published 1979
Printed in the United States of America

Library of Congress Cataloging in Publication Data
 Main entry under title:

 The Black Worker.

    Includes indexes.
    CONTENTS: v. 1. The Black worker to 1869.
1. Afro-Americans--Employment. 2. Afro-
Americans--v. 4. The era of the American Federation
of Labor and the railway brotherhoods. 3. United
States--Race relations. I. Foner, Philip
Sheldon, 1910-   II. Lewis, Ronald L., 1940-
E185.8.B553   331.6'3'96073   78-2875
ISBN 0-87722-136-7 (v. 1)
ISBN 0-87722-137-5 (v. 2)
ISBN 0-87722-138-3 (v. 3)
ISBN 0-87722-130-7 (v. 4)

TABLE OF CONTENTS

PART I

THE AMERICAN FEDERATION OF LABOR AND THE BLACK WORKER, 1881-1903

SAMUEL GOMPERS AND GEORGE L. NORTON, FIRST BLACK ORGANIZER FOR THE
A. F. OF L.: CORRESPONDENCE, 1891-1894   34

THE A. F. OF L., THE MACHINISTS' UNION, AND THE BLACK WORKER   49

PART II

THE PULLMAN PORTERS, THE RAILROAD BROTHERHOODS,
AND THE BLACK WORKER, 1886-1902

PART III

THE UNITED MINE WORKERS OF AMERICA AND THE BLACK WORKER

PART V

ALONG THE COLOR LINE: TRADE UNIONS AND THE BLACK WORKER
AT THE TURN OF THE TWENTIETH CENTURY

PART VI

CONTEMPORARY ASSESSMENTS

This is the fourth volume in THE BLACK WORKER: A DOCUMENTARY HISTORY
FROM COLONIAL TIMES TO THE PRESENT, the first compilation of original
materials to encompass the entire history of Afro-American labor. Recently
there has been a revival of interest in working-class history, but this is
the first presentation of historical documents relating to race relations
within the most important labor organizations of the 1890s: the American
Federation of Labor, the railway brotherhoods, and the United Mine Workers
of America.

THE BLACK WORKER DURING THE ERA OF THE AMERICAN FEDERATION OF LABOR
begins with the founding convention of the AFL, which came into existence
during the late 1880s as an organization of craft unions, and was destined
to become America's most powerful labor organization. During the 1890s, the
AFL leadership urged that black workers be organized even though it met with
stiff resistance from the white unions, especially in the South. Black organizers were hired by the AFL to bring black workers into the labor movement, and received strong support from the AFL national office. The Federation's constitution prohibited the practice of racial discrimination by
member unions, and in at least one celebrated case, refused to admit a machinist union which barred blacks from membership. By the end of the decade, however, the AFL had yielded to the pressures of white unions in practice, if not in rhetoric.

The determination of white unions to bar black members was dramatically
revealed by the course of action taken by the railway brotherhoods. The
brotherhoods of firemen, trainmen, conductors, and engineers not only restricted black membership, but also launched an effort to eliminate Negroes
from railroad service entirely, except as porters. Conducted by their
official organs, this attack brought forth one of the most vicious racist
assaults in the history of American race relations. The documents presented
in Volume 4 demonstrate the white racial hostility which any movement for
working-class solidarity was likely to encounter. On the other hand, some
unions were relatively open. The United Mine Workers of America, for example, accepted members without regard to race, religion, or nationality. In
fact, blacks not only were members of the UMW, but many also served as officers on local and district boards, and in one case, on the national board.
Still, blacks experienced racial difficulties even within the UMW, and a
protracted exchange between black and white miners in the UNITED MINE WORK-
ER'S JOURNAL revealed some serious grievances by black miners on the one
hand, and an insensitivity to those complaints by white miners on the other.
That exchange is reproduced in this collection.

The adamant refusal by most unions to admit blacks were part of a
broader racial hostility which prevailed in America during the early years
of the AFL. Just as the rise of racial segregation produced the need for a
new political counter-strategy, so too a new counter-strategy for circum-
venting the debilitating effects of exclusion was necessary for black workers. This volume reproduces a sampling from that wide range of opinion regarding the alternatives which seemed available at the time. Volume 4 concludes with contemporary assessments of the status of the black worker in
America, the most notable being that of W. E. B. Du Bois, a young and gifted
black social scientist.

This volume concludes the series on the nineteenth century; another four
volume series on the black worker during the twentieth century will follow.
Like the other volumes in this series, the documents presented are accompanied by introductions and notes, and original spellings have been retained
except in cases where they obscure the intended meaning.

The editors wish to express their gratitude to those who have been
generous in their assistance toward the completion of this book and the
series generally. Miss Lila Prieb once again rendered a masterful type-
script. Again we thank Roslyn Foner for designing these books, and Susan
Lewis for her many hours of tedious proofreading. Finally, we would like to
acknowledge our appreciation for the material assistance of the Black

American Studies Program at the University of Delaware, and the financial assistance provided by the College of Arts and Sciences at the University of Delaware.

Philip S. Foner
Lincoln University,
  Pennsylvania

Ronald L. Lewis
University of Delaware

I

THE AMERICAN FEDERATION OF LABOR
AND THE BLACK WORKER, 1881-1903

PART I

THE AMERICAN FEDERATION OF LABOR AND THE BLACK WORKER, 1881-1903

Even as the Knights of Labor reached the height of its success, the organization destined to supplant it had come into existence. During its early years, the American Federation of Labor pursued a policy toward black workers which contained many features in common with the K. of L. At the first convention in 1881, Samuel Gompers announced the AFL's intention to organize all workingmen who believed in the cause. Moral reasons aside, a fairly clear understanding prevailed that the exclusion of blacks was inimical to the interests of white workers themselves, since Negroes could break strikes (Doc. 1-4).

Throughout the late 1880s and early 1890s, Gompers frequently urged AFL representatives and local AFL bodies to make special efforts to organize black workers. Meanwhile, separate locals were to be organized when there was no other way to bring them into the Federation. Although his southern representatives informed Gompers that to organize blacks would be fatal to the AFL because of racial practices in the region, the New Orleans General Strike of 1892 proved that labor solidarity was indeed possible. The unions had been united in the Workingmen's Amalgamated Council, and at its call forty-nine AFL affiliated unions, about 25,000 workers in the city, ceased their labors for four days. Negroes were numerous in several of the unions, especially in the so-called Triple Alliance, composed of Teamsters, Scalesmen, and Packers. Members of the Triple Alliance left their jobs on October 24, 1892, when employers refused to grant the workers a ten-hour day, extra pay for overtime, and a union shop. The other AFL unions of New Orleans walked out in sympathy. Even though the employers attempted to use racist appeals to divide them, the strikers refused the bait and compelled their employers to arbitrate the issues. As a demonstration of interracial solidarity the strike was one of the most important in AFL history. Gompers saw it as a "ray of hope for the future of organized labor," and stated this conviction both publically and privately (Doc. 16-30). This position stimulated many local black unionists to seek help from the AFL. Gomper's early attitude toward organizing blacks is clearly revealed in his support of George L. Norton, the first black organizer for the AFL, who was hired by Gompers himself (Doc. 52-83).

Many white unionists objected to organizing blacks, and to the AFL's regulation which prohibited affiliated unions from excluding Negroes by constitutional restriction. The first significant challenge to this policy came in 1890 at the tenth annual convention, when a resolution requesting an organizer for the National Association of Machinists was rejected by a vote of 51 to 5 because the union's constitution barred blacks. Gompers himself formally requested that the NAM lift the color restriction. When they refused, he organized a rival organization, the International Machinists' Union of America, which was open to blacks, and then legitimized it with AFL affiliation (Doc. 84-98).

While this stand was commendable, it did not eliminate racial exclusion where unions remained adamant. The case of Robert Rhodes, a black bricklayer of Indianapolis, is illustrative. The constitution of the Bricklayers' and Masons' International Union set a fine of $100 for racial discrimination. Nevertheless, when Rhodes tried to obtain work on a union job, his white brothers refused to work with him. Desperation finally forced him to take a non-union job, whereupon the local union filed charges against him for "scabbing." By the time the national office settled Rhode's grievance, he was no longer a union member or a bricklayer (Doc. 99-108).

Even though white unions often regarded blacks as anti-union, many black workers demonstrated a militant adherence to labor organizations and their ideological underpinnings. The Galveston longshoremen's strike of 1898 is a case in point. When the Mallory Shipping Company cut wages in August 1898, the Colored Labor Protective Union, an AFL affiliate, established picket lines, and called for the cooperation of white workers. When the company imported black strikebreakers from Houston, fighting broke out between the two groups of Negro workers, and during the melee which followed, one man was shot. It was a clear case in which black workers placed union loyalty above racial identity (Doc. 109-114).

THE A. F. OF L. AND THE RACIAL ISSUE

1.   FIRST ANNUAL MEETING OF THE AMERICAN
FEDERATION OF LABOR IN PITTSBURGH,
1881

Mr. Gompers, Chairman of the Committee on Plan of Organization, announced that the Committee was ready to report, and submitted the 1st article, as follows:

ARTICLE 1.   This association shall be known as "The Federation of Organized Trades Unions of the United States of America and Canada," and shall consist of such Trades Unions as shall, after being duly admitted, conform to its rules and regulations, and pay all contributions required to carry out the objects of this Federation.

A motion was made to adopt the article as read, and discussion ensued.

Mr. WEBER hoped that the name of the Federation would read so as to include all laboring people.

Mr. KINNEAR--I want this organization to reach all men who labor, such as the 'longshoremen' in our seaport towns. For that reason I desire the article so amended so as to read "Trades and Labor Unions."

Mr. GRANDISON (the colored delegate), of Pittsburgh--We have in the city of Pittsburgh many men in our organization who have no particular trade, but should not be excluded from the Federation. Our object is, as I understand it, to federate the whole laboring element of America. I speak more particularly with a knowledge of my own people, and declare to you that it would be dangerous to skilled mechanics to exclude from this organization the common laborers, who might, in an emergency, be employed in positions they could readily qualify themselves to fill.

Mr. POLLNER--We recognize neither creed, color, nor nationality, but want to take into the folds of this Federation the whole labor element of the country, no matter of what calling; for that reason, the name should read, "Trades and Labor Unions."

Mr. GOMPERS--The expression of the section, seems to me to be not thoroughly understood. We do not want to exclude any working man who believes in and belongs to organized labor.

Mr. JARRETT said he was in favor of accepting all men who worked for a living and belonged to an organized body of workers, but did not want to include those who would not work and maintain themselves.

Mr. COWAN--Do you want to exclude miners? We have many thousands of them, and we want them in this Federation. You will find them to be worthy of your attention.

A VOICE--That is a trade.

Messrs. Byrne, Towelson, McKean, and Conway gave expression in favor of amending the same to include Labor Unions.

Mr. JAS. LYNCH--I think trade organizations covers the whole matter, and will reach the objects of the Congress.

Mr. POWERS--I am in favor of the report as read, as I believe it will keep out of the Federation political labor bodies which might try to force themselves into our future deliberations.

Mr. DWYER--Am I to understand that local Unions, not attached to national or international organizations, are debarred from representation by the section reported?

A VOICE--No, we want you, also.

Mr. DWYER--I represent a local organization, the Painters' Union of Chicago. Are they to be excluded because they do not belong to a national or international organization?

Mr. HENNEBERRY--I am in favor of helping anybody and every body, but let all trades join their respective national organizations.

Mr. LAYTON--I am opposed to excluding from the Federation all organizations except those of skilled mechanics. The Knights of Labor wish to be with you, and they embrace all laborers.

Mr. DOVEY--I would like the name of the Federation to read "Trades and Labor Unions."

Mr. POLLNER to Mr. DOVEY--Amend so that it be "Federation of Organized Trades and Labor Unions," and I will second it.

Mr. DOVEY--I do make the amendment as suggested.

Mr. BRANT--That suits me exactly. I wish this Federation broad enough to encompass all working people in its folds.

The previous question being called for by a sufficient number, the President (Vice-President Gompers in the chair) cautioned the delegates that, when the previous question was called for, the vote would be on the article as reported, and the amendment would be cut off.

Mr. LEFFINGWELL--Do I understand that to be the decision of the Chair?

THE CHAIR--I so decide in accordance with Cashing's Manual.

Mr. LEFFINGWELL--I appeal from the decision. Vice-President Powers assuming the chair, the question on the appeal was put, and the President's decision sustained by a vote of 34 yeas to 27 nays.

The call for the previous question being withdrawn, by unanimous consent, a motion to close debate was carried, the amendment agreed to, and the article, as amended, adopted.

Report of the First Annual Session of the Federation of Organized Trades and Labor Unions of the United States and Canada. Held in Pittsburgh, Pennsylvania, on September 15, 16, 17, 18, 1881 (Cincinnati, 1882), pp. 16-17.

2.   REPORT OF PRESIDENT SAMUEL GOMPERS TO[1]
THE A. F. OF L. CONVENTION OF 1900

Organization of Negro Labor

During the past year the question of organization among the colored workers of the South has been brought forward in several instances. Here and there a local has refused to accept members, simply upon the ground of the color of the applicant. In such cases, where there was a sufficient number of colored workers of one trade or calling, the suggestion was made that they be organized in separate unions, and a council composed of representatives of both organizations be formed to determine upon trade questions. This has generally been acquiesced in; and where similar circumstances obtain, its adoption has been recommended.

Another matter on the same line requires the consideration and action of this Convention. In some parts of the South, central bodies chartered by the American Federation of Labor have refused to receive and accord seats to delegates from local unions composed of negro workers. To insist upon a delegation from unions of colored workers being accorded representation in a central body would have meant the dissolution of that organization; and thus neither the desired purpose nor any good end would have been accomplished. This matter has been one of considerable correspondence, with the result, that the thought has been developed for the formation of central bodies composed of representatives of negro workers' unions exclusively; that they be permitted to work under a certificate of affiliation from the American Federation of Labor; that there should be a general council representing both central bodies upon any matter of importance to labor, locally or generally. Application has been received for charter from such a central body in the city of New Orleans, but the Constitution of the American Federation of Labor provides against the issuance of more than one charter in any one city; hence the matter is referred to you for such action as you may deem necessary.

Realizing the necessity for the unity of the wage-earners of our country, the American Federation of Labor has upon all occasions declared that trade unions should open their portals to all wage workers, irrespective of creed, color, nationality, sex, or politics. Nothing has transpired in recent years

which has called for a change of our declared policy upon this question; on
the contrary, every evidence tends to confirm us in this conviction; for,
even if it were not a matter of principle, self-preservation would prompt the
workers to organize intelligently, and to make common cause. In making the
declaration we have, we do not necessarily proclaim that the social barriers
existing between the whites and blacks could or should be felled with one
stroke of the pen; but when white and black workers are compelled to work
side by side under the same adverse circumstances and under equally unfair
conditions, it seems an anomaly that we should refuse to accord the right
of organization to workers because of a difference in their color. Unless
we shall give the negro workers the opportunity to organize, and thus place
them where they can protect and defend themselves against the rapacity and
cupidity of their employers; unless we continue the policy of endeavoring
to make friends of them, there can be no question but that they will not
only be forced in the economic scale and be used against any effort made by
us for our economic and social advancement, but race prejudice will be made
more bitter and to the injury of all.

Proceedings, A. F. of L. Convention, 1900, pp. 22-23.

3. COMMITTEE ON THE PRESIDENT'S REPORT,
A. F. OF L. CONVENTION OF 1900

The convention, at 4 p.m., was called to order by President Gompers.
On motion the roll call was dispensed with.
The minutes of the morning session were dispensed with.
President Gompers introduced a young union bootblack, who addressed the
convention, stating that he wanted scab bootblacks kept out of the hall. So
ordered.
Delegate O'Rourke called to the chair.
Delegate Tobin, for the Committee on President's Report, presented the
following:

Louisville, Ky., December 10, 1900

To the Officers and Members of the Twentieth Annual Convention of the American
Federation of Labor:
Gentlemen: Your Committee on President's Report respectfully presents
the following:
In the opening lines of the President's report attention is called to
the progress in freedom and organization on the part of the working class.
At the close of the last century, the working people were either chattel
slaves or serfs, tied to the soil, or members of craft guilds, the government
of which was in the hands of the masters, and, in any case, deprived of the
right of combination, mobility and migration.
By reason of the desire of the then middle class to share in the power
and privileges of the upper class, it became necessary for them to insist upon
equal freedom for all.
By and through this they were able to take the function of government
from the then rulers and to break into their circle, but they were compelled
to give to the working people--in theory, at least--equal rights with themselves, under the law.
Through these influences, chattel slavery and serfdom were abolished,
mobility and the right of migration conceded; and, the working class, feeling
its fetters dropping, insisted upon, and re-acquired, the right of combination, through which we enjoy that measure of freedom that we now have, and
which makes this international gathering possible.
We desire to remind the working people that the progress made, even
though assisted by the antagonisms above referred to, was only possible
through the unceasing struggle and the willingness to stand for human freedom, regardless of what the consequences were.
It is our purpose to warn the workers that the antagonisms and struggles

for power, of the upper classes, are now practically at an end, and that the
desire will, in the coming years, be to take from us the rights now acquired,
or, at least, to stay the progress toward that condition in society in which
no "classes" will exist. We realize that the contest will be bitter, relent-
less, and varied, and that its outcome may be disastrous, unless we shall
prove capable of a greater solidarity, mutual forbearance, and readiness for
sacrifice, than up to the present we have been able to show. . . .

In extending the organization throughout the South, the difficulties
increase by reason of the race struggle there existing, and, while we do not
in any way abate the policy laid down, by the American Federation of Labor,
namely, that the trade union is open to all regardless of race, sex, nationality, creed or color, we recommend that the laws be so amended as to permit
of charters being granted to separate unions and central bodies composed of
colored workers. . . .

> Respectfully submitted,
> ANDREW FURUSETH, Chairman,
> JOHN C. DERNELL,
> HENRY W. SZEGEDY,
> JOHN M. HUNTER,
> DENIS A. HAYES,
> L. R. THOMAS,
> JOHN F. TOBIN, Secretary.[2]

Proceedings, A. F. of L. Convention, 1900, p. 263.

4. AMENDMENT TO THE A. F. OF L. CONSTITUTION, ARTICLE 12, SECTION 6, ADOPTED IN 1900

Separate charters may be issued to central labor unions or federated
labor unions, composed exclusively of colored workers where in the judgment
of the Executive Council it appears advisable.

Proceedings, A. F. of L. Convention, 1900, p. 263.

5. BROKE UP THE UNION

The admission of colored men into the Federal Labor Union of Crawfords-
ville, Ind., has caused considerable trouble and threatens to disrupt the
organization in that city. When the Federation was organized, several local
politicians were enrolled. All Negro applicants had been systematically
black balled until one evening, owing to a small attendance, seven Negroes
were admitted for political effect. Since that time several more have been
added. Most of the whites have withdrawn and started a new union, which
announces that only whites can join.

The Recorder (Indianapolis), May 7, 1899.

6. THE INDUSTRIAL COLOR-LINE IN THE NORTH

Aside from barbers, hotel and domestic servants, and a few isolated
branches of labor along these lines, colored people find it almost impossible
to obtain employment in Northern States. Almost every branch of labor is
dominated by labor unions. As a rule, all races are eligible to become

members of these unions except the colored race. Consequently, when a
colored man seeks employment he is refused, ostensibly because he is not
a union man; if he applies to a union he is usually denied admission, either
directly or indirectly, because he is a colored man. It is only fair to
admit that it is not every labor union that makes such discriminations
against colored men, but the majority of them certainly do. Union men,
however, are naturally loath to admit that any discriminations are made by
them.

Of the thousands of miles of railway in the North, with its tens of
thousands of manipulators, the only work, as a rule, that is open to negroes
is that of porters on trains--the most menial and ill-paid occupation within
the gift of a railway corporation. Why? Because all railway unions have
laws, either written or unwritten, prohibiting colored men from work. True,
at the formation of the American Railway Union in Chicago, a hot debate ensued as to whether the constitution should contain the usual clause pro-
scribing colored men. It was finally decided in the negative, because, as
Mr. Debs argued, such an action against negroes would injure the union's
cause in the eyes of the public. A very humane and philanthropic conclusion! Of course the innocent and confiding public concludes that the doors
of the A. R. U. are thrown wide open to colored men because it has no constitutional law to the contrary. [3]

Of all the cities north of Mason and Dixon's Line there are only three
--Cleveland, Detroit, and Indianapolis--where street-railway employees are
generous enough to allow colored men to work with them, and in these cities
it is on an extremely limited scale.

In March, 1896, Superintendent Worrell of the Philadelphia and West
Chester trolley line employed two colored motor-men. The white employees
entered a protest and finally quit work. The result was that President
Shiner ordered the dismissal of the colored men. From that day to this the
management of no other street-railway in the "City of Brotherly Love" has
had the courage to employ colored men, despite the importunities of leading
citizens, both colored and white. And so it is through the entire field of
desirable labor in the North--there is no place for the colored man.

The American Federation of Labor, as is well known, is merely a union
of unions. One of its fundamental laws is that no union shall be admitted
into its domain that has written law discriminating against men because of
color. This would seem to place almost the entire field of organized labor
in the position of deprecating discriminations against color. Many, if not
most, of the great labor organizations originally had written laws debarring
colored men from membership. Now, when a labor union with such a law wishes
to enter the American Federation of Labor, all it has to do is to eradicate
that objectionable clause, and then continue to discriminate against colored
men as before.

I believe that this discrimination is due more to apathy than to wilful-
ness on the part of the masses of the laboring element. The sentiment of
most labor leaders seems to be in favor of recognizing the rights of colored
men, but there is a narrow-minded element in labor circles that favors
keeping colored men down, and right-minded men seem to lack either the courage or the manhood to oppose it. But whether a few men, or the entire force
of labor, are responsible, the result is the same.

Many attempt to explain the absence of colored people from the industries of the North by saying that colored men like, and are capable of
performing, nothing but menial work; that they are left out of labor unions
because of inefficiency and not because of color. To refute such arguments
look to the South, where colored men are to be found by the hundreds in
nearly every walk of life working side by side with white men. In some of
the mills and factories of the South it is difficult to tell whether white
or colored are in the majority. It is an every-day occurrence in the South
to see white locomotive engineers and colored firemen seated in the same
cabs. Still the North feels called upon to denounce the South for injustice
to negroes.

One argument offered by employers of the North, and accepted by many
colored persons as conclusive, is that white men will not work by the side
of colored men--a proposition as cowardly as it is absurd. I doubt if there
is one white man in a hundred who is so prejudiced against colored men that
he would absolutely refuse to work with them, if it came to a practical test.

Again, employers often say to colored people, "You have not enough
skilled mechanics among you; you have not enough educated men to compete
with white labor. Educate and train your men in the trades, and *then* come
to us, and if our white employees refuse to work with you, we will discharge
them and put on entire forces of colored men." It is my candid opinion that
such advice and promises are seldom given in good faith. And even if such
employers would do all they promise, I believe the theory is wrong. The
thought of a semi-warfare between colored and white working-men is extremely
distasteful to me. What I should like to see is this: If two colored men
are given employment in a large establishment, and twenty white men say,
"If these negroes work here we will quit," instead of raising the cry,
"Where can we find twenty-colored men to take their places?" there should
be such a spirit of justice and love of fair play fostered between the two
races that it would be easy to find twenty more white men who would be willing to work with the two colored men, and thus prove to the world that it is
the height of folly to have entire forces of colored men in one establishment, and entire forces of white men in another. The only way to create
such a sentiment is through the Christian churches. It is the work of the
church to unlock the doors of manual labor to the colored race in the North.
The church is the one earthly tribunal before which oppressed humanity may
plead for justice and sympathy.

James Samuel Stemons

The Century Magazine 60 (1900): 477-78.

7.   H. W. SHERMAN TO SAMUEL GOMPERS, OCTOBER 6, 1900

Offices of the International
Brotherhood of Electrical Workers
Rochester, New York

Dear Sir & Brother:

Replying to yours of Oct. 4th in regards to revoking of a charter held
by colored men in Jacksonville, Fla. will say, when the organizer sent in
the application for this charter he failed to mention the men who wanted it
were colored. Now, Bro. Gompers, here is the situation in a nut shell, if
we allow the charter to remain active, we loose every local in the south.
We have received protests from them all. Now, ask yourself in all candor
do you think it advisable for us to loose 12 locals in order to keep one?
Mr. Thos. Wheeler our Grand President made a personal investigation of this
matter and afterwards gave orders to revoke it. I know the A. F. of L. will
draw no color line. I therefore, suggest as a remedy that you grant a certificate of affiliation from your Body. We do not wish to antagonize any of
your laws, but we do not wish to loose all of our southern locals, for it
has cost us time and money to get them. The letter amuses me when it says
the white men of Jacksonville were not competant and the negroes was called
on to do the work. Bro. Gompers, that does not speak well for the intelligence of the white men of that section. We issued a charter to the white's
after revoking the other. Hoping this explanation is satisfactory and
wishing you continued success, I am,

Fraternally,
H. W. Sherman,
Grand Secretary[4]

A. F. of L. Archives, Incoming Correspondence.

8. H. W. SHERMAN TO SAMUEL GOMPERS, OCTOBER 10, 1900

Offices of the International
Brotherhood of Electrical Workers
Rochester, New York

Dear Sir & Brother:

    Yours of Oct. 9th, at hand and contents carefully noted. In reply will
say your ruling regards to the colored Electrical Workers of Jacksonville
is a just one and I would be pleased to know they are organized, but we have
struggled to hard to organize the south to let a matter of this kind upset
what we have accomplished. Accept my thanks. Will return the letter you
ask for as soon as I receive it from the G. P. Bro. Gompers, from the present out look it will be my pleasure to attend the next convention of the
A.F. of L. and I can assure you it will afford me pleasure to cast my vote
for the Grand Old Man of the Labor movement Samuel Gompers. Wishing you
success, I beg to remain,

                                        Fraternally,
                                        H. W. Sherman,
                                        Grand Secretary

A. F. of L. Archives, Incoming Correspondence.

9. H. W. SHERMAN TO SAMUEL GOMPERS, NOVEMBER 7, 1900

Offices of the International
Brotherhood of Electrical Workers
Rochester, New York

Dear Sir & Brother:

    I wrote you sometime ago that it had become absolutely necessary to
revoke the charter granted to the Negroes of Jacksonville Fla. and was in
hopes the matter had been amicably settled by you. I am in receipt of a
letter to-day saying the Central Body of Jacksonville refuse to seat the
delegates from our local. We are forced to draw the color line in the south
or lose the ground we have so successfully covered, as all the locals below
the Mason & Dixon Line threaten to withdraw. Kindly give this matter your
attention and Oblige,

                                        Fraternally,
                                        H. W. Sherman,
                                        Grand Secretary

A. F. of L. Archives, Incoming Correspondence.

10. TRADE UNION ATTITUDE TOWARD COLORED WORKERS

    For sometime past we have received a large number of inquiries relative
to the attitude of the American Federation of Labor toward the negro worker,
and the subject has been widely discussed by philanthropists, some negro
workers themselves, and particularly by some colored men who have advanced
to position of prominence in the realm of thought. We have endeavored upon
all occasions to give all possible information upon this as well as other
matters of interest to the workers; and while we have no desire to impugn
the motives of any one by a charge of suppression, yet for some reason or

other, the information we have furnished on this topic has not been given that same wide publicity as have the charges of insincerity or antagonism. We believe, therefore, that a few plain statements of facts here will serve to correct erroneous impressions, and will receive wider and better attention.

For years the American Federation of Labor has declared in favor of, and the necessity for, the organization of all workers, without regard to creed, color, sex, nationality, or politics. In making the declaration for the complete organization of all workers, it does not necessarily proclaim that the social barriers which exist between the whites and blacks could or should be obliterated; but it realizes that when white and black workers are compelled to work side by side, under the same equally unfair and adverse conditions, it would be an anomaly to refuse to accord the right of organization to workers because of a difference in their color.

We have more than 700 volunteer organizers and a number of organizers under salary, among which are several who are devoting their time exclusively to the organization of the colored workers. This certainly should indicate not only our desire and interest, but also the work which is being accomplished.

It need not be imagined, however, that because we realize the necessity for the organization of the colored workers that for that reason we can grant to them privileges which are denied to white workers. We want them to organize in the unions of their trades and callings, and to take their equal chance with the white workmen--they are entitled to no less, they should ask no more. We say this because there are some colored men who imagine that the organization of the colored workers comes under their especial superior wing of protection; who manifest a suspicion that the colored workers when organized will require the solicitous and fostering care of these colored "superiors" from what they indirectly intimate to be the design of the unions of white workers. We are frequently in receipt of communications from these self-constituted "superiors," who make inquiries as to "privileges" to which the colored workman would be entitled in the event of these "superiors" giving their consent or assistance in organizing the colored workmen.

The American Federation of Labor grants to national and international unions of a trade the right, autonomy and independence to make and enforce rules governing their trade, so long as they do not infringe upon the jurisdiction of other national or international unions and observe the laws, policy and principles of the American Federation of Labor.

The American Federation of Labor seeks to place the organizations of labor upon the highest possible plane of ethical, progressive, civilized and humane considerations, and among these recognizes potentially the identity of the interests of the workers irrespective of creed, sex, politics, color or nationality. Time and again have our organizations in conventions emphatically declared and insisted upon the practice of these principles; and often have white union men deprived themselves of opportunities and advantages in order to protect the rights of colored workmen. It may not be generally known that the great strike of the New Orleans white union workers some years ago was in defense and for the promotion of the interests of colored laborers.[5]

For their protection, as well as for the promotion of their interests, the colored workers should organize and in all cases become affiliated with the organizations of white wage earners or form colored workers' unions in full sympathy and co-operation of the white workers' unions.

At the Louisville Convention of the American Federation of Labor authority was granted to organize and grant charters to separate local and central bodies of colored workmen, wherever such two bodies would promote the interests of all the workers.[6]

The American Federation of Labor has a large number of unions affiliated, composed exclusively of colored workers, who feel that their interests are safeguarded by the officers of our movement as justly and wisely as the organizations of any other toilers.

Again, we have unions composed of whites and blacks, and generally these work together without any friction at all.

When a white man desires to become a member of an organization he is proposed for membership and is required to submit to rules which experience

has demonstrated to be necessary. Certainly, no greater privilege can be
conferred upon a negro simply because of the color of his skin. We repeat
that he ought to ask and be accorded equal rights and privileges; certainly,
no more.

We do not claim perfection for our movement. In a movement composed of
such immense numbers as ours, a mistake may be made, and this, too, toward
a white man. When this is done, a corrective effort is made; when, however,
it occurs with a colored man it is magnified and exaggerated by the "superiors" to whom we have already referred; and an effort is made to convey the
notion that it is the rule, not the exception, and that the labor movement
does not grant the right of the negro to organize.

The real difficulty in the matter is that the colored workers have
allowed themselves to be used with too frequent telling effect by their
employers as to injure the cause and interests of themselves as well as of
the white workers. They have too often allowed themselves to be regarded as
"cheap men," and all realize that "cheap men" are not only an impediment to
to the attainment of the workers' just rights, and the progress of civilization, but will tie themselves to the slough of despond and despair.

The antipathy that we know some union workers have against the colored
man is not because of his color, but because of the fact that generally he
is a "cheap man." It is the constant aim of our movement to relieve all
workers, white and black, from such an unenviable and unprofitable condition.

In a recent article by a distinguished colored writer, he falls into the
common error which others of his race make. Booker T. Washington, to whom
we refer, imtimated that it would be to the advantage of the colored workers
if they would be so situated in their home lives that their employers could
control them as well as the lives of their families. Certainly, if this
policy is pursued, it implies that the economic, social, and moral progress
and advancement of the negro is dependent upon the philanthropic and humane
consideration of their employers. How much can be expected from this source
is well known to any observer of economic and industrial development. Be
sides this, if workers are to rely upon the "good will and control" of the
employers, it presupposes that there is either no need or no inclination
for organization. In other words and in truth, it places the position of
the colored worker exactly as a cheap man; and it is this feature of the
problem which arouses much of the antagonism and feeling among the organized,
and more intensely by the unorganized workmen, whose very bitterest antipathies are aroused against the colored workmen because they couple them
with an instrument of their employers to force down and keep down wages to
the deterioration of the Caucasian race.[7]

If the colored workmen desire to accept the honest invitation of our
movement to organize; if those who have influence over the minds of the
colored workmen will encourage the earnest, honest effort put forth by our
fellow-unionists, we will find larger success attending their efforts, economic bitterness and antagonism between the races reduced, minimized, and
obliterated; but, if the colored workers are taught to depend entirely upon
the "good will and control" of their employers; that they can be brought
from place to place at any time to thwart the struggle of the white workers
for material, moral and social improvement; that hostility will increase,
and thus countered the very best efforts of those who are earnestly engaged
in the endeavor for the unification of labor, the attainment of social improvement of all the people, and their entire disenthrallment from every
vestige of tyranny, wrong, and injustice.

American Federationist (April, 1901): 118.

11. THE ALABAMA STATE FEDERATION OF LABOR CONVENTION, 1901

April 20

The convention was called to order at 9:30 by President Flynn, who declared the nomination and election of officers in order. President Flynn in a few brief remarks stated that the rule had been that the first vice-president be selected from the colored delegation.

He then appointed the following to act as tellers: Kemp, Richardson, Hooper, Callahan and Brooks.

Nominations for President: R. B. Howard, J. H. F. Mosley, F. B. Williams, George Barbour, Ed. Flynn, L. B. Evans, William Kirkpatrick.

Williams and Flynn declined to run.

The vote on the first ballot stood: Howard, 28; Kirkpatrick, 18; Barbour, 15; Mosley, 13; Evans, 9. No election and Evans was dropped.

Second ballot: Howard, 25; Kirkpatrick, 31, Barbour, 15; Mosley, 12. No election and Mosley was dropped.

Third ballot: Barbour withdrew from the race. The vote was: Howard, 27; Kirkpatrick, 56, and the latter was declared elected and upon motion of Mr. Howard the election was made unanimous.

Nominations for First Vice President: S. L. Brooks, R. B. Howard, L. B. Evans, J. H. Bean, A. L. Womack.

Howard, Evans and Bean declined to run.

First ballot: Brooks, 65; Womack 15. Brooks was declared elected First Vice President; J. H. Bean was elected Second Vice President by acclamation; D. U. Williams was elected Secretary-Treasurer by acclamation.[8]

April 27

The convention came to order promptly at 9 o'clock, and the committee on labels reported that union men were derelict in demanding the union label, thereby diminishing the sale of union-made goods, and the committee recommended that the convention urge union men to buy only union-labeled goods and call for the card of the clerk selling them.

Under the head of the good and welfare of the Federation R. B. Howard of Bessemer made a talk, urging unionists to throw off party yokes and carry political issues into their unions. This he believed would be the redemption of the working people.

S. L. Brooks, colored, urged that active efforts be made to organize the negro. It may be only a matter of time, he said, until the organized white crafts might have to lay down their tools in an effort to better their condition, and their places filled with the unorganized negroes. He asked whose fault it would be if they did. "The white man's," he said, "because the negro has to live, and if he couldn't get a dollar a day he would take 50 cents." "The negro, he said, was not asking for social equality, but for an equal chance to make an honest dollar. His talk was well received and his election as first vice president was in line with his request.

J. H. Bean, colored, of Selma, talked along the same line and related what had been done in the way of organization in his town.

Birmingham Labor Advocate, April 20, 27, 1901.

12. STATUS OF THE NEGRO IN THE TRADES UNION MOVEMENT

In view of the action of the Alabama State Federation of Labor in electing to its first and second vice-presidencies colored unionists, and thereby demonstrating their position toward colored workers, as toilers and wage-earners, and the mooted question in our beautiful southland of the competition of negro labor with white labor, the following from the American Federationist, the official journal of the A. F. of L., will be read with interest:

"For years the American Federation of Labor has declared in favor of,

and the necessity for, the organization of all workers, without regard to
creed, color, sex, nationality, or politics. In making the declaration for
the complete organization of all workers, it does not necessarily proclaim
that the social barriers which exist between the whites and blacks could
or should be obliterated; but it realizes that when white and black workers
are compelled to work side by side, under the same equally unfair and adverse conditions, it would be an anomaly to refuse to accord the right of
organization to workers because of a difference in their color."

This is an excerpt from a lengthy article on this subject which goes
into many of the difficulties, and it states unmistakably the position of
the American Federation of Labor.[9]

Among the difficulties mentioned are some that arise from self-exalting
meddling persons who think that the colored workers when organized should
be taken under their superior wing, given special privileges, and otherwise
fostered and fondled and given special protection from the designs of the
unions of white workers, which exist only in the imagination, or for the
fell purpose of these egoists and self-seekers.

The Federationist further says:

"For their protection, as well as for the promotion of their interests,
the colored workers should organize and in all cases become affiliated with
the organizations of white wage-earners or form colored workers' unions in
full sympathy and co-operation of the white workers' unions.

"At the Louisville Convention of the American Federation of Labor
authority was granted to organize and grant charters to separate local and
central bodies of colored workmen, wherever such two bodies would promote
the interests of all the workers.

"The American Federation of Labor has a large number of unions affiliated, composed exclusively of colored workers, who feel that their interests are safeguarded by the officers of our movement as justly and wisely as
the organizations of any other toilers.

"Again, we have unions composed of white and blacks, and generally these
work together without any friction at all.

"When a white man desires to become a member of an organization he is
proposed for membership and is required to submit to rules which experience
has demonstrated to be necessary. Certainly, no greater privilege can be
conferred upon a negro simply because of the color of his skin. We repeat
that he ought to ask and be accorded equal rights and privileges; certainly,
no more."

This is cleancut and covers the whole ground. This has been our opinion
for a long time, and as we have no copyright on our opinions we are glad to
see the Federationist express them so clearly and so forcibly. In this
district, where the whites and blacks are organized in one union or meet in
mass conclave, both parties to the arrangement are well satisfied, and it
is certain that the colored element would not change it were it in their
power, while in the case of the whites it is a problem of conditions to
which there is no other solution, and they accept the inevitable with ready
grace and strive to better the condition of the negro by every means, knowing
that in doing this is the only way to better their own condition. The only
friction that occurs or is likely to occur--and for the life of us we can't
recall a case in point at this time--is when social equality is expected or
sought, and to the credit of the colored man can it be said that those worthy
of having in the movement do not seek or expect this unobtainable boon.

The only thing that remains is for the colored race to wake up to the
benefits of unionism, and embrace the opportunity offered with a full sense
of what he is doing and a determination to live up to his obligation, without fear of discrimination on account of color, creed, or political beliefs.

Birmingham Labor Advocate, April 27, 1901.

13.   ALABAMA STATE FEDERATION OF LABOR CONVENTION
AT SELMA, ALABAMA, 1902

The local newspapers are discussing the fact that negro delegates will be seated in the convention of the State Federation of Labor, and that second vice-president J. H. Beane, a colored carpenter, has taken a leading part in making arrangements for the convention.

The State Federation does not draw the color line, and the delegates will be seated as in all general conventions under the American Federation of Labor . . . color or creed is no bar to a fair day's service. If the people of Selma for this reason turn the cold shoulder to the Alabama State Federation of Labor in the matter of hall accommodations it will not inter- fere in any way with the deliberations of the convention. . . . During the discussion of the question, Mr. McCustney of the Birmingham Typographical Union stated that he favored the motion to appoint a committee to secure a new hall because it will present an opportunity of ascertaining whether the people of Selma would turn down the representative body of 40,000 organized laborers. Rather than see one delegate, black or white, thrown out of this convention, I would go to the woods and hold this meeting.

The negro vice-president stated that he had gone to the board of revenue and other citizens trying to get a hall. "They will give you a hall gladly for your meetings but it will have a white cloth." He intimated that rather than interfere with the meeting he would be glad to withdraw and allow the whites to proceed with the business.

The information was unnoticed and Delegate Randall stated that he agreed with Delegate McCustney, and that if the people of Selma refused to give them a hall they would go out into the woods where the music of the birds would be the accompaniment of their proceedings. . . .

The hall committee reported on the afternoon of April 23, that Commandant Craight of the United Confederate Veterans, had offered the use of the hall to the convention "without regard to the color line."

Birmingham Age-Herald, April 23, 24, 1902.

14.   THE NEGRO MECHANICS OF ATLANTA

[In the Spring of 1902 seniors from Atlanta University interviewed numerous Black artisans in that city, including H. H. Pace.]

The first person from whom I obtained any real information was a brick- mason who received me cordially and who was inclined to talk. . . . He was a Union man and said that colored brickmasons were well received by the white unions "if they knew their business," although the initiation fee was larger for colored men and the sick and death benefits much smaller for them than for whites. I next saw a machinist who lived in a tumble down house in a rather poor locality. But he said he owned the house. I found a carpenter who was almost totally despondent. He couldn't get work. . . .

The next thing of particular interest to me was a gang of men, white and black, at work upon ten or twelve three-room houses. The person in charge of the work was a colored man who gave his name and address Tom Carlton, Edgewood, Georgia. He talked to me himself but refused to let me talk to his employees. . . . He said he could join the white union now, they were after him every day to do so. But he wouldn't, because once awhile back when he was working for wages he was refused admission. . . .

Of the whole number questioned . . . all had worked at some time or did work sometimes with whites in the same work. The painters said that the white painters were not very friendly disposed toward them, and did not allow them to join their union under any circumstances. The plumbers were under some- what the same ban.

Not one of the artisans in my territory had been to a trade school. Nearly every one simply "worked awhile under a first-class brickmason" or

"carpenter," etc. Several had learned their trades during slavery and
followed them ever since. . . . None answered "Yes," to the question of any
"higher training."

The most interesting bit of information in regard to color discrimination was obtained from a colored fireman on the Southern Railway. He said
the Company refused to sign a contract and wage scale with his union but
did sign one with the white union. Moreover, he said:

> If I take a train from here to Greenville, S. C., I get for that trip
> $2.60, the white engineer gets $6.00. But if that same train had the
> same engineer and a *white* fireman, the engineer would get $6.00
> just the same but the fireman would get $3.25. He gets 65 cts. more
> for doing the same work I do. . . .

W. E. Berghardt Du Bois, ed., *The Negro Artisan (Atlanta, 1902),* p. 115.

15. ATTITUDE OF A NEGRO BRICKLAYER ON UNION POLICIES

The comment of the Negro bricklayer who scoured my figures is important.
"A Negro," he says, "has to be extra fit in his trade to retain his membership, as the eye of all the other workers are watching every opportunity to
disqualify him, thereby compelling a super-efficiency. Yet at all times he
is the last to come and the first to go on the job, necessitating his seeking other work for a living. While all the skilled trades seem willing to
accept the Negro with his travelling card, yet there are some which utterly
refuse him; for instance, the house smiths and bridge men who will not recognize him at all. While membership in the Union is necessary to work, yet
the hardest part of the battle is to secure employment. In some cases in-
tercession has been made by various organizations interested in his industrial progress for employment at the offices of various companies, and
favorable answers are given, but hostile foremen with discretionary power
carry out their instructions in such a manner as to render his employment
of such short duration that he is very little benefited. Of course, there
are some contractors who are very friendly to a few men, and whenever any
work is done by them, they are certain of employment. Unfortunately, these
are too few."

Mary White Ovington, *Half A Man (New York, 1914),* pp. 98-99.

THE NEW ORLEANS GENERAL STRIKE OF 1892

16. V. SCHELIN TO CHRIS EVANS, NOVEMBER 1, 1892[10]

A. F. of L.
New Orleans Marine and
Stationary Firemen's Protective Union No. 5707

Dear Sir & Bro.:

. . . there is at present time a strike on in the city of teamster &
Loaders and warehouseman and the Amalgamated Council is about to order a
general strike throughout this City will write more fully on subject next
week.

                                        Fraternally,
                                        V. Schelin

A. F. of L. Archives, Incoming Correspondence.

17.   DEEDS OF VIOLENCE

Strikers Assault Non-Union Drivers--Record of the Day

At 1 o'clock yesterday afternoon, Thomas Young, a negro teamster employed by Labote & Co., was loading his float at the intersection of the New Basin and Liberty street, when he was set upon and brutally beaten by a negro striker, who made his escape before the arrival of the police. Young, who resides on Franklin street, near Liberty, drove back to the factory.

Half an hour later a colored driver named Chas. Crane, employed by Mr. Murphy, was passing on his float at the corner of Delord and Front streets, when a crowd of six unknown strikers, who were standing at the corner, rushed at him with brickbats in their hands and drove him away, after which they made their escape.

Wm. Crawford and Gus Ferdinand, two drivers for Mr. Douglas, were passing at the corner of Front and Calliope streets, when they were driven from their floats, by a crowd of strikers. The police dispersed the strikers and the two teamsters proceeded unmolested.

The strikers were more violent in the neighborhood of the Illinois Central Railroad depot, and at 5:30 o'clock p.m., Geo. E. Lane, a driver for Mr. Douglas, who was taking a load of rice from the corner of Spain and Chartres streets to the Illinois Central Railroad Depot, was on reaching that place, halted by a number of white men, who compelled him to proceed on his way town. They followed the float as far as the corner of Market and South Peters streets, when several of them jumped on the float and drove Lane away. They were then joined by several other strikers, with whose help they unloaded the float and spilled the rice barrels in the street. They bursted three of them open and spilled the contents in the gutter.

The police had by that time been notified and Capt. Barrett and a squad of men proceeded to the scene in the patrol wagon, but as usual, they arrived too late, and when they put in an appearance the strikers had taken flight.

At 7 o'clock p.m. at the corner of South Peters and Canal streets, one of Mr. D. M. Valon's floats, loaded with rice and driven by Henry Antoine, was stopped by four unknown strikers who ordered the driver to leave his seat. He complied with their orders, and Mr. Valon had to send one of his clerks to drive the float back.

At the same time, at the corner of Poydras and Freret streets, two floats, owned by Mr. Andrew Whalen, were stopped by infuriated strikers, who beat the drivers away and then cut the harness. The floats were placed in the Mississippi Valley yard, and the mules were driven to Mr. Whalen's stables.

At 7 o'clock a telephone message was received at the Central Police Station to the effect that there was a disturbance at the corner of Poydras and South Peters streets. A squad of police in the patrol wagon was immediately sent to the scene, and Henry Alexander, a colored teamster, was arrested and locked up in the First Precinct Station charged with threatening to assault with a rock one Ned Burke, driver of a float. When searched at the station the prisoner had on him a large rock, which was held as evidence. Notwithstanding the troubles in different parts of the city, this is the only striker arrested yesterday by the police.

At 4 o'clock yesterday, on Girod street, between Fulton and Peters streets, Ike McQuinn, a driver for Andrew Whalen, was struck in the face with a brick by an unknown white striker. McQuinn, whose lips were slightly cut, proceeded on his way up.

At 6:45 o'clock John Russell was driven off his wagon, near the Mississippi Valley Railroad depot, by some unknown negro strikers, who made their escape on the arrival of the police.

At about 1 o'clock in the afternoon a float bearing license plates No. 8225 was abandoned by its driver, on Liberty, between Perdido and Gravier streets. The mules were turned loose by some colored boys, and the harness was taken for safekeeping by Mr. Maurice Glaudne, of No. 129 Perdido street.

Thos. Dennis, a colored boy, fifteen years of age, came running into the First Precinct Station yesterday morning stating that he had been ordered off his float by two negroes, who threatened to beat him. He said that he had thus been compelled to leave the vehicle, which belongs to Mr. John Everett,

at the corner of Poydras and Freret streets. The boy, under protection of
an officer, resumed his way.

New Orleans Times-Democrat, November 1, 1892.

18. STILL GENERAL

The Amalgamated Council Adheres to the General Strike Plan--Blaming the
Failure to Arbitrate Upon the Merchants' Committee--The Wholesale Tie-Up
Fixed for Saturday--And a Meeting of Presidents of Unions Called for To-day
--To Receive Instructions as to the Conduct of the Coming Strike--The Mer-
chants Prepare to Meet the Emergency--Take Steps to Form a Protective League
of Employers--And Raise a Fund to be Expended by an Executive Committee

AMALGAMATED COUNCIL

Address to the Public by Chairman Leonard's Committee of Arbitration

The following address was furnished to the press at a late hour last
night:
"To the Public: The question of the general strike having been the
cause of a great deal of anxiety and interest to the general public of late,
we, the committee appointed by the Workingmen's Amalgamated Council to arbitrate and settle the differences, think it just and proper to make a statement in order to place the responsibility, if any, on the proper parties.
"As was published in the press of this city, the general strike was
declared off on Wednesday, pending a settlement of the differences existing
between the labor unions and the merchants and Boss Draymen's Association.
We took the matter in good faith in order to prevent any further calamity
or depression in the business of this city, and acted. Among the conditions
exacted of us in order to get a conference with a committee from the merchants' side was that we declare the strike off and order the men who had
quit work back to their former positions, which they occupied previous to
the strike, they (the merchants) to reinstate all of their old hands.
"We granted the concession to the merchants and thought we would be
able to settle the trouble on an equitable and just basis. After we had
proceeded to the point where we were impressed that a half hour's conference
would settle the difficulty, we were confronted with another strange proceeding.
"As soon as we got together and were about to get to the issue, they
asked for an adjournment to some other hour, stating that they were hungry.
But when we opposed the question it was shown that they wanted to adjourn in
order to consult on what unionism meant. We told them that was what we were
there for--to explain away the obnoxious features of unionism.
"They then claimed the right of going into executive session at any
time during our arbitration in case any important question arose; in other
words, put us out of the room and decide questions among themselves, and
bind every man's vote on their side before we could convince them of our
opinion. Queer way is this to arbitrate.
"However, the proposition to adjourn was granted by us, we thought, and
it was understood before adjournment that they were to take up the one
question of unionism.
"After reconvening, at 7:30 o'clock p.m., they once more evaded our main
agreement by a resolution stating that they could not treat with us because
all our union men had not reported for duty that morning, and some of them
who had gone to work were ordered to quit.
"We had discussed this matter in the meeting held in the evening, and,
after stating that some of our members were refused their old positions
(according to agreement) it was understood on both sides that it was a misapprehension, owing to the lateness of the hour of our conclusion on Wednesday morning, it being after 3:30 o'clock when conclusions were reached.

"Now, in order to continue negotiations with them, they required us to order the men back to work, which would naturally follow that we must adjourn until Thursday. We were there ready to settle the difficulty then, and naturally the men would be required to go to work immediately upon a settlement. They would not agree to this and consequently we had to suspend all negotiations.

"We have endeavored to bring about a settlement of the controversy by an honest and open arbitration of all differences. We were willing to give them all the points, nearly, that they asked in order to bring about the solution of the difficulty, but simply because we would not submit to a virtual adjournment for another day, which means a great deal to a working-man, they claim they will not arbitrate.

"Suppose we, on the other hand, would have acted as arbitrary in the matter, what position would it place us in with the community. They would say that we were afraid to go to arbitration.

"The question raised about the agreement of the night before can be readily understood, when it is stated that the agreement was not consummated until after 3:30 o'clock in the morning, and it was impossible for us to have over 2000 men ready for work at 6 o'clock.

"However, the following merchants were called on by the strikers for their positions and were given their answers. This will show that there was a misapprehension, which could have been settled by arbitration Wednesday night;

"Schmitt & Ziegler--Will take some men back.

"Flashpoller--Take one; leave the balance go.

"Zuberbier & Behan--Wanted to select three out of six.

"Philip Nagle--Won't hire union men.

"Chambers, Roy & Co.--Same answer.

"Jack Bokenfohr--Same answer.

"John Adams--Don't understand it and won't act until he does.

"Charles Sach--Advised his men to keep striking; would not take them back.

"Nicholas Burke--Did not know anything about it; wouldn't discharge new men until he found out further.

"C. Doyle--Some men in his employ ran the strikers away.

"We submitted these names to the committee and have since received a dozen more. It was stated by Mr. Clark in committee at the morning conference that it was a misapprehension, and that this matter would cut no figure in the arbitration.

"Another curious way to arbitrate was the fact that when we proposed to elect an umpire they stated to us that it was not necessary; we could settle matters without the eleventh man. We told them that our opinions were at variance and consequently it would naturally require the eleventh man to decide. They however refused and our committee, under those circumstances, fails to see how we could arbitrate or settle anything.

"With these facts presented, we are willing to leave our case to an unprejudiced public, and hope that they will then place the responsibility where it rightfully belongs in case the scope of the present difficulty is in any way broadened."

This is signed by John Breen, A.M. Keir, James E. Porter, J. M. Callaghan, and James Leonard, chairman.

New Orleans Daily Picayune, November 4, 1892.

19.   "SENEGAMBIAN SCHEMES"

The very worst feature, indeed, in the whole case seems to be that the white element of the labor organizations appear either to be under the domination of Senegambian influence, or that they are at least lending themselves willing tools to carry out Senegambian schemes.

New Orleans Times-Democrat, November 4, 1892.

20. A GENERAL STRIKE

The Amalgamated Council Finally Decides Upon the Step--And Orders the Arm
of Labor to Become Inert at Noon,--To Coerce the Merchants Into Making Terms
With the Strikers--All of the Unions to Go Out Except the Typographical--
Even the Cotton Labor Organizations Joining the Movement--The Merchants
Doubt the Seriousness of the Threat--But the Executive Committee Maps Out
Measures--While the City and State Authorities Take Cognizance of the Coming
Contest--The City Council Called to Meet This Morning.

THE STRIKE ORDERED

By Representatives of Some Forty-Odd Labor Bodies

HALL AMALGAMATED COUNCIL,
New Orleans, Nov. 4, 1892

At a meeting of the presidents of the labor unions and organizations
held on Friday, Nov. 4, 1892, at the Screwmen's Hall, the following manifesto was adopted and ordered submitted to all the members of labor unions
and organizations in the city of New Orleans.

To All Union Men Wherever Found Greeting: In view of the fact that in
the difficulty now existing between the Board of Trade and merchants, boss
draymen and weighers, and in view of the fact that they claim to represent
the entire employing power in the city, and claim broadly and emphatically
that they will not recognize unions or labor organizations in connection
with their business, and endeavor by their acts to prevent other employers
from either employing or recognizing union men, and, believing it for the
best interest of organized labor that we refrain from working for any
employer until the Board of Trade and others recognize the rights of men to
organize into labor unions for their own protection and defence, we issue
this manifesto to all unions throughout the city, calling on them as union
men to abstain from any work or assisting in any way in prolonging the
difficulty.

The gauntlet has been thrown down by the employers that the laboring
men have no rights that they are bound to respect, and in our opinion the
loss of this battle will affect each and every union man in the city, and
after trying every honorable means to attain an equitable and just settlement, we find no means left open but to issue this call to all union men to
stop work and assist with their presence and open support from and after
Saturday noon, Nov. 5, 1892, and show to the merchants and all others interested that the labor unions are united.

JAMES LEONARD, chairman,
JOHN BREEN,
W. M. KEIR,
JAS. E. PORTER,
JOHN M. CALLAHAN,
Committee.[11]

Louis Stachling, Bakers and Confectioners No. 185.
Geo. Buhler, Broom Makers' Union No. 5815.
J. L. Brown, Carpenters and Joiners No. 634.
E. T. Gibson, Carpenters and Joiners No. 739.
E. J. Melarober, Carpenters and Joiners No. 732.
Aug. Lumberg, Carpenters and Joiners No. 76.
Hy. Reilly, Carpenters and Joiners No. 240.
L. D. Landry, Carpenters and Joiners No. 704.
M. S. Hall, Car Drivers No. 5490.
J. A. Monier, Clothing Clerks No. 61.
Geo. Speiss, Cooper's International No. 4.
Jas. W. Kelly, Cotton Yardmen's Benevolent Association No. 1.
J. E. Boyle, Horseshoers No. 5755.
J. B. McClellan, Grain Shovelers No. 5812.
A. R. Ketchum, Marine Mates No. 5802.
Jno. H. Conners, Retail Dry Goods Clerks' Union.

Chas. Horn, Marine and Stationary Firemen No. 2707.
Lee J. Huie, Brotherhood of Painters and Decorators No. 76.
E. P. Brillault, Brotherhood of Painters and Decorators and Paper
Hangers No. 202.
F. L. Winters, Pile Drivers and Wharf Builders No. 5801.
J. W. Winfrey, Round Freight Teamsters and Loaders No. 5818.
F. Freisch, Sugar Workers' Protective Union, No. 5765.
Fred. Disque, Grain Shovelers No. 5861.
Longshoremen's Benevolent Association.
B. Moses, Musicians' Union.
E. W. Reese, Warehousemen and Packers No. 5800.
W. C. Brown, Teamsters and Lumber Yardmen.
Dorsey Moore, Scalemen's Union No. 5869.
C. H. White, New Basin Teamsters No. 5870.
Geo. Giles, Ship Scrapers' Union No. 5818.
Jos. Markey, Gas Workers No. 5894.
C. A. Lucas, Coal Wheelers No. 5814.
D. A. Ingersoll, Coachmen's Union No. 5717.
G. F. Wilson, Cotton Yardmen's Benevolent Association No. 2.
A. M. Keir, International Boilermakers and Iron Ship Builders' Union.
James E. Porter, assistant organizer, American Federation of Labor.
John M. Callahan, general organizer, American Federation of Labor.
Paul Armand, Screwmen's Benevolent Association No. 2.
Aaron Butler, Marine Firemen No. 5565.
Louis Shaeffer, Railway Workers No. 198.
Hy. Burrell, American Carriers.
O. Morice, Coachmen's Benevolent Association No. 5811.
Ed. Hale, Rice Workers' Union No. 5810.
J. Tracey, Operative Plasterers' Union No. 93.
Ed. P. Bell, Shoe Clerks No. 78.
John Breen, Screwmens' Benevolent Association No. 1.

New Orleans Daily Picayune, November 5, 1892.

21. JOHN M. CALLAGHAN TO SAMUEL GOMPERS, NOVEMBER 7, 1892

New Orleans, La.

Dear Sir & Bro.:

I suppose you see by your papers that our town is up side down. Every
one in town are on a strike. The Merchants and boss dray men combined to
"fight the union to the knife and the knife to the hilt." We accepted the
def. and now every union man in town are out of employment and are willing
to remain out until the Merchant and boss draymen take their men to work
as Union men and treat with them as such.

There are fully 25,000 men idle. There is no newspapers to be printed.
No gas or electric light in the city. No wagons, no carpenters, painters or
in fact any business doing.

We have had interviews with the Mayor and governor, and stated our case
and defined our objects.

The merchants and boss draymen are willing to meet and arbitrate wages
and hours but will not discuss Unionism in any shape. Their former proposition was they would take the men back at the positions they left, and discuss
their differences after. Their new proposition now is to discuss hours and
wages but never Unionism.

I am one of a committee of 5 with full power to act and all the power
appertaining to the Amalgamated workingmen's council. We think we will win
this strike. I am afraid that Mr. Donegan is now doing more to bring his
position and mine in discredit.

Porter and I are both on the committee. Donegan could not under any
circumstance get on. He is managing a strike of Carriage Drivers and prevents

them so I am told from accepting arbitration even the bosses are willing to
accept the president of the Amalgamated Council as arbitrator. He wants to
be arbitrator or nothing.

I am sorry you are not down here to take a hand in it. It is a strike
that will go down in history If we win we have the best union city in the
country if we lose we have none.

Yours etc.
John M. Callaghan

A. F. of L. Archives, Incoming Correspondence.

22. V. SCHELIN TO CHRIS EVANS, NOVEMBER 8, 1892

A. F. of L.
New Orleans Marine and
Stationary Firemen's Protective
Union No. 5707

Dear Sir and Bro.:

. . . at our last meeting i had the pleasure of being elected a Delegate to
represent our union at the convention in Phila on the 12th December when i
hope to have the ·pleasure of meeting you there and our fellow members of
this great and glorious institution that we owe our allegiance to, and may
we in that grand old city of historical fame and Brotherly Love cement the
Bonds of Brotherhood and Fraternal ties that will stand before the world an
everlasting monument of strength and show to the world at large that in
unionism there is strength and that our order stands preeminently at the
head of this human Race. Founded as it is on the same and glorious principle
as the great republic that we live in and who stand to day one of the greatest
Nations on this Globe so we as a band of Brotherhood in unionism proclaim to
the world that though we are laborers, we are possessed of manhood and
Principle and that the laborer is worthy of his hire and not the degraded
wretch so often portrayed in this grand universe. . . .

We are at present on a strike in which the whole city has been tied up
and commerce has been completely stopped, the point at issue is unionism and
if we fail in the recognition of the union we have lost our cause, and so
all labor organization recognizing the great point at issue have responded
nobly to the Call of the Amalgamated Council with the exception of a few and
at present writing the press has been stopped and no papers were for sale this
day the governor has been called in to arbitrate matters. . . .

Fraternally yours,
V. Schelin

A. F. of L. Archives, Incoming Correspondence.

23. A PLUCKY BAKER

Saturday night, a negro Striker visited the bakery of Mr. Lambert Frantz
on Poydras near Baronne street, and tried to persuade the men there employed
to join the strike. Mr. Frantz ordered the man off the premises but he became very insolent until he angered Mr. Frantz who struck him in the face,
giving him a black eye, after which he placed the negro under arrest. Sunday
night the establishment of Mr. Frantz was again visited--this time by a party
of six or more white men--but they were met with the information that the
first man to enter the establishment, or to attempt any interference with the

men there employed, they would be shot down. The courage of the crowd soon
oozed out, and after a few malignant looks and ugly mutterings, they went
elsewhere.

New Orleans Daily Picayune, November 8, 1892.

24. THE COMMITTEE OF FIVE

The fate of organized labor in this city, so far as the amalgamated
council is concerned, is in the hands of five men. These five men constitute an executive committee of amalgamated laborers, clothed with power to
order a general strike of laborers, which power they have exercised, and
the strike ordered by them last Saturday is still on. These five men are:
John Breen, representing the cotton Screwmen's association--the Screwmen
were working yesterday; John M. Callahan, representing the Cotton Yardmen--
the yardmen were working yesterday; A. M. Kier--representing the boiler
makers--the boiler makers were working yesterday; James E. Porter--a colored
man, clerking in the United States customhouse, and representing longshore-
men--business is going on as usual at the customhouse, and the longshoremen
are working; James Leonard--representing the Union Printers--the Union Printers are kept from their work, and from their duty to employers against whom
they have no grievance.

New Orleans Daily Picayune, November 10, 1892.

25. JOHN M. CALLAGHAN TO SAMUEL GOMPERS, NOVEMBER 13, 1892

                                                    New Orleans, La.
Dear Sir & Bro:
. . . The newspapers are down on us because we would not give them men to
print their papers and I reckon we are now the blackest men in town. We
controlled the men so well that no one was seriously injured and no one
killed. The newspapers are down on the mayor and city council for not
making the men go to work and using the police to do it with. The police
arrested every man who violated the law and he was severely dealt with.
We had several conferences with the Mayor and the governor and defied them
to point out any violence. There were lots of extra policemen and all the
militia out but they could find nothing to do, and did not dare to force us
go to work again our will.
     We now have charges against us in the U.S. circuit court for violation
of the Interstate Commerce law and about 50 of us will have to answer on
Saturday Nov 19 to some charge or another and again on the first Monday in
Dec. I dont know the charge but I know the penalty because all the newspapers
have been telling us. It is $5,000 fine and 6 years imprisonment. If they
convict us all the town will go to ---- and a man will have to beg for work
and starve when he gets it. . . .

A. F. of L. Archives, Incoming Correspondence.

26. JOHN M. CALLAGHAN TO SAMUEL GOMPERS, NOVEMBER 13, 1892

                                                    New Orleans, La.
Dear Sir & Bro.:
. . . My resignation will go into effect from and immediately after receipt
of this letter. . . .

I worked up this town from center to circumference and believe I have
the confidence of every workingman in the city. I believe I done more to
make this a union town than any man in it. I fear often when I think of
what will become of me if I lose my health or strength and am not able to be
a screwman. Even with them I feel in bad favor as a workman because they
say "He is out all night at meetings starting some nigger union and how do
you expect he can be able to work next day, and if there is a strike any
place you may not see him for a week or two" I conclude now I will have to
look to myself and endeavor to do as much for myself as I have done for
others. . . .

I remain as ever fraternally yours,
John M. Callaghan

A. F. of L. Archives, Incoming Correspondence.

27. R. P. FLEMING TO SIR [SAMUEL GOMPERS], NOVEMBER 16, 1892

New Orleans, La.

Dear Sir,
. . . It was the finest exhibition of the unification of Labor and reliance
on and obedience to leaders of men ever had in this or any other city. We
placed the opposition entirely hors du combat. . . .
    The novel sight was presented of the employers being the threateners and
the ones who hoped and hoped in vain for some act on the part of the men
calling upon its allies, the militia and the law. They were nearly maddened
and in their appeals to each other, "to do something," were met with the
saddened reply, "I cannot; we cannot arrest men for merely refusing to work."
"And there you are." The men "were quiet and firm," and there was less disturbance and conflicts, notwithstanding one of the strike days was election
day, than any equal number of days at any time. The police records fully
prove this. . . .
    From what I have learned to-day the future of Organized Labor looks
bright. . . .

Yours truly,
R. P. Fleming

A. F. of L. Archives, Incoming Correspondence.

28. SAMUEL GOMPERS TO JOHN M. CALLAGHAN, NOVEMBER 21, 1892

New Orleans, La.

Dear Sir and Brother:
    To me the movement in New Orleans was a very bright ray of hope for the
future of organized labor and convinces me that the advantage which every other
element fails to succeed in falls to the mission of organized labor. Never in
the history of the world was such an exhibition, where when every other element fails to succed it falls to the mission of organized labor. Never in the
history of the world was such an exhibition, where with all the prejudices
existing against the black man, when the white wage-workers of New Orleans
would sacrifice their means of livelihood to defend and protect their colored
fellow workers. With one fell swoop the economic barrier of color was broken
down. Under the circumstances I regard the movement as a very healthy sign of
the times and one which speaks well for the future of organized labor in the
"New South" about which the politicians prate so much and mean so little.

Fraternally yours,
Samuel Gompers

Samuel Gompers Letter-Books, Library of Congress

29.

HALL OF

WORKINGMEN'S AMALGAMATED COUNCIL OF NEW ORLEANS

November 21, 1892

To all Labor Unions and Associations of Workingmen
of the United States:

The manufacturers, merchants and capitalists, with the subsidized Press
of this city, are combined in a determined effort to crush all labor unions
and associations of workingmen existing here.

A federal Judge has been found, who, under the pretense that strikes
have the effect of interrupting commerce, holds that those who exercise their
rights to refrain from labor violate the recent act of Congress against
combinations in restraint of interstate and international commerce, and who
has made an order enjoining the labor unions and associations of this city
from engaging in any strike.

The injunction so granted is merely a preliminary injunction, which may
be set aside on the final hearing or on appeal to a higher court. The
workingmen of this city intend to carry this case to the court of last resort, and they hope that the Supreme Court of the United States will rise
above the considerations which have frequently affected the decisions rendered by many judges of the inferior courts. We believe the judges of the
Supreme Court will give us justice; but even though their decision should
be against us, it will be well to know that, under existing laws as interpreted by the courts, free men can be made slaves. If this be true, the
sooner the truth becomes generally known the better; for when it becomes
known, all men who love liberty will unite in securing the repeal of such
iniquitous laws.

The expenses attendant on the litigation in which the workingmen of this
city are thus involved will amount to a very considerable sum, and in view
of the fact that their cause is the cause of all workingmen, they feel
justified in asking not only for sympathy but for material aid from workingmen of all other localities.

Contributions, which will be thankfully received, may be forwarded to

> WM. MOAKE,
> 534 Carondelet St., or
> JAS. LEONARD,
> President Amalgamated Council
> 486 Royal St.,
> New Orleans, La.

Copy in A. F. of L. Archives, Incoming Correspondence.

30.   GOMPERS' TESTIMONY

"We had some years ago in the city of New Orleans one of the largest and
most general strikes that ever occurred in this country, and the reason of
it all was that the working people of New Orleans were becoming fairly well
organized. Some of the unions were in existence many years. The drayman,
the teamsters--Colored men--formed a union and organized labor generally
had their agreements with the employers. The colored draymen's union sent
a committee to the employers for the purpose of having their agreements
signed, and the employers would not talk to the 'niggers'. Organized labor
of New Orleans sent committees to the employers and wanted to have the agreement signed, and they would not sign it,--would not enter into any agreement
with 'niggers'. Organized labor of New Orleans went on a strike; every
machinist went on a strike; every printer went on a strike; no paper made its
appearance; the men working in the gas-houses went on a strike and there was
no illumination that night; the bakers went on a strike, and all other white
workers went on a strike for the purpose of securing recognition to the

colored workmen. And I make mention of this as being what appears to me a very interesting episode in the labor movement, and as an answer to those who have always hurled the epithet to us that we will not assist in the organization of the colored workmen. If there is any union of labor that says anything or takes any action regarding the colored man of the South it is not because of his color; it is because he has rights as an individual or because they have generally in the trade so conducted themselves as to be a continuous convenient whip placed in the hands of the employer to cow the white men and to compel them to accept abject conditions of labor. It is not a question of personal prejudice or color prejudice, and, as I tried to show by that incident of the New Orleans strike, when it comes to the interests of labor, the white men are willing to sacrifice their positions and their future in order to secure a recognition of the rights of the colored workmen."

Testimony of Samuel Gompers before Industrial Commission, Washington, D.C., April 18, 1899, quoted in Samuel Gompers, *Labor and the Employer,* (New York, 1920), pp. 166-67.

SAMUEL GOMPERS, A. F. OF L. ORGANIZERS AND OFFICIALS,
AND BLACK WORKERS: CORRESPONDENCE, 1889-1895

31. SAMUEL GOMPERS TO A. F. OF L. ORGANIZER JAMES H. WHITE,
SEPTEMBER 14, 1889

Dear Sir,
     If we fail to organize the colored wage-workers, we cannot blame them very well if they accept our challenge of enmity and do all they can to frustrate our purposes. If we fail to make friends of them, the employing class won't be so shortsighted and play them against us. Thus if common humanity will not prompt us to have their cooperation, then enlightened self- interest should.

A. F. of L. Archives, Incoming Correspondence.

32. N. E. ST. CLOUD TO SAMUEL GOMPERS, NOVEMBER 1, 1890

American Federation of Labor
Office of General Organizer

Dear Sir & Bro.:
     herafter my address will be 225 Duffy St. Savannah, Ga.
     I have failed so far to get a union here in Savannah. this is undoubtedly the worst place in the U.S. for organized Labor, but I do not Despair yet, although the remnant of the K. of L. here, are working against me, tooth and nail, I have been in Constant Correspondence with Albany for several months, and will Succeed there, although the K. of L. are working hard to beat me there, and all I can do is through the mail, as I am not able to go on uncertaintys,[12]

                                        Fraternally yours,
                                        N. E. St. Cloud, Gen. Org.

A. F. of L. Archives, Incoming Correspondence.

33.   JOSIAH B. DYER TO SAMUEL GOMPERS, NOVEMBER 17, 1890

The Granite Cutters' National
Union of the United States
Barre, Vt.

Dear Sir and Brother:
. . . In regard to the tool sharpeners there is a strong feeling in our
Richmond branch I believe against admitting colored men and Ex-convicts into
our union. . . .

Yours fraternally,
Josiah B. Dyer
NUS

A. F. of L. Archives, Incoming Correspondence.

34.   J. B. HORNER TO SAMUEL GOMPERS, MAY 30, 1891

Richmond, Va.

Dear Sir:
. . . there are 20 white trades organized here & represented in the trades
council of this city with 5 Colored labor & trades unions perhaps every trade
that has a national body has a local union here, but there is 1/2 doz or more
trades who have no national organization at all that might be organized under
the A. F. of L. if the A. F. of L. had a live hand here to organize them. . . .

J. B. Horner
District org for C & L. Un

A. F. of L. Archives, Incoming Correspondence.

35.   J. C. ROBERTS TO SAMUEL GOMPERS, NOVEMBER 8, 1891

American Federation of Labor
Nashville, Tenn.

My Dear Sir & Bro.
Enclosed please find (Eight Dollar) Postal order to pay for charter and
outfit for Clarksville mixed union. Clarksville is a city of about 4000
population in which no trade union has ever been organized owing to the
opposition of the employers, and the lethargy of the employees. When I first
visited the place I found no sentiment in favor of a union. Mechanics were
working for whatever they could get; and cutting each others throats at that,
at the first meeting called I only succeeded in getting six who were willing
to join. I put the organization off until the next night and spent the entire
day visiting the workmen the next night I succeeded in organizing with 20 members at 50 ct each, and nothing for my expenses which were $7.35, so I have
retained $2.00 out of your fees, not as a right but as a necessity. I am going
back there to organize the colored men next week and will try to do better.
Now Bro. Gompers I want you to send the new union a full outfit and charter,
and if the 2.00 must be paid, charge it to me, and I will send it on as soon
as I can, and please send me some more union literature for my own use.   I
have made a very successful break in Clarksville and shall capture the town
for union labor.   This is the third time the attempt has been made

by our union men to organize the town, but I have won I think. Please
attend to these matters at once and oblige yours Fraternally,

                                                    J. C. Roberts

A. F. of L. Archives, Incoming Correspondence.

        36. J. C. ROBERTS TO SAMUEL GOMPERS, NOVEMBER 20, 1891

                                    Office of General Organizer
                                    Nashville, Tenn.

Dear Sir & Bro.:
     Enclosed Please find Receipt for two Dollars, and Postal Order for
Eight Dollars to pay for Charter & outfit for "Clarksville Colored Labor
Union No---" organized Nov 19th 1891. I find that it is useless to attempt
to organize Labor unions and have them pay anything for organization in
this section. Where we live in the city with no expense attached except
our time at night it is all right, but to pay out from 3 to 6 Dollars for
R R fare, and nearly always remain two days to work up a union sentiment to
organize a union, and collect anything for organization it is out of the
question. . . .
     Please send charter of this new union to the Secy with the outfit, as
I have installed the officers, I cannot go back there for that purpose. . . .

                                    J. C. Roberts

A. F. of L. Archives, Incoming Correspondence.

        37. JAMES L. BARRIE TO CHRIS EVANS, DECEMBER 10, 1891

                                    Western Central Labor Union[13]
                                    Seattle, Wash.

Sec A. F. of L:
     As the following Resolutions have been drawn up in a hurry, it is to be
hoped that there will be no Hairsplitting as to their Meaning or Intention.
     The Western Central has established such a Reading Room where the more
intelligent of the workingmen by spending their Leisure, and Hours of enforced Idleness, there in acquainting themselves with all of the Alleged
Solutions to the Labor Problem The major portion of the Patrons are the
Transient Members of Organizations, otherwise called Tramps and to this
class, Organized Labor is indebted for its Foothold West of the Missouri
River, also in every Remote Section.
     It is therefore to be hoped that the American Federation of Labor will
see the Importance of such a Step, and issue Recommendation to all Central
Bodies for the Establishment of such Institutions. . . .

                                    Yours in Union,
                                    James L. Barrie, Sec W.C.L.U.

A. F. of L. Archives, Incoming Correspondence.

38.   WESTERN CENTRAL LABOR UNION SEATTLE, WASH. DEC. 10TH 1891

The Officers and Representatives of the American Federation of Labor in Convention Assembled

The Western Central Labor Union of Seattle Washington ask your consideration of the following Resolutions

Whereas, The Division that exists in the Ranks of Organized Labor throughout this country is something to be deplored and a Remedy is needed, that will Educate and bring about a Unity of Action

Whereas, Race Prejudice, The Personal Differences of Labor Leaders and the Sturbborn Opposition of Bigotry of Each Faction claiming to have the sure Solution of the Problem of Labor, Prevents any concessions for the good of the Cause, and encourages a tendency to further divide the Ranks & File

Therefore be it Resolved that it is the sense of the Western Central Labor Union, that the A F of Labor could materially enhance the Cause of Labor, by Recommending to the various Central Labor Organizations throughout the Country, The Establishment of a Labor Headquarters in their Respective Localities, connected with which should be a Non Political and No Sectarian Free Reading Room for the purpose of giving the Wage Worker an opportunity to Educate himself on the Benefits and Necessity of Labor Organizations, and acquaint himself with existing Laws and Conditions,

Resolved, That the necessity of such a movement is keenly felt by organizations engaged in the formation of good for their Members in this Western Country, and to this end, and also to the end that Race Prejudice among the working classes may be checked, The Western Central Labor Union strongly favors the Proposition of the American Federation of Labor taking the Matter in hand and upon the various Central Labor Bodies the adoption of the above or a similar Plan--

Resolutions Committee W C L U

A. F. of L. Archives, Incoming Correspondence.

39.   JEROME JONES TO SAMUEL GOMPERS, DECEMBER 15, 1891

Nashville, Tenn.

Dear Sir and Bro:

Last night I organized the colored barbers of this city, and unless I receive instructions from you to the contrary, will place them under A. F. of L. They are differently situated from the whites whom I placed under the national head, in that they work under the per centage system, which they can't change immediately. I am informed all members under the national head must adopt the wage system. The white barbers here seem to accept my idea, that is to place the colored men under the A F of L until they become sufficiently strong to demand wages and then to secure a charter from the national head.

Every union is on a solid foundation here, and we are preparing to build a temple. Could you not stop here on your return, I think you would be pleased with the condition of affairs.

Jerome Jones, General Organizer

A. F. of L. Archives, Incoming Correspondence.

40. SAMUEL GOMPERS TO R. T. COLES, APRIL 28, 1891

The sentiment of organized labor of the country is decidedly in favor
of maintaining and encouraging the equality between colored and white
laborers, so much so that at the last convention of a national union of
machinists which is particularly located in the South and which prohibited
colored machinists from becoming members, the Federation resolved to call
for a convention of all machinists' unions for the purpose of forming a
national union which shall recognize no color line.

Samuel Gompers Letter-Books, Library of Congress.

41. CHARLES P. OVERGARD TO SAMUEL GOMPERS, MARCH 23, 1892

Temple Bell, Colored Texas Union
No. 5618 (Federal Labor Union)

Dear Sir & Brother:
As one of our Brothers in good standing is going down on the S.P. Railroad and through San Antonio and other towns in Texas, I wish you would
invest him with the power of Organizing Lodges of the American Federation
of Labor. I understand the Organization is not very strong in the State of
Texas. As this Organization has undertaken to better the welfare of the
working classes. We can not do any better than have this Order as well
represented as possible, and especialy in the South. As the labouring class
there has got a very strong competition in the Negroes, and as I write to you,
I can not pass by but make a remarke on this question, for here in the
Santa Fe Railroad shops where I myself am working as a Trick Repr I can not
but observe that the Officials of the Road prefer Negroes as laborers instead
of White men here in these shops they employ about thirty negroes, and that
number is increasing while the number of White Labours is decreasing, and
during the month of Feb last they discharged to my knowledge thirty White
Labourerrs when they did not disccharge a single Negro, and here in the
yard they employ about twelve men as Section hands; and on the 19th of this
month they discharged them all in preference of Negroes, work is scarce here
during Winter, and they that have Families to support have a hard time to
get the Nessaries of life. I dont think that any of us bear any malice or
hate against any race or color of humanity But we can not let such proof as
this go by without thinking that it is only a question of time that the White
Labour will have to go to make room for Negroes. And therefore I ask you as
Our Grand Leader, to give us advice in this matter.

Yours truly,
Charles P. Overgard
Secretary

A. F. of L. Archives, Incoming Correspondence.

42. CHARLES OVERGARD TO SAMUEL GOMPERS, APRIL 7, 1892

Temple, Texas

Dear Sir & Brother:
Received your letter and contents noted. These and the Commission as
Organizer to C. C. Tabor, I am very much obliged to you for your advice in
regard to the Negroes. Reading the Globe Democrat of April 1st I see an
account of the strike on the Mississipi River! and the question has arisen

about organizing the Negroes. Please give us your opinion on the subject as
that is a very difficult question to decide and an important one. In regard to convict Labour I am very much interested as I don't think the way
it now stands the honest Labourer is not treated right neither are the
Convicts. If it would be of any importance to you, I would in my next
Letter state the Laws of Norway regarding the Treatment of Convicts, as in
that Country they are better off after they leave the Penitentiary in the
way of making an honest living than they was before Conviction. . . .

Charles Overgard,
Secretary

A. F. of L. Archives, Incoming Correspondence.

43.   C. C. TABER TO SAMUEL GOMPERS, APRIL 24, 1892

Temple, Texas

Dear Sir:
     In the Labor question I wish I could organize all of the unorganized
Labor in Texas this sumer at all shops but as I have to Work Ever Day to Live
unless I can get a smal Salry Or fee I am afraid I will not Be able to doo
as much as I wish. Now about organizing the Negroes of the South I Beg
Leave to Tell you about it If you Organize them they will compeet With the
White Labor So Strong they will Bee Compelled to give up the Shopes as they
will Stand mutch more a buse than the Whites the Negroes in the South are
not Like those in the North and Texas a speshially Hoping you will not Take
no Exception to it, I will Do all In My Power in the Field of White Labor.

Respectfully C.C. Taber, Organizer

A. F. of L. Archives, Incoming Correspondence.

44.   CHARLES OVERGARD TO SAMUEL GOMPERS, MAY 4, 1892

Temple, Texas

Dear Sir & Bro:
     I received your Letter and noted its contents. In regard to Organizing
Negroes we meet with much opposition from other Labour Organizations, that
we are afraid to make any attempt, some of our best Members are opposed to
their Organization, and the question will most assuredly separate. us, and
that would be our ruin. I am myself in favor of Organizing the Negroes, but
as the question is now regarded, we can not do anything. The White mans
attitude toward the Negroes here in the South is quite different from that
of the North and at present I think it would be best to be a little cautious
about Organizing them in Texas as that will in a measure put a stop to White
Labour Organization. . . .
     I am glad to report, that our branch of the American Federation of Labor
are more firm in their belief to day, than when we first Organized that it
is the best Organization for the Working Classes, and that is due to the
numerous pamphlets you sent us, and which I distributed among our members to
read.

Fraternally yours,
Charles Overgard,
Secretary

A. F. of L. Archives, Incoming Correspondence.

45. C. C. TABER TO SAMUEL GOMPERS, MAY 31, 1892

Temple, Texas

Dear Sir & Brother:
    Yours to Hand Thanking you Much for your In formation In Regard to
Negro Labor Must be Something Done In the South. to Day in the G.C.T.
S.F. Railroad Shop a White man Washing Boilers was Diss Charged with a
Verry Little Case and a Negro put in.   The White man was Sertainly a hard
working man and married.
    The G C & S F RR Y C. Has got a bout 3 or 4 Hundred Convicts tearing
up Track Between Temple & Galveston Texas and the good honest men out of
work. And if Imigration dont Stop coming to the U.S.A. with out capital
the Wage Workers will see a more Poverty Stricken Time.
                          I beg to remain your C. C. Taber

A. F. of L. Archives, Incoming Correspondence.

46. P. J. MCGUIRE TO SAMUEL GOMPERS, OCTOBER 24, 1892

United Brotherhood of Carpenters
& Joiners of America
Philadelphia, Pa.

Dear Sir and Friend:--Herein find a letter from Austin, Texas, from one of
our members. I wish you would peruse it and answer him. I have written
him a short note. It is my decided opinion it is unwise for Mr. Amstead
to precipitate any race disputes in the Labor movement in Austin, Texas.
Such discussions simply subordinate the greater issue of the Labor question,
and lead to no good results. . . .

Yours,
P. J. McGuire[14]

A. F. of L. Archives, Incoming Correspondence.

47. SAMUEL GOMPERS TO J. GEGGIE, GENERAL ORGANIZER, OCTOBER 27, 1892

New York

Dear Sir & Bro:
    I have read the contents of your letter very carefully, and I am free
to say that I regret very much that Mr. Amstead should do anything to arouse
race prejudice as well as practically subordinate the labor movement to the
color question. You may rest assured I shall urge upon him not only the
advisability but the necessity of acting practically in dealing with the
organization of colored wage-workers. Their full recognition in social as
well as economic equality is a matter of cultivation, development, and I
doubt that it can be forced to an earlier solution than the natural trend
will warrant. All attempts to prematurely bring this about will only result
in defeat and disaster to all concerned.

Samuel Gompers

Samuel Gompers Letter-Books, Library of Congress.

48, E. M. MCGRUDER, GENERAL ORGANIZER,
TO SAMUEL GOMPERS, MARCH 20, 1893

Paducah, Ky.

Dear Sir & Bro:

The Trades Council of this city having unanimously endorsed my appointment as organizer. I herewith notify you of my acceptance I shall
devote all the time I possibly can to the office.

I wish you would advise me up on a few points viz. Mr. Hurst some time
ago organized a colored Barbers union in this city. And later on a Trades
Council in the preliminary meetings of the council I made a bold stand
against the drawing of the color line, and wanted the negro's represented
of course this met with opposition, later on I was called a way to what was
supposed to be the death bed of my mother, and was out of town for ten days
or two weeks. When I came home Mr St came to with the papers allready except my signature which he got. Well in due time the charter came. you
can judge of my surprise when in obligating the delegates M H omitted and
surprised the word color in the obligation. I asked him afterwards by what
authority he had done so? he answered by authority vested in him, that
d--m it there was a race war existing here and he had the authority to do
so. now what I want to know is the negro's want to be admitted to the
council is it my business to force them in? and if so how is it to be done
under the circumstances?

Further the cigar makers having made it a finable offence to pattronize
a non union barber, and several organizations having followed suit, the
white barbers began to clamor for a union but they wanted a separate charter which the negroes objected to, Mr H then threatened the colored Pres
that he Hurs would revoke their charter but the negro was too sharp for him
for he already had a letter from Mr Meyers their Intl Pres. Now the
colored barbers want me to force the non union barbers in under their charter. although they have an organizer they are looking to me to do this.
And I do not feel it to be my duty. As I understand it my duty is to organize union when none now exist, and not to do the work of the organizers of
various local unions. is this the correct view of the case?

Now on the other hand the white barbers are expecting the Trades Council
through me to have the Charter of the colored barbers revoked because they
the union have several boss barbers in the union and in office. I objected
to the council considering the matter, and I believe I am here to build up
and not tear down nor have I or the Council any jurisdiction over barbers
union #96. if they are violating their constitution that is for their
Int'l union to look out for and not us, is not my possition the correct one?

I wish you would send me one of the souvenirs published for the 12th
convention also a list of 'boycotted' good that have been endorsed by the
A F of L. together with a list of affilliated unions.

With best wishes for the cause I am yours Fratt

E. M. McGruder

A. F. of L. Archives, Incoming Correspondence.

49. SAMUEL GOMPERS TO E. M. MCGRUDER,
GENERAL ORGANIZER, APRIL 3, 1893

McGruder, Paducah, Ky.
Dear Bro:

I am not in a position to state the best means to solve the question of
the white and colored barbers. I believe however, that you should write to
Mr. J. C. Meyers, Prest. Barbers Intnl. Union Box 448, St. Paul, Minn. Lay
the subject clearly before him and ask him whether it would not be advisable

under the circumstances, to allow two charters, one for the white and
another for the colored barbers union.

> Fraternally yours,
> Samuel Gompers,
> President, A. F. of L.

Samuel Gompers Letter-Books, Library of Congress.

50. JOHN F. O'SULLIVAN TO AUGUSTINE MCCRAITH, JUNE 18, 1895

> American Federation of Labor
> Office of General Organizer
> Daily Globe Office
> Boston, Mass.

Aug. McCraith, Secretary [15]

Dear Sir and Bro: One of my acquaintances in this city is interested in
the manufacture of tobacco in Richmond, and he agrees with me that his
factory ought to be organized. Whether from a business standpoint or not I
do not care, but I think if he is willing to make the shop union we ought to
be.

He employs most all negroes in the factory and came to see me to know
if it would make any difference as to the shop becoming unionized on that
account. I gave the usual reply and he feels satisfied to go ahead but he
must try to bring a pressure on his brother who is also interested in the
factory.

Wouldn't it be well to get into communication with the officers of the
Tobacco workers Nat. union to see what steps they would advise to organize
the factory. The factory is in Richmond Va and the firm is Edel Tobacco
Co.

I think that if some one was sent there they might be able to get a
partial, at least, sanction from the firm to unionize the factory.

Of course, some one who is familiar with the color question and the
environments in Va. ought to be able to do the job right, and if any in-
experienced person was sent there he might slobber over the mob and queer
us I would like to go as I think I could get free transportation through the
paper, or if I could get one of the boys on the paper in the adv. department
to work a pass for me.

But I don't think I would have the time to go, as they are getting out
a souvenir for Labor day, and it is one of the worst jobs I ever struck.

However, no matter about the going just now, so long as the officers
of the Nat union of Tobacco workers are notified. They may be able to get
us out of any fear as to the results of sending a man down there.

I am told there are about 300 men and women employed in the factory,
black and white, and as the white and black don't associate, it will be
seen at a glance that the man who does the job must be something of a diplo-
mat.

If any one is sent the officers of Union 62 cigar makers should be consulted, as they being right on the spot, would have a better knowledge of
the situation than any of us.

I am also informed that unionism might receive a big boom in other lines
if the tobacco workers union was a success.

My friend Edel seems to be struck on knocking out the color line, and
thinks that trade unionism can do more than anything else to accomplish that
result.

I don't know what he will think if the workers in his factory look for
an advance in wages, but I hope that a raise of wages will be sought for as
soon as it is possible after organization.

Attend to this as soon as you can, Thanks for promptness in sending
hoisting engineers charter.

Yours with very best wishes,
John F. O'Sullivan
General Organizer

A. F. of L. Archives, Incoming Correspondence.

51. JOHN F. O'SULLIVAN TO AUGUSTINE MCCRAITH, JULY 6, 1895

Daily Globe Office
Boston, Mass.

Dear Gus:
Yours is just at hand and contents noted I am informed that the white
hands, the males, are bosses, hence the color question will not enter into
the matter of the organization of the men.
I think, however, that the firm employs a few white women occasionally
and a number of colored women regularly and the rub will come there.
It is a great plan if it can be worked and we can give the firm the
Razzle anytime they do not do the right thing by the workers.
I talked label to my friend untill he is carried away with the scheme,
and cited some notable boycotting cases just to let him know how powerful
organized labor is.[16]
I have no doubt that the other members of the firm are not so easily
convinced of the advantages of running a strictly union plant, but would
like to tackle them on it. . . .
The machinists of this city, affiliated with I M U 28 are up in arms
here over the granting of a charter to the I H M without the knowledge or
consent of the I M U What shall I tell them John McBride wrote and told them
it was so that a charter had been issued, and they are asking how it was
that dual organizations are recognized.[17]
When you write please tell me about it.
The plan of referring the matter of the organization of the tobacco
workers of the Edel co to the Trades Council is all right, as they would be
the best ones to know how to act in the premises, provided they are furnished
with the facts in the case.
The thought of these people going in to the K of L as a result of my
efforts gives me a chill.
Holy Moses: What a narrow escape: Foster publishes the Debs Resolutions
in this weeks paper.

Yours, etc.
O'Sullivan

A. F. of L. Archives, Incoming Correspondence.

52. SAMUEL GOMPERS AND GEORGE L. NORTON, FIRST BLACK ORGANIZER
        FOR THE A.F. OF L.: CORRESPONDENCE, 1891-1894

A. S. LEITCH, GENERAL ORGANIZER, TO SAMUEL GOMPERS, JUNE 8, 1891

St. Louis, Mo.

Samuel Gompers, Pres. A. F. of L.:
. . . Mr. Geo. L. Norton, Sec. Marine Fireman # 5464, desires me

to answer the letter you addressed to him, as he is too busy. The membership of #5464 is 140 members in good standing. They have won all demands
for wages so far without recourse to strike and with but little trouble.
They are working harmoniously with the other trades here especially the
Electric Wiremen and Linemen's Union, whom they can materially assist as
firemen at the electric plants.

A telegram received here from Vicksburg, Miss., and a letter from
Memphis, Tenn. requesting an organizer for those ports immediately; men
ready to organize firemen's unions. As Mr. Norton is well acquainted along
the river, I gave him a letter to represent me at those places, and three
black applications. He states he will leave for Vicksburg to-night. The
men there are to pay his expenses.

Fraternally,
A. S. Leitch

A. F. of L. Archives, Incoming Correspondence.

53. A. S. LEITCH TO SAMUEL GOMPERS, JUNE 30, 1891

St. Louis, Mo.

Dr Sir:
Inclosed application for charter and charter outfit, and $10 for same
for Marine Firemen of Memphis, Tenn. (colored) given in through Mr. Geo.
L. Norton of No. 5464 of this city. Forward the charter and outfit *to this
office;* also the charter and outfit of the Vicksburg Marine Firemen's Union,
if the same has not yet been forwarded. . . .

I would suggest that Mr. Geo. L. Norton be given a commission either
as Asst. Organizer here, or Gen'l Organizer for the Mississippi, Missouri
and Ohio River ports. . . .

Yours Fraternally,
A. S. Leitch, Gen;l Organizer,
St. Louis

P.S. Attempts were made in Memphis and Vicksburg by K. of L.'s to "pack"
the meetings and stop organization into Federation. Mr. Norton was too
well posted on trade union matters, however.
A. S. L.

A. F. of L. Archives, Incoming Correspondence.

54. GEORGE NORTON TO SAMUEL GOMPERS, JULY 10, 1891

St. Louis, Mo.

Dear Sir & Bro.
You must excuse my delay in writing to you, for I have been so busy,
that I could not write, but I asked Mr. Leitch to write for me. I have been
working hard for the fraternity since the first day of April. I have about
(150) members in No. 1, and No. 2 and 3 are getting along finely and I think
that New Orleans will be in line before long. My trip to Memphis and Vicksburg was all that I could wish for, and I only hope that I may be as successful elsewhere. I have got a good many men, known as deckhands on steamers,
that will, I think be ready to send for its charter before long. I don't
intend to stop as long as there is anything organized. I will get them
together and Mr. Leitch or myself will try and keep them there. No more at
present.

Hoping to hear from you soon, I am,

Fraternally Yours,
Geo. L. Norton,
F. Secy.

A. F. of L. Archives, Incoming Correspondence.

55. A. S. LEITCH TO SAMUEL GOMPERS, JULY 15, 1891

St. Louis, Mo.

Saml Gompers, Pres. A. F. of L.
Dr Sir:
   The application forwarded by me from Hod-Carriers' of East St. Louis, is for a Charter for colored hod-carriers. Mr. Klinger is Secretary of the white hod-carriers, from which organization the colored are practically barred. In matter of wages, etc. the colored men are working well with the other trades. The men who make this application were organized before the white hod-carriers there, and made application for a charter to you (through irresponsible parties), but never received it. I am of the opinion that if, as the case has been presented to me, the white hod-carriers of East St. Louis do not desire to initiate colored men in their union, on account of color, then the Federation would be justified in issuing colored men a charter, with fair understanding that the two unions must work harmoniously in the matter of wages, hours, etc. I remain

Yours Fraternally,
A. S. Leitch, Gen'l. Organizer

A. F. of L. Archives, Incoming Correspondence.

56. GEORGE L. NORTON TO CHRIS EVANS, SECRETARY, OCTOBER 23, 1891

St. Louis, Mo.

Dear Sir & Bro:
   Your notice has Been Received & noted, & as to the arrears of No 5464, We will pay at once But permit me to assure you that I Did not know anything about this or I would have paid it as I have the Trades & Labor Dues of this City. I have allways kept them up Perfectly & here after will Endeavor to Do the Same By the A. F. of L. & Received 5 Doz pins & will settle for them soon. You ask the address is #3 North Levee St. St. Louis, Mo anything addressed will be ok.

Except the Best wishes
Fraternally,
Geo. L. Norton,
Gen. Orgnzr.

P.S. Please send organizers note papers as we are out entirely.
G. L. N.

A. F. of L. Archives, Incoming Correspondence.

57. G. L. NORTON TO SAMUEL GOMPERS, JANUARY 28, 1892

Dear sir & Bro:

Charter & Manuels Recd & officers Installed today & Everything is working very strong in favor of the A. F. of L. But since the Engineers has organized the white Firemans of this city wants to organized & Get a charter under the A. F. of L. But they have Been fighting us all the time untill they have nothing to fight with & now they want to join the Federation, & I told them they could come in with us if they wished to But they think they can get a charter from you. But I hope you will not grant it from any Body untill you here from No 7 of St. Louis. Leitch wrote the application for them But I will not sign it as there has Been trouble with Firemans here all the time when the Colored Fireman ask for wages the white men goes to work for what they Refuse & that is the way they have been Doing all the time.

Tell me what you think about it in you answer & Reply as soon as possible. Except the Best wishes

Fraternally yrs,
G. L. Norton

A. F. of L. Archives, Incoming Correspondence.

58. LIVING WAGES

Yesterday several thousands of strikers, Negroes and white, paraded. Numerous banners were carried by the men on parade these being among them: "Equal Rights for all!" "Fair Wages and Union Men only!" "Monopoly caused this Strike!" "We want Living Wages!", etc. After parading the principal downtown streets and visiting the Levee, the men went to Union Hall, on Christy Avenue, where they were addressed for nearly two hours by labor agitators, white and colored.

St. Louis Globe Democrat, April 5, 1892.

59. STRIKE OF ST. LOUIS NEGRO LONGSHOREMEN, 1892

The threatened river strike is on, and over 2,000 Afro-American laborers are idle on the levee. Four steamers arrived last Wednesday night and were unable to land their cargoes. A number of boats are lying at their docks waiting to be loaded, but are unable to get a pound of freight carried on board. The cause of the strike is a demand by the marine firemen that the union scale of wages be paid and none but union men be employed on the boats. This was refused by the owners, and a tie-up of the river traffic is the consequence. The marine firemen struck work Thursday morning of last week and were followed by the members of the Longshoremen and roustabouts unions. The men are quiet and orderly, and no serious trouble is anticipated. They are firm in their demands, however, and say the company must accede to their terms. As the men on strike are all Afro-Americans, thoroughly organized, and members of the Federation of Labor, it is believed they will force the company to accept their requests. The general opinion among river men is that the strike will last but a few days.

Cleveland Gazette, April 9, 1892.

60. SAMUEL GOMPERS TO GEORGE L. NORTON, APRIL 13, 1892

New York

Dear Sir and Brother:
     I am in receipt of a clipping from the "Post Dispatch" of Thursday
March 31st. which gave an account of the strike of the Marine Engineers and
Longshoremen of your city, but I find that one of the most important features has been clipped out of the centre of it. Will you kindly forward me
a copy of the paper of that date for my information, as well as to give me
any other account of it which you can and oblige.
     The men engaged in this contest have demonstrated in the plainest
possible manner that the time has come when our colored brothers of labor
recognize that their interests are absolutely identical with those of their
white brothers, that the docility of slavery has passed, that the spirit of
freedom, independence and emancipation is dawning, and the progress for the
improvement and final emancipation of the wage worker will be contested by
the white and black laborer shoulder to shoulder.
     Trusting that success may crown your every effort and asking you to
convey my kindest wishes to our fellow toilers, I am,
                                        Fraternally yours,
                                        Sam'l Gompers, President,
                                        American Federation of Labor.

Samuel Gompers Letter-Books, Library of Congress.

61.   GEORGE L. NORTON TO SAMUEL GOMPERS, APRIL 28, 1892

St. Louis, Mo.

Dear Sir & Bro:
     I Recd yours today & in Reply permit me to say that Mr. Crump wrongly
Informed you about the Boycott placed on those companys that is Being
opperated at the port of St. Louis, We never ask any of those men to help
us we ask the shippers & farmers alliance & Friends to organized Labor to
help us in our strike, for the anchor Line steamers is the only packet Line
in this city that Recognizes union Labor. The Rest take who they can get &
I must say that our Boycott is felt for the scab Boats is not Doing any
thing Like a paying Business & they Look very sad about the matter & they
also say if things are not settled Before Long they will have to Sign & I
think the next time Mr Crump writes he ought to find something to write
about for the Lines we have the Boycott on are only Local packets & ply in
the vicinity of St Louis, they also speak about cutting wages Down to the
old Rates But I Dont think it will go for the Boys are getting very strong
& when there is any thing that is worth knowing I will Certainly write to
you about it, I think you must have Enough to be troubled with without Being
annoyed with such Trash as Mr Crump has to write. I hope you will not think
hard of this writing & you will please Let me know about the Longshoremen of
Cairo, Ills I was there & Enstalled the Engineers & spoke to a Large crowd
of Laborer & I think they will Be in Line Before Long, the President from
Memphis union of Marine Firemen was here today & he says that Something has
to be Done Down there for there is a good many men there that can Be Brought
in Line. I hope the Council will Do something for those people, with this
I will close hoping to here from you soon.
     Except the Best wishes of mine I Remain as Ever

                                        Fraternally,
                                        G. L. Norton

A. F. of L. Archives, Incoming Correspondence.

62. GEORGE L. NORTON TO SAMUEL GOMPERS, APRIL 28, 1892

                                                        St. Louis, Mo.

Dear Sir & Bro:
    My trip to Memphis and Vicksburg was all that I could wish for, and I
only hope that I may be as successful elsewhere. I have got a good many
men, known as deckhands on steamers, that will, I think be ready to send
for its charter before long. I don't intend to stop as long as there is
anything organized.

                                                Fraternally,
                                                George L. Norton

A. F. of L. Archives, Incoming Correspondence.

63. SAMUEL GOMPERS TO GEORGE L. NORTON, MAY 3, 1892

                                                New York

Dear Brother:
    Convey to our brothers that you may meet and those whom you may convert
to become brothers in this grand American Federation of Labor my earnest
sentiments that they should bear in mind that there is only one way in which
they can hope to attain improvements in their condition to realize that
freedom which has been promised to them to secure these comforts of home
and independence of manhood and citizenship--through organization.

                                            Fraternally yours,
                                            Samuel Gompers, President
                                            American Federation of Labor

Samuel Gompers Letter-Books, Library of Congress.

64. ALBERT E. KING TO SAMUEL GOMPERS, MAY 7, 1892

                                                    St. Louis, Mo.

Samuel Gompers,
Pres. A. F. L.

Dear Sir & Bro:
    i taking the Obligation of writen you this Letter to Notify you How the
A. F. L. is Respected by the Inland Seamen Port U No 7 in this City the Dock
Hands & Watchmans Union Send 6 Men White to Work on the Excersion Steamer
War Eagle at the Rate of 1.75 $ per Day to 20 C Per Hour Over time Well
they Worked One Week till Capt Thoronleagon Notified officers of the War
Eagle that they Wer Hireing Union inland Seaman at 1.75 Per day from 7 a.m.
till 11 & 12 at Night With No Over time so They Made a Cut on the White Dock
Hands to 1.75 Per Day Fore 17 & 18 Hours Work about 9 1/2 or 10 c per Hour
the White Men walked of the Boat & union Black Men took thare Places With
Out Change in Wages i ask Prsident Geo Cox of inland S. U. if He War Doing
Right & told me he Could Not Help it the Men Wer Satified & Would not Call
them of the Boats i then told Him He Was taking Bad Steps to Let them Men Go
to Work in Other Union Men Places Now the Way things Look in this City the
White Unions are Sitting on the Bumpers of the Last Car and the Black Unions

are Runing Train thir Kinds of Work Will Brake up Eny Union these Excersion
Boats Grand Republic Paul Tulane War Eagle to Carrey Nothing But Union Men
to Pay Union Wages   Now this is the Results
     Well Prest Bro Hoping you will investegate this Matter at an Early
Date and Oblige Albert E. King   Representative of D D.W. Prt Un and Sec
Marine Firemen Union No 5626.   Hopin to Here From You Soon.

A. F. of L. Archives, Incoming Correspondence.

65. JOHN M. CALLAGHAN TO SAMUEL GOMPERS, MAY 10, 1892

                                                      New Orleans, La.

Dear Sir & Bro:
     You would oblige me by informing me if I am the only organizer for the
Federation in New Orleans. I hear of some others who claim to be organizers
and neglect to properly attend to business.
     I will organize a Union of Marine Firemen in a few days and they had
their applications in to a man named Lewis and he failed to properly attend.
They also told me of a man named Norton of St. Louis, Mo. who is on his way
to organize a Union of Engineers.
     Also I would wish to know if members of our Union are allowed to visit
other Unions and members of other Unions to visit our Union while in session.
. . .
     By answering at an early date you will greatly oblige me and put me in
a better condition to transact my duties as organizer.

                                        Yours etc.
                                        John M. Callaghan

A. F. of L. Archives, Incoming Correspondence.

66. JOHN M. CALLAGHAN TO SAMUEL GOMPERS, MAY 15, 1892

                                                      New Orleans, La.

Dear Sir & Brother:
     Yours of May 6th received a few days since, would have waited a few
days before writing if things did not take the shape they are in at present.
     I suppose Bro Ed J. Donigan of 5490 has notified of the advent of Bro
Norton a National organizer in our midst and the commotion created thereby.
     I have had an interview with Bro Norton. He denied point blank all the
rumors credited to him.
     I think to say the least of it, it is treating a local organizer rather
shabby to order an organizer from another part of the country in his jurisdiction without notifying him of the fact. When Bro Norton arrived in town
he made no effort to find me or give me any intimation that he was in town.
After being notified that I was an organizer and duly commissioned as such
he having been told by one of the Charter members of the Firemen's Union,
a Union I have in course of organization, having application for a charter,
he told him that he knew nothing of me and that probably I was not authorized
to organize any unions and that he knew nothing of the Union of which I am
a member and that they may be working without authority. It caused a great
deal of doubt in the minds of the members as to my reliability and authority
to act.
In the course of the interview with Bro Norton he told me that the Union of
Firemen at present in the city he thought was sufficient. Well, that Union
is composed exclusively of colored men and the Union that applied to me for

assistance is composed exclusively of white men. It would be almost impossible for them to commingle in one Union. They can and will get along
alright at work and in committees from each union can meet and confer thereby work in harmony. If they are in one Union under one set of officers and
in one meeting room they will never get along and would in a very short
while disband and form different unions and work in direct conflict. In
order to prevent such a course I would recommend that they be granted a
charter even though the present Union object. Mr. Norton may in his wisdom
think different but Mr Norton I am sure lacks the experience in labor Unions
their formation and government etc. possessed by me and learned from experience extending back for 12 years quite a length of time even you will confess for a man not yet 30 years of age.

The Car Drivers #5490 is the 29th labor union with which I have materially assisted in developing and forming.

Were it not for Labor Unions I would not have a neat sum of money on
hand and a bright outlook for my old age. As it is now I have hardly "a
dollar to jingle on a tombstone." Ever since I was 16 years old I have
earned from $1000 to $1600. per year, a nice income you would think for a
single man without any expensive or vicious habits.

I hope you will have sufficient confidence in my judgment to grant the
Firemen a charter.

Bro Norton had an engagement with me to meet me yesterday. He told me
he was sent down here *by you* on a mission that he would tell me about when
he would see me again. He failed to keep his appointment and he gave me no
address. I am utterly in the dark as to what mission he was sent here on,
and have no means of finding out. If he wishes to treat me in such careless
and indifferent manner I cannot promise him a heartly support in his undertaking.

I am offended somewhat in the manner in which I have been treated in
sending an organizer in my territory without either myself or my union being
notified of the fact. It may be the custom but for my part I think it poor
policy. . . .

I am at present engaged in trying to organize into Unions of the
American Federation two labor associations one of them has a membership of
six hundred or over and have nearly twenty-thousand dollars in their treasury. The other in a new organization of about 75 members. I will however
refrain from acting until I hear from you, perhaps you would prefer having
Mr Norton to organize them. I am pretty sure that if he attempted to organize one of them and told the members he superseded me he would get hung,
still I offer no objection nor try in any way to prevent him. I will give
him the names and locations of the assns if he wishes.

Hoping for an early and satisfactory answer I remain Fraternally Yours
etc. John M. Callaghan.

A. F. of L. Archives, Incoming Correspondence.

67. SAMUEL GOMPERS TO GEORGE L. NORTON, MAY 16, 1892

Mr. Geo. L. Norton
General Organizer, A. F. of L.,
New Orleans, Louisiana

Dear Brother Norton:
It is necessary to address you upon a subject which is of an exceedingly
delicate nature and one which probably it will hurt me more to speak of than
you even to read, for you must be aware of the fact that so far as I am
concerned I never have made distinction between the white and the black man
in the matter of our identity of interests and the necessity of organizing
and bringing them in one fold, but you are no doubt aware of the feeling
and race prejudices existing in the South and that it will take some time
before it can be abated.

For that reason I would suggest that wherever there are white laborers

who have any objection to your organizing them, then leave them to the
efforts of the organizers of their respective localitie. If I believed for
a moment that the race prejudice would be overcome, I would certainly extend your authority to all, but I am satisfied that any other course than
the one suggested would only intensify the feeling and bring about results
opposite to that which we may desire and hope for.

Fraternally yours,
Samuel Gompers, President
American Federation of Labor

Samuel Gompers Letter-Books, Library of Congress

68.   SAMUEL GOMPERS TO GEORGE L. NORTON, MAY 17, 1892

Dear Brother:
    The race prejudice exists to such an extent that it seems that it were
better under the circumstances, to give the white men and the colored men
the opportunity of organizing separate unions rather than to have them not
organize at all. It is only when men begin to organize that they also
begin to realize that their interests are much more closely allied regardless of color, nationality, religious or other prejudices.
    In any union which has sufficiently advanced in their conception of the
identity of the interests of labor regardless of color, you are fully
authorized to proceed, but in those cases where it would hurt yourself, the
colored workmen, the white workmen as well as the general interests of the
A. F. of L., I kindly suggest to you to be very discreet and allow our
agitation and time to work the desired changes.

Fraternally yours,
Samuel Gompers, President
American Federation of Labor

Samuel Gompers Letter-Books, Library of Congress

69.   SAMUEL GOMPERS TO JOHN M. CALLAGHAN, MAY 17, 1892

Mr. John M. Callaghan,
Gen'l Organizer, A. F. of L.
New Orleans, Louisiana

Dear Brother:
    I would suggest that you cooperate with Norton for the attainment of
our common purpose, namely, the organization of our fellow-workmen.
    From what I learn there is considerable antagonism to him by reason of
the fact that he is a colored man, and that the race prejudice plays considerable part in this matter, but I ask you to consider whether it is not
advisable to make some effort in the direction indicated. There is no
necessity to run counter to the social distinctions made but the wage workers
ought to bear in mind that unless they help to organize the colored men,
they will of necessity compete with the white workmen and be antagonistic to
them and their interests. The employers will certainly take advantage of
this condition and do all they can to even stimulate the race prejudice. In
many cases where the race prejudice cannot be utilized, national or religious
prejudices are harped upon or brought into play.
    As a man whom I have every reason to believe you are, serious, earnest
and honest in the desire to see our fellow wage-workers improve their condition, I ask you to examine into this question more closely to see whether

I am not right. View it in a common sense manner. Start out the investigation with the old prejudices that you have heard from infancy, but study
it in the light of the historical struggle of the people of all nations,
and you will find that I am right.

Fraternally yours,
Samuel Gompers, President
American Federation of Labor

Samuel Gompers Letter-Books, Library of Congress.

70. SAMUEL GOMPERS TO JOHN M. CALLAGHAN, MAY 24, 1892

Mr. John M. Callaghan,
Gen'l. Organizer, A. F. of L.
New Orleans, Louisiana

Dear Brother:
     . . . Geo. L. Norton, a Negro, has been appointed organizer. Being a
colored man and a man of fair ability and sincere, we believed his influence
among his own people would be greater than any other for the purposes of
organization.

Fraternally yours,
Samuel Gompers, President
American Federation of Labor

Samuel Gompers Letter-Books, Library of Congress.

71. GEORGE L. NORTON TO SAMUEL GOMPERS, MAY 25, 1892

St. Louis, Mo.

Dear Sir:
     I Recd your Last Letter Before I Left New Orleans & I think Some one
has misled you for I never went about any white Union Except the Engineers
& Brewer & they sent for me & I went. I Did all that I could for what time
I was there will Be about 3 unions Coming in that has a Large membership &
could have Did more. But you seem to listen to those Hoodlums that is organizing for political purposes & it is well known By good men of that city
& I kindly ask you to commission J. B. Baldwin president Marine Engineers &
Z. T. Reno, who are good workers & Gentlemen Now in Regards to the white
firemans the Engineers are the ones that object to too charters & not me.
it has Been a failure in St. Louis & now the colored has all of the Boats.
But the men think if they all met in one hall & had half white & half colored
officers Like the Longshoremen has it would Be Better they have never won a
strike or a point But we have to win for them & Engineers Both also we won
our Demands By ourselves, the white men says they will send their charter
Back if they Dont get more work. But there are some 15 or 20 of them will
Come in to No. 7. they want to Come now But they have a charter & told them
that 20 could hold it, I think they are all quiet down & will Do Better in
future. You will find Enclosed the Expenses of the Trip which you can Do as
think Best in the matter.
     Railroad fare to & from New Orleans 30.00. Board & Room Rent for 14 Days
28.00 at 2.00 per Day, the incident Expence I never kept an acct. of, for I had
to talk myself to Death almost & Treat & Do Everything Else to convert those
people the total I Dont know & for that Reason I have no charge to make Do
as you like. you will also find the Commission you issued me July last

Enclosed. I Tender my Resignation this 25th Day of May '92. & Beg to
Extend My Best Wishes to you & the Council.

Fraternally,
G. L. Norton

A. F. of L. Archives, Incoming Correspondence.

72.   JOHN M. CALLAGHAN TO SAMUEL GOMPERS, MAY 29, 1892

New Orleans, La.

Dear Sir & Bro:
     Yours of May 24 duly received and carefully read. I am in hope that
the ripple of Mr. Nortons arrival and stay in the city has caused no injury
to the cause of labor. I am in receipt of inquiries from Engineers residing
in Algiers as to whether I could organize a Union of Engineers then or no.
Algiers is a suburb of New Orleans and is situated on the other side of the
Miss. River. There is a Post office of their own. I told them I would make
inquiries and find out. You may remember that Mr. Norton came down to
organize and install the officers of the Marine Engineers No. 5669. By
informing whether I could organize the other Union or no you would oblige
me greatly by a speedy answer. . . .

J. M. Callaghan

A. F. of L. Archives, Incoming Correspondence.

73.   SAMUEL GOMPERS TO GEORGE L. NORTON, JUNE 3, 1892

Mr. George L. Norton, Organizer

Dear Brother:
     As an evidence of my confidence in you I reissue and extend your
commission to June 1st, 1893.

Fraternally yours,
Samuel Gompers, President
American Federation of Labor

Samuel Gompers Letter-Books, Library of Congress.

74.   JOHN M. CALLAGHAN TO SAMUEL GOMPERS, JUNE 5, 1892

New Orleans, La.

Dear Sir and Bro:
     . . . There is one thing I would like very well to know is it usual to
charge for services in organizing unions. I understand Bro. Norton done so
when he organized Marine Engineers Protective Union 5669. . . .

Fraternally yours etc.
John M. Callaghan

A. F. of L. Archives, Incoming Correspondence.

75. JOHN M. CALLAGHAN TO SAMUEL GOMPERS, JUNE 12, 1892

New Orleans, La.

Dear Sir & Bro:

Enclosed please find application of Journeymen Horse Shoers for certificate of affiliation.

The Union is composed of both white and black men. I am sure that in
the course of a few months they will have by far the greater number of the
men employed at that calling within the ranks of their Union. The Horse
Shoers are pretty well divided as to color and at my request they made a
nearly equal division of officers and as all the officers are the charter
members I would wish you would have the 8 names placed on the charter.

Inclosed also find money order for charter and charter outfit. I
would be greatly convenienced if you would have them down before the 27 inst
as that is the day of the next meeting.

There is an energetic very intelligent colored man down here who is
Financial Secretary of Longshoremens Assn. and who takes a great interest
in the labor movement. He is not in any union connected with the Federation
but I am sure if it is not against the rules to issue him a commission as an
organizer he would render a good account of himself. He materially assists
in organizing the horse shoers and I am pretty certain he could get several
of the strong colored labor organizations to enlist under the Banner of the
A. F. of L.

If not against the rules I wish you would forward him a commission.

He also was one of the arbitration committee for Car Drivers Union.

I find I have been giving his good qualities and have not given his
name, his name is James E. Porter.[18]

Hoping to receive charter and outfit in time and if not against the
rules to receive the commission of Jas. E. Porter.

I am as ever,

Fraternally yours,
John M. Callaghan,
Organizer

A. F. of L. Archives, Incoming Correspondence.

76. GEORGE L. NORTON TO SAMUEL GOMPERS, JUNE 19, 1892

St. Louis, Mo.

Dear Sir:

Matters pertaining to the trouble here have kept me so busy that I have
not had time to write, and for several days past I have been ill, and am not
now able to leave my bed.

The situation along the river front is very gloomy at present, and
there is little likelihood of a settlement soon, judging by present appearances. The policemen are acting in the interest of the employers as usual.
One of our men was shot on Wednesday night, and there have been several
cutting affrays. The purpose of the boatowners is to force the men to
abandon their unions, that they may be enabled more easily to force them back
to low wages, long hours and that (practically) state of slavery on the
river-boats which prevailed before the unions were organized. For new members the men have held out remarkably well, and it is to be hoped that they
will stick and fight it out, as the only means of forcing a recognition of
the unions.

Hoping to hear from you soon, and wishing to know whether there is any
possibility of your coming here as it is understood that the Presidents of
the Anchor and Valley lines would be willing to meet you, I remain,

                                        Yours Fraternally,
                                        G. L. Norton
                                        General Organizer

P. S. Received Sec'y Evans' letter, but have not been able to answer it.

                                        G. L. N.

A. F. of L. Archives, Incoming Correspondence.

        77.   JOHN M. CALLAGHAN TO SAMUEL GOMPERS, JUNE 28, 1892

                                                    New Orleans, La.

Dear Sir & Bro:
     Your communications to hand and carefully noted. Thanks for your
good opinion and expressions of confidence in sending commission of Mr.
Porter I have mapped out some work for him to do and I am sure he can do
where I would most likely fail. . . .
     I have been doing no work for a few weeks that is my regular work
that I make a living at but I think I have been doing some work organizing
workingmen in New Orleans and adding strength to those already organized.
My money is nearly run out now so if you do not hear from me in organizing
other unions just conclude I have gone to work and have to make a little
money to support myself for a while. I have not charged any of the unions
any thing yet that I have organized. . . .
                                        I am as ever
                                        J. M. Callaghan

A. F. of L. Archives, Incoming Correspondence.

        78.   JOHN M. CALLAGHAN TO SAMUEL GOMPERS, AUGUST 3, 1892

                                                    New Orleans, La.

Dear Sir & Bro:
     . . . I am endeavoring to get a demonstration for Sept. 19 or there
abouts, and all the unions I speak to about it seem favorably inclined. I
hope you will not make any engagements for that time until I can go further
and let you know I am about to go away for a few weeks and will also attend
the convention in Indianapolis as a delegate, and as I expect it may put
some unions about to organize to some trouble or inconveniences, I would
wish you would appoint some one as organizer for the city. I can assure
you that there is none better than Porter still I can assure you that the
race question cuts quite a figure down here yet and as many white men
would much sooner never belong to an organization than join one organized
by a colored man I would much prefer that you would commission a white man
and I know no one who would take greater pride in the work than Ed. J.
Donegan of 89 Exchange Place.
     I would like very well if possible to receive a commission as a
National organizer like one held by Bro. Norton and might possibly be able
to do something in my travels I wish you would give me the names of a few
men connected with the A. F. of L. in St. Louis, Mo. as I might stop there
for a week or so. . . .
                                        I remain fraternally yours, etc.
                                        John M. Callaghan
A. F. of L. Archives, Incoming Correspondence.

79. WILLIAM BRANNICK TO A. F. OF L. EXECUTIVE COMMITTEE, AUGUST 5, 1892

Marine Engineers' Protective Union
No. 5622, A. F. of L.
St. Louis, Mo.

To the General Executive Committee of the A. F. of L.

Gentlemen:
    We the members of Marine Engineers Assn. 5622 would Respt ask your
assistance in our lockout as we were informed by President Gompers who is
here at present that you were the proper parties to apply to about two months
ago we were notafied by the Presidents of the Mississippi Vally transportation Co. and the Anchor Lines that we would have to withdraw from the Federation of Labor or get of the Boats which we did when this order was issued.
the Fireman Inland Seaman and Longshoreman went out on a strike to assist
us and after being out about six weeks decided to return to work as the
companies were able to procure enough of scab Engineers to man the Boats
    what I want to impress on your minds is that this order virtually shuts
us out from working on any Boat in St Louis and appears that they have a
special spite against the Marine Engineers as we were the only ones ordered
to withdraw from the A. F. of L. and as a last resource we would Respt ask
your Honerabal boddy to declare a boycott against the different Boats refusing us work. now what I would suggest is that you call of the differeant
unions that are connected with steam Boating the Boiler Makers which I understand is a verry strong organisation would be of great assistance to us as
theirs is more or less Boiler work to do on the boats every trip the Harbor
Boats Pilots. could help us as the Tugs which the Pilot coals the Boats,
the Longshoremen in New Orleans is another. As that would be of untold
benefit to us as we unload the Boats in New Orleans. now there are various
unions in this city which if called out could help us in our Lockout Hoping
that you will give this due consideration at your earliest conveniance.
    I remain yours verry Respt
                                              William Brannick,
                                              Sect of M. E. Assn. 5622

    The Lines that we want the Boycott against are Anchor Line, the Miss
Valley Line, the Eagle Packet Co. the Tennessee River and Diamond Joe
Line.

A. F. of L. Archives, Incoming Correspondence.

80. JOHN M. CALLAGHAN TO SAMUEL GOMPERS, OCTOBER 26, 1892

                                                        New Orleans, La.

Dear Sir & Bro:
    . . . We are confronted with the possibility of a lively time to-morrow.
The Round freight Teamsters and Loaders, The Warehousemen & Packers, and the
Scalesmens Union are out or rather will go out to-morrow for a claim for
overtime. They all work now from 6:30 A.M. until any time after 6:00 P.M.
and very often until 11 & 12 o'clock without either time for meals or extra
pay. The Warehousemen want $2 per day. Their day to start at 7 o'clock and
end at 6 o'clock with one hour for dinner and 25¢ per hour overtime and 40 c
for Sunday work. The Teamsters want $2.50 per day to start at 6 o'clock
with one hour for dinner. Overtime the same as the Warehousemen. The Scalemen want the same pay per package during the busy season they receive in the
dull time instead of as now. 1.50 per day. Their day starting at 7 o'clock
and liable to last until 2 or 3 o'clock next morning.

As soon as the notices were served on the employers they got on their
high horses and claimed they would not submit to be dictated to and they
would not sign our countenance any such action on the part of their employees.
They formed themselves into organizations and delegated committees to wait
on the mayor to ask for police protection. They will not get it however
unless the boys go out of bounds altogether. The fight may assume proportions that I may get interested in it and leave my work to attend to
it. . . .

I know of no trade or calling that is not organized that is worth
organizing or can be organized.

Some doctor friends of mine wanted to know if they could form a local
and affiliate I told them yes before I wrote to you but when I found they
contemplated raising their rates of attending members of organizations and
their families from $2 and $5 as they are now charging to $15 and $18 and
claim as they were connected with us in a labor organization and all the
labor organizations have regular physicians, I told them it would cost them
for my fee $500 and I would not support them in their demands. I have
heard no more from them. . . .

I remain as ever,
John M. Callaghan

A. F. of L. Archives, Incoming Correspondence.

81.   SAMUEL GOMPERS TO GEORGE L. NORTON, FEBRUARY 7, 1893

Mr. Geo. L. Norton,
Sec. Marine Firemen's Pro. Union
5464 A. F. of L.
St. Louis, Mo.

Dear Sir & Brother:
You say there is some talk of the color line being drawn in the American
Federation of Labor, and I state to you that that is an utter untruth im-
material by whom circulated. I never heard the subject mooted by any one &
our record has been made up upon that subject. There are positively two
National trade unions which we could get simply by asking them, but we
refuse them admission only because they draw the color line.

The suspicion is unjust to the men who have incurred hostility because
they dared to speak for the equal Rights of the black and white men and
their equal recognition in the organization of labor.

I am surprised that you should even for a moment harbor the thought that
such a feeling prevails. At our convention not even one vote could be mustered
to draw the color line. With you and all sincere men I condemn the attempts
on the part of certain people who are in our movement simply to advance their
own personal, financial & political interests.

It becomes our duty to do all that we possibly can to help the honest
men to maintain the purity of our organizations & movement.

Fraternally yours,
Samuel Gompers, President
American Federation of Labor

Samuel Gompers Letter-Books, Library of Congress.

82. GEORGE L. NORTON TO SAMUEL GOMPERS, JULY 13, 1893

St. Louis, Mo.

Dear Sir & Bro:
    Yours Recd & in Reply will say that I have Been out of town for some
time which accounts for my Delay. In Regards to Marine Fireman #6 of St.
Louis their statement is without any foundation whatever. We have trouble
with the Valley Line Boats because they will not pay our scale of wages &
there is none of our men on them except a few Deserters or scabs. There
are some from the ports that we have nothing to Do with & cannot help it.
We have Been friendly with No. 6 all along & I Dont know what they are
kicking about Except it is the Excursion Boats & the Managers of those Boats
Did not want them because they ware to Fresh with the Ladies on said Boats
& they prefered colored Firemen I think they are Like the Rest of the River
unions & have Lost the Balance hoping to here from you soon & often I am
as Fraternally

yrs,
G. L. Norton

A. F. of L. Archives, Correspondence.

83. GEORGE L. NORTON TO SAMUEL GOMPERS, FEBRUARY 7, 1894

St. Louis, Mo.

Dear sir:
    I write to Inform you that the Marine Firemen #1 of St. Louis Mo coming
to the Front again We have 70 members now I think we will Be all Right soon.
The Low water for 6 months & the Boys have not had any work & we have Been
down to 3. But I am working hard to get the union up again, & I think I
will soon have them in good standing in the A. F. of L. you will please
send me one copy of the proceeding of the convention held in Chicago also
the Current P.W. for this year Do this & much oblige.
    Hoping to here from you soon Except the Best wishes.

I am as Ever
Fraternally
G. L. Norton

A. F. of L. Archives, Incoming Correspondence.

THE A. F. OF L., THE MACHINISTS' UNION, AND THE BLACK WORKER

84. C A L L

FOR A

NATIONAL CONVENTION

of

MACHINISTS, BLACKSMITHS AND HELPERS

To Machinists, Blacksmiths and Helpers wherever found.

Brothers:--Recognizing the urgent need of a national organization of the workers employed in the manufacture of tools and machinery, we issued in January last a call to all local organizations of our trade asking them to join with us in the formation of a national body. In reply to said call we received from 17 unions assurances of their readiness to join a national organization while others, declaring themselves in sympathy with the movement, promised to take action after the plan should have taken more definite shape.

The number and tone of the replies received show a strong and wide spread feeling among machinists that the time is ripe for consolidating the workers of our trade in a compact national organization built upon the principles of progressive trade unionism.

To effect such consolidation we invite all machinists' organizations to send delegates to a

NATIONAL CONVENTION

to convene at 85 East 4th Street

NEW YORK CITY

on Monday June 22, 1891,

at 9 o'clock A.M.

Organizations are requested to notify the undersigned committee of their action on or before June 15, 1891.

Dated, NEW YORK, April 25, 1891.

The Organization Committee of the United Machinists of New York & Brooklyn.

A. Waldinger, *Secretary Committee*
221 Broom St., New York.

85.   HARRY E. ASTON TO SAMUEL GOMPERS, APRIL 20, 1891

National Association of Machinists
Deputy Grand Lodge No. 1
Omaha, Nebraska

Dear Sir:

As I was a Delegate to the 3rd Annl Session of Grand Lodge N A M held in Louisville last year and am again selected to represent #31 (Omaha Lodge) at the 4th Annl Session to be held at Pittsburg on the 4th of May next, I would be pleased to have you write me petitioning again to have the word White stricken out of Constitution and that they would be able to consider favorably the propriety of casting their lot with us, I got the words anti-strike stricken out last year, and believe I will be able this season to have erased the word white. It may be rather late for you to have this acted upon but please try you can have the communications addressed to me at the Central Hotel in care of Anderson & Rowan Pittsburg Pa. Hoping this will meet with your favorable consideration. I am Yours Respectfully,

Harry E. Aston, D.G.M.W.

A. F. of L. Archives, Incoming Correspondence.

86. L. C. FRY TO SAMUEL GOMPERS, APRIL 7, 1892

Burlington, Iowa

Dear Sir & Bro:
    I think there will be some changes in the I.A.M. for the better at the
convention at Chicago May next, I have done considerable agitation, and I
find a circular going the Rounds of the Locals in favor of the I A of M
becoming affiliated with the A. F. of L., and fusing the 2 machinist organizations into one. You should see that some good man was at the convention
to help matters along. I will speak at the Machinist union here next Sunday.
I have already got the delegate from here to see the great necessity of
Federation, and I know that he will work that way. . . . If the proper person is at the convention I am satisfied that the 2 unions can be brought
together with Regards to all
                        I Remain Yours Fraternally,
                                        L. C. Fry

A. F. of L. Archives, Incoming Correspondence.

87. DOUGLAS WILSON TO SAMUEL GOMPERS, APRIL 14, 1893

International Association of Machinists
Birmingham, Ala.

Dear Sir & Bro:
    I am pleased to inform you that your communication came to hand this
evening, and in reply, will say that I will do all I can, to further the
cause of Union. Of course you can readily appreciate the fact that it is
very up-hill work in this section of the country, to advocate anything that
would tend to make men think that there was such a thing as the Universal
Brotherhood of Man. I do not know of anything that would make a man so
unpopular, as an advocacy of a heresy like that. Nevertheless, after a
great deal of hard work, we may now whisper it, that an educated "nigger"
is nearly as good as an illiterate though godly-say-Hibernian. I am of an
opinion that the color line will "barely" come out this time, as I am afraid
that the Southern (imagine north & south in a Trades Union) vote is the
strongest yet; though it will be a pretty close pull. Unfortunately, a good
many of our ablest men, although they know different; for the sake of
pandering to popularity, will rant and rave over the superiority of the white
race. The Southern delegation will get up on its hind legs, and swear,
"that if you take out that 'word,' accept my resignation right now," and I
cannot help thinking--are your members a source of strength to us, or a
weakness? You may count on Bro Ashe of Boston and myself to do all that is
possible in the way of consummating a union with the A. F. L., and as a
preliminary, doing our level best to knock out the word "white" from our
constitution, from where it ought never to have been. I'm no office seeker
so I can afford to express myself in Indianapolis more freely on that subject,
than I could with propriety here. Thank you, sir, for your prompt reply to
my letter, I beg to be remembered as
                            Fraternally,
                            Douglas Wilson[19]

P.S. The convention meets in Englishs Hall, in the Circle on the 1st Monday
of May at 10 A.M. Delegates will put up at the Hotel English--rates $1.50
per diem.
                                        D.W.

A. F. of L. Archives, Incoming Correspondence.

88.   NOTHING BUT PREJUDICE

President Samuel Gompers of the American Federation of Labor talked to
the International Association of Machinists in Indianapolis recently asking
them to extend the privileges and protection of their organization to the
colored man. This association and the plasterers' union are about the only
organizations which exclude the Negro. Mr. Gompers did not, however, succeed in his object. When asked what reason was assigned by the machinists
for still closing their doors to the colored man: "Now," he said, "they
have answered that this would be a step toward social equality. It's
nothing of the kind. We don't expect them to go any further, but certainly
if a Negro is good enough to work alongside of the white man, he ought to
be admitted to the trade unions. Then from another standpoint it is advisable to admit them: If we don't they bid against us, and competition in
labor is the very thing that labor organizations are agitating against.
The machinists say there are so few colored men among them that it is
not worth while to bother about them. As I said in my address yesterday,
if there are none then this article in their by-laws denying them admission
is altogether unnecessary, while if there are colored men, the article is
brutal and inhuman. They will see the effect of this too. My talk to the
association could have had no effect upon them during this session, as they
had already disposed of the question before I arrived. I am told they did
this on purpose to anticipate my endeavors. There is another association
of machinists which admits the colored man and is in the federation of labor.
It was my desire to unite the two organizations, but it cannot be done as
long as this association persists in its determination to draw the color
line. It is nothing but prejudice that keeps them out."

The Freeman (Indianapolis), May 27, 1893.

89.   JAMES O'CONNELL TO SAMUEL GOMPERS, NOVEMBER 1, 1893

James O'Connell,[20]
Grand Master Machinist
International Assn. of Machinists
Richmond, Virginia

Dear Sir:
I take this opportunity of addressing you on a subject that is of great
interest to both of us in the matter of bringing more closely to-gether the
Labor Organizations of this country, and harmonizing any differences that
may exist among them. As you are fully aware of the action taken by our
Conventions on that portion of our Constitution which is the word "white" in
it, it has been a bone of contention among our members for sometime, and at
the Indianapolis Convention we adopted a resolution to take a referendum vote
as to taking the word "white" out of our Constitution. This matter I will
lay before our Organization about the middle of this month, and knowing that
on several occasions you have said if it were not for that portion of our
Constitution there would be no rival Organization of the machinst craft in
this country, and that the I.M.U. would at once become an organization of
the past; now any assurance that you can give me on this matter will add a
great deal towards helping us to bring this matter to a speedy conclusion,
and also a successful one to all concerned.
There is no reason in the world, that I know of, why we should have
two Organizations of the same craft in this country, or in fact of any other
country. Our Organization is advancing rapidly under the present condition
of affairs in this country, and have prospects of still greater growth; and
with these facts in view I address you this letter for the purpose of having
you give me your ideas as to what would be the result if we had this word
taken out of our Constitution.

An early reply to this letter would be very acceptable.
Believe me,
                              Yours Respectfully & Fraternally,
                              James O'Connell, G.M.M.

A. F. of L. Archives, Incoming Correspondence.

        90. DANIEL J. SULLIVAN TO JOHN MCBRIDE, MARCH 26, 1895

                              International Machinists Union of America
                              Machinists Union No. 28
                              Office of International Secretary-Treasurer
                              Boston, Mass.

John McBride
President, A. F. of L.

Dear Brother:
    We would call your attention to a statement made in Boston by McConnell
Master Machinist of the Association Machinists. He stated that the A. F.
of Labor stood ready at any time to give the Association a charter of the
Federation of Labor with or without the Association doing away with the
Color-line.
    We do not believe this for we know that the Associations last Conven-
tion the Federation officials tried to get them to remove the Color line from
there Constitution.
    Please inform us is this statement of McConnell true and also try
your utmost to have the next Association Convention withdraw the Color line
so that all Machinists can affiliate under the banner of the American
Federation of Labor.

                              Yours very truly,
                              Danl J. Sullivan, Sec.

A. F. of L. Archives, Incoming Correspondence.

                        91. THIS WORD WHITE

. . . We ought to remember all these things when the Convention takes place,
instruct our delegates to that effect, make an effort to keep politics,
religion, and petty grievances out of the Convention, not strike the word
"white" out of our constitution, and so on.
    Brothers, have you ever read attentively the many articles published
in our Journal about this word "white," and especially the one in the last
issue, in which a brother says himself that there were to his knowledge only
five negro machinists in the South, and still he proposes to give the
"colored" a partial membership, restrictions which are not practicable, but
unjust. If you admit the negro you must admit him like the rest of us or
not all. Our craft, which heretofore was a white man's calling exclusively,
will cease to be; it will become flooded with negroes to such an extent
that there will be shops where a white man will be driven out and have no
chance whatever.
    The negro don't need us now, nor will he ever benefit us even if we make
him a brother. Only think of it. Not that he ain't as good a man as many
whites, no, but it is not good for us, as he is a born competitor with us,
and we will command still less pay than we are getting now. We want our
craft elevated, if not above the level of the best paid craft of the United
States, then at the same height; but we cannot do it by admitting the negro.

Progress will stop, there will be a split in our order, and if this occurs, the end will be near at hand, and some one will try and start something else until everything bursts again on the same rocky question. Now is the time, however, to meditate over such matters, and by instructing the delegates when they go to the convention it will save a good deal of trouble to decide it.

J. Best
Philadelphia, Pa.
February 5, 1895

Machinists' Journal (April, 1895): 128.

92.   JAMES DUNCAN TO W. S. DAVIS, APRIL 1, 1895

W. S. Davis
International Association of Machinists

Dear Sir:
    (As) long as you have the word "white" establishing the color line as a part of your constitution either your action must be changed or your lodges and your national body must stand debarred from all affiliation with us. . . . I believe yours is the only national union, that at present, has the color line as distinctly formed, while at the same time many crafts refused to admit a colored man without having such provision in their constitutions, the matter being left absolutely with the local unions as whether or not they admit colored applicants.

James Duncan,[21]
Acting President of the
A. F. of L.

Philip Taft, *The A. F. of L. in the Time of Gompers (New York, 1957),* pp. 309-10.

93.   EDWARD O'DONNELL TO AUGUSTINE MCCRAITH, APRIL 15, 1895

Office of Central Labor Union of
Boston and Vicinity
Boston, Mass.

Augustine McCraith,
Secretary of A. F. of L.

My Dear Mac:
    At a recent meeting of the C.L.U. I was instructed to urge your Executive Board by request of Machinists No. 28, to aid in bringing about harmony and cooperation between themselves and the National Machinists, now divided because of "color distinctions."
    No plan of arbitration and concession has been submitted upon the matter, hence I have no suggestion to make; but place it in your hands, knowing of course you will exercise your best judgment.
    Our delegate to the next convention will be fully informed and instructed thereupon.

Respectfully,
Edward O'Donnell,
Cor. Sec. CLU

A. F. of L. Archives, Incoming Correspondence.

94. THOMAS J. MORGAN TO JOHN MCBRIDE, MAY 18, 1895

International Machinists' Union
Chicago, Ill.

Dear Comrade,
Your communication relative to the action of the I.M. Assoc. received.
I have sent it on to the Executive Board of our Union for action, whatever
they advise will be submitted to the membership per the referendum.
I have not expressed an opinion, leaving the matter entirely to them.
Speaking for myself I am free to say that I could find no satisfaction
in becoming affiliated with that body. The action of their national
officers towards us in the past has been most bitter and unscrupulous,
meeting and treating us everywhere as enemies rather than fellow workmen
and members of the A. F. of L. In this they have had the fullest encouragement from the officers of the A. F. of L. a legitimate child of the A. F.
of L. we have been Bastardized, so that a more Bulky creation might be
adopted. Here in Chicago we know them personally and while of course the
rank and file are good honest machinists the Organization has been utilized
solely for the political advancement of its leaders, this characteristic
has made them hail fellow with the confidence men who rule and ruin the
Labor Movement in this city, and rather than associate with them, give to
them the benefit and indorsement of the little reputation I have I will
sever the trade union connections which I have affectionately established
and held for the last 24 years.
This is said to you alone, not a word will be used to influence our
membership, they will act upon their own judgment.
John My dear boy I would not play the part of a Gompers or a McGuire
for all the world. Nothing can be greater treason than to lull the workers
to sleep with the old trade union melody.
I am eating at the 10¢ lunch counter. My dollar and cent interest
prompts me to be diplomatic, to talk of harmony between Capitalists &
Laborers Etc. Etc. No I shall still talk war, that there is not and cannot
be peace, that the old must give way to the new even in the labor movement,
that the revolution comes nearer each year, and that our best efforts will
fail to fully prepare us to meet it. The Old World is up and doing, why
not us John. They will not let even a Burns fool them, why should we John?

Fraternally yours,
Thomas J. Morgan
General Secretary[22]

A. F. of L. Archives, Incoming Correspondence.

95. THOMAS J. MORGAN TO JOHN MCBRIDE, JULY 2, 1895

International Machinists' Union
Chicago, Ill.

John McBride
President, A. F. of L.

Dear Comrade:
The matter relative to the Association of Machinists which you submitted to the International Machinists Union, was by me referred to the
Executive Board.
I am instructed to inform you that after due consideration the conditions
upon which the members and Unions of the International Machinists would be
permitted to merge themselves into the International Association, have been
rejected, and it is fraternally insisted as a condition to the issue of a
charter to the Association, by the A. F. of L.

That the Association its officers and members be required to recognize our members as Trade union Machinists and that our members be accorded that treatment which is consistent with such relationship.

I am informed that a charter has been granted to the Association.

If so, will you kindly inform me under what provision of the constitution this act was done, and what correlationship now is with the A. F. of L.

Fraternally yours,
Thomas J. Morgan,
General Secretary

A. F. of L. Archives, Incoming Correspondence.

96. DANIEL J. SULLIVAN TO JOHN MC BRIDE, JULY 24, 1895

International Machinists' Union of America
Machinist Union No. 28
Boston, Mass.

Sir:

At the last meeting of the above union, I was instructed to find out from you on what grounds the Machinist Association were granted a charter by you as I know that it is forbidden in the Constitution of the A. F. of Labor to have two bodies of the same nature affiliated.

If you have done this and eased your conscience with the thought, that the end justifies the means, I beg leave to inform you that I hope they are but few like you at the helm guiding Labor's course. No wonder the ship strikes and is wrecked so often. On an early reply to the above depends the future action of the above Union of which I am the Corresponding Secretary.

Danl. J. Sullivan

A. F. of L. Archives, Incoming Correspondence.

97. EDWARD O'DONNELL TO JOHN MCBRIDE, JULY 26, 1895

Office of Central Labor Union of
Boston and Vicinity
Boston, Mass.

My dear Sir:

Since the granting of this dual charter, the local body here affiliated with the all powerful Association has positively refused to admit No. 28 as a body, the president tells them they will have to come in as individuals paying the regular initiation fee.

To my way of thinking this would be no reflection, and ought not to be regarded as such by 28; but human nature is so eccentric and varied in its estimation of dignity that we must refrain from censuring the smaller body for maintaining its particular standard of manhood.

The American Federation of Labor called this body into existence to bring the others into line who would not perceive that manhood could survive under a black face, and, now, forsooth, without first stipulating to both parties consolidation as the terms of affiliation, the very club we ourselves created to bring about the present consummation must be cast adrift to sink or swim.

Past indiscretion is no logical criterion to mould the action of the future upon.

Your action, to my way of viewing the situation, places the Central Labor Union in a most embarrassing position, which may possibly lead up to detrimental results.

Machinists 28 are delegates with us, small though their organization may be, and the other body is apt to apply for admission at our next meeting; and we can not refuse their admission because they and ourselves owe allegiance to the A. F. of L.

Such a policy, I care not how honorable the motive beneath it may be, must in time work destruction to the trade union movement, and dare not be pursued or tolerated much further.

It has cost too much to reach where we now are to permit of a policy fraught with such possible evil, as the present action presents itself to.

Yours sincerely,
Edward O'Donnell
Cor. Sec. C.L.U.

P.S.   Daniel J. Sullivan is Secretary of Machinists, No. 28.

A. F. of L. Archives, Incoming Correspondence.

98. I. A. M. IS CHARTERED

As the JOURNAL writes these lines, the charter is casting its fraternal beams across the paper.

Immediately after the adjournment of the convention, Bro. O'Connell and the General Executive Board made application for a certificate of affiliation to the Federation, which, in due time was granted, with the result that it now graces the walls of the headquarters office. This means a great deal to us, more than at first thought is imagined. It means that we have come to that stage in our organization's existence where both swaddling clothes and childish ideas of trades unionism are left behind. It means, that now, if we wish to show the world what sort of stuff we are made of, we have got the opportunity. We are closely allied now with the leading minds in the labor movement, and it remains with us to show both them and the world, that the members of the International Association of Machinists are equal to the occasion. To gain this end, to prove our sincerity and fealty to the cause of labor, we must forget all petty jealousies within our ranks, solidify ourselves by education; educate ourselves by fair-minded discussion, irrespective of who furnishes the subject for debate, whether he be a popular brother or not. Remembering always that the only way we can come to a fair understanding of any subject, is by listening to the opinions of others. By hearing both sides, no matter how much against the grain it goes to hear the opposition express themselves, is the only correct way to come to an honest judgment. Let us do this one thing, for a start, and we emphasize the forward step we have taken as an organization.

Affiliation with the A.F. L. also means that we have given them our strength--enlisted in the ranks to help fight in defence of labors rights. We have also gained in the transaction much more than we have given away; this will be better understood when we consider, that the mere fact of our affiliation with such a powerful combination as the A.F.L. will deter, to a great extent, that encroachment of capital that we have suffered from for the last two years.

Corporations will hesitate now, ere they announce in the same domineering manner that they have used heretofore, a cut of ten per cent. Further, even now negotiations are being entered into for the absorbtion by us of all machinists connected with bodies other than the I. A. of M. affiliated with the A. F. L.

Machinists' Journal (July, 1895): 234.

DISCRIMINATION IN THE BRICKLAYERS' AND MASONS' INTERNATIONAL UNION:
CORRESPONDENCE BETWEEN UNION OFFICIALS
AND ROBERT RHODES, A BLACK BRICKLAYER

99.

Indianapolis, Indiana
January 14, 1903

Mr. Wm. Dobson:
    Dear Sir and Brother:
    In yours of December 26, 1902, you advise that I file charges against
the striking members of our order who refused to work with me simply on
account of my color. I could not get the names of the members of the order,
but did file a general complaint against the members of the Indianapolis
Union, and presented the complaint in person. It was read by the secretary,
and on motion it was immediately tabled. Later in the meeting I moved to
take it from the table and have a committee appointed to investigate, but
could get no second to my motion, and no further action was taken. I beg
of you as general secretary to take this matter up, and make an investigation. . . . I do not want to be forced to do 'scab' work, while there is
plenty of work here for all. Something should be done at once.

Yours truly,
ROBERT RHODES

100.

Secretary's Office
North Adams, Mass.
March 17, 1903

Mr. George Frey:
    Dear Sir and Brother: Under date of February 6, I enclosed you a
complaint received from Robert Rhodes, who although a member of your Union,
claims that he had been and was discriminated against on account of his
color. I have been waiting to hear from you regarding the matter, but up
to the present time of writing you have failed to answer my communication.
. . .
    Now, I trust you will give this immediate attention, as I want to hear
your union's side before going further into the matter. . . .

Yours fraternally,
WM. DOBSON, Sec., B&M I.U.

101.

Union No. 3
Indianapolis, Indiana
March 22, 1903

Mr. Wm. Dobson:
    Dear Sir and Brother: In answer to yours of the 17th inst. referring

to R. R. Rhodes, will say that he became a member of No. 3 by card on
January 10, 1903. He had been in the city for about four weeks before his
card came, and on complying with the law was granted working pemits.

He has at all times been extended the same rights and privileges as
any other member. He procured work on the Federal building, and I am informed the men working there quit work as individuals, and after the foreman discovered the men would not work with a colored member, he was let go.
He appeared at the next regular meeting, and as he has informed you in his
letter made an appeal. He was advised then to prefer charges against the
members who had quit work, which he admits he did not do, for the reason,
he says, that he did not know the members' names.

The foregoing are the facts in the case, and if Brother Rhodes has a
grievance against members of this Union and presents his case in compliance
with the law, there will be an investigation made and he will receive the
same recognition that any other brother would get.

> Fraternally yours,
> GEORGE FREY, Corres. Sec.

102.

> Indianapolis, Indiana
> March 24, 1903

Wm. Dobson:
Dear Sir and Brother: A copy of the letter sent to you by Union No. 3
has been given to me, and I beg leave to say that as far as it goes it is
all right, but it stops a little too soon. They fail to tell you that I
tried to get them to appoint a committee to investigate my grievances and
they refused to do so. I asked them what I should do, and the president told
me to go somewhere else where I could work.

It is true that they have given me the right to meet with them, but that
is all they have done. I brought my case up several times, and the last time
I brought it up I was told that they were not going to have any more rag
chewing about it. I rose and asked the Union to set me right as to whether
they were going to work with me, and two of the brothers rose and answered
me in this way: they said, no they were not going to work with me, but said
they would not make a minute of it, for they were too slick for that, but
they would tell me as individuals that they would not work with me, and I
ought to be man enough to go somewhere else and not stay around there.

So, now, Brother Secretary, all I want is a fair and impartial trial,
and I hope you will investigate the matter and give me a chance for a living.
I have been here better than four months, and would like to know what I am
to do, as I expect to live here. . . .

> Your brother,
> ROBERT RHODES

103.

> First Vice President's Office
> New York City
> April 6, 1903

Mr. George Frey:
Dear Sir and Brother: The correspondence in the case of Rhodes vs. No.
3 has been forwarded to my office in the absence of the president. . . . I
may say that I had been made acquainted with Brother Rhodes' case through
the public press, and I could not believe that all that is printed is true.
However, all who are opposed to labor Unions have grasped at the statements
made to use as a weapon against organized labor, and it behooves us as one of

the great labor bodies of the world to place our organization right before
the public. In accordance with instructions from the Executive Board, you
will appoint a committee to investigate the matter and forward report thereon as soon as possible. . . .

> Fraternally yours,
> WM. J. BOWEN, Acting Pres.[23]

104.

> Indianapolis, Indiana
> April 10, 1903

Mr. Dobson:
    Dear Sir and Brother: I have waited quite a while for you to adjust
my matter with Union No. 3 and as yet I have heard nothing from you. Since
writing you I have been fined $25 and suspended until same is paid. I think
this an outrage to starve a man and try to force him out of the city to earn
a living when there is work for all, and for no purpose other than my
color. . . . I don't propose to be treated in this manner after paying my
money and living up to all rules and laws until forced to get work by the
wrongful acts of my brother workmen. Please answer at once.

> Yours for business,
> ROBERT RHODES

P.S. I beg to remind you of our preamble; . . . it says we hold that all
men are created equal and that honor and merit makes the man, etc., then
see what my brothers have done to me because of the negro blood in my veins.
It is simply a living lie and I propose to go to the limit of the law in
self-preservation.

105.

> First Vice President's Office
> April 20, 1903

Mr. Robert Rhodes:
    Dear Sir and Brother: In reply to your letter of the 10th inst., I
wish to call your attention to the law of the B. & M. I. U. of A. governing
appeals. If you had or now have a grievance against No. 3 Indiana why do
you not conform to the paragraphs of section 3 of article 15 of the I.U.
Constitution? Make out your appeal in duplicate according to law, setting
forth all the facts in the case; serve one copy on No. 3 Indiana and one on
the Judiciary Board of the I.U. through Secretary Dobson's office. We can
then get both sides of the case and render decision according to the evidence adduced. When you comply with the law of the I.U. we can give you the
protection that is accorded all the members.
    With kind regards, I am,

> Fraternally yours,
> WM. J. BOWEN, Acting President

106.

> First Vice President's Office
> April 20, 1903

Mr. George Frey:
    Dear Sir and Brother: . . . The Executive Board of the I.U. does not
wish to pose as reformers nor to blazon forth as the solvers of the colored

question, but we insist that we shall be prepared to repel the attacks of the newspaper critics, and to place the general organization right before the public when statements such as have come to our notice in this case of Rhodes are brought to our attention. We do not want to pass on the legality of your action in fining Rhodes, until both sides have presented their evidence, but in justice to your Union and the parent body you should take up the charges made by Rhodes in the public press, and make a thorough investigation of same. . . .

Fraternally yours,
WM. BOWEN, Acting President

107.

Bricklayers' Union No. 3
Indianapolis, Indiana
April 26, 1903

Wm. Bowen:
Dear Sir and Brother: . . . Rhodes became a member of No. 3 by card on January 1st. He has had all the privileges accorded him that any other brother has had. If he has been injured by members of No. 3 he had a redress as anyone else would have had . . . that is to prefer charges against the brothers who he says had injured him. He has repeatedly said that he would be driven to scabbing, which, in not gaining his point as he expected to do he has done, with others.
On the 2d inst. charges were preferred against him . . . of which charges he was notified and ordered to appear for trial at our next regular meeting on the 9th, at which time he appeared and entered an [sic] plea of guilty to charges, and was fined $25.00. He has been working ever since. The Union placed the extreme penalty [suspension] upon him for the reason that we were locked out by the bosses, and that he had made a proposition to one of the contractors that if they, the bosses, wish him to, he would fill our places with two hundred colored men in a week's time, which proposition later events show was not accepted as our demands were granted and work resumed. . . .
And as for solving the colored question in this locality, that we could not do, as there are too many of them here . . . and even if we are forced to do that, the Union thinks it ample time when Mr. Rhodes reinstates himself. We cannot understand why such great stress and blame should attach to No. 3 when there are other Unions throughout the country where they are not allowed to become members at all. . . .

Fraternally yours,
GEORGE FREY, Corres. Sec., No. 3

108.

Indianapolis, Indiana
April 27, 1903

Mr. Wm. Bowen:
Dear Sir and Brother: I beg to say to you that I acted under the advice of our secretary, Mr. Dobson, and filed a complaint against certain members of Union No. 3. The charges were made. The Union refused to take any steps at all. They knew I could not make specific charges against certain members whose names I could not get from the secretary, nor could I get them from the contractor. They knew this, hence I could not follow the letter of the law, nor could I get the matter squarely before the Union.
. . . If I attempt further proceedings I will be stopped because of my suspension for working with non-Union men, after a repeated effort to get work with my fellow workmen. Now I am to be handicapped and denied my rights on legal technicalities, while in fact it is simply because of my color, as they fairly said so, and wanted me to leave the city and get work elsewhere.

If I can't get a proper understanding I will pursue some other course, and
I beg of you to take the matter up, as I want no further unpleasantness.
. . .

Respectfully,
ROBERT RHODES

"Case No. 8: Rhodes vs. No. 3 Indiana as to Discrimination," in *38th
Annual Report of the President and Secretary of the Bricklayers and Masons'
International Union of America, 1903* (North Adams, Mass., 1903), 11-16, in
United States Department of Labor Library, Washington, D.C.

THE GALVESTON LONGSHOREMEN STRIKE OF 1898

109.   THE MALLORY TROUBLES

COLORED LABORERS MEET

THE SHIP AT GALVESTON--DEMAND UNION WORK AND UNION WAGES--OLD FORCE AFRAID
TO GO TO WORK.

AN ANOMALOUS condition is presented in the labor trouble which is now
on at the Mallory docks.   The men who previously worked for the line were
on hand to unload the Colorado, which arrived yesterday. A big crowd of
men were on hand, who demanded that the wages be raised from the old scale,
and who at first prevented and later persuaded the old men not to go to work.
The Mallory line's service between New York and Galveston has been suspended since April, when the war broke out.   The Colorado is the first boat
to arrive since the resumption of the service.   She left New York on August
30, and was really due here Sunday.   She had cargo and freight for Key West,
and as Key West had been branded as an infected port the company made arrangements to discharge her freight and passengers on a barge outside the harbor,
in order that she might not be forbidden ingress into Galveston harbor. An
extra crew was taken along to perform this work. They mutinied at Key West,
or rather outside of Key West harbor. Consequently there was a delay in
discharging the freight. Seven of them are now confined and will be turned
over to the authorities.
When the Colorado pulled into Galveston harbor and berthed at the Mallory
dock about 1 o'clock yesterday afternoon there were over a thousand men there
to greet her. It was not a reception committee, it was not a delegation to
welcome the return of the line, but for the most part it was a crowd of
colored longshoremen, who were there to tell the Mallory people that they
must employ none but union men, and must pay the scale of wages recently a-
dopted by the recently organized and chartered Colored Laborers' union. The
wages which the union says must be paid are 40 cents an hour for day work
and 50 cents an hour for night work. The Mallory line has paid 30 cents for
day work and 40 cents for night work. That is the scale it intends paying
again.
Many of the colored men carried billets of wood. They formed a complete
cordon guarding every avenue of approach to the Mallory docks. Some of them,
when asked as to their purpose, declined to answer; others declared that they
were just keeping their own men from blocking the gangways; others said they
meant no violence, but intended to see that no one went to work except at
the union scale. Two men who were interrogated upon the matter said it was
not the purpose to keep back the men who were to unload the ship; "but," they
added, "we are the men who will unload that ship, and we will get union wages
for it."
As a rule the discharging of a vessel begins immediately she is tied up
at the dock. Quite a crowd of spectators gathered around to await the clash

which they thought was imminent, but the afternoon wore away and there was
no clash. Neither was there any attempt to unload the vessel.

The men who stood a short distance from the Mallory sheds carrying
clubs and forming the guard line, every now and then drove back those who
pressed forward too far. It is true that some of these were of their own
crowd, but on more than one occasion this reporter saw men who professed
a desire to go to the docks for work driven back. They were told that no
foolishness would be stood and they obeyed. There was no violence.

A couple of policemen were on the ground. They said there were no acts
of violence attempted, and there was nothing for them to do. When told
that men who wanted to work had been driven back they said they had seen
nothing of the sort; that if it was going on it was not attempted in their
presence.

About 2 o'clock Harvey Patrick mounted a box or barrel on the platform
of the passenger depot on avenue A and Twenty-fourth streets and addressed
the big crowd that gathered around them. He told them that he was talking
to and for every man who has an interest in the community, and who has a
family at home to support, be he white or black. "It requires something
to subsist upon," he continued. "We are not farmers; we can not get out
and raise that on which we have to subsist. It requires spot cash. You
know what the trouble is. It is not necessary for me to tell you here. The
Mallory line steamer is here offering reduced wages upon which we can not
live. Many of you have read my letter giving the scale of wages we asked.
Now the Mallory line is charging the merchants of this town 85 cents a
hundred for freight, and they refuse to pay us 40 cents an hour for unloading
that freight. They charge the merchants 45 cents a hundred on sugar, and we
have to pay $1 for eighteen pounds of sugar -- yet they will not pay us living
wages. We have not come here to prevent the Mallory line from working, but
to ask them to pay us what we pay them through our merchants. We don't want
any trouble and don't mean to have any riotous conduct. We don't mean to
stop the Mallory line and say they shall not come into this port. We simply
ask them for liberal wages upon which a laborer can subsist. We mean to say
that scab labor from the country, which comes here for three or four months
every year after making a cotton crop to gobble our work and make a stake for
Christmas, should not be employed at reduced wages. We stay here all the year
round. We simply ask the co-operation of our white brethren. We have not
committed any violence, and we don't intend to do so. We ask this labor from
the country to disband and go back to the country. If we get more wages, we
will be able to pay them better prices for their produce and wages will be
raised in the country, everybody will be happy and we will have two children
born to one."

At this juncture Patrick explained that a more eloquent man was to speak
for them. He said he didn't know who the man was, but he would be obliged if
he would come forward. The unknown did not respond, and after a time Patrick
went on.

"I ask you all to do no acts of violence; do nothing that is against the
law or against decency. The white labor unions are ready to give us their
sympathy as long as we remain within the bounds of the law. Be cautious in
this matter. Stay away from the Mallory docks for less than 40 cents an hour.
When they are ready to consent to our terms, union men will do the work. We
don't want scabs to do the work at union wages, but we want union men and
union wages. Don't violate the law. Ask these laborers from the country not
to go to work down there, and when you ask them see that they don't do it."

This ended the speechmaking, and the afternoon wore away without particular incident.

About the middle of the afternoon a number of policemen, headed by Day
Sergeant Paul Delaya arrived on the scene. It was said they had orders from
Mayor Fly to disperse the crowds. They drove the men back into Twenty-fourth
street, south of avenue A. There many of them remained until a late hour,
evidently believing that the Mallory line might make an effort to unload the
ship if they left. It was known that this was not satisfactory to the Mallory
line; they did not consider that the crowd had been dispersed. Deputy Chief
of Police Amundsen went to the scene about 6 o'clock. By that time it had
been determined not to make any attempt to discharge the vessel until this
morning. Mr. Amundsen told the men that their assembly was unlawful. He
informed the leaders that they must not bring their men down there in the

morning, and if they did so, the police would disperse them. This had the
effect of sending most of the crowd home.

Mr. Charles Scrimgeour, superintendent of the Mallory wharf, said that
his men wanted to go to work early in the afternoon, but were prevented from
doing so. Later they demanded that he pay them 40 and 50 cents an hour.
Some of them, he said, told him they were willing to go to work on the old
terms, but they were afraid to do so.

Traffic Manager Denison was seen at the Mallory line offices last evening.

"The Mallory line has been paying its men 30 cents an hour for daylight
work and 40 cents for night work for the past five or six years," said he.
"If there has been any complaint on their part I have not heard of it.
During the suspension of the line many of the men have been out of employment. They have been going down to the dock, asking when the ship would
come in, and manifesting an anxiety to go to work. Some of them had been
turned out of their houses because they could not pay the rent. When the
quarantine was declared they were fearful lest the work which they soon
expected to get would not be forthcoming. It was our intention to give these
men our old employes, the preference. We had never been told that they were
dissatisfied; in fact, we knew that they were content to work at our scale
of wages, which we consider liberal, and which are in fact higher than we
can really afford. Many of the men were at the docks to-day, ready to go to
work, but this other crowd was down there to prevent them from doing so.
The Mallory line has been hard at work for over a month to get its service
to Galveston resumed. We have now resumed it, and were prepared to work.
Now, this is the reception we get--a mob at the dock to say that our ship
shall not be unloaded except on their terms."

"You can state," Mr. Denison resumed, "that the Mallory line cannot
afford to pay any more, and does not intend to pay more. We have paid
higher wages in Galveston than in any other port. In Brunswick, Ga., we pay
our men 15, 20, and 25 cents an hour, respectively. We are going to secure
men to unload our ships and have asked for protection. If we are prevented
from unloading them with these men we shall simply send the 'Colorado' and
our other ships to ports where they can be unloaded at our liberal scale of
wages and without interference."

"This is not our men striking. It is a lot of men preventing our men
from working. If the laboring men of Galveston do not want the employment
the Mallory line has to offer at the wages we have been paying, and at which
our men have been willing to work, we will send our ships to some other port.
We mean exactly what we say."

"I called on Mayor Fly at 12:30 o'clock to-day for police protection.
He asked me to first call on the police department. I did so. I was told
that there were two officers down at the docks, and that as no violence had
been attempted they did not consider it necessary to send more. They said,
however, that a detail of men was ready to go there at the first outbreak.
I again saw Mayor Fly and represented that the crowd was down there with
sticks and that our men were afraid to go to work. He ordered the police
department to disperse the crowd. The police drove the crowd back off the
tracks, but has not yet dispersed it."

"We have advertised for men to work on the docks, and we are going to
begin discharging the vessel at 7 o'clock this morning. Regardless of what
happens, we will not yield to the demands that have been made upon us. The
wages we are paying, as I remarked before, are the same that have been in
effect for five or six years. Our rates both to Galveston and to interior
points are lower than they have ever been before under normal conditions."

Mayor Fly was seen at his office last evening. He said that men who
desired to go to work on the docks should have the protection of the municipal
government, and would be permitted to work.

Deputy Chief of Police Amundsen said he would protect any man or men who
said they desired to work, and that he would permit no assemblies of men to
congregate as they did yesterday.

"Our men were ready to go to work. A crowd of men, most of whom, doubtless none of them have ever worked for the Mallory line, were there to say
that they should get the work and that they should get the price. Patrick
was up here in the office. I asked him if he had worked for the Mallory line.
He said he had not done so for several years, but he said his interest was

general; that if the Mallory line continued to get its labor at the scale
of wages we have been paying, he feared there would be a general reduction
for wharf labor. Now, I do not say that our scale of wages is fixed with
reference to what is paid the men who load and unload tramp steamers, but
I think the relative conditions should be taken into consideration in connection with this matter. There is a degree of permanency in the employment of our men; we have one ship every week and for several months in the
year two ships a week. It is not so with tramp steamers."

Mr. Denison has been connected with the Mallory line but a short time,
and he did not assume to speak as to the earnings of the men. So he called
in his chief clerk, Mr. DeMitt, to state to the reporter what the average
weekly wages of the men had been.

"When we have one ship a week," said Mr. DeMitt, "the minimum time
gotten in by the men is thirty-six hours a week; the maximum time is fifty
hours a week. With two ships a week the minimum time is sixty hours a week
and the maximum ninety hours. Figuring on day work only, at 30 cents an
hour, this would make the minimum weekly earnings of each man for one ship
a week $10.50, maximum $15; for two ships a week, minimum weekly earnings
$18, maximum $27."

NO CONNECTION WITH IT

It had been rumored yesterday that the colored screwmen were back of
the fight made on the Mallory line, and it was intimated that they desired
to see the wages raised, with the intention of doing some of the work themselves when there was little cotton to screw.

W. H. Davis, chairman of the board of directors, Colored screwmen's
association No. 2 called at The News office last night to disavow any connection with or responsibility for the demand made upon the Mallory line.[24]

"We have nothing whatever to do with this matter," said he. "When we,
as screwmen, worked for the Mallory line five or six years ago we were paid
40 and 50 cents an hour. When they refused to pay that we quit their employ
and joined the screwmen's association. Our employers, William Parr & Company
pay us our scale of wages, and we have no complaint to make. We have no fear
of a reduction in our wages, and have nothing whatever to do with the Mallory
line movement. It is all we can do to attend to our own business, without
meddling in the affairs of others."

Galveston (Texas) Daily News, August 31, 1898.

110. A MASS MEETING HELD

Patrick Says the Colored Union Is Affiliated With the A.F. of L.

There was a mass meeting of Mallory strikers and sympathizers last night
at the Texas press yard, Rosenberg avenue and Avenue M. No call was issued
and no notice of the meeting was published, yet from 700 to 1000 men, mostly
colored, were in attendance. The report of the meeting here given is from
the account furnished by George A. Patrick. It was late when word was received that a mass meeting was being held and the men were on their way home
when a reporter got out in the neighborhood. Mr. Patrick could not recollect
the names of all those who spoke. Two white screwmen made addresses, he said,
and he, Edward Williams, James Anderson and Bailey Sparks were among the
colored men who made short talks.

"We simply discussed the condition of affairs," said Patrick. "The white
screwmen who spoke told of the benefits of unionism. They said union labor
would stand together regardless of race, creed or color, and that prejudices
would be buried.

"The speeches of all the men were mild, calm and moderate. Oh, yes; we
discussed the affair of yesterday and we pointed out some inconsistencies. We
hope that whatever wrong was done will be righted by the law. We did not go
to the Mallory wharf with the intention of committing violence. We were not
desirous of creating trouble. We did not want a riot. We believe the shooting

was uncalled for and without provocation. We are proud to say that the
shooting of yesterday has but served to make our members firmer and more
loyal to our organization."

The speeches that were made were along that line, Mr. Patrick said.
There was no wild discussion or fierce language. It was simply the expression of men who thought a wrong had been committed.

"We want no violence and make no threats," said Patrick. "We depend
on moral suasion. We counsel peace, quietude and harmony. Of course, in
a strike like this there is always some display of bad feeling like the
attack on Abe Woods to-day. I am very sorry for Woods. Some one told me
a white screwman hit Woods the first lick and then some of the colored men
struck him."

"I hope there will be no fighting of any kind. We advocate moral suasion. We are getting good results from it. Why, twelve men have left the
Mallory shed. Two of them have joined our union. Five have received money
from us with which to pay their fare home. The others have quit out of
sympathy. There are two more we are working on to-night. I think we will
get them."

"In our meeting to-night we signified our firm intention to stick to
the scale of wages we asked for and to hold the union to its duty to aid us.
We are members of the American Federation of Labor. Oh, we will stick!"

"We tried to-day to get the Mallory line to submit the trouble to arbitration. Mr. Bornefeld, Mr. Skinner, Mr. Henderson and Mr. Kempner were
very kind in their efforts. We went as far as we could in making advances
to the Mallory line. We are very thankful to the gentlemen of the cotton
exchange."

Then with some show of mild sarcasm Mr. Patrick said they were also
thankful to Mr. Denison for his "extreme courtesy" in refusing to treat with
them.

Mr. Patrick misuses words occasionally, but on the whole speaks very
well, and has no difficulty in giving full expression to his ideas. He says
he is not an agitator, but a conservative workingman; he is a grandfather
and tries to be a good citizen. Good citizenship, he says, is the aim of
the union men, and surely it is not good citizenship to violate the law. It
was not the intention of the colored men to violate the law Wednesday, he
said, and they were not responsible for the trouble.

Galveston (Texas) Daily News, September 2, 1898.

111. WHITE OR BLACK LABOR

The Outlook for a Settlement Not Very Flattering to the Negro

The Houston negroes left for home yesterday afternoon and evening. Some
of the men quit work at noon and left on the Santa Fe, others left on the 4
o'clock La Porte train and the balance departed last night on the Santa Fe
7:30 train. Police Sergeant Paul Delaya detailed a squad of officers--Perrett,
Curtin, Plummer, Williamson, Jordan, Dave Henry and Whittlesey--to escort the
men to the trains in the patrol wagon, and some of the officers accompanied
the trains to the city limits. No attempt was made to intercept the laborers'
departure and all of them were delighted with the way they were cared for
while here and looked after on their journey home.

The Colorado is not quite loaded, but will receive the balance of her
cargo to-day and be ready to sail to-morrow morning. The ship's crew and the
extra crew carried on this trip will finish loading the steamer. The Lampasas
is expected to reach the dock this evening, and unloading will be commenced
to-morrow morning.

The Mallory line expended about $1200 in the unloading and loading of the
Colorado, which includes the crew's wages. In round numbers $500 was paid to
the Houston laborers, some of whom put in fifty hours time at 30 and 40 cents
per hour. They averaged two and three hours' night work at 40 cents per hour.

There being but the one crew, and that a small one, the work was not continued all night. One night they worked until midnight, and the other two
nights until 10 p.m.

Traffic Manager Denison, when seen by a News reporter last evening,
said he regretted that all this money was sent outside of Galveston when
the Galveston laborers could have had it. When asked if any contract had
been entered into or any agreement made by the Mallory line for letting the
work out by contract, Mr. Denison replied in the negative. He said that the
Houston men had expressed their desire to return to Galveston and be hired
for the work on the Lampasas, and unless something was done in the meantime
they will be put to work. "The places of the strikers are still open to
them, and if they wish to return to work on Monday they will be reinstated,"
was the way Mr. Denison expressed it. He said the strikers had not made
application to return to work at the present scale and he knew not what were
their intentions.

Asked if their places would be held open for them for an indefinite
period, Mr. Denison replied no. He said this unsettled state of affairs could
not be prolonged much longer. Some definite action must be taken at an
early date. He intimated that unless the strikers report for duty to-morrow
morning their places would be filled and they would be out in the cold.

There was a rumor current yesterday that the Mallory line had contracted
with a well known stevedore for the labor on the wharf, but the report was
not confirmed. A News reporter called upon the stevedore, who denied the
report and claimed he knew nothing about the matter. He was not opposed to
entering into a contract with the Mallory line to do the work and furnish the
longshoremen, but he said he had not entered into any agreement or made any
arrangements with the steamship company. If the work is let out by contract
it means that only white labor will be employed and the days of the negro
on the wharf will be a thing of the past.

Galveston (Texas) Daily News, September 4, 1898.

112. A BLACK POINT OF VIEW

The City Times, one of the organs of the colored people of Galveston,
had the following to say September 10:

"The strike situation remains about the same so far as appearances go.
Things are at work somewhere disintegrating the situation, but there is no
certain knowledge of what the forces are nor where they are at work. There
are many rumors but they are generally unreliable and hardly worth printing.
One, however, seems pretty well authenticated, and that is the Mallorys will
certainly not pay us more than 30 and 40 cents per hour, and that if they
can not obtain men at these figures they will load and unload their vessels
with their crews, difficult as it may be. It is hard to see how they can do
this unless they greatly increase the number composing their vessel crews,
and even then the work can hardly be satisfactory. The strikers should maintain a peaceable and orderly demeanor for therein is their greatest strength."

From this it would seem that the colored people feel sure of the position of the Mallory people.

In a previous issue the Times said:

WHERE WE STAND

First. We stand to uphold the law.

Second. For the protection of human life and property.

Third. We must agree with Mayor Fly in his advocacy on last Wednesday
in telling our colored laborers what the law was in cases of this nature.
But we don't by the eternal gods wash him clean for his six-shooter plays.
Nay! Nay! We further believe that if it is just and right that the rate of
40 to 50 cents should be paid our men for their labor that they should be
given it at once and the Mudcats should be immediately sent back home. But
on the other hand if it is plain that the Mallory people can't afford to pay
the 40 to 50 cents per hour then it is another consideration and it will be

to our people's own interest to be conservative, call and figure out some
plan that the matter should be at once adjusted to the interest of negroes
of Galveston and not those of Houston. This union may be all right; we
hope so, and it is never too late to do good but sometimes we make bad
mistakes by not being considerate and cool headed. Cases of this kind often
occur. We are citizens of this community. Our homes and families are
here, their support is entirely dependent upon the labor of this city. Our
earnings we spend here and not in Houston, and our cause must be given first
consideration, provided we are right in our demands. We believe the business
people of this city will see that our interest is taken care of if it is
justice, and that's all we can expect. And again we must not allow hotheaded
men to dictate our demands when they are out of reason, and if we do we will
be dumped and the result will be that every man and his brother will be
accusing each other as being the cause of them losing out. In conclusion
we are for what's just and right, fair and square, and no more, whether you
be black or white, grizzly or poor.

There is still another phase of the situation. One of the prominent men
in the ranks of the union, and a negro of more than ordinary intelligence,
who is recognized as a champion of his race and a man who has many followers
in the different negro organizations of the city, gave The News reporter a
statement in the presence of Chief Jones, which may throw a little light
upon the inside workings of the union. His name is withheld, because it
would not do for him to identify himself in the matter just at present. His
interview is substantially as follows:

"I am a negro, and am for my race first, last and always. I am with
them in their struggle for higher wages, and as a member of the union fully
indorse the organization and its aims and purposes. I do not refer to any
unlawful acts by some of its members, for the union does not preach such a
creed, but condemns riots or the use of force at any and all times. As I
said before, the union is all right in itself, and organized labor is what
the negro needs, but white politicians have made use of and are now endeavoring to use the union, or, rather, its members, as a political catspaw.
Politics is not supposed to enter into our deliberations or in anywise to
control the operations of the union, which was organized as a labor protective body and not as a political organization. We have many illiterate
men in our ranks. Ignorant negroes are to be pitied, because they are not
blessed with enough education for their own self-preservation. Certain white
men, several of them very prominent in commercial and political circles in
Galveston, have preyed upon the ignorance of our black brothers for the
purpose of feathering their own political ambitions and aspirations, at the
sacrifice of men who have stood by the negro, and in politics have received
the support of the colored citizens of Galveston. I know what I am talking
about and can furnish you with the names of men which I know would surprise
many of the good citizens of Galveston who are not aware of the scheme on
foot. (He mentioned the names of two well known citizens.) If I were a
white man I could talk plainer and make myself better understood, although
I know of what I speak, and the future will prove that I am right. When
these white men say they are heart and hand with us negroes, I know, as does
every intelligent man of my race, that they do not mean it. They may be in
hand with us and our cause, which we believe to be just, but in heart they
are only scheming for the successful consummation of their political ventures,
at the negroes' sacrifice of principle. When the negroes on the wharf organized and demanded a scale of wages which they decided upon and believe to be
reasonable and equitable, they did not consider the politics of the men who
refused to grant the wages asked for. It was a business proposition, and
the negroes never gave politics a thought. We believe we have the moral
support and the sympathy of democrats and republicans, gold and silver democrats and populists in our struggle for higher wages. But white politicians
began to work on the members, and have tried to convince the negroes that
certain political friends of theirs have indorsed the actions of certain men,
who in politics have lost a good deal of the support of the negro vote. It
is a shame that such conditions are allowed to exist in the ranks of the
organization. If the white politicans would leave us alone, I believe we
could manage our organization and let politics be cared for on the outside.
The shooting on the wharf was deplored by every sensible man in the union,

and it was and is the intention of the union to win out by their own efforts
without resort to any unlawful acts.   Unfortunately, the so-called riot
occurred, and now the white politicians are using this tragedy for their
own advancement and benefit and the downfall of the negroes."

Galveston (Texas) Daily News, September 11, 1898.

113. AFFILIATION

The colored union known as the Colored Labor protective union, was
last night affiliated with the American Federation of Labor , and will
henceforth operate under the federation charter which has been issued to the
new organization. A special meeting was held at the hall on Market street,
between Twenty-fourth street and Bath avenue, last night. An unusually
large crowd attended; in fact, the hall would not hold over one-fourth of
the membership of the union, which is claimed to be 2213. The hall was
filled early in the evening before the meeting was called to order. The
crowd packed the stairway leading up to the hall on the second floor and
extended down on Market street. There were fully 2000 negroes in the neighborhood for some time during the session. Many of them never reached nearer
to the hall than the pavement below others sweated it out on the stairway,
while many of them tired waiting around the street and went home. A system
was tried to permit every man to enjoy part of the proceedings and allow them
to sign the rolls admitting them to the organization. The system was to
admit 100 men at a time and then send them out after they had signed the
rolls, but the system was easier to suggest than to put into execution.
    With the crowd below mingled white men who were talking labor and union
to the men. Two of these men were very conspicuous and attracted no little
attention by their manner of addressing the little audiences on the street.
They believed they were doing great missionary work among their colored
brethren, but the negroes were not as favorably impressed with the preachings
of these men as appeared on the surface, for several of them remarked to a
News reporter who stood in the crowd that the white men should wait until
they were invited to come up and deliver open air services in the cause of
labor. One of the missionaries, while praying for peace with one breath,
declared war in the next. He told his hearers that they should never allow
the Houston negroes to come to Galveston and go to work. He admonished them
not to use violence or commit themselves to any breach of the law, yet he
bade them run the negroes out of town and not permit them to work. These men
did not seem to be representing any organization, but simply had taken it
upon themselves to go among the crowd and tell them what they knew about the
trouble, and incidentally a great deal that they did not know.

Galveston (Texas) Daily News, September 13, 1898.

114. POLITICAL PULLING

Lucas Luke, a prominent member of the colored screwmen's association,
was seen last night by a News reporter, and in discussing the strike situation
said:
    "Our people are determined in their demand for higher wages, because
they feel that the Mallory line can afford to pay them, and the work is well
worth the price."
    "The conditions have not changed at all, and I can not predict how it
will come out, but we all hope for an amicable adjustment of the differences."
    "Our men went into this thing as a matter of right, and with no other
object in view. I regret very much to see that some men, who are not in the
least interested in the outcome of this contention, are trying to make political

capital out of it. The other night two of these men were very conspicuous in their endeavors to persuade some of our men that Mr. Hawley is to blame for not having the strike settled in our favor, and telling us that his influence was used against us rather than for us. I hear it on the street that the negroes are not going to support Hawley. But you can say for me that these men I have referred to have axes to grind, and that our people are not going to be gulled in any such way.

"Politics cuts no figure in this strike, and the sooner these people know this the better it will be. We do not want to have anything of this sort thrust into this contention."

Galveston (Texas) Daily News, September 18, 1898.

II

THE PULLMAN PORTERS, THE RAILROAD BROTHERHOODS,
AND THE BLACK WORKER, 1886-1902

PART II

THE PULLMAN PORTERS, THE RAILROAD BROTHERHOODS, AND
THE BLACK WORKER, 1886-1902

On the surface, Pullman sleeping-car porters appeared to hold enviable jobs, with good pay and excellent working conditions. The belief was widespread that Negro porters were essentially contented cosmopolitans who traveled daily to places most people had only heard of. But life was not so glamorous for the men who tended the Pullman cars. Company spies were planted among them to report any potential union activity, and undercover inspectors worked overtime to catch porters who broke any of the innumerable rules. For infractions porters might be fined, or lose their jobs. They spent long hours on duty, and were required to perform every conceivable passenger service, for which there was no extra pay, only the possibility of a tip. In 1886, porters received about $70 per month, out of which they had to purchase uniforms and meals while on the road (Doc. 1-4).

When Eugene V. Debs formed the American Railway Union in June 1893, he intended to unite all railroad workers into one single union. White unionists, however, refused to abandon the restriction of blacks, even though Debs warned them that this policy would end in disaster. Not surprisingly, when the ARU challenged the Pullman Company in 1894, black porters and other Negro railroad men were not inclined to come to the union's aid. In fact, the Afro-American press openly urged Negroes to take the jobs which the strikers had vacated. In Chicago, some blacks formed an Anti-Strikers Railroad Union to even the score with the ARU. Apparently they succeded, for the Pullman Company defeated the strike, and the union was soon destroyed. In a Harlem speech delivered on October 30, 1923, Debs made clear his belief that the exclusion of Negroes had insured the union's collapse (Doc. 5-16).

Prior to the formation of the railroad brotherhoods (the firemen, trainmen, conductors, and engineers), blacks held many of the higher-paying positions on the railroads. From their inception, however, the brotherhoods not only excluded Negroes from membership, but they also tried to persuade the companies to eliminate those blacks who had already been employed. For example, the Brotherhood of Locomotive Trainmen called a strike against the Houston and Texas Central Railroad in 1890 demanding the discharge of black employees. When the company refused, and a strike failed, the Brotherhood went into court with a request that blacks be judged incompetent for railroad work. The court, however, refused to render such a judgment (Doc. 11-13). The Firemen and the Trainmen also launched a campaign in their official union organs to arouse support for white supremacy in the service. This campaign was accompanied by an unprecedented outburst of racist polemics in the brotherhood journals (Doc. 27-40).

With whatever contrivance was necessary, including an occasional murder, the four brotherhoods persisted in their efforts to drive blacks from the roads. It took decades to achieve their goal. As late as 1920, there were 6,595 black firemen and a total of 8,275 Negro brakemen, switchmen, flagmen and yardmen. But there was virtually no hiring of Negro replacements as the older workers retired or died, and eventually the brotherhoods achieved their aim of restricting blacks not only from the highly paid jobs, but from all job classifications other than waiters and porters.

THE PULLMAN PORTERS, THE RAILROAD UNIONS, AND RACIAL DISCRIMINATION

1. SPIES ON PULLMAN CARS

It Costs More To Watch Them Than to Pay Them

Earnings of Conductors and Porters Reduced by Fines

A New Contract Which Employes Must Sign

It is a common source of wonder among travelers who are accustomed to
buy their comfort in Pullman cars with liberal "tips" to the porter, whether
that functionary will be content to retire and live on his accumulations
after he is tired of work, or will continue his fork-over-or-suffer-for-it
system of taxation until he is rich enough to own the road. It is the
general impression that Pullman car men are well paid by their employers for
the work they do, and that whatever extortion passengers feel obliged to
submit to is additional remuneration of which the company chooses to remain
ignorant. But according to the conditions of the service, as related to a
TIMES reporter by a man who has been in it for years, this is very far from
the actual state of the case. The Pullman Company allows its porters wages
scarcely sufficient to pay for the clothes and food necessary to make their
"runs," and expects passengers, who have paid for their tickets and for the
additional accommodation supposed to be afforded in a Pullman car, to look
after the support of the porter, and his family if he has one.[25]
On the trunk lines running out of this city the pay of a Pullman car
porter is $16 a month. Out of this he is expected to pay for the clothes and
cap required by the regulations of the company, and for his meals while he is
on duty. The usual run is from New York to Chicago and return. Not allowing
for delays, he is on the road about 37 hours each way. Men who reach Chicago
in the morning start on their return trip the same night, or if they arrive
there at night they must be ready to return the next morning. If the train
is late in arriving at Chicago, it is so many hours lost from the sleep and
rest of the Pullman conductor and porters. As a general thing the conductor
can count on getting from two or three hours' sleep while his train is going
and coming, but if the cars are anything like full the porters cannot count
on so much as that. Supposing a train to be on time at the New York terminus,
the Pullman hands are allowed 88 hours off before starting on another trip.
If the train is six or eight hours late, not at all an uncommon occurrence,
it is so much deducted from the leisure time of the Pullman men.
While on the road they get their meals at reduced rates from lunch coun-
ters in railroad stations, or from a dining car if there happens to be one
on the train. The employe who gave the information for this article kept
track of his expenses for a year, and struck an average of 25 cents a meal,
75 cents a day, or at least $2.25 for the round trip. This he considered an
underestimate of each man's expenses for food in four trips out of five. A
porter usually has to buy two uniforms a year at a cost of $18 each. The
conductors have to get Winter and Summer uniforms at a cost of about $22 each.
Shabby dress or negligence of personal appearance is considered a misdemeanor.
The Pullman car conductors get a salary of $70 a month. On each train
the conductor is held responsible for the three cars on his train and the
porters under him. If the porters divide their "tips" with the conductors
as waiters do with head waiters in several New York restaurants, the company
is presumed to know nothing of it. A conductor's salary is supposed to be
sufficient for all his personal needs and his expenses in the service of the
company. Allowing $20 a month for meals bought on the road, and $4 a month
for his uniform, a conductor does well if he can get $50 a month for his
family out of his salary.
But owing to the system of inspection and fines to which the Pullman
men must submit, the chances are that the conductor will not get anything like
that sum. The conductors and porters are under the constant surveillance of

"spotters," as the train hands call them, or "special agents," as they call themselves and are called on the company's pay roll, who report at division headquarters the slightest infringement on the rules of the company. As a general thing, the Pullman conductor can no more tell a spotter from an ordinary passenger than the horse car conductors in the city can single out the company spies who are sent around to see that they do not knock down on registered fares. If a spotter sees any indications of untidiness about the Pullman cars--dust on the windowsills, scraps of paper on the floor thrown there by some heedless passenger, untidy looking berths or seats, soiled washbowls or towels--he reports to the Division Superintendent and the conductor has to pay for it. It makes no difference that the fault may have been a porter's or a passenger's, the conductor is held responsible.

The usual fine for misdemeanors of all classes is $2. A conductor considers himself lucky if he gets off with $6 in fines 10 months out of the 12. This makes a big hole in his salary. He has no chance to explain or to contradict the charges. The spotter is believed and the conductor must submit or leave the service. If the porters are not promptly on the railroad station platforms with stools to assist passengers on and off the cars when the train stops, ten chances to one the conductors get fined for not looking after them. But the greatest bone of contention and the most frequent source of complaint is with the magazines and newspapers. If a spotter finds a pile of reading matter tumbled loosely on an unoccupied seat he reports it. If the passenger happens to be temporarily chatting with someone in another seat, or smoking a cigar, and sees the conductor order the porter to straighten out or remove the newspapers, he is likely to make a row about it. Ignorant of the rules, he looks upon it as a piece of unwarrantable officiousness. Then the spotter reports the conductor of incivility to passengers.

This system of espionage hits the porters in a little different way. Unless the complaint against them is a very serious one, in which case they are suspended at the pleasure of the company, their wages are only docked for articles lost or stolen from the cars. It is not at all uncommon for a passenger to walk off with the company's comb or brush, or to carelessly smash a tumbler, and for this the porter has to pay full price. If he loses a berth check it costs him 50 cents. If he happens to have a keen appetite and an unfortunate month in losses the porter frequently finds that, aside from his "tips" he is actually paying the company for the privilege of working.

On nearly every full train with three or more Pullman cars, that runs over the trunk lines between New York and Chicago a special detective is employed to watch for graver misdemeanors on the part of conductors which may be considered outside the bailiwick of spotters. Necessarily a Pullman car conductor must handle more or less money for berths not purchased in the ticket offices. Usually a check is kept on this by a diagram, which must correspond with reports of tickets collected received from the regular conductors on the railroad. If a conductor makes an error in his diagram, a thing likely to occur at any time when passengers are dissatisfied with berths selected and desire transfers, he is fined for it, and if the offense becomes too frequent, he is liable to suspension. Until a few months ago a Pullman conductor was obliged to leave $100 or more bonds with the company as a guarantee, which was returned to him with legal rates of interest when he was discharged or voluntarily left the service. But now, in most instances, conductors' bonds are covered by the insurance system, the same as employes that handle money on the elevated railroad.

A conductor who talked with a TIMES reporter figured it. After careful consideration, he said that the Pullman Company paid three times as much money every year to spotters and detectives as their conductors' and porters' salaries amounted to. The detectives are usually employed from private agencies. To avoid possibility of their own detection they pay for their accommodation and incidental expenses of the trip the same as other passengers do. It is their business to report something and they report anything. The company's rules forbid a conductor or a porter to smoke or drink liquor while on duty. It was a common thing, THE TIMES'S informant said, for a detective to proffer a conductor a cigar or a drink and then report him for accepting it. He related this incident:

"Coming through from the west one cold Winter's day our train was blocked for three hours at a lonesome spot in the road by a snowslide. The Pullman conductor was obliged to be out in the weather a good deal, and on one occasion when he passed through a car a man was giving one or two acquaintances some liquor from what appeared to be his sample case. He called the conductor and proffered him the flask. The man shook his head, though greatly tempted, explaining that it was against the rules.

"'Oh, bosh,' said the supposed drummer, 'take a drink, man. We care nothing about the rules in an emergency like this.'

"The conductor accepted the invitation, took a drink, and went about his work. I offer no excuse for him, because he knew he was disobeying orders, no matter how strong the temptation may have been. His train arrived at its destination he made his report, and went home to bed. He had not been asleep two hours when he was summoned to the office. Very much to the company's regret, he was politely informed, he had been detected disobeying orders. It had been suspected for some time that some of the men were drinking on duty, and they had evidence beyond doubt that he had taken liquor at such and such a place, [mentioning the time and incident]. Such flagrant disobedience could not be passed over with a mere fine. He might consider himself suspended from further duty, without previous payment of the salary due him, for two weeks. The conductor afterward ascertained to his satisfaction that the man who offered him the drink was the very detective whom the company had sent out to confirm their suspicions. I merely quote this incident to show what some of the men employed as spies will do to retain their positions and earn their salaries. The conductor has no appeal. He must submit without a hearing or even an expostulation. His word counts for nothing against the detective's report."

Usually, in cases of accident where no blame could be attached to the employe, the Pullman men have been subject to substantially the same remuneration for time lost while injured as other railroad employes. Recently, however, the following iron-clad contract was issued from the general offices of the company and sent to the Division Superintendents, with instructions to obtain the signatures of the employes and return to the Secretary of the company. The italics are the same as in the printed contract:

THIS IS TO CERTIFY, THAT I, _____, have this day accepted employment by, and enter into the service of, Pullman's Palace Car Company, hereinafter called the Pullman Company, as _____, subject to the express conditions following:

First--That I may be suspended, definitely or indefinitely, with or without pay, or be discharged from such employment and service, *at the pleasure of the Pullman Company, or at the pleasure of any* General Division, or Assistant Superintendent, or authorized agent thereof, at any time, without previous notice, such notice being hereby expressly waived.

Second--That, in consideration of such employment and service, and the payment to me of the wages or salary now or hereafter agreed upon, and as a part of the agreement for such employment and service and the payment of such wages or salary I hereby undertake and bind myself to assume all risks of casualities by railroad travel, or otherwise, incident to such *employment and service,* and accordingly hereby release, acquit, and discharge the Pullman Company from any and all claims for liability of every nature and character whatever, to me, or to my heirs, Executors, Administrators, or legal representatives on account of personal injuries or otherwise.

Third--That I fully understand the meaning and effect of that part of the contracts made between the Pullman Company and the railway companies relating to the running of sleeping, parlor and drawing room cars, which is as follows:

"It is hereby mutually agreed that the said employes of the Pullman Company, named in article ___ of this contract, shall be governed by and subject to the rules and regulations of the railway company which are or may be adopted from time to time for the government of its own employees, and in *the event of any liability arising against the railway company for personal injury, death, or otherwise of any employe of the Pullman Company, it is hereby distinctly understood and agreed that the railway company shall be liable only to the same extent it would be to the person injured was an employe in fact of the railway company, and for all liability in excess thereof shall be indemnified and paid by the Pullman Company."*

I hereby undertake and bind myself to obey the rules and regulations of such railway companies in strict compliance with the terms and conditions of the contracts referred to, the same as if I were an employe in fact of such railway companies and in further consideration of such employment and service, and of the payment to me of such wages or salary therefore, by the Pullman Company, and of my transportation free of charges by such railway companies over their lines of railway, where any casualty may occur, if at all. I hereby release, acquit, and forever discharge any such railway companies from all claims for liability of every nature and character whatever, to me or to my heirs, Executors, Administrators, or legal representatives, on account of personal injuries or otherwise, *except* such liability as would accrue to me if I were at the time an employe in fact of such railway companies.

Fourth--It is distinctly understood by me that this agreement is binding upon me, while in such employment and service, whether in the United States of America, or the Dominion of Canada, or the Republic of Mexico.

The men were called to the division offices, shown this circular, and requested to sign it. Some of them did so without even taking the trouble to read it. Others who asked questions and were inclined to protest were told that all new men taken into the company's employ would have to sign it, and that old hands would be expected to sign also if they remained in the service. The compulsory contract has created a good deal of dissatisfaction among employes.

In making application for a position, either as conductor or porter in the employ of the Pullman Company, a man must face a formidable written examination involving a great deal of personal history. Among other things he must tell whether or not he has ever been married or divorced, whether he is in debt and if so to whom and how much, how long he went to school, whether he has any physical deformities, why he was discharged from or voluntarily left his last position, whatever that position may have been, whether he uses intoxicating liquors, plays games of chance or gambles in any way whatever, and whether he is willing to go wherever the company may see fit to send him, either in this world or the next.

New York Times, February 6, 1886.

2.   SLEEPER SERVICE

The Interstate Commerce Law has cut off so many railroad dead heads that the sleeping car system is on the wane. The persons who patronized the sleepers most were those who traveled on passes, but now having to pay fare they do not care to pay extra for sleepers. The poor porters who depend upon the generosity of the passengers for the tips necessary to eke out the miserable pittances the roads allow them for salary, are sufferers to a considerable extent, and some of them have already been forced to resign their positions, as they cannot pick up enough to pay their expenses. It seems that the Negro gets the worst of every deal, no matter who makes it.

There is little sympathy expressed for Pullman, however, and it is thought that he will lower his rates for berths in his cars, take off the useless conductors and place the porters in charge as conductors and porters, and pay them the same wages usually paid to conductors and, by these means, the passengers may continue to live in style. . . . .

Western Appeal (St. Paul), April 30, 1887.

3. THE RAILWAY PORTERS

The United Brotherhood of North America in Session at Chicago

The United Brotherhood of Railway Porters convened in Bryan's Hall, 446 State Street, Tuesday, at 1 o'clock. The opening remarks by Master Porter, J. P. Miller, were felicitous. Mr. D. E. Beasley, the Secretary, enrolled the following delegation:

> M. P. Miller, Chicago
> A. W. Bragg, St. Paul
> W. C. Day, Boston
> Thomas Bond, Chicago
> D. E. Beasley, St. Paul
> M. A. Charles, Boston
> Edward Grigsby, St. Paul
> M. W. Caldwell, Chicago

> Adjourned at 2 o'clock.

Evening Session

The brotherhood convened Tuesday evening at St. Paul's Church. After singing "Blest Be the Tie That Binds, Mr. W. H. Johnson, Master Porter of Garnett Lodge of Chicago, delivered an address of welcome. Grand Master Porter James P. Miller then delivered his annual address which was a masterly effort, full of logical reason delivered in a happy style. Mr. Miller is a very rousing speaker and the address was thoroughly enjoyed by all present. Mr. Miller said: "This Brotherhood of Railway Porters was organized for a moral purpose, to encourage higher associations for the porters and habits of economy. The position of porter, though lowly, should be filled by a gentleman. Some of the porters now employed are thieves, gamblers, and frequenters of the lowest dives. There are virtue destroying sharks on the cars who offer the porters from $5 to $25 not to see them carry out their hellish plans, and, I am sorry to say, the bribe is often accepted. The Company cannot rid themselves of those men unless they have the co-operation of the honest porters. Taking off Colored porters and putting on white ones would be swapping a little devil for a big one.

We don't believe in strikes, what would be the use? If we'd strike a black army one thousand strong from the hotels and barber shops would take our places. We are our worst enemies. It is a shame and disgrace that Colored porters do not receive better support than they now get. Let Colored men remember when they are shouting about golden slippers and "white wings" that God intends they should do well here. "Get education and money and all will be well."

Wednesday Morning

The Grand Lodge opened in due force with prayer by A. W. Bragg. Committee on credentials appointed, Bro. H. B. Fink moved that the present officers be retained during the session. Carried. Roll call of delegates came next. . . .

Thursday

The Grand Lodge convened at 10 A.M. with G.M.P. James P. Miller in the chair. After opening in due form the following officers were elected:

> James P. Miller, Grand Master Porter
> H. N. Valentine, 1st Asst. G.M.P.
> D. E. Beasley, 2nd Asst. G.M.P.
> J. D. Taylor, Grand Chaplain
> J. F. Morgan, Grand Treasurer
> Mark W. Caldwell, Grand Secretary
> W. C. Day, Grand Marshal

Western Appeal (St. Paul), July 14, 1888.

4.   PROPOSED PORTERS'STRIKE

There are rumors in the air of a strike of the railroad porters, and
on this fact a prominent railway official of Chicago says: "If they should
strike, we could fill their places at once, and were we unable to do this
the cars would run out just the same and neither the traveling public nor
the company would be inconvenienced a particle. Our conductors are able to
take the same care of the cars and passengers as the porters and can easily
fill their places in a pinch. If the porters should strike they would be
the most surprised lot of men that ever undertook anything of the kind. They
are the most insignificant part of our system and that is the principal reason they are so poorly paid." This is a grand bluff. The Pullman system
would be paralyzed if the porters should strike, as the conductors would
refuse to do the menial work the porters perform; not because the first are
any better than the latter, but because their pay makes them more independent,
while the porters are dependent on the public for their living, and, consequently, "stoop to conquer." This same official says: "If white men are
employed as porters there will be a chance to do away with the tipping evil.
A white person has not the same prediction for a gratuitie that a Negro has.
We would pay the white porters living wages, and the wage would be beneficial in many respects. Oh yes, they would pay the white men "living wages,
he thereby admits that Colored porters are not paid "living wages," and,
that the great Pullman monopoly forces its patrons to pay the poor porter
the wages it should pay. The APPEAL does not favor a strike, at this time
as it would work a hardship to the families or persons dependent on the
porters on account of the lack of organization, but we hope the men will see
the necessity of organizing themselves in one large union, and, then, if
the Pullman Company will not treat them like men, they can compell them to
do so.

The porters have the sympathy of the public as is shown by their tips
and they may rest assured that the public desires to have the Pullman Company
pay its workmen out of the exhorbitant fees it extorts from the traveling
public instead of being compelled, in addition thereto, to pay the wages of
the porters in tips. THE APPEAL has ever been a sympathizer with the porters
and they may count on our support to secure justice at any price.

Western Appeal (St. Paul), July 19, 1890.

5. A STRIKE THAT SHOULD NOT SUCCEED

"It really seems that the present railroad strike is unjustifiable. No
one will question that Count Pullman is a hard taskmaster, but that fact
scarcely justifies the tieing up of all the railroads of the country, the
stagnation of business and all the attendant evils. The whole public ought
not to suffer to help out the Pullman employes. Other and less radical means
of securing a settlement would probably prove equally effective."--Indiana-
polis Sentinel.

Pullman may be a hard taskmaster, that's neither here nor there, the
remedy is plain. We apprehend there was no string attached to those who
complained of his methods to the effect that they were compelled to bear them.
They had but to quit, throw up the sponges as they did, and had they gone
about their business, sought other employment, and permitted other men anxious
to work, to have done so, the stagnation of business, and general unsettling
of things complained of would not have taken place. To this color must it
come sooner or later in this country, or this country must bid farewell to
stability and future security. Either the great principle that every American citizen, whether he be a laboring man, a capitalist, a white man or a
black man shall not be disturbed in his right to life, liberty and the pursuit of happiness, must be sustained and enforced, or government of the people,
by the people, for the people must give way to anarchy, pure and simple, by
whatever name it shall elect to be known.

It is a principle as old as civilization that where justice ends, anarchy begins and it is so strange, that this great truth, emphasized so many times, and so terribly during the centuries gone, has to be learned over and over again, as though it was something new under the sun. The right to "strike," to quit work, to hunt for new fields, to seek to better one's condition, anent the material necessary things of life belongs to the sacred indisputable rights of existence and cannot be gainsayed or questioned by anyone, but beyond that, what? Because my potato crop runs short by the color of what right, am I to be permitted to forage and subsist upon my neighbor? Because of what I may deem sufficient reason unto myself, I shall determine my labor is worth more than it is bringing in market, am I to be permitted to dictate to my brother, when and how he shall dispose of his toil, and how much he shall receive for it? Because my skin is white and my brother's is black, should I deny to him in labor's name and those dependent upon him, the very thing that in the name of humanity I am demanding for myself?

Because the craft I am skilled in feels the necessity of revolt against certain conditions and forces, should there not be a length beyond which the revolt should not go, as interrupting the even tenor and prosperity of other crafts, and in the end, bringing about a general commercial and business destruction? The individual, guilty of one or all these misdemeanors is liable, and when arraigned before the bar of justice and public opinion, is made to suffer for his acts. Is it to be wondered at, and should it be different that organized individualism, confederated labor forces equally guilty, should suffer in the courts of public opinion, for similar violations of the great principles of the fatherhood of God, and the brotherhood of man? Take this American Railroad Union for instance. For one whole day, at its recent meeting in Chicago, its President, Eugene Debs, pleaded with the delegates in convention, that there should be no color line in the order, that railroad men of good standing, regardless of race, religion or color, should receive alike in the noble name of labor, the protection of the order, and the benefits to accrue from organized demand and action. But although he pleaded in vain, we honor him for his heart and judgment, just in proportion as we despise the organization for its final action. The man who cries thief, while his own pockets are crammed with stolen goods, need not be surprised, if called to an accounting. Organizations of men, whether inspired by the sacred name of labor, or what you will, who go into the court of public opinion for the purpose of demanding equality, should first learn to practice it themselves, and then other things being equal, their hope for victory is many times assured. Strikes have succeeded, and good has resulted from them, but very seldom, and then only when public opinion has backed them up.[26]

The Freeman (Indianapolis), July 7, 1894.

6. THE RELIABLE LABORER

The great strike which now deems to be sweeping from one section of the country to the other seems destined to endanger the life of the Republic itself. It is a remarkable fact that these acts of lawlessness are confined to white men. The foreign element always largely predominate in these disturbances, and the spirit of unrest is almost wholly confined to them.

Negro labor is the most reliable and contented in the world.

Throughout the southland, no alarm is heard. No declarations which do not comport with the spirit of our government go forth. The colored man labors on.

And yet but comparatively few white men realize the Negro's value and accord to him that support and recognition which he deserves. It is abuse that is his portion and the crack of the rifle, the report of the shot gun tell in no uncertain manner how with him life is brought to an untimely close.

But this situation of affairs cannot continue forever. The time will come when true merit will be recognized and the Negro's devotion to the southern white man's interests accorded the tribute which it deserves.

It is consoling indeed to know that God reigns and will bring all things right in his own time.

He knows what is best for his children, and although our fidelity to friends and faithfulness to duties committed unto us has been rewarded with stripes and followed by death the end will be all the more glorious when the divine injunction goes forth, "Well done thou good and faithful servant, enter into the joy of the Lord."

Richmond Planet, July 14, 1894.

7. THE STRIKE

The situation in the West has become alarming and the strikers seem to have been carrying things their own way. This applies however to the suspension of freight traffic. So complete has been the "tie up" that even the United States mail service has been interrupted and the mandates of the federal courts defied.

The President of the United States has accordingly through the War Department ordered troops to the scene of the disturbance, and Chicago has been to an extent at least under martial law.

A peculiar feature of the situation was the protest of Governor Altgeld against the action of President Cleveland in ordering United States troops within the confines of the state of Illinois.[27]

This is the doctrine of states' rights that this anarchistic Governor would set forth. The troops are still there and are likely to remain until the trouble is settled. As Attorney-General Olney has well put it, they are to assist the United States Marshals in executing the mandates of the federal courts, to prevent the obstruction of interstate travel.[28]

It is indeed a peculiar condition of affairs when a Democratic Governor should enter into a contention with a Democratic President as to the right to order United States troops to aid in the execution of the laws.

And stranger still ardent states' rights southern Democratic journals are supporting the President in this contention.

Richmond Planet, July 14, 1894.

8.   A LESSON THAT IS BEING LEARNED

We hope the report of an organization known as the Anti-Strikers' Railroad Union, composed of colored men, and growing, is true. Not until the Negro becomes cohesive and we may add sensible and combative enough to organize and swing together—thousands strong—for the rights, considerations and opportunities in the battle of life due him as an American citizen, will he be freed from commercial and business ostracism. The curse of past conditions, the federation of labor among the whites, and too much "come day, go day" spirit on his own part, has been against him. We hope the day of his emancipation from the aggressive hoggishness of his foes, and the lethargic, lazy incubus of his own self, is at hand.

He must do something, or he will do nothing.

If he would go up, he must get up! See?

L. B. Stevens, of Chicago, president of the Anti-Strikers' Union, in an interview in the Inter-Ocean, said among other sensible things:

"The attitude of labor unions and kindred organizations has become so aggressive as to be a serious menace to our system of government, and it is causing a revulsion in public sentiment. If capitalists and large employers of labor had given employment to the native-born American colored man instead of sending to the Old World and bringing here a class of foreign laborers who are not in sympathy with, and seem incapable of comprehending, American institutions many of the labor difficulties that now afflict the country would have been avoided."

The simple God's truth, every word of it, and more which could be said.
It took this nation two years of continuous defeat in the guage of battle,
at the hands of Mr. Jeff Davis & Co., to realize and appreciate the presence of the black man in the land, as a possible bullet stopper and defend-
er of the flag, and it may be by the time the mob spirit, now rampant, and
always present, has done its effectual work, and the smoking, gutted ruins
of factory, storehouse and business mart is all that is left of American
thrift and to mark the trail of the serpent, it may be when that time comes,
if not till then, that capitalists, those who employ help and are dependent
upon it, will learn to know the value and worth of the Negro--and learning,
dare to employ him. [29]

The Freeman ((ndianapolis), July 14, 1894.

9. THE RIGHT TO STRIKE AND THE RIGHT TO WORK

Everybody recognizes the indubitable right of people to work at their
own pleasure. Of course, people who, for any reason, being able-bodied and
able to find employment, but who voluntarily refuse to work, must not become
burdens upon the community. But in every sense the right of working people to
go out on a strike is acknowledged by the law and justified and established
in public opinion.

If any attempt were made to force a striker to work, the person or persons
so attempting would be either fuilty of assault or of false imprisonment,
and would be amenable to the law for their acts. Thus the law protects a
striker or any other person in his right to be idle, while any attempt to
reduce anybody to a state of slavery where he would be forced to work against
his or her will is expressly forbidden in the constitution of the United States.
Thus it is that a striker knows that he is free from any force or interference by any former employer.

The right to work ought to be as thoroughly protected as is the right
to be idle. But it is not. The enforced labor, which is denominated
"slavery," is expressly forbidden by the constitution of the United States,
in amendment XIII, and if any attempt were made to coerce a striker into
such servitude, the machinery of the United States courts and the entire
power of the Government, if necessary, could be put in motion to rescue the
subject of such oppression.

But there is no such protection to the right to work. The man who
wishes to earn his living by the sweat of his brow must fight his way as
best he can. Let some poor fellow attempt to work in a place left vacant by
a striker, and commonly he does so at the risk of his life. For his protection, neither Federal nor State courts are invoked, and neither Federal nor
State troops are turned out. He is denounced as a scab, and he may be
stoned or otherwise beaten by strikers every day in the week for any protection he will get from any fource. Of course, if such a man should be killed
outright, somebody might be called in question; but never, if his life be
spared, has anybody been punished for depriving, by violence and force of
arms, any man of his right to work in a place made vacant by the voluntary
retirement of a striker.

Of course, when by a strike the public are greatly incommoded; when
property is being destroyed and commerce is obstructed, and a general state
of social disorder and disorganization exists through the violence of strikers,
posses are sworn in, the troops are called out, and extraordinary means are
taken to preserve order; but nothing is ever done to protect men the right
to work. And what is the result of it? Why, plainly, that although there
may be plenty of men to take the places of strikers, they will not, as a
general thing, come forward because they know they will not be protected.
That is the experience in this city; it is the experience everywhere. The
troops will fire on mobs engaged in wrecking and burning railroad cars and
buildings; but when the outlaws confine themselves to beating and intimid-
ating men who are exercising their right to work, it is entirely another matter.

Strange as it may seem, this is a fact, and equally strange that nobody
proposes a remedy for it. Is there no sympathy for the man who seeks to
exercise his right to work?--New Orleans Picayune.

The remedy in our judgment is plain and we mistake the lesson that is
being learned every moment these days of unrest and turmoil by the justice-
loving, cool headed, fair minded people of this country if in the future
that lesson is not acted upon. The moment a trades union man, at the behest
and consent of his superior, dares to even threaten to say nothing of laying
violent hands upon a fellowman who desires to take up the work he has laid
down, that moment he should be restrained by authority and made to understand without the loss of time that the same liberty he arrogates to himself
to quit work is just as sacred to the man who desires to work.

The moment so-called organized labor becomes so solicitous for its interest that it will not stop at violence to obtain its end, that moment
organized society law and order should meet the mischievous bluff more than
half way, and in the name of human rights, and stable government, check it
before the fever to wreck trains and destroy property has been allowed its
devilish play.

To this color it is not coming, but is come, either the arrogated right
of trades unionism must be given full play, the country "be damned," or
anarchistic trades unionism must be squelched that the greater union shall
live.

The Freeman (Indianapolis), July 21, 1894.

10.   EFFECTS OF THE STRIKE

Negroes are tacitly but none the less completely excluded from railroad
positions on most Northern lines. No Negro is ever seen in a position on a
railroad which is in the line of railroad promotion. This industrial exclusion is a most serious injustice and, with other like exclusions, lies at the
bottom of much of the industrial deficiencies of the Negro. The Chicago
strike has led the Rock Island to place a number of Negroes in its yards and
switch towers. As in most great strikes the practical result of this upheaval
is to give a chance to men who had no chance or small chance before, and the
power of the Government, can be in no better business than opening a path to
work for men to whom it was before closed.

The Christian Recorder, July 12, 1894.

11.   THE RACE QUESTION THE CAUSE

WHITE EMPLOYES WILL NOT AFFILIATE WITH COLORED MEN

TERRE HAUTE, Ind., Oct. 6.--Grand Master Sargent of the Brotherhood of
Locomotive Firemen, who is President of the Supreme Council of the Federation
of Railway Employes, today issued a call for the meeting of the council at
Houston, Texas, Thursday next, to consider the threatened strike on the Houston
and Texas Central Railway. This trouble is the first instance in which the
race question has entered into the consideration of a grievance brought before
the federation. Mr. Debs said that not one of all the railway organizations
accepted colored men as members. The white railway men refuse to take the
colored laborers into their orders. There are many colored firemen, brakemen,
and switchmen in the South, but the colored man is not made an engineer or
conductor. Wages paid to such employes are not equal to the rates on Northern
roads.[30]

The white employes are endeavoring to raise wages in the South, but colore
labor can be procured cheaper. The colored railroad men have organizations

throughout the South, but they are not permitted to affiliate with the
white organizations. Owing to peculiar conditions existing in the South,
the questions to be considered by the Executive Council will be grave ones.
Mr. Sargent left tonight for St. Louis, where he will spend tomorrow with
a grievance committee of the Missouri Pacific, and will proceed to Houston
tomorrow night.

New York Times, October 7, 1890.

12.   COULD NOT DRAW THE COLOR LINE

ST. LOUIS, Oct. 10.--The trouble which has lately occurred on the Houston and Texas Central Railroad growing out of the refusal of Receiver
Dillingham to discharge negro switchmen, and which culminated in a strike,
had been satisfactorily settled. Grand Master Sargent of the Locomotive
Firemen; S. E. Wilkinson, Grand Master of the Railway Trainmen; F. S. Sweeney,
Grand Master of the Switchmen's Association, and J. W. Martin, Assistant Chief
of the Brotherhood of Conductors, arrived at Houston yesterday, and as representatives of the Supreme Council of the Federation of Railway Employes held
a consultation with the railroad officials. After a full discussion of the
situation the members of the Supreme Council concluded that the strikers had
made a mistake, that the color line could not be made an issue, and after a
promise on the part of Receiver Dillingham that the strikers should be reinstated the conference ended, and the men will return to work. The road
pays full Chicago switchmen's wages.[31]

New York Times, October 11, 1890.

13.   THE COLOR LINE IN TEXAS

The recent controversy over the color line in Texas is of interest
throughout the country. The Houston & Texas Central Railroad began to employ
black men in various departments of its service. Some of the white employees
struck, and S. E. Wilkinson, Grand Master of the Brotherhood of Railroad
Trainmen, in their behalf, applied to Mr. Dillingham, the receiver of the
road, for the discharge of the blacks. Mr. Dillingham flatly refused to comply with this demand. "The colored men," he said, "have rendered faithful
and efficient service, and I feel it would be unjust to them as it would to
any other person, to turn them out simply to put others in their places."
The question was finally carried to the Supreme Council of the Federation,
and that body decided that Mr. Dillingham was right. A noteworthy feature of
the incident is the fact that Mr. Wilkinson is a Republican, and a Grand Army
man, while Mr. Dillingham was a Confederate and is a Democrat.

The Nation, October 30, 1890.

14.   APPEAL TO NEGRO WORKERS

When we were organizing the American Railway Union in 1893, I stood on
the floor of that Convention all through its deliberations appealing to the
delegates to open the door to admit the colored as well as the white man upon
equal terms. They refused, and then came a strike and they expected the
colored porters and waiters to stand by them. If they had only admitted these

porters and waiters to membership in the American Railway Union there would have been a different story of that strike, for it would certainly have had a different result.

I remember one occasion down in Louisville, Kentucky, where we were organizing and they refused to admit colored workers to the union. A strike followed--a strike order exclusively by the white workers. After having ignored the colored workers and refused them admission, the strike came and the colored workers walked out with the white ones. Notwithstanding they had been excluded and insulted, they went out, and the strike had not lasted long until the white men went back to work and broke the strike, leaving the colored men out in the cold in spite of their loyalty to white workers.

Eugene V. Debs, "Appeal to Negro Workers," at Commonwealth Casino in New York City, October 30, 1923.

15. WILLIAM D. MAHON TO SAMUEL GOMPERS, NOVEMBER 22, 1900

                                    Headquarters
                                    Amalgamated Association of
                                    St. Railway Employees of America
                                    Detroit, Michigan.
Mr. Samuel Gompers
President, A. F. of L.
Washington, D.C.

Dear Sir & Bro:
    I received a communication from you sometime ago regarding the organization of the Order of Railway Clerks. I wrote to them for constitution and other information with the intention of calling a meeting and trying to organize a branch of their organization here. I have finally succeeded in getting a brief answer with copy of their constitution, but when we went to examine the constitution we find that it draws the color line and specifies --"any white person of good moral character, who is 16 years of age, etc., etc." I did not notice this at first but a friend of mine, newspaper man, and I were discussing the matter of trying to call them together, when he discovered the color line being drawn and would not take any interest in it, and I thought I had better write you. I told him that this might have been done in the early stages of the organization and was satisfied that they would not be admitted with the color line drawn. Then another thing, the constitution is very brief and does not specify clearly to my mind who shall be taken in. I thought it was mail clerks and such as that, but from the constitution I should judge it was all kinds of railway clerks, I wish you would make that clear to me also.
    Now, if we can take the papers as a criterion, there are going to be any amount of visionary propositions before the Federation, such as compulsory arbitration, etc., etc., at least the labor columns and the reports of the papers are full of it. One has it that a million dollar defense fund will be created. Another compulsory arbitration. Oh, I guess we will have to have our hatchets good and sharp when we get into Louisville. I received a very encouraging letter from Col. McGhill. He informs me that he has a room engaged in the 'nigger' quarters of the county jail for me, so should you not find me at the hotel, you may know where to look for me.
    Awaiting your reply on the questions above, I remain

                                    Fraternally yours,
                                    W. D. Mahon,
                                    International President[32]

A. F. of L. Archives, Incoming Correspondence.

16. JOHN T. WILSON TO FRANK MORRISON, AUGUST 22, 1903

International Brotherhood of
Maintenance-of-Way Employes
St. Louis, Mo.

Mr. Frank Morrison[33]
Secretary, A. F. of L.

Dear Sir and Brother:
    Replying to your favor of the 18th inst. I am glad to know you are
succeeding in your efforts to organize the colored workers. The Central
Bodies of colored workers organized in the southern cities will do much
towards clearing the way and making it possible for us to organize the
colored men in the small towns and along the railways. The sooner the white
men in the Southern States can be caused to realize that a labor organization
is a business enterprise, that selling labor is a matter of business, etc.,
the better it will be for them and the colored workmen. The men who buy
labor for profit care as little about the color of the men who do their work,
as a farmer does about the color of the mules used in cultivating his farm.
    In answer to your question concerning what my opinion of the attitude
of the party elected to succeed P. M. Arthur deceased towards the American
Federation of Labor will be. I see by the newspapers that his name is Stone.
I do not remember whether or not I met him, but I am of the opinion that the
policy of the B.L.E. will not be changed very much. For a number of years
they have acted upon the theory that there is a certain amount of cake in
the dish, and that if any one else gets more, they will have to take less.
I have considered the B.L.E. and the O.R.C. auxiliaries to the Railway Managers Association for some time and they wield considerable influence over
the members of the B.L.F. and B.R.T. The O.R.T. was under their influence
for some time but they discovered that their members were being used by the
older Organizations as message boys and that they were not getting anything
for their services.[34]
    Our people have suspended work on three or four different roads at
different times, and we found to our surprise that the engineers favored the
Companies.
    I prepared a brief history of the trackmens strike on the C.P.R. and
published it in book form. We will send a copy to you under separate cover.
The little book is entitled "The Calcium Light Turned on by the Railway
Trackmen." The reports and statements that appear in the book are facts. By
perusing it, I think you will conclude that it would be unsafe for us to depend upon the parties referred to, for even moral support, in case our people
are forced to suspend work in an effort to improve their conditions.

Yours fraternally,
John T. Wilson,
President

A. F. of L. Archives, Incoming Correspondence.

17.
THE BROTHERHOOD OF LOCOMOTIVE FIREMEN AND THE "NEGRO QUESTION"

W. S. CARTER TO SAMUEL GOMPERS, OCTOBER 3, 1896

Locomotive Firemen's Magazine
Peoria, Illinois

Dear Mr. Gompers:

Upon my return to Peoria, I found your circular of September 26th, also one of 9th of the same month concerning the Musician's Union. I also found a letter and a circular from Local Union #37 of the American Flint & Glass Workers. To each of these I will give space in the November issue of the Magazine.

You can well imagine how terribly disappointed I am at the results of the Galveston Convention in-so-far as an affiliation with the A. F. of L. is concerned. The negro question did it, and I fear that this same question will keep the Brotherhood of Locomotive Firemen from ever affiliating with the American Federation of Labor. I knew that there would be opposition, but I never dreamed of its bitterness. They did not care to listen to any arguments in favor of removing the word "white" from our Constitution, and you would have been surprised at the intelligent manner in which they came back at the A. F. of L. for demanding its removal. They say that the A. F. of L. *pretends* to insure autonomy to each of the affiliated unions, and then even before affiliation takes place, demands that our laws shall be changed so as not to discriminate against the negro.

There is no labor organization in the world that has suffered as much by competition with the cheap negro labor as has the Brotherhood of Locomotive Firemen. The Southern negro occupies the same relative position to the Brotherhood of Locomotive Firemen, as does the Chinaman to the Cigar Makers' Union, and you know what would be the effect if the Cigar Makers had a clause in their Constitution antagonistic to Chinese labor if the A. F. of L. demanded its removal.

Nevertheless, the question has been submitted to our subordinate Lodges, and if two-thirds of the Lodges vote in the affirmative, the laws will be changed, and the Firemen will make application for membership in the A. F. of L.

We shall do all in our power to enlighten our members upon this question, but I feel that there is nothing that would assist us as much as for the affiliated unions to help us in our fight. If Mr. Perkins, of the Cigar Makers, Mr. Prescott, of the Printers, Mr. McGuire, of the Carpenters, Mr. O'Connel, of the Machinists, etc., etc., would send a circular letter to each of our Lodges, kindly inviting the B. of L. F. to affiliate with them in the labor movement, it would have a wonderful effect. The influence would be more forcible than should you send them out, for this reason: You are looked upon as the head of the American Federation of Labor, and it is expected of you as a part of your duty to send out these invitations, while such invitations coming through others who are already affiliated, would no doubt carry the point.

In the October number of the Magazine, I have published an extract from the Grand Master's report concerning the A. F. of L., and next month, I shall take up the matter editorially, and I hope that when the "votes are counted" that "two-thirds" of the Lodges will have decided to "side-track" the negro question.

Now, Mr. Gompers, you know that my heart is set on an affiliation with the A. F. of L., negro, or no negro, and I want to ask you if you do not think that the A. F. of L. goes too far when it attempts to dictate as to who shall be eligible to membership in the component trades unions. I never looked upon this phase of the question before I went to the recent Convention, as I do now, and I believe that if you could have but heard some of the arguments made on this point, you would have to confess that the A. F. of L. does not grant autonomy to the affiliated organizations.

I sincerely hope that all will end well, but if we cannot get the necessary two-thirds vote of the Lodges, in favor of striking the word "white" from our Constitution, I will then contend that it is the duty of the A. F. of L. at its next Convention, to grant autonomy to each of the affiliated unions, so that the Brotherhood of Locomotive Firemen can become a part of the American Federation of Labor.

Yours fraternally,
W. S. Carter [35]

A. F. of L. Archives, Incoming Correspondence.

18. W. S. CARTER TO SAMUEL GOMPERS, OCTOBER 26, 1896

Locomotive Firemen's Magazine
Peoria, Illinois

Dear Mr. Gompers:

Replying to your favor of the 23d inst., will say that the exact wording
of the resolution is as follows:--"That the question of affiliation with the
A. F. of L. be referred to the Lodges and if adopted by a two-thirds vote
of all the Lodges voting, same shall be adopted." Our members will consider in voting on this question, the propriety of removing the word "white"
from our Constitution, instead of the advisability of affiliating with the
A. F. of L. To the latter proposition I have met but little or no opposition.
Our members, with but few exceptions, desire to affiliate with the A. F. of
L., but when it comes to removing the word "white" from the Constitution,
they seem to take great exceptions, and this will be the fight. If the
Brotherhood of Locomotive Firemen could be admitted to membership in the
A. F. of L. without any changes in the present Constitution, you could con-
sider the battle won. The reason I suggest this to you is that it will
perhaps aid you and our friends in offering arguments that will overcome the
opposition.

I explained thoroughly the advisability of removing the word "white"
from our Constitution and placing it in our ritual. I even said that if we
did not decide to affiliate with the A. F. of L., I believed it would be
beneficial to place the word "white" in our ritual instead of the Constitution, inasmuch as the negroes could not say we were fighting them. [36]

Mr. Sargent is on the Pacific coast, trying to reach an adjustment with
the officials of the Southern Pacific Co. I suppose he will be back by the
first of the month, at which time I understand he will take up the question
of the reference vote of our members. While I do not expect to go "out of
the way" to say much editorially on this question, I shall certainly quote
everything that other trades unions say with regard to the matter. Our
entire membership knows how I stand on the question, and anything that I
might do would have but little influence, but if they learn that the official
publications of other trades unions are interested in us and are saying kind
things of us and are desirous that we should affiliate with them, it will be
a revelation to our members.

With best wishes for the success of the movement, I remain,

Yours fraternally,

W. S. Carter
Editor & Manager

A. F. of L. Archives, Incoming Correspondence.

19. THE NEGRO QUESTION

I notice a great deal in the MAGAZINE about the American Federation of
Labor and the negro firemen. My sentiments have been spoken in nearly every
instance. I object to the proposed federation, principally on account of
having to strike the word "white" from our constitution. I don't want to be
affiliated with any organization when I have to be on an equality with the
negro. When it comes to that I will ask for a final withdrawal, and I will
not be alone on this ground, because every true Southern brother will be as
I am, and it would be only a short time until every Southern Lodge will have
surrendered its charter and I believe a great many Northern Lodges will follow
suit.

Look at the Knights of Labor. What became of them after admitting negroes
into their ranks? They collapsed, of course, just like the firemen or any

other order who will recognize the negro will do.

I was raised in the South, and still live in the South, and will always hold myself above the negro race. I have been running an engine for a little over three years. I have had white firemen and I have had negro firemen. The white firemen will burn less coal than the negro. On the same run a negro will burn from eight to nine tons of coal where the white man will burn about seven tons. The negro gets $1.80 for firing this trip. The white man gets $2.25 for the same trip and burns from one to two tons less than the negro. The least cost of coal is $1 per ton at mines. The negro gets 45 cents less than a white man and consumes from $1 to $2 worth more fuel. I wish some one could show me the economy of having a negro fireman. They (negroes) burn more coal and have less steam than white firemen and cause more delay for want of steam which frequently amounts to overtime for the whole crew. I have one (negro) firing for me, not through choice, but because I can't help myself. I wish some of the brothers who favor the proposed plan of federation could smell a sweet-scented negro just one time and I think he would change his mind when he votes. I bought a cake of soap and gave to one of them not long ago to go to the river and wash himself so I could stay on the engine with him. A skunk or a pole-cat would have been perfume for him.

I close by predicting that whenever we have to recognize a negro as a labor organization, that the Brotherhood of Locomotive Firemen will be no more in the South, and will die in the North when our Northern brothers get a little better acquainted with the negro.

                                          A MEMBER OF 426.

Birmingham, Ala.

Locomotive Firemen's Magazine (February, 1897): pp. 125-26.

                          20. HOSTILITY

     Hostility to negro labor, which has resulted in denying membership to the colored men in leading labor organizations, cropped out again last month at the convention of railroad brotherhoods held in Norfolk, Va. Press reports of an address by Grand Master Frank P. Sargent, of the Brotherhood of Locomotive Firemen, state that his utterances show "that one of the chief purposes of the meeting of the brotherhoods was to begin a campaign in advocacy of white supremacy in the railway service." A despatch to the New York *Sun* continues:

     "Mr. Sargent said that no violations of law was intended and no threats were meant, but that the white men of the South believed that the avenue to the locomotive should be open to whites alone, and these claimed the right to man the engines upon the highways of Southern Commerce. He said that the railway firemen who received in some parts of the South $30 a month, when they asked for higher wages, had been told that colored men could be secured who would work for $25. The speaker said that if this state of things continued more mutterings would be heard now in the Carolinas. He said that the South needed a civilization of intelligent workmen under the flag which has now crossed the sea. Other meetings would be held, he said, and agitation continued until the purpose of the firemen was accomplished."

The Literary Digets, December 24, 1898.

                       21. FROM LOCAL 289

     I have just received the March MAGAZINE and have read nearly everything in it, giving especial attention to the correspondence. In the February number I see a letter from "A Member of 426" concerning the "negro question."

It speaks my sentiments exactly, and I have been talking to other members of
my Lodge on the subject and they are of the same opinion. Now, I don't want
to be misunderstood in regard to affiliating with the A. F. of L., but if I
understand their constitution properly all labor must become organized to
accomplish anything, and it looks to me as if we *had* to take into our different orders *all classes* of laborers no matter what their avocation may be.
Show me a trade of any kind where there are no negroes employed! The carpenter, blacksmith, molder, trackman, or any other trade, is thrown into
competition with the negro where the law will allow. Why? Because they will
work cheaper and take more abuse than the white man! Now has the negro not
taken the place of organized labor in a great many cases? And then to think
a man who is a member of organized labor will want to take him into the order
and call him "brother." I saw a letter from Lodge 270 where the writer says,
"Why not educate the negroes and organize them?" Are we not educating them
now? What are our free schools for but to educate them equally with the
whites. And as to organizing them, how are we to do that unless we take them
into our orders and teach them the principles of organized labor? And when
once organized, even if the color line is drawn, are we not as one Brotherhood?
     I am not in favor of abusing the negro in any manner, but they should
stay in their place. I don't want it thought that he should be entirely
deprived of the privilege of earning a living at any trade he wishes to follow,
but I am not in favor of organizing him and calling him brother. Perhaps if
the writer referred to would come South and see what we have to contend with
he would change his mind. How would he feel if a Traveling Negro Fireman
should walk up to him while on duty and say, "You are burning too much coal.
I want that engine cleaned up. She is in awful shape?" What is he going
to do but do just as the negro said; for he has had his orders from his
superior officer, a negro. Such has been the case in the South. The fireman
can't say a word, for we all know what the result will be when we refuse to
obey our superior.
     When I hear a man talk as he has written it makes me want to tell him of
the experience of an old country preacher. The good old man was preaching
and in his sermon said that "the negro was as good as a white man and there
should be no distinction made between them." After the service he went home
with a good brother to spend the night and one who thought a man should practice what he preached. There was an old time "Darkey" living with this good
brother and he was well treated in every respect, but the good brother now
saw a chance to have the preacher prove his teachings; so when the hour came
for retiring he was escorted to his room by the host; There was only one
bed in the room and in this bed was the darkey. When the reverend gentleman
saw the darkey in the bed, he inquired if he must sleep there. His host
replied "Yes sir," left the room and locked the door.
     Shall we strike the word "white" out of our constitution? No! One
brother from Mt. Moriah Lodge No. 319 says: "No negro can get in our order
unless we say so." Now, how are we going to keep him out if we strike out
the word "white?" There are negroes who are just as honest and are as worthy
to be members of an organization as white men, and if they should make application how can we reject them? Only by their color? Then what is the use of
changing the constitution? Now if we should affiliate will it keep the railroad companies from hiring the negro at reduced wages? Not so long as the
law will allow it, and I think the best thing we can do is to "let well enough
alone." I have been a member of Mt. Lookout Lodge No. 289 since 1896 and
take a great deal of interest in the order, but when it comes to a lot of
nigger lovers putting me down equal with the negro I am forever done with
B.L.F. or any other order that favors negro equality.
     Should we affiliate would he not, in one sense of the word, be on an
equal with us? Will the company raise his wages to equal ours or will they
reduce ours to equal his? What have the corporations been doing in the last
few years in regard to wages? There are no negro firemen on the railroad I
work for, and I am thankful for it; but I see them every day on other roads
entering here. It is very amusing to be at the passenger depot when a train
rolls in with a negro fireman and watch the other negroes look on. The fireman would not "swap" jobs with President McKinley. Now I hope *all* members
who have the welfare of our noble order at heart will think the matter over

before they cast their ballot. It may be a serious mistake.

LYLE JOHNSTON
Chattanooga, Tenn.

[The statement is here made with the Grand Master as authority, that the present vote on the question of affiliating with the American Federation of Labor has nothing whatever to do with the negro question. The word "white" will remain in our constitution regardless of how the vote goes, in fact, the vote is not to change a single line of our present constitution, but to give each and every member an opportunity to cast his vote either for or against the proposition to ally the Brotherhood of Locomotive Firemen with the other trade unions of the country in the industrial struggle which is ahead of us. An official statement will be issued from the office of the Grand Secretary and Treasurer which will show just how many votes were cast for and against the proposition. No man can claim that he "did not understand the question" after the information which has been published in the MAGAZINE].

Locomotive Firemen's Magazine (April, 1899): 264-65.

22. THE RACE QUESTION

The race question in the South seems to be coming forward with more prominence of late than it has for years. It may be that with the acquisition of more territory people with mixed races, by this Government, is the cause of this fresh agitation; the people realizing that with the assumption of more of the "White Man's Burden" by this country, some method of controlling that burden must be established, that will prove more satisfactory than the one now in force.

It appears to thousands of Americans today that the fifteenth amendment, giving the negro the right of franchise, has not been the educator and uplifter of the race that it was designed and expected to be. The placing in office of negroes so illiterate and ignorant as to be unable to understand the first principles of law and justice has had a demoralizing influence on the race and has tended to bring them into greater disrepute, not alone with the people of the Southern States, but of the whole country. The result has been that in South Carolina, Mississippi and Louisiana laws have been passed, amendatory to the State constitutions, prohibiting illiterates from voting, and so worded as to practically disfranchise the negro voters of those States, and no others. A similar law is soon to be voted on in North Carolina, and no doubt will be adopted there. The whole tendency is to disfranchise the negro--to literally annul the fifteenth amendment. It is the logical conclusion of the relations that have existed between the white and black races for hundreds of generations, and will continue for hundreds more.

The immoral, shiftless, indolent nature of the negro, an inherent viciousness that leads to the committal of brutal and revolting crimes, their utter lack of ambition and desire to advance, are the things that are bringing about a reaction in public sentiment. Of course there are exceptions, but to the negro as a class it will apply.

It may be charged by some as a result of the conditions brought about by slavery, but while some of it may be traceable to that, and while the introduction of slavery into the United States, with its attendant evils, must always be deplored, yet the ignorant, licentious characteristics of the negro have existed through centuries in countries where he has predominated, as well as in those where he has been in the minority.

It may be classed as a step backward to disfranchise the negro, but the time is not far distant, in the light of present events, when it will be one of the leading questions of the hour. The freedom which has been permitted in the right of franchise in this country has led to much of the political corruption from which we now suffer, and has tended to degrade the right of the ballot. The ballot should be so restricted to foreigners coming to this

country that when they did become eligible to the franchise they would
esteem it as a privilege to be sought for and desired, and not as a matter
of universal license, free to all, as it is today, to the disgrace and
detriment of the American people.

While liberty and equality are the boasts of Americanism, liberty is
degenerating into license in many ways, and absolute equality, even before
the law, let alone socially or morally, have never existed even here. The
law never handles the rich, though criminal, Mr. L. as it does the poor
thief, Mr. P. It deals with the drunken debauchee, Mr. Z., vastly differently than it does with intoxicated "Weary Willie" who falls into its
clutches. Socially, legally, physically or morally there has never been
and never will be, equality between the members of the white races. Then
why talk of an equality between the white and black races, which has not,
and never will have, any existence except in the minds of theorists. It is
a condition hoped for, but which will never be realized.

In the Hawaiian Islands, where the franchise was permitted the black
race, it was but meagerly taken advantage of, and then not in a manner to
be encouraging for its perpetuation. Of course, the consent of the governed
is talked of as something that can not be overlooked, and among a people
where the capability of self-government exists it should be permitted full
sway, but that the negro of the South, or anywhere else, for that matter,
has arisen, as a race, to the opportunity offered him, cannot be demonstrated.
There is no use trying to avoid the race issue that is being constantly thrust
before the people, more and more frequently as the months roll on. Existing
conditions in the South have not proven satisfactory to the people, and while
allowance must be made for race prejudice, there is no doubt much cause for
complaint and room for reformation in the present existing relations between
the two races.

                              * * *

It would appear from the testimony of employes in the Bureau of Immigration before the Industrial Commission that our laws relative to the restriction of immigration are not properly planned and are not doing what
they were intended to do. Mr. Dobbler, chief of the Board of Immigration
Inspectors, testified that it was plain that immigrants were coached so as to
give answers to questions asked, in such a manner as to evade our laws. Dr.
Lorenzo Ullo, legal adviser of the immigration bureau, testified that the laws
were so contradictory that it was difficult to enforce the intent of the law.
For instance, a criminal, according to the law, shall be returned to the port
from which he came, and to the country to which he belongs. So a German
criminal sailing from Paris or a Chinaman from Rome, or other like cases,
would be free from the operation of this law.[37]

There is no actual law for the deportation of contract labor. It is only
by implying that meaning in the law of 1891 that this can be done, and even
means are found to evade this law by having someone who works for the corporation hire men to come and work in this country from foreign lands, and as
the man who hires them is a hired man of the corporation, the intent of the
law is evaded. It appears there is no law prohibiting the landing of girls
for immoral purposes. The laws appear on their face to fall far short of
what was claimed for them, and stand in need of radical changes.

While many newspapers and men claim the present immigration laws are all
that could be desired, it is evident they are not, and people so claiming are
either ignorant of the facts or have something to gain by so claiming.

With better times in the United States the flood of immigration has again
set in, and with apparently very little to bar its progress. Corporations
prefer the cheap foreign labor to the American article. The former is more
servile and more tractable, at least for a time. Pennsylvania receives a
large per cent of this undesirable element--Slavs, Poles, Italians, etc.--
until one can go in some parts of that State and easily imagine himself in a
foreign country. Immigration laws must be framed with due respect to treaty
rights, but this can be done and the laws so worded that a big per cent, of
this cheap labor, the criminals and paupers could be kept out, were it not for
the opposition such a law meets from the corporations that desire to retain
the club they have wielded so long over the heads of American workingmen.

Between the cheap negro 'labor and the cheap foreign labor, the intelligent American workingman is threatened in his desire to live and enjoy the benefits of our laws, to educate and raise up to some honorable calling the family about him without becoming virtually a slave himself, or permitting his family to sink into misery and squalor. The only reason that the safety of the rights of these men, who form the groundwork (and bulwark, in time of need) of the United states, is permitted to be threatened is that wealth is running the Government, without any regard to its welfare, but solely in its own interests. Possibly the coming Congress will amend the present laws so as to be more beneficial to the interests of labor, but so far all pressure that could be brought to bear on past Congresses has failed to secure legislation that was satisfactory, or if such laws as were secured appeared as if they would be of benefit to the common people they were vetoed by those higher in authority.

Locomotive Firemen's Magazine (November, 1899): 593-95.

24. MIXED LABOR

The abolition of slavery by Christian countries may be attributed to the business sagacity of capitalists, inasmuch as slavery has existed from a prehistoric period until capitalists decided that it was more profitable to use "mixed" labor.

Locomotive Firemen's Magazine (March, 1900): 195.

THE SOUTHERN NEGRO

As a part of the policy adopted by capitalists to depress their wage expense, and thereby increase their profits, negro slaves were first imported. Since the emancipation of the vast army of negro slaves, these slaves have become a part of what Hume called "mixed labor." These millions of negroes, taken with the millions of laborers imported from Europe and Asia—and the millions of Coolies, Spaniards, Hawaiians, Filipinos, Tagalos, Malays, and numerous other tribes recently annexed, provide a harvest of "mixed labor" for American capitalists. We will write of each in their turn, but now of the Southern negro.[38]
It is probable that the census of 1900 will show nearly eight million negroes in the Southern States. There is no quarrel between the white workingman and this horde of ignorant servile labor. The negro is there not by his own choosing. He is there to stay; a curse visited upon the white workingmen of the South and the North, by the sins of their fathers.
Northern capitalists, within recent years, have begun to realize the profits that can be reaped from Southern negro labor. The Civil War left but few Southern capitalists, and because of the sectional and political prejudices which came as an aftermath of the war, but few Northern capitalists ventured into the negro country. But conditions have changed; sectional prejudice is fast disappearing, and Northern capitalists are rapidly availing themselves of what is said to be the most profitable labor in the world, the Southern negro labor.
It is said that we have the Southern negro with us and we must make the best of it. Too true! But how shall we make the best of it? The ex-slaves of the South and their progeny, are of the same disposition, the same ambitions and hopes, and the same blood as that of their forefathers. While in cities more or less enlightenment has broken in upon their intellects, the vast majority are practically what they were at the time of their emancipation. This is no fault of theirs; there is no war to be made upon them; they are not

responsible for their presence in this country, but the white workingman will learn to curse the day, and the men connected with their coming!

One of the leading commercial publications, in America, is *The Tradesman*, of Chattanooga, Tenn., and one of the most interesting numbers of that journal ever published, is the January, 1900, issue. The book is largely devoted to a symposium on the South and its future. Articles are contributed by the representative men south of the Ohio and east of the Mississippi. Ex-Governor Northern, of Georgia, says of the relation between colored labor and capital:

By those who do not know, it is urged that the presence of the negro in the South will greatly hinder industrial development. This result does not necessarily follow. On the contrary, the negro is one of the South's best undeveloped resources. He is, by far, better adapted to outdoor conditions at the South than any labor now accessible to us. Properly trained, as is now the policy of the wisest of his leaders, the negro will be well fitted, technically, for all the demands necessary to meet industrial development along the lines upon which his services may be required.

The average negro is loyal and tractable. He will grow to be easily managed, as the years advance; and he will be found to endure hard labor at the South much more satisfactorily than the foreign element generally used in this way. His furnishings are very much less expensive, and his hire, therefore, requires that much less outlay. Under the system of training now commended and generally pursued for the betterment of the negro, he will grow in a degree commensurate with the South's development, and he will become, more and more, a factor for the South's successful progress. We must handle him as the negro of the future, and not as the negro of reconstruction antipathies and antagonisms.

Whilst the negro is not beyond criticism in some particulars, we cannot afford to displace him, with nothing better in sight than the prospects for supply now open.

The constantly disturbed social conditions of the North and West are unknown at the South. Because of the character of our labor, the South is practically, and in some sections absolutely, a stranger to riots, strikes and ugly uprisings among the people, in the arraignment of classes or conditions. Such business prosperity will be easily maintained if we adhere to our present relations.

In a few years, in my candid judgment, the negro will not only be worth far more, because of his better adaptation, on our farms, but he will be found working intelligently along all lines of industrial development and growth among our people. If we care for the negro properly and train him intelligently for his own profit and our usefulness, he will become a developed resource and a valuable factor in the betterment that awaits us in the future.

The Secretary of the Chamber of Commerce of Huntsville, Ala., contributes an article entitled "The South; Its Opportunities and Necessities," in which he says:

There is one prime and all-important movement needed at this time to put the South in the place where Dame Nature so clearly intended she could occupy, and that is, the creation of a stronger and more general public sentiment in this section favorable to industrial interests and industrial progress. That sentiment should establish as its first work, through proper legislation, the correct relation between labor and capital, and not leave it to the possibility of disturbance at the hands of labor agitators on the one side or political demagogues on the other.

In view of the evils that have afflicted industrial centers in the North from these sources, the South should now take this matter in hand while she can, and make it a crime to inaugurate a strike that in any way affected the general public. It is about time in the career of our common country when the rights of the public should be considered at all times, rather than see them ruthlessly trodden under foot at the behest of labor unions, as is the case in every strike of a general nature. It is the worse stain on the pages of our boasted civilization that public rights can be ignored to make way for the supposed rights of labor, under the command of disgruntled individuals. The South was whipped into giving freedom to the negro, now let her set an example to the world of not only maintaining that freedom, by giving the negro the right to work for whom he pleases and for what he pleases; not only this, but guarantee the same right to every white person within her borders.

There should be state boards of arbitration in every Southern state, and these should be charged with the duty of inculcating and maintaining proper relations between labor and capital, employers and employes; and to do this efficiently they must be beyond the reach of political influence or control. When the South puts herself in this shape she can feel that her industrial structure is based upon safe and sure foundations, and she may not feel thus if this is neglected.

There is also need of a better sentiment throughout the South toward capital invested in corporations. It should be just as easy for a corporation at any point in the South to secure justice in all matters, as it is for an individual; and if any differences should be known it should be rather in favor of than against corporations, for they are the greatest agencies available for the upbuilding of the South. These are the principal objects to which public sentiment in the South should be turned at this time, and it was to awaken sentiment in this direction that the Southern Industrial Convention was held at Huntsville, Ala., a few weeks ago.

It was noted from the above that the gentleman states that the negro should be protected from "the possibility of disturbance at the hands of labor agitators, and that the South should now take this matter in hand, while she can, and make it a "crime" for the negro to strike. It will be noted that while combinations of labor (trades unions) are to be suppressed by law, combinations of capital (corporations) are to be promoted. He believes that in matters of "justice," the corporations should have a greater share than individuals.

The President of the Agricultural College of Alabama writes of "Negro Labor and Labor Organizations," as follows:

The South has the best labor in the world. It is true that the negro is not always mindful of his obligation; but no community, with negro labor, will ever go to bed in peace and get up next morning and find its entire business paralyzed and a howling mob often making selfish and unrighteous demands.   The labor unions have been introduced into the South and unless regulated by the stern, positive sense of justice of the business community, or by legislative limitations, will bring into the South disorders which will exceed the disturbances of "reconstruction days."

As I have above stated, the South, having settled most satisfactorily all of her past problems, should not now permit the needless introduction of grave questions, which will not only injure the progress and prospects of her strongest labor element numbering millions, but which must domineer and cripple capital itself.

The South should continue to offer protection to every class of honest labor which may seek employment within her borders. The negro has a priority claim upon every class of work in the South which he is capable of doing, and he appeals to the South, through public sentiment and legal enactments, to protect him in the enjoyment of his birthright. He does not ask that others be debarred, nor does he desire such discrimination; but he asks for only a chance to stand or fall on his merits in any industrial field in the South.

Unless the Southern people regulate by law the operations of labor unions and labor organizations, as well as mark out an equitable course for capital, the best labor in the world will be ultimately driven out of her markets; and when the South permits this, her best and most loyal laborers will be gone.

When the white man brings white labor to displace his true and tried friend, the negro, then will Communism drive the white man's coach, Nihilism cook and serve his food, Agrarianism plow his fields and the red flag of Anarchy float over every Southern industry. Can the negro and can the South afford to run wild over the suffrage question? Or can both sit supinely down while these subtle serpents wind their loathsome and deadly coils around our free institutions and throttle every element of justice and liberty in them? [39]

Between this Southern gentleman's love for the negro and his hatred of white labor, he grows eloquent. Since when has the negro been his "true and tried friend?" The gentleman positively denies the right to strike to his "true and tried friend, the negro." Such ranting is laughable to any intelligent man--except a capitalist, or a henchman of capitalists, who hopes to reap wealth from ignorant colored labor, a labor that is more profitable than chattel slavery. These insane shrieks of the President of an Alabama college are like those of a wild animal which fears that a portion of his prey

will be taken away from him. This love of the Southern capitalist for his
"most loyal laborers," is like that of a hungry wolf for the sheep he has
within his power. Any person who would warn the "sheep" from his "true and
tried friend," the "wolf," is guilty of Communism, Nihilism, Agrarianism and
Anarchy!

The person who writes this article, and one other man employed in this
office, were born and grew to manhood in Southern States. They know that
the sentiments expressed in this college president's writings no more express the sentiment of Southern people (other than capitalists and their
henchmen), than do "government by injunction," and "Idaho outrages" represent the sentiments of Northern people. The white man of the South has a
burden to bear that is almost heart-breaking, because of the presence of
the millions of colored laborers whom Southern Capitalists "love" so much.
The white man in the South finds his wages regulated by this "most loyal
labor." The capitalists of the South reap fortunes and leisure from this
"most loyal labor." But let us be specific.

Within recent years, before the advent of labor organizations, white
and negro men fired locomotives for less than one-fifth the wages paid to
white men in localities where negro firemen were not employed. On the Sea-
board Air Line, the distance from Atlanta, Ga., to Abbeville, S. C., is
about 139 miles. The wages paid to negro or white firemen was one dollar
per day. If the engine went over the division twice in one day, making 278
miles, the wages remained one dollar per day. If the white man refused to
accept this pittance, a negro gladly took his place.

On what is now known as the Atlanta, Knoxville & Northern, the distance
from Marietta, Ga. to Knoxville, Tenn., is about 205 miles. The pay for firing a locomotive this distance was $1.25.

What the Alabama College president calls the "Anarchist," came--and
conditions are improving, from the workingman's point of view. The Brotherhoods have escaped the death to which capitalists would assign them, and the
firemen on these roads are now better paid.

The capitalists who owned the paper mill at Marietta, Ga., employed
white women at twenty cents per day. An "Anarchist" came into their midst,
and they struck for better wages. Forthwith these capitalists resorted to
their "most loyal labor"--the negro, but were compelled to pay fifty cents
per day to get any women to work. While that strike resulted in the sub-
stitution of colored for white labor, it also resulted in increasing the
wages in the Marietta paper mill from twenty cents per day to fifty cents
per day. What the wages are, at this time, is not known, but organized labor
left its mark.

According to the report of the Bureau of Labor Statistics of North Caro-
line, for 1897, there were employed in the cotton and woolen mills of that
State, 6,822 women, who earned from forty-seven to sixty-six cents per day,
and 6,046 children who earned an average of thirty-one cents per day. Skilled
machinists earned $1.68-1/2 per day; engineers $1.46; firemen eighty-six cents;
skilled labor (men) ninety-nine cents. If the white man, woman or child refused to labor for such profit-breeding wages, there were millions of colored
men, women and children who would gladly take their places.

The city of Atlanta, Ga., in the face of such threats as are made by the
president of the Alabama College, has become one of the best union-labor cities
of the country. The white men of the South are organizing for their own defense and are extorting legislation in behalf of humanity. The murderous convict lease system, which capitalists had adopted, has succumbed to the attacks
of the white workingman of the South. In many mills in the South, capitalists
worked little children twelve and fourteen hours a day in order to add to their
profits, until the white workingmen forbade it. The Atlanta *Journal of Labor,*
of January 27, 1900, contains the following item:

A Georgia cotton mill president communicates his fears to *The Constitution*
that another effort will be made at the next session of the Legislature to deprive the barons of their present privilege to draw fifty to ninety-three per
cent, dividends from the life-blood of little children. Poor man!

Mr. Jerome Dowd, professor of Economics and Sociology, Trinity College,
North Carolina, says in the February, 1900, issue of *Gunton's Magazine:*

Perhaps another reason for the poor wages in the South is the absence of
any labor organizations. Farm laborers are too isolated for cooperation, while
the operatives in factories, being mostly women and children, of course cannot
effect an organization.[40]

Having suggested some of the causes of cheap labor in the South, let's now look at some of the effects. First, what are the effects upon other sections of the country? The most pronounced effect is the lowering of wages in textile industries. Wages have been affected also in other lines of industry, although in a less marked and more silent manner. For instance, the employment of negroes in the coal mines of West Virginia, enabling the operatives to sell coal cheaper than could be done in any other part of the country, no doubt played a part in precipitating the cut-throat competition among operators in 1897, bringing down the price of coal and labor in other States, and inaugurating the great strike of that year.

There can be no doubt that the cheap labor in the iron industries of the South has been a factor in the decline in value in iron ore and iron fabrics within the past few years.

Shifting the point of view, let us ask: What are some of the effects of cheap labor upon the South? That many manufacturers are piling up fortunes is beyond question. That wealth is vastly augmenting itself is no less certain. But how are the masses withstanding the sudden revolution from an agricultural to a manufacturing life? How is the eleven and a half hours work-day affecting the well-being of the laborers? How is the employment of children affecting the educational progress of the country, and what will be the final outcome in respect to morals, religion, politics and civilization?

In commenting on such conditions, Professor Gunton says in his *Magazine*, the same number in which Professor Dowd's article appears:

Although the wages paid in the South are a marked improvement on what the same laborers had previously received, they are from ten to forty per cent lower for the same work than the wages paid in the Eastern States. The price of weaving, for instance, is about fifty per cent more in New England than in the South. Six and one-fourth cents a cut (fifty yards) is the price for weaving on the improved (Drapper) looms, as against ten cents in New England, where more than three-fourths of the weaving is done on looms for which nineteen and eight-tenths cents a cut is paid.

Since the South has quite as good machinery as the East, these lower wages (and, where day workers are involved, longer hours) very largely result in greater profits to Southern manufacturers. The dividends recently declared in the Southern corporations range from twelve to fifty per cent, and in some few instances more. Whenever a dull time comes and competition between the East and South sets in, Eastern manufacturers under present conditions will be very hard pressed, if not crowded to the wall. The Southern manufacturers will be able to drop prices to a point that will involve loss to their Eastern competitors and still have comfortable profits for themselves.

Now if they are able to do this at all it will be because of this cheaper labor made possible by the low standard of living, the working of babes, and the raising of a generation of ignorant, stultified citizens. The question for the economist and the statesman to ask is: When this inevitable pressure of competition comes, is it for the advantage of the South, for the advantage of the nation, that the standard of the Eastern operatives should be lowered, or that of the Southern operatives raised? One or the other of these is sure to come when this competition arrives.

The reason that white labor is cheap in the South is because if it were not cheap negro labor would be substituted.

Such conditions are the white man's burden in the South, and if the boasts of capitalists, who have their money invested there, are carried out, this burden will some day be borne by the white man of the North. During the last panic the cotton and woolen mills of the New England States reduced wages, it is reported, in some instances, as much as twenty per cent. The only reason given for this reduction was that Southern mills, with their cheap labor, could supply the demand for cotton and woolen goods cheaper than these goods could be produced in the New England States.   Southern capitalists, most of whom are Northern men, boast that in the near future the South will lead in cotton manufactures because "they have the material and labor where each are cheapest."

During the last panic, when business stagnation and wage reductions swept over the iron-producing centers of the North, ships loaded with Alabama pig iron were sent to Europe. The boast was that iron could be produced in Alabama cheaper than in any other place in the world, because of the cheap colored labor.

When the competition of these cotton mills in the "colored belt" drive those in New England into bankruptcy; when the competition of these iron producers in the "colored belt" put out the fires in the great iron plants of the North; when armies of cheap colored miners from the South overrun the mining regions of the North, then indeed will the Southern negro be a burden borne by all American white men.

Locomotive Firemen's Magazine (March, 1900): 195-200.

25. A CALL FOR THE ADMISSION OF BLACKS INTO THE BROTHERHOOD OF LOCOMOTIVE FIREMEN

The Negro and Organized Labor in the South

I call attention to what seems to be an important question, the Negro, more so in the South. He is, as he stands today unorganized in labor. There are very few unions that will take him in or co-operate with him in any way. We should take him into our labor unions, teach him and educate him. Then we can go on congratulating ourselves upon the wonderful strides we have made in organization.

The Negro, today, is rarely dissatisfied and never dissatisfied intelligently. Take for instance, Mr. Booker T. Washington, he is the best example of the Negro intellect in the United States and is undoubtedly a superior man, for he is doing his best to help to educate his fellows.

I think we can make a big improvement in the Negro by taking him into our labor organizations for, as he is, there is no ambition in him; he lacks the vital force of dissatisfaction. So let us teach him what our great organizations are for--then you will see a big improvement in his economic condition as well as that of the South. I think this will help to solve the labor problem in the South. The Negro will accept his inferiority to the white man at all times. So let us go on with whatever we have to do that means universal good, fear nothing, ignore all obstacles, and throw ourselves into the effort, and know that we are setting electric forces into action which shall surely some time bring in the results which we desire. No great worthy purpose is ever lost.

GEORGE H. PETERS.
New York, N.Y.

Locomotive Firemen's Magazine (August, 1902): 286.

26. FIREMEN RESPOND TO THE CALL FOR ADMISSION OF BLACKS

I have just read an article in the August issue of the MAGAZINE, entitled "The Negro and Organized Labor in the South." The brother's motives may be all right, but his article will receive a cup of very cold water, wherever it is read in the South.

The negro can organize on his own responsibility if he likes, but he can never affiliate with southern organizations of any kind. The fireman of the South have yet a great work to do among themselves, without crossing the color line and reaching out after Mr. "Burr Head," to assist him to a place of safety and security, protected by the mantle the Locomotive Firemen now wears with pride, bought with a great price.

What has the negro done to merit recognition by the Firemen? The brother from New York says the negro will accept his inferiority to the white man at all times. Perhaps this is so where he lives, but all southern men would laugh at the brother's ignorance of the negro, as we find him in the South, for if he is given a foot, he tries to take a block. In many, many cases, he is thick headed and non-progressive, and when he goes to school a couple of years he begins to think he knows it all, and it only makes a worthless fool of him. The southern man has done far more to advance and uplift the negro than he is given credit for, but we draw the line when it comes to taking him into our worthy order.

If the brother is really desirous of helping the organization in the South, let him use his influence toward inaugurating a system whereby subordinate lodges will receive closer attention from Grand Lodge officers, and for this, he will receive consideration and praise from Southern firemen.

Member of 522
Shreveport, La.

* * *

The Negro Problem

In the August number of the MAGAZINE, I noticed an article from the pen of a New York brother in regard to the negro problem in the South, and would like to ask the brother what he knows about the negro problem in the South? Very little, I should judge.

It is very hard for me to understand how a white man can advocate the admission of such an indolent, untrustworthy, shiftless creature into our labor organizations. To some extent he compares the average negro to Mr. Booker T. Washington, which I think is absurd. If the brother had lived in the South as long as the writer has, I am sure no such article would ever have appeared above his signature. If he is a locomotive fireman, he must at some future time hope to become an engineer and, as such, how would he like to have a negro as a daily companion. He may think now that it would be agreeable, but if he were to try it for a short while he would be of a reverse opinion.

So far as educating and elevating the negro, I think it almost as well to educate a hog, for the animal cannot accomplish any harm with his education, while the negro can. I will give you a few instances which have come under my observation, and which I am prepared to prove. In the town where I was raised, there was a young negro boy who was given the best educational advantages that the place afforded, and was also sent away to a higher school. When he had completed his education he returned home and tried his hand at forgery, and the last account I had of him he was spending a term in the State's prison. Another instance is of an educated negro preacher who was preaching in a town where I resided for awhile. He put his education to the elevating service of using, through the pulpit, every means of making the resident negroes rebellious.

I could cite other instances but for the want of space. These evidences of the negro's treachery are nothing to be compared with that of the criminal assaults, almost daily made upon our mothers, wives and sisters. I know of an instance within the borders of this state, where a northern lady came here as a missionary to the benighted negroes, and as a return for her kindness and charity, one of her students criminally assaulted her and was hanged for the crime.

We railroad people in the South are sufficiently amused with the negro as train hands and firemen, so much so that we do not want any of his antics in the lodge room. One of his characteristics is that if he feels like it he will report for duty, and if not he will lay off and "rest up."

Social equality is something that will never be tolerated in the South. When the negro presents himself to become a member of a Southern labor organization, on the day of balloting, black marbles will be at a premium.[41]

Member of 76.
Berkley, Va.

* * *

Organized Labor and the Negro in the South

I feel it incumbent upon me, in behalf of the members of the labor
unions throughout the South, to reply to the article published in the August
issue of the MAGAZINE wherein a brother from New York advocated the organization of the negro firemen of the South. If the northern brother believes
this would be a good plan, I would suggest that he introduce him into his
own lodge first. We of the South do not wish to interfere with the negro
where he is. We are content to organize white labor wherever we find it.
It is repulsive to any working man in the South, knowing the conditions he
does, to entertain such a proposition as has been set forth by the correspondent from New York. There is no point of equality existing between the
whites and the blacks as they exist in the South, and the latter are in no
way qualified to sit in our council rooms. We have the proper respect for
a negro and his labor in its proper place, but that is by no means on a
locomotive. The brothers of the North can admit the negro to membership if
they desire to do so, but he will never be admitted to membership in a lodge
south of the Mason and Dixon line, unless it is the intention to do away
with the Brotherhood in the southern country entirely.

It would be well if our New York brother would take a trip through the
South and see for himself just what the negro is. I believe such an investigation would entirely change his views with reference to the "coon" as fit
material for the upbuilding of a labor organization. It was the brother's
desire to try this first in the South as an experiment. The brothers of the
South would much prefer to have this experiment demonstrated in the North,
or at least in some other section of the country. We have some members who
come here from the North to secure employment, and after a short stay here
in contact with the negro, they invariably have less use for him than the
people of the South.

It might as well be suggested that we go to Africa and endeavor to
educate the apes as to endeavor to educate the negro of the South, especially
the class that do follow railroading. Mr. Booker T. Washington is cited as
an example, when in fact he is an exception. It would be impossible to find
another negro in the United States his equal. If the Chattanooga convention
should pass laws admitting the negro to membership, that would be the last
convention ever held in the South, for within twenty-four hours after the
passage of such a law, there would be no lodges in the South for the negro
to join.

I would recommend that the northern brother had better post up on
southern conditions before writing again on this subject, for if he knew what
a hornet's nest he has stirred up in this section of the country, and could
hear the rough criticisms that are passed on his article in the August issue
of the MAGAZINE, he would certainly have no more to say on this question. I
will conclude by saying that I do not believe there are many brothers in
the North that are in favor of organizing the southern negro.

"I. C. R. R. Fireman."
McComb City, Miss.

* * *

The Negro in the South

I notice in the August issue of the MAZAGINE, one of our northern
brothers urges that the members in the South should organize the negroes.
I wish to say that the boys of the South are too white to shake hands with
a "burr-head" and call him brother. I believe if the brother will read his
article carefully, he will see that it is a direct insult to the members in
the South to propose such a condition of affairs. If the brother would come
down into the South and study the conditions that exist, he would find that
the southern "burr-head" is no fit guest to be invited into the home of any
member of the Brotherhood of Locomotive Firemen. I believe the brother from
New York would be surprised if he could realize what the members of the lodges
in the South have to contend with, and would be perfectly willing to accord
the treatment to the negro that he rightfully receives from the southern
people. He would not wish us to be harrassed as we are, much less advocate

organizing the element that is the cause of our trouble. We might organize the monkey and teach him all that he could comprehend, but what would we have--a monkey still.

It is the same way with the negro, we cannot expect to make something out of nothing. With reference to Booker T. Washington, it is true he is a southern "coon" and he is all right in his place, but his place is in Africa. If the boys of the North would all treat the negro as he is treated in the South, calling him by the epithets by which he is known throughout the south instead of honoring him by calling him a "colored gentleman" the southern boys would not have so many of them to kill.

I believe if the northern brother will give this matter a little thought, and investigate the conditions as they exist, he will find that he was badly mistaken in his ideas as to the proper method of dealing with the negro.

Member Lodge 200.
Meridian, Miss.

* * *

The Negro and Organized Labor in the South

In the August issue of the MAGAZINE, I noticed an article by one of our brothers in which he advocated the acceptance of the negro to labor organizations, at which I was not only surprised, but sorry to learn that one of my brothers should advise equality with a race whom he acknowledges in his article to be inferior in learning, brains, and industry. If the object was simply to educate him (the negro), I would suggest that schools and colleges more suitable in which to educate him, than shoveling coal into a firebox. If it is desired to raise the standard with reference to energy, why not educate a race of our own, equal at least in color?

It is also suggested that the negro is always satisfied. This, to my mind, is one of the great reasons why he should not be admitted. Why lower the standard of labor by injecting into the union one so lazy and indolent, who has no ambition to raise himself above the condition he is now in? Let the negro do something for himself, first; then will be time enough to talk "equality."

No one is more willing than I to see the negro where he belongs and, when I say this, I believe I voice the sentiments of the South, but I am satisfied his place is not where white men are expected to take him by the hand and call him brother and take him to the bosoms of their families and introduce him to their wives and daughters as Bro.____. It may be said that this is going too far, but I do not think so, as a union, if a "union indeed," is but one great family, and if not, the sooner that union forfeits its charter the better for labor.

Ernest Martin.
South McAlester, I.T.

* * *

The Negro Problem

In reply to an article which appeared in the August issue of the MAGAZINE, relative to the negro and organized labor in the South, will say that I do not believe the brother was ever south of the State of New York, from the way he speaks of the negro.

As for the B. of L. F. taking in the negro, I hope and pray that I may never live to see the grand old B. of L. F. so disgraced as to take into its protecting folds this class of God's creation. God sent his beloved Son, our Saviour to the world to obliterate this disgraceful equalization and now, in this enlightened time for us, the grand old B. of L. F. to invoke His anger by social equalization with the negro, I must say that I am very much astonished and grieved to think that any member of this grand old organization would entertain such an idea. Besides, he could not possibly be of any benefit to us, as there is no firmness whatever in the negro; he will swear his life to support you one hour and then, if he saw an extra dollar in it, would kill you, or ruin your hopes if he didn't see the chance to kill you in the next hour

We of the South have learned by long experience not to rely upon anything a negro may say; he is a terror to our women and our homes, for we know not when we leave our dear wife and babies, to answer the summons of the caller, but that we may return to find our family outraged and murdered, and our once happy home in ashes.

I pray our Father in Heaven to protect our grand old order from such a downfall as social equalization with the negro.

> A Brotherhood Man.
> *Longview, Texas.*

* * *

Organizing the Negro

I am an old fireman and was formerly a member of Red Mountain Lodge No. 339 when that lodge was in existence in Birmingham, Ala. I am what might be termed a Southern-born fireman. I have before me the August issue of the LOCOMOTIVE FIREMEN'S MAGAZINE opened at the article signed by a brother from New York City, relative to the "Negro and Organized Labor," every word of which sets my blood on fire. I believe I voice the sentiments of every fireman of the South when I say we would rather be absolute slaves of capital than to take the negro into our lodges as an *equal* and *brother*. I do not believe that the writer of the article referred to has any personal knowledge of the negro as he exists in the South, or he would never have given expression to such sentiments. When in the South we see a negro and a white man associating together, we are always perfectly safe in deciding that the negro is the most respectable of the two. This is strictly a southern man's views and I believe if we should endeavor to take the negro into the ranks of the B. of L. F., we would deplete the ranks of the white members of the South. I could continue writing on this subject but fear I would become too radical. So long as I have been a member of the Brotherhood, I have never found the courage to send an article to the MAGAZINE for publication, but I could not let a thing of this kind go by unanswered.

> "Southern Tallow Pot."
> *Clarendon, Texas.*

* * *

The Negro and Organized Labor in the South

I noticed in the August issue of the MAGAZINE, an article from a New York brother who suggests taking the negro into our labor organizations. Now it is not my intention to cast any reflections on this brother, at all, for we presume that he is not very well acquainted with the "coon," or "burr-head," as he is generally called in this part of the world. Mr. Booker T. Washington, is a very intelligent negro and, from what I have heard, is considerably mixed with the Anglo-Saxon. Hence his intelligence.

Now, my brother, I think if you would come South and get a glimpse of our typical southern "coon," or "burr-head," and get one good sniff of that aroma he always carries with him, both winter and summer, but more especially when he is out on an excursion train, cooped up in a passenger coach when the thermometer registers about 104 in the shade, you would be in favor of sending him back to Africa, his original home and never entertain even so much as a thought of trying to organize him.

Why! My brother, you cannot get the southern "coon" organized into anything, except it be to beat the white man out of all he can, and if one of them thinks he can gain anything by giving his accomplice away he will willingly do it, and do it at the risk of getting himself into trouble.

I wish to say brother, with the best of feeling, that we are sure if you knew the negro as well as the Southern man, you would never advocate taking him into our Brotherhood; that if you wish to kill the B. of L. F., and kill it quickly and effectually, just take in a few "coons" or "burr-heads." Brother! My wife and child would not own me as a husband and father if I should

go out to attend a meeting of any order, the membership of which was partly
composed of the "coon" or "burr-head."

The negro, as I have always seen him, is most degraded, without honor,
principle, pride, or fair intelligence. His chief aim is to do just as
little as possible and undermine his fellow workers. The fact is, the negro
has ruined bright prospects of many a southern home.

"Dilar."
Mer Rouge, La.

Locomotive Firemen's Magazine (September, 1902): 427-36.

THE BROTHERHOOD OF RAILROAD TRAINMEN AND THE
DEMAND FOR BLACK EXCLUSION

27.   NEGRO DOMINATION

The JOURNAL has always contended that when a labor organization made
any distinction when the question of a general betterment of conditions was
concerned, in the race, creed or color of the people interested, it made a
mistake. The question of negro labor in the South, and of the cheapest
labor of foreign countries in the North, is one that demands careful and
thoughtful attention. The white laborer of the South does not take kindly
to the competition of its colored labor, and the intelligent labor of the
North does not take kindly to the competition of the labor forced upon it
by indiscriminate immigration, but, in both cases, it would be well for the
laborers themselves to note that the natural tendency of wages and conditions
of employment is toward the lowest point, and it is to their interest to
give to the lowest class of labor and to the poorest paid every assistance to
bring it to the higher level of wages and conditions of employment. Where
this is not done, unless some exceptional means are used to maintain wages
and conditions of employment, they will naturally drop to the lowest point.
In the South, negro labor menaces white labor, and, in several instances,
white labor has been supplanted by colored labor because it was cheaper, and
because the negro was not at all insistent upon the observance of his rights
as an employe. In the North we have the same condition in our foreign labor,
and the native laborer suffers in consequence. We have before us a case in
point in the trouble at the Atlantic Cotton Mills, in which an attempt was
made to substitute white with colored labor. The attempt is supposed to have
partly failed, although there is every evidence to prove that the owners of
the mill are quietly working to "Africanize" the plant. As it is, the conditions in the mill are now worse than those in the penal camps of the state,
and the whole result has been caused by the readiness of the negroes to take
the place of the whites at less wages. And now, the white laborer is afraid
of the attacks of the colored people, who feel that they have been frozen out
of employment, and, altogether, the condition is of a "reign of terror order"
that does not promise well for the conditions of employment, or the morals of
employes in the future. As it is, the negro controls the situation, and it
furnishes an object lesson, in this instance at least, to prove that unless
the negro is raised, the white man will have to come down. [Ed. note: The
above paragraph was reprinted as part of a larger article in the Aug. 1900
issue of the *Journal*. See below, p. 111.[

Railroad Trainmen's Journal (September, 1899): 880.

28. THE NEGRO IN TRAIN AND YARD SERVICE

Here it is at last. Please bear with me and I will endeavor to let the
readers of the JOURNAL know what I think of the above and hereby freely invite comments and criticisms from everybody, regardless of their views on
the subject. To begin, we will make the unqualified statement that the Negro
is unfit for such service. I will go a step further and say *he cannot be
fitted either by birth, education or otherwise to fill any position of trust.*
That is a broad statement, but I believe every brother that has ever worked
with the Negro will bear me out in it. Now for some facts to substantiate
the above charge. Having been associated with them in my work for the past
fifteen years, I will show you the Negro as I have found him. He is a being
of an exceedingly low order of intelligence; he is naturally vicious, sloth-
ful, filthy and indolent; has none of the finer qualities that go to make a
man and the worst feature in his nature is such that he cannot cultivate
these qualities to any noticeable extent. To prove it, look at the facilities for educating and improving him, and what is the result? Have they
advanced? No. Now I would ask any skeptical brother if it is possible for
such a being to discharge the duties of a trainman or switchman? You will
all agree with me that it requires *some little intelligence* and at *times* the
exercise of a little *judgment* to discharge your duty to yourself and to your
employer. The black man is *perfectly* devoid of these attributes. I could
cite you a dozen or more instances to prove conclusively that the above are
incontrovertible facts. Here is one: A few years ago the writer was running
a train on the T. & P. R. R. from N.O. to Baton Rouge Junction; had been on
the road eighteen or twenty hours on local; had two "Burr-heads" and a white
flagman; was going to meet the "cannon ball" at a sidetrack that would not
hold my train. About 4 a.m. everybody, very tired and sleepy, headed in and
left rear end "sticking out;" started Mr. "Burr-head" out to flag; so foggy
you could not see a headlight five car lengths so cautioned him to be sure
and get out far enough, as that place was not a stop for the "cannon ball."
I watched him till he got out of sight, which was only a short distance owing
to the fog; he had the reputation of being a *good man* (and I will say he was
as *good a Negro* brakeman as I ever saw). Not feeling safe, I followed him.
About *two telegraph poles from the switch was my flag, the flagman lying in
the bushes asleep.* Not having time to ask any questions or take any steps to
arouse him, after seeing that he was into clear (?) I picked up the red light,
which, by the way, was just about out and went after the passenger train,
which was stopped in time to avert an accident, attended with a large loss
of property and perhaps life. What became of the "Burr-head?" Oh, we made
so much noise sawing out the passenger train that he could not sleep well;
he woke up in time to catch on just as we were leaving town. Suppose you
would like to know what happened to him afterwards. If he had been a white
man we all know how he would have fared, but as he was only a poor black man
he never lost a minute's time nor was he even censured. Rest assured he was
reported "good and strong." In commenting on the case, the superintendent
(we had no T.M.) said: "Well, the poor fellow had been up so long and working
hard he could not be expected to stay awake." Now, this is not an extreme
case nor is it exaggerated in any particular, and no doubt these lines will
fall under the eye of some that are familiar with the case. Neither is this
an isolated case, and if space would permit I could mention a dozen. Omitting
details will mention one that occurred on one of our great trunk lines March
1, 1900: A freight train went in siding to meet fast mail; siding wouldn't
hold freight; "Burrhead" sent to flag "fast mail;" failed to stop them. Result: Two engines (mail train was double-header) and the postal car turned
over, seriously and perhaps fatally injuring an engineer and fireman, four
or five cars of merchandise destroyed and the cars demolished; a wreck that
will cost the company thousands of dollars in loss of property and the loss
perhaps of the lives of two men, either one of which is worth more than a
thousand "Burrheads." Now, brothers, that is the kind of labor we have in
the "Sunny South" in train and yard service. They are absolutely worthless,
in fact, are dangerous to the service. If the above case does not prove my
statement they can be multiplied many times over, for any brother in the South
that has worked with them will corroborate my statements. Now, brothers, when
such a deplorable state of affairs exists it behooves us all as Trainmen and

as American citizens to take some steps to remove this foul blot from among
us. The remedy--organize. Let us organize thoroughly and then with the
most powerful weapon--the ballot--ever wielded by man let us eliminate at
once and forever this degraded element from our chosen occupation. Once
make it clear to the traveling public that the majority of the loss of life,
limb and property is due to the carelessness, indifference, ignorance and
incompetence of the "Burrhead," and my word for it a Negro in train or yard
service will soon be a thing of the past. Come, brothers, speak out; let's
hear from somebody else on this subject. With best wishes to all, I am

                                                          S. J. WHITTAKER

Railroad Trainmen's Journal (April, 1900): 221-22.

29. THE NEGRO IN TRAIN AND YARD SERVICE

     Bro. S. J. Whittaker has so kindly invited everyone to criticize and
comment upon his article in April's issue that I will endeavor to give him
a little light on the subject.
     He probably might remark that not having the negro to contend with in
the connection he writes of, I am not a competent judge. I will leave that
to the readers to decide. The most absurd remark he makes is first italicised
statement, viz., "He cannot be either fitted by birth, education or otherwise
to fill any position of trust." This statement refers to the negro. Now,
why is he not fitted by birth? He is born in a free country, we might say,
in his native land, under laws which allow him the same privileges as Bro.
Whittaker. Why is he not fitted by education? He has the same educational
advantages that any of us have. How about Stephen A. Douglass, Washington T.
Booker, R. L. Smith, and hundreds of others? Cannot they be placed in
positions of trust? R. L. Smith has been twice sent to the Texas legislature
in a district where the white voters outnumber the negroes two to one.[42]
     There are now in the United States nearly 5,000 colored business men,
representative of millions of capital. Almost every state contains several
negroes in the professions; see the work that the agricultural college at
Hampton, Va., is accomplishing! Hundreds of young men and women are being
taught useful trades and professions every year. The college at Atlanta, Ga.,
is accomplishing wonderful things.
     Now, the question is, Have the negroes advanced? Our brother says, No.
But everyone can see that the negro has advanced, and his advancement has been
more wonderful, more rapid than any other nation on the face of the earth,
remembering that forty years ago he was in bondage in the United States, a
good subject for Edward Markham's poem, "The man with a hoe," and one he could
have defended with more ease, and today he is found in all the walks of life.
The question of color is raised very frequently by our Southern brethren.
Why is it that the negro is hired for train and yard service if he is so useless, etc? It must be because competent white men cannot be secured who will
remain in the service, consequently the negro has been placed in the train
service. The general managers have recognized this fact, and found it practicable to use him as brakeman, fireman, etc.[43]
     The boomer's day is over; his passing is in operation daily; he has been
the cause of the hiring of the negro and the recruit, while competent men are
being forced out of the business. I have a prediction to make, and that is,
that ten years from date the negro will be running trains in the South, to say
nothing about braking! He is adapted to the climate, and his physical make-up
is first-class for the service demanded of him.
     The Negro has a better opportunity in the North because of lack of pre-
judice. It was but a short time ago, in the U.S. Senate, when a senator from
South Carolina admitted that the people of his state kept the negro from the
polls, and, now, Bro. Whittaker don't want him to work. Everyday examples can
be found of men failing to do their duty on account of long hours, drowsiness,
and other causes, and the two examples cited don't prove the rule but just

notes the exceptions. Bro. Whittaker, send out your white flagman, and not
the "burrhead." "In case of doubt, adopt the safe course."[44]
Yours respectfully,
F. T. DESMOND.

Railroad Trainmen's Journal (May, 1900): 419

30. HERCULEAN LODGE, NO. 574

After an absence of a few months from our worthy JOURNAL, I am compelled
to return with a word or two as regards the arguments of the "Negro" in yard
or train service. I see where one F. T. Desmond has fully given his opinion,
and in so doing has forgotten entirely the subject he started on. F. T. D.,
you have "run off the track;" better call the wrecker out. You have gone
from railroading into educational and political standpoints. Bro. Whittaker
was speaking of railroading. Now, Mr.F. T. D., where did the negro ever
benefit you aside from a political standpoint? I dare say, nowhere. The
class of negro you name, is not by any means the railroad class on which the
subject has opened. I myself was born and raised in the South and speak the
facts only, not "theories," or imaginations. The negro is wholly unfit for
the service mentioned outside of "porter" for stations and Pullmans or parlor
cars. Where there is life at stake the negro should not be tolerated, for
if the sun is shining and he is sent back to flag, you can send somebody to
waken him up when you are ready for him to come in. It's dollars to peanuts
he will be asleep at his post. In ten years, instead of the negro running
engines, you will not find the "Burr-head" in the service at all. As the
years come, railroading is fast becoming a profession of refinement of which
everyone shall be proud. Now, Mr. F. T. Desmond, just stop one moment and
think what you have said and then think what you should have said, and see
the difference. The negro is a negro, dead or alive, and there is no dependence to be put in him; here is where Bro. Whittaker said he could not
fill a position of trust.

Railroad Trainmen's Journal (June, 1900): 499.

31. THE NEGRO NO GOOD

I don't know who F. T. Desmond is, but I do know that he does not know
anything about the negro as a trainman. If he did, he would not make such a
weak argument as he did. The idea of saying that there are 5,000 negro business men in a country with a population of 65,000,000. Why, that percentage
is so small that it is hardly worth noticing. Now, for their business; it
is peddling fish, clams and oysters, and I suppose he would place the negro
washwoman in business. Well, so be it. Now for their education; a very few
of them rise to some prominence after they get an education, but they are
very scarce. Education makes them saucy, impudent and annoying to the whites.
In the town where I live, if you go through a part of the city where there
are more negroes than whites, the negroes subject you to every petty annoyance
they can, such as passing remarks about you or your lady, or blocking the
sidewalks, so you will either walk in the street or run the risk of getting
in a street brawl. In the cars, it is just as bad. They walk all over the
white ladies' dresses and shove them and their children about because they
can. Mr. Desmond might say there is a law; have them arrested. That would
do if we wanted to be in police court every day, but we have not the time,
and the most of this lawlessness is committed by the educated negro. If a
negro who has to labor at hard labor gets in a street car, he generally be-
haves himself. It is the educated negro that causes the trouble.

We in Washington know something about the negro trainmen as we have one
division where we meet the negro in train service on a road that connects with
the Pennsylvania. . . .

Their conductors tell us they can't be trusted to set off a car without the conductor is looking at them, and when the engineer whistles for the brakes to be applied they will get on top and look to see if there is anything ahead and if they cannot see anything ahead, they will brake, but if they see anything, they will get ready to vacate the premises. A white man will brake first and find out what the trouble is afterwards. The reason some railroads hire the negro is not because he is competent, it is because he is cheap. I know of two roads that have some negro brakemen and firemen and their wages average $35 per month. On these same roads, white men in the same positions get $50 and $75. See the difference? Mr. Desmond makes the prediction that in ten years from date the negro will be running trains. Bible students tell us that there is a time coming called the "millennium," at which time the lamb will lie down with the lion. When this time comes we shall expect to see the negro running trains, but not until then.

Now, on one of these roads I have mentioned, the managers are replacing the negro with the white labor, and I make the prediction that in ten years there will not be a negro in train service in the United States. There may be some in the islands we have lately taken from Spain, but it is very doubtful. I remain yours in B.S. and I.,

SAMUEL T. GRAVES.

Railroad Trainmen's Journal (June, 1900): 505-506.

32.   LOUISVILLE, KY.

I had no idea that Bro. Whittaker's letter regarding the "Burrhead" as a brakeman and a switchman would bring to light a champion of the monkey tribe. . . .

I understand that no personalities must be indulged in when expecting the publication of a letter, and I do not wish Bro. Desmond (I say brother, but am unable to tell, as he gives no lodge number and only signs, yours respectfully, in place of the old familiar and grand preface to his name, B. S. & I., by which we understand that he is one of us). Well, to make a long story short, I will simply state that Bro. F. T. D. is on the wrong siding and his train of information is late in arriving, and in fact will never arrive unless he moves on to his meeting point. I will endeavor to make up a section of the train of information on "Burrheads" of the Sunny South, and flagging to the station where he is patiently waiting with all the courtesy and brotherly love, hand him a copy of instructions, and orders on the handling of a "Burrhead" train.

To begin with, no one is more familiar with the gentleman with the thick skull and kinky hair than myself. Why? Because I ran a yard where I was not allowed to hire a white switchman. The question comes up, why was this, and using the trainmaster's own language, when I requested him to allow me to employ white men, he said: "You could not keep them here at the salary we pay," and I believe he was right. Ninety cents per day was the pay they received. No wonder few cars of merchandise could stay in the yard over night without being robbed. Such wages is the cause of our prisons being full and overflowing. When a man works all day, "Burrhead" or white man, for 90 cents per day and feeds his family and himself, he is hoeing a hard row.

When a white brother loses his position and goes elsewhere for a job, he must have references and good ones; when a "Burrhead" struck me for an office, and I needed them almost every day, I simply obeyed my instructions and telling him to sign one of the old-time death warrants so familiar to all of us, let him go to work. If a "Burrhead" broke up a few cars, he was fired; went up town and got drunk and layed around a few days, changed his name from John to Jim and came back and I hired him over again as per instructions. Are you beginning to catch on? All they want is the "Burrhead's" cheap work, regardless of the character of any back record, and any "Burrhead" fortunate enough to escape hanging for one of the unmentionable crimes which have made them so pleasant to live with in the South, can get a job switching or braking. Only two weeks ago, a warm personal friend of my own, who was running a train on the I. C., sent his "Burrhead" back to flag. I say back, because the I. C. out of Louisville has two descendants of the babboon tribe in place of one on all trains but local. "Burrhead" goes out, takes a drink of nigger whisky out of the bottle that two-thirds of them always carry, sits down, and a rear-end collision loses the conductor his job. . . .

I could write all day and tell you incident after incident of just such as this and I have only one request to make. Let Bro. Desmond take a pleasure trip to the Sunny South, hunt me up, and myself and little wife will make things pleasant for him, and I will take him around and introduce him to Brother "Burrhead" as he really is in the South, and I will grant that for every word he has spoken in their behalf, he will go home and write a whole book on the shortcoming of the past of the southern home.

Yours in B. S. & I.,
W. R. STINBY.

Railroad Trainmen's Journal (June, 1900): 506.

33. GRAND FORK

I have just been reading my May JOURNAL, and I run across a letter from 536, regarding negroes as brakemen.

The Great Northern has pulled off a white brakeman who was getting $60 per month and put on a negro for $40 per month. Of course, they do not wear the badge of brakeman, but that of porter, and do the white man's work in every respect as near as they know how and as far as the conductor trusts them, which, I can assure you, is not far. I was standing on the corner the other day and by chance I heard one of those negroes say, the time of the strike on the G. N., in 1894, I worked two weeks in spite of the B. of R. T. men. I just give you this instance to show you what kind of negroes we have up here in this western country railroading.

I also noted the criticism of a certain F. T. Desmond. I don't know whether he is a white man or not, and if a white man, if he belongs to our order, I don't think much of his writing. No doubt there may be some very bright minds among the negroes, but you can depend on it, they are not in train or yard service, and I trust that his prediction, that it won't be many years from now before they will run trains, will never come true. His advice in the close of his letter would tend to lead a man to the impression that he himself does not trust the "Burrhead." I, for one, thank God I do not have to work with them. To think that our forefathers fought for the freedom and then have them come and take our places for less money than we get, is too much for me.

The Montana Central is out, and perhaps the entire system will go out, and no doubt our places in many instances will be filled by the "Burrhead." One thing we are sure of is that it will not be by a good B. of R. T., not even by a bad one, if such a thing exists, and a white conductor that would ask for two negro brakemen is not much.

I must now close with all the sympathy at my command for brothers who have to work with the "Burrhead."

I remain, with best wishes to all B. of R. T. boys, as usual,

THE PREACHER.

Railroad Trainmen's Journal (June, 1900): 507.

34. COLUMBIA, S. C.

In looking over the May JOURNAL, I find a lengthy criticism of Bro. Whittaker's contribution to April issue, by Bro. Desmond, in which he endeavored to give us "some light on the subject," and in which he contends that

the "Burrhead" is equally capable of holding a position of trust with the
white men of our Southland. I am sorry our brother holds such a poor opinion
of the Southern boys, and am quite sure he does not know the average negro in
train and yard service, because he has not had to contend with him. I agree
fully with Bro. Whittaker in saying the negro is not fitted by birth because
in the origination of the negro race God himself cursed the descendants of Ham,
and said they should be "hewers of wood and drawers of water," or, in short,
servants of the whites. Do you think they are your servants when you have to
work with them, and what the average negro in train and yard service knows has
to be "drilled" into his head like a poll parrot? I am glad to say there are
a few exceptions. I will admit they are free as is every one else who is
fortunate enough to be under the Stars and Stripes. If you will come south
you yourself would say, as a general rule, the negroes would be better off
if they were still in "bondage." As for education, there are some few who
have been benefited by the change, and have nobly tried to elevate the negro
race; but, come south, brother, and you will find nearly as many educated
negroes in our jails and penitentiaries, but the height of an educated negro's
ambition, and an uneducated one, too, is to go "north," and I hope to live to
see the day when the "whole push" will be north of Mason and Dixon's line,
then our northern brethren will not be so ready to condemn us when we speak.
As for the negro trains in ten years, let me ask you a few questions. Would
you be willing to trust your wife, mother or sweetheart on a line manned
entirely by negroes? Would you be willing to come down and "brake" under the
negro? I am sure you would not, and if they are capable of running trains,
and will do so, as you say in ten years, why it is they are excluded from
our order? Would you be willing to greet them with the endearing title of
brother? Come south, brother, and see the negro in his every-day life,
as we see him, and not when he is on dress parade. You say the negro has
advanced more in the last forty years than any other race. I agree with you,
brother, but in what? Immorality, drunkenness and vice of every description.
And, who is it that is keeping wages down to "scab pay?" "Mr. Burrhead."
Who is it that is responsible for most of the wrecks in our Southland? The
incompetent negro. Our brother wants to know why they are employed? Because
a negro will switch all day, twelve hours, thirty days in the month, for $20
per month. The white men will not. A negro will work "local," fifteen or
sixteen hours per day, for $1 per day. The white men will not. They are
hired at starvation wages by bosses who think they are practicing economy by
hiring cheap labor, and never think of the thousands of dollars the company
has to pay for costly wrecks, not to mention the precious lives that are
crushed out through the agency of an incompetent negro. One thing more,
brother, and I will give way to someone who will answer you more fully than
I have done. Are we not banded together, both North and South, for the
betterment of our condition? And do you think we can be bettered by having
the negro take our places for wages at which no white man can live? A negro
and a "scab" come under the same head, and I guess you know what a "scab" is.
And, the white conductors are held responsible for the actions of the "Burrhead" brakemen. I know of an instance right here in this city where a good
B.R.T. conductor is looking for an office because "Mr. Burrhead" got his job.
. . . . What became of the negro? Working every day while the worthy brother
is looking for an office. That is only one of the many instances that happen
daily where the negro is employed in train service. Come south, brother, and
if you don't agree with me in what I say, the treats are on me, and even if
you don't agree with me in every particular, you will have learned a lesson
that you will never forget, and that is the "Burrhead" can never be the white
man's equal, for "water can never rise above its level."

Yours in brotherly love,
A. D. WRIGHT,
No. 312.

Railroad Trainmen's Journal (June, 1900): 507-508.

35. MEMPHIS, TENN.

Many thanks to Bro. Desmond for his "light" on the subject, "The Negro
in train and yard service."

It is as clear as "mud." There is no mark to tell what part of the
country Brother Desmond is in, but it is a safe bet that he is *not* from any
part south of Mason and Dixon's line. The very tone of his argument (or
lack of argument) shows very clearly that he knows not whereof he speaks
when it comes to the negro question. He says: "He probably might remark
that not having the negro to contend with in the connection he writes of,
I am not a competent judge."

You are right, my brother. I certainly would make that remark if it
were not superfluous to do so, but it is not necessary for me to bring that
charge, for the brother stands self-convicted in the eyes of everyone that
has had any experience with the "Burrhead" in the connection mentioned. If
the brother has any doubt as to his having taken the wrong view of the question, let him ask his delegate to the New Orleans convention what the sentiment of that body was with regard to this subject.

With regard to "the most absurd remark he makes," (this refers to my
remark in April issue), I reiterate that statement and maintain that it is
an incontestable fact, and is sustained by the evidence.

"Why is he not fitted by birth? He is born in a free country." So are
cows, horses, pigs and dogs; yet if you wanted a cow, you would hardly buy
a horse, or if you wanted a buggy horse, would you buy a cow? Yet you had as
well do that (as absurd as it sounds), as to expect the "Burrhead" to fill
any position of trust, or one that requires the exercise of any judgment, for,
as before stated, he is perfectly devoid of that qualification; the same
comparison will apply to his educational qualification. The brother certainly
has "enlightened" me on the subject of the color of Stephen A. Douglas. I
was never personally acquainted with the gentleman (he having died about the
time I was born), but from the record, have always inferred that he was a
member of the Anglo-Saxon race; as to the others he mentions, they are rare
exceptions and only serve to prove the rule. In this connection, will say,
whenever you find a so-called negro of intelligence and refinement, if you
will just take the trouble to trace his ancestry, you won't have to go far
till you find that he is not a negro in the true sense of the word, but a
hybrid, a mongrel, a cross between the Anglo-Saxon and the African, and his
African nature has been almost eliminated by the superior intelligence and
instinct of the white race. It is useless to pursue an argument on this
question with anyone that thinks as Bro. Desmond does.

Shakespeare tells us that "A man convinced against his will is of the
same opinion still;" and indications go to show that this brother would be
convinced that way if it were possible to convince him at all. If there was
any doubt as to Bro. Desmond's incompetency to judge this question, such doubt
would certainly be dispelled when we read his prediction--"Ten years from date
the negro will be running trains in the south, to say nothing of braking."
Of all the "raw brakes" I ever heard any make, that is the "rawest." Don't
get offended, brother, but I can't help such comment when I see such dense
ignorance displayed on the subject by one who gives every indication otherwise of being a man of superior intelligence.

"The negro has a better opportunity in the north because of lack of prejudice." What line of reasoning does the brother take to arrive at this conclusion; why and where does prejudice against the negro exist in the South?
That is another instance of the brother's ignorance of the subject under discussion. Now, listen! Why is it, if the negro is treated so much better in
the north that he prefers to live in the south? Here is why: He receives
better treatment and more consideration in the south than anywhere else on
earth. Now, where the northern brother makes a mistake in the treatment of
the negro is, he tries to treat him as his equal socially and otherwise. The
negro knows better than that. He knows he is not, nor can never hope to be
the whiteman's equal in any way except it by physically.

You misconstrue my meaning, Brother D., when you say: "Now, Bro. Whitaker
don't want him to work." Such is not my desire. I know full well that he must
work, for he can't be a capitalist and he must live.

What I object to is his being employed in train and yard service of the railroads of the south to the detriment of the good, competent white men and the public welfare at large. The brother asks why these men are employed in train and yard service if they are so useless, etc. If you will come south and go to work on some of our trunk lines that employ this kind of animal for you to work with and have occasion to go before the management in the capacity of a grievance committeeman you will very soon find out why the negro is employed in above mentioned service. You will find also that it is not because he is "adapted to the climate and his physical make-up is first-class for the service demanded of him."

Bro. Desmond says: "Send out your white flagman and not the Burrhead." Who are you going to send out when they are both "Burrheads," as is frequently the case and as was the case in one of the instances mentioned in my last letter, which cost the Illinois Central company thousands of dollars in loss of property? As to the two cases cited by me being exceptions, as before stated, I can call to mind a dozen or more similar cases that have come under my personal observation, and I am only one of several thousand white men who will testify to the incompetency of the "Burrhead" in train and yard service. Now, Bro. Desmond, I would advise you to keep still on the negro question until you learn something about it. Evidently your source of information on this subject is very defective. Nevertheless, I thank you for your criticism, as I believe it will be the means of drawing the fire of some brother that does know something about the question, who is better able to handle it than I am. Come to Memphis if you want to learn something about the ebony-hued brakeman and switchman. If you will come it shall not cost you a cent, and I promise not to try to influence your opinion of the negro in any way, but will be content to let you find out from personal observation just what the "Burrhead" is.

Fraternally,
S. J. WHITAKER, Financier
347.

Railroad Trainmen's Journal (June, 1900): 509-10.

36.   MEMPHIS, TENN.

It is to be regretted that there has been so much personal feeling exhibited in the discussion of the negro question; in my letter in the April JOURNAL it was not my desire or intention to call forth personal criticism, but the chief aim and object was to air the negro question in print. To attain this end the logical starting point would be in our Official Organ.

If I have been personal, I crave the pardon of any brother who thinks or feels that he has been wronged by any statement of mine, for, brothers, I have no grievance with the B. of R. T., but with the enemies of the B. of R. T., and all other organized labor, chief among which (in my humble opinion) is the negro. As to Bro. Desmond, he is not to be censured for his views of the question, even though they are incorrect. . . .

That statement applies to white men (regardless of nationality), but does not apply to the negro at all. On the roads where he is employed he is in a class by himself; he stands alone, supreme "monarch of all he surveys;" this is not idle talk, but is a matter of record, and is supported by the facts, not "facts" as they are presented by "Mr. J. B. Killebrew, of Nashville, Tenn.," and "a southern paper" (see September JOURNAL, 1899, page 854), but actual facts as they really exist. Pardon me, brothers if my language is too strong, or appears personal, for it is not my desire nor intention to stir up strife, far from it; and I am doing my best to present this question fairly and fully before the public, feeling that in so doing I am only discharging a sacred duty to not only the B. of R. T. but all the white people of our land. I am trying to be non-partisan and unprejudiced, for the situation is bad enough without coloring or exaggeration. To quote from my April letter: Once make it clear to the public that the majority of the loss of life, limb and property on our railroads is due to the carelessness, indifference, ignorance and incompetency of the negro, it will only be a short time till a negro in train or yard service will be a thing of the past."

In conclusion, I want to sincerely thank Bro. Desmond again for his criticism, for I honestly believe that his letter has been and will be a power for good in helping to eliminate the "black cloud" from train and yard service. The issue is before us and must be met. It is "up to us" now; what are we going to do, sit idly by and watch "the white man come down?" For come down he must unless we relegate the negro to the cotton field or some other congenial employment, for it is an evident fact that he can never be raised to a degree of efficiency that will entitle him to recognition as a trusted employe in train or yard service. With best wishes to all, I am, fraternally,

S. J. WHITAKER,
Financier, No. 347.

Railroad Trainmen's Journal (August, 1900): 677.

37. NEGRO LABOR: BENEFIT OR DETRIMENT?

The JOURNAL has no disposition "to fiddle on one string," but sometimes it becomes necessary, even though the music is certain to not be pleasant.

The mention, referred to by Bro. Whitaker, did not have a word to say of the moral elevation of the negro. The entire criticsm was on the wage question, and for the benefit of the JOURNAL readers it is herewith given:

The JOURNAL has always contended that when a labor organization made any distinction when the question of a general betterment of conditions, was concerned, in the race, creed or color of the people interested, it made a mistake. The question of negro labor in the south, and of the cheapest labor of foreign countries in the north, is one that demands careful and thoughtful attention. The white laborer of the south does not take kindly to the competition of its colored labor, and the intelligent labor of the north does not take kindly to the competition of the labor forced upon it by indiscriminate immigration, but in both cases it would be well for the laborers themselves to note that the natural tendency of wages and conditions of employment is toward the lowest point, and it is to their interest to give to the lowest class of labor and to the poorest paid every assistance to bring it to the highest level of wages and conditions of employment. Where this is not done, unless some exceptional means are used to maintain wages and conditions of employment, they will naturally drop to the lowest point. In the south, negro labor menaces white labor, and, in several instances, white labor has been supplanted by colored labor because it was cheaper, and because the negro was not at all insistent upon the observance of his rights as an employe. In the north we have the same condition in our foreign labor, and the native labor suffers in consequence. We have before us a case in point in the trouble at the Atlantic Cotton Mills, in which an attempt was made to substitute white with colored labor. The attempt is supposed to have partly failed, although there is every evidence to prove that the owners of the mill are quietly working to "Africanize" the plant. As it is, the conditions in the mill are now worse than those in the penal camps of the state, and the whole result has been caused by the readiness of the negroes to take the place of the whites at less wages. And now, the white laborer is afraid of the attacks of the colored people, who feel that they have been frozen out of employment, and, altogether, the condition is of a "reign of terror order" that does not promise well for the conditions of employment, or the morals of employes in the future. As it is, the negro controls the situation, and it furnishes an object lesson, in this instance at least, to prove that unless the negro is raised, the white man will have to come down."[45]

Every letter that has protested against the negro in train and yard service has had for its basis the cheapness of the negro. And that cheapness is preferred by the companies to ability, intelligence and every other desirable quality in a railroad man. It is true that there are a very few exceptions where the negro is given the same wages as white men, in railroad employment, but the exceptions are very few. If all wages were the same it would be a decidedly contrary condition of affairs if the employer would prefer the lowest order of intelligence and worth to the highest offered him.

Cheap labor is cheap labor, and for a recent illustration the influx of Japanese to America, with their sixty cents a day for track work, is just the least convincing. If the better paid labor of America is satisfied to drop to the lowest level of wages paid, that will be its business and its mistake.

The second article referred to by Bro. Whitaker was as follows:

"It is a question of opinion whether the negro is a benefit or a detriment to the south, and in discussing its future industrial progress the worth or worthlessness of the colored brother is very much in doubt, and the question is generally settled to the satisfaction of the one holding the argument by judging from the standpoint of the worth of the negro to himself personally, regardless of the effect of the influence of the negro on the condition of his neighbor."

Mr. Polk Brown of Georgia, testified before the Industrial Commission that the negro retarded the growth of the south, and declared that without the negro the south would be open to a better class of labor. Mr. Brown believed that colonization for the negro would be for the interest of the southern States, and to the contrary, another equally good judge of the negro in the person of Mr. J. B. Killebrew, of Nashville, Tenn., says the negro is superior to anybody else in the forest and on the farm, and between the two we are no wiser on some questions than before they expressed an opinion. A southern paper sets forth its views as follows:

"The manufacturing center of the United States will one day be located in the south; and this will come about, strange as it may seem, for the reason that the negro is a fixture here. This line of argument may be somewhat startling, even to southern people who are best acquainted with the situation, for it must be admitted that the negro has been generally considered a hindrance, rather than a help, to the industrial development of the south. . . .

"Organized labor, as it exists today, is a menace to industry. The negro stands as a permanent and positive barrier against labor organization in the south. This declaration is not carelessly made. It is based upon a painstaking investigation which has extended through many years of intimate acquaintance with southern conditions, both industrial and sociological."

The idea herein expressed is evidently the whole argument in favor of the negro, and is to the effect that the negro is slow, and, perhaps, a barrier to the industrial progress of the south, but he will not listen to the labor organizer, he will always work for low wages, he is docile, sometimes, and stands in the way of increased wages and in the words of the same writer here are the prospects of the south, because of the presence of the negro.

"In a general way, it is considered that organized labor, of the vicious sort, is an evil which the south has thus far fortunately escaped. But we do not owe this blessing to the neglect of the professional agitator. He has done his best, or rather his worst, and failed. Freedom from vicious socialistic conditions is a practical and permanent advantage that the south offers today, and will always offer, to the manufacturer and to others who are seeking profitable investment. It is this tremendous advantage that will one day make the south the manufacturing center of the nations. . . ."

There is nothing easier than for a man (no matter how well read or intelligent) to get a wrong impression of the negro problem, if he relies for his information on "statistics," which are almost invariably so "crooked or doctored" that they do not convey any idea of the true state of affairs. If anyone has any doubt as to the above statement, let him look through the files of our JOURNAL for the past year; you will find statements from prominent men on this great question that are so at variance with the facts as they really exist that there can be no doubt as to their purpose to mislead; hence the northern brother, or any other brother that draws his information from this source, is not to be blamed but rather pitied, for it must be humiliating to a degree for a man to hunt up facts on a subject, get them from an apparently authentic source, then to form his opinion on said facts, and discover that it is all wrong, that his facts are not facts at all, or if they are they are so misleading as to convey no true idea of the situation. The writer does not claim to "know it all," nor does he desire to make loud and startling declarations to gain notoriety or just to hear his "head rattle," but having

had twenty-two years' experience in railroading service and having filled
every position in the operating department of a railroad, from "wiper" in
the round-house up, and his field of operation not having been confined to
any one railroad or system, but several; having worked in twelve or fourteen different states, all in the south and west, thereby being afforded a
splendid opportunity to observe the animal under discussion, in all his moods
and phases, and under almost every condition imaginable, and after making a
special study of the question, feels that his opinion should have some
consideration, even were it alone; particularly so, when his position is
endorsed and statements corroborated by every man that has ever come in
direct contact with the negro in train and yard service.

Right here the writer makes bold to take issue with our worthy editor:
JOURNAL of September, 1899, page 880. "As it is, the negro controls the
situation, and it furnishes an object lesson, in this instance at least, to
prove that unless the negro is raised, the white man will have to come down."
To this I will say, the white man may and probably will have to come down,
as the employers seem to be exerting every effort to that end, but as to the
negro being raised, that will never be, from the simple fact that there is
nothing to build on. In the name of common sense, how are we to "raise or
elevate a being that is perfectly devoid of principle, honor, integrity,
industry, ambition and every other attribute that goes to make a man? When
we can do that we can elevate the negro, not before; do your utmost, and he
will never be the white man's equal, it is not in him. . . ."

The writer is as mistaken as the one who would look for the salvation
of the north in the ship loads of immigrants that are coming yearly to compete with American labor. The man who can see industrial progress in cheap
labor only deserves to be pitied.

Cheap labor is not necessarily the most economical, and the cheap
countries of the world today are the ones that are the lowest in their social,
moral and industrial development, and the JOURNAL invites the cheap employer
to look the matter up for himself."

This is simply, in general, an argument against the organization of labor
and an argument in favor of the negro, because he will not become affiliated
with organized labor.

The cheap wages in the south stand in evidence of its lack of thorough
organization, and behind it all stands the cheap labor of the negro.

The Brotherhood of Railroad Trainmen has exerted every effort to reduce
the number of negroes in the service; the JOURNAL is with the members in their
every effort to lift the "black cloud," but after all these years of talking
and effort, the employer is found just as firmly entrenched in his favorable
opinion of colored cheap labor, with all of its influences so disadvantageous
to white labor, and with all of its faults, it does appear that the universal
law of wages and the tendency to rise or fall should not be overlooked in
this instance.

It is humiliating; no one will take kindly to it, but the other course
has been tried and its results are painfully apparent.

                                                                D. L. CEASE.

Railroad Trainmen's Journal (August, 1900): 677-78.

38. CHATTANOOGA, TENN.

Lodge No. 215 is getting along very nicely. Our goat is busy every
Sunday with two or three new candidates. We are away down in the sunny south
where the sun is always hot; but now, brothers, we are always on the go from
sun up until sun down. No. 215 is only a few in members, but those that are
members are the "proper stuff." We could have more members, but we live up
to our Grand Lodge, and when a man joins No. 215 he is the right kind of a
brother. What do we want with everyone in our lodge? Brothers, remember we
carry the Stars and Stripes in labor organizations today, and in the next ten

years we will have the say of everything, when there won't be a "Burrhead" in the train or yard service.

I have been a member for over two years and I know that the Brotherhood of Railroad Trainmen is the best in the country. I hardly ever see anything in the JOURNAL about No. 215, but I hope some of the boys will wake up and write to the JOURNAL more than they do. I remain,

> Yours in B. S. and I.,
> No. 215, "Rooster."

Railroad Trainmen's Journal (August, 1900): 684.

39.   "NIG"

Speaking of the negro question, F. T. Desmond says the boomer's day is over and that he has been the cause of the "nig" going braking, and that they will be running trains in the south. I don't think so; if the boomer has been the cause of the "nig" braking, when the boomer is gone the "nig" will go with him.

> Will B. Good.

Railroad Trainmen's Journal (August, 1900): 685.

40.   ATLANTA, GEORGIA

Replying to Bro. S. J. Whitaker's article in the April issue of the JOURNAL on the negroes serving as train and yard men, I wish to heartily endorse Bro. Whitaker and all that has been said in favor of his article. But I must say that F. T. Desmond . . . in the May issue with his article concerning Mr. Negro, is away off the track.

Bro. Desmond, I attribute your views and ideas on the negro to total ignorance on your part. You have, no doubt, often heard the old quotation that "Ignorance is bliss." You have undertaken a subject that you absolutely know nothing about, therefore it would have been better for you to have kept quiet until you become better informed on this particular question. I was born in the State of Georgia and have lived right here in Georgia and Alabama all my life, right in the heart of the south. I surely ought to know about what I am writing, and I do know, or rest assured you would have never heard from me. You ask why a negro isn't high born, etc. Well, that is an easy problem and can be easily explained. The reason that the negro is employed in the south as train and yard man isn't due to the fact that he is so reliable as you think he is. He is anything but reliable; the railroad officials know this as well as I know it. You simply cannot trust one any further than you can see him, but he can be hired cheaply; he will work for $1 per day or less. The conductor is held responsible for Mr. Negro's actions, and by his close watch and attention we manage to get along with about as few accidents as is common for railroads. But you let that conductor take his eye off that negro, go to the office to get orders, etc., which is often necessary--any railroad man understands that a conductor cannot always be right with his men. Now see what a chance the company is taking by having negroes employed; they are liable to do anything; one can't tell. You do not know a negro like I do; if you did, you would hardly allow him to walk on the right of way, much less employ him. You spoke of how the negro has come out in all lines in the past forty years; you also forgot to mention how the chain gang and penitentiary have come out, being filled every day by the negroes. They have increased more than anything I know of, and if you will please note the educated is helping more to support these institutions than anyone else. Oh, yes! he is

advancing rapidly, and so is the gallows; it is growing right along by the
side of him. Where there is one Booker T. Washington trying to do good work
for his race there are thousands upon thousands who are pulling right against
him; therefore, he has a heavy upgrade to pull a long train dragging behind
him, and I fear that it will be more than ten years before any of his converts
will be able and permitted to handle a train. Don't you ever believe Mr. Negro
will ever run trains down here; no, that he won't, and in less time than ten
years you won't find one employed on a railroad only as a porter or to wait
upon the officials. The negro is as high up in railroad circles as he will
ever be, yes, he is higher now, for I do not think it will be long before he
will be entirely dropped, or it won't be long before the negroes would own
the railroads. The negro question is being discussed more and more every day,
and it will only be a matter of time before it will come to a climax, and Mr.
Negro's fate will be settled. They are just as sure to be colonized as they
live. I can safely say that never as long as the world stands will they run
trains in the south. I know the people where I dwell too well to ever believe
they would submit to this. Now, Bro. Desmond, kindly accept an invitation
to visit the south; be sure and come by Atlanta, and be my guest, and if you
can find one single instance where I have misrepresented facts to you in this
case, then your expenses down here and back shall not cost you anything at
all. With best wishes to you, I remain yours in B. S. & I.,

W. H. HIGGINBOTTEM, No. 302.

Railroad Trainmen's Journal (August, 1900): 686-87.

III
THE UNITED MINE WORKERS OF AMERICA
AND THE BLACK WORKER

When the United Mine Workers of America was founded in 1890, it inherited a significant black membership from Knights of Labor Assembly 135.
With over 20,000 black members in 1902, the UMW had more than half the total
black membership of the AFL. In Alabama alone, blacks comprised half of
the state's approximately 13,000 coal miners. That the UMW was an industrial union from the outset had much to do with the status it offered Afro-
Americans. It was impossible to apply principles of craft unionism when
organizing coal miners because of the nature of the work. Moreover, any
attempt to organize on a racial basis in an industry which employed so many
blacks would have been suicidal. Negroes had worked in Southern coal mines
since slavery, and by 1890, they were not only solidly entrenched in this
employment, but their numbers were increasing in both northern and southern
mines. Furthermore, the UMW constitution specifically prohibited discrimination on the basis of race, creed, or nationality, making it one of the most
openly democratic unions in the nation.
     But blacks did not receive equal treatment with whites even in the UMW.
Many complaints surfaced in the union's paper, the United Mine Workers'
Journal, regarding the inadequate representation of blacks at all levels of
leadership. Also, negroes complained that they were discriminated against
in the skilled and better paying positions. Promotion was a slow if not
impossible process, and they charged that white union officials often ignored their grievances. Moreover, black and white miners frequently were
segregated into separate locals, especially in the South. Segregation also
extended inside the mines, where the two races worked in separate sections,
and often changed clothing in different wash-houses. In most mining communities, housing, education, and other public facilities were segregated
as well. Thus, local folkways inevitably found their way into the pits, and
into the union itself.
     During the 1890s, these grievances flared into a heated public debate
in the UMWJ. The most articulate of the black miners was Richard L. Davis.
Davis was born in Roanoke, Virginia, in 1864, where he worked in the tobacco
factories. After laboring in the coal mines of West Virginia for a time,
he moved to Rendville, a small mining town in southeastern Ohio. A delegate
to the founding convention of the UMW in 1890, Davis subsequently served on
the Executive Board of District 6 (Ohio), and in 1896 and 1897 he was elected
to the international executive board. Throughout the 1890s Davis helped
organize black miners in Ohio, West Virginia, Pennsylvania, and Alabama. In
his letters to the UMWJ, Davis warned white miners that if their black
brothers were not treated equally, they would provide the operators with a
vast industrial army which could enter the pits as strikebreakers (Doc. 1-61).
     Another dedicated black union miner who bluntly expressed his outrage
at racial discrimination during this debate was William R. Riley. Little is
known about Riley except that he had been a member of the Knights of Labor
Assembly 135 in southeastern Kentucky. He moved to Jellico, Tennessee, probably during the 1880s, where he continued to organize black and white miners.
Apparently Riley was successful, for by 1892, he had been elected Secretary-
Treasurer of UMW District 19, a large territory covering Tennesses and parts
of Kentucky. Riley's letters reveal the contradictory demands placed upon
black union organizers (Doc. 62-68). Although the primary loyalties of Davis
and Riley were to the broader principles of union solidarity, they were caught
between white racism on the one hand, and black racial solidarity on the other.
Their correspondence in the UMWJ indicates how profoundly black union militants
differed from bourgeois black leaders, such as Booker T. Washington, regarding
the struggle between capital and labor, and reveals black union men caught
between progressive ideals and reactionary social conditions.

RICHARD L. DAVIS, UNITED MINE WORKERS' LEADER, 1891-1900

1. A FRANK LETTER

From Correspondent Davis of Rendville[46]

GIVING THE VIEWS OF COLORED BROTHERS CONCERNING REPRESENTATION--AND DIFFER-
ING WITH THE POLICY ADOPTED IN INDIANA.

RENDVILLE, O., Nov. 20.

Work in the Sunday Creek valley, remains fair. Of course the usual
scarcity of railroad cars prevails. I might say that no doubt your many
readers are growing tired of these dull letters of mine and I am somewhat
tired of them myself, but when a fellow is writing, no matter whether it has
a deal of force or not, he is out of other mischief. This is one of the
reasons why I try to write and another reason is this, that by writing, and
especially of the things and happenings of every-day occurrences, it helps
to develop the intellectual faculties. This I need, so does every other
workingman. I have always claimed the miners, as a rule, are not as good
subscribers to labor papers as they should be; it seems that they don't want
to know the real condition of affairs. When they pick up a paper they hastily
glance at the general news and are then done with it. I was talking last
evening with some fellows about labor papers, etc., when one of them remarked,
say, that UNITED MINE WORKERS' JOURNAL is going down to nothing ain't it? I
spoke up and said that I thought it a splendid paper, Oh, h--l, he said, I
don't see a d--n thing in it of interest to me, well, says I, what do you
take a labor paper for, in answer he said that if he took a paper at all it
was so that he might get the general news which he could not get out of the
JOURNAL. I then tried to show him that that was not the real idea of the
thing and that labor paper was not intended for general news, but that its
intent should be to contain reading matter bearing on the subject of labor
that will educate us in the industrial classes, the reforms needed and the
means or ways to get them, etc. This is my version of the object or purport
of the labor paper.

Well, I see the fight is still on in Indiana, and while I do not wish to
discourage anyone, I do think that a grave mistake was made, and that is by
those miners whose employers have conceded the advance resuming work. It is
simply a repetition of the Hocking strike. This is my view of the matter, one
operator concedes the demand and as a natural consequence his mines are run
to their fullest capacity while the others are being starved into submission.
Another thing that this system brings about is this, it makes room for blacklegs. And why? Just in this way: Mr. A. says that he will pay the price,
so does B. and C., the balance hold out, and say no, we won't pay it. Well,
men will not starve when they can get anything that looks like work, and the
consequence is that the fellows from those mines that won't pay the price go
to the mines of A and B to work--see. They have left the other mine open
for blacklegs, while on the other hand had none gone to work until a sufficient number of the operators acceded to the demand this opening would have
been closed to the ignorant Polander or Hun or negro and, if necessity demands it, stop all miners in the competitive field. It wouldn't hurt to try
this plan once, if it is possible to do so.[47]

Leaving that matter I will say that it has reached my ears that my name
had been sent in to be placed on the list of nominees of District 6 for vice-
president. Now I want to have a little something to say in that matter. I
wish to say that I am not an aspirant for that office, for I do not think that
it would be possible for prejudice to step aside long enough for me to be
elected and I am one of those fellows who don't want to run for office for
the sake of running. No, no; if I run for anything I want to be elected.
While I am of the opinion that the day is past when the negro shall no longer

content himself with small things and while I am of the opinion that others
have served in such offices who were no more competent to fill then than I,
yet I don't want to be butchered in the election. I think that if I could
be elected on the board and then be given a chance that I could possibly do
something for the advantage of the organization.

Oh, yes; I came near forgetting in reading over the names sent in for
national officers I do not see the name of one negro for even a member of
the board. Now I wish to say that these things should not be left for the
colored men to mention, but you white men should see that one colored man
is elected. Some fellow might say that we can do without that; I wish to
say that it is impossible, for take the negro out of the organization and
you have a vast army against you, one that is strong enough to be felt and
feared. Some fellow might say that I am advocating for myself, but such is
not the case, for there are a great many colored men who could fill the
position as well as myself and some possibly better. So I say, by all means
let us have one of them and put him to work, give the poor negro a chance,
its high time this was being done. Remember the white people of this country in 1776 cried out no taxation without representation. I hear that cry
today among the negroes of this country and I as a negro say, take warning
and heed the cry. More anon.

                                                            R. L. DAVIS
United Mine Workers' Journal, December 14, 1891.

                            2. DAVIS HOT

REPORTS WORK IN THE SUNDAY CREEK FAIR--COMPARES THE OLD AND NEW WAY OF
ELECTING OFFICERS--AND COMMENDS THE LATTER FOR ITS PURITY--ALSO GIVES A
FORCIBLE REMINDER TO WEST VIRGINIA.

                                        RENDVILLE, O., Jan. 11.

Work in the Sunday Creek Valley still remains fair, but we have no
assurance of how long it will last. Well, as the time for the holding of
our annual conventions is drawing close to hand I suppose that a great many
have on their thinking caps. I can say that I have been thinking some myself; in fact I have thought so much that I am afraid that were I to attempt
to express myself I would make a mess of it, consequently I have come to the
conclusion to keep some of them to myself and, by so doing, others will not
have the suggestion thrown out by a great many of our leading men and think
some of them excellent. However, I would like to differ with Brother J. H.
Taylor in regard to the present plan of making nominations. I must say that
the present plan is a good one in my opinion and I will try to make an explanation. In the first place, in my opinion, it is what the miners have been
clamoring for for the last ten years, viz.: that the officers should be
elected by the popular vote and not by vote of the delegates. Secondly,
under this plan we hold our conversations in the hall and not in the hotel
corridors, as we used to do. I suppose you all know what I mean by that.
Well, I mean to say that prior to the adoption of this plan our officers were
always elected in the hotel corridor or on side street corners or, in other
words, the button holing process. Under the old plan the rank and file didn't
know who would be nominated for offices in the conventions and consequently
instructed their delegates to vote for the best man, but instead in a great
many instances they voted contrary to their own opinions and why? Well,
simply because of the rottenness of the thing; something like this: Mr. A.
would like to be elected to a certain office; Mr. B. has a man that he wants
for the same office the consequence is that they will begin to hold caucuses
and the one will say this and that about the other to defeat him, when in fact
both of them might perhaps be the greatest rascals in the whole business; see
how rotten it was. Do we have this now? No; not if we live up to the law,
but quite different, for under the present each local is at liberty to nomi-
nate who they please. The names are forwarded to the district or national
secretary and there compiled by him and sent out again to the locals. The
locals then elect their delegates and instruct them just what and who to vote
for and by so doing the rank and file does the electing and not the delegates

and for these reasons I think it a much better plan and I will vouch that
the majority of the miners think the same. Well, before closing this letter
I would like to have a word to the West Virginia officers and miners. I
chanced to go to Glouster on last Saturday on some business, and while there
I concluded to go to Jacksonville and while there I met Brother J. L. Edmunds, vice president of District 17, U.M.W. of A. I was much surprised to
learn that he was there working in the mines. In our talk I learned that
he had been blacklisted in his state and he had to come over in Ohio to
seek a livelihood. Great guns, just think how preposterous the thing is,
an executive officer being compelled to leave his own state and at that
during his term of office, to seek work elsewhere. Say Brother Moran, did
you not know this? Didn't you know it Brother Stephenson? Strange is it
not that in all your writings you never made mention of the matter. Strikes
me that some inconsistency has been used in this matter. Now then we will
see your vice president is by virtue of his office a commissioned organizer
according to your constitution, is he not? If so, then why this useless
expense of having Brother W. B. Wilson in that section. Could you have
gotten that money and paid it to Brother Edmunds to travel over the state
with. He could have done the same work and at a much less expense to the
organization. Now think the matter over and see if you have treated the
brother right. Just such things as these is what the negro is kicking
against and we are not going to have it. If your vice president is a negro
he must be treated the same as a white man and unless you do there is going
to be a mighty earthquake somewhere. Mark my words such things as these
cannot be allowed and we won't allow it either. Now I am not boasting, but
such a thing as this would not be tolerated in Ohio. Oh, no! We would have
one of the worst (I came near saying one of the d---t) strikes that you ever
heard of. Boys, you all had better come over and let us give you a few
lessons, you need it.

                                                      R. L. DAVIS

United Mine Workers' Journal, January 14, 1892.

3.   DAVIS DECLINES

Work in the Sunday Creek Slacking Off Somewhat

        Rendville, O., Jan. 18, 1892.--Work in this part of the Sunday Creek
Valley has taken a somewhat decided change. None of the mines are doing so
well as they have in the past. However, we are not the least surprised as
we had been expecting it for some time. Mr. Editor please allow me space
enough in your valuable paper to say that in your last issue I noticed my
name among those nominated for the office of vice president of the U.M.W. of
A. I would like to say to the miners of our grand old organization that
inasmuch as I am not competent to fill so important an office, I must say
frankly that I am not a candidate for said office.
        However, I wish to thank those who appreciated me so highly as to give
me the nomination. I would just say to them to wait a little while, and if
given the chances, I will certainly equip myself for some of the things that
I now must necessarily decline.

                              Yours in the cause of labor.

                                             R. L. DAVIS

United Mine Workers' Journal, January 21, 1892.

4. DAVIS APPRECIATES

THE HONOR CONFERRED BY THE OHIO MINERS, AND EXCHANGES A FEW WORDS WITH
STEPHENSON--OVER THE IMPUTED GRIEVANCE OF BROTHER EDMUNDS

RENDVILLE, O., Jan. 25.

Having just returned home from our annual convention of District No. 6,
United Mine Workers, and having nothing else to do I thought I would try to
write a few lines to your valuable paper so that they may know that I am
still in the land of the living. With your permission, Mr. Editor, I would
like a word or two in answer to my friend and brother, Henry Stephenson, of
District 17 of West Virginia. I would just say that upon my arrival home I
went to the post office and there found a copy of the constitution, District
17, as promised, which I was very glad to receive. However, before having
anything to say on that matter I would like to make a little explanation to
my beloved Brother Stephenson. In his letter he says that Davis does not
know what he is talking about when he interferes with District 17. Well,
that little piece of phraseology is the only one in his letter that I take
exception to. I will just say that I care not who it pleases or displeases.
I will always be the lad to speak my mind on anything that I think to be
unjust, whether it be national, district, sub-district, local or personal,
nor do I care whether it be Ohio, Pennsylvania, Indiana, Illinois, or West
Virginia. If I think you wrong I will be sure to tell you of it and I think
I am right in so doing.

Now then a word or so in vindication of myself in the matter. I took
the word of Brother Edmunds for the truth and I must still say that if true
the most unprejudiced mind would say that he was treated unfair. Since then
we have received the testimony of Brother Stephenson, the only thing left
for us is to weigh the evidence of both sides. This, I think, would be fair,
would it not? Well, then, if things are as stated in Brother Stephenson's
letter, then Brother Edmunds is at fault and not the district, for I do not
consider that he would be entitled to any of the benefits of organization
if he nor his local were in good standing. No, no; not for a moment would I
assume such a position. I am willing to admit that I am a little saucy,
but not unfair. I wish to do justice to Brothers Moran, Stephenson and
District 17, as much so as to Brother Edmunds, and will, and I hope that all
will be taken in a friendly spirit, and that no ill-feelings may be engendered. As for the brother being blacklisted, I have his word, only; that matter
being disputed by Brother Stephenson. The only thing that bothers my mind
is: Why would Brother Edmunds tell a bare-faced falsehood about it? I can
see no good in that, as it would only have a tendency to do him more harm
than good, for all that I want is the right thing. Give me that and you will
have no trouble with me. Brother Stephenson said in his first letter that he
did not wish to get into a newspaper wrangle with any one. I would say that
it was not my desire but simply to get an explanation. Am I right or am I
wrong? In reference to the questions asked by the brother, if as stated by
him certainly no blame can be attached to District 17 and I am very thankful
for his reply, also the copy of their constitution.

Before closing this letter I would like to say a few words to the miners
of Ohio in reference to my election as a member of the district executive
board and the handsome vote that I received. Fellow miners, your action in
your last convention fully demonstrates to me that race prejudice will soon
be a thing of the past if other states do as the grand old state of Ohio. I
must say that I have always contended that the labor organizations of this
country have done and will do more toward the placing of all men upon an
equal standing without regard to race, creed, color or sex than all others
combined, the church not excepted. This is saying a great deal, but it is
nevertheless, true. I can only say to the miners of District 6 that I am more
than thankful to them for the kindness shown me and I promise that I will do
all in my power for the upbuilding of our organization; all that I ask is,
give me a chance to develop myself to the callings of my craft. I can only
say as others that I will do my best and man can do no more. I trust that
when we again meet in annual convention that every man who works in or around
the mines in the State of Ohio will have been mustered upon the roll of

membership in our organization.

    With best wishes for the success of your valuable paper and the con-
tinued growth of the organization, I am yours in the cause of suffering
humanity.

                                                        R. L. DAVIS

United Mine Workers' Journal, January 28, 1892.

                    5.   EDMONDS HIMSELF[48]

            Takes a Hand in the Unpleasant Discussion

        Regarding the Status of the Negro in West Virginia

        Says the Whole of the Minutes Were Not Published

                                        JACKSONVILLE, O., Jan. 30.

    I have been very sick for the past two weeks and was unable to reply to
the articles in the JOURNAL of the 21st and 28th, but will now make an effort.
Brother Stephenson, in his reply to Brother Davis said, that he "did not
wish to enter into a newspaper wrangle." If that be true, why didn't
Stephenson state the matter just as it was, instead of trying to mislead?
Why did he send Davis the unfinished minutes of our convention? I say unfinished because a resolution as an amendment to the constitution offered by
Brother C. C. Wood and Brother Hogan, and unanimously adopted by that convention, "that the vice president be commissioned and put on the road as
organizer." That amendment brother miners, was left out of the constitution
and everytime that Stephenson, or any other man or set of men, say that the
executive officers have not discriminated against the colored miners of
District 17, they say what is not so.
    I see in the JOURNAL, words to this effect:
                    "APPEAL.

    To the Officers and Brothers of District 17, U.M.W. of A:[49]
    "BROTHERS--I am requested by the members of Local Assembly 2596, of
Monongah, W. Va., to ask for financial aid for their victimized brothers who
were discharged January 7 for joining the assembly when it was re-instated on
January 2, etc.
                        "M. F. MORAN, Pres. or M.W.
                        "H. STEPHENSON, Sec'y.-Treas."

    Now, fellow-miners, to show you how inconsistent these gentlemen are
and how they discriminate when it comes to color. In the latter part of
April, '91, I was discharged by M. T. Davis the third day after I was elected
Vice President of District 17, West Virginia. Local Assembly 1279 would not
take action on the matter until M. F. Moran was seen. Well, we saw Moran
after a week or two and I stated my case. He told me that he would put me on
the road to organize. In a few days after he made a trip to the Flat Top;
he was so long getting back that I commenced seeking work. I first tried
Carvers Bros., and failed. His excuse was that he had no room and at the
same time was advertising for men for his mines up the river. I also tried
to get work at Johnson's and Wyant's, with the same result. I then tried at
Union mines (T. P. Gray's mines). There I received work. I was put in an
air course to be driven twelve feet wide at 21 cents per bushel and 50 cents
a yard. In that air course was fourteen inches of slate and coal two feet
above and two feet below. I worked there for a few days and could not make
my salt. I was informed that I had to work that place or leave. Well, I
went over in the next mine, called Mount Morris, and got a place there that
a fellow-miner was just leaving. I worked there awhile and went to Black
Diamond mines from there to this place, where I have been ever since. Harry
Stephenson knew that I was discharged, for he has written to the JOURNAL and
it is on record.

The latter part of June Samuel Johnson, a man with a family, was discharged at Johnson's mine for trying to keep a boy from taking a mule in the mines, (the drivers being on strike.) The boy told the bank boss that Johnson called him a blackleg and Johnson had to go. He was a financial member of 1279 and we had not a better worker in there. Brother Johnson laid his case before the assembly and it was laid over to wait the action of the executive officers and it was lying there when I left and I guess it must have went down in the great financial scratch. I just mention these little things to show you that the negroes of District 17 have no rights that the officers are bound to respect. I will just say to T. P. Gray, that when I get through with gentlemen I will commence with others. I remain, Mr. Editor, yours unfinancially but fraternally,

JOHN L. EDMONDS.

United Mine Workers' Journal, February 11, 1892.

6.   THE WANDERERS

Should Be Brought in To Share the Burdens

Davis Explains His Work Among Colored Friends

RENDVILLE, O., Feb. 14.

Having reached home from Columbus where I have been attending the annual convention of the United Mine Workers of America and having nothing else to do, I thought I would wile away the time by writing a few lines. Well the convention being over with, I trust that each delegate will do his utmost for the upbuilding of our organization during the present year, so that when we again meet we may boast of saying that we have more than redoubled our members. This I think can be done if each one would only do his duty, and judging from the enthusiasm shown by the delegates in the convention I think they will. Boys, I can only say bring in the wanderers, that they may share the burden and help to consummate the work already begun, by stepping forward and with willing hearts and ready hands take hold of the work of ameliorating the conditions of suffering humanity. Well, to be brief, I will not have anything further to say on that score, but before closing I would like to say for the benefit of the miners of Mine 19 or Buckingham that I think there is a misunderstanding between them and me in some way. I would say that this is a matter of long standing, and to make the matter plain it originated from a rumor that colored men would not be permitted to work in that mine. This happened something like a year ago, when Mine 8 was shut down and action had been taken that as many of the men as could find places would be taken in the other mines belonging to the S.C.C. Co. About this time a rumor got afloat that the men at Buckingham had passed a resolution that negroes could not work there. Well, the colored men held meetings for the purpose of withdrawing from the organization. I went into their meeting and advised them not to be too hasty, but rather to wait and investigate the matter and find out whether it was true or not, telling them to appoint a committee and I would accompany them. Finally the miners of Mine 3 sent a committee and I went also. We met several of the miners and among them two of the committee of the mine, Messrs. Jenkins and Armstrong. We had a talk over the matter and found it to be untrue. We came home and reported it as such. Now here is where the trouble comes in, that I was not instructed to go there by President Jones. This is very true; I went on my own responsibility, but had previously written President Jones and Rae about the matter and had not received an answer. When I came back I sent my bill to President Jones, stating that inasmuch as he had not ordered me to do this work, it was left with him as to whether it was paid or not. In a few days I received a letter from President Jones stating that he had received my bill, had signed and forwarded it to Secretary Pearce for payment, etc. Now then fellow-miners of Buckingham, let me explain. When I

came to your place it was for the sole purpose of trying to keep some 300
colored men from withdrawing from the organization and I succeeded. Now
was it not worth the paltry sum of a days work? I think it was and after
having made explanation I have no doubt that you will think as I do. I
would not have written this, but it came to my ears that there was a very
bitter feeling against me on that account. I will say further that if this
is not satisfactory I would be pleased to meet the miners of Buckingham to
talk the matter over at any time that they may mention. Yours for labor,

R. L. DAVIS

United Mine Workers' Journal, February 18, 1892.

7. ENCOURAGING

Successful Campaign of Miller and Davis

Foreign Speaking Miners Join the Organization in a Body

Colored Miners Also Join Hands With the Rest

Many Thanks Due to Energetic Local Men

RENDVILLE, O., Feb. 28.

Having nothing else to do I thought I would trouble you a little with
our doings of last week. Having been ordered by President Nugent to go to
Long Run, Dillonvale and Laurelton, I accordingly packed my little bundle
and proceeded thence. Upon my arrival I met Vice President Miller and we
at once proceeded to work in the interest of the organization. It will be
remembered that at the three places there are upward of 1,000 miners and
mine laborers employed and I think I can truthfully say that less than one-
fifth of them were members of the United Mine Workers of America. The causes
of this condition of things may be assigned to various things. One of the
reasons was because of this fact, that out of the 1,000 men or more at least
two-thirds or more are of the foreign-speaking element, consisting of Hungarians, Polanders, Slavs, Bohemians and Belgians. Of course out of this
vast army of foreign-speaking people some of them were union men, but very
few indeed.

I believe the greatest drawback that these people have is the lack of
a leader. I also found a number of the English speaking people who were not
connected with the organization, and of course this was also an example for
others to follow.

In company with Vice President Miller, after scanning the fields and
taking a general survey of the ground, we got down to actual work. Having
made arrangements with the superintendent, Mr. George Atherton, to lay each
mine idle on the days of meeting we arranged our meetings as follows: On
Wednesday at Dillonvale, Thursday at Long Run, and Friday at Laurelton.
Well, I believe our visit a successful one; however, we will leave that for
others to judge. On Wednesday we held our meeting at Dillonvale, which was
very well attended. We gave the boys a short talk, after which all others
who wished had their say. At the conclusion of the discussion one was
selected from among the foreign-speaking element to explain to them the object of the meeting and as near as possible what had been said. After an
explanation had been made a vote was taken that they would join the organization in a body which was carried unanimously. So far so good. I believe
these men will work in unison with their fellow-craftsmen hereafter and this
I do know, if they don't it will not be the fault of their local officers.
However, I believe the men to be in dead earnest this time, and will signify
the same by the payment of their dues and assessments hereafter. Our next
meeting was held at Long Run, on Thursday, here we had an extraordinary good
meeting. One of the principal features of this meeting with me was the large
number of my people who were in attendance and about these people I wish to

say that they, to a man after things were explained to them, were ready to
join our organization and signified their willingness by subscribing their
names. Another feature of the meeting was the large number of foreigners
present and what I mean by that is the Polanders, Hungarians, Bohemians,
Slavs, etc. One thing that I would like to say about these people is, that
they were very attentive to the business of the meeting and especially when
one of their own number was speaking. I will just here make this plainer.
The checkweighman at this mine is a Polander, but can speak the English
language quite fluently. After Vice President Miller and myself got through
speaking this gentleman got up and interpreted it to the Polanders, Huns
and Slavs in a very able manner. It was quite interesting to notice how they
would flock around him while he was talking, in fact they just got as close
as they possibly could and looked right at him. Another noticeable feature
was this, that although the meeting was an out-door one, one could almost
hear a pin fall while he was talking. After he was through a motion was
made that they would join in a body; the vote was taken by the raising of
the hands and the motion was unanimously carried, with loud cheers from the
foreign-speaking element. At this juncture a secretary was elected from
each nationality to take their names as members of the organization, with
splendid results, after which they elected their officers, and I want to
show to your many readers the fairness of the occasion and of the officers
chosen. Among them were one Hungarian, one negro, one Polander, one Slav,
and one white, so you can readily see that these people mean business and
have started about it in the right way.

On Friday we held our meeting at Laurelton. This meeting was also
well attended and after the talk of Vice President Miller, William Nixon and
the writer a vote was taken to join the organization in a body. This was
also carried unanimously. Of course they had no officers to elect as they
had a local already in existence; oh! yes they did; they elected a Polander
on the pit committee. Now, I am not positive as to whether he was a Polander
or not, but he was of the foreign speaking element, and I think that those
people will be in line with their fellow-craftsmen and with the perseverance
of the untiring staff of officers that they have I think that this can be
made one of the strongest organized sub-districts in the State. In a word
I think that our trip in that section of the State a very successful one
indeed. Fearing this may be consigned to the waste basket I will stop.
However I would like to extend to Messrs. Thos. Wilkinson, Richard Wilson,
Joseph Curran and Matt Scott, of Dillon, and Wm. Nixon and George Reed of
Laurelton and Wm. Atwood, Wm. Fitzgerald, John Partington, M. Brooks and
Samuel Skinner of Long Run, our heartfelt thanks for their aid in the good
work, and trust that they will continue. Yes, we also wish to thank the
checkweighman at Long Run for his assistance which was invaluable and trust
that he will also continue working for the cause of suffering humanity. We
also wish to thank Mr. George Atherton for his kindness in suspending work
in the mines on days of meeting, thereby securing to us good meetings. Well
I don't suppose you have any more space to spare, wishing success to your
valuable paper and the upbuilding of our organization.

R. L. DAVIS

United Mine Workers' Journal, March 3, 1892.

8. BRAZIL, INDIANA

An Appeal to Act Impartially Toward Colored Miners

BRAZIL, Ind., March 21.--Having been a reader of your valuable paper for
the year, and seeing nothing from here, and the need of so much, I wish to
say as an Afro-American, I am pleased to hear of the stand that Brother Riley [50]
and Davis are taking for our people, and must say that I had some of the
same troubles to contend with as Brother Riley when I was at Bevier, Ky., and
the color line was the cause of losing a good strong Local Assembly there.
Now, my Anglo-Saxon brothers, why do you not keep your pledge of honor, as

you vowed when you were initiated into Knighthood? You can never get your
union strong as long as you ignore the Afro-American as a coal producer
against you.[51]
    When it becomes time for you to strike, as is too often the case, then
out of revenge we, the bulk of the Afro-Americans go to work for spite, and
because when everything is smooth you object to our color, which is unconstitutional and contrary to the will of our National, state and general
officials. I have letters in my possession from coal operators in Indiana
stating that their men had lost a strike, but still refused to work with me
and my people, but I shall try to get the Afro-Americans to reorganize here
if possible and get some readers for the UNITED MINE WORKERS' JOURNAL.

                                                    WILLING HANDS

United Mine Workers' Journal, March 24, 1892.

9.   LAND OF BONDAGE

WHERE THE BOSS TERRORIZES HONEST WORKMEN--BRUTISH DEMEANOR OF THE UNDERLINGS
IN WEST VIRGINIA--OATHS AND STONES RESORTED TO IN DISPERSING MEETINGS--TWO
HUNDRED MEN PERMIT ONE COWARD TO INTIMIDATE THEM

                                          RENDVILLE, O., June 26.
    Having got back home safely from the mountains of West Virginia, I
thought I would write a few lines for the purpose of letting your many readers know what I saw and had to contend with while here. Also the places
visited by your humble servant in that field. I will say that there is no
place that needs organization more than the miners of West Virginia, for
today those men are virtually slaves. Think of it, men working in a vein
of coal on an average thickness of three feet, take down the roof, carry
their timbers, such as props, etc., from the mountain side, mark them, then
load them in a mine car and see that they are taken to their working places;
and all for the enormous sum of 25, 40 and 50 cents per ton. When talking
with these men, most all of them say we ought to be in the organization; we
need organization, but we were in it some time back and it amounted to nothing. We were called out on strike, with the understanding that we would receive so much per week while on strike, and received nothing and were told
to resume work under the same conditions as we came out on. That they were
organized at one time and certain individuals who served as officers with
the money, etc., and in every instance it was a white man that got the money;
that when they were in the organization they never seen an officer after they
had been organized; that the officers have at all time devoted their time in
other parts and left them to shift for themselves, etc. These are only a few
of the excuses that have been made to me while in that section of the country.
Now, I will say that the cause of this state of affairs in that field is the
lack of confidence in one another. The one is afraid of the other. The whites
say they are afraid of the colored men and the colored men say that they are
afraid of the whites, so that is the way the thing goes. Another reason is
the cowardice displayed by the men toward the superintendents and bosses.
It is a fact, one man serving in the capacity of boss in any way can walk into
a meeting of 200 of those men and rip out an oath and tell them to get away
from here or there and they will shy away as though they were slaves to them.
These are plain and unvarnished truths, no lie about it. I will just here
give you a couple of incidents that happened with me while there at a place
called Claremont. We held a meeting on the 10th inst.; for this meeting we
got the school house. The meeting not being very well attended it was decided
that another meeting would be held at the same place on the 13th. Very good;
on that day I was there, went around to every house for fear the men might
say that they forgot it, as they sometimes do. Everybody was going to be
there. I went to the trustees and got the key to the building, borrowed lamps
from those who would lend them, and had everything in readiness. About this
time Mr. Roe, one of the company, learned what was going on. He went to the

trustees and told them that he wanted that school house closed up at once or
he would find out why it was not. This was about 7 o'clock in the evening,
or probably a little later. Don't you know those trustees came there almost
running and out of breath, informed me that they were compelled to shut the
house up; that Mr. Roe was awful mad about it being opened, etc., and no
talk that I could give them would satisfy them that Mr. Roe had nothing to
do with the house. So we had to close the place up. I then tried to get
the men together anyhow, but they were that badly scared that I could get
them to do nothing, so we done nothing with those men and had to leave them.
    We next went to a place a mile distant called Alaska. Here we announced
a meeting for the following night in the school house. Mr. Lawton, the superintendent, got hold of it some way and gave them to understand that they
should not meet in the school house and that he did not intend that any
meeting should be held there or anywhere. Well, we did not get a meeting
there that night, but got the promise of the men that we could get a meeting
there on Wednesday, the 22d, in the open air. Well, on that date I went there
with the full intention of establishing a local union. I notfied every man
on the place and I want to say had them at the meeting. In fact it seemed
to be my brightest meeting that I had ever gotten in the district. We were
about to open the meeting and were trying to select a chairman. Nobody would
serve. Some of the men were upon box cars and some were upon the ice house.
I heard some fellow in the crowd say, "Here comes a chairman; Brown will
serve." I didn't know who he was talking about, but I soon learned that he
was one of the head pushers of the place. Well, he came right up in the
crowd and ordered the men to get down off of the ice house. They didn't move
fast enough and he picked up a stone and pretended that he was going to throw
it and I tell you they rolled off, all except one colored boy, who remained
perfectly still and who had the manhood to tell him that he had better not
strike him. After this he went away, so we then resumed our efforts in trying
to get a chairman and seeing they were afraid, I opened the meeting, starting
my talk with boys. Everything was going lovely, I suppose I had talked about
twenty minutes or a half hour when that gentleman returned. I had noticed
some of the men shying away, but thought nothing of it; well, he walked right
up in front of me with stone in hand, and addressed me thus: "Say, look here,
you ----- ----- black scamp, I want you to get off of these premises right
away, move along or I'll knock --- out of you in a minute." I had not very
far to go; I just stepped down on the railroad track and told the boys to come
with me, and we would have our meeting anyhow. That wasn't enough, he came
again and says ----- ----- your black soul, I want you to move either up or
down this track, and that ----- quick. I then gave him to understand that I
was not on his property, and would not go any further. I tried to get the
boys to follow me, but to no avail. They were afraid, and so then I left for
home, and that night too.
    Now, I want to say that it is going to take time and money to get the
men along the New River into the organization. Flowery speeches and enthusiasm will not do it, but there must be some one there continually for some
time to come, and then mind that you don't have asoft snap of it. I said I
would mention the places visited, but as this is already too lengthy. I will
write again.
    A word on Straitsville: Here's to you. I am certainly proud of your
last move, how did you hold so long is the question that I am asking myself.
Well boys, you are in with us now, and we all know that you are a good set of
men. All that I can say is, now help us make the organization what it should
be is my prayer.

                                                              R. L. DAVIS

United Mine Workers' Journal, June 30, 1892.

10.   STILL UNSETTLED

AT RENDVILLE--TROUBLE OVER A BOSS AT NO. 8--DISCUSSES THE QUESTION OF RACE
AND CREED PREJUDICE--SAYS SPENCE WILL HAVE TO HUSTLE TO ORGANIZE WEST
VIRGINIA

RENDVILLE, O., July 11.

Work is yet at a standstill at mine No. 3 with no visible signs of an
early settlement. However, it will come bye-and-bye. No one has lost hopes
yet. There was a little trouble at mine No. 8, on Wednesday, July 6, caused
by the boss quitting, and some of the men not caring to work under a colored
boss. The consequence was the men went home and the mine was laid idle for
that day.

I say that some of the men didn't care to work under a colored mine
boss, and so expressed themselves, but I do not believe that all of them were
in that frame of mind, at the same time it came near causing trouble in our
ranks; because we have a goodly number of colored men in this part of the
country, and these men, especially those working at that mine, were hot and
swearing vengeance against everybody and everything, and a large number
threatening to withdraw from the organization at once and never have anything further to do with it if such discriminations were allowed. I knew
what that meant; it simply meant that we would go back to the same conditions
as we had ten years ago; no organization or no nothing, discord and dissen-
and strife would prevail. On the same day a meeting was called, and
the writer attended, to try, if possible, to suppress the feeling that was
prevailing. The meeting was opened and the business stated, and then the
wrangle began, and some very incendiary remarks were made on both sides.

After listening for awhile and seeing things were getting no better, but
getting worse, I got the sanction to talk to the boys awhile and, knowing the
men of the Sunday Creek valley as I did, I knew that they were too intelligent
a class of men to allow any such proceedings to be carried on. I knew that
they did not want to destroy what little organization they had. I knew that
they did not want a rehearsal of 1881-82, for it had taken years to build up
our organization to its present standing and it would be foolish and unwise
to do anything that would have a tendency to tear it down. After a little
talk we got the matter settled, as far as the boss was concerned, i.e., the
colored boss, and the threatened trouble was averted and I truly hope that we
will never have a repetition of that thing again. We have some men among us
who are members of our organization only because they are forced to be. These
men will naturally take any advantages that they can get to squirm out of it.
Don't think that these are colored men alone, for such is not the case, for
there are a few whites mixed up in the gang. Some few of our colored men
say that they will never do any good until they organize to themselves, that
is, withdraw from our present form of organization and get up an organization
of their own. Well, when I hear such stuff as that, no matter from whose lips
it comes, it makes me nervous (mad), because I think that we are too far advanced in civilization to even entertain such foolish notions. I have got it
fixed up in my brain that a man is a man, no matter what the color of his
skin is, and I don't care who thinks different. I think myself just as good
as anybody else, although the color of my skin is dark. I had nothing to do
with the making of myself, probably if I had the results would be somewhat
different.

I have had men call me a nigger, but I always call him the same kind of
a fool, so we keep even on that score. I am one of those who are looking for
a brighter day to dawn upon the working classes and it can only be attained
through the medium of labor organization and I want to do my share to that
end. It is high time for the color line to be dropped in all branches of
industry, for until then there will be no peace. The negro has a right in
this country; those of today were born here, they didn't emigrate here. They
are here and to stay. They are competitors in the labor market and they have
to live, and I think were we, as workingmen, to turn our attention to fighting
monopoly in land and money, we would accomplish a great deal more than we will
by fighting among ourselves on account of race, creed, color or nationality.

Let us learn this and we will begin to do better, for by so doing our wages
will increase. We will have better homes and our families will be made
happier.

Now, a word to Brother Spence, he says he could take me and organize
the miners of West Virginia. I am glad that the brother has that confidence. I must say that I always maintained that two men should go into
that field, the one white and the other colored. I believe more good could
be accomplished in that way. Now, my brother, there is no one who would
feel happier than I were the miners of that region brought into our ranks,
but let me say that you will have to hustle and don't you forget it. I am
one of those who are eager and anxious to do what I can for organized labor,
for it is from that source that I must live and I am only too glad to get
to do something sometimes. I think were I as good a christian as I am an
agitator, as some call me, I would surely get to heaven when I die. I will
say to the brother that I hope we will get the chance or some one else of
organizing New River.

R. L. DAVIS

United Mine Workers' Journal, July 14, 1892.

11. NUMBER THREE

Championed by the Redoubtable Davis of Rendville,

Who Wants a Satisfactory Answer to Certain Questions

In Behalf of the Men at the Above Named Mine

RENDVILLE, O., July 18.

Please allow me a little space in your valuable paper for the purpose of
making a few remarks on the conditions here:
Mine 3 is still idle and it seems that we are as near a settlement now
as we were two weeks ago. When I last wrote it seemed that the chances for
an early settlement were good, but not so now. At that time all the miners
were idle. I want to say further that it was mutually agreed that all the
mines would resume work at the same time, that is, there would be no work at
any of the mines until a settlement had been made for all concerned. We were
told this and felt easy on the matter. But in that we were much mistaken
inasmuch as the other mines started up on last Wednesday and we are still out.
Now what we want to know is this: Why were these other mines started without
our knowledge of the same? and we want a very satisfactory answer, too.
I want to say, that the only cause for organizing a sub-district was
for the purpose of more easily adjusting all grievances that might occur.
Furthermore, in this district I believe we have a rule that in cases where
one mine is locked out on account of any demand made for scale rates, that
all other mines operated by the same company be stopped until an adjustment
is made. This is why we connected ourselves with Sub-District 9. Our miners
are perfectly willing to abide by all the laws and regulations of said sub-
district so long as things are carried on in a systematic manner. Heretofore,
we have been treated very fairly by the sub-district and have nothing to
complain of, but in this case we do not think everything just right, and we
don't know where the blame properly belongs. This is what we want to find
out. There is a section in our district constitution that any mine or local
in any sub-district will not be entitled to representation in the district.
Now, then, I fear that if this thing is allowed to continue as it is we will
certainly get in bad standing in the sub-district, no matter what the consequences may be, and when I say this I am only voicing the sentiment of the
miners of Mine No. 3. The men say that there is no need of them paying to
the sub-district if one mine is allowed to remain idle while the rest are at
work, the same being contrary to the rules of the district. I have had a

hundred or more men to ask me why these mines were working, and I could not
give them an answer. Since then I have   Brother Adams, the sub-district
president, and he says that he is not to blame for it. Now who is to blame?
Speak up, we want to know, so that there will be no misunderstanding in the
matter.

Now Mr. Editor, I want to comment a little on a letter that appeared
in the Ohio State Journal on the 14th inst., by a gentleman who has been
traveling through this section of the country. He says that on account of
the Homestead trouble, that the leading disturbers among the miners are
trying to incite a general strike if possible. Right there I want to say
that this I do not believe to be true, but suppose it was, so that all
branches of industry were prepared to make the move, would it not be better?
I believe it would; such has got to come sooner or later to teach the money
kings of this country that labor has some rights that must be respected.
The gentleman goes on further to say that the miners of Sunday Creek Coal
Company seem to be ready for a strike or lay off at any time and the men in
the W. P. Rend's miners are off for the slightest grievance; they will work
one day and strike the next. This I believe to be quite untrue. He further
says that last week Mr. Rend had occasion to discharge a mine boss and put
another in his stead, he says, the miners didn't like the new boss and consequently struck and that they sent word to another mine a few miles in the
country and had them strike also, and at Rendville that they are still idle
for reasons just given. This goes to show that the so-called gentleman did
not know what he was talking about, or that he is a very noted prevaricator,
for there is not a word of truth in the statements. True, the men at Rendville are idle, but not for the reasons assigned by him, but as I have stated
in my previous letters. He even goes on to say something in regard to what
Prof. McFarland says: "That the miners are something like a bull in a china
shop using more force than judgment and obtaining about the same results."
That gentleman may have said it, if so, no one is very much surprised owing
to the position that he holds. He also says that   "About two weeks ago the
men at one of the Sunday Creek mines elected among themselves a boss mule
driver, and demanded that he be paid 25 cents extra the usual price of being
$2.00 per day." He says "the request was not granted and the whole mining
force consisting of 160 men came out on a strike but went to work next morning
with nothing but a loss to the men in wages of about $400." Note that state-
ment if you please; miners electing a boss hauler. I have been here for some
time but I have never heard of miners electing the boss hauler before. I
know this, however, that he is generally paid more than the rest of the
drivers, but so far as the men are concerned about electing him the gentleman
either lied or I am off of my base. The gentleman (a misnomer) in writing was
evidently trying to mislead the public or people, who know nothing of mining
and I have no doubt succeeded to a certain extent. He was either trying to
mislead the public by placing the miners in such a bad light or he didn't
know a thing of what he was talking about. Such statements have a tendency
to injure the reputation of the miner, but the people are beginning to learn
that we have been misrepresented and that we are not so bad after all.[52]

In conclusion I want to have a friendly rap with President McBride concerning a statement made in a speech while here in regard to the miners of
Mine 3 coming out for slight grievances, etc. Now Bro. McBride I want to
place the miners of Mine 3 in a true light and, I want to be truthful as near
as I can in the matter. Let me say that it is untrue about the miners of
mine 3 striking so much, for I cannot tell the day when the men of Mine 3 came
out until not long since, sometime in the spring, when the men thought they
were being imposed on too heavily, and it was on the docking question. Men
were being laid off a day for a single dock although we had a docking system,
yet it was never granted to our men. On this particular occasion some 26 men
were laid off, and I can truthfully say that of all that number there were
not more than three of them that could have been called a dock had it been
legally done. I say this because I am in a position to know, for at that
time I was serving in the capacity of checkweighman and seen it myself. The
men felt sore over the matter and the next morning sent the committee to the
boss to get a change. The boss said no, that he had no power in the matter
and the consequence was the men went home. This is the only strike that I
know of the men engaging in for a long while. I can say also that the men at
Mine 3 have at all other times regarded the laws as laid down in the consti-

tution, and I am sorry to say that they have been the only ones in the valley
that did do it, and they are the only ones that did not get scale rates for
break-throughs, etc. How does that strike you? Are they paid for this kind
of work now? Taking the men's word for it I would answer no. I say I take
the men's words for it because I have not been in the mine for two years,
but I believe they will tell the truth in such matters as these. If you
want to know how business is carried on say so, and I can tell you and you
will disabuse yourself of the idea that we are troublesome in any sense of
the word.

   This is supposed to not be taken in any other manner than the spirit in
which it is written and that, I will assure you, is friendly. Trusting that
when I write again our trouble will be adjusted and everything going smoothly.

R. L. DAVIS

United Mine Workers' Journal, July 21, 1892.

12. VERY PLAIN TALK

Again Indulged in by Our Correspondent Davis

Nugent's Speech Causes Some Irritation Underneath the Collar

And to Drop on Davis' Official Neck Prospects of a Tramp

RENDVILLE, O., Aug. 6.

   Since my last there has not been any great change in the conditions of
things at Mine 3. It seems that the wanderers are going to have their own
way irrespective of the consequences. They are resorting to all kinds of
trickery to carry their point, but I don't think it will avail them anything.
The writer has been classed as a very dangerous man to be with; so in walking
along the streets he can hear himself talked about by the clique. Of course
there are not many of them but they have their bearings; there are some who,
although they don't belong to the clique, are easily led, and strange to say
by men that they know don't amount to a pinch of snuff, so far as manhood is
concerned. And yet, these would-be men are most all church members, good
Christians, the lights of the world, etc. Well all that I have to say is
this, that if such men as these are the criterions for me to follow, then I
prefer going through the woods. President Nugent was here last Wednesday
night and gave the boys a good talking to. Of course I was not at the meeting
but I was told that some of them got hot under the collar. I suppose the
talk was too plain for them as people of this stripe don't like sound doctrine.[5]
   Well, it is no more than I expected in the first of this affair that the
ringleaders would get hot with me because I would not take sides with them.
Such is the case and I have been given to understand that my time is not very
long at Mine 3. They promise me that at the next election they will place
some one else on the tipple as checkweighman other than myself. They will
also make their own selections for a committee of the mine, that is if they
deem it expedient to have a committee at all. They tell me though that they
intend to be organized and all that, but does the move that they are making
indicate it? It don't seem so to me, I don't know how it looks to others. I
can only speak for myself and as far as I can see into the matter organization
will be a thing of the past. Now I don't want any one to infer that I mean
that all colored men are alike in this matter for such is not the case, for
we have some colored men here who are as true as steel, who are as good union
men as ever breathed the breath of life. These men are all right and they
will remain so, but these other--I came very near saying things I am afraid
will remain as they are. No talk, no advice will make them see a thing in
any other way than they want to see it. They haven't sense enough to reason
with a man, oh, no! if you don't believe as they do away with you, you are
nothing no how but a traitor. That is what they call me and all others who

have the temerity to speak against their ideas. Oh, if you speak you are a
crank sure. One thing that surprises me is this, that these would-be smart
men are mostly young men, with but few exceptions men who have had the chance
to educate themselves, who say that they read and keep up with the times,
but when you seek to find out their reading matter you will find that it is
the Police Gazette, the Cincinnati Enquirer or State Journal. They haven't
time to read a labor paper; there is nothing in them they say but trash, etc.
Oh, by the way, you had better be careful about publishing my letters, for
I heard that one of your subscribers of this town had threatened to write
you to discontinue his paper on account of my letter of last week, but I
hope he will be more sensible and if I write anything that is untrue, I hope
he will avail himself of the opportunity of disputing it through the columns
of your valuable journal (I cannot see how a sane man could do without it).

Well, it is simply amusing to hear some of these smart men's ideas expressed in relation to the difference between capital and labor. They claim
that capital has a right to the reins of supremacy and that labor should bow
submissively to the biddings of capital, that instead of strikes and so
forth, that if you want anything such as an advance in wages or the like, go
to the operator and ask for it. If he refuses you go to him again. If he
again refuses then I suppose you must cowardly submit. This is no idle talk
of mine, but facts, real facts; things that I have heard while sitting around
on the streets, spoken for my benefit I suppose. There are a class of men
around here who cannot get along with being led by white men I am given to
understand, and earnest prayers are going up to heaven for their early demise.
Well I don't know of any such men, but I do know of some who are anxious and
willing to do anything for the betterment of the craft be they white or black,
and we believe we are right. We also know of some who are willing to do
anything that is dirty for the sake of a smile. We believe they are on the
wrong road, in fact we know it. Now to those I have only to say that they
will find out probably when it is too late of their wrongs. I know you don't
like me because I tell you of your wicked ways. I can't help it boys. I
know you all, I can call you by name, I know your make-up and that is what
hurts you. You say you will down me off the tipple and then I will have to
tramp the ties, for you say I can't get any work here. Well boys, there is
a providence that rules the destiny of nations, and I think I can make it and
my friends also.

Brother Willing Hands, in answer to your question, that matter was
amicably settled and all went to work the next day and everybody satisfied.

R. L. DAVIS

United Mine Workers' Journal, August 11, 1892.

13. A CONTRACT

Analyzed and Criticized by Our Rendville Correspondent

The Congo Coal Company Makes Provision for Strikes

Houses Must be Given Up in Five Days After Trouble

RENDVILLE, O., Sept. 10.

Not having had anything to say in your last issue I will try to let your
many readers know what is going on around here as best I can. Mine No. 3
was idle three days this week on account of fire having been discovered in
the mine. It will be remembered that some four years ago this mine was discovered to be on fire, but after a hard struggle it was supposed to have been
extinguished. Whether it was or not I am unable to say, but it seems that
fire has generated from cause again, though not so bad as the first one. It
is now thought to be in good shape once more and I think there will be no
more trouble from that source.

Well, they say that I am a meddlesome fellow around here and I suppose if they say it is so it must be true, but it is not my intention to be classed in that light, but there is one little thing that I want some light on. Not long since the writer chanced to be aimlessly wandering over the numerous hills of Perry county and suddenly found himself in Congo. Not the Congo that we have so much read of in Stanley's works, but Congo, O., situated about one and one-half miles across the hills from this place. This is intended to be one of the most extensive workings in the state, so I understand; yes, and they are going to make a model town of it, too, so they say, and I say so, too, for they are establishing a something there that is not in vogue at any other place in the valley to my knowledge. I don't know what others may call it, but I call it iron-clad in a mild form. Some call it a house lease.[54] However, you must sign it if you want to work there. I will here give it as it is and then you can judge for yourselves. Read it carefully and see what you can make of it:

LICENSE TO EMPLOYES

This is to certify that at my special request the Congo Coal Mining company has consented and does hereby consent that myself and family may, as tenant at will, occupy their tenement house No.___, at their coal works at Congo, Perry county, O., upon and subject to the following terms and conditions and not otherwise:

First. To occupy peaceably and keep and return the said house at the expiration of said occupancy in the same good order and repair as when received, reasonable wear and tear excepted.

Second. On any pay day to pay to said Congo Coal Mining company or allow to be deducted from my earnings as they prefer, the sum of ___ dollars, as a monthly rental for said house.

Third. Without any notice within five days after I have ceased to work for said Congo Coal Mining company by reason of any strike by any employes at said coal works, to deliver up to said Congo Coal Mining company peaceable possession of said house and at any time on five days notice to quit, to me, given by said Congo Coal Mining company or their agent, by service personally or left at said house, to deliver up peaceable possession of said property to said Congo Coal Mining company.

On my neglect or refusal to comply with any one of said terms or conditions, or to deliver possession of said house within five days after I quit work, as aforesaid, or within five days after notice to quit, as aforesaid, I hereby agree that my family and myself may be treated as forcibly detaining possession of said house, and said Congo Coal Mining company, their servants or agents are hereby authorized to eject me or my family, and all personal property from said premises using such and so much force as they, the said Congo Coal Mining company, their servants or agents, or any of them, may deem proper, and I do hereby remise and forever discharge and release the said Congo Coal Mining company, their servants and agents, from any and all liability to me or my family in any shape, manner or form, for forcibly ejecting me or any of us from said house and property.

Witness our hands and seals this _____ of _____, 1892.
Signed and sealed in presence of

_____

_____

Signed:

_____ [SEAL.]

CONGO COAL MINING CO.,   [SEAL.]
           Per_____

Now, they tell me there is nothing in it. Well, this is my opinion of the matter. If there was nothing in it the Congo Coal Mining company would have never gotten it up. It must certainly be an advantage to them or they would not request each and every man to sign it. Let us see: In the first place they want all men of families, that is, enough to fill all their houses. Thus you will see that a single man will stand a very poor show to get work there. Second, unless you live in one of their houses you can't work there, so I am told. How does this strike you? Suppose a man owns his own home at a walking distance from the mines, must he give his own property and rent for the sake of getting a job? or is it fair to presume that a man should do this? I think

the man should reserve the right to live in his own property and even if
he has no property of his own he should reserve the right to rent where he
can rent cheapest.

But I am getting away from the point, I started to try to show the
little harm that there was in this article of agreement. You agree that you
must give up the house without notice within five days after you quit or
cease to work, or on account of a strike. Right there I claim is a black
eye to organization. While there is nothing said about the men organizing can
you not see a little thing in there that means to do away with the effect of
organization? For some years past the miners and operators have been meeting
jointly and formulating scales of wages, etc. These are simply mutual agreements of prices and conditions that are expected to be lived up to on the
part of both operators and miners. Now then, suppose the Congo Coal Mining
company refuses to comply with these agreements, what then? If they don't
see fit to concede to the general conditions and you strike, why, according
to this article of agreement you must get out and seek a job elsewhere. It
simply means to keep the men under submission. They know that a man is not
always prepared to pull up and move his family and men will naturally look
at this point and in some instances will submit for that reason and no other.
Again, suppose a man has within him the true principles of unionism and dare
assert his right and for those causes the company would undertake to get rid
of him by discharging him. Within five days you must get out of the house
whether you have secured another or not, eh! That is what you have agreed
to do. If the rest of the men stop work until you are reinstated then they
too must move and give room for blacklegs. Is this not so? While nothing
is said about blacklegs in the agreement it says you must peaceably give up
possession of the house. Well, if all must get out certainly they don't intend the works to remain idle. Then those who come in after you will be
blacklegs and you give them that privilege by signing that little no-harm
piece of paper. Oh, but you say that the laws of the state gives you thirty
days. Well, I don't know so much about that, not being a lawyer myself I
can't say, but it strikes me very forcibly that when you sign that document
you virtually sign away that privilege that the law gives you. I trust that
I am mistaken in this, however. In talking with a gentleman the other day
about this matter, I asked him what he would do, supposing a strike should
occur or that he got orders to quit and that his wife or one of his children
was sick, so much so that it would be dangerous to move them, and they were
forcibly ejected from the premises. Oh, he said he would kill somebody.
Does he not give them that right? I, think so, if they would be mean enough
to do it. I wish that I could discuss this matter as it should be discussed,
but being only an amateur I will leave it for those who are more able than
myself.

As this is already too lengthy I will stop for this time and will say
more in my next.

                                                              R. L. DAVIS

United Mine Workers' Journal, September 15, 1892.

14.   CONGO

Is Fast Becoming a Select Circle

A WOODEN WALL BUILT TO KEEP INTRUDERS OUT--THE COMPANY DRAWS A VERY DISTINCT
LINE OF DEMARCATION--BETWEEN NIGGER RIDGE AND THE WHITE FOLK'S HABITATION

                                              RENDVILLE, O., Sept. 18.

Work here is tolerably good at this time, though there's no telling how
long it will last, owing to the scarcity of water.

In my last I tried to give your many readers a slight description of Congo.
I must say that I only made mention of one of the evils at that place. Now,
I wish to say that there are other evils there which I do not believe would be
out of place to make mention of and while writing on the matter I hope that

none of the miners of that place will get offended, because I am not wholly
blaming them for the condition of things that are existing there, for I
fully recognize the fact that there are some good union men who are working
there and who are ready and willing to do anything that may tend to better
their condition, but somehow or other they have not taken hold as yet.
Probably they are waiting for a more convenient time when they can work with
better results. But I said I would try to give a further description of the
place, etc. Say, dear reader, did you ever in your life, especially you of
Ohio, read of the Ohio penitentiary? If so, then you know what O. P. stands
for. I know you don't know what I mean by this, but wait awhile and I think
I can make it plain in a very few words, and instead of calling it Congo it
ought to be called the O.M.P. (Ohio miner's prison).

Now then, I will give the reasons. The first place the place is fenced
in all around, with two gates, one at either side and at each of these gates,
so I am informed, they are going to have gate-keepers whose houses will be
right at the gates. The duties of these gatekeepers will be to keep out all
wagons or teams except those belonging to the company. Do you see the point?
to keep peddling wagons out. You see they don't want the honest farmer to
come in to sell his produce to the miners, no, for that would be competition
and the company would not reap the profits accruing therefrom. No, they'll
keep them out and if they have anything to sell they must sell direct to the
company, and let them get the profit. This is plain, is it not? It is to
me, yet this is a free country, eh! Well, if it is, I don't want any of it.
Now, if it was not for a railroad running through the place I don't know if
they wouldn't put up a sign board, "None but employes allowed on these
premises." But you know they can't fence the railroad in, hence the pedes-
trian manages to make his way in. I tell you that I believe in a man having
freedom of speech, freedom of thought and freedom of action, and if the
present state of things are allowed to exist he will have freedom of neither.
This is not all. Congo, unlike one of our ancient cities, sits on two hills
or ridges with a deep ravine between, access being had to either side by means
of a bridge. On one of these ridges or hills the white miners houses are
built; I don't know what they call this ridge, but on the other ridge the
colored miners houses are built; they call it Nigger Ridge, see? A distinction is made by the company, and if a colored man goes there seeking a house
he is very courteously conducted over on the other ridge you know. If he
wants one over on the white folks ridge why he is told that he can't get it,
and if he insists he is called saucy and is told that he can get neither
house nor work. That's freedom, you know.

Now, we will leave the houses alone and go down into the mine. Here we
find another distinction. On one side all the white men work, on the other
all the colored men work. This is called over in Africa, how is that, eh?
Don't suit me.

I simply make mention of these things to show how employers will do to
keep up a distinction between men for the purpose of breeding strife and
dissension in our ranks, and while we are fighting among ourselves they wag
away with the spoils, and what do we get, only the dregs? Now I think that
these things should teach the laboring man a lesson, both white and black.
They should unite and break asunder this infernal and pernicious line of
demarcation and cast it so far back into oblivion that it could never be
brought forth again, and until we do this we will never rise to that plane
that we pretend we are struggling to reach. It is evident to me that with
race distinction, church distinction or a distinction of nationalities, we
can hope for nothing, so it is time for us to learn just even horse sense
and do away with these things, then we can do something and not till then.

I cannot conceive the idea that some are so blind as to not see these
things and yet there are men, lots of them, who seem not to realize the
danger, and right here I will remind you of an incident that occurred at this
same mine:

A week or so ago there came a colored gentleman from Sand Run, Conaway
by name, a good union man, too so I am told, and I believe to be a union man
also from the little talk that I had with him. This man came to run a machine
and on account of the small number of machines or something, it was required
that two men work together. A certain white man (I won't call his name) was
told to go with Mr. Conaway, the colored man, and I am told that he refused

and when closely questioned the reason he was compelled to admit that it
was only on account of his color. Although he was a union man he would not
work with him; too black I suppose. Now, my friend, I thought you more of
a man than that, indeed I did, but I am deceived and by way of advice I
would say that it would be better for the miners as a whole were you and
your likes to return to your old avocation, viz., husking corn and rolling
pumpkins. I think you would make out better at it, for then you would not
have to work with a negro for there are not many of them around here that
like that kind of work. Yes, we must do away with this prejudice and I
for one am willing to do anything that is honorable and crush it out of
existence; then we will have good times. More anon.

R. L. DAVIS

United Mine Workers' Journal, September 22, 1892.

15. RENDVILLE

Trouble Affecting the Drivers--Misunderstanding Stops Work

A Lesson Men Should Learn: Continue Work Pending Negotiations

RENDVILLE, O., Sept. 25.

I will again attempt to let your many readers hear from our little
mining camp. Work is about as good as at my last writing. Mine No. 3 was
laid idle a couple of days last week on account of the discharge of a driver
and a misunderstanding among the drivers. The matter of the driver's discharge was placed before the committee on Monday, they at once tried to make
a settlement of the matter but failed, so on Tuesday morning a meeting was
called and the matter placed before the men. Seeing that the committee could
not make a settlement a motion was passed that the matter be placed in the
hands of the sub-district officers; by this time it was too late to go to
work and everybody went home, but I am told that they could have worked had
they wanted. On Wednesday morning a good many of the miners went to the mine
to work but the drivers did not come, hence there was no work on Wednesday.
In talking with some of the drivers they said that they understood that by
the motion was meant that the matter be placed before the sub-district and
they remain idle pending the investigation, which was just the reverse of
what the motion meant. However, on Wednesday morning Brother Adams came up
and held a consultation with Mr. McLaughlin, the mine boss, and the matter
was settled satisfactorily to all concerned. It is to be hoped that we will
not have a recurrence of this kind; we should regard the laws better. It
seems to be hard for men to learn to continue at work pending the investigation of any troubles, but we must learn sooner or later and I don't think
we will have any more trouble here on that account, our boys will try to do
the right thing. In my last letter concerning Congo I notice in the editor-
ials an article saying that unless I was largely drawing upon my imagination
or was hypnotized while writing, etc., it was the worst case heard of in
modern times, etc. Now I want to say that I always try to be truthful when
writing and I don't think that I overdrew the picture. There possibly may
have appeared some few words that were unnecessary, but it was all truth and
if you don't believe it, ask Nugent or Pearce and I think my statements will
be verified, so boys when I say a thing, although I am a little peculiar, rest
assured if I say it is true it is either true or some one has misinformed me.
     Well, as I am not feeling very well and I suppose you are already tired,
I will stop. Wishing success to the organization and your valuable journal.
I am yours for labor.

R. L. DAVIS

United Mine Workers' Journal, September 29, 1892.

16. WANTS TO KNOW

Whether They Are Asleep or Awake in Sub-District 6.

Secretary Glasgow Points Out the Courtesies Required
Between Local and Sub-District Secretaries--Bellaire Progressing

BELLAIRE, O., Sept. 24.

Well, Mr. Editor, Here I am again with a few words with your permission.
What I wish to say is regarding principles. The first thing I will
refer to is, locals within the boundary of Sub-District 6. A man claiming
the principle of union and boasting of his good works and belonging to a
local of the pure stuff, I should think should show his principles when
called on. Now, then, how can a man be so awkward and stubborn as to refuse
to answer the official call and information asked of him. In the first place,
a local should not be led by one man alone, and in the second place when a
man is secretary of a local and any correspondence is sent to him, if I judge
rightly, it is up to the local to act, not merely the secretary. I have sent
three letters and a card to C. P. Goldsmith, secretary of Maynard mine, and
have never received one word in return, and all correspondence which I have
sent to him has been of a nature worthy of recognition, and should have been
recognized. Whenever a man has the idea in his head that he is the local there
is a mistake somewhere. If he says the local has acted on these different
letters was it not his duty to inform the sender their action pro or con?
I say yes. Now there is something behind this, and now is the time to find
it out. The Maynard local is the only local of Belmont county not attached
to Sub-District 6. I thought some time ago, according to a letter in the
United Mine Workers' Journal from Mr. Goldsmith that Maynard was away up in
the top notch. But I fail to see and until I see an explanation, I can't believe it. It is claimed by the delegates that this local has been a stumbling block for Wheeling Creek. Why should it be so? I would advise Maynard
local to have a little get up about them. I know not what action the local
has taken, but I do know I have not received any word from them. I write
this to see if Maynard local is asleep or has she died and wants others to
die with her as I cannot awaken her no way. Not wishing to take any more
space on this subject I will give a few items.
    The Franklin and Trolls miners have been notified to turn rooms ten
feet in width hereafter, but have positively refused unless paid equivalent
to entry price.
    The project of forming a labor congress in this end of the district is
being worked up and will be a good thing if all men will come together and
aid the efforts being made.
    Work is quite slack in this section.
    James Holt is slowly improving and is in need of some help from his fel-
low workmen; his doctor bills will be heavy.
    We chronicle the sad death of Benjamin Dean, who was killed while re-
turning home from band practice; he was run over in the Baltimore and Ohio
yards. Benny was a miner about 20 years of age; a good, quiet, industrious
young man and was loved by all who knew him. The funeral was a large one.
    Bellaire holds her own in working of different unions. Wishing the best
of success to labor's cause and a wider circulation to the UNITED MINE WORKERS'
JOURNAL, I am

                                                        S. GLASGOW

United Mine Worker's Journal, September 29, 1892.

17.   MAY WANT A JOB

At Congo, Hence Desire to Right Things There

Work Fair Around Rendville--A Harmonious Meeting
Calls Attention to the Pending Screen Bill

RENDVILLE, O., Oct. 2.

Work around here continues fair and everybody is feeling happy.
The miners of Mine 3 held a meeting last evening for the purpose of
electing a checkweighman and committee and other business of interest. It
was one of the best attended and best conducted meetings that have been held
for quite awhile. It seemed that there was a spirit of unanimity among the
men and everything was quietly and peaceably transacted. I am one of those
who like to have peace and quietude in the ranks, for through this method I
believe more can be done for the betterment of the conditions of the workingmen of our country than any other. It doesn't hurt, however, to keep up
a little agitation now and then to keep men in mind of their duty and the
reforms needed for the emancipation of the wage slaves, for they should be
ever kept fresh in the memory of the people. It is our fight and no one can
fight it out but ourselves. I am one of those who believe that the conditions of the miner is not what they should be and I believe there are a great
many who believe the same. Then if such be true I think we should be up and
doing. I cannot see why it is that the poor laboring men can not combine
their forces as well as the rich, surely we have enough intelligence, then
why not put it into effect.

We all admit that there is something wrong with our system of government, etc. Well, then, have we not the weapon to right these wrongs if we
would only try? I think we have, then why not use them? There is one
noticeable feature among miners that I have always observed, that no matter
what the grievances, if work is good everything goes; but, just as soon as
work gets slack then they are anxious to rid themselves of the many evils
that have grown around them when times were good. In my opinion this is just
the reverse to what it should be. I have always found it easier to bring
about a reformation during the times when work was good. At any other
time the other fellow don't care whether we work or not, hence my reason for
doing these things during the busy seasons. This may not be very good judgment but I am always ready to receive instructions from those who know better
than myself.

Oh, say, boys; I don't hear anything about that question of weighing of
coal before screening. I think it about time to get this before the public,
for if we want it to become a law we must certainly have something to say or
it will be taken for granted that we don't want it. I can only speak for
myself and it's my honest opinion that it is one of the things we need more
than anything else. Let us go to work and get that, then try something else
and so on until we get all that we want, then be satisfied. Without any
jesting, the miners ought to demand in loud terms the enactment of the anti-
screen law.

Well, for a change, I will say that because of my advocating certain
things in the way of organization it is said that I am only doing it for the
money there is in it. Some say that I have got the bighead and think myself
above them and for those reasons should be relegated to the rear. In answer
to them I have only this to say, that neither of the statements are true and
as for the money part of it I would be sorry, boys, for any of you to attempt
to live on the money that I get for my little talk, for you would starve to
death. What I advocate is from a pure principle of unionism, nothing more,
nothing less. So, boys, instead of being my avowed enemies, come and let us
be friends and I will assure you that instead of working to your detriment
you will find that I am trying to do what little I can for your advancement.

Before closing this I must have a few words about Congo again. I am
informed that the superintendent of that beautiful place wanted to know or in
fact asked what in h--- that fellow Davis meant by writing such letters about
Congo? Well I think I can answer that dignitary, and by way of an answer I

will say that the bright side of Congo was being written up by some one in
our local papers describing the costly machinery, beautiful and magnificent
houses, fine tipple, power dynamos, etc., and in all his or her writings I
never saw one word about the nice fences that were built around it, or of
its pearly gates nor of the keepers of those gates and last but by no means
the least, nothing was said about the contract that they had for the men to
sign. And, seeing the bright side pictured so beautifully I thought it became me or some one else to show the dark side of the picture, and I accordingly made an effort to do it the best that I could without lying, and I
must say that there are other things that I could have written, but I thought
I had said enough. I would also say that I am one who wants to see these
things done away with, because it is possible that we may want a job over
there some time and we would like to have things in good shape. We don't
wish to sign any contracts at all unless the employer will agree to sign one
equally binding drawn up by us, and we also have a natural abhorrence to being
fenced in, and we would like to live in any house that we want, inasmuch as
we must pay the same rent. I am firmly of the opinion that it will be only
a short while when these things will be things of the past in Congo, for there
are missionaries going there most every day and I think they will get things
all right by and by. With best wishes for the paper and compliments to
Brothers Willing Hands and Riley and others, I am yours for suffering
humanity.

R. L. DAVIS

United Mine Workers' Journal, October 6, 1892.

18.   R. L. DAVIS

Takes Exceptions to Statements Made In Independent

RENDVILLE, O., April 22.

     In looking over the columns of the Miner's Independent of the 19th inst.,
headed "District 6, Convention," as we saw it, in which the writer takes some
of us severely to task, and, being sore because of the actions of the convention in connection with the official organ, etc., he seems to have lost
all regard for truth. I say this because of certain assertions which he makes.
In the first place he seems to have a poor opinion of the old board. He says
that he has been informed by a state official that it was seldom the president
could get a true opinion from his board, etc. As one of that board I take
exceptions to that statement. I do not know who the official was, but I do
know that the assertion was false of all the members of the old board, which
was composed of Chas. Call, Joshua Thomas, John Fahy, A. A. Adams and myself.
I say of all those men I do not know of one who was fraid to express an opinion, and I think an injustice is being done them by making such statements.
The gentleman then goes on to say that he don't think the president will have
that trouble this year, because of the fact that those who constitute the
board this year are men who have ideas of their own. Now, while I have the
highest opinion of the present board, I wish to say frankly and candidly that
I do not think them any more intelligent than their predecessors. The gentleman, then, after making brief sketches of the abilities and works of the newly
elected members, winds up on me, in which he says that R. L. Davis was the
only one of the old board who was re-elected. He says that Davis has been on
the board for a few years and by this time ought to be of much good to the
organization, as he has had the training of the forces that be. He then goes
on to tell of the places that I have been sent to as an organizer, etc., but
winds up by saying that no one knows of the organizing done by me. Well as
to that part I leave for others to answer.

     He then says that to know me at my best is to read my articles in the
UNITED MINE WORKERS' JOURNAL. I am sorry for this, as I wish to be known best
for the work that I have done for the organization. Lastly, he says that
Davis is a colored man, and it has been thought good for the organization to
have him on the executive board, as in that way he could hold the colored men

in line. He also says that I work at a large mine and in the convention
represented the great number of 19 men in good standing in the mine. Now,
in reference to that statement, the gentleman simply did not know what he
was talking about, for at the mine I work at every man in and round it with
the exception of engineers, carpenters and blacksmiths are in good standing,
and by way of explanation to the gentleman I will say to him that I represented the local assembly that I belonged to, and Mr. Clark represented
Local Union 398, 161 men, making a total of 180 men in good standing, instead of 19, as he would like to make people believe. And, by way of conclusion, allow me to say for Friend Thomas' benefit, that were I a white
man I would get better chances than I do, and as for my standing, ask of our
people, white or black, and he can get my pedigree.

        Thanking the miners of Ohio for their kind appreciation by re-electing
me as a member of the executive board, I am, as ever,

                                                              R. L. DAVIS

United Mine Workers' Journal, April 27, 1893.

19. GLASGOW

Gives His Ideas On a Few Things

About the Competitive Field, and a Few Things in Ohio

Addresses Himself to R. L. Davis on a Few Points

        BELLAIRE, O., May 8.--Being styled a library scholar is worthy of con-
sideration and is quite a compliment and I think I should be at liberty to
tell others of my learning and give them an idea what is taught in my school.
I have a good teacher, and when I read, write or spell I make some mistakes,
but my teacher and I never quarrel, reason, rules. There is only one drawback in our progress, which is our school is small, and such a burden to
overcome needs patience and perseverance. But I believe when the craft I
represent become acquainted with teaching from the library they will not be
in the same conditions they are today. Well, in February Sub-District 6 met
in convention, took up three days preparing a scale for the coming year.
Delegates were sent to state and national convention. With said scale time
was occupied in discussing it; it was declared the scale to present to the
joint meeting, it came back home to the miners, went into sub-district again,
then to state, back to the miners and was still declared the scale for 1893.
Tomorrow, Tuesday, another convention of miners and operators is to be held
in Columbus. What for? Why, to consider the scale presented to the operators
in April. Is it policy? Yes, for one side it is, and the other side is
policy too. Let us see, was it the intention of the miners to ask for something they did not expect to get? Surely not, or at least they did not show
it in the different conventions. Did they have any guidance in this step
forward? They surely did. Then are the miners to blame for their action?
I fail to see it. The scale as presented this year is better equalized than
it ever was before and the only cause for kicking, as I see it, is in the
localities where the miner has not been paid for his labor in equality. Let
us look at the Jackson county miners. It is true they are to blame for being
behind scale rates, but are they entitled to scale rates? is the question. If
they are, when and how will they get it? If not, why do they advocate it?
And there is the machine mines in the Hocking. For the past few years they
have advocated three-fifths of pick mining price. It is justice. They are
prepared to prove it; then why are the companies objecting? Here is Sub-
District 6. This dead work scale has been a sore of contention for time past
and the miners have agreed with operators that all such should be settled in
state convention. While I know it is true the majority of the miners are
room workers and their interest, while in their room, is more money per ton,
but when it comes to turn a room from seven to twelve feet for the coal and
a pitiful sum of from $3 to $5 then they kick. The same with entry men;

take a room man, put him in an entry six feet wide at $1 per yard and coal;
he cries not enough, he wants a room, but such is life with the real miner.
It seems the scale as a whole for District 6 is an honest one and should be
adopted as such.

Well, I must ask some of the miners and "Fairplay," also if he can tell
me where our competitive field is at now, for I am at a loss to know what
our competitors meant when they as a unit, West Virginia excepted, voted
with Ohio for the advance. The block field of Indiana has got 5 cents, I
understand, but where is the rest of the state, with Ohio, I hope. But let
me see, has Ohio won; I can only say it depends on the action of Tuesday's
convention in Columbus.

Brother R. L. Davis is still crying for help, or at least it appears so
in your issue of April 27.

Well, Brother D., if you ever expect to get more sympathy from our
craft, please let the white man get a chance to look at your race's condition.
We see no fault with the colored man, as long as he is true, because a man's
skin is black, is no reason why his principle should be so. The colored man
has the same right on this earth as any other, there is no law to prevent
them. The church is their friend, and I cannot see what Brother D. wants.
Is our union his enemy? surely not. For a man who is true to the union, the
union should be true to him. Brother D., don't let the color idea run away
with you. I don't see that you or any other of your race are kicked at, so
let us have a short rest on color line and talk about something good for us
all. I have the name of a chronic kicker, I accept it with fairness, and I
may as well say it as think it, I will kick until I am kicked out or shown
that I am kicking wrongly. A man can't persuade people to do fair and expect them to stick to him unless he is firm, and I believe what I have said
through the columns of the UNITED MINE WORKERS' JOURNAL in the past will
eventually be sustained, for the light is spreading. Nor do I wish to boast,
but I claim as I have in the past, that our craft will call for a change in
national affairs, is it not so fellow-miners? Honesty and fair consideration
is all that is needed from the miners of Ohio to convince them of what I say.
Well, I did not expect to take up so much space, but excuse me this time.
Shick's mine is running on the advance, signed for one year. Three peddling
mines are working at the advance; all others at this date are idle. Plenty
of empties going to West Virginia this week. Will close, expecting to appear
again in the future.

                                                        S. GLASGOW

United Mine Workers' Journal, May 11, 1893.

20. TO GLASGOW'S OF LAST WEEK--"NO FAIR SHAKE"

Will Discuss the Thing in a Friendly Way Later On

RENDVILLE, O., May 15.--Again I ask for a small space in your valuable
paper; this time for the purpose of trying to explain myself, also to get an
explanation from Brother Glasgow upon the lecture that he gave me in your
last issue. The brother says that I am still crying for help, etc. Well,
my brother, I always thought it manly to ask assistance from a friend or
brother if you were really in need. You say that if I expect to get more
sympathy from our craft to please let the white man get a chance to look at
my race's condition. In answer to that I have no objection to offer only
don't wait too long in making the investigation, as you have already had ample
time to have done long ago. I want to say to you, my brother, that when I
wrote my last letter, while I had no intention of trying to convey such an
idea, I say now, without fear of successful contradiction, that when it comes
to a fair shake we are not in it. Do you catch on? If not, say and I will
be more plain, as I am confident that I can sustain my argument with strong
and sufficient proof. So far as I am personally concerned I have no quarrel
as to unfair treatment, unless some one makes an attack upon me, as you have
already done, and I want to say right here that I can prove that I myself

have not altogether had a fair show. But, I do not wish to have anything
to say on that score just now; a hint to the wise is sufficient. I want to
say also that I have never said that our union was an enemy of ours; so don't
charge that to me if you please. Again, the brother says that the church
is our friend. I emphatically deny the assertion, but will defer discussion
on this point until later on; so if you wish a thorough airing on these
matters say so and I am prepared to have a friendly discussion on it now or
at any other time. I would not have said what I did in my last letter had
it not been for the unwarranted attack made upon me by Mr. Thomas in the
Independent and naturally expected Mr. Thomas to have made his own defense
and not you, my brother.

Hoping that the Journal may have a successful year I am as ever.

R. L. DAVIS

United Mine Workers' Journal, May 18, 1893.

21. THE COLORED RACE AND LABOR ORGANIZATIONS

By

R. L. Davis, Ohio

The race problem, or what ought or should be done with the negro, is a
question that has seemingly been troubling the minds of a great number of the
American people. It seems, however, plainly evident that he is a citizen of
this country and should be treated as such. This, in my mind, is the only
solution to the supposedly knotty problem. Less than thirty years ago he
was given his freedom, and turned loose to the cold charities of the world
without a dollar or an acre of land. Turned loose as he was is there any
nation of people who has made such rapid progress as the Negro has made?
No, search all history and we find them not. During all these years in a
said-to-be Christian and civilized country, notwithstanding the rapid strides
he has made, he has been looked down upon by both the church and party politics both of which should have been his best friends. Being poor and used
to it he had to obey the divine injunction, viz.: To earn his bread by the
sweat of his brow. In so doing, we find him a great competitor with the
American white labor. It is at this period that we find that the labor organizations or rather some of them, did that which no other organizations
had done, the church not even excepted, threw open their doors and admitted
him as a full member with the same rights and privileges as his white brother.
This, in our opinion, was the first or initiative step toward the equality
of mankind, and we are sorry to say that until the present day the labor
organizations are the only ones that recognize the Negro as an equal and as
a man. Recognizing this to be true it is also true that some of our people
have not yet gained enough confidence in his white brother as to trust him
very far. And yet, is this very strange? When we notice the fact that right
in our midst we have some as bitter enemies as anywhere else.

While we admit that our labor organizations are our best friends, it would
be well to teach some of our white brothers that a man is a man no matter what
the color of his skin may be. We have nothing but the best of words to say
for labor organizations, and hope they may continue in the same line of
actions, and we are confident that they will not only better the conditions
of the working classes, but will also wipe out all class and race distinctions,
and in the meantime the Negro will be found as loyal to labor organizations
as his white brother. It has been said that the Negro as a union man was a
failure, but we are inclined to think that those words were uttered more from
a prejudiced mind than as a truthful statement. Let us hope for better days
for organized labor with the Negro in the ranks doing his share in the way of
emancipating labor.

Confidence in each other is the thing lacking. This we can readily gain
if we will but try. Believing as we do that all the reform needed must and
will come through the medium of organized labor, it should be our proudest

aim to do all that we can for the upholding of our organizations. Let us
make them grand and perfect, and in so doing we will have accomplished a
noble work, and by following this line of action we will solve the race
problem, better the condition of the toiling millions and also make our
country what it should be, a government of the people, for the people and
by the people.

United Mine Workers' Journal, May 25, 1893.

22. GLASGOW AGAIN

Responds to the Rendville Man, R. L. Davis

BELLAIRE, O., May 20.--Again I come to ask for utterance in the UNITED MINE
WORKERS' JOURNAL. I had not intended appearing so soon, but believe I have
cause to reply to Brother Davis, who has become rather awakened at my last
letter. I did not intend my remarks to insult, or as a lecture, but the
brother has accepted it as such, and now I have nothing more to do than to
continue my course.

Brother D. wants an explanation; I don't know what he wants me to explain, for I tried to be clear in my former letter and I believe the brother
understands it right enough. Brother D. goes on to say he thinks it manly
to ask a friend or brother when really in need. What I want to know, what
is he in need of? He wants an investigation, soon! Well, if I had a say in
this matter the brother would not have to wait many days, for I should be on
the ground in a short time to see what is wrong with conditions where the
colored man is mining. Do they not get prices and conditions the same as
the white man? If not, Brother D., it is your place to report, and it is fair
that the blame should rest where it belongs. Let us see where are our other
races of people. Are there not many foreign-speaking people represented in
the mining craft? Why are they not crying for office and help? To be plain
and sincere, Brother D., you have been upheld by me and many others in my
section, but I will tell you, do your work at home well and I believe you,
as a member of the board, will find legal acceptance throughout the state.
Did the people support you in past conventions for fun? If so, it is dear
fun. No, they recognize and feel the need of the colored people in our union,
and I don't know of any failure on the part of union to aid you in your work.
Come and tell us where the fault lies and see if your race is in such a
deplorable condition among the mining craft, as you try to make out. What
kind of a shake is it milk shake you mean? as that is a fair shake, I believe.

No, I don't catch on to what you mean, but I have caught on to you, my
brother. If I have attacked you, defend yourself; a hint to the wise is
sufficient. I am not wise enough yet to take a hint in the style you give.

I did not say the union was your enemy, but asked you if it was. I did
say, and say so now, the church is your friend, and you cannot deny it. If
you do you are not the man in that line that you should be. I take from your
assertion that the world is the church, but it is not so.

As for a thorough airing I am ready at any time. Regarding me taking
up what you intended for Thomas, why did you seek the UNITED MINE WORKERS'
JOURNAL to inform Mr. Thomas? Why did you not send to the Independent, where
said article you refer to appeared? I thought when a letter went into the
UNITED MINE WORKERS' JOURNAL it was for the public, but if you, Brother D.,
have a special privilege over others, please make it known, for I am liable
to infringe on your special rights.

Now, Brother D., I don't want to say anything to cause hard feelings
nor do I want to take up space in the UNITED MINE WORKERS' JOURNAL to discuss personal affairs, but if the editor will permit I am ready at any time
to hear from you and will surely reply in my candid way.

With best wishes for the success of our craft, I am as ever,

                                                            S. GLASGOW

United Mine Workers' Journal, May 25, 1893.

23. R. L. TO GLASGOW

We Want Some of the Offices With Money "In It"

A Frank Letter in the Glasgow-Davis Controversy
The Latter Claims Credit for Helping the Organization

RENDVILLE, O., May 27.--Seeing that our literary friend of Bellaire is
still alive I suppose it would be no more than right that I should acquaint
him that I myself am feeling pretty fair. To begin, let me say to friend
Glasgow that I did not take his letter as an insult as he would like to have
others believe, but rather an attack from an unexpected source. The brother,
in his last, wants to know what I want, or, in other words, he asks   What
am I in need of? and right here let me say that when I made the assertion
referred to I did not mean myself individually, but all others of my race,
of which I am not the least bit ashamed, and to explain all of our needs
would require more space than would probably be allowed in this journal; so,
we pass that by for the present.

The brother says, quite good-naturedly, that, if he had the matter in
hand we would not have to wait very long, as he would be on the grounds in
a short while to see really what were the conditions of the colored men in
mining localities, etc. Let me say to you, my friend, that you are as much
on the ground as myself and can you not see the inequalities as they exist?
If not, your vision is faulty in the matter and a blind man though . . .
knows that there is something wrong so far as the Negro is concerned. Where
colored men are mining he asks, do they not get the same prices and conditions as their white brothers? I will say that possibly he does in Ohio and a
few other of the Western states, but this only applies to his work in and
around the mines. Promotion is a slow process with him; it seems hard for
him to get above the pick and shovel no matter how competent he may be. This
we believe to be unfair. Again, the brother says that there are many foreign
speaking people represented in the mining craft, and he asks why are they not
crying for office and help. I wish to say that I had heard no cry for office
from our side of the house, but since he has been so kind as to bring up this
matter and there being no conventions near at hand, I don't know as any great
harm can be done by us saying something on this very delicate question, and
before entering on it I want to ask the brother just a question or two. First,
Are not those foreigners that you make mention of classed with the whites?
Have they had better advantages for getting along in this country than I who
was born and reared in this country? Yes, and I am tempted to say that the
lazy Indian who never worked nor never will has chances far superior to mine,
although I have helped to make this country what it is, the said to be, greatest republic of the world.

We started to say something about that office business. While I have
said that I had heard no cry for office from our side of the house, we have
seen some hard scrambling on your side for office. When I say your side, I
mean the whites. Now, then, will you admit that you need us in your unions?
If so, why should we not hold offices, also? Are we not men? Have we not
the same ambition as you people have? Are we not in many instances as competent as you? Then why should we not hold office? Not office in name, but
office indeed; something that there is some money in, that we may cope with
our white brothers, as an equal? I know you will try to make it appear as
though I am speaking for myself, but such is not the case. I am speaking in
defense of a people who have been down long enough. The day has passed and
gone by that we, as a people, shall longer be content with small things. Yes,
my brother, we want some of the money, too, we have found out that it is a
good thing.

Again you say that you have caught on to me. I do not know in what way
you mean, but if it be meant for an insult, then I would say hold on also, I
have not caught on to you, but I am trying to as hard as I can and trust that
I may succeed.

You again ask of me why I did not send my article to the Independent,
where the article that I referred to appeared. Well, my brother, in answer,
let me say that I have a preference and that preference is not the Independent.

I want to be many on such matters. The Independent is not friendly toward
me and I am sure that I shall not worry about it either; I am not so friendly
toward it as you. Now, say, do you catch on again? Well, as this is already
too lengthy I will close for this time. But, by the way, there is one thing
that I forgot, and that is the brother says that I should do my work well at
home, then I will receive legal acceptance throughout the state. Well, you
make me laugh. If that is all that is required then I should have received
that acceptance long since. Do you not know I have worked ten days, weeks,
or months, but years in trying to establish an organization of our people.
Yes brother, have been out late at nights in rain and cold, have been called
everything but a gentleman, have been threatened with discharge; all for the
sake of organization and received no pay either. Would you have done it?
But this I have done with the assistance of a few others and have accomplished
our ends. We have not a man that is not a member in good standing in the
organization, and I claim a portion of the credit for the bringing about of
these results. Now, what do you want me to do? What I have said I can prove.
Now then have I not done my work well? If not, we would be very thankful to
have you come down and finish the job. Would like to hear from you again.
If you keep on you will learn after a while, so keep trying old boy. More
anon.

                                                              R. L. Davis

United Mine Workers' Journal, June 1, 1893.

                         24. ANOTHER CHAPTER

           In the Correspondence Between Glasgow and Davis

             A Friend To All Is What the Bellaire Is,

          But Doesn't Sail in the Same Boat as the Rendville Man

     BELLAIRE, O., June 3.--Seeing my friend at Rendville comes again in a
frank and earnest manner in reply to my last and bids me come again, which I
will do in the promise I made the brother, and I feel some better since I
read the brothers last letter. If I had any fear of a trouncing it has completely left me and I am as fresh as if I had been aired well and political
shower had poured upon me, while I am now truly convinced what Brother D.,
wants and what he desires for his race. Well, I don't think it would take
half the space that has been used to tell the wants which have been explained.
The brother seems to think I mean him when I write. He is strictly right,
and it is he that should take to himself first, then if any be left, cast it
abroad.
     No one has even hinted that you should be ashamed of your race, Brother
D. Go back to where I began for reference. The next answer indicates very
plainly to me that the brother has flew the track and his letter from here
should have appeared in the free debate column. I did not for a moment think
that he was dealing in politics and here I am talking organization and
Brother D. talking politics. He has acknowledged the fact I wanted to know
regarding his and his poor comrades' conditions in and around the mines.
My brother, if it is politics you mean, get up out of the rut you are in
and tell the boys about it. Why do you stick like a leach to partyism?
Come out on the side of reform and be a politician out and out. The next I
notice is where he quotes I am as much on the ground as he is. Let me tell
you Brother D., I am not in the same boat that you are outside of our labor
cause, and to be more plainly, I am not in the same boat that you ride in nor
do I desire to be. My reason is the boat has leaks and is liable to sink and
if I mistake not came near sinking in '93. Do you catch on, Brother D.? If
not, be plain and let me hear which side you swim to. I catch on to the dot-
ted space and refer it back for correction. You say, brother, that you have
heard no cry for office from your side. Let me say you have howled, and so
has your brothers from the same side and you cannot deny it. I believe you
know what I mean by this. The question asked, first, yes, they are white,

but as advantages, my brother, they are hooted at and condemned 2 to 1 to
your race, and further you and your people as you term them, have it in
your power to be free, for you can have a free ballot, have got a free
speech, and further the colored man is not what the white man made him if
he is not getting justice. The white man, I believe, shed blood to loose
the band that bound the colored man and if he would now throw back to them,
we are not satisfied and want a part of the money that is being freely spent.
My brother, if you are a candidate for governor tell it among the people.

My dear sir, I am proud to know you have won such great fame in our
ranks as a people and your labors have proven so beneficial; press on, my
brother, I will aid you what I can in honest, fair dealing to make this
grand and glorious land of liberty better. What say ye, my brother? Will
you come with me or do you want me to go with you? I don't suppose you
would be willing to split the difference.

Yes, my brother, I admit we scrambled to get who we believed were good,
true and honorable men in office, but, my brother, you were not on that side
and you cry and say you and your race are not treated right. Brother, don't
think I desire you to do what your conscience will not permit. Certainly
you should be the next president of our grand republic if the people want
you, for it is the people who elect. But it is money that wins. No, friend,
no insult intended to you, nor do I wish to wrongfully treat anyone, but if
what I say goes to the bone it would be best to rub a little salt in to preserve it.

You say, Brother D., you have a preference in papers. You are surely
welcome to it, but I deny the statement that the Independent is not friendly
to you, for I believe it is the friend of all square, honest men, or at least
I have found nothing to the contrary since I have been acquainted with it.
I have a preference to papers too, my friend, but I don't propose to seek one
to run down the other. I believe the UNITED MINE WORKERS' JOURNAL and Independent both should be working for what would do the people good. I find no
fault with the UNITED MINE WORKERS' JOURNAL and its editor and if it is good
I wish it every success obtainable, but in well wishing the Independent deserves my best. My brother, it will certainly do you good after that laugh.
My brother, why don't you present your bills for the time you have spent in
rains and cold? Why don't you sue for slander for your abuses and threats of
discharge? My brother, I suppose no other man who has been spared to live
this long has had to suffer such trials. O, no, the white man would be dead
and forgot. While I believe I have answered the questions asked as best I
can, just a word to the brother. I did think and do yet that your people
should seek reform. You are entitled to your rights and you should have them,
but now when all you have said, my brother, should have been applied, what
plan is the best to pursue to satisfy you. If you would, with your friends,
of which I have been and am yet, if your cries are not wanting too much, you
and I, my friend, are not traveling the same road, and don't expect too many
good things on the road you travel for fear you get disappointed.

While I might have condensed, excuse me, Mr. Editor.

Just a word to Brother Tyson of Danford. Your fault is faulty, my
brother, and I believe you snapped too quick. Did you gain anything at your
mine, my brother? If so tell us what. Yours for justice and the cause of
labor, white or black, foreign or American.

                                                      S. GLASGOW

United Mine Workers' Journal, June 8, 1893.

25. ALL RIGHT NOW

Says Davis, Speaking On the Question of Methods

Some Reasons for Difference From Both Sides
Man Who Kicks Most is Usually One Who Thinks Least

RENDVILLE, O., July 3.--In my last I promised that I would have a little talk with our friends Laurene Gardner and T. P. Gray, but I trust that I may be excused for the present, for there are other questions which I wish to speak of. Having seen of late a great number of letters relating to our organization and the best means of preserving it. This is a question that I have given some little thought, but think and consider as I may, I can not reach the conclusions as some of my friends have. Last week I noticed an article from the pen of President Nugent in which he at some length discusses the matter. While I like the source it comes from, viz.: a salaried officer. However, I can not coincide with his views of the matter, and while I may not be as able to explain myself as he, yet I will do the best I can in that direction with the short time I have to consider it. And to begin with let me say that we agree in so far as keeping the national organization intact, but when it comes to the dissolution of the district or state organization then we differ very muchly. In the first place, how much does it cost the miners of Ohio for the maintenance of the national? Here is what it costs per capita, 10¢ per month or the paltry sum of $1.20 per year; how much for the district? 5¢ per month or the enormous sum of 60¢ per year, or in other words we pay for state and national dues the sum of $1.80 per annum. Now the question that I wish to ask is this. Is there a sane man in Ohio who will say that he does not get $1.80 worth of benefits from it? No, I do not believe such a man can be found. Of course there may be a few sore heads who would say it but these men if such I must call them do not constitute the rank and file. Now then if it cost such a small sum to run both the state and national then I can not see the efficacy of abolishing the district for, by so doing, you would not materially decrease expenses.

Probably it might be well to explain. Suppose we do away with the district and work all together on the sub-district plan, or make our present sub-districts or couple two or three of our present sub-districts together as one district. Do you think you will lessen the expenses? No, not one iota, for under that system possibly there might be no salaried officers, but you would have several men in the field continually, would you not? These men must receive so much per day and expenses, would they not? Then, if such be true, what would be the benefit of doing away with the district, so far as dollars and cents are concerned?

Now, then, I do not think that any of our sub-districts are run on less than 2-1/2 cents per month; some more, but none less. These sub-districts officers are away from home but little, but do away with the district and you change the whole system of things. Troubles naturally arise and must be settled and money makes the mare go.

Say that Athens, Perry and Hocking counties were coupled together as a district would it lessen the cost to the miners of those three counties? I say most emphatically no. It would not decrease the per capita 25 cents in the year. I think we have a very good system of organization at present, and I would say let the present system stand and instead of raising such a hullabaloo about expenses, etc., let us go to work to perfect our organization. The one great trouble with some of our people is that no matter what is done is never in their opinion done right and to please these few we are forever changing to suit their whims and caprices. This is wrong and should be done no more, for do as we may some are never satisfied and never will be; so what is the use of paying any attention to them? In all my life I have noticed this fact, the man who is never satisfied and who does most of the kicking is the one who is generally too drunk to attend the meetings of his local; consequently nothing is done to suit him and he gives vent to himself on the street corner or with his belly up to the bar. There is where he does his talking. Ask him why he was not at the meeting on such a night and the answer you will get nine cases out of ten is "Oh, h--l, (hic) they never (hic) do any (hic) thing at their d--- (hic) meetings." These are the men who raise such a cry about the great expense of running the organization, etc.

Now, is it this class of men that we must try to please, or the honest, manly, sober and generous-hearted men? I think it should be the latter, and for goodness sake let us hear no more about the dissolution of state or national. They are both alright; all they want is the assistance of the rank and file and with that assistance I feel safe in saying that all will come out right in the end. So, boys, let us get together and work as one man, always remembering an injury to one is the concern of all. More anon.

R. L. DAVIS

United Mine Workers' Journal, July 6, 1893.

26.   A MISTAKE

Is What R. L. Davis of the Board Thinks the Board Has Made,

And Would Rectify It By Holding a State Convention

Says His Head and Not His Heart Was At Fault

RENDVILLE, O., Aug. 12.--As a member of the executive board of District 6,
United Mine Workers of America, I wish to have a few words to say by way of
vindication for the action recently taken in the matter of the acceptance
of sixty days' notes in lieu of money. Owing to the great amount of dissatisfaction existing among the miners, I feel it my duty to make my position in the matter as clear as I can. All that I can hear is, sold again;
turn the rascals out, etc., and to hear men talk I sometimes am tempted to
ask, have I been deluded into this thing or did I blindly walk into this
slough of despondency or did I do that which was right and according to the
law, as laid down in our constitution? Some say that the board overstepped
their limits when they undertook this question. I am free to admit that it
was a very grave matter to handle, and for my part, I knew nothing of such
a matter until after my arrival at Columbus, and when the letter was brought
into the room, where we were holding our meeting. A cannon ball could not
have had a more paralyzing effect upon me, and why? Because I had no dreams
of such a proposition being made. Now I am only speaking for myself; the
rest of the board can speak for themselves. However, the matter was in a
manner rejected by the board; they thought it of too great a magnitude for
so small a number of men. As I have said before, the proposition offered by
the operators was rejected and a counter proposition made by the board. Our
proposition was refused by the operators on the grounds as stated in the
circular issued by the board. Now, before going too far with this, I do not
know but that it might be well to state that we were led to believe that
something had to be done, as a great many of our men in the Hocking Valley
and other portions of the state were in such straitened circumstances that
whether we as a board agreed or not, those people would be compelled to accept any terms whereby they might be able to get enough work to get bread,
these may not be the same words, but the same meaning anyway. We thought
it unwise to take any action that would defer the money due on the 10th, and
did all that we could to secure it, but failed. We tried other plans and
failed, and what we did do, so far as I am concerned, was for the very best
without involving ourselves into trouble. I am now opposed to the acceptance
of this paper and was then, and stated in our meeting, but there were other
things brought to bear as to cause me to think that something was necessary
to be done, and that quickly, hence the action was taken as the best under
the circumstances. I felt then, as I feel now, that the step taken was a
long one, and I am only sorry that the matter was not referred to the men
and let them have taken action, whether good or bad, and if I have made a
mistake I wish to say it was one of the head and not of the heart, and I want
our miners to so understand it. I have written to all the members of the
board asking their approval of having a state convention called, but whether
they agreed or not is yet to be ascertained. I want to say that in the event
of such a convention being called, I feel confident that I can get up on the
floor of said convention and clear myself of anything that may even seem to
be crooked in regard to this matter I believe that to be the proper place and
then if the men are not satisfied there will be time enough to ask my resignation. I notice in one of our dailies that such a meeting will be called
about September 1. Why wait that long, let it be as early as possible, let
it be done at once. The matter is now fresh in our minds and may as well get
it settled now as wait. I want to rid myself of any stigma that may be resting on me as an individual for I have always tried to act honestly in my
dealings, and do not wish at this late day to be accused of crookedness. Let
those who seem to be the most angry put themselves in my place and I will
assure them that they would have done as I did. It has been said that certain
ones of our officers knew of this matter two weeks or more before it was
brought before the board. I do not know whether this be true or not, but if
they did know it they should have let it be known to the miners. Again, if such

was true a state convention could have been called as easily as the board
was called together. I do not say that these things are true and do not
make such accusations, but I simply speak these things out that all may have
a chance to vindicate themselves.

I do not write this for the purpose of trying to convince anyone that
a wrong action has not been taken, for I feel as though the action taken
was too hasty, and yet, though hasty as it was, I did not think at the time
that we had done anything other than our constituents would have done. I
am disgusted with the paper business myself, for when this matter was under
our consideration as a board we thought all business men would accept this
paper at its face value, but lo, all our business people speak in voice of
one accord saying that they will not handle it. Hence, if they will not
handle it then it is of no value to us as miners, and should not be accepted
by them, but on the other hand, why hold these indignation meetings and act
like howling demons? Why not protest against it like men and call a state
convention and do away with it if your board has made a mistake. Why threaten
their annihilation? All men are liable to err and if I have erred in this I
again say it is of the head and not of the heart. Trusting we will have a
fair chance of vindication in the near future, I am, yours,

R. L. DAVIS

United Mine Workers' Journal, August 17, 1893.

27. WRONG IMPRESSION

Deduced From R. L. Davis' Letter of Last Issue

COLUMBUS, O., Aug. 21.--As it seems that a wrong impression has gone
out in regard to my last letter, or more especially the headlines, in which
it is said that a mistake has been made, I wish to say that, when I wrote
that letter that I never intended that such an inference should be drawn.
I said that, if a mistake had been made it was of the head and not of the
heart. I could not admit that the board exceeded its authority in handling
the matter, for, according to Article 4, Section 3, of the constitution of
District 6, if you will carefully read it, you will see that the board had
a perfect right to act in the matter. So far as other parts of my letter
are concerned, I have nothing to say and leave it to the calm good judgment
of others. But do not be in anyway influenced that I even intimate that a
mistake has been made in handling the matter as a board; yet, with all that,
I truly hope that our constituents may in a short time become contented
again.

Now a few words to our friend C. H. J. of Nelsonville. In reference to
the colored men taking the places of his white brothers of Raymond, W. Va.,
and Weir City, Kans., while it is true that these men have done as said, I
want to say to my friend that the white miners are largely responsible for
this state of affairs, simply because you refuse to allow the colored men to
work among you in times of peace. If such be true, then is it any wonder
that in times of trouble these men retaliate for the treatment that they receive at your hands? Do away with this system and allow him the privilege
of working along with you and I dare say that instead of the colored men
taking your places he will be at all times to the front, doing all that he
can for the upbuilding of the craft. This is my doctrine and I care not
whether it pleases or not, I am sure that I am right and you are wrong.

R. L. DAVIS

United Mine Workers' Journal, August 24, 1893.

28. MINERAL POINT, OHIO

August 28.

. . . As I read R. L. Davis's letters, it seems to me he wants to please
everybody, and he will find it a hard job. I would advise him to give it
up or he never will please . . . take it along next time so that if you have
any more self vindication to do you can have the same member to blame, else
you would have to blame some other member and soon we would condemn the whole
structure. I just quote a few words from the latter part of your last letter:
"This is my doctrine and I care not whether it please or not." Does your
last two vindicating letters say this? No, not by a jug full.

Another thing I will just mention. How did R. L. Know that wrong impression had been drawn from his first letter when there was no issue between them? The fact of the matter of this, he thought some were displeased
by the act of the board. He wrote to try to appease those displeased ones
on his account. He then thought his first letter might have displeased some
one and so wrote again. You must keep on R. L. This only I see wrong with
the act of the board on the 8th inst.: They ought to have submitted the
operators proposals to the men before making an agreement. I have no doubt
but it would have been accepted. I think under the present circumstances it
was doing good to the operators, good to the workingmen, and good to the
country at large.

United Mine Workers' Journal, August 31, 1893.

29. FROM RENDVILLE, OHIO

As this is the first time that I have put a letter in the paper, I will
try and answer one that I saw in it lately, by a man in Murray City, O.,
telling the condition of the miners in this district. What he said about
the miners condition was all right. He said that if we could come out as
our English brother we would soon be on top. Also, our condition will improve none as long as the stream of foreign contract labor continues to pour
in upon us and lower our wages, and we will continue to drift backwards as
long as our colored brothers take our places while we are out with demands
for our rights as they did in Raymond City, W. Va., and at Weir City, Kans.
I now say to C. H. J. that there is one thing I want him to know and that is
that I know of three mines in Springfield, Ill., where a colored man cannot
work. If he thinks that the men of color are doing him an injury he can find
places to go to where colored people do not work.

In 1879, myself and four other men were refused work at Raymond City, and
if the white man would only be true to organization they would not have to
take their places when they come out on strike.

There are lots of places the colored men are debarred through ignorance,
but we, the miners, are going to stand by the officers as long as they are
in the right, which we believe them to be. We, the miners, in this valley do
not indorse the way they use the officers in the Hocking valley and Gloucester
district. O, my, I forgot something. I see where Mr. Jackson says he wishes
to see some of the officers moved. My brother consider, and see if you cannot
afford to take some of that back. I know the most of the officers myself. As
for R. L. Davis, I knew him when a boy and he always tried to act in favor of
the laborer and tried to keep them together as union men. There is Pearce,
then Nugent; we all know what they have done for us. We want them to remain,
as they are men.

LEWIS COLEMAN

United Mine Workers' Journal, August 31, 1893.

30.   JUST A WORD

RENDVILLE, O., Sept. 18.

Just a word to the union miner of Mineral Point: He seems to think
that we mean wrong in regard to color. When we pronounce color on different
subjects we are driven to it, by men who are not true to the organization
nor are they loyal citizens. What we want is one organization all under
one head, regardless of color, race or creed. No more at this time.

L. COLEMAN

United Mine Workers' Journal, September 21, 1893.

31.   NO RACE BIAS

Influenced a Mineral Point Miner In His Late Criticism

MINERAL POINT, O., Sept. 12.--I have not the slightest notion of entering into controversy with R. L. Davis. I have read his letter in the UNITED
MINE WORKERS' JOURNAL of this last week and had it not been for the last
clause I would not have replied. Brother Davis says: "It is because I am
colored that so many of you fellows jump on me." Brother Davis, if it had
been any other of the executive board I would have done just the same, and,
I suppose, they are all white, but I am glad that none of them showed their
cowardice. And, in my estimation, if you had left self-vindication alone
you would have been more esteemed. During this last five years we have had
a number of colored miners in this locality. I have worked with them, I
have lived close neighbors to some of them and their color was no offense to
me. I always held myself free to associate with any of them of good behavior,
but I am compelled to say that many of them I wanted to have as little to do
with as possible. The ill-behavior and peevishness of many of them led me to
reserve in their presence, for if anything went wrong they said: "It is because we are colored." But, if you be the man you think you are (you say you
will show any of us that you are our equal in written or oral language), show
us some wisdom in letting that old phrase, "It is because of my color," be
said only by those who are less learned. I believe it may be true in some
instances. I believe some have animosity to the colored race, but it is not
so with me. Nationality, creed or color does not effect me in the least. I
have been a reader of the UNITED MINE WORKERS' JOURNAL ever since I knew of
it and read your letters regularly and often sympathized with you when you
said you had been ill-behaved to on account of your color, but now I believe
some of these things may not have happened to you on account of color. I see
you are ready to say so whether it is or not.
      You will hear no more from me on this subject after this writing, but I
tell you I do not think it manly of you in writing these letters in question.
You acted in union with the executive board of which you form a part. Why
not stand or fall with them, instead of singling yourself out and making an
attempt to clear yourself of the seemingly wrong act to you that the board
had done, thereby casting more blame on them? (if there had been any). But
now they are justified and you will be condemned by many thinkers, if not
writers. I will say no more, I take pity on account of your color.
      I am glad to state there is a brighter outlook at this place, at least
at Huff Run mine, operated by Ridgway-Burton company. Work has been very
slack at this mine all summer, but they have paid their men regularly semi-
monthly during this panic.[55]
      At Superior and Davis mines they are only working slack, and I believe
it is a long time since they have had a pay day.
      At Van Kirk's and Holden's they have done very well during these bad
times. I cannot tell you as to their pay, but there is a general store

connected with each. I must conclude, for I think my allotted space will
be taken up. Wishing well to the United Mine Workers of America and its
officials and the paper.

A MINER.

United Mine Workers' Journal, September 14, 1893.

32. THE RENDVILLE MAN

Turns His Thoughts and Pen to Points of General Interest

When it Comes to Bread and Butter Ohio Men Are Solid

RENDVILLE, O., Dec. 17.--Work in this part of the Sunday Creek valley
is somewhat slow; mine No. 3 worked only three days last week, with very dull
prospects for the future, and even with this shortage of work the mine is
overcrowded with men. This can be accounted for because of the shutting down
of several large mines.

The question that seems to be uppermost in the minds of our men is what
shall the future be? This is because of the situation of the miners in
Western Pennsylvania and West Virginia, whose coal is said to come in direct
competition with the Ohio coal. Is it possible that the men of these fields
are so utterly destitute of common sense and reason as to be blind to the fact
that they are working injury to the Ohio miners as well as themselves. Surely
after all these years of almost incessant pleading and talking to they cannot
plead ignorance, and yet what else can it be? Surely it cannot be that they
are so niggardly mean as to endure starvation wages rather with pay a few
pennies per month for the purpose of securing and maintaining uniform and
living wages throughout the competitive field? When will the miners of this
country begin to think to study and to act for their best interest? Surely
the signs of the times indicate that without some very radical changes there
will be trouble in the near future. This is the way things look to me. It
may be that this is only an imperfection of my vision. I hope so, at least.

The press reports have it, that if there are no changes in the Pittsburg
and West Virginia fields by the time the Ohio miners hold their special convention in January, that the Ohio miners will accept a similar reduction, and
there are some who believe it. But, as one, I do not think that any such
ideas are being entertained by the Ohio miners, nor will the convention in
January be held for any such purpose, that is, if I understand the matter
correctly. I think that the January convention is for the purpose of devising
some means whereby the miners of Pennsylvania, West Virginia and other fields
may be brought together for the purpose of taking concerted action to secure
a uniform and living rate of wages.

So let us hope that this will be one of the best conventions ever held
by the Ohio miners. It has been intimated by some the organization in Ohio
is on its last legs and that it will soon be a thing of the past. Well, now,
don't entertain any such foolish notions. Although we may have our little
internal wars, petty grievances, etc., yet when it comes to the question of
wages, or bread and butter, he forgets his petty jealousies and gathers unto
himself his whole strength to resist any encroachments that may be made a-
gainst himself or his fellowman.

And now, by way of conclusion, let me say that I hope the miners of
Pennsylvania, West Virginia, Illinois, Indiana and our own proud Ohio will get
themselves together as we have never before and show to the world that we are
men worthy of the name. With best wishes, I remain yours, for the impover-
ished miner.

R. L. DAVIS

United Mine Workers, Journal, December 28, 1893.

33. R. L. DAVIS

Tells Our Readers Something About His Pocahontas Trip--No Fooling[56]

When He Says He Sincerely Believes He Would Have Become a Martyr
Had He Staid There Much Longer--Harris and Nugent Can Tell

RENDVILLE, O., May 21.--I have been asked several times why I did not
stay at Pocahontas longer than I did, and to give all the proper answer I
will refer them to ex-President Nugent and our friend George Harris of Pennsylvania, they can tell you as well as I can. I have at all times been
willing to do anything in my power in the interest of our organization, but,
boys, I am not yet ready to become a martyr to the cause, and I am confident
that had I remained there much longer that would have been the result, for
those blood-sucker operators down there will not hesitate to stoop to anything low and dirty to carry their point, and especially at this time when
the miners at all other places are out battling for their rights. It is a
picnic for these operators as long as their men continue to work, and they
will do anything rather than see their slaves stop work, or do anything else
in the way of asserting their rights as free men. I do not believe this is
so much the case in times of peace in other regions, yet a certain amount
of this spirit exists at all times they organize themselves, but when the
miner makes an attempt to organize they say no; they do not only stop there
but they might say, oh, he left because he was scared, but boys, let me say
to you that I was then south of Mason's and Dixon's line, and there is but
little justice for the black man anywhere, and none at all down there, and
for safety I thought it would be best for me to leave and even in doing this
I had to be escorted to the station, the threats being so openly made about
doing me up. Yes, and they were talking of doing Harris up, too, and he
is a white man you know. Now, I was born in the State of Virginia, and I
know that when they threaten a white man it is an absolute certainty about
the negro and he had better make himself scarce, that is, if he values his
life any. I have received several letters this week and I am told that those
men that were discharged have not been taken back yet. They say they are
still taking in new members yet, they are all colored. They request me to
ask that a Hungarian be sent there to organize the Huns and the colored will
look to their own. I will say that there you find no mixing. If a meeting
is called and the colored men attend it, very few white faces will be seen,
and vice versa, so I hope a Hungarian organizer will be sent there as soon
as possible, for if something is not done toward getting the Huns to act in
the defense of those colored fellows who have been discharged it will be
impossible to do anything in that region for a long while yet to come, and
by doing this now it will be the means of securing a good organization there,
tell them to take their tools and get out, they are disturbing the peace
and quietness of the community, or in other words, that they are keeping
bad company, etc. To prove this assertion, I, when there, organized a local
composed of those only that were known or supposed to be good men remember.
No notices were posted calling for a meeting, but it was done on the quiet by
going to each individual. We got our meeting and succeeded in organizing a
good little local. Next morning nearly all these men were picked out and
discharged, and when they asked what they were discharged for, they were
that they (the men) were dissatisfied, or that they were keeping bad company,
hence they were not wanted any longer, that they could vacate their houses
and come to the office and get their money. Now, all these men were colored,
and I believe meant business. But you might ask how they could pick out so
many and not be mistaken. I will tell you there are a number of spies throughout the region, both white and black, indeed they are so numerous that some
of them are not known. Now to prove this. I have been sitting or standing
at different places when maybe two or three strange fellows would come along
accompanied by one of the sucks of Pocahontas, when they would get to where
I was I would hear one say, there he is, or there is the s--b--. Not only
that, but I have heard myself spoken of in the same way by business men when
walking along the streets; besides I have heard threats made as to what they

would do to me if I did not leave. Trusting that success may attend the
efforts of the miners in this, their greatest effort. I am, as ever,

                                                          R. L. DAVIS

United Mine Workers' Journal, May 24, 1894.

                        34. R. L. DAVIS

          Sets Himself Right on the Question of Columbus Settlement

     RENDVILLE, O., July 22.--For sometime I have intended having a few words
to say upon the matter that I now attempt to write upon, but on account of
the storm that has been raging for the past few weeks I thought it best to
keep still, but since the storm has nearly blown over and we can only at
times hear the distant rumblings of the receding thunders I will try to explain myself or get an explanation. While at no time has anyone said anything to me personally with the exception of one, it has come to my ears
that certain ones were surprised at the stand that I took in regard to our
late settlement, or in other words that I had taken a decided stand against
McBride and his associates, permit me to say that this is untrue in the extreme. This I did do, however, I did claim that the delegates to the Cleveland convention were sent there with positive instructions to vote for 70
cents and no compromise that they had no right to leave the whole matter to
the district presidents and national board. My reasons for so claiming was
because of the fact that the delegates themselves had not the power to compromise, and consequently had not the power to delegate that power to anyone
else. So if really there be any blame it would certainly fall upon the
shoulders of the delegates themselves. However, be this as it may it is only
my opinion, and I have not accused McBride of any duplicity in the matter,
neither have I ever said that the miners had been sold, but on the other hand
have advised others who did make the charge to refrain from making such charges. The matter does not stop there, but has finally resolved itself into a
church matter. Now, there are three things in the labor question that I do
hate, and they are: 1. religious bigotry, 2. race prejudice, 3. political
partisanism.
     What right have I or any one else to question the right of another what
church he belongs to? None whatever.
     Of course at the time of the settlement, when the news first reached my
ears, I said some things that were not very pleasant, but that has passed and
is forgotten. Our friend Sullivan and myself had a little misunderstanding
over the matter. He also took exceptions to some of my sayings, but when we
came to talk over the matter and a thorough explanation we made everything
all right.
     Now, by way of conclusion, allow me to say that instead of our smart
Alecks trying to create dissension in our ranks, they should do all in their
power to heal the gaping wound and begin to get our forces together for the
next contest, for it is surely coming, and instead of doing as some of our
friends who say they will pay no more into the national treasury until those
fellows get down and out, if you would look around you and notice how closely
the employers are banding themselves together, you would drop such foolishness and come together as men and brethren, for you have no time to waste.
So, by all means, let us have an end to this strife and contention and be men.
Remember you cannot live for yourselves alone, but your fellow-men as well.

                                                          R. L. DAVIS

United Mine Workers' Journal, July 19, 1894.

35.   R. L. DAVIS

Condemns in Words of Deep Resentment the Constitution
A.R.U. in Excluding Negroes

And Issues a Challenge to Any Club In the
Hocking Valley to Play Base Ball

RENDVILLE, O., July 16.--For the past month I have had nothing to say
through your valuable paper, because of the fact that many others were having
their say in regard to the late settlement. I thought it best to keep still,
inasmuch as there is seemingly always some one ready to jump on me. During
the months of April, May and June the eyes of the entire country were turned
on the great coal miners' strike. The strike was no more than ended, when
lo, and behold, we have another;--viz., the railroad men. Surely these great
uprisings of the people mean something, and what is it? It is simply this,
that the people have been ground down by capital to that extent that they can
no longer endure it. We demand living wages, and of course if we cannot secure it by means of conciliation or arbitration, then as a last resort there
is nothing left for us to do but to strike. But when we strike, what do we
then find? We find this, that instead of having the unfair employers we have
also to fight the state and national government, or in other words the militia
and United States regulars. In fact it not only seems so but it is true,
that those whom the people have elected to enact laws have joined hands with
the money kings of the country to further oppress the already down-trodden
laborer. And yet it is all our fault. After all we will not be true to ourselves and elect men from our ranks to fill these positions, but the fellow
who has the most money and can set up the most beer and whisky, oh, he is
the man. And so it goes, year after year, the honest man has no chance whatever. Everything and everybody is against him and, of course he is elected
to stay at home. Not wishing to worry your readers further I will leave that
subject. But I cannot close this already too lengthy letter without having
a word to say about the American Railway union, which I consider to be the
best for railway men in this country, and I hope to see it grow and prosper.[57]
But there is one sad mistake that has been made in it, as the other so-
called railway organizations and that is the negro has been debarred from
obtaining membership. Why is this? Surely gentlemen, you have sense enough
to know that we were born here and intend to remain here. We are American
citizens and should be treated as such. But what can you expect of the negro
with this kind of treatment? Remember that he is as sensitive as any other
nationality or race of people. We find that the Hungarian, Polander, Italian,
Chinaman and even the lazy, shiftless Indian can be members, but an intelligen
negro who was born in this country and who has helped to make the country what
it is, is considered as naught, and is debarred. It is just such treatment
as this that has caused the negro to take your places when you were striking.
Now, if there is anything that I do despise it is a blackleg, but in places
in this country that they will not allow the negro to work simply because of
his black skin, then I say boldly that he is not a blackleg in taking your
places; he is only doing his plain duty taking chances with the world. We ask
no one to give us anything. All we want is the chance to work and we assure
you we want just as much wages as the whites. Hoping to see the day when
these things shall have disappeared, I am

R. L. DAVIS

P.S.--I wish to announce that the Rendville Base Ball club is willing to
cross bats with any club in Perry, Hocking, or Athens counties; no exceptions.
Now, who will take us up? Remember we are all church members and cannot play
for a stake.

R. L. D.

United Mine Workers' Journal, July 19, 1894.

36. THE RIGHT STEP

Is What R. L. Davis Says the Convention on the 15th is--

Wants Men to Be Men in Reality

RENDVILLE, O., Aug. 5.--I have just finished reading the call for the convention of workingmen to be held in the city of Columbus, O., on the 15th inst. I must say that this is a step in the right direction. Now, fellow-laborers, what do you intend to do? You have seen the results of past legislation. Will you now be men enough to elect honest men from among your ranks to represent you, or will you still continue to be slaves of partyism that you know has, for the past thirty years been legislating in the interest of the rich, and against the interests of the poor? Fellow-workmen, for God's sake let us be men. Let us send representatives to that convention. Let those men there adopt a platform of principles, and let us stick to them. Stop voting tickets because your fathers before you voted that way, and make one firm resolve to vote for honest men, for equity and justice. There is this about the workingman that I have noticed, he knows the best thing for him to do, but when election day comes around he forgets himself and votes the wrong way, everytime. I think that in the past year we have all learned a lesson. Now let us profit by it. Let us forget petty prejudices and come together as men working for the one common interest of all. I hope that this convention will be largely attended and that it may prove fruitful to labor throughout the whole country.

R. L. DAVIS

United Mine Workers' Journal, August 9, 1894.

37. DAVIS

Of Rendville Thinks the Organization is Too Cheap--Wants Others' Views

RENDVILLE, O., Nov. 19.--Again after a long silence I attempt to write a few lines to your valuable paper. I must confess that I hardly know upon what subject to write that would be most conducive to the best interest of our craft. However, for the purpose of drawing out the ideas of some of our modern thinkers, I will just make the claim that our organization, though the best the American miners ever had, is entirely too cheap; that is, the amount it cost each miner per month or per annum is not enough to carry on the work to a successful issue. I am well aware of the fact that while I make this claim there are many who make the counter claim that it costs entirely too much, and what surprises me most is that many of these same men came from parts of the country where they paid five times the amount they pay here, Great Britain especially. However, it is not entirely necessary to go so far as England to produce an argument in the matter. Take for instance the cigarmakers in this country who pay more into their union in three months than we pay in a year, and yet the sum paid by them is admitted by themselves to be inadquate. They are not the only ones; for instance, there are the iron and steel workers the windo-glass workers, carpenters, bricklayers and many other organizations, and yet we find none of them pay as small dues as the miners, and yet it must be admitted that to be successful in organizing the miners of this country into one organization, more field workers are needed than in any of the trades I have mentioned; nor is this all I claim that we should pay a sum sufficient to create a fund so that when we may be called out on strike that there will be something with which support those who might be so unfortunate as to be in needy circumstances, while I mention this as a precaution to be taken in case of strikes or lockouts. I also believe that had we a sufficient amount of money on hand, as we should have, we would have fewer strikes, for then the employer would not nor could he hope to depend on starving us into submission. I think no harm could be done by giving this

question a little discussion for I believe as our genial Pat does, if we have
a 10 cent organization we must expect 10 cent results, if we have a 25 cent
or 50 cent organization we must expect like results.

Now, to do the things I have mentioned can be done by chewing and
smoking a little less tobacco, and by cutting off a few glasses of beer and
bad whisky; things that we can do without.

I would like to hear from some others on this who are better qualified
to discuss it than myself. Yours for the amelioration of labor.

R. L. DAVIS

United Mine Workers' Journal, November 22, 1894.

38.   HONEST AND MANLY

Letter from Our Colored Correspondent, R. L. Davis--Defeated for Office,
But as Good Union Man as Ever

RENDVILLE, O., Feb. 25.--Times in our little image remain the same as at
our last writing--no work and much destitution, with no visible signs of anything better. With only hope it will not be long until the wheels of industry
begin to move for we are not that class of people who love idleness or who
prefer to live at the hands of charity. Now that our national convention is
over it is the duty of each and everyone of us to do our utmost to try and
heal the strained relations of the past and arise in our might to build up
our organization to what it should be. We have played into the hands of the
great corporations long enough. We say we have hard times now, but do not
forget the fact that unless we organize ourselves together as men should times
will eventually be harder with us than now. Anyone who reads the daily press
can see all kinds of reports, dissatisfaction, dissension and discord on all
sides; that the Ohio miners will dissolve their relationship with the national
organization of United Mine Workers and form an organization of their own, etc.
I desire to say, and I believe I voice the sentiment of every honest miner in
Ohio, that while it may be true that everything has not been satisfactory to
all, yet the Ohio miners are not that class of people to tear down that which
it has taken years to build up.

Having attended the last convention and having been a candidate for member of the national executive board, although I was unsuccessful, I desire to
say that I never asked anyone to vote for me or asked him anything in connection with his or their votes, I am proud to say that I was defeated by a very
small majority, which to my mind proves very clearly that the question of
color in our miners' organization will soon be a thing of the past. I now
desire to thank all of those who favored me with their votes, trusting that
the next time some great man of my race will be successful. As I said in the
convention hall, I again repeat that although defeated, I am really anxious
and willing to do all in my power for the upbuilding of the organization.

R. L. DAVIS

United Mine Workers' Journal, February 28, 1895.

39.   A STRONG PROTEST

From "Dick" Davis Against the Move Made by Some Men in the Sunday Creek--He
Never Will be a Party to an Organization Which Debars His Race

RENDVILLE, O., July 28.--In reading over the columns of your last issue,
I noticed and carefully read an article from the pen of Friend Wallace of
Hollister, giving a description of the troubles in the Sunday Creek valley;

also his opinion in reference to the national organization, and the aims
and objects of the new valley delegation as he calls it. I don't know what
it is, but some call it the labor league, others call it the screw drivers'
union while others call it the A.A. combination. I am at a loss as to what
to call it, for while writing I hold a copy of its constitution in my hand
and it begins with saying as follows:

Constitution and by-laws to govern the miners and mine laborers of the
Sunday Creek coal field, composed of the employees of the Ohio Central Fuel
company and the operators on the C.S. & H. R'y., with preamble and principles.

Now, I don't know whether this is a mistake or not, but it is the first
labor organization of the kind that I have ever heard of where operators were
one of the component parts. I cannot as yet see the utility of such an action so long as there is such a broad chasm between capital and labor. In
fact, I think the whole thing a miserable mistake, and was conceived in
fraud and born of corruption. It has been well said that the worst enemy
that the laboring man has is under his own hat. I had intended writing upon
this new organization last week, but having received a letter from Friend
Wallace in reference to it, I thought I would wait until I had more reliable
information, which I think I know have both in his article in your last issue
and in a private letter received from him by myself. I will here state that
I had written to Friend Wallace, telling him that I thought it quite essential for a combination of all the miners of the Sunday Creek valley for mutual
protection, but that, if said combination was not affiliated with the United
Mine Workers of America, then L.U. 398 would have nothing to do with it, for
we intended to remain loyal and would not intermingle with secessionists under any circumstances, and in his reply friend Wallace grows very oratorical
and thinks me a very foolish boy, although he does not say it in so many
words, yet the inference to be drawn makes results the same. I claimed that
the new something was composed of disloyalists. Friend Wallace says not.
Well, here is what the constitution says, Article 6, Section 4, while it is
necessary to be governed by a national organization, the choice shall be
left with the members of this body as to what national organization they wish
to be governed by. Now, this is just the part that I took exceptions to. I
think it is necessary to get our forces together; it is no time for divisions
and getting up new organizations to please a disgruntled few, or to suit the
whims and caprices of disappointed office seekers. Fellow miners, did it
never occur to your minds that while you are wrangling and quarrelling among
yourselves, that the operators are laughing up their sleeves at you and
quietly planning how to fleece you out of something else. Do not for a moment think that all you have to look after is the price per ton, for such is
not the case, for you have other things to look after as well, or else you
will find one of these days that you will be receiving a handsome reduction
in the way of local conditions, &c.

Now, before closing I wish to comment on another statement made by Friend
Wallace. He says that there are several national organizations that would
like to take us in and do for us, and that he thinks it is a question that
the miners of the country should consider, &c. He also says that to be
closely allied with the railway employees all over the State of Ohio, a suspension in Ohio would be equal to a national suspension. Well, well, Friend
Wallace, have you not been reading the decisions handed down of late by our
supreme court judges? If you have, you have surely forgotten yourself. Again,
are you not aware that there are as many scabs among railway men as among any
other trades? Again, I desire to know what railway union have we in the State
of Ohio that does not bar the colored man from membership? Yet you think we
should allow ourselves to become affiliated with them. Well, let old Dick
tell you something, that as long as the court knows itself I will never be a
party to the agreement, nor will any other colored man who has any sense of
respect or pride of his race, nor will he if I can bring any influence to
bear upon him. I am anxious and willing to do all I can for the advancement
of the cause of labor connected in any way with an organization; but I will
never allow myself to become connected in any way with an organization that
says I cannot become a member, and just think of it, too, I, an American
citizen by birth, and many of them are not yet dry from crossing the salt
water pond, and yet they have the unlimited gall to say that an American citizen shall not take part in an American institution because of the color of his

skin; it makes me mad whenever I think of it, and I have no respect for the man or men who steps into a thing of the kind by holding out false hopes to them. Away with such rottenness.

Now, by way of conclusion, I will say that I believe that the members of L. U. 398 are ready and willing to join in any advancement of the cause of the craft; but so long as you continue in the spirit of disloyalty, please mark us absent.

I cannot close without saying just a word to Brother Smoot of the Flat Top region. The brother seems to think they are not receiving the support from the union miners that they should. This I am sorry to learn. But I will say to the brother that while we earnestly sympathize with them in their noble flight, we are not in a position to aid them for we are slowly starving ourselves, were it within our means to do so none would respond more quickly than we, for we know their cause is just. With best wishes for all I am as ever one in the cause.

R. L. DAVIS

United Mine Workers' Journal, August 1, 1895.

40. WALLACE'S REPLY TO DAVIS

In Which a Few Very Worthy and Sensible Observations Are Made

HOLLISTER, O., Aug. 4.--Please allow me space in our craft's educator for a few remarks. While I do not believe the space should be taken up in a vain controversy, I do think it necessary to reply to the remarks made by Friend Dick Davis in his protest in the issue of August 1.

I will give you the general average of the Miners at Mine 16 first, as I believe that to be the most important No. of miners, 207; No. of days, 9 amount per day, $1.65; amount per month, $14.85. Docks and overweight that miners received nothing for was 49 tons, deducting rent and supplies there is quite a small sum left. The mines seem to be in fair condition regarding ventilation, &c; do not hear many complaints, if you excuse unmeaning language.

As to friend R. L., I am pleased to see his protest, because every one should express their opinion, but we should at all times be reasonable and use good common sense. Bro. Davis, when you refer to my letter regarding the new valley delegation, the language you use makes me believe that you are laboring under an hallucination or error. The constitution you refer to has not anything to do whatever with either of those organizations you mentioned. And as to the A.A. combination I think I perceive your meaning, which remark I think unmanly and does not reach the mark intended, as A. A. Adams has been quite a while lingering between life and death from hemorrhage of the lungs. As to the criticism of the wording of the preface you, for a purpose known to yourself and others, place thereon a misconstruction which is as unreasonable as other expressions made by you. The word "of" may have been omitted through mistake by the printer or the writer of the manuscript, but it is as reasonable for the operators to be components of an organization as to be the sole beneficiaries without helping to defray the expense of same. As you refer to the letter received from me I think you should have published the letter to give the readers a more thorough understanding and allow their own conclusions. I am perfectly willing for its publication. I do not write anything that I am not willing to see in print.

Brother Davis says he thinks it quite essential for the combination of the miners of the Sunday Creek valley, but will not have anything to do with it if it was not affiliated with the U.M.W. of A. I asked Brother Davis if that was reasonable, giving the reasons why I asked the question; told him that 21 years ago I contemplated joining a labor organization; I examined its principles; they suited me, I became a member and the first lesson I learned was to be ruled by the majority. Is that any reason for him to think that I grew oratorical or thought him a foolish boy. He claims that the new something was composed of disloyalists. I claim not, yet the new valley delegation was

composed by mutual agreement of a majority of the miners of the Sunday Creek
valley.

As I have before stated, the proceedings of every convention that has
been held for that purpose will show without regard to any of those bodies
that Brother Davis mentions in his criticisms which would infer that the
destiny of the miners of Mine 3 are solely in the hands of Brother Davis
from the responsibility he assumes.

DAN WALLACE

[TO BE CONTINUED]

[We have done our best, friend Wallace, to get your whole letter in
this week, but are forced to continue it till next.--Ed.]

United Mine Workers' Journal, August 8, 1895.

41. WALLACE'S REPLY TO DAVIS

In Which a Few Very Worthy and Sensible Observations Are Made

[CONTINUED FROM LAST WEEK]

Brother Davis's criticsm on the affiliation with the railway employees
reminds me of an individual whom the boys claim would tell continued stories.
The stories always finished up with a quart of whisky, and Davis's letters
most always close about the abuse of his race. Now, Brother Davis, this is
not for the purpose of, in anyway hurting your feelings, for I believe myself
that the race you refer to is not treated humanely in some parts of the
country. The colored man was debarred from the A.R.U., which was very in-
consistent and, if not already, should be changed, for my belief is that this
world is my country, every man is my brother and to do good is my religion,
and I belong to an organization with principles broad enough, long enough,
deep enough, charitable enough and liberal enough to embrace in its folds all
of nature's creatures, whose motto is, "An injury to one is the concern of
all." I was a member when that grand old man Uriah S. Stevens was general
master workman; was a member when Terrence V. Powderly was general master
workman, and a member when James R. Sovereign is master workman and would
still be a member if R. L. Davis were general master workman. It is not leaders of an organization that workingmen should follow but the principles.[58]

Yes, Brother Davis, I have read with sorrow the decision handed down of
late by the supreme court judges, which is enough to show you or any other
rational man that the two old political parties are the guardians of capital
and not of labor, and that Debs and his associates were sent to jail contrary
to the constitution of the United States, and sets a precedent dangerous to
the liberties of the American people, a government by injunction; and I also
read of a young woman in Washington City, D.C., daughter of a retired army
officer, or some other capitalistic fool, taking deliberate aim and shot a
colored boy, killing him, for trying to get some fruit off their trees, gave
herself up to the authorities and was acquitted. How long, O Lord, how long,
will a patient people put up with monopoly rule? Is it not about time,
Brother Davis, that we stop this nonsensical quarreling and stand by our unions
and by the political party of our own class in order that we may be able to
strike economically for our labor and politically at the ballot box for our
temporary improvement and for our ultimate emancipation?

Now, as regards THE JOURNAL, I say above all things, at all times and on
all occasions, defend, uphold and patronize our own craft paper, and all other
papers that uphold the dignity of labor, and do not support a newspaper that
does not uphold the dignity of labor. It is labor that should have the daily
papers instead of monopoly, laboring men, why not have a daily paper? Why
support the Associated Press, that is controlled by monopoly or run by some
political machine? It is only buying weapons for your enemy's army.

DAN WALLACE

United Mine Workers' Journal, August 15, 1895.

42. WHAT HAS HE DONE?

That is What R. L. Davis Wants to Know--The Company Objects to Him Being Checkweighman

RENDVILLE, O., Sept. 29.--Not having troubled you for some time I beg a small space that I may let your many readers know of the treatment that the writer has been receiving for the past few months. To do this, it will be necessary to go back to last winter. On January 26 last Mine 3 was closed down, and the miners, not having earned anything of consequence while working were in straitened circumstances. Some time during the latter part of March or the first of April, Dame Rumor had it that Mr. Rend had stated that he would start Mine 3 upon certain conditions, and those conditions were that I should be removed as checkweighman. I called President Penna's attention to the matter and he held an interview with Mr. Rend on the matter, and he informed me that Mr. Rend denied any such intentions. With this the matter dropped, and nothing more was thought of it until some time in June, when Mr. D. S. Williams, the superintendent, came here and stated to some of the men that the mine would be started if I was removed; otherwise, it would lie idle all summer. It reached my ears, and I immediately went to the superintendent and asked him about it and what the causes were. He told me that it was Mr. Rend's desire for me to be removed as checkweighman. The response he did not know, but that if he were in my place and wanted to see the mine resume work, he would get down for awhile at least. I studied and concluded that if by my getting down was the only means of getting the mine started, I would do so, provided an investigation of the matter was had. About June 23 or 24, Mr. Williams wired, asking for a meeting. The meeting was called and he was present. The chairman called on him. He arose and started off by asking the question, "How long has it been since you men have worked?" He was answered, "Five months." He then said that he had not much to say, but that Mr. Rend had two mines idle, No.'s 1 and 3; that it was optional with him as to which of them was started, but that he had a few requests to make and on the actions of the miners would rest whether Mine 3 would resume or not. His requests were as follows:

1st. That the men would send clean coal.

2d. That they would get all their supplies from the company, which they would sell them as cheap as any one else.

3d. That I should be removed as the checkweighman.

After he was through I got up and made a statement of some of the troubles that we had had at the mine, and also said that I would voluntarily get down if the starting of the mine rested on that alone, with the understanding that an investigation was had, that I had no desire to jeopardize the interest of 200 or more men for my own individual interest.

Mr. Williams promised to do all he could to secure an investigation. The miners accepted the propositions and work was resumed. June 26 a resolution was also adopted in that meeting to place the matter in the hands of officers for investigation. After this everything went on I suppose smoothly, until on or about the 20th inst., when Mr. Williams came up again and stated that he had heard that I was going to run for checkweighman, and that if the men elected me that the mine would be closed down. I did not hear him make this statement, but it got circulated, and oh! what a scare. Men who had been after me to run for the position began to take the back track. Such a stampede you never saw. I wanted to read certain letters that I had from the officers, but could not get to do it, for reasons unknown to me. So the old boy was defeated, the men most all saying they wanted me, but they wanted the question settled first by the officers.

Now, I certainly want this matter investigated. I want to know what I have done. I have done nothing that I am ashamed of. I have always tried to be honest and manly in the performance of my duties, hence I am not afraid of investigation. Some say the cause is my writing to the JOURNAL, others say it is because of my persistence in organized labor, etc. I want to know myself what it is and at that as soon as possible. I trust the officers will take the matter up, for I do not like the position I am placed in.

In conclusion, I must say to friends Costlett and Richards that they have at last taken the right step, and that all miners of the Sunday Creek valley

should join you. I shall use my every effort in this direction. Yours
for organized labor.

                                                              R. L. DAVIS

United Mine Workers' Journal, October 3, 1895.

43. COULDN'T TELL

If He Were Asked, How the People Live at Rendville, Says R. L. Davis

   RENDVILLE, O., March 9.--After a long silence I will again attempt to
write a few lines to let your many readers know how things are moving along
down here. Our mines are practically doing nothing, one and one-half days
per week is about all and turn slow at that. Were anyone to ask how we
manage to live I am sure I could not tell.
   I have just concluded reading President O'Connor's address which I
consider an able one. With such able men as this I cannot see how it is
that the miners of Illinois cannot get themselves more solidly together. I
have often thought of Indiana with her Purcell, Kennedy and others; of
Illinois with her O'Connor, Crawford, Guymon and others; of Pennsylvania
with her host of able men that are too numerous to mention, and yet seemingly all to no effect. Why is this? It cannot be other than gross negligence
and ignorance on the part of the miners, for which there is no excuse. I
hope to see the day when the miners of this country will place themselves
in a position that they may be able to command a fair share of the wealth
that they create. It cannot be done though as long as we allow ourselves
to be divided. Come boys, let us get a hustle on ourselves and get together,
it is never too late to do good. Wishing our organization success, I am as
ever for justice and humanity.

                                                              R. L. DAVIS

United Mine Workers' Journal, March 12, 1896.

44. CASE OF R. L. DAVIS

   RENDVILLE, O., March 7.--There is nothing encouraging in the local trade
to report from this end of the Sunday Creek valley. It is the same old story;
plenty of idle time. But we are in hopes of a revival of trade in the near
future.
   The case of R. L. Davis against A. B. Merser, a hotel keeper at Corning,
Perry county, O., came up for trial week before last, and P. H. Penna, W. H.
Haskins, W. C. Pearce, M. D. Ratchford and the writer were summoned as witnesses on the case. It will be remembered by the readers of the UNITED MINE
WORKERS' JOURNAL that on about August 22 last we had made arrangements for a
mass meeting in Corning, and invited the above named officers to be present.
They all arrived on the forenoon train, and R. L. Davis went down to meet
them and after a friendly shake hands all round, the officers started to the
hotel for dinner, and invited Mr. Davis to accompany them. He accepted the
invitation and was granted the privilege of registering his name, and after
doing so he was told by the clerk that he could not allow a colored man to
eat in the hotel.
   Davis asked the reason and was told that there were some people from
West Virginia staying with them and they would get insulted. Penna, Ratchford
and Haskins had by this time got seated at the table, and were waiting for
Mr. Davis to arrive, and thinking that there was something wrong, they asked
the clerk what was the matter, and he told them that he wouldn't allow any
colored man to eat at his table. It was then that our officers showed that
true union principle that should characterize all true members of our craft,

for they refused to eat dinner and went elsewhere. Davis consulted a lawyer
and was advised to enter suit at once, which he did. The case is not settled
yet and when it is the readers of the JOURNAL will know all about it.

D. H. SULLIVAN

United Mine Workers' Journal, March 12, 1896.

45.   THANKS

From Our Colored Member of the National Executive Board,
R. L. Davis, Promises to Do His Utmost

A Few Tart Words on the Conduct of the Men at Murray City, Ohio

RENDVILLE, O., April 18.--I will again ask a small space in your valuable paper to at this time thank the miners for their kind support in electing me as a member of the executive board of the U.M.W. of A. I can only
say that should I be given the opportunity, I will try to use my every effort
for the elevation of our craft. The financial condition of the organization
at this time, however, is of such a nature that other members of the board
as well as myself will have to remain at home. I trust that the miners of
the country in general will look to their interest, for, boys, you know what
it takes to make the mare go.

Let us now, since we have elected our officials, each and everyone give
to them our very best support individually and collectively; by doing this I
think that our next meeting we can find a better condition of affairs.

We have been very earnestly watching Brother Haskins's trouble at Murray City, O., and I am sorry that the men were so blind to their own interests
as to sacrifice one who had the moral courage to defend their rights. Fellow-
men do you know what you are doing? If you are honest, if you are a liberty-
loving people, then you have made the mistake of your lives in this matter.
When I first heard of this trouble and learned of its nature, I thought
surely you would not do other than give Haskins your entire support, but lo,
you supported the other fellow in whom you had no interest whatever.

If we continue on in this way it will not be very long until we cannot
get an honest man to serve as a checkweighman. We believe Mr. Haskins a
good and efficient man; in fact we know him to be such, and consequently did
not deserve such treatment as he received. Boys, let us get closer together
as miners and watch our interests better in the future than in the past.
Again thanking the miners for their kind favors, and trust that we may be
able to prove our worthiness during the next year, I am yours for the cause
of the emancipation of the wage slaves of the land.

R. L. DAVIS

United Mine Workers' Journal, April 23, 1896.

46.   R. L. DAVIS, MEMBER OF EXECUTIVE BOARD

R. L. Davis is a full-blooded colored man. He was born in the city of
Roanoke, Va., December 24, 1863. He began work at eight years of age in a
tobacco factory; and worked at that trade until he was 17 years of age, going
to school in the winter months. He began to work in the mines in the State
of West Virginia along the New River and Kanawha, and remained in that district
until 1882, when he removed to Rendville, O., where he has since remained. He
was elected a member of the executive board of District 6, United Mine Workers
of America, April 1890, and served continuously until 1895.

His education seems to be fair, at least he is a good reader, and writes

a very good hand, and as our readers know, composes a very good letter.
But it is impossible to find what there is in a man--unless you are a phrenologist, or a physiognomist-- unless he engages you in controversy, or animated conversation, or lectures you. We have never had the pleasure of
either with R. L. We cannot say whether his letters are in the nature of a
combination of well remembered phrases, impressed on the memory at some
remote time in the past, or whether they are the spontaneous utterances of
an original mind. Were Brother Davis a conversationalist, or controversial-
ist, we should long ere this have known which of these his letters manifested,
but as he has never had occasion, or perhaps we have not, to engage him in
this manner, it is difficult for us to tell. Nevertheless, his letters evince
originality or talent--talent of memory--and having cultivated it, he now
enjoys the reward of his labor in being the representative of his race on
the executive board of the United Mine Workers of America, for it would be
too much to say that he has been signalled out from among the vast number of
men of all races represented in the United Mine Workers of America, for exceptional ability. The fact is that Dick (as he is familiary known) was
elected because he is a good representative of his race and because the miners
believe that the colored men of the country should be recognized and given a
representative on the board. At the same time it is only fair to say that he
promises to give just as good service as any other man that might be elected,
for albeit he is not exceptionally talented he possesses the average ability
in the way of book learning and has other qualifications that hardly any other
man in the organization owns. He will in a special way be able to appear before our colored miners and preach the gospel of trade unionism and at the
same time will be able to prove to our white craftsmen how much progress
might be made with very limited opportunities. We have heard him speak in
conventions on several occasions, and he has generally given a good account
of himself. We trust that by the time the next convention rolls around that
Dick will have proven the wisdom of his selection. We will say this, that if
it be a good principle to recognize races or nationalities on the board in
preference to individuals, per se, the convention has done well to elect Dick,
for he has certainly merited this recognition. In fact, he has merited it
from either standpoint, for as a man, and more especially as a union man, he
has deserved well of the miners of the country. We wish him success and hope
to congratulate both him and the organization at the end of the year on the
work he will have done in its behalf.

United Mine Workers' Journal, April 23, 1896.

47. ORIGINAL

That's What Davis Says His Letters Are--He is a Representative of His Race
and Proud of the Honor and Thankful

     RENDVILLE, O., April 27.--In the last issue of your valuable paper, ye
editor, in writing concerning the newly elected officers, in my opinion, did
it well, and we must congratulate you for your very able effort. I must say,
however, that ye editor seems to know more about me than I do myself, hence,
you must be both a phrenologist and a physiognomist, i.e., if I know what
those two big words mean. In regard to my being a conversationalist or not,
I can only say that I have at all times avoided engaging myself in animated
conversation only with those whom I have a thorough acquaintance, for, I
believe that too much tongue is not conducive of any good. As conversationalist, I will say that I have been engaged in controversy in newspapers and
otherwise, and at all times tried to defend my position, but I have a dislike
for these things and have several times promised to not do it again. You
say that you cannot tell whether our letters are in the nature of a combination of well remembered phrases impressed on the memory at some remote time
in the past or whether they are the spontaneous utterances of an original mind.
I can assure you that be they ever so poor they are original, and I think
ye editor knows it well. In reference to being the representative of my race,

etc., I assure you and the miners of the country in general, that I am
proud of this manifestation of kindness in recognization of my people, and
not only am I proud, but my people also. I know that a great deal has not
been said publicly, but I do know that our people are very sensitive, and
upon many occasions I have heard them make vigorous kicks against taxation
without representation. Now, then, they cannot kick this year, for although
the representative himself may be a poor one, it is representation just the
same, and I assure you that I shall try to so act that those who elected me
shall not be made to feel ashamed.

Work here is a thing of the past. I don't know what we are going to
do. We can't earn a living, and if we steal it we will be persecuted. So
if some one will kindly tell us what to do we will be very thankful.

R. L. DAVIS

United Mine Workers' Journal, April 30, 1896.

48. BETRAYED

Is Brother R. L. Davis In the Home of His Friends-- Dick's Unionism is Too Aggressive

For Some of the People of Rendville, Who Ask For His Discharge

RENDVILLE, O., Sept. 8.--As far as we can learn all the miners that
suspended work on the 20th of last month for the restoration of scale rates
are still idle except Mine 3 of this place. It is useless to go over the
entire history of the trouble, but no sooner had the mass meeting held August 20 adjourned than the dissatisfied element who were opposed to stopping
began to scheme among themselves to break away and demanded a meeting of the
miners of Mine 3 to be held on the same afternoon. This meeting was composed almost entirely by the kickers, and they resolved to go to work next
day. It happened that the drivers and day men were not willing to go to work
at less than scale rates, and decided to remain idle until the same was
secured, so there was no work the next day, nor for a week thereafter, during
which time these uneasy fellows continued to devise ways for going to work.
They finally resolved that they would go to work at any cost and that if the
drivers and day men persisted in remaining idle then they would take their
places. They did more than this, they were mean enough to go to the superintendent and tell him that Sam Martin and myself on the part of the miners
were responsible for the actions of the drivers and day men and requested
our discharge; that if this was done everything would move along O.K.

I am sorry to say that those who did this were men of my own race. Just
how they could stoop so low I am unable to tell, and some of them, if not all,
call themselves Christians or children of the Most High God, but in reality
they are the children of his satanic majesty, for none others could commit
such a dastardly deed as to try to starve a fellow-man's wife and family because he would join with them in their nefarious work. I can only say that
it is the first time in the history of my life where men sought the removal
of one of their number to keep him from blacklegging, and I am sure that it
was quite unnecessary for them to have been so devilish particular.

I do not want it understood that all our colored men here are of this
stamp, for such is not the case. We have some good colored men here as true
as can be found anywhere, while on the other hand we have some as mean men
as ever breathed. These fellows we have been enabled to hold down until recently, by reason of a lack of interest on the part of the major portion of
our men, and the consequence is that the wrong parties now hold the reins of
government, and their ruling will no doubt tend to prove detrimental to the
interest of every miner throughout the Hocking valley and probably throughout
the state of Ohio.

I knew we had men here who were mean enough for most anything, but had anyone told me that they would have done as they have, I would have disputed him or her in the most vigorous terms. These men will some day be compelled to go elsewhere to work, and, while I do not believe in entertaining the spirit of retaliation, I do believe that miners should know with whom they have to deal. By way of conclusion I will say that a great deal has been said of a letter of mine recently containing a touch of negro and Irish dialect. It has been inferred that it was an attempt to throw or cast odium upon these two nationalities. While nothing of the kind was ever intended, it was only a conversation of two individuals, and I so stated in my letter; and again, no sane man could for a moment think that I would say or do anything that would reflect discreditably upon the negro (which race I am not ashamed to own that I belong to), and so far as the Irishman is concerned, some of my best friends are of that nationality, so why should I try to do anything to injure them? The fact is, everything was cut and dried, and when a man wants to find fault he can always find an opportunity. That's all. Will write again when we find a stopping place.

R. L. DAVIS

United Mine Workers' Journal, September 10, 1896.

49. WORKING STEADILY

At Rendville, Ohio, But Earnings Are Very Small--R. L. Davis Declines Nomination for the District Vice Presidency

RENDVILLE, O., Dec. 14.--It was with sadness that I read of the death of the esteemed correspondent known as "Laurence Gardner" in your last issue. We shall miss her valuable information given from time to time in the columns of the only miners' organ, viz: the UNITED MINE WORKERS' JOURNAL. Would to God we had a few more such women, for surely it would make the world better.

The miners here are working every day, though I have heard no complaints of too much earnings. We have been watching for results in the Pittsburgh field, and hope that something may be done to make times better. Surely the miners have had time to learn the evil effects of not being organized, for no other craft has suffered so much during the past few years; and I hope that we may get ourselves together once more so as to be in position to demand and obtain living wages.

I desire to say by way of conclusion that I have been notified that I have been nominated for member of the national executive board; also for vice-president of district 6. After carefully considering the matter, I have concluded to decline to be a candidate for vice-president of district 6, for good reasons, though I desire to thank those who were so kind as to consider my name for the position. I shall, however, allow my name to stand for a member of the national board, and place myself in the hands of my friends. I have not as yet got work; others can get all the work they want, but I, who have never harmed anyone to my knowledge, must take chances with winter and the chilly blasts without the privilege of a job so as to earn a morsel of bread for my wife and little ones. Hoping for better times soon.

R. L. DAVIS

United Mine Workers' Journal, December 17, 1896.

50. GLAD

That the Miners of Corning and Rendville Reorganized is Brother R. L. Davis

Advises All Others to Follow Their Example

RENDVILLE, O., Feb. 27.--Since the inception of the UNITED MINE WORKERS'
JOURNAL I have tried to inform its many readers of the news of this vicinity,
the mining news especially, and such other matters as I thought would be of
interest to the craft in general. I know that these letters are not at all
times enjoyed becaude they tell the old, old story, but, nevertheless, I
am compelled to follow the same old strain.

I have heard men ask the question what good has the miners' organization ever done the miner? This, in my opinion, is not a hard question to
answer, though to answer it in its entirety would consume a great deal of
time. My answer is a short one. Organized labor has been the means of
bringing about every reform that has been made in the labor world. Every
law that has been enacted in the interest of labor has been the result of
organized labor, but I think there is a better way of answering this question at least a more effective way, and that is to tell the first fellow
who asks you the same question to go to West Virginia or Pennsylvania, or
even to some mining camps in Ohio where there is no organization and if he
cannot then see for himself at a glance what the effects of being unorganized is, you may set that fellow down as being very dull of understanding.

In my mind there is no room for argument over this question, and the
man who is opposed to organization is either grossly ignorant or too niggardly mean to do that which he himself believes to be right, he would
rather stand idly by and enjoy whatever advantages that might be gained by
others, this fellow is a coward and a knave.

Then we have another fellow who has a prejudice against somebody he
won't join, and uses his best endeavors to keep others from joining. He
would rather allow himself to be robbed of from 25 to 50 cents per day than
pay 15 cents per month into the organization. This fellow is a--well, he
has no sense. Now, say, I don't want any one to take too much of this upon
themselves, for I have had too much trouble in this way already.

I am glad to note that the miners of Corning and Rendville have again
connected themselves with the organization, and I hope this time to stay.
I had never thought for a moment that they would have staid out as long as
they did, but some men had to learn a lesson, hence the delay.

I hope that some movement may be brought about to get our people out of
their present predicament. They themselves are innocent of having brought
about the present condition of things, but they were forced upon them by
others who had long established the pernicious system of cutting rates, and
these people were forced to do likewise or starve, and for the sake of their
families they chose the former.

I hope to see better times for the miners as a whole, but I fear unless
we change our tactics and take a hand as men should we may have to wait a
long while.

Hoping that I have not intruded upon too much of your space, will write
again, I remain,

                                                           R. L. DAVIS

United Mine Workers' Journal, February 11, 1897.

51. R. L. DAVIS

Of Rendville Breaks the Silence of the Last Couple of Weeks On His Part

By Once More Advising His Fellow Miners to Do Their Duty by the Organization

RENDVILLE, O., March 8.--After a long silence I again trouble you with
a few lines. Work in this part of the valley is very poor. Mine 8 is idle
on account of water in the mine, and do not know when they will do anything.
Mine 3 working a half day now and then, or in fact just about enough to make
the men sore and stiff each time they go into the mine. They are not making
a living by any means, for that is out of the question. The Congo mine, a-
bout a mile and a half from here, is the only mine in this part that is doing
anything. They are doing fairly well, and it is a pity that more men cannot
be employed there, but all men cannot expect to work in one mine. They are

now making another opening to this mine which, when completed, will give
employment to a goodly number of men in the near future. I must say that
when this mine was first opened many harsh words were said against it, and
I said my share, but I must say that in my opinion it is the best mining
camp in this part of the valley. The men are treated civilly and gentle-
manly. I have heard no complaints from this source. Our organization is
recognized, and if there is a grievance the matter is adjusted by the mine
committee and company's officials, that is, if it is not of too broad a
nature, then the subdistrict officials are called to advise in the matter.
        I say these things in justice to the company because of what I have
said in years gone by, and further because of the fact that my business
called me there not long since, and I could not have been treated better by
company or miners. Another matter is, I do not know of another company that
gave to each head of a family a big fat turkey for their dinners on Thanks-
giving day, as was done at Congo. I believe in giving the devil his due.
I have been much pleased with the letters of friend Helm of Nelsonville,
and to the establishment of a defense fund. It is the one thing needed by
the miners of this country, most of all, with one possible exception, and
that is unity. It seems that with the few miners who are organized the
greater number want something cheap. They want a defense fund if it can be
gotten up on the plan of paying 10 cents per month and drawing out $1 or
more. It is to be hoped that our people may soon get their eyes opened to
see the necessity of having an organization both numerically and financially
strong. I think the miners in this country should have an organization
second to none in the civilized world. We ought to have it. We can have it
and we will have it, if those who now proclaim themselves to be union men
will only do their duty as men should.
        Before closing this I want to say a word along the lines of friend
Incog's in reference to holidays. Yes, Incog, I am with you, but you forget
the day I love most, and that is emancipation day. By all means let us
celebrate the day when the shackles were cut loose and 4,000,000 of black men
were liberated from the galling yoke of chattel slavery. Yes, add this day
and we are with you heart and soul. Will have more to say at some future
time.

                                                            R. L. DAVIS

United Mine Workers' Journal, March 11, 1897.

                              52. R. L. DAVIS

Reviews Conditions in West Virginia and Requests the Success Met With in That
        Field in Having the Working Miners Join Their Striking Brothers.

        RENDVILLE, O., Sept. 6.--Since our long silence we will ask your indul-
gence to allow the writing of a few lines to your valuable paper. We have
just returned from the West Virginia fields, where we have been laboring in-
cessantly trying to get these people to join us in the suspension brought
about for the purpose of securing something like living wages, and when we
say that we have risked all kinds of dangers in trying to fulfill our duties
we tell no untruth, for we assure you, gentle reader, that it was like taking
one's life in his hands at times. While we never had any injunctions issued
against us, we had men and Winchesters against us which were in most cases
just as effective, and if you want proof just ask W. L. Green for he knows
all about it. I will tell you all later.
        We want to say in reference to the Virginia miners, that while they have
some men among them who are true and tried, they also have another set who
are the most ignorant and mean of all, and to call them slaves is putting it
mildly. Anything this boss says is all right, and no talk done by an organizer seems to have any effect, at least in times like these, and we know we
had some of the best men in the country down there, but all to little avail.
The miners in the Flat Top, when we first went there quit, but it was only
for a short time, and they were scared back into the mines, except in a few

cases, and these were discharged for taking part in the movement, and they
are there today without work or assistance.

Along the Kanawha and New River districts we have a goodly number of
men out, and these people have acted nobly, except at Loup Creek, Anstead,
Stone Cliff and other places where we were unable to reach them.

We will write more of this matter later on, for we don't want to be
accused of writing a long letter, so excuse us for a week, if you please.

R. L. DAVIS

United Mine Workers' Journal, September 9, 1897.

53.   R. L. DAVIS

Reports Conditions in the Kanawha Field, and Sends an Editorial That Appeared
in the Charleston Gazette of a Recent issue, in Which a Gross Injustice
is Done the Mine Workers' Association.

MONTGOMERY, W. Va., Oct. 17.--I will again attempt to write a few words
in reference to the conditions existing in the Kanawha valley. On Friday a
convention was held here, to hear the report of the committee who attended
the joint meeting of operators and miners, at Charleston, Thursday, and after
hearing of the mean treatment accorded President Ratchford and the committee
and the evident desire on the part of the operators, to whip the miners into
submission, a resolution was unanimously passed to continue the strike with
renewed vigor. The men are firm, generally speaking. There are, however,
about three at Edgewater who have been striving to get a few of the weaker
ones to make a break.

One of these things came down to Montgomery here this morning and some
of the men got after him and made him join the bird gang. He sought refuge
in the house of Mr. Montgomery and had to remain there until officers came
to escort him home, and they could not find him for some time. Some say he
found a room in the house that the owner didn't know was in it.

I do not think a break will be made tomorrow as President Robinson and
myself with others visited Edgewater this afternoon and we were assured that
such would not be the case. We will go there at 5 o'clock tomorrow morning
with the band and several hundred men as a precautionary measure.

We attended a meeting at Cannellton last evening also one at Montgomery
this evening.

Enclosed find editorial taken from the Charleston Gazette. It will show
how much sympathy these papers have for us, and yet we buy them. This is one
of the three articles, and one of the others is even more bitter than this:

"The Kanawha miners who persist in the disastrous strike can no longer
lay claim to the sympathy of the Community. The operators are willing to
deal with them on a just and honorable basis. They went on a strike without
a grievance of their own and merely out of sympathy with Ohio and Pennsylvania. The Ohio and Pennsylvania miners have returned to work. They have no
sympathy evidently with the Kanawha miners. The operators have conceded a
wage scale that is perfectly satisfactory. There is no matter of importance
in dispute between employer and employe. The men who engaged in the strike
will be taken back in good standing. No persecution, no boycott, no bad
blood. Mr. Ratchford demands that the operators shall place themselves in
the power of the U.M.W. association. The operators in the light of the past,
and in view of existing conditions, would not be justified in doing anything
of the kind. The Pennsylvania and Ohio miners might quarrel with their
bosses and the Kanawha miners who would have no quarrel with their bosses
might feel compelled to walk out again. The U. M. W. association is controlled
by Pennsylvania and Ohio, and the interests of the operators and the miners
are inimical to the interests of West Virginia so long as the Kanawha men
elect to serve a foreign controlled organization in opposition to the interests
of the local community, they cannot expect either sympathy or support. They

should go to work."
     I will not trouble you further, excuse long letter.

                                                                              R. L. DAVIS

United Mine Workers' Journal, October 21, 1897.

                              54. R. L. DAVIS

     The Sage of Rendville Gives Some Good Advice to our Fellow-Craftsmen--And
              Also Speaks a Good Word for the Defense Fund

     RENDVILLE, O., Feb. 21.--Well, ye Editor, almost all of our people are
talking war and so forth. I am free to admit that I don't know much about
war, but judging from statistics I am of the opinion that it is a very quick
way to become a little angel, so all who want to go to war with poor, old,
dilapidated but impudent Spain, can go ahead. I shall, while it is all talk,
content myself in jotting a few lines to the miners' best and--I came near
saying--only friend.[59]
     Work in any of the mines is a scarce article, one and two days being the
most, and yet you can hear some poor dunce say we don't need the eight-hour
day; that a man is free and should do as he pleases, etc. Well, such fellows
are not worth talking to or about, so we will let the matter rest at that.
     We have been trying to keep up with the Hazleton murder trial as best
we could, and would like to see every mother's son of them, Martin and deputies, get the full extent of the law, and a duty devolves upon each and
every miner, and that is to see that they are presented by the laws of the
land and not acquitted at the dictation of soulless corporations, for the
time has come when men must be men or else we must sink to a level to which
there is no hope of redemption.
     Our defense fund is another thing that should not be neglected. I have
heard a good many express themselves on the subject and most of them favor
its establishment; but, of course we must have a niggardly few to oppose it
with no other reason than that they will have to pay the 25 cents per month
more than they are now paying; but I hope that the rank and file of our miners
will see the necessity of the thing and let us have it.
     I could go on at length to give reasons for its establishment, but others
more able than I have already spoken so I will say no more on that subject.
     By way of conclusion, for I don't want to worry you too much, let me
admonish all miners to at all times give to our officers that support which
they so richly deserve, and without which it is an impossibility to succeed.
Attend your local meetings, pay your dues, don't be so dishonest as to have
200 men working in your local all paying their share and reporting only 100
or 151, for when you do this you are cheating yourselves as much as anybody
else, if not more.
     I hope no one will take offense at this, but it is free, and has been
done already, and I want to see it stopped. I shall say this before I quit,
that those who adopt this practice have always had their troubles and demanded
the attention of the officers.
     Boys, be good, don't do it any more. More anon.

                                                                              R. L. DAVIS

United Mine Workers' Journal, February 24, 1898.

                              55. R. L. DAVIS

              Briefly Reviews Conditions in Connection With Organization
                            And The Defense Fund

RENDVILLE, O., Feb. 29.--Work in this section remains as at last reported.

one and two half days per week; so, I am sure, those who are working in the mines are not making any fortunes.

Mr. D. B. Wilson, of Congo, left last week to take charge of a mine, at Poteau, I.T., I am informed. We can say for the gentleman that we wish him success in his new situation. We have known him for quite a number of years, and have always found him a gentleman in every sense of the word.

Well, in every issue of the JOURNAL, I notice a discussion as to the most successful way to establish and maintain a defense fund. Go ahead, boys, it is the best way in the world, "to be sure you are right, and then, go ahead," but let me further state, that we should not spend too much time talking now, as we know, we cannot get it arranged just now, but we can get it started and in time perfect it in all its details.

I hear a great many of our people asking, what will be the situation in Ohio, on April 1st, etc? I am still of the opinion that it is best to not cross the bridge until we get to it. Let us hope that there will be no trouble, but in the event if it does come, let us be prepared for it.

I will not trouble you longer, Mr. Editor, as I am sick, and I suppose you are tired. Will write later.

R. L. DAVIS

United Mine Workers' Journal, March 3, 1898.

56. R. L. DAVIS

Of Rendville, the Colored Sage, Writes Feelingly of the Defeat of the Defense
Fund Proposition

RENDVILLE, O., March 17.--Well! well! well! Who would have thought it? Surely it must be a mistake that the miners have by a majority vote of more than two thousand decided to have no defense fund. I did not expect a unanimous vote in its favor, but I did expect to see it established by a handsome majority. When President Ratchford in his annual address recommended the establishment of a defense fund, and assured us that if we gave to him the necessary implement of war in the way of a good, strong financial backing, he would at the expiration of the present year show to the world that the miners of an organization such as no other trade could even dream of having. While these are not his exact words, the purport is similar. I must confess my utter astonishment at the actions taken. To take a retrospective view, last July, when our miners came out on strike, what did they have? What had they to hope for, and what could they have gained had it not been for the other trades organizations and other sympathetic friends who went into their treasuries and pockets and contributed so liberally as to make success an assured fact? This alone was sufficient proof of our needs. Fellow-miners, we should look well to what we do, as our every act is watched with care by our opponents. We must lay aside selfishness, petty jealousies and prejudice, and look to our common interest.[60]

Well, I see the trial of Sheriff Martin and his deputies has ended in acquittal. It is as we expected that the miner has no rights that the coal barons are bound to respect. Surely, oh Heaven, this condition of things will not last forever. Yes, and we are all talking of going over to free Cuba. I would like to see poor Cuba freed, but would like better to free myself, the same with every other American coal miner. Boys, get a move on yourselves, for if you don't the day may soon come when it will be almost too late.

Well, I don't want to get too lengthy for, if I do, no space will be left for such eminent writers as Scalfe Kennedy and others.

Oh, by the way, to hear from our old friend D. H. Sullivan reminds one of ye good olden times. Let us hear from you more often in the future, friend Sullivan.

R. L. DAVIS

United Mine Workers' Journal, March 24, 1898.

57. THE SAGE

Of Rendville Writes Interestingly of Conditions in the Sunday Creek Valley
of Ohio

RENDVILLE, O., April 3.

That day long looked for and prayed for by the miners has come and gone,
viz., April 1, at which time the eight-hour day was to go into effect.[61]
The miners throughout the Sunday Creek valley very appropriately celebrated the event. The miners of mine 8 jollified at Corning, while the Congo
miners jollified at home. The writer was invited to address both meetings,
but owing to the roads being so muddy and being too poor to ride on the
railroad cars we could not attend the meeting at Corning. The boys of Corning had a good time and everything went off pleasantly. I am informed that
at Congo the boys had a fine time with music and speech-making, and, by the
way, they had music at Corning also. I might add that while our boys were
jubilant, all is not well, for a good deal of dissatisfaction yet exists.
In the first place the miners here have always commenced work at 7 o'clock
fast time. Now the companies insist on commencing at 7 o'clock standard
time, which is half an hour later. They also insist that one hour be given
for dinner and stop at 4 o'clock. Again, the miners have commenced firing
half an hour before quitting time. The companies now insist that they do
not fire until 4 o'clock. This means nearly ten hours for the miner to remain in the mines and is unfair. In fact, I can see no reason for these
changes, unless it be that the companies want to have the men come out late
in the evening, so that they will not enjoy the sunlight but little more than
they previously did. I see nothing it it but contrariness, that is all.
I must say that at Congo everything is moving off smoothly. They start
at 7 o'clock and work continuously until 3 o'clock, then stop. The men are
satisfied at this and it is surprisingly strange that the same cannot be done
in the other mines.
Well, I expect I had better stop, for I can't get work here today because
of my advocacy of right vs. wrong, and now for two years almost they have been
giving me lessons how to live on wind. Well, I don't care for myself, but
it is those innocent little children of mine that I care for, and yet they
say this is free America.
Hoping that all will end well for the miners of our country, if we have
one.
I am as ever,

R. L. DAVIS

United Mine Workers' Journal, April 14, 1898.

58. OLD DOG REPORTS

Work at Congo Poor and Price of Living Advancing

Also Speaks a Kind Word for a Friend and Offers Some Suggestion For His Benefit

CONGO, O., May 8.--Editor Journal: Since I do not trouble you often I
hope you will allow me a small space in the miners' friend for a few words.
Work in these parts is not so good as we would like to see it, especially
at this time of the year. Very little is earned and the cost of everything
is going up, so without a change I can't see how we poor miners are going to
make it.
Mr. Editor, I notice our old true and tried friend, R. L. Davis, walking
around. He can't get work in the mines and he says he can't get any work to
do as organizer. Why this should be I cannot see. Dick, as he is familiarly
called, has always been a staunch union man. He has done more to get the
colored miners into the organization and hold them than any other man that

I know of in this part of Ohio. He has labored long and earnestly to build
up the union, when men who now hold official positions had fallen by the way-
side and would not dare utter a word in defense of the cause for fear of
losing their jobs, but Dick always stuck to his post through thick and thin
and because of his manhood along this line he is being fought with that most
dastardly weapon, most commonly known as the black list. Knowing the man as
I do I think he should be provided for in some way. I want to say right now
that you do not often meet up with colored men like Dick, who have his grit
in them, and it is only on account of his strong union principles that he is
placed in the position he is in today. Again, in this field there is not one
colored man but who pays to the union and it is largely due to his persistent
efforts that this has been brought about, every man in this section will bear
me out in this, white and black. He has a family to keep and I think we owe
to him something. He nor his children cannot live on wind, and further, if
he was a white man he would not be where he is--mark that--but being a negro
he does not get the recognition he should have. I want to say further that
such treatment will not tend to advance the interest of our union, but will
retard its progress and cause colored men to look with suspicion upon it.
Now, as a colored man myself, I do not want any thing more than this: Give
us an equal show. Dick deserves better usage. I would not write as I do,
but I have talked with him and he feels sorely disappointed. He says he
thought that the organization would afford him something to do, and I think
so too. It will be as little as our officers could do to help him in this
way, since we know that it is because of his love of unionism that has brought
him and his family to almost want. For my part, I think if we would do right
he could either go in the mines to work or we would see to it that he was
started up in a small business or given field work. I want President Ratchford to show to all colored men that he values a man as a man irrespective of
his color and he can best do this by giving Dick a helping hand.

I hope you will excuse my bad writing and language and also method of
speaking, but I believe in calling a spade a spade. I am sure we are not
being treated just as we should be. I will write again soon if this escapes
the waste basket. I remain the

OLD DOG.

United Mine Workers' Journal, May 12, 1898.

59.   R. L. DAVIS

Of Rendville Breaks the Silence of a Few Weeks and Recounts His Experience
While Canvassing for the Journal

RENDVILLE, O., June 12.--Editor Journal: After a long silence, I will
once more attempt to write a few lines to let the readers of your valuable
paper know how things are in this neck of the woods. The mines have been
working fairly steady for the past three weeks, but don't know how long it
will continue. The writer started out a few days ago to secure more readers
for the Journal. We started at Nelsonville, and canvassed two mines, viz.,
the Hocking Valley mine and the Poston new mine, but owing to the very poor
work that they have been having, and the indebtedness of the miners we did
not secure very many subscribers, although we had the assistance of such men
as our friends Wm. Riddle, A. L. Steinrod, I. N. Coleman, Fred Powell,
Edward Lett and others who did all in their power to help us in our canvass.
Indeed men could not do more than they did. Oh, yes; I forgot to mention
the name of our big-hearted and genial German friend, Fred Weymueller, who
also assisted in making the burden as light as possible for us. I shall
never forget their kindness and hope to be able to return the compliment to
them.

We have not as yet got to canvass at Murray City or Blatchford, but hope
to in a few days.

Owing to the dullness of times, etc., we feel somewhat discouraged, but
will not give up until compelled to. Most all miners want the paper, but do

not feel able to subscribe just now, probably later on we may do better.
Every miner should read the Journal. It is cheaper than the penny dailies
and more to our interest. So miners everywhere, even if you do not like the
paper, just consider the fact that you are patronizing an enterprise of your
own. Make it what it should be by your patronage, the best trades paper
published. You can do it. Now, will you?
    Wishing success to all, we will not worry you longer.
R. L. DAVIS

United Mine Workers' Journal, June 23, 1898.

60. R. L. DAVIS

Of Rendville Makes a Plea for Proper Treatment For the Negro and Says That
Like the Mining Machine He is Here to Stay

    Rendville, O., Oct. 10.--After a long silence, not for the reason that
I esteem the organization less, but because of other things that have occurred, I felt that it was as well for me to remain silent and let matters
drift along as they might. I have been a constant watcher as to the welfare
of the U.M.W. of A. and noticing the troubles now existing in the Sucker
State among our craftsmen, prompts me to say a word at least. I am indeed
sorry to see the State of affairs as exists there, and yet it teaches us that
one lesson seemingly so hard to learn by a great many of us, viz., to organize. I do not mean to organize against the black man, as they are now doing,
for that will do no good nor will there any good results accrue from it, and
fight it as you may the result will be the same. I have watched it in the
past and have never known it to fail. I would advise that we organize against
corporate greed, organize against the fellow who, through trickery and cor-
rupt legislation, seeks to live and grow fat from the sweat and blood of his
fellow man. It is these human parasites that we should strive to exterminate,
not by blood or bullets, but by the ballot, and try as you may it is the only
way. You can't do it by trying to exterminate the negro or big black buck
niggers, as they were referred to a few weeks ago through the columns of The
Journal. I assure anyone that I have more respect for a scab that I have for
the person who refers to the negro in such a way, and God knows than a scab
I utterly despise. The negro North has no excuse, or very few excuses, for
scabbing, but the negro South has lots of them, and while I give the North
a great deal of credit, I fear that I make a mistake, for in many places even
in the North, no matter how good a union man he may be, he cannot get work only
as a blackleg. And in the South he can work almost anywhere provided he is
willing to be the other fellow's dog, and I don't mean the employer alone, but
the white laborer as well. Now, the negro, like the mining machine, is here
to stay and you may as well make up your minds to treat them right. I dare
say that you seldom or never hear of negroes being brought into a locality
to break a strike in which both white and black worked together, and even if
they were you always found the negro on the side of right. Hence, I say
treat the negro right and he will treat you right. I earnestly hope to see
the miners of Illinois win their battle, for I suppose they are like miners
elsewhere. Their pittance is already too small. A word as to West Virginia.
I hope that some day they may see the error of their ways and come within the
folds of the organization. I would like to say a word in reference to the
boycott, but this is already too lengthy. Will say something about it in my
next if this escapes the waste basket. Yours for justice,[62]
R. L. DAVIS

United Mine Workers' Journal, October 13, 1898.

R. L. DAVIS

The delegates to the eleventh annual convention received the sad intelligence that former Board Member R. L. Davis had suddenly died at his
home in Rendville, Ohio, as announced in the meeting Wednesday, as follows:

Rendville, Ohio, Jan. 17, 1900

W. C. Pearce, Indianapolis, Ind.:
    R. L. Davis died January 16th, 1900, of lung fever. G. G. WEAVER.

    R. L. Davis was born in Roanoke, Va., Dec. 24, 1863. According to the
usual custom of colored people of that age and clime he began work at eight
in a tobacco factory, working there and attending school during the winter
months until he was 17 years old. At the age of 17, he became disgusted
with the very low wage rate and other unfavorable conditions of a Southern
tobacco factory and, leaving there, he settled in the mining regions of
West Virginia, and became a miner. He worked in the mines of the Kanawha
and New River fields of West Virginia until 1882, when he moved to Rendville,
Ohio, where he has since resided.
    He was always a staunch union man and by reason of his activity in this
direction and the evidences of his latent ability he was elected a member of
the Executive Board of District 6 (Ohio) in 1890, and re-elected each year
until 1895. At the National convention of the U.M.W. of A., held in Columbus, Ohio, in April 1896, he was elected a member of the National Executive
Board, and re-elected again the year following.
    "Dick," as he was always familiarly called, was an earnest intelligent
worker, and a representative man of his race. His able assistance and timely
counsel will be missed by those with whom he associated and the United Mine
Workers have lost a staunch supporter by his death.
    We extend sympathy to the bereaved wife and orphaned children, and trust
that they will receive the assistance and support merited by the husband and
father now deceased.
    The following resolution was passed by the convention:

    "Indianapolis, Ind., Jan. 17, 1900.
    "Whereas, We have learned with regret of the death of former Executive
Board Member, R. L. Davis, of the United Mine Workers of America: and
    "Whereas, Many years of his life were devoted to advancing the interests
of his craft: and
    "Whereas, In the death of Brother Davis our organization has lost a
staunch advocate of the rights of those who toil, and his race a loyal friend
and advocate: therefore, be it
    "Resolved, That the United Mine Workers of America, in convention as-
sembled, barely expresses their deep sense of regret and extend to the be-
reaved family their heartfelt sympathy in this their hour of trial; be it
further
    "Resolved, That this resolution be spread upon the minutes of the con-
vention and a copy forwarded to his relatives at Rendville, Ohio.
                                        C. W. CAIN,
                                        J. L. CLEMO,
                                        W. D. RYAN,
                                             Committee."

United Mine Workers' Journal, January 25, 1900.

THE LETTERS OF WILLIAM R. RILEY

62. SERIOUS MISTAKE

Secretary Riley Complains of Treatment of Colored Miners

Jellico, Tenn., Feb. 27, 1892.

I thought I would write these few lines to let the many readers of your valuable paper see and know the way the colored miners are treated in this part of the country.

Before I left here to go to the Columbus convention I was called to Newcomb, Tenn., to see after some trouble there. When I got to Newcomb I found that a colored checkweighman had been elected and the white miners at that mine declared that no negro should weigh their coal. They made several excuses, such as that the man was not competent, the next excuse was that he kicked against the former checkweighman, the third was that he was not legally elected. After hearing their excuses I offered to take the colored man off that had been elected, if they would agree to support a colored man that was competent and had not kicked against the former checkweighman. Then the Master Workman of that place told me in plain words that the body of white miners had agreed to not support a colored man. After he openly told [of] the determination of the whites, the colored miners said that the white miners had promised to divide the checkweighman's office with them, the whites had promised if there was one half colored they should have the place half of the time, if there was one third they should have it one third of the time, etc., but instead of standing to their promise the whites have filled the office for more than five years, and yet they declare that the negro shall not weigh their coal. At Altamont, Laurel Co., Ky., the company put a colored man in the mine acting as assistant bank boss and the whites declare that they won't work under any negro and the drivers won't pull the coal that is dug under a negro boss. And now I would like to know how under heaven do the white miners expect for the colored people to ever feel free and welcome in the order of Knights of Labor or United Mine Workers of America, when their so-called brothers don't want them to get not one step higher than the pick and shovel. And yet, whenever there is anything in the way of trouble expected, or when anything is wanting in the way of finance these very same men will come up to the colored man and say, "Brother J. we must all stick together, for we are all miners, and your interest is mine and mine is yours; we must band together." This talk you see reminds one of the story of the spider and the fly, the majority of the white miners only need a colored brother in time of trouble.[63]

And how can you ever expect the colored people of the South to become an organized body as long as such work is carried on, which is an open violation of the laws of the order. And yet this matter is given little or no attention. When this subject was brought up by me in the convention at Columbus, that the officers should see that this color line law was fully carried out, that any place or places that made any difference in persons because of their color, and that their character should be taken away from them, they tabled the question and left it so. Now, I think something should be done about this matter. The colored people need to be organized in the South. But how can this be done by the people whom they regard as their enemies? I cannot tell. I hope some steps will be taken at once to right these matters.

Wm. R. Riley,
Sec.-Treas., Dist. 19.

United Mine Workers' Journal, March 3, 1892.

63.   A FEW WORDS FROM RILEY

The Worse Enemies Are Among Our Own Race

Jellico, Tenn., August 13, 1892.

With your permission I want to talk a little with the boys in a rambling way.   In the first place, I want to let your readers know that the miners of Jellico region are buying flour, beef steak and chicken, and the merchants of Jellico were saying this evening that they had not seen so many $20 bills in Jellico for years as were handled by the miners of certain mines.   What I mean by all this is, work is good, and there is no more eating dry bread at some of our houses for a little while, and while our work is good our men are not wasting any time with picks and shovels, and no race prejudices are heard of now as there was last winter.   Of course I don't mean to say by that that we have all good men here, for this is not the case, but the good men have got the majority on their side and they make the minority follow in line.

And now a few words to Brother R. L. Davis.   In speaking about the men at No. 3 mine, Brother Davis seems to be a little behind the times.   Did you not know that the worst enemies we have to contend with are among our own race?   Did you not know that they will seek more undue advantages over you than anyone else?   What?   A nigger?   He is the worst animal living against his race, and when I say nigger I mean nigger and not colored people.   Now, let me say, that they have surely made a man of me, I used to try to fight it out with them and I soon found out that my money would not last at that foolishness because they would take a good beating just to get a chance to have me arrested to swear against me and loud swearing some of them would do; they came near swearing me baldheaded before I learned any sense.   But now, I can laugh at their folly when they try to make war against me and say all colored and white men will consider the source it came from.   And again; I think a man that this class of men don't talk about are not worthy of an office in the labor ranks.   I am by this class like I am by my church people. When I go to a place to preach and this class of people run to me, talking about some old sister or brother over yonder, the first thing pops into my mind is, "Over yonder is the light of Christianity in this place, and here sets the hounds of h--- howling on their tracks, barking at their good name, barking at their future prosperity and barking at their religious examples that they set before them from time to time."   But when I hear of some good sister or brother that everybody likes and praises, an old Scripture passage presents itself to me: "Woe unto the person whom the world speaks well of." Now, I do love to hear of officers of our organization being spoken hard of, and I do like to hear of them having a hard time.   It will make them read the laws more carefully and fill them out to the letter.   It causes the man to try to pose himself to meet any emergency that may cross his path; and, let me say, do away with the man that everybody is well pleased with.   So Brother D., continue to press forward, make all the colored and white friends that you possibly can, and don't worry over the niggers and dogs.   "Brother Willing Hand," you must not speak a word of praise about me, I am not used to my race praising me, it might give the brain fever for ever.[64]

William R. Riley.

United Mine Workers' Journal, August 25, 1892.

64.   RILEY INDIGNANT

He Scores His Race--The Negro His Own Enemy

Jellico, Tenn., Sept. 5, 1892.

You must really excuse my delay in sending in my report of our convention

which convened on August 17, 18, and 19 last, for we have been so busy over
the Coal Creek trouble that everything else has been neglected. However,
our convention was very largely attended with delegates from all over the
district and business was carried on very smoothly until the election of
officers commenced, when Brother W. C. Webb was placed before the convention
for re-election for the office of president. He positively refused to allow
his name to come up before the convention, then it was that our convention
came to a standstill for nearly a day, trying to persuade Brother Webb to
accept of the position as president again, but he would not accept. After
trying for a day to get Brother Webb to accept the office, then Brothers
G. H. Simmons, J. W. Cox and S. P. Herron were placed before the convention
for president. S. P. Herron was elected president. A. Vaughn of Coal Creek
was elected vice president, but owing to the misconduct of A.V. the office
was declared vacant before the convention adjourned and Brother John R.
Rhodes of Coal Creek was elected vice-president in A. Vaughn's place. Our
next officer to be elected was secretary-treasurer. Brothers Mullan,
William Rhodes and myself were placed before the convention and there were
only four votes cast in the convention that I did not get on the first ballot, after which a motion to make my election unanimous was offered, which
resulted in three of my four opponents who voted for. Now I need not tell
the readers that one vote that I did not get was not a white vote, because
any white man would have been too intelligent to not vote with the whole
convention. But this was a so-called colored man belonging to an assembly
that all of the white men had drawn out of, so his colored brother told, and
the white men say the reason they did draw out was because the mine workers
of that labor assembly had not paid one cent of dues for twelve months and
the other leading officers, who are colored men, are holding from two to
four rooms in the mines working three to six men, double-shifting their
places, driving the night mule themselves for extra cars, depriving a driver
of the work where he could make his $1.75 per day, and the white men say
that they would not live in an assembly where their brothers carried on such
work.[65]
     Now, what I want the colored people to know, is simply this, that the
negro is the worse enemy to one another that they have on top of dirt; there
is a class of them that are so begrudging and jealous of their own race that
they will do anything regardless of principle or anything else to keep one
another rising one step above them. And this very class does more kicking
about the white man not letting them have a show than a Kentucky mule; and
I want to ask my people, how under heavens can you ever expect the white
man to place any confidence in them when they don't have any in one another.
If whites say that the negro is not worthy of any office or don't deserve
any, are they not paying you off with your own money? Have you not set this
example for them to go by? Have you not said by your own ways and actions
that your own race is not entitled to anything? I think you do. Now, let
me say to the colored people who are trying to be men second to no man,
continue to battle on for the right, seek wisdom and be wise, act honest men
and by so doing both white and colored men will love to respect you, and God
himself will bless you and our children, which are very apt to be the second
edition of their parents, will come on after you and take up your work where
you left off and push it on. Yes, my people, wake up and ask yourselves
these questions: How am I to live in ignorance? How long am I to be a pull-
back to my race? How long am I to be a stumbling block for the cause of
labor, justice and humanity? Say as the prodigal did: I will rise and join
the labor union and rally for its rights, defend its cause and be known
among my own craftsmen as a man among men.[66]
     Hoping that the readers will excuse this rambling letter and with best
wishes to the UNITED MINE WORKERS' JOURNAL, I am yours fraternally,

                                                              Wm. R. Riley,
                                        Sec'y Treas. Dis. 19, U.M.W. of A.

United Mine Workers' Journal, September 8, 1892.

65. NEGRO VS. NIGGER

Similar in Sound But Different In Action

Jellico, Tenn., Sept. 26, 1892.

Again Brother Editor, I shall trouble you for a little space in your
valuable columns. Times are still very lively in Jellico region, plenty of
work every day and everywhere. I visited two picnics this month, given by
Local Assembly 1855, Grays, Ky., and Local Assembly 1129, Red Ash, Ky.,
They had quite a good time at each place, financially and peacefully.
Brother S. P. Herron was with me at both places; he seems to enjoy the picnics splendidly, and wished that picnics would last forever so he could
look at the pretty mountain girls.

The Coal Creek trouble has been quite a set back to our district. We
spent all of last year getting the lower part of the district into the
union, and after we had accomplished our work there here comes this trouble
and we lose the greater part of our year's work. Our only hope is that the
national will help us a little this fall in our field work so as to put us
on the fence again.

We have great confidence in our new president and believe with the proper backing he will lead us on to victory. Our executive board is also a
cool, level-headed set, whom everyone believes will be an honor to the district.

Now just a few words to Brother "Willing Hands." My brother, you seem
to think that I was wrathy at the negroes. Now, I do think that I made a
clear distinction in spelling these two words. I never wrote any harm about
the negro at all, for I have no fight to make against them. But I wrote,
and will continue to write, against the niggers and dogs. We have tried
petting, coaxing and soft words with these curs for years, and we have gained
nothing from them only hard times. They say that we are only trying to make
a living without working, call us d---- sell outs, money seekers, etc. I believe in the saying of St. Paul, "When the child is young feed it on the
sincere milk of the breast, but when it gets old feed it on strong meat."
Now, we did believe years ago that these curs were young in the labor movement, therefore we were very tender and mild with them, but now we think it
is time for them to be grown men, and should be fed on strong meat. We can
see that it is nothing but pure niggerish, doggish principle that is in these
curs, and soft talk will do no good. My brother, I live in the South among
these people and know whereof I speak. Of course there are some as good
people in the South as there is the world, and again there are some of the
worst curs that ever lived, and Webb Riley, nor no one else can change them.
With all due respect to Brother "Willing Hands" and success to the UNITED
MINE WORKERS' JOURNAL, I am fraternally yours, [67]

Wm. R. Riley

United Mine Workers' Journal, September 29, 1892.

66. RILEY'S REPORT

Of Organizing Tour In Tennessee--Colored Men Try Again

Pioneer, Tenn., March 17, 1893.

As the evening is so bad and the boys have not got out from work I must
beg for a little space in your paper to let the boys know what the pair of
Bills are doing in District 19.[68]

Well, Billy Webb and myself started out over the district on the 8th of
March, to see if one pair of Bills could win. In our meetings in the Jellico
region we left everything wherever we met. We struck the C.S.R.R. on Saturday
morning at Junction City, and went to Barren Fork where we had a very good
meeting and the whole house voted to a man to do all they could to support the

order. This was encouraging. I parted from Billy at Hellenwood and I came
to Coal Creek, Tenn., and I went up to Briceville, where I met up with the
district vice president, standing in a small crowd, but that worthy officer
never let on that he saw me. After waiting for him to show up as though
he knew me, and then seeing that he was not going to do so, I called him
aside and asked him if he thought we could get the men together for a meeting. He said no; he thought not, as the Odd Fellows met that night, but
said that if I could get the men on the Creek together, it would be no
trouble to get the men at Briceville to organize. He further said that his
assembly had a committee [which] were out looking after the colored people
up there, and if they could not succeed in organizing them, that they would
send for me. With this kind treatment from one of our officers, I left
Coal Creek. After working there three days I succeeded in reorganizing the
colored people of that place, which I think will make a noble order. As
these colored men have always shown by their ways and actions they wanted to
be organized men, but are treated so bad by their so-called white brothers
that they don't feel like they are recognized in the order as knights. They
are willing to try the order again, thinking that the white men of Coal Creek
will yet recognize the importance of treating them as brother miners.[69]

And now I do hope that Brother J. J. Jones, vice president of District
19, will go to work and make his words true by organizing Briceville.

A few words to the many who are discussing the paper question. Boys,
the UNITED MINE WORKERS JOURNAL is good enough for me now as it is, but if
you can better it I will still read it, but for God's sake don't make it any
smaller.[70]

With best wishes to our paper and its readers,
                                        I am fraternally yours,
                                        Wm. R. Riley

United Mine Workers' Journal, March 30, 1893.

67. RILEY AGAIN

Writes About How Things Are in the South

All Good Men Will Stay Away From North Jellico

JELLICO, Tenn., May 8.--According to promise, I'll come again. I was
called to North Jellico last Monday. When I arrived at the depot I found
several of the old stand-bys there waiting. Well, they took me up to the
company's office and showed me the one-sided contract, signed by the general
manager and superintendent. Not a miner's dirty paw was allowed on this noble
piece of North Jellico clean legal cap paper. Among other things it claims
the words: A checkweighman will be recognized, but he must be approved of by
the company, or, in other words, he must be a man to suit the company, whose
wages shall be $2.25 per day; no more, no less.

Now I want the reader to read that clause carefully and think for a moment and tell me what you think of such men who could have such immense cheek
as to post up such an article in this country. They must pick the checkweighman; they must say what his salary shall be, and it shall be $2.25.
When the committee told the general manager that some of the officials of the
district were there and they would like to meet him; his reply was that he
positively would not make any contract with no labor organization; that he
had posted up the contract and that was all that he would do. He said that
he would not change nor differ from the article posted up under any circumstances. When asked if he thought the contract would stand without both
parties being properly represented, his reply was: "I'll risk it." The contract that he has posted up changes the prices on the machine men and cuts
the present prices 3 cents on the ton, so I am informed by the miners there.
This gentleman (Mr. C. S. Neill) won't meet in convention with the operators
of Jellico region nor the Laurel region. He says that the Jellico operation
throw off on him and the Laurel prices don't suit his place. So you can readily

see that he don't aim to treat his men fair at all.

I will close by asking all good men to stay away from North Jellico until things are settled, as the men are out waiting for a contract.

WM. R. RILEY

United Mine Workers' Journal, May 11, 1893.

68.   REV. WILLIAM RILEY

Ex-Secretary of District 19 Gives an Account of Some Things in the South

Jellico, Tenn. [n.d.]

I thought, as there has been no news in your valuable columns from District 19 for quite awhile, I would venture to write a few lines. Work is very good and has been reasonably good ever since the suspension, and the boys seem to be saving their little mites some better than usual. I moved down to my little farm place, near Oswego, Tenn., last month for the purpose of going into the gardening business this spring. Here I found more colored miners than there is anywhere in this region. At one place, really about two-thirds of the miners are colored.[71]

I began to talk labor to the boys, as none of them belong to the order, and some of the white miners that used to be strong labor men, or rather acted so years ago, are here, and I proposed to them that we would go to work and organize the camp, as I knew that I could do so, as the leading men here were my intimate friends and stood together in other places. The result of my efforts was this: These so-called white brothers went around to all of the weakest of the colored men and told them that Riley had left all of his property in Jellico and moved to Oswego to be checkweighman, and wanted them organized in order that the district would not go down, etc., etc., etc.

Now I want to give the whole cause of this talk. In the first place these men belong to that class of white people that I always styled as dogs; in the second place they tried to keep all the negroes away from here, but after the Indian Mountain strike in 1893 the colored people got a good footing here. These dogs kept up part of their bluff by saying that no negro should weigh coal here, like they have said at most every other place in the district by either words or actions.[72]

Now then, the black boys of course were not afraid to weigh, but just did not have the time, and when I came here they knew, first, that Riley has always been known in this country to be one of those fellows that is too lazy to run (without a leader) and plenty of time for anything that I wanted to do; and as they cared nothing for the organization, they took this step to kill the whole thing to gain one little point, viz., checkweighman. So you see what kind of cattle we have through here. Secondly, there is another who would be in the order but they don't want to be sitting in the lodge room with negroes; they want the negroes' money; they want his support in time of trouble, but as for offices they don't want Mr. Negro to have not one.

The negroes in the South are opening their eyes on this as well as other things. They want more recognition. And if the Southern negroes are ever thoroughly organized or anything like it, it must be done by men of their own race. Can you blame them, when their white brother, so-called, will come out of the lodge room with him at 10 p.m., and if, while on his way home he meets a drunken white man and the white man wants the negro to run and the negro is too lazy to run, and won't take a whipping, this drunken white man can just go to some of his brothers and tell his tale, and they will all have their Winchesters and be ready to kill the brother negro before day. Such is the case here in the South and no mistake. As you shall hear from me soon on the standing of our district in general, I will close, wishing you success, I am yours for the cause of labor.

Wm. R. Riley

United Mine Workers' Journal, February 7, 1895.

OTHER BLACK COAL MINERS

69. COLORED MINE

The Colored Mining Company of Carthage, Missouri is the only mining company owned by colored men in this country.

The Freeman (Indianapolis), March 21, 1891.

70. OUR COLORED SISTER

She Gives the Indiana Miners a Practical Tip and Says Some Sensible Things

DUGGER, Ind., June 30, 1891.

Well, Mr. Editor, I hab see some copys ob de JOURNAL and in dem I fine leters from lots ob plases teling all about how de minin business am gitin along, and I fine de invitation to ebry body to gib you information but de po niger. Now, Mr. Editor, I take de privilege to scratch a few lines dat de peple may here from dis neck ob de woods. I will jis say I hab ben acquainted wid de mines for many years an hab my eys an ears open most ob de time and I must say de business am gitin wors ebry year and it makes my ole hed whis round to see how times are gitin. De mony am just as plenty an mo so dan befo war, and dere am mo demand for de products ob de kentry dan eber befo. De rich am gitin richer, and de pore am gitin porer. I think sometimes de worl is comin to an en. De bible sais sumthin bout de las days. Der mus be purty times abot de mines in dis part. Dere am not much cole digin goin on hear now since de first ob May, de opraters fixin traps to catch de miners and de miners cusin de Zecgative Bode on de fence fund and finin falts wid ebery body. Now, de bible sais to get de beme outen your owne eye and den yer can see to get to mote in you brudders eye.

It makes my hart ake wid sadnes to see de count ob some ob my people bein shipped to de Norfwest to take de place ob good ones men fitin for dere rites. Some ob dese men gone up dere node where dey was gwine, but mos ob dem was ignant about de strike. Now, Mr. Editor, I fine dis am de fault of truble ebrywhere—not noin de facts—and I don see how tis going to get any better while de trash is coming from ebry country wid dere ignance, and de parents ob de boys an gals keeps dem home from skule wha da mite learn somethin. One thing I hab learned wif my eys open is dat de edjicated hab de money and de fine buggy and de pi and de cake, while de ignant hab de check on de compny store for one dollar wif minety cents ob dat punched out de day befo. Now, Mr. Editor, I here so much about dat man Penny. Dey saydown hear he kin jes make a coal operator think he is made outen green chese and dat he is bout to be shipped to dat land where de folks lib on cheese and kraut, and dey gib right up and sine a contract dat is about rite. I wish dat Penny would come down dis way and turn himsef into dollars and hab de same fect. But Mr. Editor, whil we hab de pennies to tos and de kany to watk wid and de rays to gil us lite we nede more good stron onions dat will bring the tears ob repentance to de eys ob some ob de rank an file. You can go no plase but yo har de organization bein cused for de faluer on de fust ob May.

Har is de pint dat gages me all de time why dese bery men dat cus de organization if dey git in trouble wid de bos dey run to de union and get dem ter strike to gane der pint and sum ob dem on metin nite wont go to de metin, but gow around to de pluck-me and talk to de stoer clerks and try to git a sof snap jus because dey git der poak and beans fer de skimp stoer. Maby I hav scratched to much already, especialy fo on ob my collah, but I see you gin Mis McNab and dat oder woman rume ter say thar little pece. Since I begin ter rite this lettah my mine has gon back ober de days whan de gals an boys useto mete in de ebman an hab a good time de dul care ob de day was lade down wid de shuvel and de ho. But in dese days massey feched de gemn to de cabin dore, den he pade docto and de bucher an get us rags ter kepe us from frezin in wintah, but since de age ob progres hab set in times am changin at de end ob de peg. Ebery dollah hab ben progresin to de opraters so fas dat an ole woman like me doan git aroun in time to see em gow into de company safe, an once dey git in dere its all day.

Wid a warnin to all, I close dis artical an urg all to wach de sines ob de times an neber make a mov when de sines is rong. Now sum foks plant dere taters in de new moon. Dere is danger in dat. Sum sindicate mite have a corner on taters up dere. Now you hear foks say when to shear sheep. De best time is when de woll is on dere back. Sum nigers say posum is de bes in de wintah, but dey am mity nice any time. But dey are de bes after yo hab dem cosched, skined and rosted.

Take de hint up dere, yo Ingiana boys. De woll will be bes on his back about de fust ob September. O, neber mine de fros, but pray fo his meditation. Mo in de futur ib dis am published.

SINTHY SNODGRASS

United Mine Workers' Journal, July 2, 1891.

71. COLOR QUESTION

Looked at From Another Point of View

When Uncle Sam Was Small--The Negro in Little Rhody

A Question of Consanguinity Propounded by Our Correspondent

JELLICO, TENN. April 28.

I have noticed for quite awhile that the columns of your most valuable paper have been open for the discussion of the so-called "race problem," which has been very ably handled by several writers, and as I have certain views in regard to the matter that no one has yet expressed I thought I would pen a few lines on the subject.

To begin with I will say that when Uncle Sam was a very small boy and did not know as much as he does at present, he allowed the "negro" to be brought into his domain, not as other nationalities came, free, but in shackles, and if I make no mistake, the State called "Little Rhody" was the[73] first place to receive the strangers; not with open arms, but unlocked fetters, which were soon securely fastened upon the limbs of this man who happened to resemble Ham a little more than he did Japheth. Well, now he is here, what next? He was worked and used to the best advantage by the people (white I mean) of the Middle and New England States, who were at that time, as well as the present, chiefly engaged in manufacturing. Now this is where the first trouble arose with the colored man. Some came directly from their native land and others only separated from it by one generation. They could hardly be learned the mysteries of the arts their owners followed, and instead of becoming a prolific source of wealth as was expected, they became unprofitable. Now, the promoters of this nefarious business, called slave trading, had too good an eye to business to send them back, so they looked around for a place to dump them and their eyes beheld the South. Yes, that's the place! This warm sunny clime will just suit these slaves, and straightway

they proceeded to dispose of their human property to the Southern planters
who saw an opportunity by making this deal, that they, instead of working
as they had previously done, could sit down and have others do their work
for them, and with the same cunning and shylock-like sagacity that has been
co-existent in all ages with plutocracy they purchased.

Well, what next? They worked them in the cotton and cane for years,
built up an aristocracy in the South with their labor, condemned them to
ignorance until the same "North" as it is termed, got jealous, (which was
caused by the Almighty, I think) and became very considerate of the condition of the slave and said that they must be set free.

Now, let us see what was the cause of this. As we have stated before,
the North had its manufacturing establishments and the South grew the cotton.
The Southern planter controlled the labor of the black man and the planter
could charge whatever price he pleased for his product and, as the Northern
manufacturer was at the mercy of the South, he became mad and jealous and
said to himself: "If these black men were free we could control their product and these Southern gentlemen would have to come down a notch." And so
the North became very philanthropic and set to work and secured the colored
man a nominal freedom.

So after centuries of primeval existence and years of chattel slavery,
we find him turned loose in 1865 without a dollar; ignorant, credulous, yet
full of gratitude, an easy prey to the cupidity and avarice of a far worse
set of Shylocks than the ones the Nazarene carpenter drove out of the temple
at Jerusalem.

Now as I proceed I will make this statement, that there is no color line
at all, but simply the slave line; and, to sustain my assertion, I will say
that I have known men and women of other nationalities who were nearly as
black, a great deal more ignorant, and four-fold more degraded than the very
meanest "nigger" I ever saw, yet they never had that infernal curse of slavery
upon them, and they were received by some of the kickers against the black
man with open arms as their social equals. "Oh, consistency thou art a
jewel." Now, the fallacy of such things is really sickening to a person of
any thought, no matter whether he be black or white.

Just to illustrate the matter I will suppose that a citizen (white or
colored) of the United States should go to Africa and happen to be nabbed as
was the colored man and become a slave for years and should then escape and
get back to his native heath, would he be received as one below the general
order of humanity or as a hero? A hero by all means. Well, why is not the
colored man as much a hero who escaped the tyranny of slavery in this country?
Now I will make another assertion, viz., that some of the smartest men we have
in this country are men whose skins are black, whether so by nature or by
climatic influences for centuries I will not discuss, but I say that a few
days ago I heard a colored man illustrate the cause of his condition in a
manner that for simplicity of understanding and correctness of detail was
ahead of any definition of the cause I ever heard. He said: "I was a bound
slave, my master controlled me and my wages, he was a smart man and they could
not fool him. Now I am a free slave, I am ignorant and at the mercy of the
rich man and cannot help myself; they made me so on purpose to rob me." But,
he said, "through organization I know I can better my condition," although,
he continued, "no man can be a true Knight of Labor man and be either a Democrat or Republican. Now I would like to know which is the best and smartest
man, this poor old slave or the white gentleman who on election day will carry
around a body full of whisky and hurrah for some low-down drunken ward politician? If I was not afraid of getting on dangerous ground I would say that
in a great many places the worst line that is drawn is the political line.
When men who are white do not like to sit in the same assembly with the colored man, yet are glad to welcome him into the political club room just before
election day and pat him on the back and call him a good fellow and then
after the election; my Lord! why they just can't stand a nigger. Another thing
let me tell you, but I want you to remember not to say anything about it, the
party that is in the majority or minority is the one that is most likely to
do this. The K. of L. declares that it abolishes races, creeds and colors
and the man who can't stand that kind of doctrine, let him just get up and
git. Now, I will say in conclusion that I would like for some one to tell me
the difference between a negro who has seven-eighths of white blood in him
and a white man with one-eighth of negro blood? "Tis place not blood that

makes the man," and if we could have a few transpositions of souls or at least the cultivated brain of James G. Blaine placed in the being of a colored man who had been blacklegging and vice versa, what would be the consequences? Why you would have a colored man with capabilities to be secretary of state and a white man who would blackleg. So I can say let politics go to thunder, stick to the principles of the K. of L., do all we can for one another, irrespective of race, creed or color. If we do this when we come to the jumping off place we will most likely go to a country where in reality there is no color line, if they do think there is one here.[74]

WM. CAMACK

United Mine Workers' Journal, May 5, 1892.

72.   COAL MINERS' BAND--EXCURSION

Blocton, Ala., Special.
    This is a small town in the Cahoba Coal Fields, with a population of about three thousand. Out of this number there are about eight hundred Afro-Americans, all engaged in mining coal for the Cahoba Coal Mining Co. We have a silver Cornet Band of which all the members are coal miners. The band ran an excursion from here to Chattanooga, Tenn., July 29th, over the East Tennessee, Virginia & Georgia R'y., and it was the most enjoyable affair of the season. Jack Robinson is running a first-class barber shop and Mrs. Robinson is feeding the hungry with all kinds of meals and vegetables. Meals served to order and at all hours. R. H. Taylor is ready to transfer a trunk or any other article with his horse and wagon.[75]

The Freeman (Indianapolis), August 20, 1892.

73.   FREE DEBATE

The Race Problem

    RENDVILLE, O., Nov. 4.--As I have been an instrument in placing the United Mine Workers' Journal in the hands of several of my race who have never read a labor paper before, I feel it my duty to write a few lines on a subject that is much talked of every day in this part of the state. That subject is, prejudice on account of color. Mr. Editor, prejudice on account of color is not a natural sentiment. There is a natural prejudice among the civilized nations to certain conditions in life incident to a state of barbarism; there is a natural prejudice to those who are given to immorality and the laws of nature; there is a natural prejudice to those who commit murder and arson; to those who lie and steal; but there is not a natural prejudice to a man simply because he is black, brown or yellow. The influence of a man's complexion is not greater than that of his moral and intellectual culture. Virtue is the highest influence that moves the heart of man, and though it may be clothed in ebony or Parian marble it will command love, honor, obedience and respect in every quarter of the civilized world. Prejudice to an individual of the Negro race can thus be easily removed, but the removal of the prejudice attached to the entire race incident to a state of slavery is a labor of centuries. The problem thereby becomes one for every individual to solve for himself, and thus solving it for himself, he solves it for his race. National progress is the same as individual progress.
    There are some writers notably Hamilton Smith, Nott and Gliddon, who deprecate the amalgamation of the races from a pathological point of view, claiming that it tends to lower the vitality and intellectual vigor of the offspring. The assertion has been denied by equally as illustrious writers and will hardly be subscribed to by any Negro American who has made a careful observation of the subject.[76]

There should be no desire to keep up race distinction in this country
or in the organization of labor when all have a common interest in it. No
benefit can come to the Afro-American by withholding himself apart from
white people, a distinctive negro community, a distinctive negro civilization, and social orders, such as churches, beneficial associations, schools,
colleges and business enterprises. These are not only not desirable, but
indeed are reprehensible, for they create class distinction and foster the
race prejudice of which we desire to free ourselves.

This principle is recognized by all other people emigrating to this
country. The Frenchman with his high sense of pride soon loses his identity
and is absorbed in American homogenity; likewise the German, the Irishman
and the Italian; even the Jew, with all his religious instincts, is relaxing
his hitherto inflexible exclusiveness and embracing the Americanisms. The
Anglo-Saxon civilization, notwithstanding the one black spot on its escut-
cheon, which has impressed itself upon the heart of the negro as a hot burning brand, must, by its grandeur and its majesty, command our highest ad-
miration. We desire to live, act and move with such a civilization and to
say to its people, as Ruth said unto Naomi, "entreat me not to leave thee,
or return from following after thee, for whither thou goest I will go, and
where thou lodgest, I will lodge. Thy people shall be my people, and thy
God my God. Where thou diest will I die and there will I be buried. The
Lord do so to me and more also if aught, but death part thee and me."

Success to the UNITED MINE WORKERS' JOURNAL.

W. E. CLARK

United Mine Workers' Journal, November 9, 1893.

74. PRATT CITY, ALABAMA

And Vicinity--News Reported By Correspondent Hannigan--Shameless White Scabs

PRATT CITY, Ala., May 28.--Our brothers of the North are aware of the
fact that we, the miners of Alabama, came on strike one week prior to them,
not because we were or wanted to be affiliated with the United Mine Workers
of America, but because we were forced to it by trickery on the part of our
employers and some of our fellowmen to help them through with their damnable schemes to put us, black and white, below the level of the slaves of
former days.

I want to be honest and above board, irrespective of consequences; when
I speak the truth I fear no man. Our employers could not accomplish one-half
what they do if it were not that some low down, mean scoundrels in our midst
helped them through. One of the worst cases we had to contend with in this
state is the contract system. When the operators could not realize enough
profit to satisfy their selfish greed they would hunt up some weak-kneed
fellow to be their tool, and sorry to say it such are too often to be found
among men who, to external appearances, are noble, but internally are rotten.
One of this class took a contract here very recently, and one who often
boasted of his true, honest principles as a union man, is now blacklegging,
the only white man of about fifty. We have nothing to fear from the colored
man in and around Pratt City; they are true and noble; it is the mean scrubs
of white men that are our enemies. All of the colored scabs we have here
are taken from other states, and the majority of them never saw a mine until
they came here.

Our victory did sometimes seem to hang in the balance, because of the
hundreds of convicts we have that fill two of the largest and best mines in
this section of the country, and also the many scabs that are coming in every
day, but now I think that evil is no longer in the way.

There was a very large meeting of the citizens and miners of this and
adjacent counties held at Birmingham on last Saturday. One of the good results of that meeting was a resolution that the local railway men refuse to
haul scab coal. They met yesterday evening to deliberate upon this very
important question. I have not yet heard their decision, but I am sanguine

of favorable results. Then victory is ours.

The men of Blue Creek were forced to vacate company houses a month ago, and now the whole of said houses are filled with scabs. Again the miners of Pratt City and vicinity are notified to do the same. What the outcome will be is hard to determine. We have any amount of guards all over this state, claiming as they do, to protect life and property. It so appears that I and my family are under their protection from the fact that they pass near to my dwelling frequently during the night--very thankful to the gentlemen, I mean, bums. They need not trouble themselves, we can take care of ourselves.

W. S. HANNIGAN

United Mine Workers' Journal, June 7, 1894.

75. A MINER

Of Alabama Writes Under Deep Aggravation at the Conduct of Blacklegs

PRATT CITY, Ala., June 25.--As I have seen a good many letters from Alabama concerning the present strike, there is one thing I never see mentioned and that is the names of white-faced, black-hearted leading scabs, these things that call themselves men, while and at the same time by their dirty actions one could not tell whether they were suckers, monkeys or long-tailed rats. One of these things is a man, who came from England to Illinois and then here, he has been at Corning, O., also. He is a general leader of scabs and moves his bed, so I am told, every night, not sleeping two nights in the same room. Next comes Bob, Robert or Rob Neil, he is a decent, canny Scotchman from somewhere near Kiliviny in Ayrshire; he was around the Panhandle awhile, he left his own mine and went to help Logan out with the negro blackleg crew, showing them how to shoot down the coal and sometimes chaining and general instructor of the negroes. Next comes George, a Pennsylvania Englishman, he is in the same gang. It's dangerous blackleg leader. These, with the assistance of John, jr., all led and instructed the imported, unskilled negro until they got enough to make a division when one split at No. 5 taking twenty of these negroes to No. 4, and then they work on till the other takes another division to No. 3 and commences on his own hook as a blackleg boss, leaving L--- and L--- as blackleg partners at No. 5, so that on the whole the company has got a good many blacklegs in the three mines not doing as much as one mine used to do with six times the expense going on; then the other side, known as the drifts, has a blackleg business, but whether it is wholesale or retail I cannot describe. One portion of it is carried on by a man from Pennsylvania and I have not much faith in him anyhow. If he sees a man coming he is like a deer, he rounds a rock in great shape to get out of the way and under cover, saying Lord save me.

Now, can we blame the ignorant negro for working, when men that call themselves white lead them to the very act that is going to ruin not only the present, but the rising generation and for generations to come, and if the devil has as much use for them as the T.C.I. & R.R. Co., well, they never will be in h--- for it's too full already of such corruption. This strike was inaugurated April 24, and the boys are still living yet, although it is a hard one, but I think they are getting along just as well as the dirty black-sheep are, and then they don't need to carry 44 pistols around nor have deputies to guard their house. H. F. DeBardeleben has at least from four to six deputies or bums to guard his carcass either by rail, vehicle, asleep or awake, which shows he is guilty of one of the greatest conspiracies against his own color and labor that ever was enacted by any firm. Besides he is plunging the company into thousands of dollars of expense.[77]

I will now conclude, wishing your valuable paper success and hoping the victory may be ours.

W. J. KELSO[78]

United Mine Workers' Journal, July 5, 1894.

76. ALABAMA NEWS

Blacklegs of the Worst and Meanest Kind Prevent a Settlement--All Tricks
Tried--And Thousands of Dollars Spent to Defeat the Miners--Still Firm,
However.

PRATT CITY, Ala., July 16.--Since my last writing the situation is unchanged except with regard to a few of the blacksheep who are dropping off,
not being able to sustain themselves on the price paid. On Friday there
was a negro boy killed at the drifts aged 8 years. The state law of Alabama reads, "that no boy shall be employed in or around the mines under 10
years." What will they do with this case? I would like to see Mr. Hill-
house out here to investigate, but I expect, like the Mary Lee disaster, he
will have to see mamma and stay two or three weeks, allowing the company
time to fix all things right again. Thank God they cannot break the ranks
of the miners this time as they are as solid as the first day they came out.
This Debardeleben has tried every conceivable plan, first by bringing imported negroes with the white gulls to lead them and deputies to guard them;
second, by throwing the people out of the houses, and thirdly, by offering
free transportation to the whites to thin and weaken our ranks; fourth, by
hiring a scoundrel to buy the men with beer. By this kind of business
Debardeleben has spent thousands of dollars, and all to no purpose. Still
the white blacklegs are pulling along showing the "ignorant" negro how to
dig coal. Now, I would ask, who is the worst, the negro or the white blackleg? Had it not been for the exertions of these white leaders we would have
long ago gained what we were striking for, and that is simply living wages.
The T.C.I. company has spent more money now to try and break up this strike
than would have paid their miners to cents per ton for the next five years,
and the miners ask no more than the old scale of 45 cents per ton, with all
coal weighed as usual. Of all the blacklegs I ever saw these men have been
the meanest of mean. Neil and Rutledge left their own mines and went to No.
5 as that was the first recruiting depot of Pratt mines; No. 4 next, and No.
3 next. I think that all honest miners should give them the cold shoulder
wherever they meet them, as I guess we will have no use for them after all
is settled and the company will have just as little. There are none of them
but what are mean enough to blackleg the devil if they only thought they
could get smiles from the imps. All right, blacklegs, we will see the day
when the poor hungry honest man's child, who is crying for bread today, may
smile at a well furnished table, while you are hunting for something to give
yours. The protection of armed deputies will not always be with you to guard
you in your sleeping and waking hours. A day of reckoning will come, and
before you know it. The insults and slurs you have thrown out to these poor
miners when you had the governor, the sheriff and the company at your back
will surely be remembered against you. Wishing your noble paper success,
and hoping I will have better news next time."[79]

WM. J. KELSO

United Mine Workers' Journal, July 26, 1894.

77. CLARK

Of Rendville Writes on Many Things

Affecting the Laboring Man--Politics and Strikes

RENDVILLE, O., Aug. 8--Once more I would ask space in your paper, by
request, as I have been asleep so long. Well, I could only say for the craft
that we are only living here today. We are crowded up to the last notch and
dissatisfaction seems to be the ruling power here now. Well, Mr. Editor,
some new ideas have sprung up in the minds of the Northern Pacific Coal company of Roslyn, Wash. They have two agents here after colored men, only they

have a contract or agreement for each man to sign before going. I tried to get hold of it, but it was impossible. It is a corker.

I see that the national officers want a change in politics. Well, that is good. When men like McBride are willing to leave their old parties and try others, what ought the colored laborers do?[80]

Now, Mr. Editor, as a colored man, I may have a different view of this matter, and I know I will find many a one to oppose me in what I want to say on this subject. Since August last there has been a year passed into eternity that the nation will not soon forget. It has told its tale; of its few joys to the many and oppressed of this country, and of its sorrows and bereavement to the same. Monopoly has been against them and the government also in the last few months. My mind has wandered from world to world. My first wonder was, I wonder if the other worlds were inhabited? Did they have the same kind of law and government that we have? and my next wonder was, was this world of ours the hell we read about in the good book? If it is not, how can a man stand the punishment twice and then live through eternity. They burn men alive, skin them, lynch them, shoot them and torture them in a way inconceivable under both administrations. I would ask those of my race who shall read this to study and see if at this late date, do you owe any political party a debt of gratitude? I claim not. The past has taught its lesson, the present is ours, and the future we know not of. Since the year of 1881 there has been over 500,000 immigrants yearly to our country until we are so thick they can't stand it. The government could afford to have a million or two pushed off the side of the earth and not miss them.

Well, with regard to a new party, could not the colored people of America afford to join a new party if it would pledge itself to them or adopt a plank in the platform for protection of its citizens and see that they are not discriminated against. What will you gain by voting with the same old parties. As long as you do you will make millions of men rich yearly who will not legislate against their own interest. But I want to say, as one, I am in favor of the black man of America forming a party of his own. Some will say that will do no good. What good are you doing now with the old parties? If you do that you will be recognized as citizens, as it has been said, in a body we can elect or defeat.

I know that the colored voters are discriminated against, and can prove it by letters in my possession, from the best so-called Republican in Perry county.

A word to friend Colman: Go slow and learn to trust and keep your powder dry. I am tired of strikes and don't think much can be done on that line until we come in unity as a class of laboring people; all look one way, think one way, do one way and vote one way; and then I think victory will be ours. I think all men ought to work on this plan for the betterment of all concerned because if you advocate strikes you will have the operators to fight and the bankers, the state officials, the soldiers and a portion of your own craft who toil beside you every day. So, be careful, for restraint and injunction will be in order next locally. I have had a hint, so I will close hoping that much good may be accomplished on the 15th of August at the convention.

W. E. CLARK.

United Mine Workers' Journal, August 9, 1894.

78. A LITTLE HISTORY

And a Pathetic Appeal by a Colored Man of Hackett, Pa.

As I have lately subscribed for your paper, and finding it to be very interesting, and more than this, valuable, I desire to occupy a little corner of your space. On the 21st I saw a little piece in your paper which, it would seem, our American people have forgotten. Let me call their minds back to the year 1856, when President Buchanan was inaugurated on March 6. Two days after additional provocation was given to the political opponents of

slavery by a judgment of the supreme court in the "Dred Scott" case. It
was decided that a negro was not a citizen, and it was held by two-thirds
of the judges that the Missouri Compromise was contrary to the constitution.
This decree increased agitations; "personal liberty" bills and other proceedings were taken to neutralize the fugitive slave laws in the northern
states. Indeed, some of the most sanguinary conflicts took place under Mr.
Buchanan's government.[81]

So, my friends of labor, will you not dwell on these things. Look at
the negro who is not considered a citizen, though he goes to the ballot-
box and votes, and pays his taxes. We are not good enough to have a good
job if we are capable of fulfilling its duties. Friends, consider how long
the old negro has been in this new world; ever since the year 1528 on April
14. We preach union; let us sustain it. Look at the A.R.U. I have been a
railroad man though my skin is dark. I cannot get a job if I desired one
with other American railroad men. But we will look to the Lord. I thank God
that the day is getting brighter. Laborers the darkness is just what we
have made.

May the Lord bless the entire world and forgive them for their many sins.

R. A. SCOTT

United Mine Workers' Journal, July 26, 1895.

79. MONTHLY MASS MEETING

Social Democracy Defended--Sensible Remarks by a Colored Minister

WEST PRATT, Feb. 25, 1898.

On Thursday last the miners of West Pratt held their regular monthly
meeting. After the usual routine of business had been transacted, Mr. T.
Dickey gave a very interesting and instructive talk on the rise, progress
and future prospect of Social Democracy and advised the miners to look in
that direction for deliverance from the slavish conditions which exist,
rather than to the labor organizations that now exist.

J. M. Morton, pastor of the A.M.E. Church, was requested to make a few
remarks and made the following enigmatical address:

Fellow Workmen, some preachers say dat we is livin' in troublous times;
dat de time am come when no livin' man may, and no dead man can, speak de
trufe and nuffin but de trufe, 'less he's prepared to walk fru de garden of
Gesseminy by he self. De bible tells us we must not talk deceitfully or
shores you born de good Lord will one day get eben with us an' some folks
naturally buck agin talkin' dissimulatively.

Methinks I hear some old ignant nigger ask, "What is our tongue good for
anyhow?" Why to squirt out ob your mouf day nasty terbacker juice and so on,
"But musn't we walk?" Ob course you can. De good Lord has given us feet
an' legs for locomotion. These to be healthy and useful must be exercised so
we can walk, run an' kick football, an' should we dread an attack of gout,
to prevent dat, we must kick each other. So its just de same wid our tongues.
Let us talk but only for tongue exercise.

Ten months ago, President Baxter came out here and told us dat he an'
his 'sociates wuz in trouble; dat owin' to de high price which dey was a payin'
us for diggin' dis coal dat dey couldn't compete successfully wid de other
firms an' dat unless, we ob our own free will an' proverbial goodness of the
heart, conceded to them a 5 cent a ton reduction, de mines would necessarily
hafter shut down indefinitely an' de grass would grow green on de streets of
de Magic City of our loved an' beautiful southland.

Dat is a specimen of tongue exercise which only de ignant or captious
will say is not an admirable one, but to make sure let me ask which one of us
all can lay his hand on his heart an' say, wid conscience void of offense,
"President Baxter spake all words of trufe an' soberness." Take another
specimen. A voice once said, "I couldn't advise you men to send a representa-

tive to examine the books in de office of de T.C.I. & R.R. Co., because dat's where all de deviltry is done an' I knows it." Two months later de same voice said, "the privilege of examining de books is one not to be lightly esteemed," seeing we have so few--by all means let us hold on to it. Now who of us all can lay his hand on his heart an' say dat de words means dat de company's officials an' our leaders meet once a month to plot agin us, concoct schemes to deprive us of our liberties as our lives instead of its true meaning, dat is, dat dey meet to consider what is best an' most pro- fitable to all parties so dat peace an' happiness may abound--tongue exercise.

In conclusion let us just take another example. 'Spose on leavin' de company's office one of our most trusted leaders should feel a gentle tap on he shoulder an' a sweet gentle voice whisper in he ear, "you is gettin' old Father William, your hair is a growin' gray, your knees is becomin' weak, your hands hang feebly down when you go home. Dear frien' study your bible for there you shall fin' written in letters of gold dat' "He dat fails to pervide for he own household is worser an infidel," an you must not hastily construe it as meaning necessarily dat de only way one can do dat is by dig- gin' coal at 35¢ a ton."

Tongue exercise. Now, de logical conclusion of de whole matter am dat if de daily study of de bible am profitable to de plutocrat, it hadn't orter be unprofitable to de plebian.

PETER TIDWELL

Birmingham Labor Advocate, March 5, 1898.

80.   COLORED ODD FELLOWS

The colored Odd Fellows paraded around our camp in uniform. They made a splendid showing. They are a very intelligent body, progressive and ardent supporters of unions pertaining to their interests.

Birmingham Labor Advocate, March 5, 1898.

81.   A COLORED

BROTHER FROM GRAPE CREEK ILLINOIS SENDS AN INTERESTING LETTER

The Rat That Killed the Cat, and Got a "Dead Baby" and Says That Their is No
Discrimination Against the Colored Man at That Mine

GRAPE CREEK, Ill., Nov. 3.--Editor Journal: Please permit me space for a few words in your valued paper. I will first introduce myself as a colored miner in the Danville district. There has been a few of us trying to effect a permanent organization in this field for several years, and of course the operators rewarded us by keeping us on the move. But, thanks to James Murray, formerly of Spring Valley, now of Westville, Ill., he came in our district in the year 1897, as it were, by night, and inquired for my old comrade, R. H. Noel, and I. As we were then the only fool negroes in the district, neverthe- less we went around and notified a few of the friends, Hungarians and Luthi- vanians, and held a little meeting. Then they called upon the rat that would volunteer to bill the cat. The trouble was that we had an old charter up in town and who would venture to bring it down? When the operators had then been informed of Brother Murray trying to rent a hall in the town, but of no avail. The operators owned the moon. Then I went up in town, got the box with the charter in it and on being asked what I was carrying my answer was "dead baby." I carried it in the hot sun to a hall about three miles away, on Grape Creek, and there organized what is known as L. A. 310, with a vast membership and a local treasury of over $1,000 cash now. She was then a dead baby, but if you

could once be in one of our meetings and hear us discussing the many questions that concern labor you would think it a ten-year-old boy now.

Now, Mr. Editor, there seems to be a misrepresentation of our union
among some people, which I term as enemies to the organization, in saying
that the colored men are discriminated against. I don't know how other
districts are, but I term this one fair from the very fact that our district
vice-president, Henry Rector, is colored, and very deeply colored. This
district is about, I will say, less than one-fourth colored, and not a local
in the district that has any colored members is there but has colored local
officers. As for myself, I hold more offices than I know what to do with.
I have served on one tipple nine months as check weighman without removal
and resigned on my own account; was off a little over three months and am
now at the same job. Now, does this look like discrimination and only three
colored men in the mine out of a total of 300 miners?

I will say we have a few men of the foolish, jealous, "bum" element
that would, if they could, find enough such to back them up, but if such
people as that had been in the majority we would have had no union at all.
So we follow the old people's advice, "When you hear nothing say nothing."

Now I hope that all my colored brothers will take my advice, knowing
that they are free men. They should not enslave themselves by making themselves the tools of monopoly, but should rise up and assert our rights as a
free people in a free land, demand our rights and if not granted make a
stand for them, and don't stop standing until our demands are granted. God
hates a coward, anyway. Think of Patrick Henry the Great, as I term him,
when this country was a dense wilderness, when he, having a brave heart
within exclaimed, "We will not fight our battles alone. But there is a just
God that looks down upon the destinies of all nations and He will raise
friends to fight our battles for us." This country then rose up, threw off
the yoke of tyranny and oppression, unloosed the shackles of slavery and
became a free and independent people. Now we are the greatest, most industrious, most Christian-like, most free people on earth. But they did not
gain it by cowardice, neither did they gain it by listening to the ingenious
lie manufactured by their oppressors.[82]

My dear brother, this must be the policy sooner or later, and let it
come, that we may be more able to provide for our families, whom we promise
an all-wise God we will love, nourish and cherish. On listening to the
other fellow's pitiful plea we throw ourselves in this channel, "A man that
don't provide for his own household is worse than an infidel."

Yours truly,
S. C. ARMSTRONG

United Mine Workers' Journal, November 10, 1898.

82. CHASM OF PREJUDICE

Bridged By the Plank of Common Sense in Iowa

A Colored Brother Who is Pained by the Actions of His Race in Other States--
An Excellent Letter by O. H. Underwood

MYSTIC, Iowa, July 10.--Editor Journal: As Mystic is one of the largest
mining camps in the low coal field, and never seeing anything from Mystic in
your paper, I thought it would be a good idea to let you know how the Mystic
breezes were blowing in this part of the moral vineyard. We have a very good
local here. While it is not in as prosperous a condition as we wish yet,
and still the miners here and in fact in the State of Iowa are awakening to
the benefit of the organization, while some mistakes have been made, yet they
are nothing to compare with the benefits gained.

Appanoose county is proud of one thing and I think we are justified in
our pride, and that is, it was the first county in the State of Iowa to unfurl
to the breeze the eight-hour concession. I believe it is now nearly general[83]
throughout the State. The next greatest need of Iowa is the check-off system,

and we think we will have that also before another year. I have read considerable in your paper regarding the colored men, but I can proudly say
that in the low coal field (and in nearly all of the State) that the chasm
of prejudice has been bridged with the plank of common sense, and we are
marching side by side, hand in hand, to accomplish the same great object.
Visit the different locals with me if you will and all the colored men
presidents, secretaries and members of the executive boards and then in my
pride at seeing these things would I be disloyal if I should say I believe
that the United Mine Workers has done more to erase the word white from the
Constitution than the Fourteenth Amendment. And as a colored man, I am
speaking from a colored man's standpoint and can say that the sting is more
bitter to us when some of our race go wrong. But as all things cometh to
him who waits, we are waiting for the day when they shall see as we see and
shall walk in the true light as we do.[84]

The State convention will be held in Oskaloosa on or about August 16,
and we shall offer as candidates for office two of our brainiest and best
young men, H. G. Street, of Mystic, and Joe Sharp, of Brazil. Believing, as
we do, that they have stood up for the rights of the miners through thick
and thin, and they should be written of as one who loves their fellow men,
the miners of Iowa will make a mistake if they don't indorse them and a
greater mistake if they do not re-elect John F. Ream as State president. He
is a man among men and has done more to keep the organization up than any
one man in Iowa.

Wishing success to the mine workers and may West Virginia speedily awake
to her true condition, respectfully,

O. H. UNDERWOOD[85]

United Mine Workers' Journal, July 29, 1899.

83. F. A. BANNISTER

The Colored Orator Makes An Eloquent Plea For Organization[86]

President Smith, Board Member Stephenson, Organizer Scott and O. T. Wilkins
Also Contribute to the Success of the Montgomery Meeting

MONTGOMERY, W. Va., July 26.--Editor Journal: The mass meeting held
this date on the ballground was addressed by Messrs. Smith, Scott, Bannister
and Wilkins. Brother Farry being very ill could not be present.

President Smith opened the meeting with a short address, stating, among
other things, that this meeting was called for the purpose of perfecting the
organization and to select delegates to the convention to be held here on the
8th day of August, 1899.

Mr. F. A. Bannister, ex-vice-president, was then introduced and presented
in his usual style a forcible argument in behalf of organization. The principal parts are as follows:

"Fellow miners, it is always a pleasure to meet with you on such an occasion as this. I know your pleasure and I know your disappointments, and
share them with you.

"You should consider this a day of pleasure. You should consider the
questions that come before you, such as the cost of production of coal, cost
of living, price of coal in the various markets, etc.

"How will you meet the emergency? How will you meet your employers unless you prepare yourselves for the task?

"I appeal to you to look around you. Take a view of your surroundings.
It is no crime for the monopolists to unite. Then why not you as miners and
mine laborers unite for self-protection?

"We have a short life. Then we should improve the time. You have the
right to go to any other State and find plenty of work at good wages, brought
about by organized effort, by your fellow mine workers, while you have been
asleep neglecting your duty. Have you got those conditions here? No, and it
is because your spleen is not long enough. I can talk plain to you today.

One year ago you would say I could talk this way because I was paid $2.50
per day. Today I am here without pay and talk with sincere motives. Some
men are afraid to be at this meeting for fear the bosses will see them.
    "Ask them if they are afraid to attend a mass meeting. Are they will-
ing to accept a one-fourth cent advance in place of one-half cent, which
they are entitled to? Miners, what made the operators offer the one-fourth
cent? It was the efforts put forth by the mine-workers to secure what is
justly due you. My advice to you is to join the organization and attend the
meetings of your local unions, and you will always find your humble servant
ready to lift his voice in your behalf."

United Mine Workers' Journal, August 3, 1899.

84. TWO BLACK MINERS PRESENT CONTRASTING VIEWS
AT THE ILLINOIS STATE U.M.W. CONVENTION, 1900

Cal Robinson

    This grievance was given to me by some of my colored brothers here. There
are five shafts in and around Springfield, all supposed to be managed by
good union men, and in these shafts no colored men work, simply on account of
their color. Because their faces are a little dark they cannot work in these
shafts. I claim that when that man (Pointing to the painting of Abraham
Lincoln) emancipated the black race he gave them all privileges and equal
rights. I think when a colored man pays his money into the union and conducts
himself as a good union man should, he is discriminated against when he has
to walk two or three miles to his work when there is a shaft at his door. If
you do what is right in this matter, gentlemen, you will have none of your
Virden and Carterville riots, and no blood will be spilled. If this discrimination is blotted out you will never hear of such riots as we have had
in this State. This discrimination means that when the negroes are barred
from these shafts and if there is a strike ordered at these places, the
operators will say they will get negroes from the South and that they will
run the shafts. Gentlemen, we should get closer together; it behooves all to
do this; it will stop all friction. When a man takes an oath to make no
discrimination against another man on account of race, creed or color he
should keep that oath. At the two east shafts, the New North and the Two
Citizens, my people are discriminated against. Even the co-operative shift
here that is run by labor itself, where all men are supposed to be laboring
men who run it, the negroes cannot enter that shaft. We want to abolish all
of these evils, and then we shall not have to get out our Gatling guns, we
will have no fights along these lines, and we will have no riots. I hope you
will help to abolish this thing here and now. [87]

George Durden

    I cannot find words in the language that will do justice to my expres-
sion of thanks to you and to the organization. Up to 1619 the African was
happy and contented under the shadow of the palm leaves of his own home. Then
he was kidnapped and brought here and sold into slavery and shackles. Then
in 1865 we were turned loose, four and one-half millions of us, without a
place in which to lay our heads. We were without money, without friends,
without education. We took up our lives then without any of these things,
without anyone to help us. Today the value of the negro can be seen in all
the States from Virginia to the Gulf of Mexico. We have made applications to
organizations to help us time and again. You know how even the Masons and
Odd Fellows have discriminated against us. There has been no organization
that has come to our assistance with such outstretched arms as has the United
Mine Workers of America. We are sensitive, it is true. There is a certain
class of men in some localities who will not allow the black man to work side
by side with his white brothers. No such discrimination is made by the constitution of the organization. There are many places in this State where no

color is known when it comes to work. I have seen this organization reach
out its arms for my race. They have given them homes and friends; they have
helped them when they most needed help. This organization has extended to
us more help than we have received from any other organization in America.
There are places in this State where colored men have been told that they
could not stay at all, where when we were without friends, almost without
clothes, where the moment we presented our union cards we were taken in and
helped and given work. We knew it was not the United Mine Workers of America who fired the shots that shed our men's lifeblood at the riots in Virden
and Carterville. Those shots were not fired by Mine Workers; the first shots
were fired by my own people, they were fired on the non-union men, and it
was the non-union who fired upon us. Let us have no break between the white
and the black. Your constitution has not made any discrimination against
anyone. The organization is strong, and we love it, and we know that it is
only individuals who make objection to our working, and we should not get
sensitive over this and attack the union. I thank you, gentlemen, for your
attention.

Herbert G. Gutman, "The Negro and the United Mine Workers of America," in
Julius Jacobson (ed.), *The Negro and the American Labor Movement (New York,
1968), pp. 114-15.*

85. THE JOINT CONVENTION IN ALABAMA

Shortly after 9 o'clock President Young called the convention to order
and stated that the operators would be in the hall in a few minutes. He
suggested the scale committee do the talking for the operators.
A delegate thought it would be better for each delegation to have a
spokesman.
A colored delegate said the negotiations should be conducted as they
were last year.
President Young said if the convention decided that the scale was to be
open to general discussion, every delegate, as a matter of course, could
participate.
A motion was offered that if the operators in their arguments selected
one particular place, the delegates from that place be allowed to make
remarks.
National Committeeman Fairley said he was in favor of allowing every[88]
delegate to speak his mind, but the matter of the scale would have to be
talked over between a committee of the operators and the committee at the
convention. At all events, the scale would have to be ratified by the convention. All this discussion was unnecessary, because there will be no limit
to free speech at the seasonable time. But if it is not wise to break into
the negotiations of the joint scale committee. He called the attention of the
convention to the fact that if every delegate intends to exercise the right
to talk, the convention will not adjourn before Christmas. The matter will
come down to what it did last year and previous years, a number of men will
have to be appointed to discuss and defend the rights of the miners. (Ap-
plause.) He concluded by saying the spirit which seems to be manifest, that
rights of delegates were to be curtailed, had no substance. When the convention adjourned every delegate should feel that he had a share of the responsibility of making the scale.
The question recurred upon the motion and it was adopted.
While waiting for the operators Delegate Scott sang "The Honest Workingman," in fine voice.
Some of the delegates joined in the chorus:
"It's a glorious union,
    Deny it who can.
That defends the rights
    Of a workingman."

Mr. Fairley then called for a song from one of the colored brethren.

Charley Farley, colored, ascended the rostrom and sang "We are Marching to Canaan." It had the old-time camp meeting lilt and the colored delegates crooned the lines and broke into the chorus:

"Who is there among us,
The true and the tried.
Who'll stand by his fellows,
Who's on the Lord's side."

Delegate Jack Orr responded to the call of the convention with "Silver Bells of Memor." The convention took up the refrain with gusto.

There was a storm of calls for "Bill Fairley," to sing a song. "I'm never bluffed," he said with a smile. "I hope the reporters will not take down my song." He sang "Give Me Back My Heart."

Birmingham Labor Advocate, June 30, 1900.

IV

BLACK COAL MINERS AND THE ISSUE
OF STRIKEBREAKING

PART IV

BLACK COAL MINERS AND THE ISSUE OF STRIKEBREAKING

Patterns of conflict in the southern Illinois coal fields during the 1890s present an excellent microcosm of working class race relations in the mining industry. In 1897, twenty mine operators, led by the Chicago-Virden Coal Company, objected to the wage settlement established by an industry-wide agreement that same year, complaining that high labor costs was pricing Illinois coal out of the Chicago market. When the UMW rejected their appeal for an exception to the agreement, the Chicago-Virden Company decided to operate its Pana and Virden mines, two of the largest in the state, with nonunion labor. After several unsuccessful attempts to use white scabs, the company began to recruit poor black workers from Alabama (Doc. 1-12).

The Afro-American Labor and Protective Association of Birmingham opposed the recruiting of Negro strikebreakers for the Chicago-Virden Company in its struggle with the United Mine Workers, but to no avail. Once the Alabama recruits discovered that a strike was in progress, however, most of them refused to work, but according to a Chicago weekly, armed guards threatened to "shoot Negroes who attempted to leave." Determined to keep out all black scabs, well armed Illinois miners opened a steady fire as the trainload of strikebreakers arrived at Virden. Company guards returned fire, killing fourteen white miners and wounding twenty-four others. A few blacks were also wounded. Illinois Governor John R. Tanner called out the National Guard, and promised the white miners that he would not tolerate the importation of blacks into Pana and Virden (Doc. 13-29).

The white miners applauded the governor for his stand, as did the AFL, but to most black spokesmen, "Tannerism" symbolized a racial conspiracy between white politicians and trade unionists. "They bar the Negro from the benefits that unions are designed to confer," the Colored American raged, and the Christian Recorder expressed sympathy for the striking miners, but chastised the strikers for barring black miners from the "employment by which they can earn bread." Not even the fact that blacks numbered among the strikers reduced the bitterness voiced in the black press. Trade unions could not be trusted, went the argument, not even those which admitted blacks, for "as soon as unionism was strong enough in these United States, it joined forces with the colored man's enemy and cried 'no quarter.'" The Freeman of Indianapolis and the Recorder of Philadelphia were the only two black papers to take a different view of the events in Illinois. The Freeman condemned the mine operators "for the introduction of Negro workmen for the express purpose of defeating white workmen," and caustically suggested if the employers were so concerned about the employment opportunities for blacks, "let them employ Negro workmen in times of peace; put them in wherever they can and as many as they can until the faces of black men excite no curiosity." At the same time, it urged the trade unions to contribute toward "the relaxation of the high-tensioned relations between the races" by proving that "they are for the Negro workmen." The Recorder concurred and added its own plea for the union movement "to lower the bars and allow Negro labor to enter. Give us a chance" (Doc. 30-55). A liberal white paper pondered the dilemma of the black worker: "If nonunion men are not permitted to work and colored men are not permitted to join the union, where does the colored man come in? Or does he stay out?"

IMPORTATION AND BLACK STRIKEBREAKING

1. TWO ADVERTISEMENTS

WANTED COLORED coal-miners for Weir City, Kans., district, the paradise
for colored people. Ninety-seven cents per ton. September 1 to March 1;
87-1/2 cents per ton March 1 to September 1, for screened coal over seven-
eighths opening. Special train will leave Birmingham the 13th. Transportation advanced. Get ready and go to the land of promise.

Colored Coal Miners Wanted for Weir City district, Kansas. Coal 3 feet
10 inches high. Since issue of first circular, price paid for mining has
been advanced to one dollar per ton in winter and ninety cents in summer,
for lump coal screened over seven-eighths inch screen. Payday, twice a
month, in cash. Transportation will not exceed ten dollars, which will be
advanced. Special train leaves Birmingham Tuesday night, June 13. Leave
your name at Kansas City railway office, 1714 Morris Avenue.

Sterling D. Spero and Abram L. Harris, *The Black Worker: The Negro and the
Labor Movement (New York, 1931), p. 211.*

2.   COLORED MEN REFLECT

Southern Labor Against Northern Labor[89]
From John Swinton's Paper

A short time ago our correspondent at Bevier, in Missouri, told of the
suffering of the coal miners, who, during their strike, were supplanted by
colored men, anxious to work for such pay as is given to the dogs of Con-
stantinople. In the case of the striking miners of Grape Creek, in Illinois,
gangs of poor colored men were transferred from the South, by the corporation,
to take their places. During the Hocking Valley troubles in Ohio, two years
ago, colored men were brought from the South, as well as Huns from across
the ocean, to break the strike; and Miner Smith has just sent a letter from
Ohio to the Pittsburg *Labor Tribune*, in which he says: "Our district is
visited by fifty-six blacklegs (colored men) from Richmond, Va., and there
are rumors of one hundred more on the road for No. 9 district, Ohio. This
is the remuneration they are giving us, the boys in blue, who served one to
five years in the Union army to make them free citizens!"[90]
There have been other examples of the same kind in Western Pennsylvania.
In fact, as the *Labor Tribune* says, the transfer of Negroes from the old
slave States to the North for the purpose of breaking down wages, may grow
into fashion until it will rival or even excel the importation of contract
labor. It is hard to find fault with the poor colored men for the part they
have taken in these inroads; but for the capitalists who have brought them
to the North there should be nothing short of positive popular condemnation.
In the country districts of the South, the Negro laborers are held in a
condition akin to slavery. They are paid so little wages, receive so little
cash after their fifty or seventy-five cents a day suffers from the "pluck-
me" system, that they are easily lured to the North at wages disgustingly
inadequate for white workingmen. The imposition on the Negroes is systematically carried on. An illustration of this lately came from the Georgia
mines of the "pious" Senator Brown, where the practice of the old slavery
devices raised revolt among the convicts employed--all Negroes--who had been
supplied by the courts who habitually sentence Negroes to ten and even twenty
years imprisonment (convict labor) for petty crimes which would go unwhipt

of justice committed by white men.   They are pushed to the wall by the same
spirit that struck the Union to maintain slavery, and every year indicates
that the old slavedrivers who retain this spirit are getting the Negro in
trim to degrade the laborer of the North.   The action is systematically to
this end; it is not found in spurts, but sticks out everywhere outside the
cities of the South. [91]

Here is work for the colored press, which we especially commend to that
champion of the colored roll, the *New York Freeman*, edited by our brilliant
friend, T. Thomas Fortune.   While every effort must be made to assert the
rights of the colored laborers of the Union, they should be loudly warned
against being used as tools to break down the white labor of the North. [92]

New York Freeman, December 4, 1886.

3.   WHITE AND COLORED LABORERS DETRIMENTAL

In another column we print an article from *John Swinton's Paper*, headed
"Colored men, Reflect," which should be carefully read by every colored man.
The charge is there made that colored men are imported from the South by
labor contractors to take the place of Northern white Laborers who are on
strike.   In other articles on the labor question we have placed ourselves
squarely on record as opposed to this sort of thing as being opposed to the
common interest of laboring men and as yielding only a temporary benefit to
the colored man.   We desire here to emphasize this important fact.

The labor organizations of the country have shown a most magnanimous
and fraternal disposition to put colored men on equal footing with white
members, and to stand by them in all their efforts to better the common lot
of the laborer.   This being true, colored men, in the North or the South,
cannot afford to undermine white laborers when they make organized resistance to unjust wages or treatment at the hands of employers.   There is no
obstacle in the way, therefore let the colored laborer make common cause
with the white laborer.   They cannot pursue any other course without mutual
loss and permanent disadvantage.

Nobody will dispute that the lot of the colored laborer of the South is
as severe as it can be made, and that the wages paid are not such as to im-
part to the physical man the sustenance absolutely necessary to enable the
laborer to live and produce up to the normal standard.   This being true, it
is not to be marvelled at that colored men should embrace the inducements to
better their condition held out to them by labor agents.   These laborers are
not always acquainted with the real condition of things in a district until
after they have reached it, and when they have either to go to work or break
the contracts and starve or suffer the effects of starvation in their efforts
to reach again their Southern homes.   It is a work of self protection for the
labor organizations of the North to educate the colored laborers of the South
on the true conditions of the labor problem in the North.

In the meantime we have no doubt *John Swinton's Paper* will read a severe
lesson to those white New York laborers who went to Virginia last week to
take the places of dissatisfied colored stevedores.   This conduct of the white
men is as reprehensible as the conduct of the colored men; indeed more so, as
Northern labor is supposed to be more intelligent than Southern labor.   Lay
on the lash, Mr. Swinton; lay on the lash.

New York Freeman, December 25, 1886.

4. NEGRO MINERS IN DEMAND

Good Wages Earned

EVANS, Iowa, special to *The Freeman:*
    There are now about 200 Negro miners at Evans and more are coming. But few white men are employed here, most of them having gone out on the recent coal miners' strike. I am glad to say that the black miners used good sense in holding their jobs, for the result is that Negro miners are now very popular with the mining operators, and the prospect for future work is very good. About 200 Negroes came to this county last week from West Virginia, and 300 more are expected to arrive this week. Jobs are waiting for them all in the various mines throughout the county, and good inducements are offered. The miners of this county make from $40 to $75 a month. Those who are inclined to save their money are doing well; many of them own their homes, and some have houses to rent or money to loan.

The Freeman (Indianapolis), July 11, 1891.

5. THE NEGRO AND STRIKES

    For some time past the warfare between labor and capital as shown by strikes has been confined to whites.
    The Negro has to a great extent kept aloof and given no trouble, in sometimes taking the places, of white strikers and finding thereby avenues of labor open to him through necessity, which had formerly been closed.
    But the indications are that he is not to continue in this passive attitude from certain events which have recently transpired.
    Whether it will be for his best interest or not the trend of things seem to be that he will be swept into the general movement and array himself on the side of labor. This is but natural and proves that the Negro in this, as in every other case in this country where general interest are involved, takes ground outside of racial lines.

The Christian Recorder, June 7, 1894.

6. THE MINING RIOTS

    The daily press the past week had teemed with specials from different sections of the land which bespoke a condition of things the next door to bloodshed and a reign of civil strife and anarchy. Indiana's brave volunteer force, some hundreds strong, was ordered out by Gov. Matthews and for a number of days have been at the seat of the "coal war" in Clay, Sullivan, Parke and other counties. At this writing (Tuesday noon), the reports are not encouraging. The miners seem savagely in earnest, and, if reports are true, will stop at nothing to gain their point. It is a most unhappy condition of things, and if nothing more serious grows out than has already, nevertheless the amount of damage done to invested capital and its twin brother labor, will reach a great sum, to say nothing of other damaging results to all concerned, not to be readily computed by dollars and cents. Without attempting at this time to enter into a discussion of the probable causes of these outbreaks that are multiplying so fast upon the surface of the body politic of the country, one thing is plain to the dullest observer, something is wrong, the times are out of joint, and he is a wise man and a statesman out of the ordinary who can anywhere near accurately forecast the outcome. A good book for contemporaries and observers to read these days is

Carlyle's French Revolution. There is much in the growing conditions a-
round us to remind us of the lurid intimations that preceded that awful
period of bloodshed and horror as depicted in that great work.[33]

The Freeman (Indianapolis), June 9, 1894.

7. LABOR OUTLOOK FOR COLORED MEN

Seldom does an ill wind blow upon this nation without conveying some
good to the Negro. The industrial agitations and upheavals that have not
quite subsided seem to forcibly illustrate this fact in point of tendency
and indications, to say the least. What the outcome may disclose is not
quite so certain, but at present, Negro labor which has hitherto been at a
discount, if not generally ignored as an industrial factor, has clothed
itself with a prestige and promise which none but the unobservant need
gainsay or deny.

At the centre of the great Western strike we have already shown to what
extent the colored workman has been invited to enter new industrial avenues.
Positions which he has never been able to reach in the line of promotion or
competency, has been thrown open to him by considerate railroad companies.
In the State of Illinois, mining corporations have agreed to employ him as
never before. So encouraging is the premium placed upon his industrial
worth and trustworthiness even as a skilled laborer, that numbers of his
race are now being trained by a railroad enterprise in Texas, to whom
permanent employment has been guaranteed in the event of dissaffection or
uprising on the part of the white labor forces now mastering that situation.

The duty of the colored workman under the circumstances and in the light
of the logic of the situation is sufficiently clear and incumbent. He must
acquire competency as a workman and skillfulness as a laborer. As a skilled
laborer he will sooner be in greater demand than ever before. As a reliable
factor attention will be taken from foreigners and turned to him. He must
become the subject of systematic management. He must become organized, not
to control labor but to control himself. Self-protection and self-direction
can never be his, as long as he remains outside of methodic and organized
government. As he operates so successfully as a religious power in virtue of
self-governing institutions, he will serve himself best as an industrial force
by standing together with his kind in a judicious manner.

Let the leaders of the race enjoin upon their followers the duty of biding
their time with patience and fitness. Let them be shown the folly and danger
of co-operating with labor malcontents in their fight against capital. As the
balance wheel of industrial power in this country there is an encouraging
future for the colored man, if he be cautious and politic in his approach
thereto.

The Christian Recorder, July 19, 1894.

8. THE SPRING VALLEY RIOT

The Philadelphia *Telegraph* says:
The rioting, the attacks on person and property at Spring Valley, Ill.,
should not be considered too seriously by anyone who believes that our immigration laws are so nearly perfect as to need no revision, radical or otherwise. The outrages inflicted upon the negro miners of Spring Valley are some
of the natural outgrowths of these laws, which the Congress of the United
States finds so nearly perfect as to render any material alteration of them
undesirable. The colored American citizens were formally notified by the
non-English-speaking mob that if they, their women and children, did not leave

Spring Valley within the limits of a single day "they would be shot down in their tracks," all of them, without discrimination as to age or sex. Prior to the holding of this meeting, at which it was resolved by 2,000 Italians to issue the notice of expulsion, a number of the negro miners had been shot or clubbed down in their tracks by these non-English-speaking foreigners. Of course they did as they were warned to do, and when later 500 American miners adopted a resolution that they should return and be permitted to work unmolested by others, the Italians again declared that they should not be allowed so to do.

The outrages perpetrated upon the colored workingmen, their women and children, the practical confiscation of their property, the denial of every one of their rights of citizenship, and the terrorism exerted to banish them, were not the acts of the American white miners; they were the acts of the Italian miners, of those ignorant, vicious, morally degraded immigrants from Italy to whom this country has thrown open its generous doors in welcome, and after a brief period, before they can speak the language of the country, to the highest privileges of citizenship--namely, the suffrage. Not only these scum of Italy are voters at Spring Valley, but one of their number is Mayor of the city, and he has been again and again, by the most reliable authorities, charged with sympathizing with his murderous countrymen in their assaults upon the persons and property of the colored miners. This affair would serve as a convincing object-lesson to any body of men who cared to learn the truth, but from the manner Congress has so long faltered with the demand for a revision of the Immigration laws, it is obvious that body does not want to learn anything on the subject.

The Detroit *Tribune* says:

It is not a labor strike, but a race riot. These Italians, who are still so un-American that they require to have the mayor's address interpreted to them, have taken it upon themselves to say that no colored man, born upon the soil, shall work or even live in that community. We are told in the dispatches that "The foreign element, which dominates the situation, declares that no man, black or white, shall return to work until the coal company agrees to discharge every colored man in its employ, and also to hire no new men of either race; that all idle men"--whom they approve-- "in Spring Valley shall be given employment." This is their modest demand. What country is this, anyway? Can this be America, "the land of the free and the home of the brave?" Is it possible that there is law in Illinois, and peace officers, and a militia, and a governor? Aye! there's the rub! Illinois has a governor, but someway the impression has gone out, since he pardoned the Haymarket anarchists, that his sympathies are not strong for law and order.[94]

The Memphis *Commercial Appeal* says:

So they are learning something of the nature of the negro up in Illinois now. It is well. When they become thoroughly acquainted with him they will know that it is his disposition not to stay in his place, but to take an inch if allowed an ell. They will also come to the conclusion that he knows how to misrepresent the situation--an accomplishment he has probably learned from overzealous coon-bussers north of Mason and Dixon's line. He is putting up the plea of persecution now in the Spring Valley affair, when his side was really the aggressor.

The Chicago *Dispatch* says:

Nothing in the Spring Valley situation warrants the assumption that war is being waged against the negro race. The negro miners at that point belong to the "tough" classes, and they unfortunately have become embroiled with equally "tough" aliens in a riotous outbreak. A handful of lawless negroes are quarreling with a handful of lawless Italians. But there is no discrimination against the colored man and brother here.

The Jacksonville *Times-Union* says:

This is the most disgraceful piece of business that ever soiled the records of a State. It is not a mere case of mob violence. It is the indorsement of mob violence and the protection of mobs by the authorities of the town, county, and State.

Public Opinion (Chicago), August 15, 1895.

9.   THE SPRING VALLEY AFFAIR

The FREEMAN is certainly delighted to know that justice is being meted out to the perpetrators of the Spring Valley outrages. The mayor has been indicted on several counts. The main charge is, that, he knowing the intentions of the mob failed to order them to disperse. This in itself, would amount to complicity. It is very likely that he will be removed from office. A number of other persons are indicted, including aldermen of the city. We see no necessity for any unusual demonstration because of this justice. We expect it in this latitude.

The Freeman (Indianapolis), September 14, 1895.

10.   SOME DAY

Some day men and women who labor will form an universal association for the purpose of world-wide co-operation and there will be no lines or divisions because of creed, nor of distinction because of color, and the only requisite of membership will be a good character, and the fact of being a toiler. Toil then will be an honorable sign, and men and women will more readily embrace it.   No false notions, nor erroneous opinions, as to whom the wealth produced belongs to will then prevail, and it will be very easy to separate the drones from the industrious people, and just as easy to determine "that if any do not work, neither shall they eat."

United Mine Workers' Journal, October 13, 1898.

11.   WORK FOR NEGRO MINERS

A car load of Negro miners left Ft. Scott, Kans., Monday for the mines at Ft. Yule and Ft. Fleming. A special train followed, bearing Deputy United States Marshalls who will promptly arrest the strikers should they interfere with the new men.   Three hundred Negro miners from West Virginia have been sent to work in the mines in Indian territory.

The Recorder (Indianapolis), June 24, 1899.

12.   INTERVIEW WITH A WHITE U.M.W. MEMBER

As far as we are concerned as miners, the colored men are with us in the mines. They work side by side with us. They are members of our organization; can receive as much consideration from the officials of the organization as any other members, no matter what color. We treat them that way . . . there is only one particular objection, and that is they are used to a great extent in being taken from one place to another to break a strike. . . .

W. E. Burghardt Du Bois, ed., *The Negro Artisan (Atlanta, 1902), pp. 161, 177.*

IMPORTED BLACK MINERS AND THE PANA-VIRDEN STRIKE, 1898-1899

13. WANTED

100 Colored Laborers

Colored laborers--coal miners, drivers, and laborers--for mine work in Illinois. Steady work and regular pay every two weeks. The coal is 7 feet high. Pay 25 cents per ton run of mine; $1.75 per day for drivers; $1.50 for mine laborers.

No charges for blacksmithing. All coal weighed on tipples before being dumped.

The company has no commissaries.

Want nothing but first-class men. Bring your tools well tied up if you wish to carry them. Transportation will be furnished and ample time given you to pay the same; which will be very cheap. We will leave here on the Kansas City train Monday night at 10 o'clock. You be at the Union Depot promptly at 9 a.m. if you wish to go. For further information apply to Kansas City passenger office. 1914 Morris avenue. Men living in the city need not apply.

J. J. Sullivan
Adger, Ala.

United Mine Workers' Journal, September 1, 1898.

14. MISREPRESENTATION

Benj. and Jack Anderson being duly sworn, upon their oath say they are residents of Birmingham, Ala., resided at Birmingham for 11 years; occupation coal miners; say that on Monday Aug. 22, 1898, they were approached by two white men and one colored man who represented that they were from Pana, Ill.; that most of the miners had gone to the war for two years; that there was a new mine opening there and a great demand for labor, and they wanted 150 men; and there was no trouble there; said about eight or nine months ago there had been a little trouble but that was all settled; affiants said they were working . . . but on being told that they could make from $3 to $5 per day were induced to give up their jobs and go to Pana.

Victor Hicken, "The Virden and Pana Mine Wars of 1898," *Journal of the Illinois State Historical Society 52 (Summer, 1959): 267.*

15. NEGROES IN STRIKERS' PLACES

The Arrival of 200 Alabama Miners May Cause a Crisis at Pana

PANA, Ill., Aug. 25--Sheriff Cobb assembled 125 deputies today, swore all in and gave them instructions to reassemble, armed with Winchester, and meet a number of negroes expected to arrive from Alabama to work here in the coal mines. Ten negroes arrived at Pana last night to take the place of white miners here who have been on a strike here for several months. The negroes were escorted to the city limits by a committee of miners and induced to leave town. The strikers are reinforced by union miners from over the state.

The strikers assembled today in large bodies awaiting the arrival of the Alabama negroes. The train arrived in Pana from Birmingham, Ala., with 200 negroes, but was rushed through the city to the Springside coal mine, outside the city limits, where the negroes were unloaded under the guard of deputy sheriffs.

Several hundred miners were at the Union depot to meet the negroes and talk with them, but were unable to do so. All the grounds at the Springside mines are heavily guarded, and no citizens are permitted to pass the lines.

The strike leaders have requested Governor Tanner to take action regarding the mining efficiency of the negroes, and he has answered that he will send state mine inspectors to examine the men.[95]

The American (Coffeyville, Kansas), August 27, 1898.

16. AFFAIRS AT PANA

The effort to start the Pana, Ill., mines with imported southern colored labor seems to have been a failure, and we sincerely hope it will continue to be. We are sure that all that can legitimately be done will be done by the state authorities of Illinois to prevent an undesirable, incompetent, illegal class of employees from being employed in any part of that state. This is proven by the action of Governor Tanner in sending the Secretary of the Bureau of Statistics, Hon. David Ross, down to Pana, to make an investigation of conditions there and determine whether or not the military were wanted. Secretary Ross made his report, and the militia are at their homes. He (Ross) it will be observed by reading Scaife's letter, instructed Mine Inspector Rutledge to see that the requirements of the two years' mining experience law was fully complied with and as a consequence many of the imported men can only work as laborers for the more experienced ones. In addition to the above we publish a clipping from there which shows that the National Vice President and State Secretary-Treasurer as well as Sub-district Presidents Cartwright and Topham, were, and we presume are, actively engaged in the work of assisting the Pana miners, with the best advice and with the sinews of war as far as their limited resources will permit, so that it is safe to say the ground will be stubbornly contested and every advantage will be quickly seized to gain the victory for the men, who should not have been compelled to suspend at last not since they made a reasonable proposition and which proposition was endorsed and recommended as the price to be paid by the State Board of Arbitration who also investigated the trouble. The clipping referred to reads as follows:

Contrary to predictions no lawlessness is resorted to by the striking white miners, although they have been reinforced by the arrival of numbers of union miners from over the state. John Mitchell, of Spring Valley, Ill., National Vice President of the United Mine Workers; John W. Russell, of Danville, State Vice President; W. D. Ryan, State Secretary-Treasurer; President Cartwright of Springfield District; and President Topham, of the Danville District are here advising with the strikers.[96]

The officers express the opinion that the remaining blacks, some fifty in all, will leave the city in a few days after learning the real situation. Mine owner Penwell stated today, however, that it is the intention of the local coal operator's association to have shipped in 150 more negroes from Alabama as soon as possible. The sixty-five negroes who left the Springside mine camps yesterday have notified their friends at Birmingham, Woodward and Bessemer, Ala., of the conditions existing here, advising them to have nothing to do with the propositions to come to Pana. The union miners sent 37 of the negroes to Chicago last night in a special car, and 20 back to Alabama, while several walked out of town in different directions on the railroads during the night.

State Mine Inspector Walter Rutledge, of Alton, arrived here today and examined the Alabama negroes remaining at the Springside mine. He found only a part of them to be competent miners.

It will be noticed by reading the "dodger" sent us by Sullivan, of Adger, Ala., and which was plucked by him from a telegraph pole near that place, and which we reproduce in another column, that it is a "decoy duck" from beginning to end; that the real destination in Illinois is not given, and that many other items of information which would want to be known to a person seeking employment for an honest, honorable purpose before he would consent to emigrate even though his railroad fare was cheap and ample time given to reimburse the company for the advance to pay it with. It is evident that the originators depended for success not so much on the promises held out as they did upon the ignorance of the parties whom they wished to secure through deception to enable them to defeat the striking miners.

We anticipate that more trouble will be experienced in securing black legs in Alabama than formerly, if, indeed, they can be secured at all among the experienced mine workers, such as will be permitted to do mining in Illinois, for the reason that President Ratchford has notified State President Fairley, of Alabama, and Board Member Dilcher, who is also in that state, of the efforts being made to have colored men from that state go to Illinois. The following message was sent to the officials named:

Indianapolis, Aug. 26, 1898

To W. R. Fairley, Pratt City, Ala:
Negro miners are being imported from your State to the striking districts of Illinois. Those who arrived have refused to work, and have joined the union or left the state. Further importation must be stopped by yourself and Dilcher. Illinois miners are striking against reduction since April 1st.
M. D. RATCHFORD.

From reading the above it will be seen that it will be no easy task to start the Pana mines with imported labor of any kind, and we believe that the strikers will come out victorious. Natural requirements will soon add strength to their position by creating a greater demand for coal, and this fact is recognized and appreciated by the mine owners, hence their persistent effort to start the mines at any and all hazards. Idleness means loss of money at any time, but in a month or so later the loss will become greater and the demand of such a character that they can not afford to ignore it because of maintaining an unwarrantable attitude toward scale prices.

United Mine Workers' Journal, September 1, 1898.

17. MISUNDERSTOOD "DODGER"

Some misunderstanding has occurred because of our publication last week of a dodger furnished us by J. J. Sullivan, of Adger, Ala., concerning the importation of negro miners to Illinois. Just why the matter should be misunderstood we are unable to say. The object of the circular was clearly stated by Mr. Sullivan and its deceptive character was pointed out by us, and for fear that any would be deceived we concluded that it would be the proper thing to do to publish it just as it was sent to us and to draw attention to its iniquity in our columns. We trust that the circular and Mr. Sullivan and our remarks pertaining thereto will be read by all, for we believe that no mine worker so doing will be induced to go to any part of Illinois to work during the pending trouble.

United Mine Workers' Journal, September 8, 1898.

18. EX-CONVICTS POOR MINERS

The ex-convicts are not a success as coal diggers by any means. The

Springside mine, according to the Beacon Light, a paper published in the
interest of the conspirators against the peace and welfare of Pana, worked
four weeks and hoisted thirty-five cars. Fifty-four ex-convicts were employed all this time, so that it will readily be seen that the coal is costing
them a trifle over 40 cents per ton. Penwells have worked eight days and
have averaged one car per day with fifty scabs, nine of which are "white
niggers." From this it will be seen that beyond aggravating the men who
are locked out, the coal they produce cuts no figure.

United Mine Workers' Journal, September 29, 1898.

19.   AFFAIRS AT PANA

We think the Governor can and will find means to right affairs at Pana
and restore peace and tranquility to the troubled community. That such is
needed the following clipping from a Pana paper . . . proves:

"Saturday night will long be remembered in Pana, not from the fact of
riots or anything of the kind, for on that score everything is quiet, but
from the indignities that are being heaped upon our citizens by not only
the sheriff and his deputies, but by the black convict negroes themselves.
These negroes have, by their treatment received from the hands of the operators and the officers, become so insulting in their actions that the same
state of affairs would not be allowed in any other city but Pana. It does
seem to us that an indignant public should rise up en masse and put a stop
to the present state of affairs.

It is patent to all good citizens that the sole object of the operators,
aided and abetted by the sheriff, is to create a riot if possible and in
that event they hope to induce the Governor to send troops here, but so far
their efforts in that direction have all been for naught.

Negroes continue to parade the streets both day and night and insult
both ladies and gentlemen. These negroes are heavily armed and if any reply
is made by the citizens to these insults the negroes will run their hands to
their hip pockets with the words: "We will kill all of you white trash if
you fool with us." Is there another community, unless it is Rosemond, which
would tolerate this state of affairs for a day? This state of things can be
laid at the door of Overholt, Penwell, Broehl and Sheriff Coburn, who are
backed up by three or four of Pana's wealthy men, who if it comes to the
worst can leave town and who cares no more for the town than a rat does for
an ant. Our best citizens are jerked up and put under bonds for not serving
as deputies where no riots exist. The grand jury has been prevailed upon to
bring in indictments against parties who have violated no law and but for the
inference of three or four of our citizens would have been compelled to go to
Taylorville and be locked up in jail over Sunday, for that was the scheme,
but it did not work. How long Pana is going to stand this we do not know.

"Last evening while Ex-Alderman Ed Molz was going home he was stopped by
two big black niggers and when resenting their insults, they knocked Mr.
Molz down and then left him. Again while Louis Broadman was passing Penwell's
he was ordered to get "out of the way, you d--d cripple, by a big black
scoundrel, as the same time kicking at his crutches to injure the boy. The
cripple was bothering no one, and the black buck's actions entitled him to
arrest, which should have been done."

"At the time the insult to young Broadman was offered, nearly all of the
negro convicts had been brought to his place of business by George V. Penwell
himself, so it is rumored, for the purpose of inciting a riot, and yet during
all of the time there was a line of deputies in close to the front of the
store building and not a hand was raised by them to interfere with the black
brutes. The only reason that there was no riot was through the efforts of A.
B. Corman, Sr., Mose Finerock and Officers Smith and Lee, who went among the
outraged union miners and spoke words of wisdom and cautioned them to hold
themselves in check. We believe in equal rights to all when used in a proper manner, but right now it seems to be all one-sided. If a riot could be
started by the operators and sheriff that fact would relieve them of all

responsibility for the payment of the big deputy bill.

While Sheriff Coburn and deputies were marching their prisoners to dinner Saturday the biggest strike of the season occurred when it was learned that arrangements had been made by the sheriff for dinner at the New Grand Bakery and Restaurant. The prisoners gave notice that they would go without anything to eat for a week before they would eat in any "scab" shop. They were marched back to the city hall and later given a dinner by State Secretary W. D. Ryan of the U.M.W. of A., and still later while Sheriff Coburn was in Baker's saloon taking a drink he stated that when he ordered the dinner at the New Grand he did not think anything about it being a non-union shop.

"As we go to press all is quiet."

United Mine Workers' Journal, September 22, 1898.

20. CARRY THEIR POINT

Virden Miners Refuse to Permit Negroes to Land There

Men Brought Here and Fall Into John Hunter's Hands--President of United Mine
Workers is Eloquent and Prevails on Men to Return

The negroes from Birmingham, Ala., who were to take the places of the striking miners of the Chicago-Virden company at Virden, are in this city and are in the hands of the United Mine Workers of America. A special train carrying 100 negroes, including sixteen women, arrived in Virden early yesterday morning, but the track was lined with striking miners, armed to the teeth, and no attempt to stop them was made.

The train was run to this city and it was met there by a number of labor men, among them President John Hunter of the United Mine Workers of America. Several speeches were made and the men were induced to leave the cars and march to the executive mansion where it was expected Governor Tanner would address them. The Governor had not been notified of the coming of the miners and he was not at the mansion when they arrived. Colonel Tanner appeared for him and briefly thanked the miners for the visit, but he said he would not discuss the mining situation in the absence of the Governor.

President Hunter then induced the negroes to visit the headquarters of the United Mine Workers where several addresses were made, urging them not to take the places of the Virden strikers. The negroes were fed and the president assured them that they would be furnished transportation to their homes if they would desert Operator Lukens and stand by the union. This the negroes voted to do, not a vote being cast against the proposition.

The Alabama miners claim that they were deceived into coming to Illinois with false representations made by the men who hired them, and by circulars, which stated that they could make as high as $4 a day in the Virden mine. They say they knew nothing of the labor trouble at Virden until they came to the town and found the railroad tracks lined with armed men. They were very indignant at Thomas Hayward, who came with them as their leader, and there was talk of lynching him. Hayward insisted that he had acted in good faith not knowing that there was a strike on at Virden.

The negroes, numbering over one hundred, left Birmingham about midnight Thursday night. They were in special coaches attached to a regular train. The trip was a slow one to East St. Louis and that point was not reached until Saturday night. The train was side-tracked at East St. Louis and it was long after midnight before the start for Virden was made. It was shortly after 6 o'clock when the train reached Virden.

It was the intention to side track the train on a switch near the coal mine at Virden and march the men and women to the houses situated along the siding leading from the mine, but the miners of Virden knew for two days that negroes were coming from the South to work and they were on the alert for them. For the last two days and nights the miners were on watch and were

determined that the imported miners should not get off the train.
When the news that they were coming was first made known, a meeting of
the miners was held at Virden and it was decided that they would use no
violence but would approach the negroes in a friendly way, but the miners
armed themselves with clubs and some carried revolvers. The men stood
armed all through the heavy rain of Saturday night, awaiting the arrival of
the train for they were confident that it would reach there during the
night. The train consisted of a baggage car and two coaches and it was
sighted in the early morning. The engineer had been given orders not to
stop at the depot but to make a running switch and back in at the mine.
As the train neared the depot the detectives who were on it looked out
and on seeing the mob lined along the track, concluded it was not policy to
carry out the original plan. The engineer had the train under control and
when he saw the crowd, he began looking back for signals. Directly two
detectives gave him a forward signal and he opened his throttle. The train
darted past the switch and was run to Auburn. Here a consultation was held
between the detectives and the representatives of the mine on board and it
was decided to proceed to this city. The train was started and there was
no further trouble until this city was reached.
A coal miner from Virden came to the city on the first train and spent
the day here. In conversation with a representative of the Journal he
describes the situation at Virden when the train went through as follows:
"The miners had been informed that the negroes were coming and were
determined they should not get off the train. We had agreed not to use any
violence but to argue with them and make clear the real situation. There
were over three hundred miners in the crowd when the train reached the city.
We were lined up along the railroad track. We saw that the train was reducing speed and we were preparing to surround it when it stopped. We saw
several men poke their heads from the platforms and give the engineer a
signal to go ahead. The train then started out at full speed and passed the
crowd like a shot out of a cannon. We then were at a loss to know what the
intentions of the railroad people were. One of the men telephoned to Auburn
and found out that the train left there for Springfield. We then knew we
had gained our point and there was general rejoicing among the men."
As the train was nearing Virden a number of men in the cars looked out
of the windows and on seeing the crowd, they became greatly excited. In one
of the coaches there was great turmoil until one of the detectives assured
the men that there was no danger of any trouble and that they would be protected. One of the negroes said:
"I can tell you I was might scared this morning when I looked out dat
window and saw all them men there, I wished I was back in old Birmingham.
I dun thought we was all gwine to be hurt. I tell you I was might glad when
dat train started goin' fast."

THEY REACHED SPRINGFIELD

The train bearing the negroes arrived at Springfield at 8 o'clock. The
train was side-tracked at the freight depot on North Third street and the
presence of the miners soon became known to the leaders of the local labor
unions. The men were in charge of Thomas Hayward, who had hired them at the
insistence of the Virden operators. He was at a loss to know what to do with
the men when he got them here and it was an easy matter for the officials of
the United Mine Workers of America to secure control of the men.
Will Fannon of the Black Diamond shaft was one of the first of the union
men to learn of the arrival of the negroes and he posted off to the Collins
House to notify President Hunter. In the meantime President Hinman, of the
State Federation of Labor, had heard of the coming of the negroes and he was
at the depot when Hunter came up. With Mr. Hunter was J. A. Crawford, the
former State President of the United Mine Workers, and George Dunman, a labor
leader of Lisbon, O., who was in the city consulting Hunter.
President Hunter was almost out of breath when he reached the depot, for
he had run almost all of the way from the hotel to the depot. Pale with excitement, he pushed his way through the crowd to the train and addressed the
men in the cars. "I would like to talk to you men," he said. "I want to say
that we do not come here to mob you or to injure you in any way. We only want
to talk to you and reason with you. We would like for you to come from the
cars so that we can talk to you. I will give you my word as State President

of the Illinois United Mine Workers that you will not be hurt. We will see
that you are protected. Only give us a chance to explain the condition of
affairs at Virden."

The benevolent Scotch face of the labor leader beamed on the crowd of
frightened negroes in the cars and reassured them. "Come on out," urged
the President again. "I give you my word that you will not be harmed. We
are your friends. All we want to do is to prevent you from making a mistake
that you will regret. We believe you are honest men and that you have been
imposed on in coming north."

The appeal had its effect and there was a general movement toward the
car doors. A large crowd had gathered by this time, but it was a peaceable
body of churchgoers and the negroes seeing that there was no danger of a
hostile demonstration, began to file out and gather around the President of
the miners' organization. One of them, who appeared to be a sort of leader,
said were ready to hear what Mr. Hunter had to say.

Then the veteran agitator made one of his characteristic speeches. He
reviewed the history of the trouble at Pana and Virden in his own way, told
of the struggles of the Illinois miners in pathetic appeal to the negroes
to return to their homes. He was satisfied, he said, that they had been
deceived in coming here and he assured the men that if they would stand by
the union, it would protect them and see that they got home safely. President Hunter was careful to avoid threats and his speech took well. When he
concluded, there were murmurs of approval from the crowd.

J. A. Crawford followed up this advantage in short order and supplemented what his brother Scot had said with a further appeal to the negroes
to stand by the union. He told the men that preparations had been made at
Virden to house them near the mines like so many cattle, where they would
have to live as chattel slaves shunned and despised by their fellows. He
hoped, he said, that there was too much manhood about them to submit to
this and he insisted that the only thing for them to do was to return home.

OPERATORS ARE SCORED

Crawford vigourously scored the coal operators and told the men that if
they stood by them it would be to their undoing. They had deceived them in
getting them to Illinois, he said, and they would not hesitate to further
deceive them after they reached Virden. Once they were within the stockade
he said, they would be at the mercy of masters as hateful as the slave
drivers of the South and their condition would be no better than that of their
fathers in slavery days.

By this time the negroes were showing unmistakable signs of wavering to
the side of the strike leaders and Hayward made a feeble effort to stem the
current of opinion. He insisted that he had acted in good faith and that
the conditions he had promised would be complied with if the men went to
Virden. Hayward denied that he knew anything of the labor trouble when he
induced the men to come to Virden and he said that he believed there would be
no trouble. The coal mine people, he insisted, were reliable and he felt that
every agreement made with him would be carried out. He was in favor of giving
them a chance, anyhow, he said, and he appealed to the men to stand by their
new employers. They were in a strange country, he reasoned, and they knew
nothing of the merits of the controversy at Virden other than what they were
told by men they did not know.

State President Hunter closed the speech-making at the depot. He declared that he had correctly outlined the condition of affairs at Pana and
he defied anyone to successfully contradict what he had said. The miners of
Virden, he insisted, were in the right and their cause was a just one. For
the negroes to take their places, he said, would rob them of places they
were entitled to and this he did not believe the Alabama men wanted to do.
More than that he said that for the negroes to do so would mean the demorali-
zation of the local business throughout Illinois and would result in a
general cut of wages and hardship on every miner in the State.

President Hunter said that if any of the miners doubted what he said,
he would refer them to the Governor of Illinois. It was evident that the
Alabama men had heard of the Governor's friendship for the negro soldiers of
Illinois, for the mention of his name was received with approval. If you will
go with me," he said, "I will take you to Governor John R. Tanner. He is a
man you can rely on. He will tell you the exact condition of affairs at Virden.

He is a fair man and you can believe what he tells you. If he says that I
have not told you the truth, then I will have nothing more to say."

At Mr. Hunter's suggestion, a vote was taken by the negroes on the
question of going to see the governor. Every man was in favor of the proposition and so a procession was formed with Hunter at its head. Directed
by the labor leader, the crowd marched Madison street to Fifth street, and
then south to the Governor's mansion. Many of them had bundles and they
presented a novel appearance as they marched into the grounds of the executive mansion and lined up in front of the north entrance.

GOVERNOR NOT AT HOME

President Hunter acted as spokesman and informed the surprised inmates
of the mansion of the purpose of the visit. Governor Tanner was not at home
and Colonel Tanner appeared in his stead. He asked Mr. Hunter to notify the
crowd of the Governor's absence, but the President insisted that he talk to
the Negroes. "They might not believe me," he said, "and they will be better
satisfied if you explain the situation to them."

Then Colonel Tanner addressed the men. "Gentlemen," he said, "President
Hunter, of the United Mine Workers of Illinois, has informed me that you have
called here for the purpose of seeing the Governor and having him make a talk
to you about the condition of affairs at Virden. I regret very much that he
is not here and I am not able to say when he will return. I can only say
under the circumstances that if you will follow the instructions of Mr. Hunter
you will be taken care of properly while you are here."

After briefly thanking them for the visit, Colonel Tanner turned into
the mansion and the miners decided to follow Hunter. He asked them to fall
in line again and this they did the women leading. "I always like to see
ladies in the lead," said the gallant old Scot, and with a polite bow he urged
the women to come forward and occupy the place of honor. Then the word was
given and the strange procession started on its way to Allen's Hall, the headquarters of the United Mine Workers.

The march from the mansion was from the west entrance to Capitol Avenue,
east to Seventh Street and North to the hall at Seventh and Washington streets.
A large crowd had congregated by this time and it was augmented by people returning from church, so that several hundred people were following the negroes
when they went up Seventh street. There was some cheering as the men and
women trudged along the street, but most of the crowd appeared to be actuated
by idle curiosity and there was little demonstration.

HUNTER WAS ELATED

President Hunter was in high spirits when he got the negroes into the
hall, and he proceeded to make them a speech. He said that the men were now
to decide whether they would stand by him or by Operator Lukens of the Virden
mine. "We will stand by de ole man," shouted one enthusiast and Hunter replied, "Well, we will take a vote; all who are in favor of the union will
stand."

Instantly a hundred men were on their feet and then the president, as a
matter of form, asked those who favored the operator to stand. One man
arose, but there was a howl of disapproval from his companions and he subsided. He explained that he did not understand and supposed he was voting
in favor of deserting Lukins.

After this several speeches were made by representatives of the local
sub-districts, all of the speakers urging the Alabama men to stand by the
union. Then lunch was served. It consisted of crackers and cakes and a
half-barrel of beer. Later a more substantial meal was served. It consisted
of beef, bread and butter and vegetables, together with coffee. President
Hunter gave orders that the miners be given all they wanted to eat and said
the union would stand good for the cost.

There was one sick man among the negroes, Doc. Allen, of Birmingham,
and Hunter ordered that he be taken to St. John's hospital and cared for.
Allen is suffering with malarial fever and is a very sick man. He was slightly
ill when he left Birmingham and he suffered with headaches all the way to
Springfield. He made the march to the Governor's mansion, but after he
reached the hall became faint. It is believed that others of the party will
become ill after the excitement of their present position wears off.

The miners are in bad shape as regards clothing. Evidently they have
had little work at home, although most of them say they left positions to
come to Virden, and they are entirely without funds. Altogether they are a
sorry looking lot. The women, as well as the men, are poorly clad but most
of them appeared to be in good spirits.

THEY WERE INDIGNANT

After the negroes had listened to the speeches of the officers of the
miners' union and had been assured that they would be protected and cared
for, they began to feel that they had been the victims of misplaced confidence and many of them were loud in their denunciations of the men who had
prevailed upon them to leave their homes and come here. They said the agent
for the company was in Birmingham several days and distributed circulars
that read as follows:

"WANTED--One hundred and seventy-five good colored miners for Virden,
Illinois. Pay in full every two weeks, 30 cents per ton, run of mines. Miners
can make from $2.75 to $4.00 per day. Want twenty skilled drivers, pay $1.75
per day; fifteen good top men and outside laborers, $1.35 per day; fifteen
good timber men, $1.75 per day; two first-class blacksmiths, $2.25 per day;
thirty-five experienced miners with families; eight first-class machine
runners, $2.00 per day; ten boys for trappers, 75 cents per day. Coal is
seven to eight feet thick. Twenty cagers, $1.75 per day; no charge for black-
smith; no commissions; want nothing but first class miners; all coal weighed
on top. Bring your tools well tied up if you wish to carry them. Will leave
Birmingham Thursday night at 8 o'clock, September 22. Transportation will be
furnished and ample time given you to pay the same. For information call at
1905 Third avenue."

The negroes say that they were told before they left home that they would
be paid 30 cents a ton but when they got on the train they heard they would
get twenty cents per ton. They claim that they were informed also that the
strike had been ended for the past six months and that the men had gone to war.
They were also told that there was no danger after they had been landed at the
coal mine and that they could go to work at once. One young negro, with
scarcely enough clothes on to cover him said:

"This is pretty tough. I wanted to come here and work right off as I
only got 90 cents a day for driving. Now I have lost my job at home and don't
know what to do. I guess all I can do is stick with the rest of the crowd.
These miners here are all right and I wish I belonged to the union."

WILL BE SENT HOME

All the negroes will be sent back to Birmingham as soon as arrangements
can be made for their transportation. This was decided upon by the leaders
of the miners' union last night. The negroes are all anxious to get back
home and when they signified their willingness to return without going to
work, the union took steps to provide for their transportation. While the
miners will send them home, they will also endeavor to have Mr. Lukins pay
for their transportation.

United Mine Workers' Journal, September 29, 1898.

21. LIVE WIRES PLACED AROUND THE STOCKADE KEEP MEN IN PRISON

Thursday morning at 8 o'clock one of the colored men, Jim Walker of the
group who left Birmingham a short time ago for Pana, Ill., walked into the
ADVOCATE office. He confessed that he was a prodigal but was willing to
return without having a drop of blood spilt on his account.

Jim gives a blood-curdling account of his experiences in the coal regions
of the . . . Virden coal company which had deceived him. Most all the miners
had gone to the war. It looked to him as if all the soldiers were stockaded
at Pana when he got there. Company tried to switch them off into a stock yard
but were thwarted in their purpose by the miners. Alabama Negroes were
promised 30 cents per ton to go to Pana but when they got there were told

that they were to receive only 20 cents per ton.

Jim Walker says large stock yards are built and once a negro gets in there he belongs to the company. Several guards are on duty continuously and wires heavily charged with electricity are run all around the stocks so as to make escape impossible. He who attempts to escape is a dead man.

Jim says the miners are orderly and as clever a lot of men as he ever met. Compliments President Hunter very highly. Says when the negroes learned the truth, that the miners were trying to force the company to carry out the contract with them, the Alabama delegation joined the strikers and refused to work.

As soon as the company learned of the action of the negroes, says Jim, it sent a representative to the sheriff to prefer charges against President Hunter of intimidation. A deputy sheriff was sent to the meeting hall of the miners, where a conference with the negroes was being held, and notified President Hunter of the charges that had been preferred against him. In presence of the deputy sheriff and the men whom it was claimed by the company had been intimidated by the miners of Pana, President Hunter arose and asked the imported also, if they had come to that hall of their own free will and accord or if they had been forced to come there by threats of miners, force or other undue influence of Mr. Hunter or his agent or agents. The negroes, to a man, declared that the company had allured them to Pana by misrepresentations and for that reason, they had refused to work, and that they were in the miners' hall because they were in sympathy with them.

Whereupon the deputy sheriff declared that the intimidation was on the other side and left the hall.

Birmingham Labor Advocate, Oct. 1, 1898.

22.   SLOW TO GO AWAY AGAIN

The negroes who went to Pana with the exception of one or two who remained to accept work at other callings, have returned to their homes and will be slow to go away again until they know definitely what they are doing. They say there are a few negroes in the stocks who will stay there the balance of their days unless they are rescued by process of law by outside friends.

Birmingham Labor Advocate, October 1, 1898.

23.   TIMELY ADDRESS

R. L. RUFFIN OF BIRMINGHAM TO THE COLORED MINERS AND MINE LABORERS OF THE BIRMINGHAM DISTRICT--SAYS NEGROES SHOULD STAY AWAY FROM PANA, ILL.

Following address was received last week too late for publication:

To the Colored Miners and Mine Laborers of the Birmingham District: Dear Sirs: In reply to the several communications received by me, both written and personal, with regard to the recent exportation of miners and mine laborers from this section and their location in Pana, Illinois, and other sections of the country. I think it a very unwise thing to do; and it is not in keeping with the interest of labor and common sense. Besides, it is an infringement upon the rights of labor and a trespass in the premises of a brother workman with no permanent advantage to the colored miner.

I have made some close examinations into the matter and find the follow facts and conditions:

The miners at Pana, Ill., are asking for a legitimate and equitable sca price for digging coal which should be given them. This district had the go fortune to settle at the last annual meeting of operators and miners in this

city and we feel justly proud for men who were instrumental in bringing
about a peaceful adjustment of a very grave question peculiar to their
interest. The same presents itself to their brother workmen in Illinois.
To be the means of depriving them of actual necessities is within itself a
crime of treason against labor and at the same time disqualifies them from
any just consideration whatever as a friend of the daily toilers or supporters of law and order and good government. . . .

We have noticed recently a petition to the governor of Illinois published in the St. Louis Globe-Democrat, Sept., signed by R. H. Pringleton,
J. T. Shaw, and T. P. Haraldson, in which they pray the governor of Illinois
for protection and sight many reasons for the same.

With reference to the above we wish to state that the petitioners with
the exception of T. P. Haraldson, are very familiar in Jefferson county, Ala.
Neither of them ever dug coal or are in any way connected with any labor
interests. Neither did they identify themselves with any regular occupied
class of labor in this section and have been residents here for fifteen years
and we do not believe either of them today have mined a single ton of coal
since they found it to advantage to go to Pana. Mr. Haraldson is familiar
on immigration topics of negro labor and needs no comment.

J. T. Shaw and R. H. Pringleton are plausible talkers and were carried
there by Haraldson to be used as an instrument to persuade the colored miners
from this section.

The negro should not intermingle to break down wages but should stay
away from Pana and other sections where he is not wanted until a strike and
will not be equally retained after the strike is settled. He should act as
an example of manhood and not one of a scullion, for if anybody needs more
money for his labor it is the negro.

Hoping this will suffice, I remain, respectfully,

R. L. Ruffin

Birmingham Labor Advocate, October 8, 1898.

24. DESERTED BY THEIR EMPLOYERS

The two carloads of negroes from Gilchrist who were held in the yards
here two days last week were deserted by their employers and left without
food or money. All the victims had was a few crackers. The railroad company
finally hauled the negroes back to Mercer county and dumped them off at Aledo.
These negroes were imported from the south to take the place of strikers.
Now they are out of a job, broke, and the Mercer county taxpayers can care for
them, and of course they will like this arrangement. As for the employer,
who by means of a bogus contract evades the responsibility of caring for the
dependent negroes and their families, no one is concerned. He was 'running
his own business,' which, as many assert, is not the business of the public.

Galesburg (Illinois) Labor News, October 8, 1898.

25. ON THE BANKS OF THE RAILROAD

(To the tune of "On the Banks of the Wabash.")

Away down in our homes in Alabama,
Us coons we were contented to stay.
'Till Mr. Lukens come and told us what he would give us
If we would come with him to Virden far away.
When we arrived in Virden Sunday morning
We found that things were not what Lukens say,
The miners were all lined up along the railroad

And you bet us coons was glad to get away.

CHORUS

The moon is shining brightly along the railroad,
And the miners are situated there to stay.
The candle lights are gleaming in the stockade;
Mr. Lukens thinks he's having things his way.
He told us the miners were all in Cuba,
And there wasn't only eight men there to stay;
He didn't tell us what a pen he'd put us into,
When he got us down to Virden far away.
Then good-by to Mr. Lukens, we are bound for Alabama
     there to stay;
If Mr. Lukens ever comes to Alabama
We will show him what us coons will do that day.

United Mine Workers' Journal, October 13, 1898.

26.   AFFAIRS AT VIRDEN AND PANA

In the absence of direct information and depending for our news from Virden and Pana upon the reports as contained in the dispatches to the "dailies," we can see no material change in the situation at the above places from that reported last week. It appears it's a stand off between the miners and operators and so long as that condition remains the mine workers must be regarded as at least holding their own, if not actually gaining an advantage. We believe that the action recently taken by the Alabama miners' division of the Afro-American Labor and Protective Association, will be productive of much good, for the reason that the colored men who are being duped and deceived into going to Virden and Pana and elsewhere by slick-tongued white scoundrels who pose as labor employing agents, and too often by fraud, deception and misrepresentation, induce the colored men to leave their sure employment and homes, to go to places where the representation made to them partakes largely of the character of Utopia, but, which when they arrive there more resembles in actual experiences "Hades," than anything they formerly had seen or heard of, for this reason, as before said, we believe that the action of the African Industrial and Protective League will do much good in restraining the colored people from going to places where their presence and their labor is only wanted for the purpose of enabling unjust and unscrupulous employers to reduce wages and destroy conditions of employment at the points to which they desire them to emigrate, or be imported to.

President Fairley, of the Alabama miners, sends us the following account of and the whereas and resolutions passed at a recent meeting of the league before referred to:

"At a meeting of the executive committee of the Coal Miners' Division of the Afro-American Labor and Protective Association was held last night at Jackson Hall, Birmingham.

"It was called for the purpose of taking action in the matter of colored miners going from this district to Pana, Ill., to replace striking miners.

"The committee was called to order by R. L. Ruffin, President of the association, who made a full statement of present conditions at Pana. He dwelt upon the perilous situation in which the colored miners had placed themselves up there. He was surprised that any colored miner had been beguiled into going to Pana. He urged that immediate steps be taken to discourage the movement. The association should show to the world that the negr is not the enemy but the friend of labor.

"A committee on resolutions, consisting of Brooks, Mayfield, Swinney, Hutchinson, Alexander, Thomas, Starks and McCray, was appointed.

"Pending its report speeches were made by several of the committeemen.

"The committee submitted the following resolutions:

"Whereas, The miners of Pana, Ill., and vicinity have asked a fair, legitimate and living scale of prices for digging coal; and

"Whereas, We believe such demands are just and realize that a reduction in wages at Pana means to this district a reduction of wages or the shut down of our mills, furnaces, mines, etc; and,

"Whereas, A large number of colored miners are being ignorantly carried to take the places of the so-called striking miners; therefore, be it

"Resolved, That we deplore the conditions now prevailing at Pana, and that we condemn the action of the colored miners in going to Pana, remaining at Pana or participating in any manner to aid the operators in carrying out their tyrannical designs against labor.

"Resolved, That we use every effort to intercept the movement of negro miners from this section to Pana, and that we join our efforts and arguments with J. M. Hunter, W. R. Fairley and others to relieve Pana mines of all colored laborers carried there and retained there by reason of the strike.

"Resolved, That R. L. Ruffin, President of the Afro-American Labor and Protective Association, is hereby authorized and requested to confer with all labor leaders and friends of labor as to the carrying out of this plan; that a copy of these resolutions be sent to Presidents J. M. Hunter and W. R. Fairley and others, and that a conference be sought with President Hunter at the earliest possible date."

From the above it will be seen that the negro miners are in earnest in their efforts to prevent the further importation of colored men from Alabama to Illinois, and we opine that an organized body of that kind will be very influential in establishing their desires. In the meantime let the whites stand firm as a stone wall. Scabbing is just as vicious, deplorable and damnable when practiced by a white as it is when done by a colored man. What is villainy in the one cannot and is not commendable in the other. Scabbing when done by anyone should be unmercifully condemned, and the scab of any color, creed or nationality execrated by his fellow men. The crimes of Judas Iscariot, who betrayed his Master, and of Benedict Arnold, who betrayed his countrymen, are not more execrable and do not deserve more condemnation and punishment than does that of the scab, who, while their fellows are striving by a suspension of work, to secure greater pay and better conditions of employment, come in and like thieves in the night, rob them of employment and in order to do so, must live like cattle in pens or prisoners in a jail, inside of a stockade, while they are doing the dirty work of an employer, who in nine cases out of ten, discharges them after they have served his purpose.

United Mine Workers' Journal, October 13, 1898.

27. THE SITUATION

At Pana, Illinois and Washington As Told in the Daily Papers

WE GIVE THE REPORTS WITHOUT KNOWING AS TO THEIR ACCURACY, BUT REPRODUCE THEM FOR THE BENEFIT OF MINE WORKERS WHO DEPEND ON THE JOURNAL FOR THEIR NEWS FROM THE POINTS MENTIONED

PANA, Ill., Sept. 28--. Striking union coal miners and imported colored men engaged in a pitched battle in the main street of this city tonight. Several hurried shots were exchanged.

No one was wounded in the ranks of the union men. The colored men were driven from the city to the stockades carrying with them, it is believed, a number of wounded comrades. One of the colored men is reported to have died soon after reaching the stockade. Desultory firing continues at midnight in the vicinity of the stockades. The trouble which has been narrowly averted between the striking coal miners of this city and colored men imported from the south to work the mines, was precipitated at 8:30 o'clock this evening.

As usual the colored men, from the stockades at the Springside and Penwell mines, were making demonstrations on Second and Locust streets, the principal business streets of the city, by parading heavily armed.

The union miners were in session at their hall where a Chicago labor leader was speaking. One of the negroes appeared at the foot of the miners hall and engaged in a quarrel with a union white miner. Officer Samuel Smith immediately arrested the black, and was escorting him to jail, when he was closed in on by a posse of negroes, who, pointing their revolvers at Smith, threatened to kill him if he did not release his prisoner. Smith continued on his way to jail with his prisoner. Union miners and others meanwhile went to Smith's assistance, and the negroes were driven back. Smith took the prisoner to Operator George V. Penwell's store and upon Penwell's standing for the negro's fine he was released.

Before Smith had released his prisoner, however, the negro posse had been recruited and assumed a threatening attitude toward the white men. David McGavic, leader of the union miners, clubbed one of the blacks over the head with a revolver, it is said. For half a block McGavic forced the negroes to retreat and several shots were fired.

The negroes retreated double quick to their stockades, secured rifles, returned to Locust street, and challenged the miners for a fight, the opposing forces lined up on the street, the negroes with Winchesters, and the miners with shotguns, rifles, and revolvers. Neighboring business houses were immediately closed, lights extinguished, and citizens generally sought their homes. At the word of command firing commenced. The first volley it is said, came from the negroes. The union men responded with a volley, and heavy firing continued for five minutes. Much of the shooting was wild and entirely harmless to the white men, who finally drove their enemies in full retreat to the stockades. The negroes are thought to have carried several men with them, and one is reported dead.

A second encounter between white and blacks occurred twenty minutes after the first battle near the Penwell stockade, but the firing was scattered, and it is not believed to have been a serious engagement. The miners had full charge of the business streets at midnight. Desultory rifle reports could be heard from the Penwell and Springside stockades, but no person would venture into the streets near the mines, and very few are loitering about the business or residence sections. The union miners say the battle of tonight is only a foretaste of what may be expected to follow. They blame Operator Penwell for the trouble, and say they will tomorrow swear out warrants charging him with inciting tonight's riot.

Governor Tanner will be asked to send militia to protect property in this city and to remove the negroes.

TOWER HILL, Ill., Sept. 30.--Several hundred striking union miners from Pana City held up a special Baltimore and Ohio Southwestern train, conveying 50 Washington (Ind.) negro miners to Pana to take the place of the union miners. The negroes were taken from the cars and compelled to walk back to Tower Hill, where they were locked in the depot until 10 o'clock tonight. At that hour the negroes were placed on board an east-bound train and taken back to Indiana at the expense of the miner's union.

The holdup of the train was perfectly executed and was a bold stroke on the part of the union miners. Engineer George Worsham, of Pana, was in charge of the train, and on being flagged brought the train to a stop. The miners were all armed and masked. The engine was uncoupled from the coaches and run a short distance, the enginemen being kept under guard of guns. Masked men then entered the front doors of train while their associates surrounded the coaches. The negroes were then marched out back doors and walked down the track to Tower Hill. News of the capture of the blacks having reached Sheriff Coburn at Pana he sent an armed posse of deputies, including negroes from Springside camp, toward this town to intercept the miners on their return. Sheriff Coburn's force had not arrived at a late hour. In case they fail to appear the miners will remain here overnight and take a roundabout way home. It is believed that a battle will be precipitated if the Coburn forces show up in this vicinity. The sheriff of this county refused to interfere with the union men.

PANA, Ill., Sept. 30.--Last night was a terrorizing one for the people of Pana. Two-thirds of the residences were unoccupied. Each of the houses occupied contained a group of families. In some cases all the residents of an entire block spent the dark hours in one house, armed, terrorized and

awaiting attacks expected to be made on their homes by the negroes imported
from Alabama.

All night the striking miners, re-enforced by brother union miners from
other towns, armed with shotguns and rifles, paraded the streets, and in
some cases lay in ambush on housetops and in alleys awaiting the coming of
the blacks from Springside and Penwell stockades, who had announced an intention to march into the city and drive out the whites. But the deputy
sheriffs were successful in keeping the colored men under control and within
the stockades. Many shots were fired in the vicinity of the mines throughout the night but with what results could not be ascertained. Sheriff Coburn in wiring for troops last evening, reported one black killed in Wednesday's riot and several wounded.

Mayor Penwell, son of Operator Penwell, spent last night inside the
stockades. He said he was afraid of being mobbed by the miners, and that
for fear of mobs his father and mother have left the city.

PANA, Ill., Sept. 30.--Light battery B, of Galesburg, arrived on a
special train from Springfield this afternoon. The battery consists of two
Gatling guns and 68 men with side arms and Springfield rifles, in charge of
Captain Craig. Two camps of the Sons of Veterans from Aurora and Elgin, in
command of Colonel Hamilton, arrived this evening. They were equipped with
guns at Springfield and mustered in as national guards.

Governor Tanner's instructions to the troops before their departure
from Springfield were to arrest all persons carrying arms and hold such persons until further orders; protect citizens and their property, maintain
order, but lend no assistance to operators in operating their mines with
imported labor.

The militia are in full charge of the city tonight, and are parading
the business streets. The utmost quiet prevails.

SPRINGFIELD, Ill., Sept. 30.--In answer to queries regarding a report
that he had refused to send 300 rifles to the sheriff at Pana, Governor
Tanner today said:

"Yesterday I received an urgent telegram from the sheriff asking for
troops and saying he had done everything to protect life and property, but
the conditions had reached a point where he was unable to cope with the
difficulty any longer, and that a serious riot was imminent unless he received state aid by or before Friday evening. After several telephone conversations with him I became so impressed with the importance and needs of
the situation that I ordered the Galesburg battery and two companies of the
Sons of Veterans regiment to report at Pana for riot duty by the first train.
I directed Captain Craig in command to arrest and disarm all persons until
further orders, to protect citizens and their property, and to maintain
order, but not to allow any portion of his command to aid mine owners in
operating their mines with imported scab labor.

"This habit of importing labor into our state to take the places of our
citizens has to stop if I have the power to abate it."

WASHINGTON, Ind., Sept. 30.--A crowd of about 30 colored miners who
were brought here from Kentucky last fall to take the places of the striking
miners left for Pana, Ill., this morning to aid the colored men in the
threatened riot with strikers. All who left here were armed, some with revolvers and shotguns, others with Winchester rifles.

PANA, Ill., Oct. 1.--Owing to the heavy rain, which has been incessant
since the state troops went into camp here, the troops left the camp this
afternoon and are now quartered in the Haywood opera house, where they will
remain during their stay here. Captain Craig has given out orders for the
closing of all saloons until further notice. Lieutenant F. C. Henry, of
Battery B., said today: "We will put on a provost guard of fifty men this
evening, which will be continued indefinitely. I will have charge of the
guard. We will make a searching investigation as to location of the state's
guns, which are said to be in the hands of the blacks, placed there by the
sheriff, and we will take them in charge."

Six members of Battery B., who for some cause failed to make the train
at Galesburg Thursday night, were arrested and brought here to camp today
by a deputy sheriff.

The striking union miners returned here today from Tower Hill, after their exciting experiences in forcibly turning back the Indiana negroes imported by the mine operators to break the coal strike here. The miners guns were boxed up and smuggled into town in wagons filled with hay. Large crowds congregated on the streets of Pana, but they were orderly. Not a negro appeared in the city, and the quietness was only broken by the cheers accorded the soldiers as they marched through the streets. Last night Sheriff Coburn requested the militia commander, Captain Craig, to go to Tower Hill and arrest the union miners there who had captured the negroes and release the latter. Craig flatly refused to do so, saying he was here to protect the lives of citizens and property. He was not here for the purpose of obeying the sheriff's instructions or orders. His orders were from Governor Tanner, and there would be no foolishness in the matter, either. The militia are patronizing only the union butchers, bakers and merchants.

WASHINGTON, Ind., Oct. 1.--Guarded by four white miners heavily armed, the crowd of negro non-union miners who left this city yesterday to work in the mines of Pana, Ill., where a big strike is on, returned this morning, having been intercepted on the way by strikers, who, at the point of Winchesters, compelled the colored men to return to Washington. They did not resist and none were injured.

WASHINGTON, Ind., Oct. 2.--The elements of war are very much in evidence in this city tonight, and a bloody battle between white and colored coal miners is expected before morning. At 10 o'clock tonight a crowd of armed whites corralled about 20 non-union colored miners and started with them toward the B. and O. S. W. yards, where the strikers intended to force the negroes to board a freight train and leave the city. Many of the blacks were armed, in fact, most of them have never been without arms since being brought here from Kentucky a year ago, and when within a few blocks of the yards some of them turned upon the whites and fired. The union miners quickly returned the fire, and eight shots were exchanged.

One negro was wounded, but owing to the intense excitement his name can not be learned. Chief of Police Thomas Call, anticipating a riot, turned in three alarms of fire in quick succession, and this brought hundreds of sleepy citizens from their beds. Officer Call organized a posse, and with the entire day and night police force started for the scene of battle. The crowd of strikers and crowd of imported laborers are now stationed upon Lower Main street, one block apart and hostilities are expected to be renewed at any moment. The negroes are the same that went to Pana, Ill., Thursday, and were escorted back to this city by armed Pana strikers Friday.

WASHINGTON, Ind., Oct. 3.--The sensational reports sent from this city last night that 150 miners from Pana, Ill., had come to this city and last night as sited in forcing the colored scab miners out of the county at the point of their pistols is wholly without foundation in fact.

The Washington striking miners met the scabs last night at 10 o'clock and peaceably invited them to leave the county, which several of them promised to do, and because a number of the striking miners congregated and went from house to house where the scabs were housed, the police force that has just been appointed took alarm and turned in the fire alarm. This aroused great excitement and brought many citizens on the streets, but no injury to property or person was committed. Although it was rumored last night that one of the colored scabs was beaten into a jelly. . . .

Today everything is quiet. Of course the entire sympathy of the city is with the striking miners. Those of the colored miners who left last night at the solicitation of the strikers have all returned today with the exception of two. They are determined to remain, and it is thought there will be no further trouble.

Midnight--Ed Myers, one of the negroes run out of town last night, has just returned. He was terribly beaten by the strikers, and is in a bad condition. An affidavit may be filed against a certain member of Company D. One Hundred and Fifty-ninth Indiana, who was alleged to have been in the mob, Mrs. Steve Young, a negress, says this soldier insulted her while he held a gun in her face. All is quiet at a late hour tonight.

SPRINGFIELD, Ill., Oct. 3.--Assistant Adjutant General Ewert today outlined the status of the military at Pana, Ill.

"Martial law," said Mr. Ewert, "can be proclaimed only by the governor of the state in public proclamation. No such proclamation has been issued, and martial law does not exist at Pana. It is a common error to suppose that every time troops are called out martial law exists. As a matter of fact the soldiers when they are called out as they have been at Pana, are subordinate to the civil authorities."

WASHINGTON, Ind., Oct. 4.--Isaac Harris, a member of Company D, One Hundred and Fifty-fifth Indiana, was fined in a justice's court this afternoon for entering the residence of Louis Young, one of the negro miners, on the night of the riot, and threatening to blow out the brains of Young's wife, while a crowd of masked men were dragging her husband from the house.

After the trial, Captain Ross Smith ordered Harris taken to Camp Mount, Indianapolis, where he will be turned over to a military guard. No other arrests have yet occurred.

Sheriff Bowman tonight received a telegram from eight of the negroes who were driven from the city Sunday night. They are at Vincennes. They ask that the sheriff, with deputies, be at the depot to protect them when they return to Washington for their families and household effects. They promised to move away.

This afternoon the Enquirer correspondent started for the Cabel Company's mine to interview Bank Boss C. C. Rowland, who, with about fifteen negroes, reside in shacks, surrounded by a stockade. When within 400 yards of the mine two men stepped out of the bushes and ordered him to halt. Each man was armed with a Winchester rifle. When the men learned that it was not an enemy that stood before them they lowered their rifles, and became more sociable.

They said they were looking for an attack and were fully prepared for it. Sentinels are stationed about the mine and it would be an impossibility for anyone to get near the mine without being discovered.

The families of some of the colored men who were driven from the city are in destitute circumstances and the township will soon be compelled to provide them with the necessities of life. All is quiet tonight.

PANA, Ill., October 4--The Baltimore and Ohio Southwestern carried from this city two coaches and cabooses which the trainmen were ordered to leave at Cowden, where the Clover Leaf Railroad crosses the B. and O. They concluded that the cars were to convey more Southern negroes to Pana to take the places of strikers in the coal mines here. A movement was inaugurated to intercept the train. Later it was reasoned that the sending of the coaches was a ruse of detectives to induce the miners to attempt another hold-up and to effect a capture of the entire crowd of unionists. The miners who were preparing to leave town were ordered not to do so by the union officials.

The sheriff of Shelby County arrived today and is working on the hold-up of last Friday. It is probable arrests will follow.

A number of shots were fired by deputies at the Pana Coal Company's mine last night. The militia commander, Captain Craig, immediately dispatched fifty men to the mines. The soldiers went on a run. On the arrival the deputies said the mine had been attacked by strikers with stones. The militia divided in squads and searched the neighborhood, but no strikers were apprehended and no arms found.

Two labor agents left the city today for Alabama, being escorted to the train by an armed deputy sheriff. It is expected that the 500 negroes will arrive from Birmingham before the close of the week.

PANA, Ill., Oct. 3.--The military were actively engaged today disarming the deputies, negroes and any person found with arms, Captain Craig, commanding the militia, has notified all stores to sell no more firearms.

United Mine Workers' Journal, October 6, 1898.

28.   STRIKERS SHOT DOWN BY GUARDS AT VIRDEN.   MILITIA ORDERED OUT

A Bloody Battle Over Train Load of Negroes

Governor Says Mine Owners Are Murderers

Tanner Would Indict Owners

These men--the president and officers of the company, who precipitated this riot by the bringing in of these imported laborers, are guilty of murder, and should be and will, I believe, be indicted by the Grand Jury of Macoupin County, and tried and convicted for this heinous crime, statement by Governor Tanner, of Illinois.

Mine President's Statement

We shall take proper steps to secure redress against all who prompted, aided, abetted or participated in the riots of today, whether they are miners, officials, State officials or others. We shall determine for ourselves and others in this State just how far a Governor can annul and evade the duties placed upon him by the Constitution and statutes of this State.--PRESIDENT T. C. LOUCKS, of the Chicago Virden Coal Company.

Virden, Ill., Oct. 12--The climax in the mining troubles at this place came shortly after the noon hour today. The expected clash between the striking miners and armed guards on a special train bearing imported negro miners to the mine developed at that time, with very serious results. Several hundred shots were exchanged, with the result that nine men were killed, probably eighteen wounded, some of them fatally.

The Dead and Wounded

THE DEAD AT VIRDEN

Frank Hilyer, miner, Springfield
Joe Kutlin, miner, Mount Olive
Ed Greene, miner, Mount Olive
Ellis Smith, miner, Mount Olive
Abe Brennaman, miner, Girard
D. H. Kiely, Chicago & Alton detective, Chicago
A. W. Morgan, guardian stockade, Chicago
Thomas Preston, ex Lieutenant of police at Chicago,
    killed by militia

DEAD AT SPRINGFIELD

W. W. Carroll, deputy of train, Chicago

FATALLY WOUNDED, SPRINGFIELD

William H. Clarkson, deputy on train, Fort Leavenworth
Ervin Ryan, negro miner, from Alabama, through head

Six of the strikers were killed by the guards, while three of the guards, two on the train that conveyed them to the town and one within the stockade, lost their lives. One innocent man, a Chicago detective, who came here to guard the Chicago & Alton switches, was shot down by the first fire, and another man, who was mistaken for Manager Lukens, was shot and then stamped almost to death.

Shot by a Striker

Late tonight another death was added to the list when ex-Lieutenant Tom Preston, of the Chicago Police Force, who was acting as a guard at the stockade, was shot and killed by a striker just as the militia companies arrived. Preston was within the stockade and as the train bearing the troops pulled in he opened one of the big gates and stepped out. As he did so the sharp report of a revolver was heard. It was followed quickly by another shot and the ex-policeman fell, mortally wounded. He was carried within the stockade, where

he died. The shots at first led to the belief that the soldiers had been
fired upon and a skirmish line was formed to charge the miners congregated
about the stockade, but the order was not given and the miners fell quietly
back when the soldiers advanced.

The train then pulled down to the town and the troops were disembarked.
While they lined up on the platform guards were sent in to bring up the
striking miners and disarm them. There was no opposition by the miners,
who one after another fell into line and held their hands high above their
heads, while the soldiers went through their clothes. Adjutant General
Reece is in charge here tonight, and the troops are acting with a promptness
that is giving a reassurance this town has not felt since the arrival of the
Alabama negroes at St. Louis was announced.

The crisis of today was not unexpected. The trouble became more and
more aggravated every day this week, and the culmination is no surprise to
those who have kept in touch with the miners and have known their temper.
At 12:40 this afternoon a special train of five coaches bearing negro miners
and armed guards, who kept watch from the platforms, made its appearance in
the view of a large crowd assembled at the village station. The striking
miners and their friends had been advised through telegrams from Carlinville
and informed when the train was on the way and would arrive here about the
time men would be in anticipation of it. Hundreds of people were assembled
on the depot platform. The train went past the station at the rate of forty
miles an hour.

GUARD FIRED FIRST SHOT

As it arrived opposite the station one of the armed guards from the
platform of a car discharged his rifle presumably into the air. It did no
damage, but it was the signal for a volley of shots from the remainder of
the guards.

The exchange of shots suddenly grew into a fusillade, but the fatalities
in this first skirmish were miraculously small. Robert Kiley, watchman for
the Alton road, was shot through the head and fell forward on the depot
platform. He died soon afterward.

The special train was whirled away toward the stockades which surround
the mine property of the Chicago Virden Coal Company, and when that barri-
cade was approached the speed was slackened, the purpose being to stop and
land the negroes within the stockade under cover of the armed guards.

On the way between the station and the mine the miners who were stationed
along the track sent volley after volley after the train and many shots took
effect.

BATTLE AT THE STOCKADES

It was at the stockades, however, where the fiercest and most disastrous
encounter of the day occurred. When the armed deputies within the wooden
enclosure saw the train bearing down to the mine they emerged from within to
assist the armed guards in protecting the negroes while the latter were being
transferred from the train to the enclosure. Another battle with the miners
was the result.

Across the railroad track in a field within easy gunshot distance a
considerable body of striking miners was drawn up in order for deputy conflict.
Upon seeing them the deputies, it is claimed, opened fire.

Hundreds of shots were exchanged, this time with serious results. It is
the assertion of the miners who were in this attack that the most deadly fire
from the coal company's property came from the tower at the shaft. In the
meantime, the force on the train decided that the conflict was growing entirely too hot, and instead of coming to a dead stop the throttle was pulled wide
open and the train was hurried on to Springfield with whatever dead and
wounded it had on board.

Shortly after the last battle the word went out that Mr. Lukens, the
mine manager, had come from the stockades and was on his way to the company
store. A large crowd of determined miners made an immediate rush on the
store. Mr. Lukens was not there, but the manager, Frank Eyster, was in the
building. Eyster retreated to the roof of the building. While in that ex-
posed position a shot, alleged to be from the miners' hall, near by, brought
him down. Later he was taken from the building, and, once outside, was kicked
and trampled upon until he sustained fatal injuries.

NEGROES AT SPRINGFIELD

SPRINGFIELD, Ill., Oct. 12.--The train on which the negroes were brought to Virden, arrived in this city at 1:30 this afternoon.

The men injured consisted of six of the armed train guards and one negro. The other passengers escaped the balls by throwing themselves in aisles or under the seats.

In an interview with Governor Tanner this evening regarding the Virden riot he said:

"T. C. Louck, president, and Mr. Lukens, superintendent, of the Virden Coal Company, at 12:30 today made good their threats to land a trainload of imported laborers from the South, and attempted to put them to work in their mines at the point of the bayonet and the muzzle of the Winchester, such laborers being drawn largely if not entirely from the criminal class, ex-convicts who learned their trade while doing terms in the penitentiary of Alabama, after having been fully advised, and having full knowledge that the landing of such imported laborers, would precipitate a riot. I had wired them that if they brought these imported laborers they did so at their own peril, and under the circumstances would be morally responsible and criminally liable for anything that might happen.

THROWN FROM TRAIN BY GUARDS

John M. Hunter, president of the United Mine Workers of Illinois, was the victim of a brutal assault at the hands of two of the deputies on the train. He had boarded the train to ride north from this city, his object being to talk with some of the negroes and induce them not to go to Virden. He was struck and pushed from the train while it was in motion, and sustained severe injury. Tonight he swore out warrants for the men, charging them with assault with intent to kill. Mr. Hunter blames Operator York, of Chicago, for the attack, charging that he set the deputies on him. He was kicked in the mouth and stomach.

William Messer, one of the wounded detectives who was left here for medical attention, is authority for the statement that there were fifty-four guards on the train, and that thirty-eight of them are missing tonight. Where they are is unknown here, but it is believed some of them may have been pulled from the train near Virden, and that others watched for an opportune time and made good their escape from the striking miners of Virden.

Governor Tanner tonight wired the War Department asking if the Fifth Illinois Infantry could not be placed at his disposal for use at Virden. Colonel Culver, the commander of the Fifth, has tendered his services and those of the regiment to the Governor.

"Instantly on learning of the trouble I directed Adjutant General Reece to order Captain Craig, of the Galesburg battery, and one company of the Sons of Veterans' regiment, now stationed at Pana, to proceed at once by the quickest route to the scene of the trouble."

Undated newspaper clipping, A. F. of L. Archives, Incoming Correspondence.

29. PANA AND VIRDEN

Since the terrible affair of two weeks ago the quietness at those places has assumed the proverbial graveyard quietness, a quietness that would never have been disturbed or broken had not the operators seen fit to break it by the importation of ex-convicts from Alabama. The locked-out men in Illinois are to be congratulated for their staying qualities. From April 1st to November is quite a stretch for men to stand a siege that were in very poor circumstances financially to start with. Their stamina, pluck and endurance is highly commendable to them and worthy of emulation by all miners. The manner in which the miners at work in Illinois are responding to the call for help is also highly creditable to them but then, Illinois miners have been fighters from away back, and have contributed thousands of dollars to the cause

of boys in the same straits as are the Pana, Virden, Auburn, Green Ridge,
Nilwood, Sandoval and other locked-out miners in the Sucker State. With
such heroes as those, and the help they are receiving, we predict a con-
tinuance of the struggle until victory perches on their deserving banner.

United Mine Workers' Journal, October 13, 1898.

30. THE VIRDEN RIOT

It is a common thing when riots take place, to appeal to the public to
disregard all pleas tending to excuse or justify, and to insist, regardless
of every other consideration, upon the immediate and unconditional suppression
of disorder. But when we remember that in communities that are habitually
peaceful, riots seldom take place unless provoked by some injustice which
ought to be removed, we should ask ourselves whether, notwithstanding their
importance, peace and order are after all the sole consideration at such a
time. We should at any rate be disposed to consider the facts, rationally
and calmly. Let us discuss, then, the Virden riot in that spirit.

Virden is a coal mining town in central Illinois. Most of the miners
usually employed there live in or near the town, and many of them own their
homes. These miners are dependent for a living, upon employment at digging
coal in the mines of that region.

But the mines there, like mines everywhere, have been turned over to
private owners, just as if they had been produced by the owners instead of
having been given to mankind by nature. Consequently, the Virden miners
cannot dig in the mines unless the mine owners hire them. A question necessarily arises, therefore, as to the amount of wages which the corporation
can afford to give and the miners can afford to accept.

The same question having arisen from similar conditions in other parts
of the coal mining region of Illinois, the mine owners and the mine workers
of the state recently met in joint convention and agreed upon what they regarded as fair terms. But for peculiar local reasons these terms were not
satisfactory to the Virden mine owners, who shut down their mines.

The local miners, whose homes and livelihood were now at stake, offered
to compromise; but the mine owners ignored them. The miners then offered to
submit the issue to the decision of the state board of arbitration. This
proposition, also, the mine owners ignored. And when the board, upon its
own motion, thereupon investigated the issue and advised as to the sum which,
under all the circumstances, would be a fair rate of wages, the mine owners
still refused to allow their mines to be worked. They enforced what is commonly known as a "lockout," as distinguished from a "strike."

Affairs having remained in this state for some time, the mine owners
sent agents into Alabama to engage gangs of negro miners to come into the
Virden mines. These agents represented to the negroes that in consequence
of the prosperity of the country, which had made the coal business active,
and of the war which had drawn large numbers of white miners into the army,
there was a brisk demand for miners at Virden.

The negroes, thus deceived, were brought to Virden by the car load, and
when they arrived the local miners took up arms and threatened to prevent
their landing. Meantime the mine owners had employed bodies of private
detectives, organized and armed in military fashion, some of whom were placed
upon the railroad trains to guard the negroes, and some at the mines to cover
the landing.

The mine owners also called upon the mayor, the sheriff and the governor
for assistance. The governor, who is a republican, refused assistance. He
said that he would send troops to preserve the peace if necessary, but that
he would not allow the troops to be used as a guard to facilitate the landing
of the Alabama negroes.

This was the situation when, on the 12th of this month, a train load of
negroes was brought into Virden. The riot or battle then ensued. Who fired
first is not yet established; but the battle was between armed mine workers,
and armed private detectives employed by the mine owners. Many men on both
sides were killed and wounded.

As soon as he received word of the violent outbreak the governor threw
troops into Virden, disarmed both sides, and enforced the peace; but he
refused and has ever since continued to refuse, to allow the mine owners to
unload the gangs of miners imported by them from other states.

These are all the material facts, in substance, that have as yet been
disclosed.

The first question to which these facts give rise is the legality of
the acts of the miners and of the position of the governor. But no one can
positively answer that question until the courts decide. For we have fallen
upon times when neither legislatures nor custom, but judges make our laws.
Since a bare majority of the supreme court of the United States overruled
the precedents of a century to nullify the popular income tax law, and other
courts began to overrule the principle of trial by jury, by issuing injunctions in restraint of anticipated crime in labor cases, it has not been
easy to know the law in a given case, in advance of the decision, without
first knowing which side retains the judge who has the casting vote. Before
a Tanner court, it is not improbable that the action of the miners and the
governor's position, in the Virden matter, would be approved as legal; but
before a corporation court it is even more certain that it would be condemned.

In our own humble opinion the latter decision would be right. Legally,
it was a breach of the peace for the miners, by arming and threatening violence, to prevent the landing of the negroes from Alabama, even though the
negroes were poor dupes of the mine owners, and not citizens of one state
seeking, in good faith, work in another state. And we should say that both
in refusing to respond to the call of the sheriff with troops to preserve
the peace, even though that involved protection to the coal mine owners in
landing the gangs of negroes, and in preventing the landing of those negroes
after he did send troops to Virden, the governor was without legal justifi-
cation. Good reasons might be advanced, no doubt, for regarding Governor
Tanner's action as illegal. It might be said, for instance, that the coal
mine owners were entitled by law to pursue their business in their own way
in peace, and that if prevented by lawless force with which the local authorities could not cope, they were legally entitled to protection from the
state. So it might be urged that the negroes had the legal right to come
into the state as they did, and to be defended with all the power of the
state against lawless force. It might be argued also that the railroad company had legal interests in the matter which it was the duty of the governor,
which properly called upon to protect with every power at his command. But
this question need not be pursued. It is doubtful if any lawyer, whatever
his personal sympathies, would undertake to defend the disorder of the miners
or the position of the governor, upon purely legal grounds.

But the governor and the miners are not the sole violators of law in
connection with the Virden riot. The mine owners, too, are guilty.

The employment of private guards, as they were employed by the mine
owners at Virden, is distinctly forbidden by the statutes of Illinois. These
guards were no part of the police force, either of the county or of the state.
They had not been called into service by any legal authority, and their acts
of violence were as much outside the law as were those of the miners.

Whether this fact renders the guards and their employers liable for
criminal homicide in connection with the loss of life in the riot, will depend upon the sentiment of the judges who have the last say in the case.
It is to be hoped, however, that it will be found that they are liable.
Peaceable people who are also sensitive to injustice, would like to see the
law less discriminating in its assertions of majesty. If miners are to be
punished for violating it, let mine owners, railroad managers, and those
detective agencies that make a speciality of furnishing private troops in
the teeth of the law--let them be punished, too. Much has happened in recent years to excuse if not to justify the feeling of workingmen that the law
discriminates against them, and there would be no disputing it if the governor were censured and the miners punished for the Virden riots while the
corporation managers were allowed to defy the law without question.

If we pass from the domain of mere legality to that of public morals,
the whole force of the condemnation for the Virden riot must fall not upon
the governor nor the miners, but upon the mine owners. Had they cherished
the slightest interest in the public welfare, there would have been no riot.

In this aspect of the question, it makes no difference whether they were strictly within the pale of their legal rights or not. Keeping out of the penitentiary is by no means the best test of good conduct.

They are in the attitude of the man who deliberately excites his adversary to anger, so as to have the law of him for some overt act that his passion may prompt. When they brought gangs of negroes into Virden from a distant part of the country, they did so for the purpose of angering men whose homes were at stake, and of provoking them to violence, in order that a necessity might be created for military interference. Peace, order, life, were nothing to them. They were ready and eager to disturb the peace, to overturn order, to sacrifice life, provided they could make the blame appear to rest upon some one else. All they cared for was the object they pursued, which was to reduce a community of American workingmen to a village of serfs. For no one believes that they expected these negroes to be satisfactory miners. At half the ordinary wages the negroes would have been dear workmen. They were imported to serve the temporary purpose of making the lockout successful. That accomplished, the negroes would have been thrown upon the town as paupers. Even if the mine owners had been strictly within the law, as in fact they were not, their conduct would have been as reprehensible as Shylock's, who also was within the law.

Going still further back of the question of legality, we meet the most important issue of all. It is that of abstract justice. For laws are but a species of arbitrary force, except as they promote justice; and though all agree that order must be preserved, that is because we regard order as a necessary condition of justice. When its preservation is made a bulwark of injustice, it ceases to be order, and becomes anarchy in the very worst sense of that much abused word. There is no worse conception of anarchy than legalized injustice.

Yet it is impossible to consider the circumstances of the Virden riot, fully and candidly, without recognizing the truth, that in deep-seated legalized injustice it had its origin. Why did these men kill each other? From race or class antipathy? Not at all. The miners had no deadly race feeling against the negroes. Neither had they any deadly hostility to the armed guards who garrisoned the mining grounds. Nor had the negroes nor the guards any such feeling in return towards the miners. As men, they could all have met in good fellowship; and under almost any other circumstances they might have done so. Yet under these circumstances they killed one another. Why? For a chance to work. Think of it! They killed one another for a chance to bear the curse of Eden!

And are opportunities to work so scarce as that--so scarce as to set men at killing one another? By no means. Opportunities to work, unless something be done to diminish them, are limited only by the general desire to have work done and to give work in exchange for it. And that is limitless.

But something does diminish these opportunities. The one thing without which no work at all can be done is monopolized, and the owners shut workers out from it. That one thing is the land, upon which and out of which we live, and without which no one can live who does live.

The Virden miners needed access to the buried coal, they needed that and nothing more, in order to live. But the coal mine owners, in whom the law has vested authority to open or close the mines at their own will and in their own way, exercised their authority by locking the miners out. It was against this that the miners rebelled, and it was this that led on to the riot.

The miners felt that in justice they had a right to earn their living by working in those mines. Were they wrong? The burden is upon those who assert that they were. What better right in justice had the mine owners to close the mines than the miners to insist upon working them? What better right in justice had they than the miners to fix the terms upon which the mines should be opened? Did the title of the owners give them the better right? Trace their title back, even to the state or to the federal government, or to the French or English crown, and you get no nearer to anyone who had a just right to deed the earth away from those who are born in dependence upon using it for a living.

There is no just title to the Virden coal mines. Society itself is without the right in justice to control them, except by regulation to promote their use. It has no just right whatever to authorize them to be closed

against use. Yet society did authorize them to be closed; and it was against
that authorization that the miners rebelled. Who is most at fault for this
rebellion? The miners themselves who fought for their natural right to earn
a living, or society which empowers a favored few of its numbers to close
God's cellar door?

The Public Opinion (Chicago), October 5, 1898.

31.   UNDER THE THUMB OF UNIONISM

The Colored American has had many complimentary things to say of Governors Tanner, of Illinois, and Mount, of Indiana, because of their generous
treatment of the Negro volunteers of their respective states; but we cannot
condone their failure to come to the relief of the Negro miners who are now
being persecuted in those states by white strikers. Sympathy with the contentions of labor is out of place when the majesty of the law is assailed.
It is the governor's prerogative and imperative duty to preserve order, and
to protect life and property at any cost. It is the Negro's privilege to
accept work from contractors anywhere and under any circumstances, if the
wages are satisfactory, and the state must secure him against molestation in
the performance of that labor. Members of unions who interfere are law-
breakers and enemies to the peace and dignity of the commonwealth, and should
be dealt with as such. To stand aloof in awe of their political power is
cowardly in the extreme, and deserving of nothing but contempt.
There is too much fear of these tyrannical labor trusts on the part of
public officials, anyway, and the people's welfare is bartered away year after year to satisfy the ever-increasing demands of these selfish cormorants.
They bar the Negro from the benefits that unions are designed to confer, and
then proceed to terrify capitalists and politicians into connivance with their
indefensible schemes. Governors Tanner and Mount can best subserve the ends
of justice, as well as their own political future by protecting these poor
Negro miners in their efforts to earn an honest living, and rely upon the
good sense and moral courage of the more intelligent and Christian workingmen to sustain them. To alienate the friendship of the faithful and patient
Negro to court the illusory favor of a lot of kickers and strikers, the
majority of whom are ignorant foreigners, is like saving at the spigot and
wasting at the bunghole.

Colored American, October 8, 1898.

32.   TANNER OF ILLINOIS

Governor Tanner of Illinois is another executive specimen of extreme
color prejudice. In his zeal to cater to the striking miners and win favor
with the laboring classes for political advantage he refuses to do his sworn
duty in maintaining peace, order and tranquility in his state. He is a
pusillanimous, villainous imbecile with a severe case of Negrophobia of the
Ben Tillman type. He refers to Negroes who seek honest employment in his
state, by which they can earn bread, as "ex-convicts and scalawags." He is
following step by step the path that led Altgeld to the political guillotine.
And it is a consolation to know that as soon as the liberty loving citizens
of Illinois get a whack at him his political head will be chopped off. He
is a disgrace to the Republican party and they ought to see to it that he is
immediately impeached. Such proceedings are certainly in order.

The American (Coffeyville, Kansas), October 15, 1898.

33. THE ILLINOIS STRIKE

The situation in Illinois is very serious indeed. The miners have
been on a strike for nearly six months, and they have been resorting to
their usual tactics in trying to prevent others from taking their places.
An unusual feature of the situation is the attitude of Governor Tanner, of
that State. He apparently sympathizes with the lawless methods of the
strikers.

For some time, the owners of the mines have been threatening to supply
the places of the striking miners with colored men, and they have actually
attempted to do so. This, of course, brought matters to a crisis, for the
greatest injury that can be done to the average white striker of America is
to fill his place with a colored workman.

As a result of the attempt to import colored laborers into the State,
on Wednesday last, fourteen men were killed outright and twenty seriously
wounded. Many of the wounded are expected to die of their wounds.

The state of anarchy which prevails, and the fearful loss of life, can
and will be charged against the Governor of the State, for his words and
attitude gave encouragement to the rioters, and led them to believe that the
sympathies of the head of the State were enlisted on their side. This
Republican Governor of a very important State has plainly intimated that
colored laborers were not wanted in that State. This is the man who, a few
weeks ago, received the plaudits of the entire country for enlisting a regiment of colored soldiers, and commissioning colored officers to command it.
He was perfectly willing that the colored citizens of his State should risk
their lives on the field of battle in defense of the nation, but was not
willing that those same colored men should have an equal chance on the field
of labor within the boundaries of his State. It is an inconsistency which
has cost the shedding of blood, and has intensified the feeling between the
races, particularly in that section, and has done the cause of labor irre-
parable injury. His objection is not against the importation of laborers
into the State, but is against the importation of *colored* laborers. This
attitude of the Governor should be indelibly written on the memory of every
member of our race.

The cause of the striking miners may be a just one. They struck against
a reduction of their pay. Every fair-minded man is in sympathy with them
there, for we all know that labor does not receive its rightful compensation.
But, have these men a right to prevent others from taking what they have
refused? Have they a right to take the law in their own hands and destroy
and shed blood at will? Has the Governor a right to encourage such a condition? Certainly not, and for the present lawless condition in Illinois,
Governor Tanner will have to answer at the bar of public opinion. The *Press*
of this city concludes an editorial on this subject in these words:

"There may be some sympathy felt for the deluded miners in this situation, but there will be none felt for Governor Tanner. His unwise course
has misled the miners, resulted in bloodshed and murder, brought disgrace
upon a great State and injured the cause of labor irreparably. Instead of
upholding law and order he has encouraged riot and crime. Of this charge he
will stand accused at the bar of public opinion."

Every word of which is true.

The Christian Recorder, October 20, 1898.

34. GOVERNOR TANNER RESPONSIBLE

The murderous conflict which occurred last week at Virden, between
the striking coal miners and the representatives of the companies, was not
only lamentable in itself, but it was a bitter disgrace to the State of Illinois and to American civilization. Some eight or ten men were killed in
this fight and twenty wounded, but these casualties, much to be regretted as
they are, do not measure the injury upon civilization which such an affair
inflicts. Responsibility for what has occurred must be apportioned in varying

amounts, doubtless, among the contesting parties. We have not the full
information which enables us to do this work of apportionment with accuracy,
and therefore we shall go no further in that direction than facts, which
are clearly in sight, warrant. One conclusion will be plain to every dis-
passionate man who reads the published accounts of the trouble and who
reflects upon the utterances made concerning it by Governor Tanner. He must
be held to largest responsibility for the insurrection and for the murders
which accompanied it.

What are the essential facts of the case? There was dispute between
the miners and the operators as to the amount of wages that the former would
receive. This difference should have been settled by peaceful and reasonable conference between the contending parties. We believe it could have
been so settled if both sides had fairly endeavored so to dispose of it.
There is a right and a wrong in all such cases which can usually be made
clear if only both sides are willing to "talk it over" face to face. But
this mutual adjustment failing, from whatever cause, it became incumbent on
Governor Tanner before the first bloody warning, which occurred at Pana the
day before the Virden battle, to adopt prompt measures for keeping the peace.

Had Governor Tanner been a wise man, as well as a loyal maintainer of
law and order--which latter he was bound to be,--he would personally, or
through some judicious representative have gotten face to face with mine-
owners and strikers preceding the first bloodshed, and have used his strongest
influence to settle the difference between them. He would have said to them
first: "Men, can you not settle your trouble amicably and reasonably? If
not, I will suggest a board of fair-minded and responsible men, who will have
the confidence of both sides, in whose hands you can place the matter, if
both sides will agree to accept their decision." If the miners and their
employers had accepted so reasonable a proposition, well and good; that would
end the trouble. If not, then it would have been the Governor's plain duty
to say: "Very well, my friends; I now stand toward you simply as the Governor of Illinois; I shall enforce the law with every power at my disposal.
I shall suppress every unlawful act, by civil means, if possible; by the
military, if it is necessary." It is perfectly clear that the company had
a full right to bring in laborers from the State, or outside it, to fill the
places left vacant by the striking miners. Employees, under all ordinary
circumstances, have a legal right to strike, and the converse is true of
employers, that under all ordinary circumstances, they have a right to get
other men to take the vacant places of strikers. That is a game at which
both sides must be allowed to play fairly. It is a bad game at best, but at
least it must be played fairly. For the strikers to use violence to prevent
the work which they give up being taken by others is to use foul play. Such
foul play has always been the greatest injury to the cause of organized labor.
The cause is doomed which turns to violence for its advancement. But what
did Governor Tanner do when the workmen at Virden asked red-handed murder into
their ranks? He took a position and uttered words which ought to brand him
as a demagogue of the most dangerous description, and make him a political
impossibility for the future. On Sunday before the fight the Sheriff of
Macoupin County telegraphed to Governor Tanner for troops to preserve the
peace, as there was imminent danger of an encounter between the opposing
forces, and he had not deputies enough at his command to maintain order. The
Governor, upon learning that it was the intention to import laborers from the
South, refused to comply with the sheriff's request. Although he was obliged
to acknowledge that the mine-operators had a legal right to follow this course,
he refused to give them and the public the force necessary to preserve the
peace. In a word, he refused to maintain law and order, which it was his
plain official duty to do, because he was personally opposed to the importation of extra-State labor.

These are Governor Tanner's words as they are reported:

"I told him that they were undesirable citizens; that as soon as they
got a few dollars ahead they would quit their jobs, enter upon crime, and
find places in our poor-houses, jails, and penitentiaries, and become a burden on society and the taxpayers of Illinois; that I was opposed to this system; *that while it is true there is no law that would authorize the Governor
to keep them out of the State, yet at the same time I did not feel it my duty
as the Governor of Illinois to use the arms of the State to give protection*

to mine-operators in operating their mines with this class of citizens,
thus depriving our own citizens of the opportunity to labor; that I was not
much of a State-rights man, yet was elected by the people of Illinois, and
am employed as their servant, to look after their interests; that I felt it
my duty to give the citizens of our State a shade the best of it, and that
I could not use the army to operate mines with imported labor."

After considering the fact we have stated and reading the above, we
believe the readers will concur with us in the opinion that the Governor
of the State of Illinois signally failed of his duty at a critical juncture,
and that he is morally responsible for the shame and misery of the Virden
conflict, and for the lives of miners and of the employees of the operators
lost in it.

City and State, October 20, 1898.

35.   THE ILLINOIS RIOT

October 12 a conflict at Virden, Ill., between striking coal miners and
a force of deputies and detectives who were guarding the property of the
Chicago-Virden coal company, resulted in the death of nine miners and three
deputies. Twenty were wounded. The immediate cause of the outbreak was the
arrival of a trainload of Negroes who had been engaged to take the place of
the strikers. Governor Tanner, replying to a notification by the mine-
operators that their property was in danger and that they were entitled to
protection, sent the following dispatch:

Under the present well-known conditions at Virden, if you bring in this
imported labor you do so, according to your own messages, with the full knowledge that you will provoke riot and bloodshed. Therefore, you will be morally responsible, if not criminally liable, for what may happen. In my
opinion the well matured sentiment of the people of Illinois is largely opposed
to the pernicious system of importation of labor, and I am not wedded to any
policy which is in opposition to the will of the people of Illinois. Hence,
while I do not suppose that you care to listen to a suggestion from me, yet I
venture to advise you to abandon the idea of importing labor to operate your
mines.

Chicago *Chronicle* (Dem.)

The men, union or non-union, whom the coal company chooses to employ are
entitled to full protection if their lives or limbs are menaced by persons
whose places they take. They have been guilty of no crime; their necessities
doubtless have compelled them to accept what wage a tariff-protected company
chooses to give them. There ought not to be any confusion in the popular mind
concerning the relative duties of the company and the state. The state must
preserve order. But the state is under no obligation while preserving order
to run the business of a private corporation. That business may be conducted
as its responsible owners see fit as long as it is done without tumult or
disorder or trepass upon the rights of any one else. The government's sole
duty in the premises is to preserve order.

Chicago *Journal* (Ind.)

When Governor Tanner tells the Virden mine-operators they will be morally,
if not criminally, responsible for what may happen if they carry out their
determination to import Alabama ex-convicts to work Illinois mines, he gives
the operators the worst of the argument. If they don't want the riot and
bloodshed let Loucks and Lukens abandon their attempt to set up in Illinois
the labor standards of the convict camps of Alabama and Georgia. They have
no moral right to do that, no matter what their legal rights may be. Any
official who, by legal means, opposes their attempt, is acting in the interests
of the people of this state, and his services deserve recognition, even
though he be John R. Tanner.

New York *Press* (Rep.)

The president of the company informed the governor that he was acting
entirely within the law, and demanded protection. This Governor Tanner refused, averring that the performance of his duty, in conformity with his
oath of office, was opposed to "well matured sentiment of the people of
Illinois." Thus relieved from all legal restraint and restored by the action of the executive to a state of nature, both sides, previously conduct-
ing a peaceful struggle, flew to arms. Their forces met, and in the battle
that ensued the losses were heavier than those of the regiment which bore
the brunt of the much-discussed action of La Quasima. The events which led
to this bloody affair lay the guilt for these deaths at the governor's door.
If there is no law in the state of Illinois to reach this arch-criminal and
wholesale murderer, then God help the state of Illinois!

New York *Journal of Commerce*

It is the right of every owner of property in Illinois to employ on
that property any person he chooses to, and both he and that person are
entitled to ample protection by the state or its subordinate political divisions in carrying on any lawful occupation. If any citizen of Illinois
refuses employment on terms offered and the employment is accepted by any
person not a citizen of the state--a person who went there, as a great part
of Governor Tanner's constituents went there to seek employment--the town,
the county, and the state are under obligations to protect the man who
offers the employment, the man who accepts the employment, and the property
on which the work is done. In denying this, in refusing to restrain Illinois mobs from assaulting men who come from Tennessee or elsewhere to obtain
work, Governor Tanner is undertaking to incite a new movement of secession.

Brooklyn *Eagle* (Ind. Dem.)

The state of Illinois must hang its head in shame at such an exhibition
of demagogism on the part of its chief officer. When Governor Tanner declares that he will not protect the citizens of Illinois in their right to
employ the citizens of Georgia he is false to his official oath. When he
charges the coal company with bringing a blot upon the name of the state he
is guilty of sophistry. If he had done his duty in the first place there
would have been no bloodshed. The strikers may have had grievances against
their employers, but they had no right to use force to prevent other men from
working under conditions which they had found intolerable. It is a fatal
error for strikers to conclude that violence can ever be effective in the
settlement of disputes. The moment they fire a shot the whole organization
of orderly society is arrayed against them. They can not win in any contest
with the forces which insist on the peaceful conduct of business.

The Public Opinion (Chicago), October 20, 1898.

36. TANNERISM

Tannerism, as it relates to the Illinois situation, is synonymous with
cowardice and hypocrisy. As we have said before, a governor has no rightful
alternative than to preserve order, and is in duty bound to protect the
liberty, life and property of every person within the borders of his state.
He cannot go into the character of the individuals making up the population,
and has no power to judge of their qualifications or desirability as citizens, as long as they outwardly conform to the requirements of the law.
Courts and juries must settle disputed points as to criminality or admiss-
ibility of persons into the state. Gov. Tanner, in his treatment of the
colored miners who came up from Alabama to work for an honest livelihood,
has truckled miserably to a set of tyrants, inoculated with the poisonous
virus of trades unionism. In running after the uncertain labor vote, he
alienates the faithful Negro who has stood by the party in season and out of
season. Gov. Tanner has chosen to serve the mammon of deceit and demagogy.
Let him take the consequences, and the insulted and outraged Negro will see

to it that those consequences are bitter and far-reaching. If his head
isn't hit by the black voters every time it pops up with a bid for support,
we greatly mistake the temper and manhood of the Afro-American electors of
the state of Illinois. Tannerism is a fungous growth that should be extir-
pated at the earliest possible moment.

Colored American, November 5, 1898.

37. GOV. TANNER REVOLUTIONARY

We have entertained the kindliest feelings towards Governor Tanner of
Illinois, and have been loath to believe that he would in any manner reflect
upon or injure the people with which we are identified.

His action, however, in the matter of dealing with the colored laborers
brought from the state of Alabama to take the place of the striking miners
is a mystery to us, so far as a proper explanation of it is concerned.

While we regret that these colored men even went there, and had we been
consulted, should have advised otherwise, still, we cannot see where the
authority to keep them out rests.

In other words, he has undoubtedly transcended and set aside the law
and from the tenor of his remarks, he is not in consultation with the Attorney-
General of his state.

This comment was occasioned by remarks attributed to him, which are as
brutal as they are cruel. He is quoted as saying at Madison, Ill., October
26, in a public speech:

"I reiterate that I will not tolerate this wholesale importation of
foreigners into Illinois, and if I hear that a mob is to be brought into
this State, such as was taken into Virden, I care not on what railroad it
comes or for whom, I will meet it at the State line and shoot it to pieces
with Gatling guns."

This would be murder. The men, whom he would blow out of existence have
committed no crime against the laws of the state of Illinois. He is quoted
further:

"When the United States government found it necessary and deemed it just
to forbid importation of foreign labor into this country, I felt that I was
fully justified in the course I took at Virden. That trouble never would have
occurred if the Negroes had not been brought here to take the place of white
men."

But the United States' government acted under laws previously passed by
the Congress of the United States.

The legislature of Illinois has enacted no such measure, and the people
have granted no such authority to its Governor. What is the explanation?
Well, the disregard of the Constitution by the officials of the southern
states has caused a like action in the northern ones.

Richmond Planet, November 5, 1898.

38. NO DIFFERENCE

"When Governor Tanner spoke of the negroes who were brought from Alabama
into Illinois to take the place of the striking white miners as 'ex-convicts
and the scum of creation,' he was simply indulging in wild and foolish talk.
It is possible that some of these colored men had been criminals; but, as far
as we have been able to discover, the majority of them are hard working and
law-abiding citizens. After they were hustled out of Illinois under guard,
and kept for several days in jail at St. Louis, a Memphis contractor, who

was acquainted with many of them and had already had them in his employment, came forward and offered them work at one dollar and a half a day,
and they were glad to accept his proposition. It is a little remarkable
that a Southern man should have rescued them from their pitiable condition."
--*Christian Advocate. (Nashville, Tenn.)*

The butchery of colored laborers in Illinois, and the massacre of colored voters in North Carolina only illustrate that race prejudice is not
confined to either section, but that North or South bad white men will rob
or murder to gratify their avarice or passion, and then try to escape public
condemnation by criminating their helpless victims.

The Christian Recorder, December 1, 1898.

39.   FIGHTING FOR A JOB

I regret the necessity of the Virden event, but I do rejoice that in
America there are thousands and hundreds of thousands of men who would rather
go to their graves fighting for a job and to save their families from starvation than to have an inferior intelligence forced upon them. Under our
present monopolistic conditions, where three men are looking for one job,
the man who can live on the least gets the job and the other two can tramp
the streets. President Loucks says his men can earn $6 a day. I know that
when I was labor commissioner under Gov. Altgeld the 38,000 miners in Illinois never averaged apiece $300 per year or $1 per day.

George Schilling, ex-State Commissioner of Labor in Illinois, quoted in
The Literary Digest, December 24, 1898.

40.   COLORED MEN

OF ALABAMA AND ELSEWHERE ADVISED NOT TO GO TO PANA TO TAKE THE PLACES OF
UNION MINERS

BIRMINGHAM, Ala., Dec. 19.--Editor Journal: Mr. Fred Dilcher, member of the
national executive board of the U.M.W. of A., and William Fairley, president
of the Alabama district of the same body, take a different view of their
errand and do not hesitate to condemn it. A news reporter saw Mr. Dilcher
this morning. Mr. Dilcher said the labor agents now in this district want to
get colored men to take the places of striking coal miners at Pana, Ill.
There has been a strike there ever since April 1, and the colored men wanted
to go there as blacklegs. The colored men should not go there. In the first
place they will find it very uncomfortable to go to work at Pana. There have
already been rows at that place and they would not be entirely safe from
personal collision with the men whose places they are to take. In the second
place they are needed at home in Alabama where much better conditions exist
than in Illinois and where they are practically assured steady work for some
time to come. The Birmingham district needs all the labor it has and bids
fair to give its labor a better return for its work than it can get elsewhere.
In the third place the Alabama colored labor has not been informed of the true
situation. He is told that he will get 25 cents a ton for run of mines coal;
he is not told, however, that the regular scale in Illinois is 40 cents a ton
for machine-mined run of mines coal. He is offered 15 cents less than the
Illinois price, and that on a different basis. You can see that there is
nothing very flattering in the offer. The Illinois agents are employed by a
Chicago bureau which is engaged in placing blackleg labor wherever union labor
is on a strike. There has been a strike at Pana since April 1st, and it would
be foolish in the extreme for men to quit good jobs with steady work in Alabama

for this uncertain employment. You can say in conclusion (and I am res- ·
ponsible for what I say) that I, as a member of the national executive
board of the U.M.W. of A., thoroughly, cordially and heartily condemn any
movement of Alabama labor to the strike district at Pana, Ill., as unwise,
unprofitable and disloyal to all union labor. Mr. William Fairley, who was
present when Mr. Dilcher spoke, said: "I heartily endorse every word Mr.
Dilcher has said as truth and wisdom. He has stated the plain sober facts
and we can easily show that he knows whereof he speaks." It would be
foolish in the extreme for Alabama miners to leave a section where there are
practically no mine troubles for the uncertain and even personal danger,
attending the taking of union strikers' places in the North. I join Mr.
Dilcher in the condemnation and disapproval of such movements.

> Yours fraternally,
> GEO. BARBOUR,
> Pratt City, Ala.

United Mine Workers' Journal, December 29, 1898.

41. GOV. TANNER'S "NIGGERS"

Gov. Tanner's offensive "niggers" at Pana, Ill., are now being shipped
out of the state to take the places of strikers at some Indian territory
coal mines. This will, presumably, end the labor troubles which disgraced
the state last summer. Gov. Tanner then served notice that he would use
guns to make Illinois too hot for black men guilty of coming into the state
to earn their living by honest labor, and the victory seems to be his. But
when it comes to taking up the white man's burden where consolidated capital
thinks it, sees a profit, Tanner is ready to show approval along with all
the rest.

Springfield Republican, March 4, 1899.

42. ILLINOIS IN REBELLION

Gov. Tanner, however, through his own unauthorized acts placed the
state of Illinois in rebellion against the federal constitution and laws. He
undertook by force to deprive citizens of the United States of rights, privileges and immunities guaranteed by the federal power. He ventured to deny
to them the constitutional right to enter the state of Illinois from other
states and work at lawful labor for an honest living. And there was no
power in Illinois at the moment to call him to account.

Obviously the president of the United States was not to expect that his
attention would be called to the case by the Illinois state officials. But
was he, therefore, to remain necessarily in constructive ignorance of the
matter? Must he blind his official eyes to what his natural eyes have seen
in the public prints, or in letters and appeals from private citizens? Was
President Lincoln to remain in official ignorance of the outbreaks in South
Carolina until some United States marshal chanced to inform him, or the state
authorities themselves, who were in rebellion? Sworn faithfully to execute
the laws, and instructed specifically by the federal statutes (see Revised
Statutes, section 5299) to preserve the rights of citizens against insur-
rectionary attacks within the states, was Mr. McKinley to affect an ignorance
of the Illinois situation and refuse to move until called upon by some particularly authorized person or agent of government?

Courts of justice, in the nature of the case, do not move themselves.
But we are hardly to entertain with patience a suggestion that the executive
power occupies a similar position in the state. It is evidently the opinion
of our questioner that if, perchance, the Filipino rebels should manage

to capture or kill the whole United States force at Manila, the president[97]
must remain in official ignorance of the matter and refuse to stir until
some officer there rose from the dead or escaped from the enemy, to inform
him, so that he could "constitutionally take cognizance of it." We venture
to say, however, that no matter how hard it might be for President McKinley
to learn officially of rebellion against the rights of negroes in Illinois,
led by a republican governor, he would find no difficulty in hearing of
this colored suppression of white invaders in the Philippines, and would not
be slow in asserting the power of the national government accordingly.

Springfield Republican, March 13, 1899.

43. WOMEN AMONG THE KILLED AND WOUNDED

A Negro Miner Said to be the Cause of the Affair

A deadly riot, the most serious disturbance that has occurred at Pana,
Ill., since the union miners instigated a strike in April, 1898, was enacted
yesterday, resulting in seven persons being shot to death and nine wounded,
as follows:

THE DEAD

FRANK COBURN, citizen
XAVIER LE COCO, Frenchman, union miner
Three negro men.
One negro woman
Unidentified negro, found last night near shaft
    No. 2 of Pana coal company.

THE WOUNDED

Frank Landsworth, shot in head
Mrs. Henriet, shot in left arm
Will Kuhn, laundryman, shot in legs and hands
Cyrus Strickler, shot in back
Albert Vickers, shot in hand
George Kimball, farmer, of Rosemont, shot in arm
Henry Stevens, negro, shot in neck
Cass Proffitt, shot in foot
Carrie Felix, shot in breast

The situation quieted down at nightfall, and no more trouble was looked
for. Adjt. Gen. Reece, Col. A. E. Culver and three companies of infantry
arrived at 6 o'clock last evening on special trains, and perfect order was
maintained throughout the town from that time on. The troops at Pana are
Co. H, from Decatur, under Capt. Castle, Co. G. from Springfield, under First
Lieut. Bauman, and Co. B from Taylorville, under Capt. B. Prish. The soldiers
immediately began patroling the streets throughout the entire town. Miners
stood about in groups talking, but there was no outward manifestation of
excitement, although it was evident that great indignation existed, especially
among the townspeople over the shooting of the citizens and women.
Henry Stevens, a negro miner, who has long been considered a leader among
his associates, is declared to have been the direct cause of the riot. It is
said he was also the leader of the riot that occurred in September. Stevens
has long cherished hatred for Sheriff Downey, and has openly made threats
that he would kill him on sight. He was on the street Monday with a revolver,
saying he was looking for Sheriff Downey. He continued this yesterday, and
Sheriff Downey came upon him on Locust street. The sheriff commanded Stevens
to deliver the revolver, and told him he was under arrest for carrying concealed weapons. Stevens without a word instantly leveled his weapon and fired
at the sheriff. The bullet went wild. The sheriff immediately opened fire
on the negro. Deputy Sheriff Cheney hearing the shooting rushed to join

Sheriff Downey, Stevens took to his heels and succeeded in gaining Penwell's general store in Locust street, the principal thoroughfare, two blocks distant, and took his stand in the entrance. He hesitated there an instant and then stepped to the pavement, leveled his revolver down the street toward his approaching pursuer and fired.

Springfield Republican, April 11, 1899.

44. ANOTHER STAB

The following is what John Mitchell, president of the United Mine Workers of America, says concerning the employment of colored labor in the mine:

"Colored labor has been and is being used for the purpose of reducing wages of workingmen. They are imported from the South to the northern states and frequently are kept working under guards. To prevent this, laws should be enacted, making it a criminal offense for employers to induce laborers to leave their homes under misapprehensions. Colored laborers are used to work in the mines of Illinois more than in any other industry there."

Coming from such a source, these statements and recommendations are no doubt designed and certainly calculated to arouse opposition to colored labor in the mines of the North. It is another instance of the employment of specious forms to mislead the people and grossly misrepresent the colored laborer. There is no truth whatever in the statement that the underlying motive on the part of the mine owners is to reduce wages. The reduction may follow as the result of the law of supply and demand, as where the supply of colored labor is greatly in excess of the demand and where organization has not been effected by which the fluctuation of wages may be prevented or regulated. But that this is the controlling motive of the employer is not true. The fact is that colored labor in the mines is becoming more desirable on account of the absence of colored labor agitators, walking delegates, mischievous demagogues and manplots, whose pleasure and pride it seems to be, to foment discord, encourage idleness, develop insubordination and array labor against capital. The colored miner is satisfied to take what he actually earns, because it is more than he can get in the South where colored labor is poorly paid and because it is but fair. Moreover he is no intruder, he does not seek to dislodge other classes of miners. He accepts the opportunities of labor at fair wages only after they have been ignored or lost by the whites who insist upon unreasonable demands. On more than one occasion his timely assistance in the mines has prevented a coal famine and thus insured moderate prices and home comfort to the masses. Nor are the wages the colored miner receive much less if any, than were received by the whites. The difference is so inconsiderable as not only to justify them in accepting the wages, but constitutes no reason for strikes. When a mine owner has colored labor, whether paid scheduled wages or somewhat less, he is satisfied that the output will be fair and the demands reasonable. The opposition to enact a law to prevent colored people from seeking or accepting labor wheresoever they see fit, is another indication of the spirit of ostracism and injustice on the part of white labor organizations. These labor organizations while professing to be advocating the cause of labor and ameliorating conditions, are seeking to restrict the labor rights of the colored people by a prostitution of the legislative power to the worst forms of prejudice, tyranny and injustice. They would have the law deny to the colored people the right of free locomotion and circumscribe his opportunities for self support. The proposition in itself is enough to show that labor organizations are more grinding and unreasonable than the power of monopoly which they are constantly opposing. It is needless to state that the Congress will be too just to pass so unjust and unconstitutional a measure; but the attempt to secure it indicates the unfriendly spirit of labor organizations toward colored people. Between the policy of refusing to employ colored labor in North Carolina and the proposed legislation to force it to remain there is to place the colored laborer between the upper and nether millstones. Even

if it is desirable to displace the colored laborer, it is ungenerous and
criminal to seek to do so through the law-making power. The colored
people are denied labor by white organizations and he is justified in obtaining it under the best terms possible.

Washington Bee, April 22, 1899.

45.   PANA STRIKE TO END

It is stated on good authority that the Pana, Ill., strike is at an
end. At a conference held last week between the mine workers and mine
owners, it was agreed to recognize the union and send the Negro miners
back to Alabama. This strike, which has been on for the past thirteen
months, has resulted in the loss of thirteen lives and cost the State of
Illinois thousands of dollars in the maintenance of a military guard
around the mines.

The Recorder (Indianapolis), May 7, 1899.

46.   600 NEGRO MINERS TURNED OUT

Late last week a trainload of negro miners going to take the places of
some striking negro miners near Carterville, were fired upon and one woman
was killed and several men wounded. While marching to the mine later on the
negroes retaliated by setting fire to the village where the striking miners
live. Troops, at last accounts, were being ordered to the scene. The battle
at Pana, which has been going on with much shooting and a pretty constant
reign of disorder and terror for a year, has ended finally in a victory for
the strikers. The mines have been operated by negroes imported from the
South, and protected by stockades against a regular siege from armed striking
miners. The latter have been encouraged in their stand by Gov. Tanner, who,
last year declared that he would stop the coming in of black labor if he had
to use the guns of the militia to do it. After a long struggle the mine owners
have now closed down their works. The black men thrown out of work are left
penniless, and the governor of Illinois has undertaken to send them back to
their homes at the expense of the public treasury. Some 600 negroes will thus
be turned out of the state.

Springfield Republican, July 4, 1899.

47.   EMPLOY NEGROES IN TIME OF PEACE TOO

The Pana, Ill., incident is closed at last. Whether its finale was fitting is a question that will be debated and settled by different standards of
right and wrong and according to the respective methods employed in solving
the race problem. But as The Freeman has said it thinks it can afford to say
again, that the introduction of Negro workmen, for the express purpose of
defeating white workmen of attaining their ends when a controversy arises between proprietors of mines, mills, shops, or what not and the white workmen
is a dangerous expedient. It will not contribute anything to the relaxation
of the high tensioned relations between the races. The workingmen of the
country have settled convictions and they are in the vast majority. They, it
is true, are not for the Negro workmen, but this hostility cannot be broken
down by brute force. These men swear by the principles of their orders and

in many instances they are right from their standpoint--self-preservation.
It is but fair to assume that there will always be some kind of compact
between workingmen. The iron heel of the bosses and multi-millionaired
trusts may crowd down as swift and hard as avenging gods, but in some form
they will endure.

If these bosses are sincere, let them employ Negro workmen in time of
peace; put them in wherever they can and as many as they can until the face
of black men excite no further curiosity.

Every Northern State could repeat the Pana, Ill., incident if they were
so disposed. The thousands of shops in the North do not swing their doors
inward to Negro workmen. There need be no expression of holy horror at this
affair; it is in embryo elsewhere.

There are shops in Indianapolis that work night and day to keep pace
with their orders. These men do double duty. They are all white men. Why
not run in a few hundred starving Negroes who would be glad enough to work
either night or day? Strain not at a gnat and swallow a camel.

The same reasons that actuate these institutions in our own midst actuated the miners of Pana, Ill., and the Governor of that state. But cannot
the whole thing be changed? Can not these institutions slowly introduce
Negro workmen even if it be in the lowly places? Or shall Negroes be compelled to set up their own institutions and patronize them? Is there any
reason Negroes should not set up institutions and employ their own people?
Is there not very great reason for doing something of the kind?

The Freeman (Indianapolis), July 8, 1899.

48. THE NEGROES MUST "GIT"

The edict from Kansas--"bleeding Kansas,"--is that there is no room or
opening there for the negro who wants to work for his living. We have seen
how the republican Governor of Illinois had negroes shot down because they
wanted to work in the mines of that State. The following telegram shows how
hospitable Kansas is to the "ward of the nation."

IMPORTATION OF NEGROES STOPPED

Striking Miners Stop Operators From Bringing Them In--Say They Are Criminals

Pittsburg, Kan. June 18.--The striking union coal miners appear to have
temporarily stopped the importation of southern negroes by the mine operators.
The hearing of the injunction cases brought by strikers to prevent the importation of miners from other States has been postponed until June 26. The
miners set up that the negroes are criminals and affected with contagious
disease and that their coming would be a menace to the health of the community and the good order of the public.

Booker Washington is right when he says that the negro has a better
chance in the South than in any section of the Union. The South does not
coddle him or deceive him like the sentimentalists of the North. It lets
him work, give him employment, pays him for it, and supports public schools
for his children. It says plainly and bluntly that he shall not govern, but
does not prate hypocritically of his "rights and privileges" and refuse him
admission to places where there is work on the ground that they "are criminals and affected with contagious diseases and that their coming would be a
menace to the health of the community and the good order of the public."

Washington Bee, July 8, 1899.

49.   THE MURDER OF THE MINERS

The trouble between the white and colored miners at Cardiff and Bloss-
burg, Ala., resulted in the cold-blooded assassination of Edward Ellis, the
leader of the colored men, and also the murder of Adam Samuels, June 27th.

It was found that both men had been shot in the back, and in the body
of Ellis as many as twenty five buckshot had been fired.

The white men secreted themselves in a box car, and the shooting was
done at close range. The colored men are armed and it is alleged that
trouble is feared.

If colored men had shot down white men in this cowardly manner, all of
the machinery of the state would have been put to work to apprehend the
cowardly murderers.

Colored men have no protection whatever, and self-reliance must be
their main dependence.

It it unfortunate indeed that these white men were not punished, not
by the officers of the law, but by the colored miners themselves. The
coroner's jury returned a verdict that they were killed by unknown parties.

The only way now to make them known is to punish them at the time that
they are committing crimes which disgrace modern civilization.

Richmond Planet, July 8, 1899.

50.   NOT SETTLED

Pana, Ill., Situation Unchanged

Pana, Ill., July 10.--Editor Journal:
The situation remains unchanged in Pana since sending in our last communication, with the exception that the negro and white scabs have vacated
the city and left the situation in control of roundheads and their sympathizers. The report has gained circulation that the Pana operators have
settled and the mines are going to resume operations. Such is not the case.
There has not been any overtures made toward a settlement as yet. It is
useless for idle miners to come here in quest of work. The Pana mines will
be unable to give all their old employees work immediately after resuming
operation on account of entries being caved in and the mines being in bad
condition generally.

PRESS COMMITTEE

United Mine Workers' Journal, July 20, 1899.

51.   A WARNING VOICE

ECHOES THROUGH THE IRON BARS AT CARTERVILLE PRISON

A Colored Union Miner Now Incarcerated in Williamson County Jail, Writes Upon Ex-convict Labor and its Evil Effects

Carterville, Ill., July 12.--Editor Journal:
The seemingly irresponsible conflict existing between the U.M.W. of A.
and the mine operators is a source of much needless suffering through the
land. Why is it that two such potent elements so dependent upon each other
for their mutual existence and support are continually at daggers' points is
a problem. It certainly arises from an extremely morbid condition of affairs
that is wrong is evident from the conception of the fundamental principles

existing between bodies naturally allied to each other by bonds of mutual
interest. There is a tide in the affairs of man, which if taken at the
flood, leads on to peace and harmony. We believe that tide today is recognition of the U.M.W. of A. and their principles as they exist for the
better interests of the wage earner and justice to the mine operator. The
miner is fully aware of the obstacles with which our pathway is strewn.
We are also convinced of the fact that we are pitted against brains, money
and prejudice. So from a financial standpoint in the interest of gigantic
corporations that are daily filling the laborers' homes with hunger and
pain. The grim wolf of starvation is at the door of 90 per cent of every
miner's home in America today from the fact that capital and capitalists
have banded together in reducing wages and the advancing of commissary
articles so essential to the comforts of the laboring masses. Then the
working man must do likewise, and sooner or later these principles will assert themselves, for heaven knows that the golden order of the U.M.W. of A.
will be found advocating the cause of the miners, even until time on earth
shall cease to be and silence holds sway over the universe. Ere this remote
day the strong arms of the U.M.W. of A. will be felt from the Atlantic to
the Pacific oceans, regardless of the consequences. It seems an utter impossibility to suppress the daily importation of ex-convicts and criminal
labor into the fair State of Illinois. The class of labor mentioned is
criminal beyond question. These facts were ascertained at Pana and Carter
ville, Ill. Even among their associates murder and bloodshed run riot. In
May 1898 these people came to Carterville. They had been in Carterville
only four months until Will Prentice had killed Chas. Miller, Alex Boy shot
James Shen, George Cloud killed Sam Duckens. This with many other cutting
scrapes goes far to satisfy the public that this class of labor would be
better in their native haunts than in Illinois. The women, like the men,
are veteran criminals, and boast of their many visits and stays in Knoxville,
Tenn., and other jails. As visitors these women and men have but one place
to go calling their homes--to saloons. And to say the least the parties
thus styled women, go staggering home to return on the morrow. Is this
conduct not demoralizing to society, and are they not dangerous to public
good? Yea, the dumping of the unwelcome people in Illinois has robbed honest
men of all that is dear to human existence--employment that feeds their wives
and babes, and today the little barefoot children know not where their tomorrow's bread will come, whilst mothers in agony groan.

Even the wholesale issuance of warrants which has filled the Williamson
county, Illinois, jail with union miners, is but in part demonstraging the
untiring persistency with which the unprincipled agency seeks to intimidate
and drag down the wage earner. Intimidation is a dread to every true miner
that lives, and the prisons of Siberia with all their sorrow could not cause
us to depart from our course.

The U.M.W. of A. only ask peace and recognition and living wages. Rioting, bloodshed and murder is as far from their principles as the east is from
the west. Were it not so, the U.M.W. of A. would not hazard so dangerous an
undertaking as devolved upon them in assuming the leading lights of the land.
The miner is not blind to the ways of operators or officials. Together we
stand, and no unprincipled agency or disappointed or successful office seeker
shall invade our quiet ranks and contaminate its pure virtue with subter-
fuges and empty promises.

Where was his excellency in the time of our lamentable distress? And
what can Williamson county's sheriff say about the burning of the U.M.W. of
A. homes on June 30, 1899? He even smelled the smoke as our homes went up
in ashes, leaving men, women and children with no where to lay their heads
nor shoes or clothing, and why did the sheriff not deputize the citizens to
arrest the perpetrators of that crime? Was the sheriff ever in need of
assistance? Who did he deputize? The evening of June 30th, 1899, when he
had Eli Sucker, Ed Richard and Jim Hicks, three union men arrested and Mr.
Brush's ex-convicts and fired upon them? The sheriff saw it, was there,
knows the parties. Why is there no arrest or efforts to do so? How long
will justice sleep? Even the State troops are playing a prominent part in
arresting union miners, charged with offenses weeks before the troops came
to Carterville.

The above is just the opposite to the Pana and Virden trouble in which
the governor never once lost sight of the sheriff's duties. Had Williamson

county's Sheriff exhausted his resources in deputizing citizens of his
county to serve him as deputies? Even the offered services of law-abiding
citizens were not in accordance with the sheriff's views, and his much
abused friend Brush. Let us see how Mr. Brush has suffered. In May 1898,
he imported 200 men and families from Jellico, Tenn., to Carterville, Ill.,
arriving at place named. Brush deliberately entered the union miners' homes
(whites) and bundled their beddings, wives and children together and cast
them out in the rain and mud, knowing at the time that those poor unfortunate miners with their families had nowhere to look for shelter. At that
time the mud was eight inches deep at and around Brush mines. The brutal,
cruel and inhuman treatment perpetrated upon the union by this Christian
(?) gentleman has no parallel--no not in the history of the mining industry,
and for more than a year those men robbed of home and employment have sat
idle and saw their families move from place to place, pale, haggard and
hungry. This without a protest or demonstration of violence. Mr. Brush's
fatherly kindness to his ex-convicts scab labor is a direct repetition of
the monkey that weighed the cheese for the cat. He was their host at and
around Jellico, Tenn., a distance of 461 miles from Carterville. Notwithstanding, transportation rates Mr. Brush charged his criminals nine dollars
and twenty-five cents ($9.25) per head. These people were in transit one
day and night. During this time he furnished his men with one loaf of bread
and one pound of sausage, for which Mr. Brush charged $1.25 per man or woman.
Each receiving the same, the total cost for bread and sausage was about $360.
00. His second act of kindness was to open a general merchandise store for
the benefit of his children. On articles purchased: Stool bottom chairs
that cost 25 cents in Carterville, cost 50 cents at Brush's store; chickens
that cost 20 cents at Carterville, cost 40 cents at the mines. The grip
drill at the mines cost $10.50. The (Thompson make) needle, $1.75; tamper,
$1.75 and thus the accounts run. The three-ton cars that formerly weighed
5,500 dropped to 4,000, notwithstanding the miners filled and cribbed the
cars to their utmost capacity. After Mr. Brush had worked his men a few
months at these figures he struck on a new and novel idea. He took from
each and every car 200 pounds per day for one month. When his men investigated, Mr. Brush told them that he (Brush) had weighed the cars 200 pounds
in excess for six months on their first arrival, and every man that came
in Brush mines more than a year ago is in the same or sadder condition today than when they left the Jellico mines many owing today transportion.
    The convict spirit is still fresh in their bosoms, from the fact that
they go to work under guard, come home under guard, sleep and eat the same,
and are content. If this is not prison then I am lost.
    In speaking of this class of labor, they do not represent the better
class of the Southern Afro-American. The evidence of this is seen from the
slightest observation. They have no furniture, few clothes and no money,
showing that they had sold their household effects. They had no ties of
friendship that could induce them to stay at home. Why homes? They have
none. The better element of Southern colored people have a few hogs,
chickens, furniture, etc.; also friends and no labor agent or transportation
could cause them to leave their homes. These facts are consistent, notwithstanding the actions of the officials or I.N.G. or their services or object
at Carterville, and all fair impartial thinkers are today at a loss to know
the cause and are praying for an explanation.

COLORED UNION MINER,
Now in jail.

United Mine Workers' Journal, July 20, 1899.

52. COLORED MINERS IN A FRENZY--COMPANY OF STATE TROOPS
ARRIVES TO PRESERVE ORDER

    Carterville, Ill., was the scene about noon yesterday of a bloody riot
in which six negroes were instantly killed and one fatally wounded, while two

others received slight wounds. Trouble has been brewing since the militia
was recalled by Gov. Tanner Monday. The white miners of the place have refused to allow the negro miners to come into town, always meeting them and
ordering them back. Yesterday, however, 13 negroes, all armed, marched
into town going to the Illinois Central depot, where they exchanged a few
words with the white miners. Then the negroes pulled their pistols and
opened fire on the white men, who at once returned the fire. A running
fight was kept up. The negroes scattered, some being closely followed by
the white men up the main street, while the rest fled down the railroad
track. After the fight was over six dead bodies were picked up and another
man was found mortally wounded.

The Killed

> Rev. T. J. FLOYD
> HUSE BRADLEY
> JOHN BLACK
> JIM HAYES
> HENRY BRANUM
> One unidentified.

Mortally Wounded

> Slim Cummins

Trouble has existed at Carterville off and on for over a year, but no
fatalities occurred until June 30, when a passenger train on the Illinois
Central railroad was fired into and one negro woman was killed. These
negroes were on their way to the mines, having come from Pana. A short time
afterward a pitched battle ensued between the union and non-union forces,
during which the dwellings occupied by the non-union negroes were burned.
Several arrests were made, and the accused are in jail at Marion awaiting
trial on the charge of murder. Superintendent Donnelly of the Brush mines,
where the negroes live, reports that the negroes are worked into a frenzy
and that while he is doing all in his power to hold them in check, he is
afraid that he cannot do so much longer. Co. C. 4th regiment, Illinois
national guards, arrived at Carterville last night, and will endeavor to
preserve order. Forty miners from the Herrin mines are reported to have
left that place for Carterville armed with Krag-Jorgenson rifles and determined to assist the white miners.

Springfield Republican, September 18, 1899.

53. THE MINE RIOT AT CARTERVILLE, ILL.

Chicago (Ill.) *Inter-Ocean*

The riot which broke out at Carterville on September 17 could have been
no surprise to any person familiar with the conditions prevailing at the Brush
coal mine. About two and half months ago a train load of Negroes on their
way to that mine were fired on near Carterville, and troops were ordered to
the town. They stayed there ten weeks--until September 11. During all that
time the peace was unbroken, but only one week later came murderous riot.
The militia were ordered away from Carterville by Governor Tanner at the urgent solicitation of the leading citizens, who pledged themselves to maintain
order, but who were powerless to do so. As subsequent events showed, this
solicitation was absolutely unwarranted. It was unreasonable and indefensible.
What has occurred was just what might have been expected--just what has oc-
cured elsewhere under similar circumstances. More than twenty lives have been
sacrificed in this state during the last year in the coal mine controversies.
The deaths have been about equally divided between whites and colored men.

Chicago (Ill.) *Times-Herald*

After his summary of the accounts that had reached him

of the slaughter of Negro miners at Carterville by white union laborers, Governor Tanner says: "It seems to me from the brief facts reported and the further fact that no one was killed except the Negro miners that it was prearranged, preconcerted, premeditated murder." Murder it undoubtedly was. The white miners were moved by a murderous intent as soon as the Negroes joined the loitering throng at the railroad station. They were the aggressors, and they were mad with the thirst for blood.

The race problem of the south and the labor problem of the north have both been factors in this shicking tragedy which will make the name of Illinois a byword and a hissing among the states of the union. The white miners joined "nigger" and "scab" among their epithets, showing that they were as quick to raise the one issue as the other, so that there is some point in the speech of the Georgia planter who warns his hands against coming to this commonwealth. For the present, at least, we cannot protest against his charges. But there is still a way out of our disgrace and degradation. Let the murderers be brought to justice with all the promptness that the courts can command. Let the scaffold proclaim that the laws of the state may not be defied with impunity.

Macon (Ga.) Telegraph

Strife between the white American laborer and the Negro or any other laborer belonging to an inferior alien race whose standard of comfort is pitched upon a lower scale, and the representatives of which can, therefore, thrive on lower wages--strife between the American white laborer and all such is a foregone conclusion, and may be looked for more and more in every part of this union as time goes on. Up to the present time there has been more strife in the northern than in the southern states for the simple reason that the southern white laborer is born to the yoke, so to speak, and is thus less quick to resent unequal competition. But there are signs that he is growing more and more restive, and when the old slave owners and old slaves are gone (both of which elements tend to preserve the peace), it is to be feared that he may become as violent and implacable in his attitude toward Negro competitors as are his white brothers in Illinois at the present time.

Charleston (S.C.) News and Courier

The announcement that South Carolina farmers had resorted to violence to rid themselves of Negro competition aroused our esteemed western and northern contemporaries to righteous indignation. Their comments upon the Greenwood incident ran the gamut from pained protest to intemperate invective. We have no inclination to defend the Greenwood whitecaps, but we do wish to call attention to the fact that they are less guilty than the men who shot Negro laborers down in cold blood in Carterville. The northern press will kindly observe that while the whitecaps of South Carolina contented themselves with beating and otherwise maltreating their colored competitors, their Illinois confreres killed their opponents outright. These matters are of little moment to the unfortunate victims of northern prejudice and brutality, but they are worth mentioning just now in view of the abuse to which the people of the south are constantly subjected.

Pittsburgh (Pa.) Post

Governor Tanner's action when the previous riots occurred must in the nature of things have incited the outbreaks of Sunday, with the resulting killing. Last spring he justified the forcible exclusion of Negro citizens from the state and this stirred hot blood and many were killed. The Carterville tragedy flowed legitimately and inevitably from the governor's action at that time. It illustrates the danger of placing incompetent and reckless men in positions of high executive power and responsibility.

Public Opinion (Chicago), September 28, 1899.

54. BRUTAL MURDER

Carterville, Ill., was this week the scene of as disgraceful affair
as ever falls to the lot of man to witness. It was the same story--racial
difficulties.

The Carterville incident, where six Negroes were shot to death, is no
more nor no less than a complement to the affair at Pana, Ill., of several
weeks ago and now supposed to be closed. It never will be closed! It's
the story, we repeat it, it's the story of the strong against the weak.
White miners of that region have combined and sworn that a black man shall
not exist if they can have anything to do with it. They call themselves
having a union, which is no more than an abominable "trust" so far as it
relates to the still poorer blacks. In spite of the determination that
Negroes should not "light" in the town, thirteen of them defied the threats
of the white miners and their sympathizers and marched boldly into the town.
The courage was commendable enough--but the result six Negroes, who but a
few minutes before marched exultingly into the town with heads erect,
breathing a defiance justifiable in the sight of God, warranted by the
spirit of the laws of the land, hearts beating firm with high hopes and
manly resolves, have been shot to death. The hot blood that leaped and
surged as it coursed its way through its portals has been stilled by the
assassins' hands. Those wounds, poor dumb mouths, if they could speak would
they say, "Forgive them, for they know not what they do," or would they curse
their souls?

At any event, the shooting down of six Negroes for dare entering a town
will mark a racial epoch--the beginning of the end, whatever the end will be.
It may be well held that there was not the usual case of provoke as it sometimes happens. The white men felt outraged that the Negroes dared act against
their orders. It is but another evidence how cheap Negro life is held on
the Continent of America. The Negroes now have a faint idea as to what the
future may mean. The laws are powerless to cope with this class of evils.
What does it mean? It means that Negroes must hold their lives dearer. It
means the Negroes must create a valuation if one does not exist.

Washington Bee, October 7, 1899.

55. A COLORED MOTHER

Who Has Witnessed the Benefits of Our Organization

Springfield, Ill., March 26.--Editor Journal: I wish to say a few words
in your valuable paper, as I read a few letters in your last issue of some
ladies, and thought if any woman had any heartfelt thanks or gratitude to
the United Mine Workers, it is me. First, my husband is one of the men that
was arrested and put in prison because he refused to work when he had been
called out by the officials of the union. You may know I was at a loss to
know what to do. I was in Danville, Ill., and my husband was in jail. I
picked up the paper and saw that they had put him in jail, and it was but a
short time until I saw Mr. W. R. Russell, our Vice President, coming to my
rescue. So they took me and my children to Springfield and placed us nearby
the jail and convenient to the schools, and put clothes on my children's
backs, shoes on their feet, books in their hands and started them to school.
They handled all just as if we were children of their family. They also
treated my husband while he was locked up just as kind as if he had been in
a hotel locked up. So I hardly know how to thank the U.M.W. of A. for its
kindness to me and my husband and children. We certainly enjoy reading the
Journal and will not be without it in our house if we can help it. Again, I
must say that my husband would have been in prison yet had it not been for
the officials of the U.M.W. of A. He was sentenced to six months from Sept.
19, 1899, to March 19, 1900, but through the officials of the U.M.W. of A. he
was released on Dec. 25, 1899. So you see, my husband is with us since Dec.

This is my first letter to the Journal, and I guess I am the only colored
lady writing, so I will close at this by saying good luck to the United
Mine Workers. I remain, yours truly,

MRS. WM. CANSLER (colored).

United Mine Workers' Journal, May 22, 1900.

V

ALONG THE COLOR LINE: TRADE UNIONS AND THE
BLACK WORKER AT THE TURN OF THE
TWENTIETH CENTURY

PART V

ALONG THE COLOR LINE: TRADE UNIONS AND THE BLACK WORKER
AT THE TURN OF THE TWENTIETH CENTURY

In 1891, a Cincinnati newspaper reported the results of a questionnaire distributed among Southern employers by The Tradesmen, a commercial paper of Nashville. The questionnaire was designed to evaluate the "efficiency of the Negro as a skilled worker, as a factory operative, and as a free laborer generally." The results of the survey led the paper to conclude that black economic progress was "truly marvelous." Black spokesmen generally contradicted this sanguine assessment, however. Racial discrimination among white workers, unions, and employers, along with the rising tide of legal segregation , worked in unison toward eliminating Negroes from many traditional occupations and prevented them from entering new ones. Afro-Americans who worked as compositors thus encountered stiff opposition from white workers who wanted them removed. And at the Bureau of Engraving in Washington, D.C., black women were being eliminated even as additional whites were being employed, and the civil service increasingly passed over qualified black applicants (Doc. 1-6).

Even Birmingham, Alabama, which was a virtual boom town in the 1890s, did not provide equal opportunity for Negro employment. Birmingham was "The Negroes' paradise" according to one black newspaper editor, yet even this optimist was forced to recognize that there was "little demand for skilled colored labor." Indeed, thousands of blacks wandered about the streets "in fruitless search for something to do," and to make matters worse, the foundries recruited whites from the North to take their places (Doc. 5, 14). Southern textile manufacturing, which had grown dramatically since the Civil War, also excluded blacks in most instances, and became the special preserve of poor whites. Usually, attempts to employ black workers caused trouble. Such was the case in 1897 at the Fulton Bag and Cotton Mill of Atlanta. When the company hired black women spinners, their presence precipitated a spontaneous strike by the white operatives, who refused to return until the black women were fired. Again in 1899, the entire plant went out on strike when Negroes were introduced onto the shop floor (Doc. 7, 12).

Unsurprisingly, a wide range of opinion prevailed among southern blacks regarding the best strategy for economic improvement. While some, such as Lizzie Holmes, spoke for many unionists who argued for working class solidarity against the "capitalistic oppressors" (Doc. 9, 16), most blacks enlisted in the ranks of the industrial education movement led by Booker T. Washington. From Tuskegee Institute, Washington won widespread support with the rationale that Negroes should be schooled for skilled occupations since unions would not open their doors for black apprentices (Doc. 3,8,10,19). A small core of blacks resisted complete reliance on industrial education, however, arguing instead for the elimination of racial barriers in the trade unions (Doc. 20).

Compared with the North, however, blacks found a cornucopia of skilled occupations open to them in parts of the South. One black New Yorker visiting Jacksonville, Florida, for example, noticed that the carpenters and brickmasons were nearly all black, a dramatic contrast to the situation in his hometown (Doc. 27). Afro-American leaders publically commented that it was easier for intelligent northern blacks to become professionals than skilled tradesmen. John Durham of Philadelphia noted that blacks simply wanted work, and suggested that wealthy businessmen provide them with jobs rather than philanthropy (Doc. 23, 29, 30). Most northern blacks agreed that labor unions were the real culprits. Even The Freeman of Indianapolis, which heralded the cause of labor as a "sacred one," blamed the unions for poverty among blacks, and charged that they were controlled by "Negro-haters." Unions exploited the most oppressed workers of all while, at the same time, they bellowed against capitalist exploitation. The Freeman thus called for black workers to break strikes where white unions excluded them, and most black publications in the North supported the assertion that "trade unions must be brought to terms or made to suffer the consequences " (Doc. 31-36, 39, 43, 45).

THE COLOR LINE IN THE SOUTH

1. OPPOSITION TO NEGRO COMPOSITORS

From the Atlanta Constitution

COLUMBIA, S.C., July 17.--The State press is very much agitated over
the discovery that one of the leading county papers in the State, the Abbeville *Press and Banner,* is printed exclusively by negro compositors. A very
hot editorial was written upon the subject by the editor who made the discovery that "for the sake of cheap labor young white men were crowded out
of a field of industry peculiarly their own." Another newspaper thought it
a degradation of an honorable business, and declared its intention of having
"nothing to do with a newspaper edited by a white man and set up by negroes."
Several other journals have followed the lead of the paper which started the
boycott, and much editorial space is devoted to the matter. These journals
consider the *Press and Banner* particularly unjustifiable, as it has always
been a ferocious enemy of negro education. The *Press and Banner* declared it
was working for the almighty dollar, and proposes to have the cheapest and
most satisfactory labor without regard to the boycott. It is somewhat singu-
lar that the *Baptist Tribune,* the largest colored organ in the State, edited
by two colored men, should be printed exclusively by white compositors.

New York Times, June 20, 1887.

2. NEGRO COMPOSITORS IN THE SOUTH

From the Montgomery (Ala.) Dispatch, July 21.

Several negro papers in this state have been set up and printed by white
compositors. In 1870-71 the *Alabama State Gazette,* edited by James T. Rapier,
who was at that time a prominent politician, was set up and printed in a
Democratic newspaper office in this city. The *Gazette* was probably the first
newspaper edited by a negro ever published in Alabama. The *Herald,* a negro
paper now published in Montgomery, until recently was published in a well-
known job office in this city. Of course this was all right. But on the
other hand a prominent and influential weekly, published in the black belt,
and edited by one of the most uncompromising Democrats in the State, who did
more to bring about the race issue in 1874, when Houston was elected Governor
and the State was freed from negro Republican domination, than any man in
Alabama, was set up and worked off a Washington hand press by a negro for
several years. The negro got a pretty fair education in the office, and afterward represented his county in the Legislature one or more terms. The paper
in question was the *Wilcox Vindicator,* and it was edited by Major Charles L.
Scott, now Minister to Venezuela. Major Scott was one of the rabid Democratic
editors in the State during the memorable campaign in 1874, and his paper was
quoted far and near. A forcible writer and a man of courage, and as fearless
as he was honest and sincere, he made a brilliant record, both through his
paper and on the stump by his able advocacy of white supremacy during that
dark period of the State's history. The articles which were characterized
by the most scathing abuse and ridicule of the negro as a dupe of unprincipled
men, "fools, and thieves," were set up principally by a negro compositor.
Nobody cared then to kick at the employment of the negro by the *Vindicator,*
and although there was a strong opposition paper published in the same town,

Camden, at the time, it never referred to the *Vindicator's* printer, and this publication of the facts is doubtless the first that has ever been made.

New York Times, July 24, 1887.

3.   SKILLED LABOR

Mr. Editor:--

   Dear Sir:--In your last weeks issue you were kind enough to publish an article relative to the importance of skilled labor among the colored people of our city and state; and the advisability of establishing mechanics institutes in our several communities for the benefit of the colored youth. I see no reason why we should not begin at once a movement, looking forward to the establishment of such an institution in the city of Richmond. Talking about what should be done is vain, unless we act. Now is the time for action.
   Can the colored people of this city erect a building suitable for the purposes aforesaid, and meet the expense necessary to the support and maintenance thereof? No man who has a growing family could reasonably object to contributing, at least, one dollar per annum to such a human cause, and all important object. By a little effort we have succeeded in building very many respectable--if not costly and splendid temples of worship. Is it not reasonable to conclude that with determination, and effort commensurate with the importance of the cause, we can succeed in achieving the desired object?
   Now we must show ourselves men by sacrificing something for the future welfare of our people, or accept that inevitable alternative resulting from the law of the survival of the fittest in the race of life. Unless we take steps looking forward to the education of our people in the mechanic arts, the future will be a gloomy day for the Negro.
   There is every reason to believe that the Southern whites prefer Negro skilled labor to the foreign born mechanic. The Negro is, by nature, peaceable, thoroughly American, and opposed to all revolutionary and dangerous methods in any endeavor to obtain redress for wrongs; and he is satisfied with fair wages.
   The opposition to the Negro in the mechanic shops come mainly from the employees, who are, for the most part, foreign born, and, who knowing that the Southern whites have a preference for Negro labor, when efficient, see that it is to their interest to keep up a constant warfare against Negro mechanics. We will never be able to make a successful fight against such prejudice, until we have enough mechanics to take possession of a shop, I am for action along the line indicated.

W. H. SMITH,
May 7th, 1891, Richmond, Va.

Richmond Planet, May 30, 1891.

4.   THE NEGRO AS A WORKER

   The efficiency of the Negro as a skilled worker, as a factory operative, and as a free laborer generally, is a question of general interest, especially interesting to southern states. *The Tradesman* recently sent out to extensive employers in the south, a circular asking the following question among others:
   "4. What degree of efficiency do you find in common and skilled Negro labor as compared to white labor in like work?
   5. Do you intend to continue the employment of Negro labor?
   6. Are your Negro laborers improving in effeciency?
   7. What effect has such education as the younger generation has acquired

on them as laborers?

8. Does it add or detract from a Negro's efficiency as a laborer, in your opinion, to educate him?"

The replies received indicate that the wages now paid the Negroes in the south equal, if not exceed, the average wages of white factory operatives, as shown by the census of 1880.

The Negroes, moreover, are as yet generally exempt from the curse of child labor in mine and factories. The summary of answers received by *The Tradesman* are thus given:

"Replies were received from 106 persons residing in all the southern states, and employing 7,835 colored workers, of whom 978 are reported to be skilled laborers. The highest wages reported as paid to skilled laborers is $3 per day, the lowest $1.10, and the average wages of skilled laborers $1.75 per day. The highest wages received by unskilled laborers, as shown by these replies, are $1.50 per day, the lowest .60 cents per day, and the average $1.10 per day.

The replies to the fourth question . . . are not so general as the answer to some of the others. Briefly stated, 27 employers of 1,879 colored workers see no difference as to their capacity as compared to white labor; 35 employers of 1,491 colored men prefer white labor, and 49 employers of 5,214 Negroes prefer them to white laborers in the same capacity.

To the inquiry: Does it add to the Negro's efficiency to educate him? the answers are very interesting. To questions 7 and 8, concerning this topic, there were received 139 answers, most of which were quite brief. Employers, 30 in number, having 2,800 colored employees say that the amount of education which the younger Negroes have received has been of benefit to them, and that it adds to the efficiency of a Negro to educate him."

From the answers received there is left no doubt that the Negro is becoming capable of doing better work, and that where the opportunity is given him to do skilled labor, as it is in the south, he is capable of developing so as to improve it. There has been some fear on the part of a few that the Negro was not holding his own, or gaining ground in the industrial or mechanical line. However, in spite of his many drawbacks, he is steadily going forward and to one who has made his progress a study, in this line his advancement is truly marvelous. *The Tradesman's* inquiries were directed to employers in the Southern States only. In the north the wages run considerably higher. For instance, I have been investigating the wages received by Negroes in the North and their acceptance as employees and find that the highest wages paid to skilled Negro laborers in the North is $4.50, $1.50 in excess of what is paid to skilled Negro laborers in the south. The lowest wages paid to skilled colored laborers in the north, $1.75; the average $2.50 per day. For unskilled Negro labor in the north, the average wages per day $1.35; .25 cents in excess of that in the south. I also find that the skilled Negro laborer, when given a chance, is as preferable, if not more, as the whites, and that there is no difference between the efficiency of a skilled Negro laborer and a skilled white laborer.

                                                                            LARPH

Cincinnati Gazette, September 12, 1891.

5. TRADE EXILES

A City Swarming With Idle Negro Mechanics

Birmingham, Ala. Special

Birmingham is the metropolis of Alabama and the Negroes's paradise. It is to the South what Pittsburgh is to the North, a great mining and manufacturing center, made up of a heterogeneous population. Branded as the "Magic City," its growth within the past eight years has been wonderful. It is a town of machinery, mills, furnaces and a net work of railroads and electric cars. The majority of the laboring class is colored, filling such places as the proud

Caucasians refuse. Like most other undertakings, the whites have a union which leaves the Negro out when it comes to building. There is little demand for skilled colored labor here. It is safe to say not less than five thousand idle men and hungry women and children wander around the streets in fruitless search for something to do. White supremacy and corrupted Democracy, the prevailing powers, often force the Negro to act the part he otherwise would not. The overplus of broken down farmers and bankrupt merchants from the rural districts, who come daily hoping to find something better, only make it worse for the inhabitants. The twenty-eight furnaces in the Birmingham district, besides rolling mills, factories and hundreds of shops. The city furnishes more attractions than work for these labor seekers. Notwithstanding the bitter opposition to "negro domination," (the interpretation the Bourbon gives to the fact that the Negro is trying to rise), some have arisen above the common level. Birmingham has five colored mail carriers, one jeweler, one undertaking establishment, one inventor, one author, one photographer, one silk grower, the only one in the State, one bank, five editors, three lawyers, two M.D.'s, one S.D., one L.L.D. and D.D.'s by the score.

The Freeman (Indianapolis), October 22, 1892.

6.   COLORED WOMEN NOT WANTED

The front page picture of THE FREEMAN last week was accompanied with an argument deploring the American disposition to close the doors of commercial and industrial employment against the youth of the race. This week we are called upon to record as shameful a story of Democratic disposition to militate against some score of worth qualified women of the race as can be found within the annals of political meanness. Since Chief Johnson of the government Bureau of Engraving and printing at Washington, took charge of that office in July '93, not two years, there have been eighty women removed. Of this number eighteen were white and seventy colored; leaving only ten colored women remaining in the service. Of the whole number dismissed, eighteen white and seventy colored, twelve of the white women have been reinstated and but one colored woman. Another fact, all these women received their appointment through competitive civil service examination. But let the Civil Servic Commission that has recently given publicity to the correspondence with the secretary of the treasury upon this matter, finish this story of small beer politics ergo Democratic narrowness and wrong, and after, kick yourslf for not voting that ticket last fall if you can. Said the Commission, writing secretary Carlisle under date of Dec. 15, '94:
  This nearly clean sweep of colored women extended also to appointments from the certifications of the Civil service Commission from the regular eligibles. In the year ended June 30, 1894, forty-five women were passed over upon certification without selection, of whom at least ten were colored. Under Mr. Johnson's predecessor, Mr. Meredith, appointments were made in the order of grade, practically none being passed over. Under Mr. Meredith there were only eighteen dismissals out of about 158 women employed between 1888 and 1893, as compared with 88 dismissals to 543 employed in a year and a half under Mr. Johnson. At present there are only eight colored women remaining. Of the women dismissed by Mr. Johnson twelve white were reinstated and one colored.
  "The fact of this large number of discharges of colored women and of passing them over on a certification has greatly reduced the number of colore women applying for examination. During Mr. Meredith's term under President Harrison's administration, there was only one colored woman removed. No allegations have been made to the commission that the colored women were removed for any misconduct." [98]
  In stating these facts to the Secretary of the Treasury, the commission said:
  "From these facts it would appear that under the administration of the present chief of the Bureau of Engraving and Printing there have been very

marked discriminating on grounds of color merely, not only in the making of
appointments from the eligible register, but the dismissal of persons already
in the service.

The Freeman (Indianapolis), February 23, 1895.

7. SPONTANEOUS PROTEST

In 1897 a strike against the employment of Negroes occurred in Atlanta,
at the Fulton Bag and Cotton Mill. The strike was a spontaneous protest
against the employment of twenty Negro women spinners who were to work along
with white women. Fourteen hundred workers quit, and formed a union that
afternoon. The strike lasted only a day. The employers agreed to discharge
the Negroes, and the employees agreed to work overtime when necessary. When
the workers returned, however, they presented an agreement to Mr. Elsas, the
manager, which called for the discharge of all Negroes employed by the company except janitors and scrubbers. Mr. Elsas refused to sign the agreement,
stating that it involved more persons that he had verbally agreed to discharge, and adding that he did not see any reason for the discharge of the
additional Negroes. Thereupon the workers went on another strike. This
strike lasted only one day also, for Mr. Elsas agreed to discharge all Negro
employees and to discriminate against none of the strikers. He refused,
however, to sign any written agreement. The strike was called off and the
workers returned to their places.

Atlanta Constitution, August 5-8, 1897.

8. THE NEGRO: HIS RELATION TO SOUTHERN INDUSTRY

By Will H. Winn, Columbus, Ga.

The oration at the celebration of Emancipation Day at Columbus, Ga., was
delivered by Richard R. Wright, head of the State college for negroes, and
one of the best informed representatives of his race in Georgia. Referring
to the importance of the negro to the South, and the evidence of his progress,
he said:[99]
"We care for our sick; we bury our dead; we build our churches; we are
supporting our ministers; we are rearing our families; we are educating our
children, and we are gaining property. In the South we are doing 57 per cent
of the agricultural work and over 90 per cent of the manual and domestic
services; we are doing for the South over one thousand million dollars' worth
of work every year at lower wages than is paid to any other class of laborers
in America. We are doing this without strikes and without labor organizations
and riots. It is admitted that we are the most peaceable and patient laborers
in the world."
No one with a knowledge of the negro's condition in the South will question the above statements. While his percentage of labor shows a tendency to
decrease in the agricultural districts, the negro is making rapid advances in
the mechanical industries of the South—a fact due, in great measure, to the
conditions described in the closing sentence of the quotation.
Practical and general trade organization among the negroes of the Gulf
States has never been attempted, to my knowledge, and were the initiative to
begin at once, with all the forces at our command, it would be a matter of
doubt to many minds if the dawn of the 20th century would witness any material
progress.
While there are many exceptions, of course, to the general rule, it is a
fact patent to every observing man who has studied the negro from contact that
as a race, he does not give evidence of a possession of those peculiarities

of temperament such as patriotism, sympathy, sacrifice, etc., which are
peculiar to most of the Causasian race, and which alone make an organization
of the character and complicity of the modern trade union possible--suffi-
ciently to warrant a hope that his condition might be improved by organization corresponding with the good results obtained through white organization.

Those well-meaning but misguided philanthropists (and others) who would
attempt a solution of the negro problem in the South on the supposition that
his character, his needs and adaptabilities are similar to those of the
white race, do not appear to take into consideration certain well-known
traits of negro character, prominent among which is his distrust of his
fellows in black and his deep-seated prejudice against the white workingman,
the ignorance of the adults, and his abandoned and reckless disposition. I
said that there were many exceptions to this, but, as applicable to the
race, the truthfulness of the above is universally recognized in the South,
and may be easily verified.

It would be well for all union men, irrespective of section or opinion,
to understand correctly the negroe's position in the Southern labor movement,
as, I believe, he is yet to bring about a complete readjustment of the
Southern industrial problem. We must deal honestly and fearlessly with conditions as they are, and not as we would have them be.

At present the negro has a decided advantage over the white man in the
Southern industrial field. There is but little if any excuse for an idle
negro. If he cannot find employment in the cities, there is always an
opening in the country--farmers sometimes having to hold out extra inducements to obtain his labor, as they much prefer him to the white man. In
most of the cities he has a practical monopoly in such trades as carpentering,
brick-laying, blacksmithing, etc. He does the bulk of the labor at cotton
warehouses, compresses, lumber and raw mills. Porters, hotels and restaurant waiters, domestics, coachmen and driver, longshoremen, river hands,
corporation hands, firemen and tenders of stationary engines, "day laborers,"
etc., etc.--the bulk of them are negroes. Why? Simply because he works
for what he can get, as many hours as may be required of him, and is the
happiest and most contented individual imaginable. Now who ever heard of a
contented people descanting upon burdensome conditions. Is not the "agitator"--he who points out and rebukes error and injustice--the forerunner
of reform? And what reform, pray, came about except through the workings
of the inseparables--discontent and agitation?

Outside a few of the more skilled and organized trades, if a body of
workmen generate sufficient temerity to ask for less hours or an advance in
wages, the Goliath in command has only to utter the magical word "negroes!"
to drive them back into the ruts in fear, and trembling for their positions.
The fact of their not being organized is a sufficient comment on their sub-
missiveness; they know that, in addition to the swarms of white men that
may be "shooed" up from the farms, where 5-cent cotton has played hide and
seek with their appetites, there are also hordes of negroes ready to drop
the plow-shares for work at almost any price in town for the sake of the
education which the State gratuitously offers their children. There is
hardly any sacrifice of the comforts that the negro will not willingly and
cheerfully make in order to educate his children--very commendable, indeed,
but alas for expectations! the records show an increase of crime along with
it.

I will say, also, that some of their distinguished educators have
developed quite as much oratorical ability in denouncing and villifying the
trade unions as they have business sagacity in disposing of the large school
and charitable donations from the land of the Puritan, in distilling into the
young hopefuls a sense of equality and even superiority over the "poor white
trash" and "factory tads," (euphemisms easily recognizable by all who have
journeyed Southward). And the ease and dexterity with which they continue
to elongate the philanthropic leg forms a study in metaphysics.

Recently, several hundred white textile employes have been discharged
to make room for the negro, on the plea of economy. Cotton mills have a way
of going to the cheapest market for labor. It is the opinion of many that,
in the no distant future, unless the unforeseen should happen, negroes will
be worked almost exclusively in the cotton mills of the South--and then what?
But that's another subject.

I have myself anticipated in the organization of several unions that

were, in time, forced to disband because their members could not procure
work at a union wage in the face of negro competition. Unfortunately,
there are but few unions in the South which have the negro as an active
competitor that can truly lay claim to stability; and inasmuch as he is an
active competitor in 90 per cent of Southern industry it would appear that
time and money spent in a general organization of white workingmen is, at
best, experimental--notwithstanding that there are industries which public
sentiment will not permit the negro to engage in that are not organized,
but which should and could be had we the organizers with time and money to
accomplish it.

I shall not attempt to discuss a general organization of the Southern
negro. In a few local instances it might and doubtless has proven advan-
tageous, but, generally speaking, I doubt if there be a hundred native
Southerners who would seriously entertain such a proposition; and as these
believe, so would the people of other sections doubtlessly believe with
like information on the subject. Public sentiment (an all-powerful factor
in such matters) argues that it is impracticable, if not impossible, and
altogether out of question, albeit with a due respect for those of different ideas, whose environment, possibly, is not black and yellow on the
horizon.

But even admitting as possible a thorough organization of the negroes,
it is hardly probable that the white workers generally could be induced
to recognize them as union men--that is, brothers in a common cause--and
without such recognition or federation or understanding between the two
organized races whereby concerted action might be engendered, I submit that
organization would be worse than worthless.

From a Southern view, colonization would be a practical and mutually
agreeable solution of the negro-labor problem. Bishop Turner, of this State,
and many others of the prominent negro divines and educators, all over the
South, favor the emigration or colonization scheme, and are now working to
that end in favor of the negro republic of Liberia. The only opposition
these men encounter is from the capitalistic class (of course), and its
chief tool--a hireling press. The negroes themselves are friendly to the
proposition, as witnessed by the fact that some 19,000 of them have emigrated to the black republic, although the prosperity of Liberia has been
very obvious, it a poor country; its climate is bad, and its native surroundings unfavorable to the purpose.[100]

The country most suitable in every respect, and at present the most
available for negro colonization, is Cuba, "Queen of the Antilles," and
the garden spot of the continent. There the negro would thrive and prosper
as he would nowhere else on earth. And with this end in view the United
States might well afford to put an end to the horrible conditions now
prevalent on that unhappy isle. I believe 90 per cent of the Southern
negroes would hail with delight this opportunity.

And the white toilers of the South, once freed from this disorganizing
competition and a consequent wage and hour system the most demoralizing
of any section of America, would easily demand and receive a just compensation for a reasonable amount of labor.

Reader, this article is not intended to influence your opinion against
the negro. No fair-minded man would blame him for that which he cannot
help, considering that he, like all humanity, derives his natural character
from a source which we dare not assail. I would place him on a higher level,
open his way for greater possibilities and rejoice with him in his happiness,
but I would also help those whom his competition unwittingly injures.

I have thus laid before you an unprejudiced statement of the negroe's
position in the southern industrial problem.

American Federationist (February, 1898): 269-71.

9. THE LABORERS' WAR

Shall the Poor Longer Fight the Battles
of the Rich

OBLITERATE THE COLOR LINE

THE ONLY JUSTIFIABLE WAR IS THAT OF THE OPPRESSED AGAINST THE OPPRESSOR--
THE LATTER ARE UNITED THE WORLD OVER; WHY NOT THE FORMER ALSO?--IT IS THEIR
ONLY HOPE OF VICTORY.

A few days ago I listened to an address from a young colored man before
an audience of thoughtful men and women, where he acquitted himself remarkably well. He made a strong plea for the obliteration of the color line
between laborers. He showed that unless the white labor unions were willing
to fraternize with the black people working in the same trades they must all
sink into a condition of hopeless slavery nearly as bad as that from which
his race had been rescued.

It seemed to me that the young speaker struck the key to the situation,
which cannot be too strongly emphasized. The interests of the working people
are the same the world over. Their common cause is of more importance than
any other issue that can possibly arise. Difference in race, religion,
nationality, are minor matters they must be willing to forget and clasp hands
over the one cause common to all or give up the struggle for an opportunity
to live as human beings should live.

The capitalists, the great moneyed men of the world, understand this
perfectly well. So well do they comprehend the fact that already they are
practically one. Observe closely, and you will perceive that the money powers of the different nations differ very little on questions of a national,
religious, philosophical or even of a strictly political nature. They simply
watch each other like hawks to see that one does not get an undue financial
advantage of the other. They realize that no question on earth is of as much
importance to them as their economic hold on the world. They know, also,
that the common people do not realize the solidarity of their own interests
and that it is very easy to intensify their differences and keep them fighting
with each other over non-essentials. They are perfectly well aware of the
sort of stories to fling among them in order to keep them engaged in destroying one another.

It is pitiful to see the faith that the working people put in the importance of their little differences and how little they realize that the
"bread and butter question," the economic question, the question of how to
live at all, lies at the bottom of every other question. They are so loyal
in their patriotism and so innocently trust that this virtue is shared by
all their good countrymen, rich and poor alike. They guard their religion
so devotedly, as though it mattered to the exploiters of the earth after what
form they worshipped. And that old prejudice, born of the superstitious times
when everything strange or foreign was feared or hated is still cherished with
a faithfulness worthy of a better cause. For it they turn away from the worker of another color who needs help and who is able to help. For it they
follow political leaders into faraway paths, where they lose themselves in a
labyrinth of sophistries which bring up nowhere. And therefore it is that
the one power which we have to fear is well organized and ready for work in
any direction, while we are scattered, distrustful of each other and unable
to resist their encroachments.

The critical situation between the United States and Spain illustrates
this truth very strongly. The diplomatic action, or, rather, inaction, of
the leaders in the two countries proves that principle has nothing whatever
to do with a war should one occur, for if love of justice and a desire to
defend the helpless is the incentive, why have we waited so long? If ever
interference were justifiable, it is in this instance, where women and children, the sick and the wounded, the old and the helpless, have been treated
with a ferocity that would put to shame the most savage tribes of the most
savage ages. If the honor of the nation is to be the cause, why have we
waited so long? American citizens have been insulted over and over again and
American rights trampled upon. If Spanish rapacity and cruelty need punishing,

why have we waited so long? Why have we waited until an expensive warship
is blown to atoms and 250 lives have been sacrificed thereby before we move?[101]
    Even now there will be no war if there are greater values at stake than
those involved already, for with the great capitalists of the world there
are no national boundaries, no national interests. This may be a startling
statement to make, but I believe it is true. They together compose a power
that is neither English, German, French or American, and the interests of
neither country are considered when compared with the interests of their
values which are centered in all lands wherever labor power and natural resources exist. While there is nothing to be gained by a war and much to be
lost in the way of the unsettling of values, of stocks, bonds, etc., there
is little likelihood of war, unless--which is not likely--the sentiment of
the people should rise to an overwhelming force. Race prejudice, patriotism,
superstition hatred, any of the emotions always swelling to the surface of
the common people, would be appealed to, and the poor working folks of two
countries would be set to work butchering each other. But no money lord or
politician would get where he would be hurt.
    It is a terrible thing to think that the poor workers of this country
should be sent out to kill and wound the poor workers of Spain merely because
a few leaders may incite them to do so. If there are men brave and strong
and good enough to go to Cuba and help the Cubans to gain their liberty, who
will drive the mistaken soldiers of Spain, who are themselves poor and are
only willing at their rulers' command, out of the island and then let them
go and also come home and let the Cubans arrange their own affairs. I would
say, "God speed!" But a war that is to be waged so the verge of destruction,
that will blacken and ruin the land and sacrifice countless numbers of lives
of innocent people for the sake of a big gunboat or even for the sake of the
poor soldiers sacrificed with it, who could not be brought back to life by
it, I deeply hope will not come to pass. I wish the common soldiers on one
side would send such a message as the soldiers of the commune in 1871 sent
to the common soldiers of the Prussian army. In those days it might be
answered in a greater, a higher, spirit than it was then.[102]
    The workers on one side of a sea or a river can conceive of no laudable
excuse for hating and wanting to murder the workers on the other side of it.
They are the producers of the world's wealth, and they are all suffering
alike from a common wrong. They have but one genuine enemy on earth, and this
is the united money power that is fleecing them systematically wherever they
are. When they once realize this and refuse to fight for the property of the
rich, for the wounded honor of some petted parasite, for the possession of
territory out of which capital may wring fresh tribute, for the defining of
a boundary line that signifies nothing to any one except a few fleecers, wars
will cease, for the world's great men will not declare war when they see that
no one will fight them. They do not want wars that must be waged personally--
they only fight by proxy. It is one thing to get up a quarrel in which millions of common men are sacrificed and millions of dollars can be "made" and
quite another to precipitate a struggle that must be fought out by oneself.
    No, the only laudable, justifiable kind of war that can ever be waged
again is one of the oppressed against the oppressor, of the producers against
their exploiters, the slaves against the tyrants. Even such a war, let us
hope, need never be. Intelligence has spread over the world so rapidly, so
widely, that this mighty and vital question of the right of labor to its own
productions may be settled peacefully. If the workers of the world will awake
to the fact that their interests are the same, and if they will refrain from
quarreling with one another about the color of their skin, the places where
they happened to be born, the political and religious faiths of their grand-
fathers, it will be. For rulers and exploiters who will not fight their battles unless they can do it with substitutes will not fight the common people
if they can find none among them who will do it for them.
    It is not necessary that the people all agree as to theories and remedies,
for that would imply that some among them must be hypocrites or that they
should crush down their honest convictions. But it is necessary that they have
for each other's opinions the utmost tolerance. It is above all necessary
that they recognize that the needs, aspirations and wrongs of the people in
all other nations are similar to their own and that if anybody must be killed
it isn't that kind of people.

Don't, workingmen, be too anxious to load yourself up with killing machines and march away to kill a lot of poor fellows just like yourselves. If you feel the inspiration to help the Cubans, go and do just enough killing to accomplish your purpose--no more.   Then come home.

LIZZIE M. HOLMES

Birmingham Labor Advocate, April 2, 1898.

10.   HOW OUR EDUCATED YOUNG MEN AND WOMEN CAN FIND EMPLOYMENT

By

Booker T. Washington

The whole question of textile manufacturing and the making and fitting of clothing is largely a new one in the South and the race must have leaders along this line also.   In short, in the laying of a foundation of any race, the needs are largely along the three cardinal lines that I have mentioned: food, shelter and clothing.   In order to be more helpful to the young men and women who are being educated, I will be more specific.   Any young man or woman who prepares himself thoroughly in any one of these lines will not be long in securing a position at a good salary; agriculture, horticulture, landscape gardening, dairying, stock raising, poultry raising, architecture, mechanical engineering, electrical engineering, mining engineering, brick masonry, carpentry, house decorating, house contracting, cooking, dressmaking, millinery, textile manufacturing, tailoring, etc.   The fitting of one's self along any of these lines will either enable him to find a place, or, what is better, to make a place.

The Christian Recorder, September 29, 1898.

11.   COLORED LABOR IN COTTON MILLS

"The unfortunate result of an experiment at negro labor at Columbia, S.C.," says the Louisville *Courier-Journal,* "is another answer to the oft-repeated query why the colored man is not a skilled laborer."   The paper continues:

"That he does not become a well-paid mechanic instead of a mere hewer of wood and drawer of water is certainly not due to the existence of race pre-judice in the South, however it may be in the North.   In the South the few blacksmiths or carpenters or bricklayers or trainmen of African descent find ready and remunerative employment.   The reason there are not more of them is chiefly to be found in the negro himself.   At least this is the opinion of the writer in *The American Wool and Cotton Reporter,* who details the failure of an enterprise which it once was thought would go a great way toward solv-ing one of the various phases of the race problem.

"The correspondent in this case refers to the failure of a cotton mill at Columbia which was started with the intention of utilizing negroes as operatives.   Of course, the mill was to be managed by whites, but it was thought that colored help was equal to the requirements of the machines.   The mill has proved a costly loss and will now be sold under foreclosure pro-ceedings.   The kind of work the hands did leads to the following bitter obser-vations from *The Reporter's* contributor:

"I here take occasion to repeat what I have said before, viz.; that negroes will not make good cotton mill operatives; indeed, now that the experiment has fully tested in two or three instances, it can be stated that they have not

made even fair operatives, and there is no reason in the world for believing
that they ever will, for I know the average Southern darkey well--his habits
and predilections, his instability and love of "freedom." They will not,
as a rule, submit to the application and confinement required of the successful mill operative. They demand too many "holidays." They must attend
their "festerbuls" and lodge and other secret society meetings, to some half-
dozen or more of which most of them belong; and even if they were good work-
men--which they are not, on machinery of any character, being clumsy and
listless at the best--they woefully lack the quality of application (as
stated by me at the time, and as has been shown so conclusively by the fre-
quency with which the superintendents of this mill and the one at Charleston have had to hunt new hands) to make successful mill-hands."

"The writer has a good deal more to say, part of which is undoubtedly
true and part of which may be prejudice. One thing, however, can not be
controverted, the negro is not disposed to train himself for skilled employment, and to make him do so requires an education which shall dispose him
to labor and self-denial. This is the task to which Booker Washington and
his fellow workers and students have set themselves, and it is worth their
noblest efforts. If professor Washington and such as he can train the negro's hands to skill and can induce him to live cleanly, soberly, and honestly,
they will do a far greater work than the men who put the ballot in his
possession."

The Chattanooga, Tenn., *Tradesman* says:

"There is no difference of opinion among real business men concerning
the cause of the failure. The men at the head of the concern had far more
hope, enthusiasm, and theory about them than business sense, an article they
seem to have been very short on. Their attempt to do a business of that
kind with negro help showed lack of judgment. They began deeply in debt.
They enlarged the debt by turning the mill into a sort of textile school,
with scholars who went and came as they pleased. The enterprise is hope-
lessly swamped, tho it might now be prospering, had not its nominal owners
gone about to force nature, and in violation of the sound canons of business,
undertaken to make mill-operatives out of people who have hardly passed the
corn-hoeing, rock-quarrying, and dirt-shoveling stage of civilization. We
are glad the failure is complete and final. Being so it will probably deter
other cranks from fooling away some money."

The Literary Digest, October 15, 1898.

12. STRIKE OF MILL WORKERS AT FULTON COTTON MILLS[103]

ATLANTA, Ga., July 20.--
The Mill slaves were organizing when a number of them were discharged
and supplanted by negro labor, because it was cheaper and unorganized.
Thereupon the entire force of Mill workers struck, and after being out several days, won the strike, although the active participants in the strike were
later discharged and their union crippled. While the strike was in progress,
the Executive Committee issued a manifesto to the people, and this manifesto
is such a strong indictment against capitalism that it is herewith reproduced.

Manifesto of the Strikers Issued by Textile Union

The Strikers Declare they are not Fighting the Negroes, but are Contending Only for Their Rights--Plain Talk About the Mill Owners.

To Whom It May Concern:
We, the employees of the Fulton Cotton Mills, herewith present to the
public the attitude of the cotton mill workers in the present controversy.
Notwithstanding the fact that 1,000 wage-workers, composed mostly of women
and children, have for years been compelled to have their flesh and blood
counted in dollars and cents by the mill owners, owing to excessively long
hours of work and extremely long wages, they are now subjected to such

indignities as would meet the condemnation of every loyal white citizen of
Atlanta, and also of the majority of self-respecting black citizens.

The efforts of the Fulton mill owners to force the white women and
girls employed there to work with the negro women who were placed among
them, is a deliberate attempt to eliminate the white wage-slaves from this
avocation and substitute black wage-slaves because they will work cheaper,
although the white wage-slaves do not live but simply exist. The real
question at issue now is one of wages and not of prejudice. The mill owners
know that the white workers are organizing and becoming more intelligent,
and they are making an effort to keep them in subjection by employing cheap
labor and forcing the white workers out of employment. . . . The published
accounts of the controversy make it appear to the public that it is a strike
originating in racial prejudice, but such is not the case. It is a strike
against the introduction of cheaper labor; against forcing those people out
of work who have held the positions for years, and against the damnable
wage-slave system which is building up this cotton mill and the cotton
industry of Atlanta on the bodies and souls of the daughters and sons of the
fair southland.

We realize that under the system of competitive capitalism conditions
cannot be permanently improved and that this system must be supplanted by
a co-operative system in which all shall have the opportunity to apply their
labor power properly, before permanent relief can come to the people.

                                                    Executive Committee

Daily People, August 6, 1899.

13.   COLORED PEOPLE'S PLEA

Plea-Address Issued By Afro-American Convention

Disfranchisement of Negroes

Lynching of the Black Man of the South--
Inconsistency of the Trade Unions Deplored

The committee appointed by the Indiana Afro-American convention to prepare an address to the public, today gave out the following to the people of
America.

We, the colored citizens of Indiana in convention assembled, for the
purpose of considering the many forms of injustice to which we are subjected,
on account of our color, and believing the great heart of the American people
still beats in sympathy with the spirit of liberty and justice for all men,
and believing further, that the apparently sleeping conscience of the major
portion of the people is largely due to a lack of information concerning our
real condition and the wrongs that are heaped upon us as a race in all sections
of our country--we deem it wise to issue this address, setting forth the facts
which we wish considered appealing to the sense of justice of the American
people.

The greatest injustice which we suffer is the taking of human life without trial by jury, at the hands of mobs, which is a violation of the most
sacred right known to civilization.

We call the attention of the world to the appalling fact that more than
thirteen hundred human beings have been lynched in this country within the
past seven years.[104]

The ingenuity of thousands of a refined civilization has been taxed to
its utmost to devise methods of inflicting the most excrutiating tortures
upon helpless negroes, surpassing often the practices of savages in barbarity.
Hanging and shooting have become too tame--they are flayed alive and left to
die, fingers and toes have been "pounded to a jelly," and then the victims
hanged, they are tied to stakes, dismembered and burned, and the roasted remains cut and sold to eager purchasers as souvenirs; they are shot and scalped,
etc.

The apologists for these horrible outrages claim defense of pure
womanhood as the prime cause of these outbursts of savagery, but we call
attention to the fact that, according to the press dispatches from the daily
papers published in the sections of country in which these lynchings occur,
less than one-third of the 1,300 lynched were not accused of assault or of
rape. During last year (1898) according to President Dreher, of Roanoke
College, Virginia, out of 127 Negroes lynched, twenty two were accused of
assault or attempted assault.

We do not condone crime, and do especially condemn that of rape and
favor the punishment of those guilty of it by the death penalty, according
to law. We stand ready to unite with all law-abiding citizens for the en-
forcement of the law.

The category of crime as narrated above, fills us with horror unspeak-
able, and we feel that it is high time that pulpit and press should unite
in an earnest crusade against the terrible American crime of lynching.

We point with sadness to the gross violation of the United States
election laws, by statutory enactment, in the states of North and South
Carolina, Georgia, Mississippi, and Louisiana, whereby three-fourths of the
Negro voters of those states are disfranchised under the guise of an educational qualification.

We do not protest because of an education qualification, but we do protest against the law because it is only applied to the Negro, and we call
upon all citizens who believe in a fair ballot to join us in this protest.
Laws should be general in their application, and apply alike to all citizens.

We call upon all men, regardless of race or political faith, who believe
in equal rights before the law, to use all honorable means in their power to
have the representation in Congress from those states reduced to the basis
of their actual voting strength.

Discriminating laws having for their purpose the humiliation and degradation of our people under the thin guise of giving to us the same rights
and privileges that are accorded to other citizens, have been enacted by
various states.

Those laws--among which may be mentioned the election laws, the separate coach act, school laws in several states, the provisions pertaining to
public places of entertainment and amusement--work upon us great hardships
and injustice.

As a race of laborers, we sympathize with every honorable and lawful
movement or combination, now perfected, or to be perfected, which has for its
object the betterment of the condition and environment of honest toil, whether
skilled or unskilled, regardless of race or the political and religious creed
of those who go to make up the great army of the world's producers. We,
therefore, contemplate with regret the impression that seems to be general
throughout our country that for the benefits, protections, encouragements
and guarantees vouchsafed to labor through and by the direct influence of the
trades unions, no colored man need apply.

It seems to us, with all deference to those earnest and consecrated men
who have, and are, devoting their lives to the organization and marshalling
of the forces of labor, they are guilty of great inconsistency. It is an
axiom of the law, as old as jurisprudence, that "he who seeks equity should
first himself be willing to do equity, if he would come into court with clean
hands and a prima facie claim that justice be extended him."

How can the trades unions continue to demand and expect to receive without question or challenge, sympathetic approval and endorsement of public
opinion when the very things it is demanding for itself--justice, fair treatment and a living chance to secure through honest toil bread and protection
for their loved ones--they refuse to extend to some millions of other laboring men, whose only crime is that of their unfortunate environments, and that
Jehovah in his wisdom dowered them with dark skin.

Again, if all labor was organized black and white, skilled and unskilled,
such spectacles as have been afforded the world within the last month in the
cities of New York, Brooklyn, Cleveland and Evansville, would seldom be witnessed. The "scab" workman black or white not existing could not be used by
the oppressors of organized toil to thwart the union in its just and humane
demands.

Sincerely hoping that the time will not be longed delayed when union
labor will insist upon taking the broad and humane view of this great question,

and that every lover of humanity, of justice and of fair play will join us
in bringing about the result so anxiously desired we rest our complaint
with the conscience and judgment of the great American Nation. Signed by
the committee:

                              EDWARD L. GILLIAM,
                                            Chairman.
                              JNO. J. BLACKSHEAR,
                                            Secretary
                              GEO. W. CABLE,[105]
                              W. E. HENDERSON,
                              S. A. ELBERT,
                              LANDONIA WILLIAMS,
                              L. E. CHRISTY,
                              W. ALLISON SWEENEY,
                              D. A. GRAHAM

The Freeman (Indianapolis), August 12, 1899.

14. TO REDUCE NEGRO LABOR

White Men Are Being Imported to Take Their Places

     BIRMINGHAM, Ala., March 16--The first batch of workmen from the Niles,
O., district, who will be employed in the Bessemer and Ensley districts,
arrived today. There are 24 men in the party, all of whom will go to work
in the puddling department of the Bessemer rolling mills. Several other
large parties of skilled laborers from Ohio will arrive during the next
few days to complete the quota needed at the Bessemer mills, after which the
remainder will go to Ensley to work at the steel plant and furnaces. It is
stated that at those places hereafter negro labor will be used for only the
rough work, such as loading cars, breaking iron and other heavy drudgery in
the furnace yards.
     This is part of a general movement which has been inaugurated by the
large labor employing corporations of this district to reduce the number of
negroes employed to a minimum.

Birmingham Labor Advocate, March 23, 1901.

15. LABOR UNIONS ASSAILED

An Alabama Leader Declares Them Treasonable Organizations

     WASHINGTON, June 13.--Before the industrial commission yesterday N. F.
Thompson, secretary of the southern industrial convention, of Huntsville,
Ala., made a somewhat sensational attack upon labor unions. "Labor organizations are today," said Mr. Thompson, "the greatest menace to this government that exists inside or outside the pale of our national domain. Their
influence for disruption and disorganization of society is far more dangerous
to the perpetuation of our government in its purity and power than would be
the hostile array on our borders of the armies of the entire world combined."
     In support of his statement he said that on every hand, and for the
slightest provocation, all classes of organized labor stand ready to inaugurate a strike, with all its attendant evils, and that in addition to this
stronger ties, of consolidation are being urged with the view of being able
to inaugurate a sympathetic strike that will embrace all clases of labor,
simply to redress the grievances or right the wrongs of one class, however
remotely located, or however unjust may be the demands of that class. He
maintained that "organizations teaching such theories should be held treason-

able in character, and their leaders worse than traitors to their country."
He urged a law making killing in self-defense of any lawful occupation
"justifiable homicide," and said that negro labor was essential to the
prosperity of the south.

Richmond Planet, June 16, 1900.

16. THE COLOR LINE IN ORGANIZATION

BIRMINGHAM, Ala., June 25, 1900.
    I will say before entering this controversey that I am a democrat and
as far from social equality as any man living. Yet after the other Constitutional amendments made the colored man a citizen of the south, I voted
for the Fifteenth amendment to give him an equal right in all the states,
so he would not be a citizen in one state and an alien in another.
    In the labor question, the colored man earns his bread and meat by the
sweat of his face, just like I do. His bread and meat, like mine, stops
when he ceases to work. In a word, both white and black have to work for a
living, whether organized or not. Now, the only question for consideration
is, will Organized Labor admit the black man, not only thereby benefiting him,
but adding strength to organization; or will it leave him to the tender
mercies of the sweatshops?
    I may dig coal on one entry and the black man on another some distance
away, yet we work together; you may work in one shop and he in another, yet
you work together; you may work in a rolling mill and he may fire the engine
that runs on the rail you forged into shape, yet you work together. This
being an unalterable fact, will organized Labor take him under its protection
for mutual benefit, or will it leave him out to be used by the enemies of
organization as a powerful force against us. If we act wisely and conserva-
tively in this and all other matters, we will gain the esteem and confidence
of all wise, conservative men. If we can do this, we shall have gained all
we need.
    Intelligence and honesty has ever governed the world. Like the Hebrews,
men may have suffered for a time, but an honest, intelligent Moses has
always come forth to right their wrongs. "The pen is mightier than the sword,"
and now that the dollar has taken the place of the sword to a great extent,
the pen is mightier than the dollar. "The fool and his money are soon parted"
is an old saying, but is as true today as it ever was.

                                                        W. T. WESTBROOK

Birmingham Labor Advocate, June 30, 1900.

17. NEGROES IN ATLANTA

    In reply to Mr. W. L. Scarborough, a colored professor in Wilberforce[106]
University, Ohio, the Atlanta *Constitution* denies the story which appears
to be going the rounds of the Western press, that there is a newsstand in
Atlanta at which negroes are not permitted to buy papers. The *Constitution*
adds:
    "Here in Atlanta we have negro lawyers, physicians, and dentists; negro
merchants, tailors, undertakers, shoemakers, tinners, painters, carriage-
makers, blacksmiths, and wheelwrights; negro contractors, who employ white
as well as colored workmen; negro machinists, carpenters, cabinet-makers,
brick-masons, plasterers, and plumbers; negro workers in shops, in every
trade and business for which their ambition and their ability fit them; and
opportunities open to them in every direction that their capabilities may
suggest."

Where can anything like this be found in the East or in the West? We happen ourselves to know of the negro dentist in Atlanta. He resigned a good position in the Treasury Department a few months since in order to practice his profession in that city. But think of negro contractors who employ white workmen--and in the South, too! Can Senators Hoar and Chandler name many--or any--such instances at the North, or such a diversity of industries among the colored population as that shown by the *Constitution?*[107]

The Nation, August 28, 1900.

18.   TRAINING NEGRO LABOR

The experiment of employing colored labor in textile mills in the south is one of peculiar interest, as the ability for skilled workmanship is looked upon as of peculiar interest, as the ability for skilled workmanship is looked upon as in an important degree a measure of the capacity for the development of the race. So far none of the numerous tests have resulted satisfactorily, and yet it is admitted that in no case has a fair trial been given. Negroes have become good mechanics, such as carpenters, bricklayers, and engineers, but in work which requires delicacy of manipulation and taste he has not shown much aptitude. Whether this is from lack of training and opportunity or from indolence or other fault has not yet been determined, and will not be until the negro has been given a fair trial in this respect. A staff correspondent of the New York "Journal of Commerce," who has been investigating the textile industries of the south has made the subject of negro labor in mills the text for one of his articles. He does not appear much encouraged. In alluding to the mill erected at Concord, N.C., by negro capital and in which negro labor is to be exclusively employed, he says the mill is ready for work, but had not at that time any money to buy cotton. Its equipment of 5,700 spindles and 140 looms is adequate, but second-hand, and hence could not offer a very satisfactory text. A number of white capitalists are interested in the mill and not only hold a large amount of stock, but had loaned the company $10,000 to complete the plant. White carders, spinners and weavers had offered to teach negroes the work, so there will be no trouble on that score if money can be raised to start the mill. When Negro girls are whipped in the silk mills of Fayetteville, N.C., the superintendent a Negro man says:

"No one desire more than I do to see the portion of my people improved; but I have no false ideas as to the present condition of the majority of them. They lack responsibility, and are like children where money is concerned. That may be kept in view when dealing with them."

Certainly this belief of a colored man as to the only way to make his race work skillfully and work regularly differs but little from that practiced in the factories of the North; the difference being one of method only. Northern capitalists are not adverse to brutalities, especially when they use police and militia to club and shoot their workers into submission.

Daily People, November 12, 1900.

19.   INDUSTRIAL EDUCATION IS THE SOLUTION

by

Booker T. Washington

At Tuskegee, Alabama, starting fifteen years ago in a little shanty with one teacher and thirty students, with no property, there has grown up an industrial and educational village where the ideas that I have referred to are put into the heads, hearts, and hands of an army of colored men and women, with the purpose of having them become centers of light and civilization in every part of the South. One visiting the Tuskegee Normal and Industrial Institute today will find eight hundred and fifty students gathered from twenty-four States, with eighty-eight teachers and officers training these students in literary, religious, and industrial work.[108]

Counting the students and the families of the instructors, the visitor will find a black village of about twelve hundred people. Instead of the old, worn-out plantation that was there fifteen years ago, there is a modern farm of seven hundred acres cultivated by student labor. There are Jersey and Holstein cows and Berkshire pigs, and the butter used is made by the most modern process.

Aside from the dozens of neat, comfortable cottages owned by individual teachers and other persons, who have settled in this village for the purpose of educating their children, he will find thirty-six buildings of various kinds and sizes, owned and built by the school, property valued at three hundred thousand dollars. Perhaps the most interesting thing in connection with these buildings is that, with the exception of three, they have been built by student labor. The friends of the school have furnished money to pay the teachers and for material.

When a building is to be erected, the teacher in charge of the mechanical and architectural drawing department gives to the class in drawing a general description of the building desired, and then there is a competition to see whose plan will be accepted. These same students in most cases help do the practical work of putting up the building--some at the sawmill, the brick-yard, or in the carpentry, brickmaking, plastering, painting, and tinsmithing departments. At the same time care is taken to see not only that the building goes up properly, but that the students, who are under intelligent instructors in their special branch, are taught at the same time the principles as well as the practical part of the trade.

The school has the building in the end, and the students have the know-ledge of the trade. This same principle applies, whether in the laundry, where the washing for seven or eight hundred people is done, or in the sewing-room, where a large part of the clothing for this colony is made and repaired, or in the wheelwright and blacksmith departments, where all the wagons and buggies used by the school, besides a large number for the outside public, are manufactured, or in the printing-office, where a large part of the printing for the white and colored people in this region is done. Twenty-six different industries are here in constant operation.

When the student is through with his course of training he goes out feel-ing that it is just as honorable to labor with the hand as with the head, and instead of his having to look for a place, the place usually seeks him, be-cause he has to give that which the South wants. One other thing should not be overlooked in our efforts to develop the black man. As bad as slavery was, almost every large plantation in the South during that time was, in a measure, an industrial school. It had its farming department, its blacksmith, wheel-wright, brickmaking, carpentry, and sewing departments. Thus at the close of the war our people were in possession of all the common and skilled labor in the South. For nearly twenty years after the war we overlooked the value of the antebellum training, and no one was trained to replace these skilled men and women who were soon to pass away; and now, as skilled laborers from foreign countries, with not only educated hands but trained brains, begin to come into the South and take these positions once held by us, we are gradually waking up to the fact that we must compete with the white man in the industrial world if we would hold our own. No one understands his value in the labor world better than the old colored man. Recently, when a convention was held in the South by the white people for the purpose of inducing white settlers from the North and West to settle in the South, one of these colored men said to the president of the convention: "'Fore de Lord, boss, we's got as many white people down here now as we niggers can support."

The negro in the South has another advantage. While there is prejudice against him along certain lines,--in the matter of business in general, and the trades especially,--there is virtually no prejudice so far as the native Southern white man is concerned. White men and black men work at the same carpenter's bench and on the same brick wall. Sometimes the white man is the "boss," sometimes the black man is the boss.

Some one chaffed a colored man recently because, when he got through with a contract for building a house, he cleared just ten cents; but he said: "All right, boss; it was worth ten cents to be de boss of dem white men." If a Southern white man has a contract to let for the building of a house, he prefers the black contractor, because he has been used to doing business of this character with a negro rather than with a white man.

The negro will find his way up as a man just in proportion as he makes himself valuable, possess something that a white man wants, can do something as well as, or better than, a white man.

I would not have my readers get the thought that the problem in the South is settled, that there is nothing else to be done; far from this. Long years of patient, hard work will be required for the betterment of the condition of the negro in the South, as well as for the betterment of the condition of the negro in the West Indies.

There are bright spots here and there that point the way. Perhaps the most that we have accomplished in the last thirty years is to show the North and the South how the fourteen slaves landed a few hundred years ago at James-town, Virginia,--now nearly eight millions of freemen in the South alone,-- are to be made a safe and useful part of our democratic and Christian insti-tutions.

The main thing that is now needed to bring about a solution of the diffi-culties in the South is money in large sums, to be used largely for Christian, technical, and industrial education.

Booker T. Washington, "Signs of Progress Among the Negroes," *Century Magazine* *37 (1900): 476-77.*

20.   INDUSTRIAL EDUCATION NOT THE ONLY SOLUTION

I am heartily in favor of the industrial and mechanical training for such Negroes as may feel that their calling is on the farm or in the factory, but I challenge the assertion of those who claim that the only solution of the so-called race problem lies in the direction of the industrial and mechanical training of the Negro.

Surprisingly strange, perhaps, but nevertheless true, slavery itself furnished the race with valuable lessons in industrial and mechanical train-ing, and produced a race of high-class mechanics, skilled workers in wood and iron and metals of all kinds, many of whom remain until this day, and, I regret to say, far more than can obtain employment, caused by the unreasonable and unfriendly attitude of the trade-unions toward colored mechanics. How, then, can the multiplication of Negro mechanics help to solve the so-called race problem, when those who are already skilled cannot obtain employment? In this city, to my personal knowledge, there are a score or more of skilled Negro mechanics who are subject to enforced idleness by reason of the color-phobia which dominates the trade-unions. Those who are disposed to advance the Negro's best interests can render him invaluable services by demanding, in tones of thunder loud and long, that the trade-unions shall cease to draw the color line, and that fitness and character shall be the only passport to their fellowship. When this barrier shall have been removed, the time for the multiplication of Negro mechanics on anything like a large scale, will have become opportune but not until then. [109]

I know full well the argument of the contra-contendents--how that an appreciable increase in the present number of Negro mechanics would make a white contractor independent of white mechanics when his interests might war-rant the employment of Negro tradesmen. But it cannot be justly claimed that this argument rises to the force and dignity of an argument. It is at the very best but a mere theory, and one shorn of plausibility for the reason that it apparently overlooks the fact that the trade-unions, by the power of the boycott, could influence the dealers both in raw and manufactured material not to sell to said contractor, and thus abort his designs to defy them by the employment of Negro artisans. The trade-unions constitute a most potent organization, and it is very difficult to thwart its will. Therefore, the primal and essential accomplishment is to influence its directors to abandon the cruel and frigid color line.

But, then it can be answered that if the Negro mechanic cannot find employment for his skilled hands, let him go to the farm and engage in agricultural pursuits--learn how to scientifically raise sweet potatoes, as the present chief revivalist of the industrial training for the Negro is wont to urge.

When in the unregistered aeons of the genesis of creative development-- when prehistoric man roamed at will, and before God had fixed the bounds of man's habitation--in what recorded cycle of time was it written on the tablet of divine fiat that the universal position of the Negro should be that of a tiller of the soil? It may not be a self-evident truth that all men are created free and equal, but it is an axiomatic verity that all men, other than imbeciles and idiots, are endowed with mental and spiritual capacities capable of varied and illimitable expansion; and the Negro being a man, is irremovably within the sphere of this axiomatic verity. Hence, unless it can be established that the Negro is not an integral and component part of the original plan of man's creation, but the increment of a mere accident, the crystallization of the particles of the surplus dust that marked the creative place of generic man, it must be accepted as the corollary of the axiomatic verity that the Negro, in common with all the other race varieties, is endowed with mental and spiritual capacities, capable of varied and illimitable expansion; and that, as a whole, his sphere of operation cannot be limited to the tilling of the soil; but that his development will be marked by variety of attainments and accomplishments, thus proving himself to be an originator as well as an imitator.

Moreover, the acquisition of scientific agriculture cannot possibly profit the masses of the Negroes to any great extent, seeing that they are not the owners of the soil. By this I refer to the diversification of crops as the result of a knowledge of scientific agriculture. The diversification of crops is not dictated and controlled by the tillers of the soil, but by the owners. The plantation hand in the South exercises no choice whatever as to the number of acres he shall plant in cotton or the number he shall plant in corn or wheat or any other cereal. In this regard he must obey the mandate of his employer. In view of this is the suggestion valueless that so far as the utility of a diversification of crops is concerned, that this advice should be pressed upon the owner of the soil rather than upon the tiller? It is the owner alone who can change the existing conditions of things. The advice which Secretary of Agriculture Wilson gave to the young white men of the South, in his address at the McKinley banquet in Savannah, Georgia, was most opportune and should impress the present chief revivalist of industrial training for the Negro with the fact that in insisting on the study of scientific agriculture by the masses of the Negroes, he is building a cage for a bird that is yet to be caught; unless, perchance, the Negroes should become the owners of the soil. There can be no doubt that the practical application of the principles scientific agriculture will increase the yield of a given crop in a stated area; but if by this it is meant that a knowledge of scientific agriculture is essential to teach the Negro how to hoe cotton and plant corn, such is as far from the reality as the east is from the west; as the Negro has long since graduated in the accomplishment of hoeing cotton and planting corn, and his diploma was stamped on the great majority of the ten million bales of cotton which were marketed in this country last year. Therefore aspire to add to the Negro's present limited fund of knowledge by teaching him how to do something which he does not now know how to do.[110]

The necessity of the Negro's training in industrial pursuits, either as a theory or a dictum, did not originate with this generation, but is coeval with his existence on the American continent. With equal propriety might one term John Wesley the apostle of Christianity as to term the Master of Tuskegee the apostle of industrial training for the Negro. The former was simply the revivalist of a long-existing doctrine; the latter is merely the revivalist of an ancient dictum. "Teach the Negro how to work," and in reechoing this dictum has struck a popular chord in the minds, if not the hearts, of a large element of the American people, some of whom emphasize their approval by throwing dollars into his open hands. . . .[111]

When the present chief advocate of industrial training for the Negro as the speediest and most effective solution of the so-called race problem shall have gone outside of his own bailiwick, as I have; when he shall have placed himself in a position to observe the present status of the various elements of mankind, notably in Europe, West and Southwest Africa, South America, and the Caribbean Archipelago; when he shall have seen a woman and a dog hitched together and drawing a loaded cart through the streets of Antwerp, Belgium; when he shall have seen Hungarian women digging coal in the mines of their own native land; when he shall have looked upon the peasantry of Europe so poorly fed, poorly clad, poorly housed, and poorly paid; when his attention shall have been directed to the fact that three fifths of the inhabitants of the earth live in a one-room hut, that scientific agriculture is as little known to the peasantry of Europe as it is to the plantation hands of the Southland, and that the farmer has no more to do with the diversification of the crops than do the latter, he may at least find some of his views modified thereby, come to realize that the doctrine of the survival of the fittest will shape and govern the destiny of the Negro as it does that of all other race societies, that the Negro cannot be limited to any one sphere of physical or mental operation, but will ramify every nook and corner of Americanism and add his quota to its strength, perpetuity and adornment.

Nashville American, January 29, 1899.

21.   TRUSTS SMILE

Now, any labor leader of intelligence will admit that labor cannot afford to fight labor, that antagonisms should not be promoted between any classes of workmen, be they black or white.

Whenever this is done, trusts smile and enjoy the situation hugely. So long as the colored laborers are careless of the welfare of the white laborers and vice versa, the breach thus made and kept open makes the enemies of labor certain of success in any attack made upon the divided ranks of labor.

Richmond Planet, September 8, 1900.

22.   CRITICAL POSITION OF THE NEGRO

Is The Race Losing Ground?

DARK VIEW OF THE PRESENT INDUSTRIAL STATUS OF THE NEGRO OF THE SOUTH--OPINION EXPRESSED THAT THE RACE HAS GONE BACKWARD IN CIVILIZATION AND EFFICIENCY SINCE SLAVERY--A VERY STRIKING TESTIMONY BY A SOUTHERN MAN.

To the Editor of *The Republican*:--

In an editorial article in *The Republican* of November 20 in criticising the study of "The Negro in Africa and America," by James Alexander Tillinghast,[112] you accuse him of "inherited bias against the free blacks," and ask the question:--

"Taking southern agriculture as a whole how was it possible for its farm values to increase in greater percentage in the two decades mentioned (1880-1900) than the farm values of the whole country, if the negro labor, upon which southern agriculture largely depends, was all that time degenerating in quality? Obviously, there is a conflict between Mr. Tillinghast's conclusion and the broad fact of the southern uplift in agricultural wealth."

There is no conflict between Mr. Tillinghast's contentions and the fact

of Southern prosperity and development. These are due to the white man, not
to the negro, to the immigration of white men from the West and to the up-
lifting of the poor white of the South, whose progress during these two decades has been as rapid as the decay of the negro as a laborer and a producer.
These statements of Mr. Tillinghast are substantiated by the census and every
other statistical report published which lets in any light on the subject,
and they cannot be brushed away by the general and vague statement of a North
Carolina banker as you suggest.

    You very properly take agriculture as the industrial field in which the
negro makes the best showing, for he has been an agriculturist for generations. Of all the southern crops, that in which he makes the best showing
is cotton. The cotton industry is based on negro (slave) labor. The negro
was believed to be the best cotton laborer in days of slavery, and the planters even pretended to find that his hand was better made to pick cotton than
that of any other race. Originally the entire cotton crop was raised by
negro labor; and, at the death of slavery, certainly nine-tenths of it was
raised and picked by the negroes. If, however, you return to the census of
1900, statistics of agriculture, volume II, you will find that the two counties producing the largest amount of cotton in the South, over 80,000 bales
each, are Ellis and Williamson counties in Texas. The negro constitutes
only one-tenth of their population, and produces less than one-tenth of their
cotton. Of the 19 southern counties producing over 50,000 bales of cotton
each, 17 are overwhelmingly white, nearly all the cotton in them being raised
by white labor, and only two are black--Washington county, Miss., and Orange-
burg county, S.C. A comparison with former censuses will show that the cotton
production is drifting away from the black belt to the white counties in
nearly every southern state. Thus, in North Carolina the big cotton counties
are white. Louisiana the center of cotton production has shifted from the
rich alluvial lands of the Tensas Basin where the cotton is raised by negro
labor, to the central district, where the population is mainly white. . . .

    Such is the negro in the field of agriculture, where he appears to the
greatest advantage. In manufactures no one claims anything for him; in the
mechanical trades he is losing ground steadily. In spite of the optimism
that you and others feel, the industrial horizon of the negro is growing
steadily narrower, and is now actually more limited than in the days of slavery. To those who look only at the surface it seems different, for they see
new industrial schools established for negroes, and the old ones enlarged and
better endowed. The New Orleans school board has established the higher grades
in the negro public schools and will use the money for industrial education
of the negro youth, which is proclaimed the panacea for all negro ills.

    But when we study the trades, a very different condition of affairs is
found. The negro's field of labor is each day more circumscribed. Slavery,
as is well known, is not conducive to manufactures, and it was inimical to
mechanical work by the whites. "Mechanic" became a word of reproach to a
white man in the South of old; in addition to which he found himself placed
at a great disadvantage in competing with negro and perhaps with slave labor.
As a consequence, nearly all the mechanical work in the Southwest in ante-
bellum days was done by negroes. The gas company imported white mechanics
from Philadelphia, but discharged them and replaced them with negro slaves,
finding that the raising of pickaninnies paid 20 per cent on the investment
in addition to getting the work done cheaper. Most of the mechanical work,
however, was done by the free men and women of color. They were the mechanics,
the carpenters, blacksmiths, painters, tailors, dressmakers, etc., and originally the policemen and firemen of New Orleans. Their descendants have been
crowded more and more out of the trades, until now, their main source of income is shop work for the clothing factories. They have retrograded immensely
during the last 40 years in health, education, labor and social standing, and
have drifted back almost to the condition of the plantation darkey. Those
who believe that the negro is advancing have but to wander through the rear
of the 2d district of New Orleans, where probably 25,000 mulattoes and quad-
roons, "Creole negroes," descendants of the free people of color of ante-
bellum days, live today. He will see at once a retrogression to the African
type, for these negroes, having ceased all intercourse with the whites, and
marrying among the purer blacks, are growing darker. Some of them were
wealthy in old days, nearly all had independent means. Scarcely any of them
have anything worth mentioning today.

During this period, as compared with even the days of slavery, the negroes have lost ground industrially. They have ceased to be carpenters, painters, engineers, tailors, cigar-makers, shoemakers, except a few who work mainly among their own people. Their labor has become more and more the roughest manual work, and even in the fields they occupy they are each year more circumscribed. In only one trade have they maintained their former standing--a bricklayer's. Those who are not bricklayers and outside of domestic service are teamsters and loaders, longshoremen who unload and load vessels, or section hands on the railroads. The closing of city contract work to negroes and the division of the ship-loading business between the races has had the effect of crowding a number of negro men out of New Orleans. As a consequence there are more than three negro women to each man, the former supporting themselves by washing and domestic labor. The census figures will probably show fewer negro men at work in New Orleans than 10 years ago, although the colored population of the city has increased.

The statistics read at negro meetings of the property accumulated by negroes in the South are utterly misleading. The negroes own less property in Louisiana than they did in slavery time; the slight increase reported by the auditor is due wholly to improvements in value from greater general prosperity, and it does not keep pace with the general growth of the community or the percentage of increase among the negroes themselves. The proportion of taxpayers among the negroes is growing smaller, and so is the per capita wealth; and if the assessors' tables be examined, it will be found that the bulk of the property with which the negroes are credited is in the hands of a few of the race, who, although called negroes, are nearly white in color, and altogether white in their ideas, character and aspirations. One-fourth of all the assessed wealth marked "belonging to negroes" in New Orleans, belongs to a half a dozen persons, who would pass for white in any part of the world save the South, who secured much of this wealth through inheritance and have added to it by their energy and diligence. And yet these millions have figured before every negro convention, and in speeches of white sympathizers, as evidence of the progress the negro has made since slavery.

Mr. Tillinghast declares that slavery civilized the negro and that since the withdrawal of slavery the race has gone backward. This view is sharply substantiated in Louisiana where the deterioration of the negro is mainly due to the separation of the races, which is so marked a feature of the South today. Intermarriage between the races is prohibited in Louisiana; even miscegenation was made a crime by the last Legislature, and that influx of white blood which was at least improving the negro mentally has ceased. The separation is growing more marked every day. The law separates the races in the hotels, theaters, restaurants, on the cars, street railways and boats, even in the penitentiary and insane asylum. The trend of affairs has separated them in other respects. The negroes now occupy distinct quarters of the town. In politics, religion and social affairs they are separate. Visitors to New Orleans are always surprised at the small number of negroes they see on the streets, the reason therefore being that the negroes do not visit the white suburbs or patronize white stores. With this separation, the white control and discipline of the negro race has been lost, the negro is thrown more and more on his own resources and the civilizing work of slavery is being undone. The segregation of the negroes is better for the white man, but it has proved a most unfortunate setback for the negro.

But I do not want to wander off into discussion of the negro problem, but merely to call your attention to the fact that there is a flaw in the line of argument you pursued in criticising Mr. Tillinghast, and that because the South is improving today it does not follow that the negro is improving. If you look over the census more carefully and see in what sections of the South there has been prosperity you will see a disproval of your statement. If you do not I shall be glad to furnish it.

NORMAN WALKER,
New Orleans, Louisiana.

The Springfield Republican, December 1, 1902.

THE COLOR LINE IN THE NORTH

23. DOUGLASS ON WORK

It is easier today to get a colored lad into a lawyer's office to study law, than into a blacksmith shop to hammer iron. . . . The effects of being ruled out of all respectable trades at the North, has compelled the colored people there to crowd the cities, lanes and allies (sic)--and live by work which no other class of people will do. This work being occasional, coming at intervals, and never long continued exposes them to the ten thousand evils of enforced idleness and poverty.

Frederick Douglass, Oration . . ., Delivered on Friday, October 1st, 1880, quoted in the *African Methodist Episcopal Zion Church Quarterly 5 (July, 1895)*: 165.

24. ENCOURAGING

It is very encouraging, as we look over our exchanges, to note that colored barbers in different parts of the country are exhibiting manhood enough to obliterate the color line in their shops. The discriminations which colored men have made in their establishments against colored men, have been one of the biggest stumbling blocks in the way of our obtaining civil rights. No other race of people on Gods green earth treats its members as some of ours do each other.

Western Appeal (St. Paul), April 30, 1887.

25. COLOR LINE

A correspondent to the *Chicago Conservator* writing on the "color line," seems to think it is because colored men do not apply for places that they do not get them, but that is a mistake. Colored men are constantly making applications for places, but without success.

There have been several instances in this city where colored men have answered advertisements and been requested to call at the advertisers place of business, but when they put in their appearance they would be put off with some lying excuse. And when he does get a place he seldom gets a promotion, but he is kept in the same place he starts in. The correspondent doubtless means well, but he certainly does not know anything about the trouble, trials and tribulations that a young colored man has to undergo in endeavoring to get the commonest clerkship in mercantile circles. There are very few white men who have the nerve and back bone to employ a colored clerk in opposition to the wishes of his other employees, and when they begin to put on airs they at once give in and the obnoxious man and brother is discharged. If the heads of business firms would not look at the color of the applicants but only at their qualifications and when they happened to get a colored man or woman would give him or her support there would be thousands of applications from colored people where not a dozen are now made.

Western Appeal (St. Paul), August 13, 1887.

26. THE COLOR LINE IN BASEBALL

The St. Louis Browns Refuse to Play With the Cuban Giants

PHILADELPHIA, Sept. 11.--The Philadelphia *Times* will say tomorrow that
for the first time in the history of baseball the color line has been drawn,
and that the "world's champions," the St. Louis Browns, are the men who have
established the precedent that white players must not play with colored men.
There have been little dissensions before, but only about a player here and
there. The Browns were in open revolt last night. Some time ago President
Von Der Ahe arranged for his club to play an exhibition game at West Farms,
near New York, with the Cuban Giants, the noted colored club. He was promised a big guarantee, and it was expected that fully 15,000 persons would
be present. The game was to have been played today, and President Von Der
Ahe yesterday purchased railroad tickets for all his players and made all
the arrangements for the trip. While he was at supper at the Continental
Hotel last night thinking over the misfortune that had befallen Capt. Comiskey, he was approached by "Tip" O'Neill, the heavy slugging left fielder,
who laid a letter on the table and then hastily slipped out of the room.
The letter read as follows:

PHILADELPHIA, Penn., Sept. 10.

To Chris Von Der Ahe, Esq.:
DEAR SIR: We, the undersigned members of the St. Louis Baseball Club,
do not agree to play against negroes tomorrow. We will cheerfully play
against white people at any time, and think, by refusing to play, we are only
doing what is right, taking everything into consideration and the shape the
team is in at present.
W. A. Latham, John Boyle, J. E. O'Neill, R. L. Caruthers, W. E. Gleason,
W. H. Robinson, Charles King, Curt Welch.
President Von Der Ahe did not wait to finish his meal. He left the
table hastily and went down stairs into the corridor, where he found the
players talking in a group. The sudden appearance of their manager among
them surprised the players and they acted like a ship's crew about to mutiny.
When Von Der Ahe asked the meaning of the letter he had just received, nobody
answered him. "Yank" Robinson hung his head and sneaked to the rear of the
crowd. "Silver" King opened his mouth, but his tongue refused to move, and
even Artie Latham, whose jaws are always going, couldn't get out a word.
Receiving no reply, President Von Der Ahe said quietly: "As it seems to be
a matter of principle with you, you need not play tomorrow."
President Von Der Ahe said to a TIMES reporter tonight: "I am sorry
to have disappointed the people of West Farms today, as I always fulfill my
engagements. I was surprised at the action of my men, especially as they
knew a week ago that the game was arranged, and yet they waited until the
very last minute before they informed me of their opposition."
The St. Louis players were not disposed to talk of their action. Latham,
Boyle, and O'Neill were the leaders, it is said, and they had considerable
trouble in securing the signatures of some of the men. Capt. Comiskey didn't
know anything about the matter, and Knouff refused to sign the letter. They
had played with the Cuban Giants before last season, and they seemed to
enjoy it better than a contest with white players. Curtis Welch, the centre
fielder, played with the Toldeo Club when The Walker, the colored player, was
a member of the team, "I think some of the boys wanted a day to themselves,"
said Capt. Comiskey. "They have played against colored clubs before without
a murmur, and I think they are sorry for their hasty action already."
The Cuban Giants were originally organized at Trenton about two years
ago as an independent club. This season they have been in various places in
close proximity to New York City. They are good players and the team has
made money. They have played games with the Chicago, Indianapolis, Detroit,
Louisville, Athletic, and other prominent clubs, and this is the first time
that any club has refused to play with them on account of their color. The
International League recently adopted a resolution prohibiting the employment
of colored players by its clubs. This was caused by opposition from the

players, who objected to playing with Second Baseman Grant, of the Buffalo
Club, and colored Pitcher Stovey, of the Newark Club.

New York Times, September 12, 1887.

27. BLACK TRADESMEN NORTH AND SOUTH

JACKSONVILLE, March 9.--To persons coming South from any Northern city, a
deep impression is made upon them if they notice, as they cannot help from
doing, the change which confronts them in the laborers who do the work requiring brain and muscle. If you stand upon one of the wharfs of the large
cities of the North, and watch one of the great steamships as it is being
loaded, you find that the work is done entirely by white men. But when the
steamer reaches a Southern port, it is unloaded and reloaded by colored men.
What is true in this instance is likewise true in many others. The carpentering, bricklaying and machine work which are done in the North principally by white men, are performed in the South chiefly by colored men.

The questions are often asked, Why do we not find more colored men than
there are doing this work in the North? Is the North entirely devoid of
colored men who possess trades? I think not, and still, so few are the
colored men who follow these trades in the North, that if one should go to
work upon a building in New York as a carpenter or brick mason, the street
in which that building might be situated would almost become impassable by
the congregation of people who would stop to behold the strange sight. I
mention this to call attention to and emphasize the fact of the scarcity of
colored men working at these trades in large cities of the North like New
York. No doubt this scarcity is due to the trades unions there. I feel
certain that if colored men in the North possessing these trades had an
opportunity to demonstrate their capabilities to do the work done by white
men, it would be found that their work would lose nothing by comparison
with the work done by their white brethren.

The greater part of the carpenter and brick mason work done in this city
is performed by colored men. Their work reflects credit upon them and demonstrates that colored men can do as good work in this line, and in fact in
any other line, as white men. The only thing they need is the opportunity.
It is only a pusillanimous prejudice which prevents them from entering into
all of the avenues of life and succeeding as do white men.

New York Age, March 16, 1889.

28. ACCEPTED AS CO-WORKERS

How the New Century Guild of Philadelphia
Was Opened to Colored Women

From the Philadelphia Tribune

Some weeks ago through the instrumentality of Mr. John Durham, President
of the Workingmen's Club, the question was submitted to the ladies of the
New Century Guild for Discussion, whether they would accept colored women as
co-workers with them in the more exalted avocations of life--as clerks, type-
writers, bookkeepers, saleswomen, etc. It is very well known that the New
Century Guild is a very strong organization of white working women, possessing among its members some of the ablest of the sex in this city. The question was set for discussion on the first Saturday night in March. Mr. Durham
himself opened the debate, and was followed by Counselor Mint, Dr. Wayland
and Mrs. Fannie Jackson Coppin; the time being consumed, the matter was continued for the next regular meeting, April 6.[113]

At that meeting, after a liberal discussion of the question by the ladies of the guild, a vote was taken which stood 28 in the affirmative and 7 in the negative.

All fair-minded persons--and especially our own people--will highly appreciate this act of the Ladies' Guild. Those who are not tinged with color can little appreciate the difficulties that beset a young man or woman of color in obtaining employment above the grade of the ordinary laborer. Employers, in order to escape their responsibility, frequently attribute the cause of their refusal of employment to the prejudices of their employees. The action of the Ladies' Guild has removed from themselves any responsibility for this injustice. We congratulate them upon their ability to rise above sordid prejudice and accord to all women the right to win as honorable a living as they demand for themselves and, to a great extent, enjoy. It is a cheering mark of the advancement of times.

New York Age, May 3, 1889.

29. WHAT OUR WORKING MEN WANT

BY

John Durham

I have come here to ask you to help the colored man to get a job. That is all he wants, a job, work,--not occupation in some line to which he is restricted by present customs, but work in any line of employment for which he may have a special liking or ambition. In the North he will soon be out of work. He has been the American janitor, waiter, and barber; but the army of foreign immigrants is gradually thrusting him from these occupations into the higher departments of work. In applying for a trade, the workshops are closed upon him. On seeking a place behind a desk or counter, there is no opening for him. In consequence he turns to the learned professions; and many a half educated fellow who would have made an excellent blacksmith or carpenter or commercial drummer, is now failing most successfully in the pulpit, and selling his independence and real manliness for the money which he receives from kind-hearted, but misguided white philanthropists.

I cannot in the time allotted me, do more than hint at the demoralizing influence this system of encouraging dependency is exerting upon some of the brightest young men of my race. Nor can I tell you of the half-made doctors and lawyers, who, emulating the work of the race's well-trained professional men, aimlessly struggle and suddenly sink in this sea of human competition and oppression. It is sufficient if I have succeeded in indicating to you my belief, that the real want of the Negro today is freedom of entry into industrial and commercial competition. Give him a chance; if then he should not succeed, dub him, as Bob Toombs did,--the scrub race,--but not till then. Fourteen months ago our club began making personal appeals to employers, in behalf of deserving and promising colored men and women. We have placed one man, a stenographer, who holds his own in a prominent establishment in Phila- delphia. Not one girl has secured the humble position of saleswoman. Quietly and earnestly we will keep employers thinking about this question; for we can never become a business people until we shall have an opportunity to acquire business habits and business education.[114]

Our clubs in this congress are composed of all classes of workers, from the humblest, unskilled laborer to the wealthy capitalist, who is probably the harder worker of the two, and who can see that in seeking communion with what Matthew Arnold calls the universal human spirit, in impelling himself and his fellow to high thinking and high doing, he urges forward true civili- zation much more than by running his mill or his store or his railroad. As representatives of these industrial extremes, and their intermediate classes, then organized for the moral, intellectual and social well being of the community, you must be interested in this very important phase of the color question. Its appeals to your judgment, your sense of fair play, and--what

is a great draw-back to your success--your social aversion--I feel safe in
asking you to follow the dictates of your sense of justice, even though you
should be compelled to stifle the persistent protests of your inbred prejudices. If you are a workman, do not hesitate to declare your perfect
readiness to work by the side of a colored man, who is honest, clean and
capable. If you are employers give applicants for work a hearing, and give
your colored porter or messenger the same opportunity to learn your business
and to rise as you extend your white apprentice or cash boy. If you are
accustomed to appropriate a thousand dollars a year to Negro education or
Negro Christianity, try the experiment of paying another thousand to the
right kind of colored salesman, or bookkeeper, even if you should be compelled to train him yourself; and I assure you that you will have made the
first step toward solving the Negro Problem. [115]

If you are a Northern man be careful how you criticize your Southern
neighbor. In the section of the South where caste-feeling is densest, where
Negroes dare not attempt to vote, there are human relations between the white
man and the black man which are not known in the North.

There is an industrial freedom, which is today threatened by the introduction of Northern capital and labor. Hesitate therefore in your denun-
ciation of political intimidation and reflect upon our own system of industrial caste. Weigh the two, and determine if you can which is the more
to be condemned, the beam or the mote.

Though the colored people have but indirect participation in the gains
which accrue from National Tariff system, I am a Protectionist of the Pennsylvania brand; but I do insist that the colored workman, a native who has
earned his title to American citizenship by sweat and blood, should enjoy
the same opportunities to learn and to rise in every department of work, as
are so freely extended to unskilled foreigners.

In closing I beg leave to remind you, that the Negro asks simply to
learn. We have no army of prodigies to recommend. Our boys and girls must
rise by the same process as your own. We simply ask a square start and a
fair field. If then we do not succeed, we deserve to fail. In every city
represented in this congress most noble work may be done by the Workingmen's
Clubs, as organizations and individuals. Encouraged, conditionally moved,
emboldened by our relations to members of this congress, we ask you to go
further in co-operating with us in this movement. Do we ask too much?

New York Age, June 8, 1889.

30. JOHN DURHAM ON UNIONS AND BLACK WORKERS

We know that the most degraded foreigners refuse to work with us; but
will you not follow the example of these two Pittsburgh firms Parke Brothers
and Company and Clarke Solar Iron Works. Every strike offers you the same
opportunity that they have seized to their profit; will you not give our men
a chance instead of Hungarians and Italians. Our vote is not a thing to be
despised.

New York Age, October 10, 1888.

With the trades-unions closed against our boys, and the business houses
against our men and women, it is a curious thing to me that our schools and
colleges have not turned out an annual crop of thieves and gamblers, men who
are determined not to do menial work.

New York Age, December 1, 1888.

If one will go to the root of the matter, I think that he must decide
that the industrial education of the Negro is not due to the fact that he is
the American Negro, that he was once a slave, or that he is black. It is
merely an application of the law of supply and demand which impels combined

workmen to keep everybody out that they possibly can. . . . The Northern
Negro knocks at the door of the trade union and says that a poor Negro begs
permission to have his boy taken in as an apprentice. Why can we reasonably
expect our boys to be accepted when there are thousands of white fathers,
members of the union, who are denied the privileges of having their boys
learn their own trades, and for the very reason that the members of the
unions have determined to sacrifice the interest of their own children in
deference to this law of supply and demand.

New York Age, July 21, 1889.

31.   ILLITERATE NEGRO-HATERS

No doubt labor unions are excellent things in their way, and serve many
good purposes in protecting the interests of the wages-earner, but when such
organizations are controlled by narrow-minded, illiterate Negro-haters who
deny an industrious colored man an opportunity to learn a trade, they deserve no encouragement at the hands of our race. When they fail to respect
the principles of justice and humanity their usefulness is fatally crippled;
their mission is ended. The Chandler & Taylor "color strike" is a burning
shame and should bring a blush to the brow of every liberal-minded white
man in the community. There is yet work for the missionary in Indiana.

The Freeman (Indianapolis), January 18, 1890.

32.   COLOR LINE IN TRADES UNIONS

One glaring wrong which has been passed over too lightly is the sense-
less, inexcusable color proscription practiced by the trades unions of this
country. We heartily endorse any project which points to the elevation of
our working people, and admire the zeal and earnestness displayed in their
many protective unions, but denounce, with all our might, that project if
based upon a principle, wrong in the sight of God, and detestable in the
eyes of honest and fair-minded men. Race proscription is this, and nothing
less. In circles where wealth is the magic countersign, the moneyless man
must wait until he can purchase the pass-word. He waits patiently, without
murmur. No such excuse can be urged in the case of unions of artisans. They
are poor men, working for their daily bread. The Negro's status has been
fixed by public opinion as a laborer. It is manifestly unfair, then, since
he must labor, to further restrict his efforts by confining him to particular
classes of labor, contrary to his tastes and adaptability. It is poor economic policy to spoil a good machinist to make a poor coachman, or to force
a natural-born compositor into the awkward roll of table-waiter. This question should be agitated by the press. Our boys must be given a chance in the
trades, and they must not be denied the profit derived from membership in the
various unions. The interests of the white man and the black are the same.
The sun is too high in the heavens to allow the wheels of national development to be clogged by so small and trivial a thing as color for skin.

The Freeman (Indianapolis), April 19, 1890.

33.   LABOR UNIONS AND THE NEGRO

The St. Louis Union Record, a labor paper, in an editorial intended to reflect upon non-union labor, calls attention to the fact, that within the last fifty years the working marts of America, have been supplied at different times with laborers from Ireland, England, Wales, Norway, Sweden, Hungary and Italy. Referring to the trouble and strikes that each one of these nationalities have had with their employees, including the Italians, who of late have been mixed up in strikes and lockouts, the Union says: "Who is to replace him (the Italian) is a question, which now is driving the employers of cheap labor almost crazy. The Darkey won't answer."

Why won't the "darkey," using the Union Records term of opprobrium in referring to the colored man, why won't he answer?

Is it because he is outside the pale of necessity, is he independent, and has no need of employment? As a slave, an enforced tiller of the soil and bondman, is it possible that he cultivated such habits of indolence, became so run down and emaciated physically, that his descendents of this day are not equal to the drain that toil would make upon their strength and general health, hence he wouldn't answer as a substitute for striking white labor?

None of these reasons exist. The Negro as a class are laborers, his past conditions, and present outlook suggests no time for many years to come, when he will not be a laborer, a toiler, depending upon the sweat of his brow for a maintenance and support.

Such are his conditions and prospects, but strange to say, since his emancipation from enforced thralldom, he has been met upon the very threshold of his new found estate, by the opposition, not of capital, not of the men and syndicates who employ labor, and diffuse the benefits of invested wealth amongst the ranks of the "toiling millions," but by labor, organized systematized labor itself.

Where he should by right, and the bond of similar conditions, expect succor co-operation and a spirit of brotherly encouragement, he has been met with organized opposition and a virulence of hate and hostility, that is a blistering reproach to American institutions, and for which, organized labor, so-called will yet hang its head with shame and enforced humiliation.

The cause of labor is a sacred one, and its demands when inspired by the broad spirit of "fair play" and consideration for the rights of all its votaries, regardless of race or past and present conditions, must sooner or later appeal to the great power of public opinion to such a degree, as will in the end, right the inequalities complained of, and so recently emphasized in the lamented Homestead tragedy, and the subsequent attempted murder of Mr. Frick.[116]

But before this condition is assured, the spirit of equity must prevail. How can organized labor consistently demand what it steadfastly refuses to extend?

Are not the wants, the necessities of the black man as sacred and crying as are those of white men surrounded by like conditions?

Granted that the Negro has been a slave, more's the pity, and that the curse of past conditions still pursues him, and is nourished and kept alive by sectional interpretations of the law, and the partisan hatred of locality, the sacred cause of labor, intelligent organized labor, should spurn to become an ally of his foes. Clothed in the habiliments of its great mission, standing as a mediator between capital's inordinate greed, and labor's pinching necessity, like the fabled goddess of justice, it should be blind to the color of its beneficiaries, and open-eyed only to their wants.

Until the high priests of organized labor, its advocates, its newspapers and leaders can comprehend this great truth, and be fitted with it, they cannot expect, and should not look for the allegiance and co-operation of black men in the long struggle that is yet before it with the powers of corporate and invested wealth.

Instead of such sneering remarks, as the "darkey won't answer," "no nigger need apply," etc., etc., all things being equal, no field should be barred against him, no opportunity closed to his approach. Less than this is not the Fathership of God, the brotherhood of man.

The Freeman (Indianapolis), July 30, 1892.

With the change in the management and affairs of the Indianapolis Street Railway Co., soon to be consummated, by which the old proprietary interest and management will be succeeded by a new, and we are told more progressive deal all along the lines, comes a query to THE FREEMAN's mind, which without further ado we propose to air. Inasmuch as it has never been done, why should not this new management about to take possession celebrate its entree to the control of Indianapolis' richest and most generally patronized corporation by the employment of colored men in a fair and proportionate sense, as conductors, motormen and drivers upon its lines? Presuming that the management will be keenly alive to the fact that the prosperity of its well-established and growing plant is predicated solely upon the support extended by the generous public of Indianapolis, of which the colored people constitute about one eighth of the whole, a sense of justice to its patrons and supporters, ought to urge the management, if applied to properly, and in a due considerate spirit, to at least look with favor upon our proposition as indicated above. We undertake to say that since Indianapolis first boasted of a Street Railway System, the money contributed to its support through the patronage given it by colored citizens of Indianapolis would, if the actual figures could be known, amount to many thousands of dollars. It follows logically that as the city spreads and grows in population from year to year, this condition of facts must be continually enlarged upon, in the matter of dollars and cents contributed to the company through the patronage of the continually growing colored population. There are two lines in particular, Indiana avenue and Mississippi street, that on account of the proximity of hundreds of homes of our people, have been for years, and will continue to be, largely sustained and supported by colored travel, and it would seem to be the simplest justice on the part of the Street Car Company to recognize this fact by the employment of an occasional colored man, in one of the other capacities of driver or conductor. Several Northern cities have already set an example and preceded Indianapolis in this respect, one of the most notable being the city of Cleveland, Ohio, there being no less than a half dozen colored motormen, doing good work, on her electric lines, and drivers in a fair proportion. In everything else very near, as far as the status and treatment of her colored population is concerned, Indianapolis is a shining mark, and has set an example that no city in the Union has surpassed, and very few have come up to. In the matter of recognition in municipal affairs, the colored people of Indianapolis have been for a number of years extended such consideration as has been enjoyed by the colored people of few cities throughout the land, but nevertheless, we must beware of the inaction that comes of satisfaction; we must look ahead, push forward, deem nothing beyond us or too good for us along the lines of manly, upright, persevering action. What the city has done, is done. So much, so good, and we are sure that we appreciate it. We appreciate the recognition extended to us on the police force, in the fire department, and at odd times in the different city and county offices, but should we be content to stop here? We cannot all be policemen, cannot all run with the "fire laddie," cannot all be selected to go to the county or city desk in different clerical capacities. The city and county governments having shown so fair a spirit to give us employment, why should not the government of some of our great private institutions and corporations be requested to do so? Starting with the Street Railway Co., has there ever been an appeal made to it by the colored people of the city, asking a fair recognition in the ranks of the hundreds of men employed to conduct its service? If not, why not? Its a poor plan to fold your hands and argue because you're a colored man, was a slave, or the son of a slave, have suffered, that the good chances should come to you because you deserved them. The black man who takes such chances is generally left. The community of Negroes that stakes its growth and improved circumstances on such dissolving hopes, is very liable to remain a community of whitewashers, janitors, carriage drivers and waiters. The thing to do, individuall and collectively, is to "git up and git," cultivate a move and go after what you want. A trick untried remains a trick unknown. "Knock and it shall be opened to you, ask and you shall receive," is a good rule to go by, in business as well as spiritual matters. How many times have we heard colored men

on the street corners in Indianapolis abusing the Street Car Co., and other
rich corporations because they employed no colored men. Wasted breath. Why
should the Street Car Co., taking it for an example, why should it put itself
out of the way, tear its cost to put dollars in the pockets of colored men,
until colored men go to them first and signify a desire to put day's works
upon their lines that the dollars may come after? Without desiring to make
a scape-goat for attack out of the Street Car Co., and hoping that we may
yet see the day in Indianapolis when all men desiring to work may obtain it
when qualified, regardless of color, we repeat why should not the Street
Car Co. of this city give employment to a fair number of colored men upon
its different lines as conductors, motormen and drivers? If it has ever
been asked to do so by the colored people of Indianapolis, we do not know
it, hence do not know that it would refuse. Is the matter worthy of the
consideration of the colored people of Indianapolis, and, if so, will they
say so through the columns of THE FREEMAN. Who will be the first one to
speak and offer a suggestion for the proper course to be taken in this very
important matter? Make your communication short and pointed. THE FREEMAN
is with you.

The Freeman (Indianapolis), December 10, 1892.

35. THE RACE NEEDS AN EXAMPLE--SHALL INDIANAPOLIS SET IT?

Our recent editorial, the Indianapolis Street Railway vs. Colored Men,
is commencing to bear fruit. The appended communications on another column
of this page from reputable, solid citizens of our city, are of the right
ring, and we gladly give them the space desired. But the good work begun
so auspiciously by The Freeman, should not be allowed to go ahead and blaze
the way, but we can do but little unless we are backed up and supported by
the race. Four of our leading citizens have spoken, but let thirty and
three, or more, speak along the same line, and thus shall you convince the
onlookers, the community, that you are a unit in this matter. One newspaper,
or two or three men, contending for a just cause, may attract a passing attention, but when twelve or fifteen thousand people speak, all swing at once,
with right and justice on their side, something has to come. Send in your
communications, The Freeman will take pleasure in publishing them, and when
the time comes for other steps to be taken, The Freeman will be found at
your back in the spine of right and the race. Sometime between now and early
spring, it might be well enough to hold a big mass meeting, in some one of
the spacious churches or halls of the city, that a general expression of the
people could be heard on this very important question. What the race needs
today, not only in Indianapolis, but everywhere in the Union is emancipation
from the cruel and unjust burdens of commercial and business caste. Of what
value is manhood, liberty, and citizenship, if the privilege and blessings,
that rightfully go with them, are denied or taken away? Or taking another
view, should a people who are too indolent, too ambitionless, to wake up
and try to better their chances in life, be surprised, and rail at fate, because they are continually sucking the hind test? God helps him who helps
himself. The Negro has been all and more than he will ever be again in this
country politically. That field has been worked, and to death. In the future
if he would be an ornament, a help to himself and race, and a force in the
affairs of his country, he must expect only to rise and expand, along the
beaten paths of manual and industrial effort. We must seek and insist on
employment for head and hand. Recognizing the utility and power of organized
labor, let him strive to enter its guarded portals and be benefited by the
potency of its prestige. If those who should hold out their hands, turn their
back upon him, the exigency will surely suggest a remedy, it never falls.
In a conversation with statistician Kennedy of the Central Labor Union of this
city, we were informed by that gentleman, speaking of the street car question,
that should the Street car drivers and conductor's Union refuse to admit colored men to membership, their charter would be revoked by the powers in authority, as one of the conditions attending the granting of the same, was that no

man should be refused admission because of race or religion. If this be
true, and it certainly must be for Mr. Kennedy spoke with authority, what
might have been an obstruction does not exist, and the blame for refusal
to employ colored men, if the request is ever made, it would rest entirely
upon the company, which blame we do not think the Company would willingly
assume. In the meantime, men of Indianapolis agitate! Agitate! Give us
your views and suggestions. There is wisdom and good in council. Once
given employment by the Indianapolis Street Car Company their example
would be followed by a dozen other great corporations in the city and
township. That's the point. We have no grievance against the street car
Co. specially, our grievance is against all who refuse to give us employment. We have simply picked this corporation out on which to test the
efficacy of our persuasions, succeeding here, why should we not succeed
all along the line? Indianapolis, setting the example, why should not
other cities be benefitted accordingly? Speak out, let us hear from you.

The Freeman (Indianapolis), December 31, 1892.

36.   SPEAKING FOR THEIR RACE

     The following communications from well known and leading Indianapoli-
tians were drawn out by our recent editorial on the justice of the Indianapolis Street Railway Co. giving employment to colored men. They speak for
themselves, and well, and will no doubt be followed by others on the same
line of complaint.

EDITOR, THE FREEMAN;

     I wish to say that your editorial on the Indianapolis Street Car ques-
tion, is a step in the right direction. You should be encouraged by all
good people, and I think both races will concede the justice of your request.
I have often wondered why some one has not spoken of it before. I have been
talking the matter quite awhile, and during the last street car strike, got
myself in bad form with some of our citizens for urging that colored men
should be employed to take the places of the "strikers." I cannot see why
it is that you find so many white people opposed to giving such work to
colored men, and yet are willing to employ them in other spheres far more
important and particular. Nine out of ten of the elegant "turnouts" of the
city are handled and driven by colored drivers. Their ladies and children
are entrusted to the care of colored coachmen, but when it comes to putting
a street car under their control, it is something else. It may be that the
company is not solely to blame for this tardy recognition of simple justice,
for I don't think the Negro as a class in the city has ever asked for employment on its lines. I shall rejoice, and be exceedingly glad, when the
time comes, as I believe it will, when the members of my race shall be given
the same chance, everywhere, to work for an honest living, as is accorded
to white men. Yours for the race,

                              J. A. PURYEAR, Councilman 4th Ward,
                              Indianapolis, Ind.

EDITOR, THE FREEMAN:

     Sir:--In reading the editorials of the last issue of your progressive
and enterprising paper, my attention was attracted to an article entitled,
"Indianapolis Street Railroad--Colored Men." I think colored men should be
employed as motor men, conductors and drivers for the following reasons:
(a) The company is daily enriched by our people, not only from the patronage of the Indiana avenue and Mississippi lines, but from Virginia, Massachusetts and College avenues. (b) Other cities are employing colored men,
and we have as many intelligent and competent men in the city of Indianapolis
as can be found in any city of the same population in the Union. A few of
our intelligent men have been given an opportunity to prove their ability
in the city offices, the postoffice, the fire department, the police force
and can boast of one of the best detectives in the land. And last but not

least, men who have the ability to be a success on the turbulent sea of
journalism. I am with THE FREEMAN and believe that if a few of the prominent colored men of the city would form a committee and wait upon the new
managers of the City Railway, they would put some colored men on the different street car lines of the city, and the colored man would be no longer
conspicuous on account of his absence. Yours for the race in opening avenues for its development.

THEOPHILUS PRICE,
Pastor of Allen Chapel,
Indianapolis, Ind.

EDITOR, THE FREEMAN:
    I desire to say that I am with you in anything that is for the good of
my race. My opinion is that the doors of no corporation or industry should
be closed to the colored man. Time and again has he demonstrated the fact
that he is fully able in everyway to hold his own in any place and at any
time, and I hope some good colored men will go to the new Indianapolis
Street Car Co. and apply for work, as there should be some employed in every
department. Let them start as extra men and by promptness, work their way
upward. I am glad you have taken up the subject and hope you will speak of
others that are of great importance to the community. Yours truly,

DON D. WELLS,
Indianapolis, Ind.

EDITOR, THE FREEMAN:
    It is my opinion that the Citizens R. R. Co. of Indianapolis should
give some employment on their lines to the Afro-American. He is part of
the city in interest on the improvements, and contributes largely every day
of his means to keep the electric wheel moving. The company should consider our case and give us a chance with the balance in the future.

W. T. FLOYD,
G.M., F.A.A.M., of Indiana.

The Freeman (Indianapolis), December 31, 1892.

37. THE NEW GOSPEL OF ORGANIZED LABOR

    "A little study of the matter will convince any one that many avenues
to work are being steadily closed against the colored people in this city.
Some labor unions are shutting them out by adopting a cast-iron rule that
the acceptable applicant shall be "white." There are thousands of living
citizens who can remember when there were many colored carpenters, bricklayers and other mechanics employed in the building trades in Philadelphia.
Now there are none, or so few as not to count."--Philadelphia Telegraph.
    The Negro problem is a serious one, and will be until it is solved and
settled in those courts of equity that hold their sessions in the conscience
of men. Rightly understood and spoken of, there's no such thing as a Negro
problem, which has its life and being in the Negro himself. As far as his
special entity and actions are concerned, he is no better or worse than
other American citizens, and by all the laws of right and equity should
share and be treated alike in the battle for life and the pursuit of happiness. The problem, the real problem to be solved, and which may yet shake
this nation from centre to circumference, when the time for settlement comes,
as come it will, is found in this simple proposition, namely, through what
influence, by what means, can the white man of America be induced, persuaded
or driven to treat his brother citizen, the Negro, right? Apologize, hope,
theorize, speculate as we may, the most serious problem before the American
people today resolves itself at last into this simple direct proposition,
to this color must it come. Not the Negro's sins, for as a plain mortal, as
God created him, anxious only to live, and let live, he has committed no sin,
but the white man's sins, and his alone, has caused all this trouble between
the races, and as sure as there is a God in heaven, sooner or later, somehow

and somewhere they must be past upon and expiated at the tribunal of exact and rigid justice. What has become of the many mechanics and skilled artisans of color, that the Telegraph refers to, who in other days made Philadelphia their home, and were given work and countenance by her citizens? All dead think you, or has their hands and brain lost their cunning? Not a bit of it, but of late years the Telegraph might have added, the tyranny and prejudice of "trade unions" and "leagues," controlled by and for white men, have done their complete work, and today, not only in Philadelphia, but in every considerable Northern city, the Negro mechanic of former days has been driven to the wall, made to feel the stigma of his color, in the name of "union" when there was no union, and in the interests of white men alone, who ninety-nine times in a hundred, had no better claim upon the consideration of the employing classes of the American public, than that other foreign parasite and blood sucker, the detested and hunted John Chinaman. The picture drawn by the Telegraph of the changed condition of the Negro, and his opportunities, as he exists in Philadelphia, is sad enough and true, and contains much food for reflection. Between the mandates of organized labor and the fawning humbleness and sycophancy of capital, with a very few exceptions, who hasten to sneeze when the labor barons of unpronounceable names take snuff, the Northern Negro, from an industrial, bread and butter standpoint, is having a rocky road to travel. Every cloud has its silver lining, hence THE FREEMAN derives a keen satisfaction in directing attention to the brave words of President Gompers, of the American Federation of Labor, delivered before the International Association of Machinists, which convened in Indianapolis a few weeks since. Said Mr. Gompers:

"If a Negro is good enough and smart enough to work alongside of a white man, he ought to be admitted to the trades unions. Then, from a selfish standpoint, it is advisable to admit them. If we don't they bid against us, and competition in labor, the very thing that labor organizations are fighting against, comes in.

"The machinists say there are so few colored men among them that it is not worthwhile to bother about them. As I said in my address Thursday, if there are none, then this article in their by-laws denying them admission is altogether unnecessary, while, if there are colored machinists, the article is brutal and inhuman. They will see the effect of it, too."

This is talk of the right ring, and we honor the man who uttered it, and until organized labor, so-called, is imbued through all its ranks with the same lofty ideal of unselfish right and justice, it will always find itself half armed, handicapped, in its battles for its rights. The Labor Signal, of this city, in its issue of May 12th, imbued with the same broad spirit that filled President Gompers, said:

"As education extends among the colored race, and the taste and ambition for the higher and better things of life are cultivated, the young colored man and woman will never be satisfied to pursue the heavy drudgery slavery imposed upon their fathers and mothers. They are bound to enter the skilled trades, as they have a perfect right to do. It is wrong to impose a single barrier to their advancement."

Keep it up, gentlemen, this better gospel of united labor, you are building right and well. Organized labor, real organized labor, that knows no American citizen by his color, past condition, religions or politics, would be such a force as could stand against the world. In the very act of demanding justice, be great enough to extend it to all men alike, black or white, Jew or Gentile, Catholic or Protestant, and you will have entrenched yourselves behind a barrier, too high to be scaled, too strong to be pierced.

The Freeman (Indianapolis), May 27, 1893.

38.   AN OPEN LETTER TO JOHN BURNS, ESQ. [117]

Sir:

You have arrived in the United States as the representative of organized labor in England to participate in the general labor conference which will

open at Denver on Monday next. In the name of the rights of labor, we ask
you to make some notes for your countrymen at home concerning more than
eight million workmen in this country who suffer the gravest injustice at
the hands of organized labor in the United States. In the name of these
colored workmen, we urge you to report upon the conditions which exist in
this country and to recommend that there be no co-operation on the part of
British trades unions until American trades unions shall give all workmen
in this broad land equality of opportunity.

The people for whom we speak, Sir, are not foreigners. They are not
the Poles and Huns and Italians, whose condition has already provoked your
compassionate and fraternal interest. They are among the first comers.
They arrived with the other first families of Virginia early in the seven-
teenth century; and, like a large number of their English associates, they
were not voluntary exiles from home. Their labor has contributed to the
growth of the nation. In every war, colonial, foreign or domestic, their
lives have been given freely and bravely in the common defense in peace and
war. Suffering every injustice that a cruel, ingenious caste feeling can
invent, they have displayed a Christian forbearance and humility beyond the
average American comprehension. Their great and only crime consists in
having been born black.

In your home in England, you have doubtless read the horrible stories
of midnight lynchings in the South; the crime to which we invite your attention is organized throughout this broad land, perpetrated in open daylight and is ten-fold more horrible. Think, Sir, of eight million beings
under the boycott of the American people! Not one, says the boycott, shall
be a locomotive engineer, a printer, a mechanic. As you travel through the
country, verify what we say. The colored man must be the menial, no matter
what his capabilities. Mr. Powderly made a magnificent stand for justice
at Richmond and his influence began to wane from that moment. Mr. Gompers
has attempted to do something; but he stands almost alone. There are a few
leaders like these who, unable to inaugurate an agitation for equality,
would welcome from you a fraternal word of warning to the effect that they
who would demand their rights must respect the rights of others.

If you can spare the time, visit the schools in which colored children
study. Visit our churches in which black men preach. Think as you talk to
them that the organizations you meet at Denver are striving to starve those
souls. And, Sir, in the fire of British love of fair play, raise your voice
at Denver, raise your voice in London! Proclaim the truths that the right
to work is God-given and that he who steals a man's birthright to make the
best of himself, cannot command the confidence and respect of justice-loving
men.

The Christian Recorder, December 6, 1894.

39. EXCLUSION IS WICKED

"Two wrongs never make one right," and "the tit for tat," "if-I-can't,
you-sha'nt" methods are not wise because unjust. Again, more laborers are
unorganized than are found in unions. These also should have an open field
and a fair chance. Barring men by violent means from the right to earn a
living when and where their labor is needed, because they do not belong to a
union, is usurpation. The exclusion of a person from the benefits of Labor
Unions on account of color is wicked and condemnable. . . . Many of these
white Labor Unions complain of the monopoly of capital being tyrannical, yet
they themselves seek to monopolize employments to the exclusion both of non-
Union men and of colored men. In drawing the color line upon labor they become dictatorial, exclusive, and tyrannical. This is a free country, whose
sentiment is an open field and a fair chance for all. It is evident, therefore,
that along these lines organized labor is wrong in theory, wrong in method.

J. T. Jenifer, "The Labor Question, North and South," *AME Church Review 13,
(1896-97): 377.*

40.   THE INDUSTRIAL COLOR LINE IN THE NORTH AND THE REMEDY

Possibly no graver problem confronts the colored race in the states North of the Mason-Dixon line, than the one indicated by the subject of this article. Colored people are being rapidly educated in the North, but it is with scarcely the shadow of a hope of obtaining positions for which they are being fitted. To the contrary, no difference what their capabilities are, they are, as a rule, relegated to the most menial and ill-paid labor, and compelled to be servants of servants. Go to the South, where colored people are allowed to be diversified in their industrial pursuits; take the State of Georgia, for example, and we find that in Georgia only 28 per cent of the colored people actually at work are engaged in domestic and personal service. But coming North, and taking a few states at random, we find that in Kansas 57 per cent of the colored people who find anything to do, are engaged in domestic and personal service; in Ohio 61 per cent, in Massachusetts, 65 per cent, in Pennsylvania, 69 per cent, and in New York, 70 per cent, of the people who find anything to do, are engaged in domestic and personal service; and 68 per cent of those domestics are males, showing conclusively that instead of being allowed to engage in the manly, elevating pursuits of labor, as they are in the South, in the North colored people are tied down to a few ill-paid menial occupations.

We may be satisfied, if we will, with the few civil and political privileges that are doled out to us in the North, but I say that no matter how fine a hotel or theater we are allowed to enter to *spend* money by the side of white men, until we are allowed to enter workshops and factories, steam and street railways, and *work* and *earn* money by the side of white men, we are in a more baneful and a more unreasonable state of slavery than that from which we were emancipated in the year 1865. "Oh yes," argue some people, "colored people are debarred from work in the North, to a great extent, but time alone will settle this question. The colored race has made wonderful progress in the last thirty years." As for this assertion, progress on the part of colored people against tremendous odds is one thing, and progress on the part of public sentiment to give them opportunities commensurate with their acquired qualifications is quite another. And I defy any person to prove that the industrial conditions of the colored race in the North are a bit better today than they were thirty years ago; but I assert, and defy any person to refute the assertion, that the industrial conditions of the colored race in the North are worse, and much worse than they were thirty years ago, and thirty years is time, a long time, a lifetime to many people.

Even fifteen years ago there were to be found a few colored brakemen on freight trains in the North, and especially in the Northwest a few, very few, colored firemen, conductors, etc. But time, to which so many people flee for refuge, has given birth to railway unions, and they have clutched with octopus fingers for all of these branches of labor. Every race of people is admitted to these unions, exclusive of the colored race, consequently, when you seek the colored man in railway circles in the North today, he is only to be found (thanks to time) in the humble capacity of porter, the most menial and ill-paid position within the gift of a railway corporation.

This is what time is slowly, but surely doing for the colored race in the North, along almost all of the broader avenues of labor. This is an age of combines and organizations. We can scarcely conceive of a branch of labor that is not hampered by organizations. Coal miners, boiler-makers, iron-ship builders, iron moulders, iron workers, brass, tin-plate and sheet-metal workers, street-railway men, railway trainmen, mercantile clerks and salesmen have all organized and discriminate against the colored man; and, as though to cut off his last retreat, the tramps, bums and hoboes of the country have organized and discriminate against him. Oh yes, time will settle this problem, but the colored man will doubtless be at the bottom of the settlings.

"Well," urge many persons, "since white men are organizing so strenuously against colored men, the only thing for colored men to do is to organize among themselves and be prepared to compete with those white organizations." I have, so far, been unable to see any common-sense in such a proposition. The white people are, figuratively speaking, on top, and I believe that they are going to stay there just as long as we fight them, or try to rival or measure arms with them. I believe that every effort of the colored race to obtain broader industrial privileges is doomed to an ignominious defeat unless we get the

Christian white people and liberty-loving white workingmen, to co-operate
with us in each and every effort.

We must organize *with* the white people, but *against* them--Never!

There are, to my mind, so many false views and theories as to the
industrial condition of the colored race in the north, that I am afraid my
limited space must be taken in an effort to clear up the debris of false
ideas.

One nonsensical argument, and one which, strange to say, I have heard
from none but colored people, is that we have no financial interest in the
great industries of the country, and for that reason should not expect to
be allowed to share in the profits that accrue from them through the medium
of manual labor. ·How intelligent colored persons can be so uncharitable
to their own race, is a mystery of mysteries to me.

Only a short time ago an intelligent colored man told me that there was
a time in Philadelphia when street railway stock was low, and many colored
men might have purchased shares; they failed to do so, and for that neglect
on their part, colored residents of the city have no strong point upon which
to urge their rights to be conductors, motormen, trolleymen and linemen on
the street-railway lines. Well, if colored residents do not own shares in
the street railways, they faithfully patronize all of them.

But even though they own no stock and do not spend one cent as patrons,
I fail to see in what way that would be an argument against their right to
be employed. Such corporations have never been conducted on the spoils
system.

I doubt if one man in a hundred, who does ordinary work for those
corporations, could trace the remotest relationship to any of the stockholders.
But to the contrary, it is an every day occurrence to see aliens, those who
can trace no relationship to the nation, and who have no desire to do so,
working for those corporations. How, in the face of this, sane men can see
colored citizens crowded out of such work, and contend that it is justice,
because we own no shares in the industries, is a mystery to me.

How are we ever to own anything unless we are permitted to secure it by
honest toil at any kind of labor that we are capable of performing?

We added to the wealth and resources of this country by two hundred and
forty-seven years of ceaseless toil as slaves, for which the most conspicuous
remuneration was to be cast ignorant, penniless and homeless upon the mercies
of a cold and prejudiced world, with a stigma upon us more cruel than the
brand of a felon.

Yet the colored man from the earliest conception of this government,
has been one of the most reliable and potent factors in the laying of the
foundation upon which rests the great institutions and industries of which
this country boasts. And I believe that though colored men have no script
to attest the fact, they own a share in every railway, every factory, every
mill , and every business house that has ever been, or ever will be erected
on American soil; at least to the extent of entering such establishments,
and working to make an honest living the same as white men do.

Another argument that employers of labor produce, and which many colored
persons accept as conclusive, is that white working-men will not work by the
side of colored men--an argument as cowardly as it is absurd. I doubt if
there is one white man in a hundred who is so prejudiced against colored men
that he would absolutely refuse to work with them if it came to a practical
test. The threats that white men make to "quit work" if colored men are
employed, are bluffs, pure and simple, and if met by a particle of manhood,
and moral courage on the part of the employers, would soon be made a thing
of the past.

There is, however, little inducement for employers to take this advanced
step unless they are brimful of Christianity and love of fair play. If objections are made to colored men, it is easy for the employer to find white
men who are just as desirable in every respect as colored men are, or perhaps
ever will be. If the natives of America cannot meet the demand it takes
the slums of Europe but a short time to make up for the deficit. As for the
admonition often given colored men to make themselves so thorough and proficient in the mechanical trades that they will create a demand for themselves
because of their superior worth, I see no common sense or reason in it.

With the trades and professions carried almost to the zenith of perfection by a race of people that has had centuries for development, as our competitors, and with only a few years of civilization back of us, how we can be

expected to surmount race prejudice and force for ourselves a place in the industrial arena from sheer superiority of ability, is a nut that is too hard to crack.

I think that the colored man has accomplished untold wonders when he can stand by the side of white men and be recognized as their *equals* in the trades and professions, without being expected to so far excel them that he will overbalance the scale of prejudice and create a demand for himself because of his *superior* ability. This would be proclaiming the black man the superior of the white man to an extent that our most ardent friends and admirers would not admit.

But, reverting again to the employers, many of them say to colored people: "You have not enough skilled mechanics among you; you have not enough educated men to compete with white labor. Educate and train your men in the trades, and *then* come to us, and if our white employees refuse to work with you, we will dismiss them and put on entire forces of colored men." It is my candid opinion that such advice and promises are seldom given in good faith; they are only a ruse and a subterfuge to keep from employing colored men in the first place. If a man has so little backbone as to allow his employees to dictate as to who shall and who shall not work for him, he is the last one who is going to summon enough moral courage to dismiss those men, in the face of public sentiment, to make room for a down-trodden race. But even though he should do all that he promises, I believe that the theory in itself is wrong. The thought of a semi-warfare between colored and white workingmen--colored men entering establishments with the understanding that if white men refuse to work with them, they will be dismissed, and entire forces of colored men substituted--has always been extremely distasteful to me. This is a grave and solemn problem--one that must be solved on the broad principle of Christianity and brotherly love. Just as soon as colored men begin to supplant (?) white workingmen because of the prejudice that exists between the two races, just that soon will this prejudice be kindled into a flame; Christinity set aside; brotherly love trampled under foot; and we shall begin to wield a sword of retaliation that has two edges--one for our enemies, and one for ourselves. And again, such a course would only strengthen the belief of some people that colored and white people cannot and will not work together in harmony.

So, what I would like to see is this: if two colored men are given positions in a large establishment and twenty white men say, "If those Negroes work here, I'll quit," instead of raising the cry, "Where can we get twenty colored men to take their places?" there should be such a spirit of justice and love of fair play fostered between the two races that it will be easy to find twenty more white men who will be willing to work with the two colored men, or twenty colored men as the case may be, and thus prove to the world that it is the height of folly to have entire forces of colored men in one establishment and entire forces of white men in another.

I have endeavored to show what I think are some of the false methods and doctrines regarding our condition. I now want to set forth what I think are some practical methods; measures which, if adopted and prosecuted, will free us from industrial subjugation and bring to us the full enjoyment of these, our most precious rights. One of the prime requisites is for us, as a race, to become thoroughly alive to our condition and intensely interested in ourselves. The voice of the race must be lifted as the voice of one man in a plea for justice along these lines. We must unite through our churches with the Christian white people through their churches.

It is the work of Christian churches to solve this problem; it is the work of the church to unlock the doors of manual labor to the colored race in the North. Let Christian people, colored and white, unite through their churches and let the clergy educate the people from their pulpits on this question, and there will soon be such an outburst of public sentiment that such outrages will be made an impossibility. I feel that this article would be incomplete, if I failed to give my ideas of a method by which all liberty-loving churches, white and colored, may soon be united in this cause.

I speak of it with great assurance, because it has been highly approved by some of the leading churches and clergymen of the country, and is now being successfully prosecuted in Philadelphia (as many readers will know), and is doing more, perhaps, to unite the two races than any move has ever done before. The "Industrial Rights League" is the medium through which this reform is being conducted, the object of which is to combine all Christians and lovers of justice, both colored and white, through the churches, into a systematic association whose influence will be used to break down the color line in the various branches of labor.

It is expedient that this organization should be supported by every church and by every member of that church, yet no person is expected to join this organization who would in any way make industrial discriminations against men because of their color. To this end, every person who joins is requested to take the following pledge:

"I do solemnly promise to exert my influence to break down the barrier of prejudice that prevents men, because of color, from engaging in various branches of manual labor in this country. To this end, I pledge myself never to employ, or work with, as occasion demands, any person because of his, or her color."

It is a well-known fact that the majority of the dominant and better class of laborers are professed Christians and the leading business men and employers of labor want to be looked upon by the world as being devout Christians and large-hearted philanthropists. Yet they degrade the name of Christianity by peremptorily refusing to employ colored men except in the most menial capacities. The object of the above pledge is to incite all Christians and fair-minded persons to mix a little manhood and moral courage with their Christianity, by persistently refusing to make industrial discriminations against men because of their color--a step that no Christian can possibly refuse to take, and if one-fourth of the Christians will take this stand, this problem is solved.

Since the majority of the employers of labor and of the dominant and better class of laborers are professed Christians, it is easy to be seen that this method will bring the majority of those upon whom colored people are dependent for work to the point where they must demonstrate the practical part of their Christianity to the world by strenuously refusing to make industrial discriminations against men because of their color, a refusal which they cannot deny without denying their interest in the most sacred rights of men.

I have expounded this plan in hundreds of white, as well as colored, churches, and they heartily approve of the method, and with very few exceptions, stand ready to give their hearty co-operation. Such a move will receive but little opposition from our most bitter foes, because it is easy to see that it is based upon the broad principle of Christianity and Christian brotherhood.

The move was highly endorsed by the Central Labor Union of Cleveland, Ohio, the most powerful body of organized labor in that State, and it is safe to say that the majority of the thinking class of laborers will give such a cause as this their hearty approval. In the great struggle of the masses against the classes, workingmen are anxious to appear in the role of the oppressed and not the oppressor, consequently they are anxious to appear before the gaze of a sympathetic public as liberty-loving, and considerate of the rights of the most humble sons of toil.

The industrial discriminations made against us are possible only because the public conscience is asleep. Once arouse and awaken the public as to these conditions, and it will be as difficult to find a sensible man who will stand up in defense of such barbarity as it now is to find men who will employ or work with colored men. Let all Christians, white and colored, unite through their churches and throw their combined influence against this outrage, and in a very short time, when it comes to work and wages in this country, men will be recognized not by their race or color, but by their merit and manhood.

JAMES SAMUEL STEMONS

AME Church Review 14 (1897-98): 346-56.

41.   A NEW INDUSTRIAL APOSTLE

Mr. J. S. Stemons, founder of the Industrial Rights League, Philadelphia, contributes a paper in this issue on the labor question. It is a well-considered, clear-cut argument addressed to the reason and justice of those who have it in their power to open up the factories and fields of labor to colored laborers as well as to white. Mr. Stemons' views are novel in one respect; he argues against putting on solid colored crews to the exclusion of whites, claiming that the idea that a working force must be all white or all colored is engendering and strengthening the antagonism of the two races by making them believe they cannot work together. He says if one colored man has the requisite skill and one man is needed, that man ought to be employed and his white co-laborers ought to receive him beside them. It is unjust, he contends, to the few Negroes who may be fitted, to tell them that the employer would willingly give them work if there were enough of them to fill all the places; thus not only counting for naught all the time and hardship passed in fitting themselves, but holding them accountable for the failures of others whom they in no way control. Mr. Stemons' views are right and well presented—there should be no color line in labor and strange to say, in the South there is little of it, except what the Northern people have introduced. But are his views practicable?

One would think at first they were not, but his plan of accomplishing this revolution (for it would verily be one) is eminently practical. He proposes to present the matter through the churches, whose mission is to advance the brotherhood of man. No one is asked to go out of his way or do any special thing to remove this taboo on colored labor. He is simply asked to agree not to refuse to work himself, or engage others so to do, beside a colored man. In Mr. Stemons' opinion, when the churches go on record as striking this attitude, the opposition will weaken and vanish, for the public sentiment behind it will be gone. The Christian people of this country have its reforms in their hands. We say with shame and regret, however, that it is by no means certain that the Christians of this country are willing to do justice in this matter to the Negro. The churches are honey-combed with worldliness, and in some cases consenters to wickedness where the rights of this much-suffering race are concerned. Let us hope for an awakened conscience soon, and a realization of all that justice and sympathy with hearts willing to work for an honest living, demand.

AME Church Review 14 (1897-98): 373.

42.   BECAME A WHITE MAN IN ORDER TO SUCCEED

Two brothers, who were printers, came to Philadelphia several years ago to work at their trade. There was nothing in their appearance to indicate their African descent. One secured work in a large office where white men were employed, and the other obtained a place in the composing-room of a paper published by colored men. At the end of two or three years' faithful service the first of the brothers had become the foreman of the office where he worked. Then one of his subordinates learned that he was a colored man, and promptly communicated the startling news to his fellows at the cases. They immediately appointed a committee to warn the employer that he must at once discharge the colored printer, or get another force of men. The foreman admitted that he was a colored man, and protested that no discrimination should be made against him because of his race.

The employer said: "I agree with you, and your work is entirely satisfactory. Besides, I do resent this dictation by men who have worked with you all this time in perfect harmony. You know more of my business than any of the others,—the contracts which I have on hand, and the loss which I would suffer if these men should suddenly leave. If you can find me a force of colored men as efficient as yourself, I'll let the others go, and take your force, retaining you in your present position." The foreman replied:

"I cannot get such a force, but I can suggest a plan which will insure my obtaining work. I have a red-haired brother who is a first-class printer. Discharge me, and take him. I can then secure his place."

The plan was adopted; the brothers changed places, and harmony reigned in the printing office until the fair-haired brother's identity was discovered. But the first brother finally gave up the struggle in despair. He left his friends and family one day, and entered a wider world. He became a white man among strangers, and is now successful.

About three years ago I advised a colored printer to apply for admission to one of the unions. As the place of his residence he named a street on which many colored people live. A week or two later three men called at his house, and were received by his mother, who offered to take any message they might have for him. They gave her a sealed envelope, and departed without a word. The envelope contained the same sum of money that the colored printer had sent with his application for admission to the union. He cannot say that the money came from the union. He cannot say that he was denied admission.

At the time of the last strike of streetcar conductors and motormen in Philadelphia, the question of employing colored men was presented both to the company's managers and to the labor unions. The managers declared that they feared the resentment of the men, and the labor leaders declared that they would make no discrimination in their organizations. Yet, although applications have been filled for more than a year, no colored men are employed in this work in a community one twentieth of whose residents are colored people.

Atlantic Monthly 81 (February, 1898): 228-30.

43. THE RACE PROBLEM AGAIN

Bishop Walters Wants His People to Protest Against Outrages

The colored citizens of New York will soon hold a mass meeting for the purpose of ventilating grievances. Bishop Walters of the African Methodist Episcopal Church has just come out with a statement to his people in which he says that the outrages perpetrated against Postmasters Loften of Hogansville, Ga., and Baker of Lake City, S.C., were for no other cause than their race and color, and, judging from past experience, he does not believe that the perpetrators will be brought to justice.[118]

The Bishop goes on to say that there is a determined effort on the part of the white labor unions of the country to exclude the negro from the industrial avenues in which he can make an honest living, and, therefore the colored people must organize for self-protection. The Bishop suggests that T. Thomas Fortune, the President of the National Afro-American League, should call a meeting of the leaders of the race at an early date to consider the present condition of affairs and find a remedy. All who unite with him in the request are to communicate with Mr. Fortune.[119]

Several efforts have been made in past years to get colored men into trades unions, and District Assembly 49 in its palmy days made special efforts in that direction. But only a few colored men comparatively were initiated into the order, as somehow or other white and colored men did not get on very well in any union.[120]

Comparatively few of the skilled trades have unions of colored men. A colored waiters' union was once organized, and affiliation with white waiters' unions was promised, but the union met with very weak support.

Edward McHugh, the organizer of the American Longshoremen's Union, made it a special feature of his propaganda to try and abolish all race and national feeling among longshoremen, and to unite whites, blacks, and Italians in one body. He was obliged to organize separate unions for the Italians,

on account of their ignorance of English, but it is said that the bonds of
Union between white and black longshoremen are not strong.[121]

New York Times, March 14, 1898.

44.   LABOR DAY

The first Monday in September is generally observed as Labor Day. It
is a day devoted to the interests of labor, when workmen of all grades as-
semble in public gatherings, listen to speeches of various kinds and presumably make plans for the future benefit of labor. The states generally
have made this day a legal holiday so that there can be no demands of
business which would detract from the interest of the day. It is pleasant
to think that this recognition is given labor by the authorities, for the
time was when the laboring man's interests were of no account whatever with
the monetary powers of the country.

Philadelphia is looked upon as the embodiment of things patriotic, but
the demonstration made by labor in this city last Monday did not in any way
sustain the claim. The procession was anything but representative. At its
head we noticed a banner bearing a socialistic motto and other devices which
savored more of the anarchistic idea than of the freedom of American institutions.

The personnel of this procession was decidedly foreign, and what attracted our attention most was the entire absence of the Negro from the
ranks of the processionists.

Is he not a laborer? Has he not an interest in the celebration of
Labor Day as well as the foreigners whom we saw? It can be plainly seen
that as far as the existing labor organizations are concerned, the Negro is
not recognized as a part of the laboring element of this country. These so-
called Labor Unions are organized against him, and as far as possible they
make their purpose plain.

The Christian Recorder, September 8, 1898.

45.   BRING TRADES UNIONS TO TERMS

Disguise the situation as we may, the Negro is losing ground in the
industrial world. This is one particular reason for indorsing the labor
propaganda of Booker T. Washington, for the cause which he strives to promote,
is the race's weakest spot.

The potent influence that retards the Negro's progress industrially is
the Chinese wall erected by the trades unions. They form a labor trust, as
it were, and prescribe that a white skin shall be one of the necessary
qualifications for participation in its benefits. They deny the black boy
the right to become an apprentice at a trade, and freeze out the black man
who in some way has managed to acquire a fair degree of skill as a workman.

Organization is everything to those who are not rich in this world's
goods. The white man is an adept at combining, and his superiority along
this line, coupled with his prejudice against the Negro, is driving the
latter to the wall, and crowding him out of pursuits heretofore monopolized
by the darker race. The whites are daily encroaching upon the territory
preempted by the Negro and the latter is not making any appreciable gains in
the white man's territory to offset it.

The Negro is still an artist in the catering business. He is a painstaking printer, a faithful laborer, a dignified coachman, an expert waiter,
an unsurpassed bootblack--but he is being crowded out of these pursuits by
the poor whites and foreigners. Labor unions are absorbing these callings,
and by the force of organization are filling up the places with men of their

own choosing, shutting out the Negro. The union card, instead of a reliable
"reference" has become a shibboleth of success in securing employment. By
a bluff and fictitious show of strength these unions have terrified politicians into doing their bidding, and many influential men of affairs are
held down by the theat by them, not daring to give a day's work to an individual distasteful to the tyrannical combine. They go so far as to attempt to overrule the dictum of the general government, and cases have frequently been reported where the Public Printer has been unable to keep a man
in the service of the nation because the man in question did not belong to
the labor trust. Today the street car service, the shops and mills are
afraid to put on a faithful and tried Negro because the white employees
would strike and tie up the road, causing financial loss to the business.

It is time for the Negro to strike back. The Negro cares nothing for
the labor union that denies him the opportunity to earn bread for his family.
He cares nothing for a cabal that throttles the freedom of employers favorably inclined toward him, and that terrifies politicians who would otherwise
undo the legislation that restricts the black man's prosperity to the nar-
rowest limit. We are no nearer the solution of this labor problem that we
were ten years ago, and the labor unions show no signs of hearkening to the
enlightened sentiment of the times. If the unions will not open their doors,
they should be fought with all the strength our numbers and influence can
command. If we unite and decline to purchase union-made goods, decline to
support candidates who will not repudiate union tyranny, pass by the stores
of men dominated by union prejudices, and give our tremendous patronage to
the alleged "outlaw" or "rat" establishments, we can make ourselves felt.
Why shouldn't we do it? We have nothing to lose. Think over this, colored
friends. Something must be done to give our boys and girls a chance. Trade
Unions must be brought to terms or made to suffer the consequences.

Colored American, October 29, 1898.

46. ITEM

We don't care how wide Uncle Sam opens the doors in his new possessions
if he will only induce the white labor unions in America to open their doors
to Negro workmen.

The Recorder (Indianapolis), January 7, 1899.

47. ITEM

They hang the negro in the south but they are not so bad in the north;
they just simply starve him to death by labor's union.

The American (Coffeyville, Kansas), March 11, 1899.

48. ITEM

If non-union men are not permitted to work and colored men are not permitted to join the unions, where does the colored man come in? Or does he
stay out?-- *Indianapolis News*.

Most assuredly he stays out. But why? The abilities of the non-union
colored man are never measured by those of the union white man; but 'tis the

color of their respective faces that causes the Negro to remain on the
outside.

The Recorder, Indianapolis, August 5, 1899.

49.   ITEM

What is it to us if the wages of factory employees are increased if
over the doors of them the sign hangs out, "No Black Man Wanted Here," no
black boy or girl shall enter here that they may become skilled artisans.

The Christian Recorder, August 17, 1899.

50.   THE INDUSTRIAL SITUATION

The New Age, of London, England, has this to say of the industrial
situation:
"But the evil American influence is being exercised upon us in ways
far more subtle. American so-called, "Socialists" are permeating among our
working men, trying to instill into them that the whole world is made for
"the white man,"--that there is "a Negro question," and "a labour question,"
instead of the simple fact that there exists everywhere the question of unskilled and skilled labour, and that the Negro of America finds himself ruthlessly pushed back into the former rank, because the Trades Unions will not
receive him! It is said that there are already in America more skilled negroes than can obtain work at proper wages--which, if a fact, tells against
Booker T. Washington's hope to "elevate" his race by means of "technical education."
Again we are to understand that America beyond its borders is making
the doctrine manifest that the whole world is made for the white man?
Even England with its conservative ideas admits that the American idea
of a white man's country is obtaining foothold there. The information is
scarcely less than astounding.
But there is great hope for salvation in America. If the Negroes are
to be saved they must save themselves. This mighty fabric of ours--our
commonwealth of states is founded on the almighty dollar. It is the panacea,
the battering ram that will breach the most formidable walls.
It is absolutely essential that the Negroes learn to mass their wealth,
and employ their kind or else demonstrate the world's accusation of incapacity and forever be the caste class of the Western Hemisphere. It is evident
that from a standpoint of business policy alone, regardless of color and race,
that those are to be employed who can in some way contribute greatest to the
success of a business undertaking.
Sentiment has never entered the world of business and it never will. The
dollar is the actuating motive and no man is willing to impede its progress
to his exchequer. Who is the better fitted to promote this flow? It is quite
apparent.
It is useless to discuss the relations of unions to Negro workmen. These
unions are with us. We know to the Negro's hurt what they mean. Sentiment
or charity will not batter down these walls. The relief lies in the power
to compel by the reason of financial sufficiency. Will the race profit by the
writing on the wall?

The Freeman (Indianapolis), August 26, 1899.

51.   UNIONISTS REFUSE TO PARADE BECAUSE NEGROES ARE BARRED

A sensation new to this section was sprung in Montgomery on the 23rd in the labor circles. A street fair and trades display will be held here, commencing Monday, with a street parade, in which the trades unions were to participate. Today the unions announced that they would take no part in the parade because the committee of the fair decline to allow the Negro trades union a place in the line. The street fair people and the unions appointed committees to confer and try to arrange matters, but without results. The white union men take the position that, as a regularly organized trades union, the Negro organization is entitled to a place in the parade, and that the refusal of the fair committee to give the Negro a place shows disrespect to organized labor rather than to the Negro race.

The Recorder (Indianapolis), October 28, 1899.

VI

CONTEMPORARY ASSESSMENTS

Albion W. Tourgee was a carpetbagger judge in North Carolina during
the Reconstruction who had earned the undying enmity of conservative whites
for his views on racial equality. After the state was redeemed, however, he
moved to New York and became a novelist. Even though Tourgee abandoned the
South, he had not forgotten the black struggle for equal rights. During
the 1890s Tourgee became a leader in the National Citizens Rights Association, a civil rights organization founded to combat the passage of segregation laws. Tourgee became active in a campaign to challenge their con-
stitutionality, but ultimately lost the Supreme Court decision of Plessey
v. Ferguson (1896), which validated the principle of "separate but equal."
Because of his close association with the civil rights cause, many blacks
wrote to him of the intimidation, the violence, and the general disregard
for basic rights in the South. Several of the more poignant letters received
by Tourgee are reproduced in Document 1.

Another contemporary political reformer-novelist, Ignatius Donnelly,
denounced the southern racial system. His Doctor Huguet: A Novel (1891),
published to deservedly dismal reviews, was a story about a young southern
white physician with radical racial views. Through a rather contrived
Faustian transfiguration, the doctor's mind and soul are placed inside the
body of a brutally coarse Negro, who in turn assumes possession of Huguet's
body. The novel then follows the failures of this transfigured mind, which,
because its is housed in a black body, is perceived as a threat by the white
community. Huguet is finally released from captivity when the Negro slays
his own body, and Huguet's body and soul are reunited. The book was a hard-
hitting satire on the southern caste system, in which social status was acquired only through the color of one's skin. Document 2 reproduces a
chapter from the novel which describes the failures of Huguet's mind to find
employment.

The late nineteenth century was a time of remarkable economic growth
in the United States. During this period the nation was transformed from a
preeminently agricultural nation to an industrial colossus, and although
this enormous economic expansion produced significant benefits for capitalists and workers alike, the extent of the growth, coupled with the speed at
which it came, also created severe social and economic dislocations. The
nature of the problems created was not clearly understood at the time, however, and several federal commissions were established to define the difficulties and to propose solutions. The most important such commission of the
1890s was the Industrial Commission on the Relations of Capital and Labor,
which convened in 1898, and heard testimony from witnesses from all walks of
life over a period of several years. Eventually, the testimony and findings
were published in a nineteen-volume report, prepared by experts on the subjects addressed. Some of the testimony relating to black labor is reproduced
in Document 3.

In 1897, W. E. B. DuBois, the prominent black intellectual and protest
leader, accepted a teaching position at Atlanta University. While at Atlanta
between 1897 and 1914, he took it upon himself to supervise sixteen mono-
graphic studies which came to represent a valuable contribution to Afro-
American sociology. One of the best of the series, The Negro Artisan (1902),
was based on data derived from questionnaires distributed to hundreds of black
artisans, union officials, and local "correspondents" throughout the nation.
The questions, responses, and DuBois' assessment of racial patterns affecting
black workers are partially summarized in Document 4. DuBois was prepared
for the Atlanta monographs by research for his now classic study, The Philadelphia Negro (1896). His study was founded upon door-to-door interviews
with black families of the Seventh Ward, the center of Negro life in Philadelphia, from which emerged a vivid picture of the social pathology resulting
from poverty and discrimination. Document 5 partially reproduces DuBois'
analysis.

STATUS OF THE BLACK WORKER AT THE TURN OF THE TWENTIETH CENTURY

1. LETTERS TO ALBION W. TOURGEE[122]

                                                    Wayneboro, Miss.
                                                    December 17, 1891

Mr. Albion W. Tourgee. . . .
    We are women of Wayne County Miss. and we thought we would write and
let you know what is going on as the men was afraid to do it for fear it
would not be very good for them to let it be known we are continuly haveing
some trouble the white peope of this county are taking the colored men and
beating them and putting them in jail they beat a young man nearly to death
this week and put him in Jail and said they would take him out and mob him
the men have to pay a too dollar Poll Tax and them that cannot vote a colored
man cannot get any charge made against a white man here they take the colored
man and send him to the penitensiary and the law is not executed on the white
man at all too houses was robed Sunday night and they said some Negro done
it and they beat this man monday and put him in Jail there were three other
towns robed and the citizens never taking any colored man up for it I cannot
tell how it is all done down here We will have to have some protection or
else go away from here We cannot live here much longer at this I cannot write
any more now.
                                                    Yours truly
                                                    Jane Evans
                                                    Minnie Evans

                                                    Austin Tex Feb 21th 1892

Dear Sir it is with much pleasure that I take this opportunity of giving
vent to my appreciation of your Common Cence articles which are the best and
most timely that I have had the good fortune to read concerning my Race God
knows we need all the help we can possibly get to pull us through and am
very much afraid that unless we can get Friends to stand by us we are lost or
if we were able to arm our selves for self Protection but we have no chance
and we are satisfied that State nor Federal government can not protect us in
our lives and Property they cant do it They never did nor never will protect
the Life of a poor unarmed inofensive niger from the Blood Thirsty Deamons
of the South look if you please at Chili Two white men got killed out there[123]
and the Government spent over two millions of money in Bringing Chilli to
account for the Crime Committed. There has been killed in round numbers
since the serender of 17711 nigers in the south and not as much as a finger
has bin raised in our behalf Could you or any man or men love such a Country
or such a government no no Sir the Federal government is not able for the
Task nor never will be able we have found that out long ago so we will go to
Mexico as the only accesable Country where we will become Citizens and be
protected as such and as we go we will sing

                    My native land from thee
                    Oh land of misery from thee I fly
                    Land where we have often tried
                    Thy harsh laws to abide

But we will now let you slid and go to Old Mexico where we will become
Citizens and soldiers if she wants us. . . .

                                            I remain very Respectfully

                                                    Jos. W. Smith

La Fayette, Ala March 23 1892

Dear Sir Language cannot express the warmth of heart I have for you and the
earnestness with which I pray that God may long let you live, give you
strength and Courage to continue to battle for righteousness and justice
for the oppressed race with which I am identified.   I do not believe that
the Republican party will have done its duty toward God or man till the end
for which you are laboring will be reached. . . . Under the present situation we down here can't be of very much help but we are in full sympathy
with you and are ready to act in anything that we can with safety.   Why,
Sir, the Colored people in some localities are as slaves in this very state
--they are knocked and cuffed and kicked around and are afraid to leave
their homes to even come to town.   They are simply not their own and if they
resent this treatment the mob steps in and its the end of that person.   What
is true of Alabama is true of every other Southern State.   I should be happy
to live to see the day when this would be indeed the land of the *free*. Again
I believe the National Government should enact a marriage law; our women
are degraded by white men raising families by them and then the whole race
is scorned for it and the white man, of course retains his purity (?)   In
many cases, no doubt, the white men would marry the colored woman and raise
a respectable family if the laws would permit.   If one of our men look at
a white woman very hard and she complains he is lynched for it; white men on
the high ways and in their stores and on the trains will insult our women
and we are powerless to resent it as it would only be an invitation for our
lives to be taken.

The South is a pretty good organized mob and will remain so until bursted
by the Federal Government.   It is strange to me how some of the northern
people can make so much ado over the goodness of the South when all of these
outrages are going on against a helpless people and not one of their newspapers will condemn them but rather encourage them.   A good law would be to
prohibit these newspapers, publishing these outrages seemingly endorsing
them, from passing through the mails; such only encourages others to do likewise. . . .

Sincerely yours,

A. N. Jackson
Pastor M.E. Church

Duncan Miss Bolivar Co   July 4th 1892

Dear Sir: In your notes to the Interocean June 7th last, you give notice to
all Lovers of Liberty, Justice and Freedom, and especially to those belonging
to the National Citizens Equal Rights association to Form what is to be
known as Local unions, accordingly We have met and considered the matter carefully, you are satisfied that there is no Law in this State to protect a Black
man who makes any attempt to enlighten his Race on any political question;
Surely you do not realize the situation as we do, who lives here, the man or
Woman who attempts to strike a Blow here for Freedom must be killed out right
--or he must be Exiled from all he possesses at once as Miss Ida B. Wells of[124]
the Memphis Free Speech have been.   In a word he must be made such an example
of, untill no other Negro will attempt to do such a thing again, We are a
little tired of having to show our Corpse to prove to the world that the Laws
of this Country is not sufficient to protect the Black man as well as the white
We read your notes Regular and Readily, our liberty have been taken from us
so long untill we have almost got use to it, In a word we see no *possible*
chance of ever being Free under The Flag of Liberty and christian civilization.
Do you know my Dear sir, that there are standing armies in every county in
every Southern State called Malitia, and are at the command of the Governors
of the different States, who are Negro haters and who are willing to sacrufice
everything even Life in order to give the negro to know that he *must* obey the
white man, These armies are always ready to go to any scene where a negro resist a White man no matter how small the case may be, or however wrong the
white man may be, The *Negro must submit* It is no use to try the Law, Now what
can people do who are Situated as we are, Just as complete into the hands of
our Enemies in 1892 as we were in 1852 It is possible that something can be

done, but how it is to be done, is as fare out of our sight as the God who
created the heavens & the Earth, It took this government Four yrs with all
of the modern artilry and the most skilful men of war, With as much money
as they needed and more men than they did need, to drive these same men
from the same power they have now, and how can we ever do such, with no men
of war, no artilery, and no money. It is simply absurd, but we have deciden
to do what you have requested even if we are exterminated we shall hope to
hear from you as early as possible stating what you further will have us do

Very Respectfully

S. R. Kendrick

These letters were reproduced from Otto H. Olson (ed.), "Albion W. Tourgee
and Negro Militants of the 1890's: A Documentary Selection," *Science &
Society 28 (Spring, 1964): 191-95, 198.*

2. DOCTOR HUGUET: A NOVEL[125]

CHAPTER XXV

FREE AGAIN

> "Where am I now? Feet, find me out a way,
>   Without the counsel of my troubled heart:
> I'll follow you boldly about these woods,
> O'er mountains, through brambles, pits and floods.
> Heaven, I hope, will ease me. I am sick."
> > --*Philaster (Beaumont and Fletcher).*

The day arrived on which my sentence expired. I shook hands with the
jailer and his assistants. They regarded me with a species of awe. I
certainly had not acted like the notorious Sam Johnsing. I think they were
rather glad to get clear of me: there was to them something mysterious and
uncanny about the whole business. They could not understand it.

Ben was on hand to take charge of me. He insisted that I must go to my
own house; and there he would secrete me, and care for me, until the "hoodoo,"
as he called it, terminated. But I declined his kind offer. I told him that
the spell had been placed upon me because I had not done my duty according
to the lights of my own conscience, my inmost monitor; and that I could only
escape from the curse under which I suffered by going out into the world and
laboring for the welfare of the black race. If I hid myself and lived a life
of pampered idleness, the spell would remain upon me forever.

Then he wanted me to agree that I would receive a certain sum of money
from him every week--enough to pay my board and other expenses of living. He
would take it out of my own income. But this offer also I declined. I told
him that I desired to show the negroes that the fault of their not rising to
greater heights of distinction, and so overcoming the cruel prejudices which
surrounded them, was because they did not address themselves to the task of
success with a white man's brain and energy. I proposed, I said, to throw
myself, bare-handed, into the shock and battle of life, and win by sheer force
of intellect. In the day of my success it would not do to be subject to the
reproach that I was indebted, for my triumph, to the fact that I had been in
receipt of an income which placed me above want, and gave me an advantage over
other black men. No! I would go into the conflict as a negro, and win as a
negro, or fail as a negro; but I had no fear of failure. I felt so confident
of the advantages which my thoroughly equipped intelligence gave me that I was
sure I should revolutionize the whole social status of the negroes of the
entire world. Yes, I said, the new era for the black man of America would
date from my going forth from these walls to-day, even as the calendar of the
Moslem begins with the Hegira of Mahommed from Mecca to Medina.

And so, shaking hands warmly with my faithful friend, we parted, and I started forth upon my mission.

I had given the subject a good deal of thought, during my imprisonment, and it had seemed to me that, if I was to teach the colored people, it would be well to seek a place as a professor in some college or university. This would give me a vantage-ground--a standing--from which I could readily move to a higher level of statesmanship and statecraft.

There were two institutions of learning in C_____, both of prominence. I would make my first applications there.

I sought out the president of the most important of these first. I found him a pleasant, smiling, affable gentleman, with gray hair, and gold spectacles on his nose, an eminently respectable, scholastic-looking personage; a minister of the gospel and a pillar of society. He received me courteously and asked my business. I told him I wanted an opportunity to teach in his college, in however humble a capacity, or for however small a compensation. His face broke into a broad smile, which he politely tried to suppress.

"What can you teach?" he asked, good-naturedly.

"Latin, Greek, French, German, Italian, music, English literature, or medicine," I replied.

He looked surprised and handed me a copy of a Greek work, and requested me to translate a few lines of it into English. I did so readily and correctly.

His astonishment was great, and his manner became more respectful. He asked me several questions as to where I had been educated, all the time studying my rude, black features with a bewildered expression. He offered me a chair. I inquired whether there was any place in his institution I could secure, in which I could make use of my knowledge to earn a living.

He politely told me that he regretted to say there was none; that his institution was purely and solely for the education of white students, and that they would not receive learning from one of my color. He added that such prejudices were foolish, he was ready to acknowledge, but they existed, and as a practical man he had to recognize them; if he employed a single negro tutor in his school he might just as well close up his doors. He said they needed a servant, however, to look after the stables, and --

But I interrupted him, and replied that I did not want to do menial work; and, thanking him for his courtesy, I bowed myself out.

I was not discouraged; I expected rebuffs. I made my way to the other institution. The head of it was very unlike the gentleman I had just seen. He was beetle-browed, dark--dark as a mulatto--with great quantities of black hair on his hands and arms; in fact, his hands were *furred*, so to speak, except on the palms and knuckles. I could not help but think of Darwin and Evolution and the great apes. His voice was coarse and gruff, and manner brusque. He had none of the sweetness and suavity of the other gentleman. He roared with laughter, in my very face, when he heard my proposition; and did not even trouble himself to test my attainments, or make any explanations, but rudely ordered me out of the room. He told me he had no time to waste in such nonsense.

Still I was not discouraged. If I could not get employment in any institution of learning, at least the merchants' stores were open to me. I must find a resting place, a fulcrum, for the Archimedean lever with which I proposed to move the world.

I walked past several stores and scanned the proprietors and the establishments carefully. At last I came to a large dry-goods shop, with many salesmen. A benevolent-looking old gentleman seemed to be in charge of the place. I entered. I think the employer was of Quaker stock, for he used the "thee" and "thou" of that quaint, interesting and admirable people.

I told him I wanted a situation as a salesman; that I would work for the first month for nothing (I had money enough to carry me along for a time); and after that I would ask such small stipend as he thought would be reasonable, sufficient merely to pay my board.

The old gentlemen smiled on me blandly and replied:

"Thee cannot belong to this place, friend, or thee would know that people of thy color cannot be employed, side by side, with white people, in such an establishment as this. If I employed thee, and thou wert ready to work for nothing, still it would not do. The mere sight of thy black face (I say it kindly, friend), behind this counter, would drive away every white customer from my store and bring me to bankruptcy."

"Is there no store in which I can get employment?"

"No," he replied; "not one. The line of color is clearly drawn."

"Are there any negro stores?" I asked.

"No," he replied; "thy people are generally poor and would scarcely be able to maintain stores; and if they were established the better off among them would probably prefer to patronize the white stores, for they are, naturally enough, ambitious to be something higher than their fellows. The aristocratic distinctions are as clearly defined among thy people as among the whites, as thou art probably aware."

My heart began to sink. What a dreadful and all-pervading thing this race-feeling was. No outlet for a black man among the whites, and none among his own color! No wonder they were forced down into servile places, such as waiters, barbers, etc. But I would not be driven in that direction. I would continue the fight. I thanked the pleasant-looking old gentleman for his courtesy and politeness, and started out again.

I walked for some time before I had the courage to make another attempt. At length I passed a lumberyard. In the office a fat man sat perched upon a high, three-legged stool, making entries in a book. I bowed politely to him, taking off my hat and standing humbly before him, and asked him if he needed a clerk.

"A clerk!" he replied, in a loud voice, staring at me insolently.

"Yes," I replied; "I am a book-keeper and have a thorough education. I can speak French and German as well as English. If I could make myself useful to you I would work for a very small compensation."

He hopped down off his chair, and, pointing to the door, yelled at me:

"Get out of here! It's a pretty state of things when d--d niggers, like you, can speak French and German and know more than their betters, and ask to be bookkeepers! Go down to the levee and yank cotton bales. That's the kind of work you are fit for! Out of here!"

I retired before this burst of vituperative bigotry, perfectly overwhelmed.

But why pursue further the wretched narrative of rebuffs and disappointments? All day long I passed from place to place, trying to find employment fit for a gentleman. Sometimes I was treated civilly, sometimes insolently, and sometimes canes and yard-sticks were raised over my head.

I had the money to pay my board in a comfortable hotel, but all such were shut in my face; and I had to put up for the night in a low, dirty haunt of men of my own color.

It was a long time before I could get to sleep. The high hopes and aspirations with which I had started out in the morning were all blasted and withered. I began to lose confidence in my own theories. The Archimedean lever would not work. I could not find a fulcrum for it. It seemed to me that the eloquence of Daniel Webster or the learning of William E. Gladstone, wrapped up in a black hide, would amount to nothing. The saddest part of the business was the dreadful revelation of the baseness of human nature which I had witnessed; for, during the day, I had made applications for employment to several of my intimate friends, whose faces had never before been turned to mine save when wreathed in obsequious smiles, and I had started back before the dark and scowling brows with which they greeted a helpless inferior. The world is a wretched-looking object viewed from below, but grand and gaudy as stage scenery to him who can contemplate it from above. The highest test of a true gentleman is gentleness to servants and courtesy to the unfortunate. The man who can address a begger with the same tones of voice which he will use toward a prince is one of nature's noblemen,--yea, a species of demi-god, and fit to be worshiped by common humanity.[126]

I had also found that it was impossible for me to force my way into many of the trades and mechanical pursuits, even as an apprentice. They all had their laws limiting the number who could learn the business.

What was left for me? I must either resort to servile employment or hard physical toil. . . .

Ignatius Donnelly, *Doctor Huguet: A Novel* (Chicago, 1891), 197-201.

3. HEARINGS BEFORE THE INDUSTRIAL COMMISSION, 1898-1900

Washington, D.C., *April 17, 1898*

TESTIMONY OF MR. JOHN HEALY,

First General Vice-President, National Building Trades Council of America

FORM OF CONTRACT ADOPTED BY THE BUILDING TRADES COUNCIL,
WASHINGTON, D.C., AT ITS MEETING, FEBRUARY 25, 1896

In consideration of the organizations represented in the building trades council, a central representative body of the District of Columbia, pledging their support and assistance to the undersigned concerns and individuals, the latter hereby agree and pledge their faith to employ none but local union labor, recognized as such by the said building trades council, on all their work in the District of Columbia, in the lines of business sought to be protected and assisted by the said council, whether such work be in the construction, repair, or remodeling of buildings owned by said undersigned concerns or individuals.

It is expressly understood and agreed, however, that if any local union, whether it be a member of the said council or not, refuses to ratify this agreement by entering into a contract similar to the foregoing and relating to its particular trade or craft, then the employment by said concerns or the said individuals, or either of them, of any person or persons not members of the said nonratifying or refusing union, shall not be the basis or form an excuse for the calling off of the hands of the unions which have ratified and accepted this contract, or for any strike or boycott on its or their part against said employing concerns or individuals, or either of them.

And in cases of differences growing out of the failure to observe the foregoing undertakings, or which may arise in the employment of any unfair labor, and which can not be settled between the said organization and the concern or individual complained of a board of arbitration shall be elected, as follows:

Three arbitrators shall be elected by the said building trades council and three by the concerns or individual complained of, and if necessary, these six shall elect a seventh impartial man.

The decision of this board of arbitration shall be binding on all parties concerned.

This contract shall go into force on the _____day of_____,A.D. 1896, and remain so until the____day of____, A.D.____.

In witness whereof the said building trades council has caused these presents to be signed with its name by its president and secretary, and its seal annexed, and the said concerns and individuals have on their part caused same to be signed with their names, on this_____day of_____,A.D. 1896.

_____.

_____.

Q. Do you have any colored men in your organization?--A. Not in the local organization; but the national organization does not prohibit colored men from becoming members. There are colored bricklayers in Washington, but not connected with our organization.

Q. (By Representative Gardner.) For what reason? Why are they not connected with you?--A. Because we do not permit them; we do not admit colored men to our organization.

Q. (By Mr. KENNEDY.) Have you affiliated with the hod-carriers' union, who are largely union men?--A. We affiliate with them in the building trades council.

Q. (By Representative GARDNER.) What latitude have the local organizations the country over in the admission of members; that is, the grounds on which they arbitrarily decline to admit persons as members? For instance, you said awhile ago a bricklayer had to be vouched for by 2 people, and so on.-- A. I stated also he had to be a citizen of the United States or Canada.

Q. It seems to be true that the local organization here has power to draw the color line absolutely, without regard to the qualifications of the applicant. To what extent does that power generally go with local organizations

Is it absolute? Could it extend to a roman nose, gray eyes, wart on the chin, or must it rest upon some reason? What is the law about it?--A. Such a condition might be possible, but not at all probable.

Q. You mean then that all those things rest absolutely upon the will of the local organization?--A. Why, yes; they rest upon the will of the majority, but I want to say that this method of excluding the colored men is not adopted all over the country in every organization affiliated with the national union. In the cities of New York, Boston, and all through the east they are admitted to membership to any local and admitted to membership in the national union.

Q. (By Mr. FARQUHAR.) You say that the local union does not admit the negro?--A. Yes.

Q. Suppose a negro comes from a local union with an international card; what is this union going to do?--A. We will admit him; we recognize his card all the time.

Q. Is it not common that a great many of the unions south of the Potomac and Ohio rivers draw the color line?--A. South of the Potomac River.

Q. And the Ohio.--A. South of the Potomac River it is common for white and black to be mingled in the same organization. That has been forced upon them as a matter of necessity, because in some localities, especially in the far South, the colored mechanic is in the majority.

Q. Then the farther north you go the line is closer drawn?--A. I can not say that, but when you get to Washington the line is drawn, and before you get to Washington, Norfolk and Richmond, and those places not so very far south of the Potomac, the line is very distinctly drawn, and as far as Washington and Baltimore. But when you get as far as New York--I do not know about Philadelphia--but when you get to New York the colored man is on a par with the white man, and so it is farther east and north. You go to Chicago and they are on an equality with the white mechanic. While the laws of our organization exclude colored men, I want to say that we have less trouble, less opposition from the colored man than we have had from those few white men who have remained outside of the pale of our organization. We have worked in entire harmony with the colored men. The colored men, I believe, understand, as we do, one of the most important reasons for excluding them from membership in our organization, and that is that 99 per cent of the colored bricklayers, especially those in Washington, are not qualified to hold their own with the white man, and of course we could not admit them to membership unless we regulate that as a whole.

Q. Bring down your own standard?--A. We would have to bring down our own standard; we recognize that fact.

Q. (By Mr. A. L. HARRIS.) Is that from natural qualities, the want of efficiency?--A. They have never had the opportunity to become efficient, as has been stated here before, like those people who have served apprenticeships and worked in the larger cities.

Q. (By Representative GARDNER.) They are admitted in New York and Boston?--A. Yes.

Q. Probably have a pretty good standard of work there?--A. Yes.

Q. Now, do you know whether those colored men generally belonging to the unions in New York and Boston are freed slaves, or are they the descendants of colored people who have lived in the North for generations?--A. I do not know, but I would presume that they are the descendants of people who have lived in the North for generations.

Q. That is to say, they become competent, more competent mechanics by being more thoroughly de-Africanized?--A. Yes, by being constantly in closer touch with the white men of their particular trade or calling. . . .

Washington, D.C., May 5, 1899

TESTIMONY OF MR. G. W. PERKINS[127]

President of the Cigar Makers International Union

Q. (By Mr. FARQUHAR.) How does he get any particular benefits?--A. Increased wages, shorter hours generally, and improved shop conditions.

To bring out more clearly the point I made a short time ago regarding

expenditures for out-of-work benefits, let me say that in 1893 the expenditures for out-of-work benefits, in round numbers, was $89,000; 1894, $174,
000; 1895, $166,000; 1896, which was the banner year, $175,000; then the
decline commenced; 1897, $117,000; 1898, $70,000.

Q. Explain this out-of-work benefit.--A. We pay $3 a week to any
member who is unemployed and in good standing.

Q. (By Mr. KENNEDY.) Do you make any distinction between married and
unmarried members?--A. No distinction whatever. Every member is served
precisely alike. We make no distinction regarding sex, color, creed, nationality, whether married or single.

Q. (By Mr. PHILLIPS.) Have you many female members?--A. Very few,
comparatively speaking, to the large number of females employed in the trade.
We have probably, not over 5,000, all told, and they are largely located in
New York and through Pennsylvania.

Q. How many colored members have you?--A. Quite a few in the South.
That is, I say, quite a few when compared with the members that are in other
trades. Regarding the colored question, I want to say now, if it is per-
missible: Our constitution makes it obligatory on the part of local unions
to accept journeymen cigar makers as members. Any journeyman cigar maker
who has served 3 years at the trade can come in, and by paying his initiation
fee in installments, if he wants to, he is regarded as having been initiated.
It requires no vote; the constitution makes it mandatory. . . .

Washington, D.C., April 7, 1899.

TESTIMONY OF MISS CLARE DE GRAFFENRIED

United States Department of Labor

Q. (By Mr. SMYTH.) Do you not think that the cost of living is very
much less in the South?--A. Very much less in every way. In the first place,
the expense of fuel is inconsiderable. At the North it has to be used at
least 8 months in the year; in the South, probably 3 or 4. Next, the clothing
is entirely different; the heavy expensive wool stuffs used in the North are
not needed in the South. As to food, not only is the dietary less varied and
extensive than it is in the North, but many kinds of food are cheaper. I
should like to see a better dietary among certain Southern mill operatives,
who now use no sugar, no milk, few fresh vegetables and meats, and live on
pork and corn bread. There are many Southern mills where the dietary is good,
where pasturage is provided, where cows are kept, where the people have plenty
of milk, and raise vegetables and fruit. That is true of the mills along the
Patapsco. The corporations not only furnish certain land for a garden, but
they also have a sort of communal garden, and each family is allowed to have
a strip in that garden which they may tend and cultivate. Of course this
enables them to live better than they could otherwise. In other parts of the
South the same is true. I know a mill in Athens, Ga., where the superintendent has a garden plot for each family. It is just as much a part of his work
to have those gardens ploughed and those houses whitewashed as to pay dividends
to the stockholders. At other mills no attention is paid to that sort of thing,
and the operatives do not work in the gardens, being tired with their tasks
in the mills. Those are the districts where the families are so poor that
they use no milk or sugar. On the other hand, you will find that many poor
farmers do not feed their cows and they are without milk, except in summer,
when the pasturage is good.

Q. (By Mr. FARQUHAR.) Is it mainly the local population that is employed
in those mills?--A. It is altogether a local population--that is to say, local
within a radius of fifty or a hundred miles. You know, of course, that no negro
labor is employed in the mills of the South except in the picker room. Negroes
also are employed as porters and teamsters, but they do not tend machines.
Columbia has a cooperative mill owned and worked by negroes.

Q. (BY Mr. SMYTH.) Has that not failed?--A. So I understood. I understand there is a mill in Charleston that employs only negroes. The reason I
call attention to the fact that there are no negroes employed with whites on
textiles in the South is that in the course of some remarks I was making in
Boston on the subject of Southern spinners I was interrupted by a man who said

that all that work was done, of course, by negroes. He was a mill owner
himself, yet was under that false impression. . . .

Washington, D.C., April 21, 1899

TESTIMONY OF MR. J. W. BRIDWELL

Secretary of the Atlanta Federation of Trades

Q. (By Mr. KENNEDY.) You say there are very few strikes in the South.
Do you attribute that to the fact that organization is comparatively weak in
the South?--A. Yes; that is one of the reasons.

Q. You consider organized labor in its infancy in the South almost,
do you not, and struggling to get to the front?--A. Yes; but gaining very
rapidly.

Q. (By Mr. RATCHFORD.) Do you think the number of strikes would increase
or diminish if the organizations were strengthened?--A. I think it would
diminish.

Q. (By Representative LIVINGSTON.) If we had the same proportion of
foreign labor mixed up in Atlanta as they have in Chicago, would you have
more strikes or less?--A. We would have more strikes.

Q. (By Mr. FARQUHAR.) What reason can you give for that?--A. It is the
restless condition of the foreign element.

Q. How long have you been acquainted with Southern unions of all kinds?
A. I have been a member of unions for sixteen years.

Q. Has there not been, proportionately to the number of members in the
Southern unions, as many strikes there as there have in the North or West or
East?--A. Proportionately, we have our share of them.

Q. (By Mr. PHILLIPS.) Have you any strikes of the colored labor in the
South?--A. Yes, occasionally; unorganized strikes, and sometimes organized.

Q. Do the colored people belong to any organizations in the South?--A.
Yes; they have members in a number of organizations.

Q. (By Mr. KENNEDY.) If you pay the same proportion of dues that are
paid by the membership elsewhere, and you have occasional strikes in Georgia,
is it probable that you get your full share of the benefits from the international organizations?--A. Yes; we get our full share.

Q. You have no fault to find?--A. No.

Q. (By Representative LIVINGSTON.) Do you suppose you have as many as
5,000 or 6,000 laborers in Georgia in organizations of different kinds?--A.
Yes; in good standing, exclusive of the railroad organizations. The cotton
mills' operatives organized in Augusta with 1,500 or 2,000 alone, and Columbus
has just been organized. We have 5,000 or 6,000, in round numbers, outside
of these just organized. . . .

Q. What relations have you with nonunion labor? For instance, in the
typographical union, does the nonunion man have the same rights and privileges
there in Atlanta as a union man would have?--A. There are some printing establishments he can not work in at all, not being member of the typographical
union. The same rule applies to other organizations.

Q. (By Mr. KENNEDY.) Can he work in the Constitution office or the Journal office?--A. The Constitution is an open shop; the Journal is a union shop
or office. [128]

Q. It is said the Constitution does not recognize the union at all. Is
that so?--A. We have a majority at the present time--members of the typographical union.

Q. (By Representative LIVINGSTON.) Have you had much trouble with non-
union labor?--A. We have had no more than our share that you will run across
around the country.

Q. As a rule, are the negroes able to pay the initiation fees and dues?
A. No; but the unions always provide a way where they can pay the initiations
and dues. They can pay the dues more easily after they get into the union on
account of the higher rate of wages.

Q. In the first instance, how could they get in?--A. There are different
rules in the organizations; most organizations give them an opportunity to
pay as they earn. Some organizations will not admit them to membership.

Q. Do they have the same facilities and opportunities that our white people have?--A. Yes, excepting the railroad organizations.

Q. Do they get the same money?--A. They get the same amount of money in trades they are employed in. The railroad organizations debar them from membership.

Q. How about the typographical union; does it debar them?--A. I can not answer that; we have no colored typographical men in the South that I know of.

Q. Stonecutters--they can cut stone?--A. No; we have no colored stone-cutters. We have quite a number of stone masons. I have heard of two stone-cutters in the State, but they are not connected with the union.

Q. Do you fight nonunion men, oppose them, browbeat them, or fight them out of employment, as a rule?--A. We keep them out of employment in certain shops where they get in our way. . . .

Q. (By Mr. KENNEDY.) Can you state the sentiment of organized labor in Atlanta as to the question of immigration; are they in favor of restricting it; have they considered it; passed resolutions on the subject?--A. They are in favor of restriction.

Q. (By Representative LIVINGSTON.) Why?--A. So as not to put so many laborers on the market.

Q. Which is to get rid of competition they would naturally bring in? A. Yes.

Q. Do you not think your social standard would be lowered if they were tumbled in on you there?--A. Undoubtedly; yes.

Q. Have you any suggestions to make on this immigration question?--A. No; except we believe it should be restricted.

Q. You want to make that an educational restriction?--A. Educational.

Q. Colored labor?--A. Colored labor is most unskilled labor in the South. There are quite a number of them engaged in trades, and some are organized. In Augusta, Ga., for instance, they have a carpenters' colored local and painters' union, and seem to take care of themselves as well as any other organization.

Q. What about convict labor; do they affect you in any way in the South?--A. They affect the miners seriously, and common labor considerably in the manufacture of brick and work on farms. I believe these are the only industries where they are used in that section. It takes the employment out of the hands of that much free labor. I do not know as it seriously affects farmers as much as it does the miners.

Q. (By Mr. KENNEDY.) Have your organizations petitioned the legis-lature to provide noncompetitive employment for convict labor?--A. They have not, so far; but they will through the legislative committee this coming convention.

Q. (By Representative LIVINGSTON.) In other words, where manufacturers are selling their goods made by convict labor, you propose to have something to say about that?--A. Yes; in several ways; to have them branded as convict-made goods, for instance, is one way.

Q. (By Mr. RATCHFORD.) Has the organized labor which you represent taken action, giving their representatives and officers of the association instruc-tions, through this State convention, to bring this matter up and finally have it referred to the legislative committee, which will appear before the legislature, to have these bills properly introduced?--A. Yes.

Q. Are you satisfied that the sentiment of free labor is against the employment of convicts in the mines and in the trades which you mention?--A. Yes.

Q. Are there any suggestions offered by the organization as to how the situation can be relieved?--A. It could be relieved by working convicts on public roadbeds, putting public roads in better condition, and keeping them in repair after once made.

Q. Is labeling the product of prison-made goods regarded as being a cure for the situation, or simply a remedy that will relieve it to some extent?--A. It would be a way. We could relieve ourselves to some extent by not patronizing convict-made goods of any description.

Q. (By Mr. FARQUHAR.) Have you an acquaintance with the convict-labor law in the State of Georgia?--A. They let the convicts out through a lease. The system was changed a short while back, I believe; a certain number to be worked in the mines and a certain number on the farms.

Q. Are these leases determined by the penal sentences of the prisoners, for instance, 5, 10, 15 or 20 years?--A. Yes. They are leased according to

the crime. In the State of Georgia certain prisoners are governed by the
county authorities, and others are governed by the action of the prison
commission, and a law as to how they shall lease these fellows.

Q. (By Representative LIVINGSTON.) A man that is sentenced for life;
what do you do with him?--A. Usually send him to the mines. . . .

Charlotte, N.C., March 14, 1900

TESTIMONY OF MR. JAMES L. ORR

President and Treasurer, Piedmont Manufacturing Company,
Graniteville, S.C.

Q. Your place of residence?--A. Greenville, S.C.

Q. And your business?--A. President and treasurer of the Piedmont
Manufacturing Company, situated on the Saluda River, 11 miles south of
Greenville, on the Southern Railroad.

Q. The Piedmont Company is a cotton mill corporation?--A. Yes; we
manufacture sheetings and drillings; we have about 60,000 spindles and looms.

Q. It is one of the first and one of the largest cotton mills established in South Carolina after the war?--A. Yes; it was one of the first
mills established. It is not one of the largest now, though it is probably
fifth or sixth.

Q. Do you use entire white labor?--A. Yes; we use no negro labor at
all, except scavengers and firemen, and all our teamsters are white.

Q. (By Mr. C. J. HARRIS.) Do you not employ negro labor in the mills?--
A. I do not think it is desirable to work the two together. I think that
the preference should be given to the white labor, as long as we can get it,
because they have had a hard time in the South for a long time in competition
with negro labor, and this is the only sphere, as it was, set aside for their
benefit. As long as I can use the white labor to any advantage I intend to
do it.

Q. Is that the custom in all the cotton mills you know of?--A. Yes.
There are some mills--there is one mill I know which is using negro labor
exclusively, except the overseers. Negro labor was used in the South for a
number of years before the war, to a limited extent. One of my superintendents worked before the war in the late Saluda mill near Columbia, where some
negro labor was employed.

Q. Is there anywhere a mixture of white and colored labor? It is either
one thing or the other?--A. Yes, except in some of the mills they use negroes
for scrubbers and outside hands, and such as that; but inside the mills, some
of them use negroes as picker hands in the picker room.

Q. (By Mr. RATCHFORD.) Why is it not desirable to mix the races in
their employment?--A. In the first place, between the class of hands that
work in the mills and the negro labor there is considerable feeling; that is
one objection. Then another, the social feature that it would bring about.

Q. What feeling is it--race feeling?--A. Yes.

Q. Would it, in your opinion, do justice to both races to have them come
into closer contact with each other, both in their employment and in social
matters?--A. Hardly socially, sir.

Q. Would it tend to elevate the lower classes?--A. I think not. I
think the history of the world shows it is rather dragging down than bringing
up.

Q. (By Mr. SMYTH.) The whites would resent it?--A. Very much.

Q. It would be very hard to force them to work together?--A. Yes.

Q. (By Mr. RATCHFORD.) Do they resent it in other occupations?--A. Not
on the farm; not in the mines; but there, you see, there are principally males
occupied, whereas if the negro was allowed to work in the cotton mills, generally, they would be mixed up with the women, too.

Q. (By Mr. C. J. HARRIS.) I should like to ask you in regard to the supply
of labor for mills; is it plentiful, or the reverse?--A. Up to this time we
have had ample labor for the mills. You know, in the upper part of South
Carolina, and the upper part of Georgia, and western part of North Carolina
the white population largely predominates, and we get our help principally
from these three sections. There will be some scarcity until the hands are

trained, in consequence of the number of new mills going up now, I apprehend.

Q. (By Mr. SMYTH.) What work does this white labor come from?--A. From farms almost exclusively.

Q. Why do they leave the farms? Are the attractions and opportunities better?--A. Yes; they have much better facilities for schools. The mills, so far as I know, everywhere run their schools longer than they do in the country. For instance, we have for a number of years at Piedmont supplemented the public school fund so that we teach 10-1/2 months in the year. Then they have the advantages of churches. We have 5 churches in Piedmont regularly supplied. Being close together, they have social advantages which they do not have in the country. Probably a more weighty reason than any of the others is that they can have employment 310 days in the year at fairly good wages, much better than they can make on the farm. . . .

Q. Is there always a plentiful supply of colored labor?--A. Yes.

Q. What have you to suggest as an improvement for that condition?-- A. Nothing suggests itself just now to me.

Q. The colonization of the negro has been advocated by witnesses before this commission. What is your judgment upon that?--A. I think it would be the greatest misfortune that could happen to the South. I think the negro labor is the best for the farm that we can get. They can live on less and they can do more work when properly treated than any class of labor that we can have. But for the negro labor we could not live on 5 cent cotton, and but for 5 cent cotton the South would not be able to control the cotton markets of the world. So I am utterly opposed to taking the negroes away from the South.

Q. Do you think that ultimately the assimilation of the races will result in the building up of a higher standard among that class?--A. By assimilation I do not suppose you mean miscegenation. That would be the greatest curse on earth to this or any other country. They are an imitative people, and I think their condition has improved very much through association with the white people. What satisfies me of that is the condition of the negroes in the upper part of the State where they come into contact with the white people, and that of those of the lower part of the State, where they live by themselves very much. The negroes in the upper part of the State are very much more intelligent, I think, sir.

Q. As the result of the influences surrounding them?--A. Yes, environments.

Q. (By Mr. SMYTH.) Is it a fact that the negroes in the lower counties of the State have actually retrograded in intelligence?--A. That seems to be the universal judgment of everybody down there.

Q. That is, since the control of the whites has been removed where they gather in large bodies by themselves?--A. Large bodies by themselves, and have no association with the white people; I think they have deteriorated mentally, morally, and physically, from what I can see and hear.

Q. In your neighborhood the negroes are working as carpenters and bricklayers with the whites, are they not?--A. Yes, particularly in the building of new enterprises--mills and warehouses and stores--you will see negro carpenters, negro bricklayers, and negro plasterers working along with the white people.

Q. In that way they come into competition with the white mechanic?-- A. Yes.

Q. And force them to take lower wages?--A. Yes.

Q. In other words, the wages are based on the lowest stratum?--A. Not only with us, but, I think, with everyone in the world.

Q. That is one difficulty with the laboring class in the South--the competition with negro labor, which forms the basis of comparison?--A. Yes; the white people in the South of that class have found that they could go to the mills where the negroes have not been able to go. They have had that sphere to themselves heretofore.

Q. But the negro has followed them there in Charleston?--A. Yes; they are running the mill entirely by negroes, except the bosses.

Q. (By Mr. RATCHFORD.) Admitting that the lowest wages paid do much to fix the standard for all, is it not also true in thus fixing a low standard of wages the low standard of living follows, and all that accompanies a low standard of living?--A. The amount of wages received, of course, regulates the living. . . .

Charlotte, N.C., *March 14, 1900*

TESTIMONY OF MR. THOMAS H. RENNIE,

Superintendent Graniteville Manufacturing Company, Graniteville, S.C.

The subcommission of the United States Industrial Commission met at the Southern Manufacturers' Club at 10 a.m., Mr. E. A. Smyth, presiding. Mr. Thomas H. Rennie, superintendent of the Graniteville Manufacturing Company, Graniteville, S.C., was introduced as a witness at 10:35 a.m., and, being duly sworn, testified as follows:

Q. (By Mr. SMYTH.) Please give your name.--A. Thomas H. Rennie.

Q. Your place of residence?--A. Graniteville, S.C.

Q. What is your business?--A. Superintendent of the Graniteville Manufacturing Company.

Q. That is a cotton mill?--A. Yes.

Q. That mill was established a good many years before the war by Mr. [129] Gregg, I believe?--A. In 1845.

Q. It is about the oldest mill in South Carolina?--A. The oldest.

Q. As well as one of the most successful?--A. Yes.

Q. How long have you been connected with that industry in South Carolina?--A. Eighteen years.

Q. Are you a native of South Carolina?--A. I am a native of the State of New York.

Q. Were you in the cotton-mill business before coming to Graniteville? A. Yes.

Q. For how long a time?--A. Sixteen years.

Q. You were for 16 years engaged in cotton manufacturing in the North, and you have been for 18 years, you say, in the South?--A. Yes.

Q. You are therefore somewhat conversant with the labor conditions on both sides of the line?--A. Yes.

Q. Do you employ any colored hands in your mills?--A. In the picker department, roustabouts around the yards, etc.

Q. You employ none in the mill proper?--A. None in the mill proper except to carry water, wash floors, and that class of labor.

Q. Would it not be practicable to employ the races together in the cotton mill?--A. It would be impracticable.

Q. It would be resented by the white operators?--A. It certainly would. They would not work side by side.

Q. That is a matter of race prejudice--race feeling?--A. Yes; that is older than we are, I suppose.

Q. (By C. J. HARRIS.) In the mines and in other work here in the South we work whites and blacks together without friction; that is, where only males and adults are worked. I do not see that there is any particular friction in other employments?--A. Your question answers itself because you state "where only males are employed."

Q. (By Mr. SMYTH.) There are a large number of mechanics, colored bricklayers, etc.--A. Yes.

Q. They work side by side--A. They do.

Q. What effect does their wage have on the white mechanics?--A. It affects them.

Q. (By Mr. RATCHFORD.) Do they offer themselves for less wages than the white mechanic?--A. They do.

Q. What is the difference in wages?--A. The white journeyman bricklayer in our section gets $2.50 a day, and we are able to employ a colored bricklayer for $1.75.

Q. Skill being about equal?--A. Skill being about equal.

Q. Does it not follow that the colored bricklayer is usually employed and gets the preference where there is not a market for the labor of both?--A. I should say yes.

Q. (By Mr. SMYTH.) It has been stated here that the mill in Charleston is employing colored labor with white overseers. Do you know whether this is working successfully?--A. The managers of the enterprise say yes, and skilled manufacturers who have gone in and examined the work say no.

Q. Do you think there is any reason why the colored people cannot be taught cotton manufacturing?--A. I do not know of any reason.

Q. They work for less wages than the whites in Charleston?--A. About two-thirds of the wages of the whites. The only difficulty they have experienced so far is regularity of work. They stay away from their work a great deal, and it takes a great many more hands to operate a mill with colored labor.

Q. If that becomes successful to any great extent it will have its effect and bearing upon the wages of the white operator, will it not?--A. Most assuredly.

Q. (By Mr. RATCHFORD.) Do we understand that the colored labor is not as attentive to the work and does not work as regularly as the white labor? A. That has been the experience at the Charleston mill, sir.

Q. (By Mr. SMYTH.) From your testimony, then, you think the colored laboring class as a rule are a drag on the white laboring class in the South, and tend to cut down their wages?--A. They are, most assuredly.

Q. And in South Carolina you have about two blacks to one white?--A. That is about the proportion. The white journeyman represents about one-third of the labor of South Carolina.

Q. (By Mr. RATCHFORD.) The employing class are invariably the white class, are they not?--A. Always. I say "always;" I will change that by saying it is almost the invariable rule. There are some colored contractors in our section.

Q. Then if the employers of your State would pay the same rate of wages and the same scale, whether to the black or to the white man, would it not remove that evil of which the white man complains, to white labor?--A. It would create another inequality. The colored man does not expend for his living or for his family what the white man does. It costs the white laborer more to live. The result is that if the colored labor received the same wages as the white man, he would have the advantage of the white man, even in his living.

Q. Do you not think he would spend it if he made it--if not for the necessaries of life, for something else?--A. Always. He would surely spend it, but it would not be spent as the white man spends it, on his family and on his home.

Q. (By Mr. SMYTH.) You think it would be squandered--wasted?--A. It would be most assuredly squandered. That has been my experience of 18 years in the South with colored labor.

Q. (By Mr. RATCHFORD.) What truth is there in this claim, which has been made by witnesses before this commission, that, in order to get the best service out of a colored man, his wages must not exceed the living point very much because if it does he will lie idle until the surplus is spent?--A. I have had some very bitter experience myself along that line.

Q. (By Mr. SMYTH.) Supporting that testimony?--A. Supporting that testimony. In other words, where a negro makes a living, just a living, he is a better employee than where he makes a surplus.

Q. He is more regular in his work?--A. He is more regular in his work and a better citizen.

Q. You think, then, that he lacks ambition to accumulate; that he wants a sufficiency, and will not work beyond what will give him that sufficiency? A. I do not know whether that exactly covers the ground. As soon as the negro gets money to spend he wants to make a great big showing and spend it. In other words, as soon as a young negro man commences to earn money he wants to be a sport and a flashily dressed man, and to cut a large figure in colored society, and he usually does it if he gets anything more than a living.

Q. (By Mr. RATCHFORD.) Does it not seem plain to you, in view of these conditions, that the lower rate of wages paid to the colored labor will necessarily reduce the standard of living as well as the wages of white labor?--A. It will tend to regulate the wages of white labor in the South. It would not tend to lower it any from the present standard.

Q. (By Mr. SMYTH.) The price of labor, I suppose, is regulated by supply and demand?--A. I think so.

Q. (By Mr. RATCHFORD.) Let me ask for a moment; If a white bricklayer in your State asks for employment and makes known his rate of wages, which is $2.50 a day, I believe you stated, the employer may say to him in return I can employ a negro bricklayer who has as much skill as you, and will do as good service for $1.75. Now, I will put you on at $2.25. Have you known of any instances of that kind?--A. I have not, in our section.

Q. Are such things not likely to happen?--A. It might happen, but all
the white bricklayers in our section are union men with a regulated standard
of wages which they never break.

Q. Then you believe the union is a preventive against that particular
departure from their rate of wages?--A. I do.

Q. (By Mr. SMYTH.) But as a result a good many jobs go to the negro
bricklayer?--A. A good many jobs go to negro bricklayers.

Q. And the white bricklayers are idle?--A. A part of the time.

Q. I mean in consequence of these jobs going to the colored laborers?
A. I say they are a part of the time.

Q. (By Mr. RATCHFORD.) Are the negroes unionized?--A. They have recently formed two unions in Augusta, just across the river from us. We are
13 miles from Augusta.

Q. Will the white men accept their membership in their union?--A. They
have separate unions.

Q. Separate branches?--A. Separate branches. The object of the white
men in organizing the negroes is to get the negro workmen to demand the
same wages that they demand, in order to equalize them.

Q. To make them uniform?--A. Yes. . . .

Charlotte, N.C., March 14, 1900

TESTIMONY OF MR. S. B. TANNER

Treasurer Henrietta Mills

The subcommission of the United States Industrial Commission met in the
rooms of the Southern Manufacturers' Club at 10 a.m., Mr. Smyth presiding.
At 1:03 p.m. Mr. S. B. Tanner was introduced as a witness, and, being first
duly sworn, testified as follows:

Q. (By Mr. SMYTH.) What is your name?--A. S. B. Tanner.

What is your occupation?--A. Treasurer of the Henrietta Mills.

Q. These are cotton mills?--A. Yes, sir.

Q. How long have they been established?--A. Since 1888.

Q. How many hands do you employ?--A. We employ about 1,300 hands.

Q. Are they all white?--A. All white except the scrubbers, cotton
handlers, etc.

Q. Any operatives in the mill colored?--A. No.

Q. Why not?--A. It has never been the custom to work them that way.

Q. The white operatives would not submit to it?--A. Would not submit
to it. We should have to build a separate mill if we worked whites and
negroes. Especially the women folks, the whites will not work with the negro.

Q. Notwithstanding white carpenters and mechanics work with colored
carpenters and mechanics?--A. On outside work; yes, sir.

Q. But more particularly on account of the females being in the same
room and working together?--A. Yes, sir.

Q. (By Mr. RATCHFORD.) Are there any special reasons why they refuse
to work with them?--A. They have different reasons.

Q. (By Mr. SMYTH.) Race feeling, I suppose, predominates?--A. Race
feeling is the trouble. . . .

Charlotte, N.C., March 14, 1900

TESTIMONY OF MR. BENJAMIN R. LACY

Commissioner of Labor, and Cashier of the Dime Savings Bank, Raleigh, N.C.

Q. Are you familiar with what has been done for other branches of
organized labor?--A. I am sorry to say I do not think the others have taken
the same stand. We have done it on account of the danger to the public and
the company's property. We have no fireman's organization. We had one, but
it went out.

Q. (By Mr. SMYTH.) Were the firemen organized?--A. Some few that ran
into the State. We have so many negro firemen; that is the only place where

they come into competition with the whites.

Q. Railroad employees?--A. Yes.

Q. (By Mr. RATCHFORD.) Have there been any strikes?--A. No, sir. The truth of it is, a great many engineers like negro firemen best. They had negroes, first and are only working white men in now; the white men are taking the places of negroes.

Q. (By Mr. SMYTH.) The negroes are not admitted into the fireman's brotherhood?--A. No, sir. In most instances they do not pay the same wages.

Q. They will not admit colored members into the fireman's organization? A. No, sir.

Q. There are no colored engineers on the railroad at all?--A. No, sir.

Q. Most of the firemen have been colored and are preferred by the white engineers?--A. A great many of the old engineers prefer negro firemen. They can treat them differently--make them wait on them. The white man does not do that. . . .

Charlotte, N. C., *March 14, 1900*

TESTIMONY OF MR. J. H. MC ADEN

Cotton Manufacturer, and Banker, Charlotte, N.C.

Q. Do you employ any colored labor?--A. No, sir. Not on account of any prejudice. I have a kind feeling for the negro. I used to own a good many before the war, and I have always felt a deep interest in the colored man. But I do not think it advisable to work them together and I do not think you could do it satisfactorily, and therefore I would rather not try. I have no colored men about the mill who are employed by the mill. There are some few women around there--washerwomen--who do not live inside the corporation, and a few men who chop wood and work for the different families; but they have no employment in the mill. Even my teamster is a white man. . . .

Charlotte, N.C., *March 14, 1900*

TESTIMONY OF MR. S. WITTKOWSKY

President, Chamber of Commerce, Charlotte, N.C.

Q. (By Mr. RATCHFORD.) Do I understand you to say that today they get more wages than then?--A. Yes.

Q. In what particular lines?--A. I think in all lines. I think wages in all lines have advanced.

Q. The wages then were 65 cents a day?--A. That is what he got.

Q. Common labor?--A. Yes; in the foundry as a laborer.

Q. We had testimony before the commission today that the average wages for unskilled mill operators is 65 cents a day.--A. Yes; this man was in a foundry--an iron foundry.

Q. They pay better wages there, do they?--A. Yes; I presume they do, because it is mostly skilled labor.

Q. (By Mr. C. J. HARRIS.) What would be the wages of common labor in the city of Charlotte?

The WITNESS. Today?

Mr. HARRIS. Yes.

The WITNESS. Day labor?

Mr. HARRIS. Yes.

The WITNESS. Well, about 75 cents. I have not been doing a great deal of building the last year, but that is what I have been paying.

Q. (By Mr. RATCHFORD.) To both colored and white labor?--A. Yes.

Q. (By Mr. C. J. HARRIS.) Do you make any distinction in the carpenters that you hire? Do you pay them and the bricklayers less than the whites?--A. That depends on how skilled the labor is. If I want a common job, I get a colored man, and if I want a better job I get a white man.

Q. Suppose they are of equal skill, do they get the same wages?--A. Yes. I had a foreman and gave him $2 a day, and I had a colored man recently who asked me $2 a day and I gave it to him.

Q. It depends mostly on the skill of the individual man, does it.--A.
Yes. In this connection I will say that I have been a director in a cotton
mill for quite a number of years. I can not speak as to details as well as
Dr. McAden, but the labor is getting along very peaceably, very pleasantly,
and they are all saving up a little money. I will venture to say that of
the $325,000 we have today in our building and loan from $75,000 to $100,000
runs to colored people.

Q. (By Mr. SMYTH.) That applies to the city, of course?--A. Yes; I
know nothing about the country.

Q. Wages of course, are higher in the city than in the country?--A.
I presume so. Farm labor is always less.

Q. Do you think that because the colored man can make more in the city
than in the country is one reason why he crowds to the cities?--A. Yes, and
their facilities for schooling are better. They see more sights; they get
certainly better wages, and they love to live in the city--dress better and
acquire more. I was president of the savings bank for awhile, and the colored
people deposited a good deal of money in proportion to the whites here in
this city.

Q. (By Mr. C. J. HARRIS.) Do you find that the Southern working people,
white or colored, are thrifty in the way of saving? Are they not rather
careless?--A. They are becoming so gradually more and more. As they become
educated they become more saving. I know some colored people who are just
as saving as any white man could possibly be, and as thrifty, but as a class
they are not. They part with their money very freely.

Q. This is the greatest drawback to the South?--A. They go and spend
their money in any fake thing that comes along. . . .

Atlanta, Ga., March 19, 1900

TESTIMONY OF HON. RUFUS B. BULLOCK[130]

Cotton manufacturer, Atlanta, Ga.

The subcommission of the United States Industrial Commission met at the
Kimball Hotel at 10 a.m., Senator Kyle presiding. Hon. Rufus B. Bullock,
233 Peachtree street, Atlanta, Ga., was introduced as a witness at 2:35 p.m.,
and, being duly sworn, testified as follows:

The WITNESS. I wish to say, Mr. Chairman and gentlemen, by way of pre-
mise, that my relation with manufacture began here with the pioneer mills in
Atlanta in the year 1877, and I was actively in charge of the mill as treasurer and president until 1892. Since that time I have not given it any
personal attention, although I am still a director of the company; but Mr.
Fisher, vice-president of the company, is here, who, I may say, was raised
in a mill from boyhood. He knows all there is to be known about it.

I have read very carefully your paper which was sent me by your secretary, but have not prepared a written paper, and I shall be very willing to
answer any questions you may see fit to ask.

Q. (By Senator KYLE.) Yours is distinctively a Southern enterprise?--
A. Yes.

Q. This is not New England capital invested in the South?--A. There
was some Northern capital originally invested in starting the mill, but not
New England capital. Mr. Fisher has been here with us 7 or 8 years--9 years.

Q. You being one of the pioneers, it would be very interesting to have
your testimony.--A. I am only the pioneer in this immediate vicinity. Of
course, there were plenty of cotton mills in the South before ours. Ours
was the first one that started in this immediate vicinity. I think we were
the pioneers in using steam power in this Southern country.

Q. (By Mr. SMYTH.) Are your mill employees white?--A. White labor,
except the colored labor for rough work--sweepers, coal heavers, firemen, etc.

Q. You never attempted to work colored labor in with the white labor?
A. No, sir; except when the white help goes out to get a can of snuff the
colored sweepers run the loom.

Q. Would the white labor be willing that the colored help be employed
in the mill?--A. No, sir.

Q. They would not work together?--A. I should say there would be very

serious objection to it. They might consent to it if a person pushed them
for the experiment, but it would be wiser to either have all colored or all
white in spinning, weaving, carding, etc.

Q. That is a matter of race prejudice, I suppose?--A. Altogether race
prejudice, and social prejudice perhaps more than race prejudice.

Q. Do you know of any cotton mills being run by colored help?--A.
Only by newspaper report, in Charleston.

Q. There are none of them you know of your own experience?--A. No,
sir; none at all.

Q. Do you think the colored people are competent to serve as employees
in cotton mills?--A. Perfectly so; that is, you could make up a corps from
colored people.

Q. You think they could be taught as readily as the white population
that come to the mills--some of them?--A. As you know, some of them are
more intelligent, some are less so; the same as white people. . . .

Atlanta, Ga., *March 19, 1900*

TESTIMONY OF MR. H. E. FISHER

Cotton manufacturer, Atlanta, Ga.

The subcommission of the United States Industrial Commission met in the
parlors of the Kimball House at 10 a.m., Senator Kyle presiding. Mr. H. E.
Fisher was introduced as a witness at 3:35 p.m., being duly sworn, testified
as follows:[131]

Q. (By Senator KYLE.) State your name, post-office address, and voca-
tion.--A. H. E. Fisher, manufacturer, Atlanta Cotton Mills, Atlanta.

Q. You may begin by telling us something about the labor in the factory
for a period of years, kind of labor, wages paid, and number of female employees, male employees, and number of children employed, school facilities,
houses furnished by the company, freights, and so on.--A. The labor, of
course, is all white, and as far as the proportions are concerned it is about
30 per cent male, and the rest female and children. The only colored labor
that we have is the roustabouts, firemen, and sweepers in the mill. I will
say, that we have one colored girl that has worked in the cloth room ever
since I have been here, and I think ever since the mill was begun, right
along with the white hands, and that is old Carrie Hall. The wages average
more than has been stated per week. We employ about 275 hands and have a
pay roll of $1,300 a week. You will see it is very nearly $5 a week.

Q. (By Mr. SMYTH.) An average of nearly $1 a day?--A. Yes.

Q. (By Mr. RATCHFORD.) That includes overseers?--A. Includes all the
help we employ.

Q. Can you give an average without overseers and bosses?--A. Taking out
our engineer and 4 overseers, the pay roll will average about $1,175.

Q. (By Senator KYLE.) For 275 men?--A. Two hundred and seventy employees.

Q. (By Mr. SMYTH.) What is the name of your mill?--A. Atlanta Cotton
Mills. . . .

Atlanta, Ga., *March 20, 1900*

TESTIMONY OF HON. A. D. CHANDLER[132]

Governor of Georgia

Q. (By Representative LIVINGSTON.) For the betterment of the negro race
would you prefer an industrial education or a literary education?--A. Our
situation is peculiar here. Industrial education is preferable, confined to
certain lines. Now, we have this difficulty to encounter: The poorer class
of white people engaged in our industrial enterprises are jealous of the negro.
They do not work together well in the same factories. Now, I do not think
it would be to the interest of either race to mix them in manufacturing establishments, because of these race prejudices which crop out. We may deny

it, but they exist in every human being. The negro is the best farm laborer
I ever saw; no question about that. He is a skillful and successful farm
laborer when under intelligent direction.

Q. (By Mr. RATCHFORD.) You believe that is his natural sphere?--A. I
believe he is more useful there than anywhere else.

Q. Do you believe it is a mistake for him to enter the professions?--
A. Well, yes; I do. Of course he can preach; that is all right. He is
useful there. There is no reason that I see why he sould not practice medicine among his own race. He should be prepared for it though.

Q. (By Mr. SMYTH.) You would prefer the establishment of manual schools
for colored boys?--A. The best school I ever saw for the negro, or white boy
either, was the corn patch.--to learn the art or science of farming.

Q. I mean manual training for such occupations as bricklayers and
carpenters.--A. I doubt if it would be to the interest of either race for
them to be trained in these schools.

Q. (By Senator KYLE.) Have you many such colored tradesmen?--A. The
bricklayers' trade is very largely in the hands of the negroes in Georgia,
and there are a good many carpenters. While I was a contractor I employed
both and found as a rule that the whites were better carpenters than the
negroes, but as bricklayers some of the best I ever had were negroes.

Q. (By Mr. RATCHFORD.) Do they usually receive the same wages from contractors?--A. Always the same, so far as my observation goes. There are
small contractors that do odd jobs, and there is a good deal of cutting there,
and negroes frequently do that kind of work lower than white men, but when it
comes to building a large house and the contractors employing them to do the
work, I know of no discrimination in wages where the skill is equal.

Q. (By Senator KYLE.) Now, if they are to be relegated to the farm, is
there an opportunity for their advancement along that line? Is there a future
before them as owners of the farm?--A. I think so. They now frequently buy
and own farms and are as successful as white men. For a number of years nobody, white or black, has been successful on the farm on account of the low
prices of farm products; but when farm products brought good prices, I knew
quite a number of negroes that bought land and did well.

Q. (By Mr. SMYTH.) To go back to the educational question, have you a
compulsory school law in Georgia?--A. No, sir.

Q. Would you favor such a law? Is it needed?--A. I hardly think so,
because our people are disposed to go to school all they can now.

Q. You do not think there is an apathy on the part of the parents of
some of the white children as to the schooling of their children?--A. So far
as my observation goes there is not a great deal; of course there is some.
The negroes have manifested a great eagerness for school privileges since
they were freed.

Q. Really more than the whites?--A. Yes sir, I think they have more than
the whites. They had an idea that education would lift them at once to a level
with the whites, and hence they seize on school opportunities.

Q. (By Senator KYLE.) They are not successes as managers, you think?--A.
No, as a race they are not.

Q. That is something that is acquired with long experience?--A. That is
it exactly.

Q. (By Mr. RATCHFORD.) Parents usually send them to school until what
age?--A. The schools are open to them until they are 18, but after they get
to be 15 or 16 years old they have a roaming disposition and usually drift
away from the parents and go to town and hire out for manual service or work
for wages.

Q. (By Mr. SMYTH.) That is the colored children?--A. Yes, sir.

Q. (By Mr. RATCHFORD.) Is it not the general custom among the white
families in Georgia as well as the colored, to take the children out of school
and put them to work at the age of 12 or 13?--A. They have to do that even
earlier--8 or 10 years years--during the crop time, from planting time to
lying-by time--up to the middle of July.

Q. (By Mr. SMYTH.) Boys of 10 plow in Georgia?--A. Sometimes they do.
I plowed at 10.

Q. (By Mr. RATCHFORD.) You would favor a law restricting the employment
of children until they attain a certain age?--A. In factories?

Q. In factories or other works.--A. Well, I do not know. There are
families--for instance, widows who cannot, at the wages that they can command,

support themselves and children without the aid of the children. Under these circumstances, it seems to me the children ought to be allowed to help the mother earn the food, even though under 12 years old. . . .

Atlanta, Ga., *March 20, 1900*

TESTIMONY OF MR. H. F. GARRETT

President, State Federation of Labor, Atlanta, Ga.

Q. What can you tell the commission as to any trade--any of the skilled trades in which both white labor and colored labor is employed? Are their wages equal?--A. Yes; in some trades they are; among the stone masons and the brick masons they are equal; the carpenters in some places are and in some places not.

Q. Will the white tradesmen admit negroes into their unions?--A. Well, no; but they organize in separate unions.

Q. They cooperate with them in that way?--A. Yes; and skilled labor in the South has no fear of the negro at all. The negro is a good citizen when you can control him, and you can control him when organized better than the white man. That has been my experience with them.

Q. (By Mr. SMYTH.) Are there any colored men in your shop?--A. No, sir; I never worked in a shop with a negro machinist.

Q. You spoke about apprentices. Those boys, if they were discharged as all-around machinists, would there be any demand for their work?--A. The demand for machinists is great now for the simple reason that nearly every one is running double time, day and night, so there is employment for all skilled labor in the South today.

Q. At the present time?--A. Yes.

Q. (By Mr. RATCHFORD.) Is it not a fact that 30 per cent are only temporarily displaced, or thereabouts; while they may be displaced from the shop temporarily, they move from one department to another?--A. Yes. That is by a different method, from one department to another. The rule of the International Association of Machinists is as to apprentices--1 to the shop and 1 to every 5 journeymen.

Q. I am speaking of 30 percent which you say is displaced. To illustrate that point, when the Merganthaler typesetting machine was introduced, each machine did the work of 5 men. When the coal-cutting machine was introduced, probably 40 per cent of the labor in mining a ton of coal was done by machinery, and each of these trades held that men were displaced. Now, the fact remains that there are more printers and miners working than ever. Does not that disprove that labor has been displaced by machinery?--A. Well, to a certain extent, yes.

Q. Is it not because of machines that there have been more machinists employed than ever before?--A. Yes, on account of the business of the country picking up, but you take conditions as we have had them in the last 5 years --there were at least 30 per cent of the machinists walking the streets, and that is a menace to those men at work.

Q. During the last 5 years there has been an unusual depression of labor?--A. Yes; there has.

Q. (By Senator KYLE.) Not only machinists, but all other trades?--A. Yes; that is true. Now, as to negroes in the South, as regards to skilled labor, we never come in contact with them to amount to anything at all, because skilled labor in the South had rather have the negro than any foreign element--Poles or Hungarians.

Q. You prefer the colored man?--A. We prefer to have the negro than to have the Poles and Hungarians that you have around Pittsburg.

Q. (By Mr. SMYTH.) You can control him better?--A. Yes, for this reason; the negroes, very few of them, save their money. They make it and spend it. The foreign immigrants that come to the country--their money is banked in some other city, and there is no tax put on it at all, and I do not consider them good citizens.

Q. (By Mr. RATCHFORD.) And for the additional reason that you can always get the negro to understand you?--A. Yes.

Q. That is a very important reason, too, is it not?--A. Yes.

Q. The tendency, I believe, in the unskilled branches of industry has been to supply colored labor for a less rate per day than white labor can be supplied. Is that right?--A. Yes; that has been the case.

Q. What effect has that upon the wages of the white labor?--A. Well, of course it has this effect; it brings the wages of white labor down. The simple reason is that the labor of the South had never been organized. When they become organized, as they are in the North and East and West, then the negro will get as much pay in proportion as the white man gets for equal work--as much for the same class of work; but there has never been any organization to build those people up and to protect them.

Q. It is claimed by some that if the negro gets a rate of wages higher than the amount that is actually required to sustain him he will not work? A. Well, that may be true.

Q. In other words, it is claimed that if the negro will make enough of money to support him a week in 4 days' work that he will not work more than 4 days a week?--A. Well, you may find some; it will be rare instances. I do not believe that, for the simple reason that negroes used as helpers around where I have always worked are very steady negroes. The trouble is that the negroes like to run after women and spend their money that way. The majority--9 out of 10--have always got 1 or 2 women. What makes the negro loaf around the streets is simply this; if you have a girl cooking around your house, she will steal enough to feed this fellow who is loafing around and doing nothing. This class of negroes is of no benefit to the country at all, but the negro that works is a good citizen in this country. There is no doubt about that part of it.

Q. (By Mr. RATCHFORD.) Are the organized trades of the South hopeful that the negro will be unionized with them?--A. Yes.

Q. In separate branches?--A. Yes.

Q. To what extent are they unionized now, if any?--A. Well, in this city the carpenters are being organized and they are making an effort to organize brick masons.

Q. You speak of the colored class now, do you?--A. Yes. The white carpenters are well organized, but the negro carpenters--there is an effort being made to organize them, and an effort being made to organize the brick masons, both white and colored.

Q. What are the social advantages of your organization, if any?--A. Well, a great deal. Organization makes better citizens. Where a man does not belong to an organization, and does not study nor read, he does not become a better citizen as to the needs and wants, but where he belongs to an organization and hears discussion on economical points, it causes him to think and read, and the consequence is he becomes a better citizen; it makes him more steady and more sober. and gives him an insight into how he should vote and everything of that kind.

Q. Are there any requirements needed in membership--any man with good moral character can join the organization?--A. Yes.

Q. Without it can he join?--A. Some can and some can not.

Q. That is regulated by the local unions?--A. Yes.

Q. It is not encouraged, however, that men who have not a good moral character become members?--A. No, sir. Now, in machinists, he must be a skilled workman and a good moral man. We have considerable trouble in organizing the negro on account of preachers and politicians. They claim it is a political scheme when we organize them, but politics are never discussed in the union at all. The discussion is on economical questions, and they leave it to a man's own judgment how to vote. The rules of the organization do not allow any politics in it at all. . . .

Atlanta, Ga., *March 20, 1900*

TESTIMONY OF MR. C. C. HOUSTON

Editor of the Journal of Labor, Atlanta, Ga.

Q. (By Mr. RATCHFORD.) Do you care to take up the subject of colored labor briefly and deal with that in its relation to white labor?--A. My obser-

vation of the colored labor in the South, so far as it relates to the
trades where skilled labor is required, is that it is held over the head
of white labor to the extent of holding down wages, except in instances
where there are organizations of colored labor. They are required to receive the same wage scale that the white men do. In the building trades,
for instance, where more or less skilled labor is required, the wages paid
to white labor are based primarily on the wages to colored labor; and in
every instance in which an increased wage scale has been secured, with one
or two exceptions, it has been reached only after the colored man was
organized and a combined effort of the two was made. Of course, as far as
unskilled labor is concerned, there is no competition between the white and
colored here. That is controlled exclusively by the colored men.

Q. Is there not competition on the farms in the unskilled lines?--A.
Well, as to farm labor I am not prepared to say. So far as the manual labor
on the farm, the drudgery work is concerned, it is nearly done by colored
labor.

Q. Is there not competition in the cities in the unskilled lines?--A.
Very little; it is usually done by colored labor.

Q. What is the tendency of colored labor--to endeavor to rise to the
same plane as the white labor, both as to wages and standard of living,
etc?--A. Yes, sir. They have an ambition to receive a wage equal to that
of the white man, and to live on a plane relatively equal to that of the
white man. The industrial schools of the South, I think, have had something
to do with that; that is, the colored industrial schools. In Alabama, I
believe, there are two of them, and they turn out colored mechanics.

Q. Your trade union does not admit them to membership?--A. Yes, sir.
They are admitted. There are very few mixed unions, but, for instance, in
the building trades the carpenters' union will organize a branch of the
colored carpenters.

Q. Do you not think mixed unions--by mixed unions I mean unions that
admit trademen, journeymen, without reference to their color--would encourage
that very ambition that you speak of?--A. To acquire a wage equal to that
of the white men, and a social standing?

Q. Yes--A. Certainly it would.

Q. Why is it not done?--A. The white men of the South do not have any
disposition to do so.

Q. (By Representative LIVINGSTON.) Do you not think it would encourage
the white men to quit the union?--A. Yes; they won't mix.

Q. (By Mr. SMYTH.) Oil and water won't mix?--A. The white laborer does
not recognize the colored laborer as a social equal. He recognizes him as a
factor in the competitive market and will do as much or more than anybody
else to elevate him in his class.

Q. (By Mr. RATCHFORD.) The white man has been forced to recognize the
competition of his labor?--A. Yes.

Q. His muscles are as strong?--A. Yes.

Q. He is able to do as much for a dollar as the white man?--A. He has
as much capability, comparatively speaking, as the white man, and the white
man in order to protect himself has to consider the black man.

Q. Yet you believe that that is among the things that are not likely to
occur, to say the least, that the white man and the black man will organize
and attend to trade affairs jointly?--A. Not in the same union. They do it
through conferences. The black man has his union of carpenters, for instance,
and the white man has his, and they will meet together in conference and
regulate matters, but not in a general mixed union. They will not accept them
in membership. There have been a few instances where it has been attempted,
but for only a temporary effect.

Q. You understand the strongest trade union in the world draws no color
line?--A. I understand that.

Q. (By Mr. SMYTH.) That is not located in the South?--A. No. we are
affiliated with it, but we get around that in a way. We organize them, of
course, in separate branches. There are some branches of skilled labor in
the South where we can not afford to encourage the colored man at all. In
the building trades here they have got a hold that they are bound to retain,
and on the railroads.

Q. (By Mr. RATCHFORD.) What would you suggest as a means to the elevation of the colored man to the same standard as the white man--anything in
particular?--A. I would not make any suggestions along that line because I

do not think there is any means by which the colored man could be raised to
the same standard. However, I think, as I explained a moment ago, the white
man in order to retain his wages and in the hope of increasing his wage
scale, has not only to recognize but assist the black man, and unless you
do assist him and raise him up, he is going to pull you down to his standard. In that way and for that reason the white mechanics of the South are
assisting the colored men to organize.

Q. (By Mr. SMYTH.) That is from the selfish motive of self-preservation?--A. Not altogether.

Q. (By Mr. Ratchford.) Do you think that the colored man is a less
hindrance to the advancement of organized labor than is the Hungarian and
Pole in other States?--A. Oh, yes. I would rather deal with the colored man
of the South in the labor field than I would with the Pole or Hungarian or
Italian. They are more susceptible to teaching and they will act fairly.
You get a colored man organized, get him in the trades union, and he will
stick to the last ditch.

(Testimony closed.)

Memphis, Tenn., *March 22, 1900*

TESTIMONY OF MR. EDWARD B. MILLER

Secretary of the Memphis Industrial League

"There is a great surplus of common muscle labor in the South. The
walking delegates of the labor union can not force the negro into their
trades unions, nor grade common molding and foundry work to the standard of
the higher grade, nor in woodworking to the scale of the cabinetmaker or
turner. In the South before the war each plantation was an empire in itself; 'Bill' was the blacksmith, 'Mose' was the carpenter, 'Jim' was the
painter, and 'Sam' the brickmason and plasterer. The pickaninnies who
clustered around each boss of his trade in those days are today carpenters,
masons, blacksmiths and painters throughout the South. The working negro
in iron and steel and in the woodworking plants of the South is today filling
the sphere of this common muscle or semiskilled labor. He is contented at
receiving his 75 cents to $1 a day. In fact, Carroll D. Wright, Commissioner
of Labor, asserted that the average work of the Southern negro was 30 hours
a week; but his was the best paid, best fed, best clothed, and most tractable
and contented labor of this country. Hence the 10,000 Southern negroes are
here in the South to stay. When the negro has been enticed North he has
been shot down by the labor unions in strikes and refused work in all the
trades save that of servant or barber. If 500 or 1,000 in any Southern city
are induced to join the unions their employers have 5,000 or more as a supply
within 50 miles, who are field hands at $8 to $10 per month, anxious to come
in and take their places at $20 to $30 per month, and in a few months these
new recruits to the industrial and mechanical field will be equipped by their
quick imitative ability to fill the required spheres of labor made vacant by
the strikers. The Southern laborer is industrious and tractable when properly
directed, and of immense importance at this period as a factor of Southern
manufacturing development. The South needs 1,000,000 skilled men from the
North and the owners of small factories in all lines to remove here and
supply the South, Mexico, West Indies, and soon the Orient with manufactured
wares, because commerce sooner or later will demand the shortest distance
between two points."

Q. (By Mr. RATCHFORD.) You have laid special stress upon one subject
there that I wish to ask you a few questions relating to--one of the advantages of the South compared with the North is the fact that labor is cheap as
a result of cheap living, and it is also nonunion labor. Is that right?--
A. Yes.

Q. Do you find that is an advantage to the Southern country to have
labor unorganized?--A. Of that class, yes.

Q. Of any class?--A. No; very careful distinctions.

Q. What are they?--A. I said in this that the hewer of wood and the
drawer of water that comes on to fill the sphere of semiskilled labor, of
muscle, the moment he has obtained a little more skill he has got to be paid

a little more, and somebody must come in behind him and take his place in
the making of chains, common, heavy, irregular iron, and structural iron,
heavy grades of foundry work, the molder of the South. The negroes around
the Birmingham district--40 or 50 per cent of them--have been taught molding in 4 months in that character of work. The unions that are in existence
there of a higher grade of labor have considered that they were infringing
upon their rights. The vast number of planing mills and sawmills operating
all through the South, a good many of them in swampy districts, have men
that handle swing cut-off saws, planers, and rip saws, and the heavy work,
and the negro they pay from $1 to $1.25 a day.

Q. The purpose of your paper, as I understand it, is to encourage
capital enterprises to come to the South?--A. Yes.

Q. I want to know whether it is any advantage to that capital you wish
to encourage in the South to come here and find labor--any branch of labor--
unorganized? Whether the interests of employers are best served by having
labor in such a state or otherwise?--A. Permit me to answer that question
in this way, if you please: For many years to come the South will not enter
into the skill of the North, not even mechanism; but in the handling of
lumber and heavy foundry work the negro answers every purpose, and I do not
think that he can be ignored and set aside.

Q. Well, that does not seem to answer my question. Could he answer
every purpose equally as well if he was a member of a trades union, with
the same skill, same ability, same willingness as an employee, instead of
dealing with the individual man if the employer would deal with the organization, or its committee officers?--A. I simply contend that the labor is
governed by supply and demand. If you admit that negro into your trades
union you say he must work for $2 a day, and he must quit work unless he
gets wages according to the scale paid for that class of work.

Q. Who makes that scale?--A. The trades union.

Q. Who composes trades unions?--A. The organized labor.

Q. Of individual units, is it not?--A. Yes.

Q. Then the scale you speak of is made by the individual unit. What
is the reason it can not be assigned to a committee?--A. Nothing, except
it might be cornered.

Q. Now, you speak of the walking delegate. What are we to understand
by walking delegate?--A. In my experience of the past few years a number of
men from the coal-mining districts of Illinois, men that have been noted as
organizers, have been sent into the north Alabama coal-mining districts.
They have spent considerable sums of money going around and holding meetings
--I have been present at them--trying to organize negro labor into trades
unions, and to raise the price of coal mining and of foundry work, and they
have failed.

Q. Have not the Alabama miners recently received an advance in wages?
--A. Yes.

Q. As a result of what?--A. As a result of increased prices.

Q. What had their growing organization to do with it; anything?--A. Had
everything to do with it.

Q. You believe organization was--- A. (Interrupting.) I believe organization was concerned in that.

Q. Responsible for that?--A. Yes.

Q. Then by walking delegate we understand you to mean the organizer of
trades unions, do we?--A. There is a distinction between organizer and what
I would term an agitator.

Q. What is it?--A. The organizer is the party delegated from the
federation of unions to organize labor under their direction. The agitator
comes down into a community that really does not demand any interference with
the trade, that has no particular white labor that is in competition, that
is ground down by low wages, and simply for the sake, possibly, of a difference of wages in localities, makes an attempt to organize labor that is
unorganized. For instance, in the Birmingham district there have been thousands of negroes that would be glad to get $1 and $1.25 a day, and, of course,
if they are organized and the union says they can not work for that, it is
going to breed dissension and strife and trouble with those who do want to
work.

Q. The question that I asked you was to describe the walking delegate.
What is he; is he an agitator or organizer?--A. Both.

Q. He is both?--A. Yes.

Q. Delegated by his union?--A. That I do not know.

Q. Have you seen any of those agitators in the Birmingham district?
A. Yes.

Q. Among the miners?--A. Yes.

Q. Who were they?--A. I do not remember their names. I attended one of their meetings.

Q. Do they advise strikes?--A. No.

Q. Simply encouraged organization?--A. Yes.

Q. And because of that they are agitators, so classed? Let me ask if the free miners of Alabama do not have to fight the convict labor in mines?
A. Yes. How do you mean?

Q. Compete with convict labor.--A. Not for the last few years; no.

Q. When did it exist?--A. There was a time when convict labor was done there, but in recent years there has been too much demand for coal and iron.

Q. Is convict labor still pressed into the mines?--A. Yes.

Q. Is it not a fact that the cheapest part of a commodity does much toward fixing the price of the whole commodity?--A. I do not understand the question.

Q. For instance, 10 per cent of the coal of Alabama might be convict mined. Does that 10 per cent if sold at a lower price than the 90 per cent, do much toward reducing the price of the other 90 per cent?--A. It is not sold lower.

Q. Are you sure of that?--A. Yes.

Q. At the same price?--A. Yes. The men who have the benefit of that convict labor simply have the benefit of the profit.

Q. Now, you take the negroes; you say many of them are willing to work for less wages than the union prescribes. If such a condition existed, would the union men not be obliged to come down and work for the same rate of wages in competition with the cheap labor of the negro?--A. If in that class of work, yes. I will explain this whole thing in one sentence. In my work and efforts, in all talks I have given in my experience of 11 years in the South, I have gone before the Northern people universally and deprecated and advised against labor coming South; there is plenty of common labor; there is a demand for skilled labor in all classes and all grades, but what I mean to say is this: That there is no demand for common semiskilled labor --shovelers, muscle labor--in the South, and a man is wasting his time to come from the North and compete with that class of labor.

Q. (By Senator KYLE.) What you mean by walking delegate is this, a man who takes it upon himself to go down to Alabama from the Northern States and advise organization and talk of organization without being sent for?--
A. Yes.

Q. (By Mr. RATCHFORD.) Do you know any man who took it upon himself to do that?--A. Yes.

Q. Pay his own expenses?--A. That question was thoroughly discussed there, and I am positive of that. A body of 7 came down there and labored 3 months, and they held meetings every night over all the district, and the Cornishmen and English coal miners positively refused to go into a strike that they were trying to get up.

Q. Were you familiar with the mining conditions in States adjoining Alabama at that time?--A. No, sir.

Q. Did you know that at that time the miners of Tennessee were offered a reduction when Alabama was brought up to the level?--A. No, sir.

Q. Did you know that if the miners of Tennessee suffered a reduction the miners of Alabama would also suffer one?--A. No, sir.

Q. Those are things you might well give consideration to.--A. I am a firm believer in organized labor. I believe the highest standard that an American citizen can conceive of in a democratic-republican form of govern-ment, such as we have, is the elevation of labor to a higher grade of con-sideration and respect. In speaking of the South, I am speaking of an abso-lute condition of 10,000,000 of negroes that have muscle, to a certain degree intelligence, who are here. On the plantations they do not work over 5-1/2 months of the year. There is an enormous loss of muscle. They are idle 6-1/2 months of the year, and it takes the sum they have earned in 5-1/2 months entirely for fuel and food. It is the intent of all industrial negro schools

of the South to bring the negroes into a plane of industrial work. In the
North they generally won't admit them or allow them to work with them, but
they are here in the South as necessary economical factors in the upbuilding
of the South. There are only two solutions of the negro question. One is
absorption and the other is deportation, and they won't go away, and the
Southern people don't want them to go away. Now, I contend that the Southern
people by heredity are a pastoral and agricultural people, that will not
engage in manufacturing; they do not understand it, and if the section and
country is developed on factory lines, it must be by Northern capital. A
strong element of saving and greater profit for that capital is the negro
labor of the South at its command.

Q. (By Mr. SMYTH.) Do you think it would be attractive to Northern
capital in the South if the labor of the South was organized?--A. No, sir;
I do not.

Q. On the other hand, is that not rather an attraction for Northern
capital to be invested in the South, the fact that we have no organized
labor as a rule?--A. I have so found it.

Q. Therefore you think it would be a detriment to the South, seeking
Northern capital, foreign capital, a detriment to the Southern people to
have organized labor?--A. Yes. I can show you letters received in the
past few weeks from several piano manufacturers of Chicago taking up this
question of labor.

Q. (By Mr. RATCHFORD.) We have testimony before this commission from
the president of the Georgia Federation of Labor stating that the trades-
unionists of the South would prefer to have the negro to deal with rather
than to have the foreigner of the North; that he is not as much a hindrance
to the growth and prosperity of organized labor as is the Hungarian, Slav,
Pole, and Italian of Pennsylvania, for instance.--A. I believe that, too.

Q. Do you concur in that belief?--A. I do. I have had experience
with both classes.

Q. (By Senator KYLE.) The only question of difference, now, is as to
the advisability, in your judgment, of organizing the negro; that is the
point in this stage of the proceedings?--A. Yes. We can not tell what 10
or 20 years hence will give.

Q. In fact, you are trying to build up manufacturing industry in the
South, and you do not think the time has come to organize the negro?--A.
That is it.

Q. (By Mr. SMYTH.) Do you think that if there was organization of
labor in the South it would retard the development of its manufacturing
industry?--A. I most certainly do.

Q. Therefore the direct interests of the South is in not having labor
organized?--A. Yes. I have said it and give it as my opinion that there
is the greatest demand for a million skilled men.

Mr. RATCHFORD. I believe you.

(Testimony closed.)

Washington, D.C., *April 18, 1900*

TESTIMONY OF MR. SAMUEL GOMPERS

President, American Federation of Labor

Q. (By Mr. CLARKE.) The emergence of European labor from barbarism
through servitude to wage-earning--you said that was not the condition of
American workingmen. I would ask you if you would make an exception of the
colored people who were emancipated from slavery?--A. Yes; of course, it
would be necessary to do that. Of course, we have a population variously
estimated now at about 80,000,000.

Q. And their condition has greatly improved, has it not, in certain
things?--A. Oh, yes; certainly; but there are still numbers of them who are
working at day labor at 50 cents a day, on which they are required to sustain
themselves and their families. I say that in the South, some few years ago--
the men working on the plantations. Their conditions have not very materially
improved around there.

Q. To what extent is labor organized in the South?--A. Rather poorly, comparatively, to the workers of other parts of the country. Good, for instance, in the iron and steel; they are very well organized. In coal they are only fairly organized. In the printing trades they are very well organized. In the finer class of clothing they are very well organized.

Q. (By Mr. FARQUHAR.) How is it in the cotton manufactures?--A. In the cotton and textile industries they are only barely organized; and as I indicated some little time ago in my testimony, we have a number of organizers in the South specially trying to organize the textile industries, and we are meeting with a very great deal of success. I look upon the present movement of the workers to organize with a good deal of hope. I think it may not be amiss for me to say to you that, without being in a position to give you accurate figures, we have organized not less than 400,000 workingmen within this past year, in addition to those who were organized before that time.

Q. Do you speak of the whole country now?--A. I am speaking of the entire country; yes.

Q. (By Mr. CLARKE.) This does not include agriculture labor, I suppose?--A. Only to a very, very limited extent. There are some of our friends--the farmers--who are now making a very serious effort to organize, and there are men engaged in this work--very serious, earnest men--and I am in hopes that an American Joseph Arch has been developed or discovered by whom the agricultural workers of the country will be organized in a great national union, and affiliated and in full touch with the American labor movement.[133]

Q. Do the Southern unions take in colored people as well as white?-- A. Often; but when they do not they encourage their organization in separate unions. Of course, the color line is drawn socially, and often they do not care to meet with them socially or in the meeting rooms, even though they work side by side.

I may be permitted to relate an incident which may be interesting for you gentlemen to know as well as for the students hereafter to have available. We had some years ago in the city of New Orleans one of the largest[134] and most general strikes that ever occurred in this country, and the reason of it all was that the working people of New Orleans were becoming fairly well organized. Some of the unions were in existence many years. The draymen, the teamsters--colored men--formed a union and organized labor generally had their agreements with the employers. The colored draymen's union sent a committee to the employers for the purpose of having their agreements signed, and the employers would not talk to the "niggers." The organized labor of New Orleans sent committees to the employers and wanted to have the agreement signed, and they would not sign it--would not enter into any agreement with "niggers." The organized labor of New Orleans went on a strike; every machinist went on a strike; every printer went on a strike; no paper made its appearance; the men working in the gas houses went on a strike and there was no illumination that night; the bakers went on a strike, and all other white workers went on a strike for the purpose of securing recognition to the colored workmen. And I make mention of this as being what appears to me a very interesting episode in the labor movement, and as an answer to those who have always hurled the epithet to us that we will not assist in the organization of the colored workmen. If there is any union of labor that says anything or takes any action regarding the colored man of the South it is not because of his color; it is because he has as an individual or because they have generally in that trade so conducted themselves as to be a continuous convenient whip placed in the hands of the employer to cow the white men and to compel them to accept conditions of labor. It is not a question of personal prejudice or color prejudice, and, as I tried to show by that incident of the New Orleans strike, when it comes to a question of the interests of labor, the white men are willing to sacrifice their positions and their future in order to secure a recognition of the rights of the colored workmen.

Q. Now, I would like to inquire, when white people and colored people are organized in the same trade, whether or not the union insists upon the same wages irrespective of color?--A. Yes. It may be an interesting incident for you to know that about 2 weeks ago there was a strike in Kansas City, Kans., in one of the large establishments where the colored hod carriers, the building laborers, would not work with the white men [laughter] because the white men were not demanding the same wages that the colored men were

receiving. So you see it was not the colored man's prejudice against the
white man; it was his prejudice against the cheap man. [Laughter.]

Q. (By Mr. A. L. HARRIS.) May I ask you what the numerical strength
of organized labor is in this country today?--A. Well, this is just about
the close of our fiscal year. I sent out about 2 months ago, blanks to
all of our affiliated organizations, and they are only just coming in to
our headquarters. They will be in in about 10 days, completed. We are
required to make a report to our annual convention of the American Federation of Labor that is to take place on December 11, at Detroit, Mich., and
I might hit wide of the mark by making some haphazard guess; and then it
would be a discourtesy, even if I knew, to my colleagues who have made me
their executive officer, to report to any other body prior to reporting to
them; I should be glad to furnish that information to the commission later
on.

Q. (By Mr. FARQUHAR.) What were the numbers for the last year?--A.
The number for the last year was about 700,000.

Q. (By Mr. A. L. HARRIS.) I understood you to say that the increase
for this year would be in the neighborhood of 400,000?--A. Well, you can
draw your own inference now. [Laughter.] Let me say that this does not
include all organized labor, because I regret to say that the steam railroad organizations are not yet affiliated with the American Federation of
Labor, although within this past month one of the railway organizations,
the Order of Railway Telegraphers, has become affiliated; so the first break
in that line has been made, and I look forward to good results in that line.
And since I gave my testimony here last April, the International Bricklayers
and Masons' Union has voted in favor of becoming an affiliated body. We
have now indeed the most comprehensive and general federation of labor that
has ever existed in the world.

There is something that I had in mind that I ought to have said in
connection with the color question, and that is the attitude of the American Federation of Labor upon that subject. We have consistently and persistently insisted that organizations which become affiliated or desire to
become affiliated with the American Federation of Labor must of necessity
eliminate the color clause from any constitution or laws which the organization may have. We have gone so far, in our convention in Birmingham, Ala.,
to refuse courtesies such as banquets which had been offered, which had been
arranged in honor of our gathering. We declined to participate in a banquet
because we had three colored delegates who were not included in the invitation. The Cigar Makers' International Union, of which I am a member, refused, or at least boycotted a hotel. We quitted a hotel because our treasurer, who was a colored man, was given a room, a place for his meals, outside of the dining room--the ordinary or dormitory or some other old place.
We insisted that if he could not sit at the table with us, why we declined
to be in the hotel. We had to take inferior accommodations at some other
place, but we simply desired to attest our adhesion to a principle. The
American Federation of Labor declares positively and unequivocally that it
is the organization of the working people without regard to politics,
nationality, sex, color, or any other condition. The only qualification is
that of a wageworker desirous of improving his own condition and the condition of his fellow workmen.

Q. (By Senator KYLE.) And you stated a moment ago that you have hopes
of organizing the farm labor?--A. Yes; I have very ardent hopes.

Q. Do you mean the farmers themselves or the laborers on the farms?--
A. More particularly the farm laborers, the wageearners on the farms. I
believe in organization. The more and the better we are organized in every
form for the purpose of accomplishing a good and material and moral purpose,
the better will it be for all mankind. And I believe in the organization
of the employers; I believe in the organization of labor. I believe that
the organized forces meeting with each other will be governed by reason,
and that they will respect each other by reason of the power that they have.
In the beginning they will fear each other, but in time that fear will wear
off, and they will begin to respect each other, respect each other's strength,
respect each other's motives, and try to avoid by every means within their
power any open hostilities, the cessation of work, strikes, or lockouts. . . .

Washington, D.C., *June 12, 1900*

TESTIMONY OF MR. N. F. THOMPSON

Secretary of the Southern Industrial Convention,
also Secretary of Chamber of Commerce, Huntsville, Ala.

Q. (By Mr. FARQUHAR.) That was given out at your industrial convention, on the question of arbitration?--A. Yes.

Q. Have you in the Southern country now any trouble in respect to
strikes?--A. Yes.

Q. In what classes of labor do they usually occur?--A. All classes.
The Birmingham district--I might state that I was secretary of the Birmingham Commercial Club and secretary of the Alabama Commercial Association 10
years ago. From there I went to Pennsylvania and was 5 years in Johnstown,
Pa., returning to Alabama a year ago. I was secretary of the citizens committee at Birmingham, Ala., during the strike in 1894, in which we had
occasion to have before that committee all the labor elements of the dist-
rict--the labor leaders. The tendency was very general; there was no particular class among them. The leaders there were vicious. They got unfortunately a class of organizers around Birmingham, and it seemed to be that the
first thing, after they got a class of labor organized, was to assert themselves by striking. That occurred very frequently. I know of one coal
mining company that was in operation there 12 years peacefully and harmoniously. Their labor was organized, and they struck within 60 days--one of
the most serious strikes in the district. The plumbers' association organized, where they had been nonunion for a number of years without any
difficulty, and a strike occurred there almost immediately. There is quite
a number of these instances that have come to my observation. So the tendency is not with any class; there is a tendency very prevalent among all
classes.

Q. What you call the unskilled labor--is that organized in the South
in any number?--A. Well, not to any great extent. Around the Birmingham
district the negroes are being organized. That is regarded as the unskilled
labor of the South. Negroes now are taken into the unions practically on the
same basis with all others; but there is still a discrimination against them.

Q. Well, in the matter of mining, do the blacks work by themselves or
with the whites?--A. Both.

Q. Both ways or both together?--A. Both together. . . .

Washington, D.C., *June 14, 1900*

TESTIMONY OF MR. JOHN P. COFFIN

Vice-President of the Southern Industrial Convention

Q. Your industrial convention and your officers there have widened the
discussion of industrial labor in the South. Have you anything to state to
the commission independent of what you had in your paper there, as to the
advance in the industrial education of the black man, and how much your States
cooperate with it, the public bodies?--A. Well, I did not look that up definitely as to details, but there are several industrial institutions in the
South. I mentioned two of the leading ones. There is another at Charlotte,
N.C., and there is one for girls at Concord, N.C., and they are doing great
good, I consider, in the line of educating them industrially. I have no
special figures to give regarding it. I do not know of any.

Q. Do you know what the sentiment of your convention was on this question?--A. Yes. The question has been discussed. We were the first convention that permitted colored men to speak before white men on the subject,
and they were both men that had made it a practical life study, both able
men, and they are working along these lines.

Q. That was Washington and Council?--A. Washington and Council. I
was talking with Council as I came up from Knoxville on this trip. He wants
to get manufacturers to locate there and employ different sets of his people
at a cheap wage, simply a living wage, simply what they can barely subsist on,

to give them the principle of mechanics, in some different lines, in shoe
manufacturing and things of that kind that they can handle, and says he will
guarantee all the labor and good labor, steady labor, to anyone who will
come and locate there and try it in that way.[135]

Q. I believe you have a standing committee in your organization on
Southern education?--A. There is an educational committee; yes. I am on
the industrial.

Q. What is the real meaning of the expression in your paper there, of
having in the negro of the South a reserve force in case of strikes and
labor troubles and combinations against capital in the South?--A. The real
meaning that I intended to convey was that he would be a buffer against injustice; that the negro is absolutely loyal to his employer; he is not given
to strikes; he does his work faithfully, and can be depended on. Now, while
I do not believe it is going--in the near future--to be necessary to use
this buffer, in my opinion it is a thing that will keep out much of the
agitation of labor in the South, because the Southern people and manufacturers of the South will, before they submit to unjust domination by unions,
negroize their industries. They will not want to do this, and they will
not do it if labor is at all reasonable. They do not desire it. Many of
them today do not think they would do it under any circumstances, but you
bring them to the test, and it will be done. If labor is reasonable, if
labor will work for anything within reason, white labor will dominate the
South forever; but they will not submit to such outrages as have been frequently committed by organized labor.

Q. (By Mr. KENNEDY.) That would bring negro domination in industry
then, would it not?--A. It will bring negro domination of the labor market
if labor is unjust.

Q. And the white man will dominate the social and political conditions
of the South, and the negro will dominate the labor market of the South?--
A. The negro will never dominate the labor market of the South, and when I
said negro domination, I only had reference to it as far as negro labor was
concerned. In other words, he would dominate the labor that he did, but
would never dominate the market. The white employer would simply put him in
place of unjust white, probably foreign, labor.

Q. If they dominated white labor, white labor would be suppressed?--A.
They will never dominate white labor. He will take their places, but domination will rest with the whites. There is no fear of negro domination in
the South.

Q. I do not mean domination over the employer, but domination over the
white labor. They would be eliminated, would they not?--A. No; the employer
would dominate the labor, not the negro. The negro never will dominate the
Anglo-Saxon. He may take his place in work under certain conditions, but
the Anglo-Saxon was not created to be dominated.

Q. If the Anglo-Saxon who works with his hands, whose capital is his
muscle, believes that he is suffering injustices, and he makes demands to have
those injustices righted, and the employer will not accede to them according
to his idea, then the employer is going to negroize the labor in these factories; and then it seems to me that the negro certainly does dominate that
Anglo-Saxon labor?--A. The first question that will come in will be, according
to my idea, compulsory arbitration between the white man and the employer.
If the employer is in the wrong he will be compelled to right it; if he is
not in the wrong, he ought not to be compelled to accept the situation. . . .

Report of the Industrial Commission on the Relations of Capital and Labor,
Vol. 7 (Washington, D.C.: Government Printing Office, 1901), pp. 162-790,
passim.

4. THE NEGRO ARTISAN

By W. E. B. Du Bois[136]

Every trades union affiliated with the American Federation of Labor, and all others that could be reached, were asked to answer the following questions. Ninety-seven answered; eleven males made no replies after repeated inquiries:

1. Name of Union.
2. May Negroes join this Union?
3. If not, how is their membership prevented?
4. If they may join, how many Negro members have you at present?
5. How many had you in 1890?
6. How many Negro applicants have been refused admission to your knowledge?
7. Can local Unions refuse to admit a Negro if he is otherwise qualified?
8. Can local Unions refuse to recognize the travelling card of a Negro Union man?
9. Do Negroes make good workmen?
10. What are the chief objections to admitting them to membership in your Union?
11. Are these objections likely to be overcome in time?
12. General observations (add here any facts or opinions you may wish. They will be held as strictly confidential, if you so desire).

The central labor bodies in every city and town of the Union were sent the following schedule of questions. Two hundred of these, representing 30 states, answered:

1. Name of Council or Assembly.
2. Are there any Unions affiliated with you which are composed of Negro members?
3. If so, how many, and what is their membership?
4. Are there any Negro members in any of the local Unions?
5. If so, how many, and in which Unions?
6. Do any of the local Unions bar Negroes from membership?
7. Have Negro applicants ever been refused admission to any of the Unions?
8. Do local Unions ever refuse to recognize the travelling card of a Negro mechanic?
9. Do Negroes make good workmen in any of the trades? In which trades are they the best?
10. What are the chief objections usually raised against admitting them to the Trades Unions?
11. Are these objections likely to disappear in time?
12. General observations (add here any facts or opinions you may wish. They will be held as strictly confidential, if you so desire).

To the state federations a letter was sent asking for whatever general information was available on the subject. Most of them answered these requests.

To the industrial schools the following schedule was sent. Many of the schools were not able to answer definitely, and some returned no answer at all. The principal schools reported:

1. Name of institution.
2. Address.
3. How many of your graduates or former students are earning a living entirely as artisans?
4. How many of the above mentioned are:

Carpenters,	Dressmakers,	Tailors,
Blacksmiths,	Iron and steel workers,	------------
Brickmakers,	Shoemakers,	------------
Masons,	Painters,	------------
Engineers,	Plasterers,	------------
Firemen,	Coopers,	------------

5. Where are most of these artisans located at present?
6. How many of the rest of your graduates or former students are
     earning a living partially as artisans?
7. What trades and other work do they usually combine?
8. What difficulties do your graduates meet in obtaining work as
     artisans?
9. Do they usually join Trades Unions?
10. How many of them teach industries in schools?
11. Can you furnish us with a list of your graduates from industrial
     courses, with occupations and addresses?

In 1889 and 1891, the *Chattanooga Tradesman* made interesting and exhaustive studies of skilled Negro labor in the South. The Corresponding
Secretary of the Conference invited the Editors of the *Tradesman* to co-
operate with Atlanta University in a third investigation. In 1902, each
bearing half the expense. . . .

The Negro and Organized Labor. It would be interesting to know if
Crispus Attucks, the Negro who fell as the first martyr in the Revolution,
was a member of that roistering band of rope walk hands whose rashness precipitated the Boston Massacre. If so, then the Negro's connection with
organized labor, like his connection with all other movements in the history
of the nation, dates back to early times. There appeared, too, in early
times that same opposition to Negro workingmen with which we are so familiar
today. This opposition came chiefly from the border states where the free
Negro mechanics came in contact with white mechanics. On the other hand in
the actual organizations of workingmen which began in the North nothing is
usually heard of the Negro problem except as the labor movement avowedly made
common cause with the abolition movement. The Evans brothers, who came from
England as labor agitators about 1825, put among their twelve demands: 10th.
Abolition of chattel slavery and of wages slavery.   From 1840 to 1850 labor
reformers were, in many cases, earnest abolitionists; as one of them said in
1847: [137]

"In my opinion the great question of labor, when it shall come up, will
be found paramount to all others, and the operatives of New England, peasant
of Ireland and laborers of South America will not be lost sight of in sympathy
for the Southern slave."

"Indeed, the anti-slavery agitation and the organization of the mechanics
of the United States kept pace with each other; both were revolutionary in
their character and although the agitators differed in methods, the ends in
view were the same, viz., the freedom of the man who worked."

Along with this movement went many labor disturbances which had economic
causes, especially the series of riots in Philadelphia from 1829 until after
the war, when the Negroes suffered greatly at the hands of white workingmen.
The civil war with its attendant evils bore heavily on the laboring classes,
and led to wide-spread agitation and various attempts at organization. [138]

"In New York City, especially, the draft was felt to be unjust by laborers
because the wealthy could buy exemption for $300. A feeling of disloyalty to
union and bitterness toward the Negro arose. A meeting was called in Tammany
Hall and Greeley addressed them. Longshoremen and railroad employees struck
at times and assaulted non-unionists. In New York Negroes took the places of
longshoremen and were assaulted." [139]

The struggle culminated in the three days' riot which became a sort of
local war of extermination against Negroes.

There had been before the war a number of trade unions--the Caulkers of
Boston (1724), the Ship-wrights of New York (1803), the Carpenters of New York
(1806), the New York Typographical Society (1817), and others. There had also
been attempts to unite trades and workingmen in general organizations as the
Workingmen's Convention (1830), New York, the General Trades Union of New York
City, (1833 or earlier), the National Trades Union (1835) and others. In all
these movements the Negro had practically no part and was either tacitly or
in plain words excluded from all participation. The trade unions next began
to expand from local to national bodies. The journeymen printers met in 1850
and formed a national union in 1852; the iron molders united in 1859, the

machinists the same year, and the iron workers the year before. During and
soon after the war the railway unions began to form and the cigar makers and
masons formed their organizations; nearly all of these excluded the Negro
from membership.

After the war attempts to unite all workingmen and to federate the
trade unions were renewed and following the influence of the Emancipation
Proclamation a more liberal tone was adopted toward black men. On Aug.
19, 1866, the National Labor Union said in its declaration:[140]

"In this hour of the dark distress of labor, we call upon all laborers
of what ever nationality, creed or color, skilled or unskilled, trades
unionist and those now out of union to join hands with us and each other to
the end that poverty and all its attendant evils shall be abolished forever."

On Aug. 19, 1867, the National Labor Congress met at Chicago, Illinois.
There were present 200 delegates from the states of North Carolina, Kentucky,
Maryland and Missouri. The president, Z. C. Whatley, in his report said
among other things:

"The emancipation of the slaves has placed us in a new position, and
the question now arises, What labor position shall they now occupy? They
will begin to learn and to think for themselves, and they will soon resort
to mechanical pursuits and thus come in contact with white labor. It is
necessary that they should not undermine it, therefore the best thing that
they can do is to form trades unions, and thus work in harmony with the
whites."

It was not, however, until the organization of the Knights of Labor
that workingmen began effective co-operation. The Knights of Labor was
founded in Philadelphia in 1869 and held its first national convention in
1876. It was for a long time a secret organization, but it is said that
from the first it recognized no distinctions of "race, creed or color."

Nevertheless admission must in all cases be subject to a vote of the
local assembly where the candidate applied, and at first it required but
three black balls to reject an applicant. This must have kept Northern
Negroes out pretty effectively in most cases. On the other hand the shadow
of black competition began to loom in the horizon. Most people expected it
very soon and the Negro exodus of 1879 gave widespread alarm to labor leaders in the North. Evidence of labor movements in the South too gradually
appeared and in 1880 the Negroes of New Orleans struck for a dollar a day but
were suppressed by the militia.

Such considerations led many trade unions, notably the iron and steel
workers and the cigar makers, early in the eighties, to remove "white" from
their membership restrictions and leave admittance open to Negroes at least
in theory. The Knights of Labor also began proseltyzing in the South and by
1885 were able to report from Virginia:

"The Negroes are with us heart and soul, and have organized seven assemblies in this city (Richmond) and one in Manchester with a large membership."

So, too, the Brotherhood of Carpenters and Joiners said about 1886 that
they had Negro unions as far South as New Orleans and Galveston:

"In the Southern States the colored men working at the trades have
taken hold of the organization with avidity, and the result is the Brotherhood embraces 14 unions of colored carpenters in the South."

Even the anarchists of this time (1883) declared for "equal rights for
all without distinction to sex or race." By 1886, the year of "the great
uprising of labor," the labor leaders declared that "the color line had been
broken, and black and white were found working together in the same cause."
That very year, however, at the Richmond meeting of the Knights of Labor,
ominous clouds arose along the color line. District Assembly 49 of New York
had brought along a Negro delegate, Mr. F. J. Ferrell, and he was the source
of much trouble in the matter of hotels and theatres and in a question of

introducing to the convention Governor Fitzhugh Lee. Mr. Powderly had to
appeal to the chief of police for protection, the press of the nation was
aroused and the Grand Master Workman issued a defense of his position in
the Richmond *Dispatch:*

"You stand face to face with a stern living reality--a responsibility
which cannot be avoided or shirked. The Negro question is as prominent
today as it ever was. The first proposition that stares us in the face is
this: The Negro is free; he is here and he is here to stay. He is a citizen and must learn to manage his own affairs. His labor and that of the
white man will be thrown upon the market side by side, and no human eye can
detect a difference between the article manufactured by the black mechanics
and that manufactured by the white mechanics. Both claim an equal share
of the protection afforded to American labor, and both mechanics must sink
their differences or fall a prey to the slave labor now being imported to
this country.

"Will it be explained to me whether the black man should continue to
work for starvation wages? With so many able-bodied colored men in the
South who do not know enough to ask for living wages it is not hard to guess
that while this race continues to increase in number and ignorance, prosperity will not even knock at the door, much less enter the home of the Southern
laborer.

In the field of labor and American citizenship we recognize no line of
race, creed, politics or color."

This was high ground for a labor leader to take--too high, in fact, for
the constitituency he led, since the history of the labor movement from 1886
to 1902, so far as the Negro is concerned, has been a gradual receding from
the righteous declarations of earlier years.

The Knights of Labor, after a brilliant career, having probably at one
time over a half a million members, began to decline owing to internal dissensions and today have perhaps 50,000-100,000 members. Coincident with the
decline of the Knights of Labor came a larger and more successful movement--
the American Federation of Labor which has now nearly a million members.
This organization was started in 1881 at a meeting of disaffected members of
the Knights of Labor and others. From the beginning this movement represented
the particularistic trade union idea as against the all inclusive centrali-
zing tendencies of the Knights. And although the central administration has
grown in power and influence in recent years, it is still primarily a federation of mutually independent and autonomous trade-unions, among which it
strives to foster co-operation and mutual peace. The declared policy of
such a body on the race question is of less importance than in the case of
the Knights of Labor, since it is more in the nature of advice than law to
the different unions. The attitude of the Federation has summed up as follows:

"It has always been regarded as one of the cardinal principles of the
Federation that 'the working people must unite and organize, irrespective of
creed, color, sex, nationality or politics.' The Federation formerly refused
to admit any union which, in its written constitution excluded Negroes from
membership. It was this that kept out the International Association of
Machinists for several years, till it eliminated the word 'white' from its
qualifications for membership. It was said at one time that the color line
was the chief obstacle in an affiliation of the Brotherhood of Locomotive
Firemen with the Federation. The Federation seems, however, to have modified
the strictness of the rule. The Railroad Telegraphers and Trackmen have both
been welcomed and both restrict their membership to whites.

"In a considerable degree the color line has been actually wiped out in
the affiliated organizations. Great Unions controlled by Northern men have
insisted in Southern cities on absolute social equality for their colored
members. Many local unions receive whites and blacks on equal terms. Where
the number of Negroes is large, however, national unions usually organize
their white and their colored members into separate locals. In 1898 the
Atlanta Federation of Trades declined to enter the peace jubilee parade because colored delegates were excluded.

"The convention of 1897 adopted a resolution condemning a reported
statement of Booker T. Washington that the trades unions were placing obstacles in the way of the material advancement of the Negro, and reaffirming

the declaration of the Federation that it welcomes to its ranks all labor without regard to creed, color, sex, race or nationality. One delegate from the South declared, however, that the white people of the South would not submit to the employment of the Negro in the mills, and that the federal labor union of which he was a member did not admit Negroes. President Gompers said that a union affiliated with the Federation had no right to debar the Negro from membership.

"With increasing experience in the effort to organize the wage earners of the South, the leaders have become convinced that for local purposes separate organizations of the colored people must be permitted. President Gompers said in his report to the convention of 1900, that here and there a local had refused to accept membership on account of color. In such cases where there were enough colored workers in one calling, an effort had been made to form a separate colored union, and a trades council composed of representatives of the colored and the white. This had generally been acquiesced in. In some parts of the South, however, a more serious diffi- culty had arisen. Central bodies chartered by the Federation had refused to receive delegates from local unions of Negroes. The Federation had not been able to insist that they be received, because such insistence would have meant the disruption of the central bodies. President Gompers suggested that separate central bodies composed of Negroes be established where it might seem practicable and necessary. The convention accordingly amended the constitution to permit the executive council to charter central labor unions as well as local trade and federal unions, composed exclusively of colored members."

The attitude of the American Federation of Labor may be summed up as having passed through the following stages:

1. *The working people must unite and organize irrespective of creed, color, sex, nationality or politics.*

This was an early declaration but was not embodied in the constitution. It was reaffirmed in 1897, after opposition. Bodies confining membership to whites were barred from affiliation.

2. *Separate charters may be issued to Central Labor Unions. Local Unions or Federal Labor Unions composed exclusively of colored members.*

This was adopted by the convention of 1902 and recognizes the legality of excluding Negroes from local unions, city central labor bodies, &c.

3. *A National Union which excludes Negroes expressly by constitutional provision may affiliate with the A.F.L.*

No official announcement of this change of policy has been made, but the fact is well known in the case of the Railway Trackmen, Telegraphers, and others.

4. *A National Union already affiliated with the A.F.L. may amend its laws so as to exclude Negroes.*

This was done by the Stationary Engineers at their Boston convention in 1902, and an (unsuccessful?) attempt in the same line was made by the Molders at their convention the same year. The A.F.L. has taken no public action in these cases.

This is a record of struggle to maintain high and just ideals and of retrogression; the broader minded labor leaders, like Samuel Gompers, have had to contend with narrow prejudice and selfish greed; it is a struggle parallel with that of the Negro for political and civil rights, and just as black Americans in the struggle upward have met temporary defeat in their aspirations for civil and political rights so, too, they have met rebuff in their search for economic freedom. At the same time there are today probably a larger number of effective Negro members in the trade unions than ever before, there is evidence of renewed inspiration toward mechanical trades and a better comprehension of the labor movement. On the other hand the indus-

trial upbuilding of the South has brought to the front a number of white
mechanics, who from birth have regarded Negroes as inferiors and can with
the greatest difficulty be brought to regard them as brothers in this battle
for better conditions of labor. Such are the forces now arrayed in silent
conflict.

If we carefully examine the various trade unions now in existence, we
may roughly divide them as follows:

1. Those with a considerable Negro membership.
2. Those with few Negro members.
3. Those with no Negro members.

The first two of these classes may be divided into those who receive
Negroes freely, those to whom Negroes never apply, and those who receive
Negro workmen only after pressure.

Unions with a Considerable Negro Membership. These unions are as
follows:

Trade Unions	Negro Membership 1890	Negro Membership 1900	Total Membership 1901
Journeymen Barbers' International Union	200	800	8,672
International Brick, Tile and Terra-Cotta Workers' Alliance	50	200	1,500
International Broom-makers Union			380
United Brotherhood of Carpenters and Joiners Carriage and Wagon Workers' International Union	240	500	2,025
Cigar-makers' International Union			33,954
Coopers' International Union		200	4,481
International Brotherhood of Stationary Firemen	0	2,700	3,600
International Longshoremen's Assoc.	1,500	6,000	20,000
United Mine Workers of America		20,000	224,000
Brotherhood of Painters, Decorators and Paper-hangers of America	33	169	28,000
International Seaman's Union			8,161
Tobacco Workers' International Union	1,500	1,000	6,170
Brotherhood of Operative Plasterers			7,000
Bricklayers' and Masons' Union			39,000

These unions represent the trades in which the Negro on emerging from
slavery possessed the most skill, i.e., the building trades, work in tobacco,
and work requiring muscle and endurance. Most of these unions deny any
color-discrimination, although the secretary of the carpenters merely says,
"None that I know of;" the carriage and wagon workers: "None that has been
reported;" the coopers: "If any, it was many years ago;" and the painters'
secretary: "I do not know." The carpenters and coopers both admit that
local unions could refuse to receive Negroes, and the carpenters and plasterers are not certain that the traveling card of a Negro union man would be
recognized by all local unions.

The following note in the barbers' official journal throws light on the
situation in that craft:

"At a previous convention of our International Union a resolution was
passed, calling upon our General Organizer to make a special effort to
organize our colored craftsmen in the South. Today, we have, at a fair estimate, about eight or nine hundred colored members. My experience with them,
both as General Secretary-Treasurer and President of a local, has shown that
when they become members they at once become earnest and faithful workers.
I find, however, that during the past term an unusual amount of friction has
taken place in the South and that some of our white members, who still have
the southern objection to a colored man, have sought to bring about class

division. It is, of course, known to all of us, that the labor movement
does not recognize class, creed, or color; that the black man with a white
heart and a true trade union spirit is just as acceptable to us as a white
member. Hundreds of letters have reached me asking if the colored man could
not be kept out of the union. In every case I have answered that if he is
a competent barber our laws say that he must be accepted. If below the so-
called Mason and Dixon line where the color line is still drawn, they have
the right to form them into separate unions, if above that line they can
join any local.

"A question of the color line, and one which must be acted on in some
way by this convention, is the trouble now existing in Little Rock, Ark.
Bro. Pinard was in that city in February of last year and organized a union
of colored craftsmen. No white union could be formed as they would not
attend a meeting. In October following, however, a white union was formed.
From that time on there has been trouble. The whites want to control the
situation and want our colored local to adopt their laws. The colored local,
however, was organized first and refused. This has brought on a heated
correspondence and when the photo of delegates was asked for, the delegate
from the white union stated distinctly that his photo must not appear near
any colored man, as he was a white man and must not be placed near any burly
Negro. In a number of places he refers to them as black demons. I know
nothing definite as to their trouble, as it is a question of law and as
such comes under the jurisdiction of the General President, but I felt that
as No. 197 is a union in good standing in the International they were entitled
to protection."

The trouble is not confined to the South; in Northern cities barbers are
sometimes refused admittance into unions, and one secretary in Pennsylvania
writes:

"We have to recognize them to hold our prices and short hours, but we
find it very hard to get along with them."

The Negro membership seems, however, to be increasing rapidly and members are reported in nearly every state.
The secretary of the brick-makers writes:

"We have had a number of strikes where the colored man was imported to
take the place of any man, therefore, there is more or less prejudice against
them but we hope that will be removed in time."

They have but few of the large number of colored brick-makers.
The secretary of the broom-makers writes:

"I am informed that some organizations refuse membership to the Negro.
I consider it a serious mistake, as white labor cannot expect the Negro to
refrain from taking their place unless we will assist him in bettering his
condition."

Nine-tenths of the black membership of the carpenters is in the South
and mostly organized in separate unions from the whites. In the North there
are very few in the unions; there are a few in the West. In great cities
like Washington, Baltimore, Cincinnati, Philadelphia, New York and even Boston
it is almost impossible for a Negro to be admitted to the unions, and there
is no appeal from the decision.
The cigar-makers' is one of the few unions that allows its local little
discretion as to membership:

"Our constitution makes it obligatory on the part of local unions to
accept journeymen cigar makers as members. Any journeyman cigar maker who has
served three years at the trade can come in, and by paying his initiation fee
in installments, if he wants to, he is regarded as having been initiated. It
requires no vote; the constitution makes it mandatory."

Colored cigar makers can be found in small numbers in nearly all Northern
cities and in large numbers in the South. Florida alone reports 2,000.

The secretary of the coopers' writes:

"We have local branches composed entirely of colored coopers at Egan, Ga., Norfolk and Lynchburg, Va. At New Orleans, Hawkinsville, Ga., and other places they work together in the same local union."

Practically no Negroes have been admitted to Northern unions--Trenton, N.J., alone reporting a single union Negro.

The stationary firemen in 1899 requested the St. Louis union to stop color discrimination and they have organized a number of Negro locals, especially in the mine regions. They assert that Negroes are received in all locals and this would seem to be so in most cases.

Among the longshoremen, who may be classed as semi-skilled artisans, the Negro element is very strong. From the great lakes a secretary reports:

"We have many colored members in our association, and some of them are among our leading officials of our local branches. In one of our locals that I can call to mind there are over 300 members, of which five are colored; of these two hold the office of President and Secretary; so you can see that nothing but good feeling prevails among our members as regards the colored race, and when you consider that our people average fifty cents per hour when at work, you can readily imagine that our people are not half-starved and illiterate."

From the gulf another writes:

"In New Orleans we have been the means of unity of action among the longshoremen generally of that port, both in regards to work, wages and meeting in hall together. I believe that we are the only craft in that city who have succeeded in wiping out the colored question. Our members meet jointly in the same hall and are the highest paid workmen in New Orleans."

Still the color question arises here and there:

"In 1899 a color line difficulty arose among the longshoremen of Newport News, Va. The local unions there of longshoremen were composed entirely of colored men. White men refused to join them. The colored men were finally persuaded to consent to the issue of a separate charter for the white men."

The membership of Negroes is very large; Florida alone reports 800; Detroit, Mich., 60, and large numbers in Virginia, Louisiana and Texas.

The United Mine Workers receive Negroes into the same unions with whites, both North and South; Secretary Pearce testified before the Industrial Commission:

"As far as we are concerned as miners, the colored men are with us in the mines. They work side by side with us. They are members of our organization; can receive as much consideration from the officials of the organization as any other members, no matter what color. We treat them that way. They are in the mines, many of them good men. There is only one particular objection, and that is they are used to a great extent in being taken from one place to another to break a strike, as we call it, in such cases as we have here now at Pana, where this trouble is going on, and that trouble they had at Virden, Ill."

In the Alabama mines, 50% of the miners are black, still the whites are said to

"Recognize--as a matter of necessity they were forced to recognize--the identity of interest. I suppose among miners, the same as other white men in the South, there are the same class differences, but they have been forced down, so that they must raise the colored man up or they go down, and they have consequently mixed together in their organization. There are cases where a colored man will be the officer of the local union--president of a local union."

The state president of the Federation, however, reports considerable dissatisfaction on the part of the whites at the recognition of Negroes. Negro union miners are reported in Pennsylvania, West Virginia, Alabama, Illinois, Iowa, Kansas, Kentucky and Missouri. There are also a few members of the Northern Mineral Mine Workers Progressive Union, a kindred organization operating in Michigan.

The secretary of the painters' union writes:

"The only difficulty we find with Negroes is that there is a disposition on their part to work cheaper than the white man. This is due largely to want of education and the influence of men of their own race who are opposed to the Trades Union movement. The Trades Union movement is the only movement that will ever settle the Negro question in America, and men who are interested in the advancement of the Negroes should thoroughly investigate the whole question of Trades Unionism, as it relates to the Negro and the working people in general."

There would seem to be other difficulties, however, as there are almost no colored union painters in the North--one or two being reported in Portland, Me., Cincinnati, O., and Trenton, N.J. They seem to be pretty effectually barred out of the Northern unions, and in the South they are formed usually, if not always, into separate unions. Florida reports a considerable number, but there are not many reported elsewhere.

The secretary of the seamen writes:

"We are exerting every effort to get the Southern Negroes into the union at present, and if we can once convince them that they will have an opportunity for employment equal to the white man I believe that we can succeed. We have nearly all the Portuguese Negroes in the union at present. And they get the same wages as the white men, and the same opportunity for employment. The Negro seaman is now becoming a menace to the white seaman since the ship owner is endeavoring to use him against the union to break down wages, and they take the pains to impress on their minds that if they join the union and demand the same wages as the white men they will not be given employment. The Negro seaman being somewhat more illiterate than his white brother believes this, rather than believe us. We may in time be able to convince them that this is not so, but at present it is an uphill fight. The most of the colored sailing out of New York are union men and we have increased their pay from $16 and $18 to $25 and $30. Our worst ports are Philadelphia, Baltimore and Norfolk."

The following quotation from the testimony of the secretary of the tobacco workers is characteristic of the labor union attitude:

"Probably one of our greatest obstacles will be the colored labor, for it is largely employed in the manufacture of tobacco in the South. It is pretty difficult to educate them to the necessity of organization for the protection of their interests. In the South I suppose 75% in the tobacco business are colored, although there are a number of white people it seems, going in from the country to work in the factories, as I have been told. A number of manufacturers told me they did employ and would employ one wherever they could, either male or female. . . .

"There was one colored tobacco workers union organized in Winston but the white men resisted the organization and I do not think it succeeded. I do not think there is any colored organization in the state now."

Opposition on the part of Southern white workmen, and the eagerness of union organizers to replace Negro by white laborers explains the difficulty of extending the union movement and the justifiably suspicious attitude of Negroes toward it. The tobacco workers' constitution especially prohibits color distinctions, but separate locals are organized. The colored union men are chiefly in Kentucky, Virginia and the Carolinas.

The plasterers have a good number of Negro members. In Memphis, Birmingham, Atlanta, Richmond, Danville, Savannah and New Orleans they are said to outnumber the whites, and in the South there are some "in most, if not in all, of our locals." They are scarce in the North, however, 2 being in Pennsylvania, 1 in Massachusetts, and a score or more in Illinois. The Southern unions are often mixed.

The masons and bricklayers also have a large Negro membership in the South and often in mixed unions. Considerable numbers are reported in Texas, Tennessee, Virginia, Louisiana and South Carolina; there are some 200 in Florida, and at least that number in Georgia, and probably in Alabama. In the North, however, it is very difficult for Negroes to enter the unions. The First General Vice-President of the National Building Trades Council testified before the Industrial Commission that "we do not permit" Negroes to join our organization in the city of Washington--"we do not admit colored men to our organization." He said, however, that the national organization "does not prohibit colored men from becoming members" and that there were members in some other cities. A Negro bricklayer and plasterer of St. Mary's, Ga., who has long worked as foreman, and can read and write, has travelled over a large part of the country. Although he had his union travelling card he was refused work and recognition in Tampa, Fla., Norfolk, Va., Washington, D.C., Baltimore, Md., and New York City. He was allowed to work in Boston and Chicago and most other Southern towns. In Cincinnati, a report says:

"We have some colored bricklayers here but those that work on buildings with union men and who belong to the unions are men so fair in complexion as not to be noticed, among sun-burned and brick dust covered white men, as colored men. I have a distinct recollection of an experience I had with a black bricklayer who came to this city in 1893 from Chicago. He was a member of a union there and worked with white men in that city. He came to Cincinnati with a band of white bricklayers who vouched for him. They were given, by the local union, union cards and immediately got work. He, the black man, was kept dancing attendance on the master of the local union and delayed upon one pretext and other until he was driven from the city without being permitted to follow his trade because the local union did not give him his card. I was remodeling a building of ours and I gave him work as a plasterer. The union hod carrier, an Irishman, refused to carry mortar for him because he did not have a card from the local plasterers' union as a plasterer. He was compelled to work as a scab to get money enough to get out of town."

The Knights of Labor claim 6,000 Negro members at present, and 8,000 in 1890, a decrease of 25 per cent. This report came too late for insertion in the table.

To sum up we may make the following list in the order of increasing hostility toward the Negro:

Miners--Welcome Negroes in nearly all cases.
Longshoremen--Welcome Negroes in nearly all cases.
Cigar-makers--Admit practically all applicants.
Barbers--Admit many, but restrain Negroes when possible.
Seamen--Admit many, but prefer whites.
Firemen--Admit many, but prefer whites.
Tobacco Workers--Admit many, but prefer whites.
Carriage and Wagon Workers--Admit some, but do not seek Negroes.
Brick-makers--   "   "   " "   "   "   "
Coopers--   "   "   " "   "   "   "
Broom-makers--   "   "   " "   "   "   "
Plasterers--Admit freely in South and a few in North.
Carpenters--Admit many in South, almost none in North.
Masons--   "   "   "   "   "   "   "   "
Painters--Admit a few in South, almost none in North.

The evidence on which the above is based cannot all be given here; it is, however, pretty conclusive; there are, for instance, numbers of competent Negro painters, carpenters and masons--yet who has seen one at work in a Northern city? There are numbers of brick-makers, wheelwrights and coopers, but few have been brought into the unions and in the North few can get in.

The seamen, firemen and tobacco workers have many Negroes, but Negroes fear
to join them lest, by demanding union wages, their white fellow-workmen will
hasten to supplant them. This has virtually been admitted by labor leaders
and others. A South Carolina employer says that among bricklayers of equal
skill Negroes receive $1.75 and whites $2.50 a day and "the object of the
white men in organizing the Negroes is to get them to demand the same wages
that the whites demand." Messrs. Garrett and Houston, President and Secretary of the Georgia Federation, confirm this, as do many others, and the
Secretary of the Southern Industrial Convention adds: "There is discrimination even in the union. The white members try to get employment for each
other and to crowd out the colored members." The same thing occurs in the
North; now and then a Negro is admitted to a union but even then he stands
less chance of getting work than a white man.*

   Unions with Few Negro Members: The following national unions report a
few Negro members:

Trade Unions	Negro Membership	Total Membership†
Journeymen Bakers and Confectioners' International Union..................	"Several."	6,271
International Brotherhood of Black-smiths............................	"Very few."	4,700
National Assn. of Blast Furnace Workers and Smelters of America.............	100 or more.	
Boot and Shoe Workers' Union..........	A few.	8,037
Nat'l. Union of United Brewery Workers	12.	25,000
Amalgamated Society of Carpenters and Joiners‡..........................	A few.	2,500
Nat'l. Soc. of Coal Hoisting Engrs....	4.	950
Amalgamated Society of Engineers......	"Several."	1,779
Intern'l. Union of Steam Engineers....	A few--1 local.	4.409
United Garment Workers of America.....	10.	15,000
Granite Cutters National Union........	5.	6,500
United Hatters of America.............	Very few.	7,500
Int'l. Un. of Horse Shoers of U.S. and Canada............................	?	2,100
Hotel & Rest. Employees' Int'l. Alliance & Bartenders' Int'l. League of Amer.	100.	10,962
Amal. Assn. of Iron, Steel & Tin Wkrs.	"Practically none."	8,000
Shirt, Waist & Laundry Wkrs. Int. Un..	2 locals.	3,066
Tube Workers' Int'l. Union............	"Some."	
Amal. Meat Cut. & Butcher Workmen of North America......................	A few.	4,500
Int'l. Assn. of Allied Metal Mech.....	?	2,400
American Federation of Musicians......	A few--1 local.	8,100
Journeymen Tailors' Union of America..	10.	9,000
National All. of Theatrical Stage Emp.	10.	3,000
International Typographical Union.....	A few.	38,991
Watch-case Eng. Int'l. Association....	1.	285
Wood, Wire & Metal Lathers' Int'l. Un.	25-50?	
Amal. Woodworkers' Int. Un. of America.	?	14,500
Amalgamated Assn. of Street Rlwy. Emp.	-10.	4,000

* Possibly the hod-carriers ought to be mentioned under this division as semi-
    skilled laborers. They have a predominating Negro membership in all parts
    of the country, but have no national association. The local bodies are
    usually associated with the various city central labor bodies. The team-
    sters have a national body and many Negro members.
† Based mainly on actual paid membership tax. Cf. Report Industrial Com-
    mission: Vol. 17.
‡ Not the same as the Brotherhood of Carpenters and Joiners, but a smaller
    independent body allied with English unions as well as with the A.F.L.

The small Negro membership in these unions arises from two causes:
the lack of Negro mechanics in these lines, and color discrimination.
Probably the first is the more important in the case of boot and shoemakers,
brewers, granite cutters, hatters, metal workers, watch-case engravers and
metal lathers. In these cases the real discrimination is in keeping Negroes
from learning the trades. In the case of most of the other unions, however,
especially blacksmiths, blast-furnace workers, engineers, horse-shoers, hotel
employees, iron and steel workers, musicians, street railway employees and
printers, the chief cause of the small number of Negroes in the unions is
color discrimination. Without doubt incompetency plays some part here, too,
but it is doubtful if it is the leading cause. The granite cutters say that
"employers do not care to employ Negro apprentices, hence the few Negro
journeymen." The steam engineers say through their secretary:

"The Trade Union movement is based upon the broadest lines and recognizes
that every wage worker ought to be within its ranks. There is, of course,
an unfortunate feature, one that will take time and education to remove, and
that is the biased opinion held in regard to the Negro. Our organization
grants charters to Negroes when same is requested and there are a sufficient
number of them to support a self-sustaining local. We have some difficulty
with the accepting of a card when presented by a Negro but headquarters has
always taken action in the matter and endeavored to have the card recognized."

The prejudiced element prevailed, however, at the last meeting in Boston,
1902, of the Stationary Engineers (an organization formed under the Steam
Engineers,) and it was voted to have the word "white" placed before the word
"engineers" in one of the articles of their constitution. The motion was
made by a Mr. Grant of New Orleans, and was the cause of a most passionate
debate. The vote was carried by a large majority, but not until there had
been many strong speeches, the Southerners of course taking the affirmative
and the Northerners opposing. Mr. Grant said that if the association granted
"the Negro this social equality he did not deserve," it would lose all standing in the South, and that the Negro belonged in Africa. Mr. Optenberg of
Wisconsin said if he voted to shut out the Negro he would be ashamed to look
any Grand Army man in the face. Mr. Babbitt of Worcester said he knew colored
engineers who deserved respect and he would stand for the colored man. But
when Mr. C. Eli Howarth of Fall River declared that there were men present
whom he would rather discard than the Negro, he was hissed for a full minute,
and the Southerners had their way.
The secretary of the iron and steel workers thinks it is "only a question
of time when it will be necessary to accord the Negro the same privileges as
are extended to the white brethren." In the recent strike of steel employees
against the Steel Trust the color line was broken for the first time and
Negroes invited into the union. Few, if any, seem to have entered.
The hotel employees and bartenders have spent $525 "in a futile effort
to organize colored locals," no Negro being allowed in a white local. "The
main objection from our membership against Negroes appears to come from locals
in the southern part of the country." The printers usually exclude Negroes;
there are a few individual exceptions here and there, but not many. The
secretary of the Atlanta Federation of Trades when asked if the printers there
barred Negroes said: "I cannot answer that; we have no colored typographical
men in the South that I know of." There are from 50 to 100 black printers
in Georgia alone.
The metal lathers report a few members in Birmingham, Savannah, Asheville,
Augusta, Memphis, Nashville and Jacksonville, but none in the North. Three
colored shoemakers are reported. There was a local in New Orleans which barred
Negroes but this is now defunct. The meat handlers have colored members in
Kansas City and Boston. In the latter city they took part in the strike of
the freight handlers of last summer. In one local a Negro has held office,
and the last convention had several Negro delegates. The bookbinders say:
"Some of our people refuse to recognize Negroes as mechanics," but there are
no actual discriminating statutes.
When asked how many Negro applicants had been refused admission to the
unions, the Amalgamated carpenters, musicians, blacksmiths, street railway
employees and brewers returned no answer; the engineers, granite cutters and
glass workers were evasive, saying that they were without official data or

did not know. Most of the others answered, "None." Many acknowledged that
local unions could refuse to recognize a traveling card held by a Negro,
although several said the action was "illegal." . . .

These unions fall into three main groups: those say that they admit
Negroes but have no Negro members; these include the goring weavers, trunk
workers, tile layers, leather workers, metal workers, plumbers, plate
printers, car workers, paper workers, oil well workers, ladies garment
workers, special order clothing workers, chair makers, upholsterers and
piano workers. Their explanation is that no Negroes work at these trades
and they consequently have no applications. This is true except in the
case of plumbers and upholsterers. The plumbers have a semi-secret organization and there can be no doubt that they practically never admit a Negro,
although one Negro member is reported in Flint, Mich. The organizer says
that most Negroes are incompetent.

"Such Negroes as have shown a greater ability than others have usually
found their way into a small business and are patronized by the Negro residents of our Southern cities. There is no general law in our organization
to exclude Negroes but as before stated none have ever joined and to the
best of my knowledge but one has ever made application to us."

A prominent official of the chain makers reports that they had 6 Negro
members in 1901, but that they refused to strike which "naturally would
cause hard feelings." The general secretary of the metal workers thinks
"there would be no difficulty in initiating a colored metal worker into one
of our local unions," but adds, "I am speaking from a personal standpoint
on this question. There is no doubt but what we have some members who are
prejudiced against the Negro."

The second class of unions is those which are undecided or non-committed
on the Negro question. These are the various glass workers, the potters,
stove-mounters, jewelry workers, wood carvers, textile workers, stereotypers
and electrotypers, printing pressmen, metal polishers, steamfitters and lace
curtain operatives. As no Negroes work at most of these trades the question
of their admission has not been raised or decided. The textile workers are
exceptions and have very clearly drawn the color line, North and South,
although they do not acknowledge it. The Negroes working at the trade have
never been allowed to join the union, and the attempt to introduce Negro
mill labor in Atlanta a few years ago so strengthened the Textile Union in
the South that "it is doubtful whether in the future a Southern cotton mill
can employ any Negro labor unless it is ready to employ all Negro labor."
There appear to be one or two printing pressmen in Rhode Island and Illinois.

The last class of unions includes those who openly bar the Negro. These
are the great railway unions--the engineers, firemen, telegraphers, car men,
switchmen, trainmen, track men, and conductors; and the stone cutters,
machinists, electrical workers, boiler makers, and wire weavers. The editor
of the organ of the engineers attributes the exclusion of the Negro to the
prejudices of Southern engineers, but thinks that most of their fellows agree
with them. Mr. E. E. Clark, Grand Chief Conductor and member of the Coal
Strike Arbitration Commission, writes:

"I think wherever any opposition to the colored race on the part of
organized labor is manifested, it can generally be traced to the fact that
colored men are always willing to work for wages which white men cannot, and
should not be asked, to work for."

The Grand Master of the Trainmen says:

"The Brotherhood has no plans for the organization of colored men employed in railway occupations. Some ideas have lately been proposed along
these lines, but as yet they have not met with any general favor among our
membership."

Mr. John T. Wilson, president of the trackmen, was once addressing some
Negroes in St. Louis on the advantages of unionism. They reminded him of the
attitude of his union and he replied that

"I was employed to execute laws, not to make them, and if they could see themselves as I saw them, they would not be surprised at my inability to annihilate race prejudices."

And he added that

"Concerted action on the part of practical and intelligent Negroes and white men of character who really desire to see the conditions of the down-trodden masses improved without regard to race, would eventually cause the white and Negro workmen to co-operate in industrial organization for their mutual advancement."

The Negro locomotive firemen are still active competitors of the white, although forced to take lower wages and do menial work. The Commissioner of Labor of North Carolina testified before the industrial commission that

"The truth of it is, a great many engineers like Negro firemen best. They had Negroes at first and are now only working white men in; the white men are taking the place of Negroes. . . . A great many of the old engineers prefer Negro firemen. They treat them differently--make them wait on them. The white man does not do that."

The Grand Secretary of the Boiler-makers says:

"There is not one man in this order that would present the application of a Negro for membership. This without laws forbidding him. Hence we have none. Being a Southern man myself, having lived 30 years in New Orleans, I know that no Negro has worked at boiler making since the war."

The secretary of the wire weavers says:

"Our laws, up to a few years ago, provided that only white males were eligible, but it at present makes no distinction, but at the same time I am satisfied that our men would not work with a Negro. We work partners and coming in such contact with one another no white man would take a Negro for a partner. And I am frank enough to say that I don't think any of the men would allow a Negro to start at the trade."

The International Association of Machinists was organized in 1888:

"Almost alone among national labor organizations, excepting the rail-road brotherhoods, it put a clause in its constitution excluding colored men. It desired to join the American Federation of Labor, but the Federation re-fused at that time to admit unions whose constitutions recognized distinctions of color. . . .

"At the Federation convention of 1892 the president of the Association of Machinists appeared before a committee of the Federation, expressed satis-faction with the action of the executive council, and stated that the next convention of the Machinists' Association would eliminate the color line from its constitution. It was not until 1895 that affiliation with the Federation was finally effected.

Notwithstanding this the secretary of the Washington lodge writes us in 1899 "the Negro is not admitted to the International Association of Machinists," while the secretary of the National Union refused to answer questions as to the eligibility of black men. A labor leader when asked by the Industrial Commission if he had ever worked with a Negro machinist, answered:

"No, sir; I never worked in a shop with a Negro as a machinist."
"Would you not?" "No, sir; I would not."

The president of Turner Brass Works tells how the machinists in his establishment objected to a colored workman, but the Negro "was so good-natured and did his work so well" that he was permitted to stay--but not to join the union.

"Right there is my objection, and right there is my reason for declining

to treat locally with unions, because the men out of the union should have
as good a right to employment as the men in the union. We do not ask them
if they are Methodists or Democrats, or whether they are Masons or union men.
We ask them, "Can you do this work!"

There may possibly be one or two Negroes in the machinists' union in
Boston.

The secretary of the electrical workers reports:

"I will state that we have no Negroes in our organization. We received
an application from Jacksonville, Fla., but it was thrown down by our locals.
We are in favor of the colored men organizing, but we believe that they
should have locals of their own, and not mixed with the whites."

In the Jacksonville case it is said that the local was granted a charter;
then it was learned that they were colored and the charter was revoked. There
are one or two Negro members in Massachusetts and New Jersey.

The reasons adduced for discrimination against Negroes vary:

"Unfit for the business."--Telegraphers.
"Not the equals of white men."--Boilermakers.
"Color."--Electricians, Locomotive Firemen.
"Race prejudice among the rank and file of our members."--Trainmen.

When asked if these objections would disappear in time, the answers were:

"No."--Locomotive Firemen.
"Eventually; co-operation will come."--Trainmen.
"We hope so."--Electricians.
"Not until prejudice in the South disappears."--Engineers.
"Time makes and works its own changes."--Boilermakers.
"Think not."--Telegraphers.

Finally the Railway Educational Association writes:

"Usually the railroad service is open from the top to the bottom for
promotion to those who enter it, but your race seems to be discriminated
against and barred from promotion. I understand that you are working on the
idea that education is the power that must advance your race, and finally
break down opposition to the progress of its members. In this you are surely
right, although the time for the realization of your hopes may be more distant than you expect."

There are a number of unions from whom repeated inquiries secured no
information, as, for instance, the bridge workers, core makers, table knife
grinders, iron molders, paving cutters, tin plate workers, marble workers,
lithographers and sheet metal workers. The addresses of others were not found
in time, as the powder workers, brickmakers, spinners, box makers, marine
engineers and firemen, and stogie makers. Most of these, however, have none
or very few Negroes, except possibly the core makers and molders, in which
trades many Negroes are employed. In the last Toronto meeting of the molders,
1902, it is said that:

" warm discussion was precipitated in the iron molders convention this
morning by a delegate from the South touching the admission of Negroes to the
Iron Molders' Union. The delegate thought they should be excluded, but those
from the Northern States, ably assisted by the Canadian members, championed
the Negro. They thought there should be no difference made. They objected to
the making of a race question."

Repeated letters to the secretary of the molders' as to the result of this
proposal and the general attitude of the molders, have elicited only this
response:

"You will have to kindly excuse me from giving such matters any more of
my time as I am very busy with my office work!"

Local option in the choice of members. The general attitude of the
Federation of Labor, and even of the National Unions, has little more than
a moral effect in the admission of Negroes to trade unions. The present
constitution of the Knights of Labor admits members "at the option of each
local assembly." The real power of admission in nearly all cases rests
with the local assemblies, by whose vote any person may be refused, and in
a large number of cases a small minority of any local may absolutely bar a
person to whom they object. The object of this is to keep out persons of
bad character or sometimes incompetent workmen. In practice, however, it
gives the local or a few of its members a monopoly of the labor market and
a chance to exercise, consciously or unconsciously, their prejudices against
foreigners, or Irishmen, or Jews, or Negroes.
The following unions require a majority vote for admission to the locals:

Boot and Shoe Workers	Amalgamated Engineers
Amalgamated Carpenters	Metal Polishers
Bottle Blowers	Stove Mounters
Glass Workers	Bakers
Wood Workers	Barbers
Coopers	Steam Engineers
Stogie-makers	Coal Hoisting Engineers

The woodworkers, coal hoisting engineers, and coopers, require an examining committee in addition.
The following require a two-thirds vote for admission to the locals:

Brotherhood of Carpenters	Sheet Metal Workers
Painters	Pattern-makers
Tile Layers	Tin Plate Workers
Flint Glass Workers	Broom-makers
Iron and Steel Workers	

Nearly all these require also the favorable report of an examining committee. Among the iron and steel workers and tin plate workers two black
balls can make a second election necessary.
These unions require more than a two-thirds vote for admission:

Electrical Workers, two-thirds vote, *plus* one, and examination.
Molders,   "   "   "   "   "
Core-makers,   "   "   "   "   "
Boiler-makers, three black balls reject.
Blacksmiths,   "   "   "   "   two require second election.
Street Railway Employees, three-fourths' vote.
Leather Workers, (horse goods), three black balls reject.

The Typographical Union and printing pressmen and many others leave all
questions of admission to the local unions absolutely, except that an appeal
lies to the National Union. In nearly all cases save that of the cigar-makers
the adverse vote of a local practically bars the applicant. It is here, and
not, usually, in the constitutions of the National bodies, that the color line
is drawn ruthlessly in the North.
The colloquy between the Industrial Commission and the First General
Vice President of the Building Trades Council brought this out with startling
clearness:

Question--"It seems to be true here that the local organization has the
power to draw the color line absolutely, without regard to the qualifications
of the applicant. To what extent does that power generally go with local
organizations? Is it absolute? Could it extend to a Roman nose, gray eyes,
wart on the chin, or must it rest upon some reason? What is the law about it?
    Answer--Such a condition might be possible, but not at all probable.
    Q.--You mean that all those things rest absolutely upon the will of the
local organization?
    A.--Why, yes; they rest upon the will of the majority."

In like manner the methods regulating apprenticeship militate against Negroes in nearly all the trades. Many unions, like the hatters, trunk makers, printers, stone cutters, glass workers, and others, limit the number of apprentices according to the journeymen at work. Very often, as in the case of the hatters, the union prescribes the terms of apprenticeship and oversees the details. In the case of the coal hoisting engineers, elastic goring weavers, and some others, the consent of the local must be obtained before any particular apprentice is admitted. In other cases there are age limits, and there is very general demand among the unions for still more rigid regulation and the use of articles of indenture. Strong unions go so far as to refuse to recognize a workman who has not served his apprenticeship in a union shop or begun it between the ages of 17 and 18. The tin plate union especially enjoins its members from teaching their trade to any unskilled workingmen about the mills. The black boy who gets a chance to learn a trade under such circumstances would indeed be a curiosity.

Strikes against Negro workmen. It is impossible to get accurate statistics on the number of cases where white workmen have refused to work with black men. Usually such strikes, especially in the North, are concealed under the refusal to work with non-union men. Strikes for this cause have occurred in 2,751 establishments in this country in the last 20 years, and nearly 70% of them have been successful. It is thus possible in some trades for three men absolutely to bar any Negro who wishes to pursue this calling.

There are a number of cases where the object of getting rid of Negro workingmen has been openly avowed. These, by causes, are as follows:

STRIKES FROM JAN. 1, 1881, to DEC. 31, 1900.

	Total	Succeeded	Failed
Against employing colored girls...................	1		1
" " " men.....................	23	5	18
" " " men and for increased wages	1		1
" " " foreman.................	1	1	
" working with Negroes......................	7	1	6
For discharge of Negro employees..................	16	5	11
" " of foreman and vs. colored laborers journeymen's work.............................	1		1
Total..	50	12	38

INDUSTRIES IN WHICH STRIKES AGAINST NEGRO LABOR HAVE OCCURRED

	No	Succeeded	Failed
Agricultural Implements............................	1		1
Brick..	1		1
Building Trades....................................	4		4
Clothing...	1		1
Coal and Coke......................................	6	3	3
Cotton Goods.......................................	3	2	1
Domestic Service...................................	2		2
Glass..	2	1	1
Leather and Leather Goods..........................	1	1	
Machines and Machinery.............................	2		2
Metals and Metallic Goods..........................	3		3
Public Ways Construction...........................	2		2
Stone Quarrying and Cutting........................	1	1	
Transportation.....................................	18	3	15
Wooden Goods.......................................	1		1
Miscellaneous......................................	1		1
Total..	49	11	38

STRIKES BY YEARS

Year	Cause	Establish-ments	Succeeded	Failed
1882	Against employment of colored men......	2		2
1883	" " " " "	2	1	1
1885	For discharge of colored employees.....	1	1	
	Against employment of colored men......	1		1
1887	Against working with colored men.......	1		1
1888	For discharge of colored employees.....	5		5
	Against employment of colored men and for increased wages.................	1		1
1889	Against working with colored men.......	2		2
	For discharge of colored employees.....	1		1
	Against working under colored foreman..	1	1	
1890	Against working with colored men.......	1		1
1891	" ' " " " "	1		1
1892	" " " " "	1		1
1894	For discharge of colored employees.....	2	1	1
	Against employing colored men..........	12		12
1897	For discharge of colored employees.....	1	1	
1898	Against employing colored men..........	1	1	
1899	Against certain rules and for discharge colored head-waiter.................	1		1
1899	For discharge of colored employees.....	4	1	3
1900	Against employment of colored girls....	1		1
	" " " " men......	5	3	2
	Total...........................	47	10	37

Detailed information as to all of these strikes is unfortunately not available for the last ten years; for the first ten years 1,458 men were engaged in such strikes, involving 21 establishments and entailing a pecuniary loss to employers and employed of $215,945. If the strikes of the last ten years were similar in character we may say that in the last 20 years 3,000 white workingmen have fought against the employment of other workingmen for the sole reason that they were black at a cost of nearly half a million dollars. And that moreover this probably is only a small part of the strikes against colored men, since usually the strike is technically against "non-union labor."

The greatest strike of which we have record before 1891 is that which took place in a steel works in Pittsburgh in 1890. The Iron and Steel Workers Union ordered out 400 of the 500 employees because Negroes were employed. The strike lasted over eight months and failed. The wage loss was $15,000, toward which labor unions contributed $8,000. The employers lost $25,090 and eventually 300 new hands were hired in place of the strikers.

Summary of the Attitude of Organized Labor. Putting the strength of organized labor in the United States at the conservative estimate of 1,200,000, we may say:

Unions with 500,000 members, include 40,000 Negroes.
Unions with 200,000 members, include 1,000 Negroes.
Unions with 500,000 members, include   No Negroes.

The rule of admission of Negroes to unions throughout the country is the sheer necessity of guarding work and wages. In those trades where large numbers of Negroes are skilled they find easy admittance in the parts of the country where their competition is felt. In all other trades they are barred from the unions, save in exceptional cases, either by open or silent color discrimination. There are exceptions to this rule. There are cases where the whites have shown a real feeling of brotherhood; there are cases where the blacks, through incompetence and carelessness, have forfeited their right to the advantages of organization. But on the whole a careful, unprejudiced survey of the facts leads one to believe that the above statement is approximately true all over the land.

It is fair, on such a vital point, however, to let the white labor leaders speak for themselves and the opinions of a few are here appended.

Views of Labor Leaders--(By C. C. Houston, Secretary of the Georgia Federation of Labor, Samuel Gompers, President of the American Federation of Labor, and others).

"A labor union is primarily a business institution and very little sentimentalism enters into its make-up. It is for the collective bargaining, conciliation and arbitration of labor. It is to the working man what the Chamber of Commerce is to the business man. It differs from a commercial trust in that it is not a close corporation, but its influences for good are world-wide, and its membership is restricted only to those qualified to perform the work of any special calling in a workmanlike manner. It gives greater liberty and independence of action to the workman and insures not only a higher standard of wages but a higher standard of living.

"Dr. George E. McNeill, author of a volume entitled 'The Labor Movement,' says: 'There is no such thing as liberty of contract between a single wage-worker and an employer. It first becomes possible through the efforts of trade unions. The union is to the laborer what a republican form of government is to the citizen--it gives him freedom. Unions have first made labor problems a matter of interest to the people generally, and have increased respect for labor. They have brought back self-respect and have a strong educational influence. Drunkenness and other bad habits are frowned upon by labor unions.'[141]

"Were it not for the labor unions the working people of this and other civilized countries would be in little better condition than were the chattel slaves of this section before the civil war, and this is the only power that can resist the great and growing combination of capital. There are in the United States today over 2,000,000 skilled working men and women enrolled in the ranks of the various labor organizations. The system comprises local, state and national unions. Each local union is a self-governing body, and is to the national body what a single state is to the United States. Each local union has complete trade autonomy, and regulates its own internal affairs. These local unions range in membership from seven to over six thousand, the last being "Big Six" typographical union of New York City, the largest local labor organization in the world.

"The older trade unions, which have practically complete control of their trade membership, such as the printers, stone cutters, tailors, and engineers, conductors and cigar makers, have comparatively few strikes and it is only the newer organizations that are usually forced to resort to strikes to gain recognition of demands for wage scales and regulation of hours. In the case of the older trade unions they have local and sometimes national agreements with associations of employers as to wages and hours of labor. Through the efforts of trade unions few skilled workmen now work over ten hours, while in a great majority of instances eight and nine hours constitute a day's labor at a greater wage scale than formerly prevailed for ten and eleven hours.

"In this general trade union movement the Negro artisan has been a beneficiary in proportion to his membership. It is only during the past ten years that the colored workingman has become in any great measure a factor in organized labor affairs, for there are very few unions among unskilled laborers.

"With the possible exception of the railway orders, none of the trade unions of this country, North and South, exclude the Negro, and his connection with the labor movement is becoming more apparent every year, and he is fast finding out that it is to his individual and collective interest to become affiliated with the organization of his craft. In this the white artisan is lending encouragement and assisting the Negro, giving him a seat, with voice and vote, in the labor councils, local, state and national. The feeling that formerly prevailed among the Negro skilled artisans that the white laborer's sympathy for him was for a selfish purpose is being rapidly dispelled by the mutually beneficial results of organization."--C. C. Houston.

The President of the American Federation of Labor writes:

"It has been and is now our endeavor to organize the colored workers whenever and wherever possible. We recognize the necessity of this if it is hoped to secure the best possible conditions for the workers of every class in our country." Later, on reading §53, he replied: "I should say that your statement is neither fair nor accurate. After careful perusal of the summing up of the attitude of the A.F. of L. toward colored workmen, I should say that you are inclined, not only to be pessimistic upon the subject, but you are even unwilling to give credit where credit is due."--Samuel Gompers.

The following opinions are from various states:

VIRGINIA.--"One of the greatest drawbacks to the labor movement in the South is the ignorant prejudice against the Negro on the part of the whites in trades unions."

MASSACHUSETTS.--"I always considered a Negro as good as a white man, in any labor union, provided they live up to the obligations."

KANSAS.--"Unions do not bar Negroes by their laws but do not solicit them. If they would apply they would be rejected."

IOWA.--"There are only a few Negroes here but they are not discriminated against according to my knowledge except in the Federation where a Negro cannot act as a delegate legally."

FLORIDA.--"The Negroes in this city have no need to complain, as the white men work, smoke, eat and drink together with them, meet in Central Union and hold office together. I organized and installed the Central Union, as General Secretary, and I am a Negro, and have held the same for two elections and was elected by the whites, who are in majority. I have presided over the same body, but do not visit their daughters and have no wish. The white painters do in a way draw a line, but not openly; the boiler makers also, but none others."

ILLINOIS.--"We have but one Negro in this town and don't need him."

IOWA.--"The Negro in the world is fast learning to overcome superstition, race prejudice, etc. He is 90% a better citizen than the semi-civilized pack of humanity that is being imported into this country by capitalists from Asia Minor and Syria."

MASSACHUSETTS.--"I have met Negroes in the printing trade who were rapid compositors and good union men."

ILLINOIS.--"There is only one union here but what the Negro stands on a level with whites, and they would take them in when they apply; but the Negro knows better than to apply."

INDIANA.--"It is my opinion that if a Negro proves himself a mechanic and a man, and holds up trades rules, he has a right to work and make an honest living, the same as any one else; but don't understand by this that I am in favor of this class of people in general, for I am not."

PENNSYLVANIA.--"The working people do not believe in distinctions of races at all."

WASHINGTON.--"I want to say under this head that the Negroes as a race are bigoted and should not, in my opinion, be allowed to associate with whites on an equal basis. Although they do not follow my line of business, I have had enough experience with them to convince me that any time they are treated as equals by whites they go too far and apparently consider themselves entitled to more consideration than a native born white American citizen."

PENNSYLVANIA.--"I have known cases here where colored men were refused admittance to a trades union, the reason being that there are so many of them who are unreliable; which is due to a great extent to their want of education, and this but points more forcibly to the need of the 8 hour day for the colored

workman, and their organization into some body which will awaken them to
the greater possibilities of elevation, both material and intellectual,
offered them by trades unionism."

OHIO.--"I am of the opinion that the Negro in common labor pursuits is
far ahead of the whites, and many in trade occupations. One Negro friend of
mine holds a very responsible position with this union--has been presiding
officer since its organization three years ago, and the organization has
about 200 members, white and black."

INDIANA.--"We have had no test here in regard to admitting Negroes to
our local unions. How they would be received is hard to tell at present."

TEXAS.--"Color discrimination must disappear, if the trade union movement succeeds."

TEXAS.--"The Negro question is the one drawback to the success of the
labor movement today, especially is this true in the South. The Negro has always been the stumbling block in the way of success, in many cases; this, however, is not the fault of the Negro, but until the white men realize that it
is with the organization and assistance of the Negro, that they can and must
win, the labor movement will not be as successful as we hope for. I believe
that if the Negro was organized thoroughly, then the solution of the labor
problem would be found. They are laborers, in a larger percentage, than their
white brothers; they are the ones used to whip the white men into line when
striking for their rights or demanding recognition from their employers, whereas,
if they were organized, no inducement could be made to cause them to falter in
their duty to mankind."

MICHIGAN.--"In my opinion it is only a question of time--the evolution
which will bring with it the higher civilization--when a colored man will be
recognized and entitled to all the rights and privileges now enjoyed by the
whites, and by such enjoyment proving the claim that it is civilization and
education that makes the man."

The Employer, the Artisan, and the Right of Suffrage. A few quotations
throw an interesting side light on the suffrage question in the South and its
relation to the Negro. The last Southern Industrial Convention at Chattanooga said:

"We recommend that every possible means shall be used to educate the
public sentiment of the South to regard the Negro as a factor in the upbuilding of the South, and that as such we should use all possible means to make
him as efficient as possible, and pledge him the fullest guaranty of earning
a living in every honest field of honest endeavor, and protection in his God-
given right of self-support."

A prominent Southern man said before the Industrial Commission:

"I believe that in the Negro labor of the South lies the panacea for the
wrongs frequently committed by organized labor, and a reserve force from which
can be supplied any needed number of workers when the time shall come when
they shall be needed."

Most workingmen in the South laugh at such threats because they are certain the Negro cannot become a formidable competitor in skilled labor. A
writer in the Molder's Journal makes considerable fun of the exaggerated predictions as to the Negro molder and writes him down as a "dismal failure."
Another writer, however, takes him to task and asserts that the writer

"Will not woo us into a sense of fancied security and induce us to look
upon the Negro problem in our trade as one that will solve itself by the
Negro's demonstrating his incapacity and being ignominiously dismissed from
the foundry.
"That is very flattering to our vanity, but it is contrary to facts. I
believe I am well within the mark when I say that in the last twenty years
Negro molders have increased 500 per cent, and that excluding the Negro pipe

molders, whom I do not class as skillful mechanics, I know of two foundries, at least, where the molding is done entirely by Negroes--three if we include the Ross-Mehan annex in Chattanooga. There is the one at the foot of Look-out Mountain, and another in Rome, Ga. A few years ago a mere handful of Negroes worked at molding in Chattanooga, today there are over two hundred; and I am convinced that the question of what shall be done with the Negro molder is one which, in the very near future, will demand more of our attention if we would maintain for ourselves fair wages and condition in the South."

On the other hand a white speaker in the 10th Barbers' Convention said: "Is the disfranchisement of the Negro the first step toward making history repeat itself? I for one will not believe it, as I have too much confidence in American manhood to think that they will allow it. Those of you who live in the South may feel, you may even say it is right, and then I will say to you, if it is right to deny the right of franchise to any American citizen, though his color or nationality be what it may, then it may be your turn tomorrow, because those who seek to disfranchise the Negro today will seek to extend their power by disfranchising you tomorrow. Our protection for tomorrow calls on us to protest in favor of the disfranchised Negro of today."

Here, then, are the four great forces: the Northern laborer, the Southern laborer, the Negro and the employer. The Southern laborer and the employer have united to disfranchise the Negro and make color a caste; the laborer is striving to make the whites unite with the Negroes and maintain wages; the employer threatens that if they do raise labor troubles he will employ Negroes. The Northern laborer sees here the danger of a disfranchised, degraded and yet skilled competitor, and raises the note of warning. Is not this a drama worth the watching?

The Employment of Skilled Negroes in the South. The Chattanooga *Tradesman* made, in 1889 and 1891, inquiries into the status of Negro labor in the South. The employers questioned in 1889, employed 7,000 Negroes of whom possibly 2,000 were skilled or semi-skilled. "The general tenor of the replies indicated perfect satisfaction with Negro labor." In 1891 replies were received from the employers of 7,395 Negroes of whom 978 were skilled and many semi-skilled and the editor concluded that "the Negro, as a free laborer, as a medium skilled and common worker, is by no means a 'failure;' that he is really a remarkable success."
In 1901, a third joint investigation into Negro skilled labor was made by the *Tradesman* and the Sociological Department of Atlanta University. It was not an exhaustive inquiry and there is no way of knowing what proportion of the employers of skilled Negro laborers were reached. In 1891, twelve per cent, of the Negroes employed by those written to were skilled or semi-skilled; in 1901, twenty per cent; 344 firms answered in 1901, employing 35,481 men, of whom 16,145 were Negroes, and 2,652 of these were skilled or semi-skilled workmen. Negroes were employed at given occupations as follows in the various establishments:

KINDS OF EMPLOYMENT FOLLOWED BY NEGROES, BY ESTABLISHMENTS

Shipping clerk,	1	Plasterers,	1
Saw sharpening,	5	Edgers,	14
Pan shoving,	3	Setters in planing mill,	9
Farmers,	2	Trimmers,	2
Engineers,	23	Teamsters,	1
Sawyers,	20	Graders,	4
Wood workers,	2	Lumber inspectors,	2
Pressmen,	29	Cupola tenders,	6
Meal cooks,	40	Stove mounters,	1
Linters,	17	Molders,	14
Handlers Cotton Seed Products,	1	Log cutters,	1
Handlers of Machines,	26	Watchmen,	1
Firemen,	45	Planers,	5
Huller men,	4	Raftsmen,	1

Grinders,	3	R. R. engineers,	2
Cake millers,	5	Wood turners,	2
Ginners,	14	Boiler makers,	2
Pipe fitters,	2	Furnace men,	3
Mill wrighters,	1	Core makers,	5
Pump men,	4	Electric linemen,	1
General oil mill men,	5	Painters,	3
Stockers,	1	Stone Cutters,	1
Truckers,	1	Inspectors of castings,	1
Sackers,	1	Drillers,	1
Ice plant men,	1	General saw mill workers	1
Cake formers,	3	Barrel makers,	1
Oilers,	4	Stave makers,	1
Machine repairers,	1	Plow polishers,	1
Strippers,	2	Stove tenders,	1
Foremen,	4	Pattern makers,	1
Blacksmiths,	14	Iron pourers,	1
Blocksmen,	5	Riveters and drillers,	1

. . . *Summary.* We have studied in considerable detail the history of
the Negro artisan, the industrial schools, the condition of Negro mechanics
throughout the country, the attitude of organized labor toward the Negro,
the opinions of employers, and Negro inventions. On the whole the survey
has been encouraging, although there is much to deplore and criticise. Our
conclusions may be summed up as follows:

1. Slavery trained artisans, but they were for the most part careless
and inefficient. Only in exceptional cases were they first-class mechanics.
2. Industrial schools are needed. They are costly and, as yet, not
well organized or very efficient, but they have given the Negro an ideal of
manual toil and helped to a better understanding between whites and Negroes
in the South. Eventually they may be expected to send out effective artisans, as they already have begun to do.
3. There are a large number of Negro mechanics all over the land, but
especially in the South. Some of these are progressive, efficient workmen.
More are careless, slovenly and ill-trained. There are signs of lethargy
among these artisans and work is slipping from them in some places; in
others they are awakening and seizing the opportunities of the new industrial
south.
4. The labor unions, with 1,200,000 members, have less than 40,000
Negroes, mostly in a few unions, and largely semi-skilled laborers like
miners. Some labor leaders have striven against color prejudice, but it
exists and keeps the mass of Negroes out of many trades. This leads to
complicated problems, both industrial, political and social.
5. Employers on the whole are satisfied with Negro skilled labor and
many of them favor education as tending to increase the efficiency of Negroes.
Others think it will spoil the docility and tractableness of Negro labor.
The employment of Negro skilled labor is slowly increasing.
6. The Negro evinces considerable mechanical ingenuity.
On the whole this study of a phase of the vast economic development of the
Negro race in America but emphasizes the primal and emphatic need of intelligence. The situation is critical and developing swiftly. Deftly
guided with the larger wisdom of men and deeper benevolence of great hearts,
an outcome of good to all cannot be doubted. Muddled by half trained men
and guided by selfish and sordid interests and all the evils of industrial
history may easily be repeated in the South. *"Wisdom"* then *"is the principal
thing; therefore, get wisdom, and with all thy getting, get understanding."*

W. E. Burghardt Du Bois (ed.), *The Negro Artisan* (Atlanta: Atlanta University
Press, 1902), pp. 10-11, 153-180, 188. Footnotes have been eliminated from
the text by the editors.

5.   THE PHILADELPHIA NEGRO

By W. E. B. DuBois

THE CONTACT OF THE RACES

Color Prejudice.--Incidentally throughout this study the prejudice
against the Negro has been again and again mentioned. It is time now to
reduce this somewhat indefinite term to something tangible. Everybody
speaks of the matter, everybody knows that it exists, but in just what form
it shows itself or how influential it is few agree. In the Negro's mind,
color prejudice in Philadelphia is that widespread feeling of dislike for
his blood, which keeps him and his children out of decent employment, from
certain public conveniences and amusements, from hiring houses in many sections, and in general, from being recognized as a man. Negroes regard this
prejudice as the chief cause of their present unfortunate condition. On the
other hand most white people are quite unconscious of any such powerful and
vindictive feeling; they regard color prejudice as the easily explicable
feeling that intimate social intercourse with a lower race is not only undesirable but impracticable if our present standards of culture are to be
maintained; and although they are aware that some people feel the aversion
more intensely than others, they cannot see how such a feeling has much influence on the real situation, or alters the social condition of the mass
of Negroes.

As a matter of fact, color prejudice in this city is something between
these two extreme views: It is not today responsible for all, or perhaps
the greater part of the Negro problems, or of the disabilities under which
the race labors; on the other hand it is a far more powerful social force
than most Philadelphians realize. The practical results of the attitude of
most of the inhabitants of Philadelphia toward persons of Negro descent are
as follows:

1. As to getting work:
No matter how well trained a Negro may be, or how fitted for work of
any kind, he cannot in the ordinary course of competition hope to be much
more than a menial servant.
He cannot get clerical or supervisory work to do save in exceptional
cases.
He cannot teach save in a few of the remaining Negro schools.
He cannot become a mechanic except for small transient jobs, and cannot
join a trades union.
A Negro woman has but three careers open to her in this city: domestic
service, sewing, or married life.

2. As to keeping work:
The Negro suffers in competition more severely than white men.
Change in fashion is causing him to be replaced by whites in the better
paid positions of domestic service.
Whim and accident will cause him to lose a hard-earned place more quickly
than the same things would affect a white man.
Being few in number compared with the whites the crime or carelessness
of a few of his race is easily imputed to all, and the reputation of the good,
industrious and reliable suffer thereby.
Because Negro workmen may not often work side by side with white workmen, the individual black workman is rated not by his own efficiency, but by
the efficiency of a whole group of black fellow workmen which may often be
low.
Because of these difficulties which virtually increase competition in
his case, he is forced to take lower wages for the same work than white workmen.

3. As to entering new lines of work:
Men are used to seeing Negroes in inferior positions; when therefore, by
any chance a Negro gets in a better position, most men immediately conclude that

he is not fitted for it, even before he has a chance to show his fitness.

If, therefore, he set up a store, men will not patronize him.

If he is put into public position men will complain.

If he gain a position in the commercial world, men will quietly secure his dismissal or see that a white man succeeds him.

4. As to his expenditure:

The comparative smallness of the patronage of the Negro, and the dislike of other customers makes it usual to increase the charges or difficulties in certain directions in which a Negro must spend money.
He must pay more house-rent for worse houses than most white people pay.

He is sometimes liable to insult or reluctant service in some restaurants, hotels and stores, at public resorts, theatres and places of recreation; and at nearly all barbershops.

5. As to his children:

The Negro finds it extremely difficult to rear children in such an atmosphere and not have them either cringing or impudent: if he impresses upon them patience with their lot, they may grow up satisfied with their condition; if he inspires them with ambition to rise, they may grow to despise their own people, hate the whites and become embittered with the world.

His children are discriminated against, often in public schools.

They are advised when seeking employment to become waiters and maids.

They are liable to species of insult and temptation peculiarly trying to children.

6. As to social intercourse:

In all walks of life the Negro is liable to meet some objection to his presence or some discourteous treatment; and the ties of friendship or memory seldom are strong enough to hold across the color line.

If an invitation is issued to the public for any occasion, the Negro can never know whether he would be welcomed or not; if he goes he is liable to have his feelings hurt and get into unpleasant altercation; if he stays away, he is blamed for indifference.

If he meet a lifelong white friend on the street, he is in a dilemma; if he does not greet the friend he is put down as boorish and impolite; if he does greet the friend he is liable to be flatly snubbed.

If by chance he is introduced to a white woman or man, he expects to be ignored on the next meeting, and usually is.

White friends may call on him, but he is scarcely expected to call on them, save for strictly business matters.

If he gain the affections of a white woman and marry her he may invariably expect that slurs will be thrown on her reputation and on his, and that both his and her race will shun their company.

When he dies he cannot be buried beside white corpses.

7. The result:

Anyone of these things happening now and then would not be remarkable or call for especial comment; but when one group of people suffer all these little differences of treatment and discriminations and insults continually, the result is either discouragement, or bitterness, or over-sensitiveness, or recklessness. And a people feeling thus cannot do their best.

Presumably the first impulse of the average Philadelphian would be emphatically to deny any such marked and blighting discrimination as the above against a group of citizens in this metropolis. Every one knows that in the past color prejudice in the city was deep and passionate; living men can remember when a Negro could not sit in a street car or walk many streets in peace. These times have passed, however, and many imagine that active discrimination against the Negro has passed with them. Careful inquiry will convince any such one of his error. To be sure a colored man today can walk the streets of Philadelphia without personal insult; he can go to theatres, parks and some places of amusement without meeting more than stares and discourtesy; he can be accommodated at most hotels and restaurants, although his treatment in some would not be pleasant. All this is a vast advance and augurs much for the future. And yet all that has been said of the remaining discrimination is but too true.

During the investigation of 1896 there was collected a number of actual cases, which may illustrate the discriminations spoken of. So far as possible these have been sifted and only those which seem undoubtedly true have been selected.

1. As to getting work.

It is hardly necessary to dwell upon the situation of the Negro in regard to work in the higher walks of life: the white boy may start in the lawyer's office and work himself into a lucrative practice; he may serve a physician as office boy or enter a hospital in a minor position, and have his talent alone between him and affluence and fame; if he is bright in school, he may make his mark in a university, become a tutor with some time and much inspiration for study, and eventually fill a professor's chair. All these careers are at the very outset closed to the Negro on account of his color; what lawyer would give even a minor case to a Negro assistant? or what university would appoint a promising young Negro as tutor? Thus the young white man starts in life knowing that within some limits and barring accidents, talent and application will tell. The young Negro starts knowing that on all sides his advance is made doubly difficult if not wholly shut off, by his color. Let us come, however, to ordinary occupations which concern more nearly the mass of Negroes. Philadelphia is a great industrial and business centre, with thousands of foremen, managers and clerks--the lieutenants of industry, who direct its progress. They are paid for thinking and for skill to direct, and naturally such positions are coveted because they are well paid, well thought of and carry some authority. To such positions Negro boys and girls may not aspire no matter what their qualifications. Even as teachers and ordinary clerks and stenographers they find almost no openings. Let us note some actual instances:

A young woman who graduated with credit from the Girls' Normal School in 1892, has taught in the kindergarten, acted as substitute, and waited in vain for a permanent position. Once she was allowed to substitute in a school with white teachers; the principal commended her work, but when the permanent appointment was made a white woman got it.

A girl who graduated from a Pennsylvania high school and from a business college sought work in the city as a stenographer and typewriter. A prominent lawyer undertook to find her a position; he went to friends and said, "Here is a girl that does excellent work and is of good character; can you not give her work?" Several immediately answered yes. "But," said the lawyer, "I will be perfectly frank with you and tell you she is colored;" and not in the whole city could he find a man willing to employ her. It happened, however, that the girl was so light in complexion that few not knowing would have suspected her descent. The lawyer therefore gave her temporary work in his own office until she found a position outside the city. "But," said he, "to this day I have not dared to tell my clerks that they worked beside a Negress." Another woman graduated from the high school and the Palmer College of Shorthand, but all over the city has met with nothing but refusal of work.

Several graduates in pharmacy have sought to get their three years required apprenticeship in the city and in only one case did one succeed, although they offered to work for nothing. One young pharmacist came from Massachusetts and for weeks sought in vain for work here at any price; "I wouldn't have a darky to clean out my store, much less to stand behind the counter," answered one druggist. A colored man answered an advertisement for a clerk in the suburbs. "What do you suppose we'd want of a nigger? was the plain answer. A graduate of the University of Pennsylvania in mechanical engineering, well recommended, obtained work in the city, through an advertisement, on account of his excellent record. He worked a few hours and then was discharged because he was found to be colored. He is now a waiter at the University Club, where his white fellow graduates dine. Another young man attended Spring Garden Institute and studied drawing for lithography. He had good references from the institute and elsewhere, but application at the five largest establishments in the city could secure him no work. A telegraph operator has hunted in vain for an opening, and two graduates of the Central High School have sunk to menial labor. "What's the use of an education?" asked one. Mr. A____ has elsewhere been employed as a traveling salesman. He applied for a position here by letter and was told he could have one. When they saw him they had no work for him.

Such cases could be multiplied indefinitely. But that is not necessary; one has but to note that notwithstanding the acknowledged ability of many colored men, the Negro is conspicuously absent from all places of honor, trust or emolument, as well as from those of respectable grade in commerce and industry.

Even in the world of skilled labor the Negro is largely excluded. Many would explain the absence of Negroes from higher vocations by saying that while a few may now and then be found competent, the great mass are not fitted for that sort of work and are destined for some time to form a laboring class. In the matter of the trades, however, there can be raised no serious question of ability; for years the Negroes filled satisfactorily the trades of the city, and today in many parts of the South they are still prominent. And yet in Philadelphia a determined prejudice, aided by public opinion, has succeeded nearly in driving them from the field:

A____, who works at a bookbinding establishment on Front street, has learned to bind books and often does so for his friends. He is not allowed to work at the trade in the shop, however, but must remain a porter at a porter's wages.

B____ is a brushmaker; he has applied at several establishments, but they would not even examine his testimonials. They simply said: "We do not employ colored people."

C____ is a shoemaker; he tried to get work in some of the large department stores. They "had no place" for him.

D____ was a bricklayer, but experienced so much trouble in getting work that he is now a messenger.

E____ is a painter, but has found it impossible to get work because he is colored.

F____ is a telegraph line man, who formerly worked in Richmond, Va. When he applied here he was told that Negroes were not employed.

G____ is an iron puddler, who belonged to a Pittsburgh union. Here he was not recognized as a union man and could not get work except as a stevedore.

H____ was a cooper, but could get no work after repeated trials, and is now a common laborer.

I____ is a candy maker, but has never been able to find employment in the city; he is always told that the white help will not work with him.

J____ is a carpenter; he can only secure odd jobs or work where only Negroes are employed.

K____ was an upholsterer, but could get no work save in the few colored shops, which had workmen; he is now a waiter on a dining car.

L____ was a first-class baker; he applied for work sometime ago near Green street and was told shortly, "We don't work no niggers here."

M____ is a good typesetter; he has not been allowed to join the union and has been refused work at eight different places in the city.

N____ is a printer by trade, but can only find work as a porter.

O____ is a sign painter, but can get but little work.

P____ is a painter and gets considerable work, but never with white workmen.

Q____ is a good stationary engineer, but can find no employment; is at present a waiter in a private family.

R____ was born in Jamaica; he went to England and worked fifteen years in the Sir Edward Green Economizing Works in Wakefield, Yorkshire. During dull times he emigrated to America, bringing excellent references. He applied for a place as mechanic in nearly all the large iron working establishments in the city. A locomotive works assured him that his letters were all right, but that their men would not work with Negroes. At a manufactory of railway switches they told him they had no vacancy and he could call again; he called and finally was frankly told that they could not employ Negroes. He applied twice to a foundry company; they told him: "We have use for only one Negro--a porter," and refusing either further conversation or even to look at his letters showed him out. He then applied for work on a new building; the man told him he could leave an application, then added: "To tell the truth, its no use, for we don't employ Negroes." Thus the man has searched for work two years and has not yet found a permanent position. He can only support his family by odd jobs as a common laborer.

S____ is a stonecutter; he was refused work repeatedly on account of color. At last he got a job during a strike and was found to be so good a workman that his employer refused to dismiss him.

T____ was a boy, who, together with a white boy came to the city to hunt work. The colored boy was very light in complexion, and consequently both were taken in as apprentices at a large locomotive works; they worked there some months, but it was finally disclosed that the boy was colored; he was dismissed and the white boy retained.

These all seem typical and reliable cases. There are, of course, some exceptions to the general rule, but even these seem to confirm the fact that exclusion is a matter of prejudice and thoughtlessness which sometimes yields to determination and good sense. The most notable case in point is that of the Midvale Steel Works, where a large number of Negro workmen are regularly employed as mechanics and work alongside whites. If another foreman should take charge there, or if friction should arise, it would be easy for all this to receive a serious set-back, for ultimate success in such matters demands many experiments and a widespread public sympathy.

There are several cases where strong personal influence has secured colored boys positions; in one cabinet making factory, a porter who had served the firm thirty years, asked to have his son learn the trade and work in the shop. The workmen objected strenuously at first, but the employer was firm and the young man has been at work there now seven years. The S. S. White Dental Company has a colored chemist who has worked up to his place and gives satisfaction. A jeweler allowed his colored fellow-soldier in the late war to learn the gold beaters' trade and work in his shop. A few other cases follow:

A____ was intimately acquainted with a merchant and secured his son a position as a typewriter in the merchant's office.

B____, a stationary engineer, came with his employer from Washington and still works with him.

C____, a plasterer, learned his trade with a firm in Virginia who especially recommended him to the firm where he now works.

D____ is a boy whose mother's friend got him work as cutter in a bag and rope factory; the hands objected but the friend's influence was strong enough to keep him there.

All these exceptions prove the rule, viz., that without strong effort and special influence it is next to impossible for a Negro in Philadelphia to get regular employment in most of the trades, except he work as an independent workman and take small transient jobs.

The chief agency that brings about this state of affairs is public opinion; if they were not intrenched, and strongly intrenched, back of an active prejudice or at least passive acquiescence in this effort to deprive Negroes of a decent livelihood, both trades unions and arbitrary bosses would be powerless to do the harm they now do; where, however, a large section of the public more or less openly applaud the stamina of a man who refuses to work with a "Nigger," the results are inevitable. The object of the trades union is purely business-like; it aims to restrict the labor market, just as the manufacturer aims to raise the price of his goods. Here is a chance to keep out of the market a vast number of workmen, and the unions seize the chance save in cases where they dare not as in the case of the cigar-makers and coal-miners. If they could keep out the foreign workmen in the same way they would; but here public opinion within and without their ranks forbids hostile action. Of course, most unions do not flatly declare their discriminations; a few plainly put the word "white" into their constitutions; most of them do not and will say that they consider each case on its merits. Then they quietly blackball the Negro applicant. Others delay and temporize and put off action until the Negro withdraws; still others discriminate against the Negro in initiation fees and dues, making a Negro pay $100, where the whites pay $25. On the other hand in times of strikes or other disturbances cordial invitations to join are often sent to Negro workmen.

At a time when women are engaged in breadwinning to a larger degree than ever before, the field open to Negro women is unusually narrow. This is, of course, due largely to the more intense prejudices of females on all subjects, and especially to the fact that women who work dislike to be in any way mistaken for menials, and they regard Negro women as menials *par excellence*.

A____, a dressmaker and seamstress of proven ability, sought work in the large department stores. They all commended her work, but could not employ her on account of her color.

B____ is a typewriter, but has applied at stores and offices in vain for work; "very sorry" they all say, but they can give her no work. She has answered many advertisements without result.

C____ has attended the Girls High School for two years, and has been unable to find any work; she is washing and sewing for a living now.

D____ is a dressmaker and milliner, and does bead work. "Your work is very good," they say to her, "but if we hired you all of our ladies would leave."

E____, a seamstress, was given work from a store once to do at home. It was commended as satisfactory, but they gave her no more.

F____ had two daughters who tried to get work as stenographers, but only got one small job.

G____ is a graduate of the Girls High School, with excellent record; both teachers and influential friends have been seeking work for her but have not been able to find any.

H____ a girl, applied at seven stores for some work not menial; they had none.

I____ started at the Schuylkill, on Market street, and applied at almost every store nearly to the Delaware, for work; she was only offered scrubbing.

2. So much for the difficulty of getting work. In addition to this the Negro is meeting difficulties in keeping the work he has, or at least the better part of it. Outside of all dissatisfaction with Negro work there are whims and fashions that affect his economic position; today general European travel has made the trained English servant popular and consequently well-shaven white men-servants, whether English or not, find it easy to replace Negro butlers and coachmen at higher wages. Again, though a man ordinarily does not dismiss all his white mill-hands because some turn out badly, yet it repeatedly happens that men dismiss all their colored servants and condemn their race because one or two in their employ have proven untrustworthy. Finally, the antipathies of lower classes are so great that it is often impracticable to mix races among the servants. A young colored girl went to work temporarily in Germantown; "I should like so much to keep you permanently," said the mistress, "but all my other servants are white." She was discharged. Usually now advertisements for help state whether white or Negro servants are wanted, and the Negro who applies at the wrong place must not be surprised to have the door slammed in his face.

The difficulties encountered by the Negro on account of sweeping conclusions made about him are manifold; a large building, for instance, has several poorly paid Negro janitors, without facilities for their work or guidance in its prosecution. Finally the building is thoroughly overhauled or rebuilt, elevators and electricity installed and a well-paid set of white uniformed janitors put to work under a responsible salaried chief. Immediately the public concludes that the improvement in the service is due to the change of color. In some cases, of course, the change is due to a widening of the field of choice in selecting servants; for assuredly one cannot expect that one twenty-fifth of the population can furnish as many good workmen or as uniformly good ones as the other twenty-four twenty-fifths. One actual case illustrates this tendency to exclude the Negro without proper consideration from even menial employment:

A great church which has a number of members among the most respectable Negro families in the city has recently erected a large new building for its offices, etc., in the city. As the building was nearing completion a colored clergyman of that sect was surprised to hear that no Negroes were to be employed in the building; he thought that a peculiar stand for a Christian church to take and so he went to the manager of the building; the manager blandly assured him that the rumor was true; and that there was not the shadow of a chance for a Negro to get employment under him, except one woman to clean the water closet. The reason for this, he said, was that the janitors and help were all to be uniformed and the whites would not wear uniforms with Negroes. The clergyman thereupon went to a prominent member of the church who was serving on the building committee; he denied that the committee had made any such decision, but sent him to another member of the committee; this member said the same thing and referred to the third, a blunt business man. The business man said: "That building is called the _____ Church House, but it is more than that, it is a business enterprise, to be run on business principles. We hired a man to run it so as to get the most out of it. We found such a man in the present manager, and put all power in his hands." He acknowledged then, that while the committee had made no decision, the question of hiring Negroes had come up and it was left solely to the manager's decision. The manager thought most Negroes were dishonest and untrustworthy, etc. And thus the Christian church joins hands with trades unions and a large public opinion to force Negroes into idleness and crime.

Sometimes Negroes, by special influence, as has been pointed out before, secure good positions; then there are other cases where colored men have by sheer merit and pluck secured positions. In all these cases, however, they are liable to lose their places through no fault of their own and primarily on account of their Negro blood. It may be that at first their Negro descent is not known, or other causes may operate; in all cases the Negro's tenure of office is insecure:

A____ worked in a large tailor's establishment on Third Street for three weeks. His work was acceptable. Then it became known he was colored, and he was discharged as the other tailors refused to work with him.

B____, a pressman, was employed on Twelfth street, but a week later was discharged when they knew he was colored; he then worked as a door-boy for five years, and finally got another job in a Jewish shop as pressman.

C____ was nine years a painter in Stewart's Furniture Factory, until Stewart failed four years ago. Has applied repeatedly, but could get no work on account of color. He now works as a night watchman on the streets for the city.

D____ was a stationary engineer; his employer died, and he has never been able to find another.

E____ was light in complexion and got a job as driver; he "kept his cap on," but when they found he was colored they discharged him.

F____ was one of many colored laborers at an ink factory. The heads of the firm died, and now whenever a Negro leaves a white man is put in his place.

G____ worked for a long time as a typesetter on Taggart's *Times*; when the paper changed hands he was discharged and has never been able to get another job; he is now a janitor.

H____ was a brickmason, but his employers finally refused to let him lay brick longer as his fellow workmen were all white; he is now a waiter.

L____ learned the trade of range-setting from his employer; the employer then refused him work and he went into business for himself; he has taught four apprentices.

M____ is a woman whose husband was janitor for a firm twenty years; when they moved to the new Betz Building they discharged him as all the janitors were white; after his death they could find no work for his boy.

N____ was a porter in a book store and rose to be head postmaster of a sub-station in Philadelphia which handles $250,000, it is said, a year; he was also at the head of a very efficient Bureau of Information in a large department store. Recently attempts have been made to displace him, for no specified fault but because "we want his place for another [white] man."

O____ is a well-known instance; an observer in 1898 wrote: "If any Philadelphian who is anxious to study the matter with his own eyes, will walk along South Eleventh street, from Chestnut down, and will note the most tasteful and enterprising stationery and periodical store along the way, it will pay him to enter it. On entering he will, according to his way of thinking, be pleased or grieved to see that it is conducted by Negroes. If the proprietor happens to be in he may know that this keen-looking pleasant young man was once assistant business manager of a large white religious newspaper in the city. A change of management led to his dismissal. No fault was found, his work was commended, but a white man was put into his place, and profuse apologies made.

"The clerk behind the counter is his sister; a neat lady-like woman, educated, and trained in stenography and typewriting. She could not find in

the city of Philadelphia, any one who had the slightest use for such a
colored woman.

"The result of this situation is this little store, which is remarkably
successful. The proprietor owns the stock, the store and the building.
This is one tale of its sort with a pleasant ending. Other tales are far
less pleasing."

Much discouragement results from the persistent refusal to promote
colored employes. The humblest white employe knows that the better he does
his work the more chance there is for him to rise in the business. The
black employe knows that the better he does his work the longer he may do it;
he cannot often hope for promotion. This makes much of the criticism aimed
against Negroes, because some of them want to refuse menial labor, lose
something of its point. If the better class of Negro boys could look on
such labor as a stepping-stone to something higher it would be different;
if they must view it as a lifework we cannot wonder at their hesitation:

A____ has been a porter at a great locomotive works for ten years. He
is a carpenter by trade and has picked up considerable knowledge of machinery;
he was formerly allowed to work a little as a machinist; now that is stopped
and he has never been promoted and probably never will be.

B____ has worked in a shop eight years and never been promoted from his
porter's position, although he is a capable man.

C____ is a porter; he has been in a hardware store six years; he is
bright and has repeatedly been promised advancement but has never got it.

D____ was for seven years in a gang of porters in a department store,
and part of the time acted as foreman. He had a white boy under him who
disliked him; eventually the boy was promoted but he remained a porter.
Finally the boy became his boss and discharged him.

E____, a woman, worked long in a family of lawyers; a white lad went
into their office as office-boy and came to be a member of the firm; she
had a smart, ambitious son and asked for any sort of office work for him--
anything in which he could hope for promotion. "Why don't you make him a
waiter?" they asked.

F____ has for twenty-one years driven for a lumber firm; speaks German
and is very useful to them, but they have never promoted him.

G____ was a porter; he begged for a chance to work up, offering to do
clerical work for nothing, but was refused. White companions were repeatedly
promoted over his head. He has been a porter seventeen years.

H____ was a servant in the family of one of the members of a large dry
goods firm; he was so capable that the employer sent him down to the store
for a place which the manager very reluctantly gave him. He rose to be
registering clerk in the delivering department where he worked fourteen years
and his work was commended. Recently without notice or complaint he was
changed to run an elevator at the same wages. He thinks that pressure from
other members of the firm made him lose his work.

Once in awhile there are exceptions to this rule. The Pennsylvania
Railroad has promoted one bright and persistent porter to a clerkship, which
he has held for years. He had, however, spent his life hunting chances for
promotion and had been told "You have ability enough, George, if you were not
colored____."

There is much discrimination against Negroes in wages. The Negroes have
fewer chances for work, have been used to low wages, and consequently the
first thought that occurs to the average employer is to give a Negro less
than he would offer a white man for the same work. This is not universal,
but it is widespread. In domestic service of the ordinary sort there is no
difference, because the wages are a matter of custom. When it comes to
waiters, butlers and coachmen, however, there is considerable difference made;
while white coachmen receive from $50-$75, the Negroes do not get usually
more than $30-$60. Negro hotel waiters get from $18-$20, while whites receive $20-$30. Naturally when a hotel manager replaces $20 men with $30 men
he may expect, outside any question of color, better service.

In ordinary work the competition forces down the wages outside mere
race reasons, though the Negro is the greatest sufferer; this is especially
the case in laundry work. "I've counted as high as seven dozen pieces in
that washing," said a weary black woman, "and she pays me only $1.25 a week
for it." Persons who throw away $5 a week on gew-gaws will often haggle over
twenty-five cents with a washerwoman. There are, however, notable exceptions

to these cases, where good wages are paid to persons who have long worked for the same family.

Very often if a Negro is given a chance to work at a trade his wages are cut down for the privilege. This gives the workingman's prejudice additional intensity:

A____got a job formerly held by a white porter; the wages were reduced from $12 to $8.

B____worked for a firm as china packer, and they said he was the best packer they had. He, however received but $6 a week while the white packers received $12.

C____has been porter and assistant shipping clerk in an Arch street store for five years. He receives $6 a week and whites get $8 for the same work.

D____is a stationary engineer; he learned his trade with this firm and has been with them ten years. Formerly he received $9 a week, now $10.50; whites get $12 for the same work.

E____is a stationary engineer and has been in his place three years. He receives but $9 a week.

F____works with several other Negroes with a firm of electrical engineers. The white laborers receive $2 a day: "We've got to be glad to get $1.75."

G____was a carpenter, but could get neither sufficient work nor satisfactory wages. For a job on which he received $15 week, his white successor got $18.

H____, a cementer, receives $1.75 a day; white workers get $2-$3. He has been promised more next fall.

I____, a plasterer, has worked for one boss twenty-seven years. Regular plasterers get $4 or more a day; he does the same work, but cannot join the union and is paid as a laborer--$2.50 a day.

J____works as a porter in a department store; is married, and receives $8 a week. "They pay the same to white unmarried shop-girls, who stand a chance to be promoted."

3. If a Negro enters some line of employment in which people are not used to seeing him, he suffers from an assumption that he is unfit for the work. It is reported that a Chestnut street firm once took a Negro shop girl, but the protests of their customers were such that they had to dismiss her. A great many merchants hesitate to advance Negroes lest they should lose custom. Negro merchants who have attempted to start business in the city at first encounter much difficulty from this prejudice:

A____has a bakery; white people sometimes enter and finding Negroes in charge abruptly leave.

B____is a baker and had a shop some years on Vine street, but prejudice against him barred him from gaining much custom.

C____is a successful expressman with a large business; he is sometimes told by persons that they prefer to patronize white expressmen.

D____is a woman and keeps a hair store on South street. Customers sometimes enter, look at her, and leave.

E____is a music teacher on Lombard street. Several white people have entered and seeing him, said: "Oh! I thought you were white--excuse me!" or "I'll call again!"

Even among the colored people themselves some prejudice of this sort is met. Once a Negro physician could not get the patronage of Negroes because they were not used to the innovation. Now they have a large part of the Negro patronage. The Negro merchant, however, still lacks the full confidence of his own people though this is slowly growing. It is one of the paradoxes of this question to see a people so discriminated against sometimes add to their misfortunes by discriminating against themselves. They themselves, however, are beginning to recognize this.

4. The chief discrimination against Negroes in expenditure is in the matter of rents. There can be no reasonable doubt but that Negroes pay excessive rents:

A____paid $13 a month where the preceding white family had paid $10.

B____paid $16; "heard that former white family paid $12."

C____paid $25; "heard that former white family paid $20.

D____paid $12; neighbors say that former white family paid $9.

E____ paid $25, instead of $18.

F____ paid $12, instead of $10.

G____ the Negro inhabitants of the whole street pay $12 to $14 and the whites $9 and $10. The houses are all alike.

H____, whites on this street pay $15-$18; Negroes pay $18-$21.

Not only is there this pretty general discrimination in rent but agents and owners will not usually repair the houses of the blacks willingly or improve them. In addition to this agents and owners in many sections utterly refuse to rent to Negroes on any terms. Both these sorts of discrimination are easily defended from a merely business point of view; public opinion in the city is such as the presence of even a respectable colored family in a block will affect its value for renting or sale; increased rent to Negroes is therefore a sort of insurance, and refusal to rent a device for money-getting. The indefensible cruelty lies with those classes who refuse to recognize the right of respectable Negro citizens to respectable houses. Real estate agents also increase prejudice by refusing to discriminate between different classes of Negroes. A quiet Negro family moves into a street. The agent finds no great objection, and allows the next empty house to go to any Negro who applies. This family may disgrace and scandalize the neighborhood and make it harder for decent families to find homes.

In the last fifteen years, however, public opinion has so greatly changed in this matter that we may expect much in the future. Today the Negro population is more widely scattered over the city than ever before. At the same time it remains true that as a rule they must occupy the worst houses of the districts where they live. The advance made has been a battle for the better class of Negroes. As ex-Minister to Hayti moved to the northwestern part of the city and his white neighbors insulted him, barricaded their steps against him, and tried in every way to make him move; today he is honored and respected in the whole neighborhood. Many such cases have occurred; in others the result was different. An estimable young Negro, just married, moved with his bride into a little street. The neighborhood rose in arms and besieged the tenant and the landlord so relentlessly that the landlord leased the house and compelled the young couple to move within a month. One of the bishops of the A.M.E. Church recently moved into the newly purchased Episcopal residence on Belmont avenue, and his neighbors have barricaded their porches against his view.

5. The chief discrimination against Negro children is in the matter of educational facilities. Prejudice here works to compel colored children to attend certain schools where most Negro children go, or to keep them out of private and higher schools.

A____ tried to get her little girl into the kindergarten nearest to her, at Fifteenth and Locust. The teachers wanted her to send it down across Broad to the kindergarten chiefly attended by colored children and much further away from its home. This journey was dangerous for the child, but the teachers refused to receive it for six months, until the authorities were appealed to.

In transfers from schools Negroes have difficulty in getting accommodations; only within comparatively few years have Negroes been allowed to complete the course at the High and Normal Schools without difficulty. Earlier than that the University of Pennsylvania refused to let Negroes sit in the Auditorium and listen to lectures, much less to be students. Within two or three years a Negro student had to fight his way through a city dental school with his fists, and was treated with every indignity. Several times Negroes have been asked to leave schools of stenography, etc., on account of their fellow students. In 1893 a colored woman applied at Temple College, a church institution, for admission and was refused and advised to go elsewhere. The college then offered scholarships to churches, but would not admit applicants from colored churches. Two years later the same woman applied again. The faculty declared that they did not object, but that the students would; she persisted and was finally admitted with evident reluctance.

It goes without saying that most private schools, music schools, etc., will not admit Negroes and in some cases have insulted applicants.

Such is the tangible form of Negro prejudice in Philadelphia. Possibly some of the particular cases cited can be proven to have had extenuating circumstances unknown to the investigator; at the same time many not cited would

be just as much in point. At any rate no one who has with any diligence
studied the situation of the Negro in the city can long doubt but that his
opportunities are limited and his ambition circumscribed about as has been
shown. There are of course numerous exceptions, but the mass of the Negroes
have been so often refused openings and discouraged in efforts to better
their condition that many of them say, as one said, "I never apply--I know
it is useless." Beside these tangible and measurable forms there aré deeper
and less easily described results of the attitude of the white population
toward the Negroes: a certain manifestation of a real or assumed aversion,
a spirit of ridicule or patronage, a vindictive hatred in some, absolute
indifference in others; all this of course does not make much difference to
the mass of the race, but it deeply wounds the better classes, the very
classes who are attaining to that to which we wish the mass to attain. Notwithstanding all this, most Negroes would patiently await the effect of time
and common sense on such prejudice did it not today touch them in matters of
life and death, threaten their homes, their food, their children, their
hopes. And the result of this is bound to be increased crime, inefficiency
and bitterness.

It would, of course, be idle to assert that most of the Negro crime was
caused by prejudice; the violent economic and social changes which the last
fifty years have brought to the American Negro, the sad social history that
preceded these changes, have all contributed to unsettle morals and pervert
talents. Nevertheless it is certain that Negro prejudice in cities like
Philadelphia has been a vast factor in aiding and abetting all other causes
which impel a half-developed race to recklessness and excess. Certainly a
great amount of crime can be without doubt traced to the discrimination
against Negro boys and girls in the matter of employment. Or to put it
differently, Negro prejudice costs the city something.

The connection of crime and prejudice is, on the other hand, neither
simple nor direct. The boy who is refused promotion in his job does not go
out and snatch somebody's pocketbook. Conversely the loafers at Twelfth and
Kater streets, and the thugs in the county prison are not usually graduates
of high schools who have been refused work. The connections are much more
subtle and dangerous; it is the atmosphere of rebellion and discontent that
unrewarded merit and reasonable but unsatisfied ambition make. The social
environment of excuse, listless despair, careless indulgence and lack of
inspiration to work is the growing force that turns black boys and girls into
gamblers, prostitutes and rascals. And this social environment has been built
up slowly out of the disappointments of deserving men and the sloth of the
unawakened. How long can a city say to a part of its citizens, "It is useless to work; it is fruitless to deserve well of men; education will gain
you nothing but disappointment and humiliation?" How long can a city teach
its black children that the road to success is to have a white face? How
long can a city do this and escape the inevitable penalty?

For thirty years and more Philadelphia has said to its black children:
"Honesty, efficiency and talent have little to do with your success; if you
work hard, spend little and are good you may earn your bread and butter at
those sorts of work which we frankly confess we despise; if you are dishonest
and lazy, the State will furnish your bread free." Thus the class of Negroes
which the prejudices of the city have distinctly encouraged is that of the
criminal, the lazy and the shiftless; for them the city teems with institutions
and charities; for them there is succor and sympathy; for them Philadelphians
are thinking and planning; but for the educated and industrious young colored
man who wants work and not platitudes, wages and not alms, just rewards and
not sermons--for such colored men Philadelphia apparently has no use.

What then do such men do? What becomes of the graduates of the many
schools of the city? The answer is simple: Most of those who amount to anything leave the city, the others take what they can get for a livelihood.
Let us for a moment glance at the statistics of three colored schools:

1. The O. V. Catto Primary School.
2. The Robert Vaux Grammar School.
3. The Institute for Colored Youth.

There attended the Catto school, 1867-97, 5915 pupils. Of these there
were promoted from the full course, 653. 129 of the latter are known to be in

positions of higher grade; or taking out 93 who are still in school, there
remain 36 as follows: 18 teachers, 10 clerks, 2 physicians, 2 engravers,
2 printers, 1 lawyer and 1 mechanic.

The other 524 are for the most part in service, laborers and house-
wives. Of the 36 more successful ones fully half are at work outside of the
city.

Of the Vaux school there were, 1877-89, 76 graduates. Of these there
are 16 unaccounted for; the rest are:

Teachers	27	Barbers	4
Musicians	5	Clerks	3
Merchants	3	Physician	1
Mechanic	1	Deceased	8
Clergymen	3	Housewives	5
	47		

From one-half to two-thirds of these have been compelled to leave the
city in order to find work; one, the artist, Tanner, whom France recently
honored, could not in his native land much less in his native city find room
for his talents.[142] He taught school in Georgia in order to earn money enough
to go abroad.

The Institute of Colored Youth has had 340 graduates, 1856-97; 57 of
these are dead. Of the 283 remaining 91 are accounted for. The rest are:

Teachers	117	Electrical Engineer	1
Lawyers	4	Professor	1
Physicians	4	Government clerks	5
Musicians	4	Merchants	7
Dentists	2	Mechanics	5
Clergymen	2	Clerks	23
Nurses	2	Teaching of cooking	1
Editor	1	Dressmakers	4
Civil Engineer	1	Students	7
			192

Here, again, nearly three-fourths of the graduates who have amounted to
anything have had to leave the city for work. The civil engineer, for instance, tried in vain to get work here and finally had to go to New Jersey
to teach.

There have been 9, possibly 11, colored graduates of the Central High
School. These are engaged as follows:

Grocer	1	Porter	1
Clerks in service of the city	2	Butler	1
Caterer	1	Unknown	3 or 5

It is high time that the best conscience of Philadelphia awakened to her
duty; her Negro citizens are here to remain; they can be made good citizens
or burdens to the community; if we want them to be sources of wealth and
power not of poverty and weakness then they must be given employment according to their ability and encouraged to train that ability and increase
their talents by the hope of reasonable reward. To educate boys and girls
and then refuse them work is to train loafers and rogues.

From another point of view it could be argued with much cogency that the
cause of economic stress, and consequently of crime, was the recent incon-
siderate rush of Negroes into cities; and that the unpleasant results of this
migration, while deplorable, will nevertheless serve to check the movement
of Negroes to cities and keep them in the country where their chance for
economic development is widest. This argument loses much of its point from
the fact that it is the better class of educated Philadelphia-born Negroes
who have the most difficulty in obtaining employment. The new immigrant
fresh from the South is much more apt to obtain work suitable for him than
the black boy born here and trained in efficiency. Nevertheless it is undoubtedly true that the recent migration has both directly and indirectly increased crime and competition. How is this movement to be checked? Much

can be done by correcting misrepresentations as to the opportunities of
city life made by designing employment bureaus and thoughtless persons; a
more strict surveillance of criminals might prevent the influx of undesirable elements. Such efforts, however, would not touch the main stream of
immigration. Back of that stream is the world-wide desire in the world, to
escape the choking narrowness of the plantation, and the lawless repression
of the village, in the South. It is a search for better opportunities of
living, and as such it must be discouraged and repressed with great care
and delicacy, if at all. The real movement of reform is the raising of
economic standards and increase of economic opportunity in the South. Mere
land and climate without law and capital and skill, will not develop a
country. When Negroes in the South have a larger opportunity to work, accumulate property, be protected in life and limb, and encourage pride and
self-respect in their children, there will be a diminution in the stream of
immigrants to Northern cities. At the same time if those cities practice
industrial exclusion against these immigrants to such an extent that they
are forced to become paupers, loafers and criminals, they can scarcely complain of conditions in the South. Northern cities should not, of course,
seek to encourage and invite a poor quality of labor, with low standards of
life and morals. The standards of wages and respectability should be kept
up; but when a man reaches those standards in skill, efficiency and decency
no question of color should, in a civilized community, debar him from an
equal chance with his peers in earning a living.

     Benevolence.--In the attitude of Philadelphia toward the Negro may be
traced the same contradictions so often apparent in social phenomena; prejudice and apparent dislike conjoined with widespread and deep sympathy;
there can, for instance, be no doubt of the sincerity of the efforts put
forth by Philadelphians to help' the Negroes. Much of it is unsystematic
and ill-directed and yet it has behind it a broad charity and a desire to
relieve suffering and distress. The same Philadelphian who would not let a
Negro work in his store or mill, will contribute handsomely to relieve Negroes
in poverty and distress. There are in the city the following charities
exclusively designed for Negroes:
     Home for Aged and Infirm Colored Persons, Belmont and Girard avenues.

W. E. Burghardt DuBois, *The Philadelphia Negro:A Social Study* (Philadelphia,
1899), pp. 322-55. Footnotes have been eliminated from the' text by the
editors.

NOTES AND INDEX

1   Samuel Gompers (1850-1924) was born in London, England, immigrated to the United States in 1863, and settled in New York City. A cigar-maker, he joined the Cigarmakers' International Union, and rose through its leadership ranks to become first vice-president from 1896-1924. He helped organize the Federation of Organized Labor Unions, and in 1886 was a founder of the American Federation of Labor. Gompers served as president of the AFL, with the exception of 1895, from 1886 to 1924. His importance as a shaping influence on the American labor movement can hardly be overemphasized. Distrustful of industrial unionism, he ignored unskilled workers and stressed organization of the crafts. Stressing business unionism, craft autonomy, and voluntarism, Gompers opposed eight hour laws, unemployment compensation, independent political action, com-pulsory arbitration, and other policies more radical labor leaders con-sidered of prime importance. Initially he refused to support discrimi-nation against black workers, but gradually yielded to the enormous pressures of "Jim Crow." Gompers' *Seventy Years of Life and Labor* (2 vols.) was published in 1925.

2   Andrew Furuseth (1854-1938) was born in Norway and became a seaman. During the 1880s he shipped out of ports along the west coast of the United States. In 1887 he became an officer of the Sailors' Union of the Pacific. During the 1890s he served in Washington, D.C., as legislative lobbyist for seamen's unions as well as the American Federation of Labor. His more than twenty-year struggle for legal protection of American seamen resulted in the La Follette Seamen's Act of 1915. From 1908 until his death in 1938, Furuseth served as president of the International Seamen's Union.
     Denis A. Hayes was an official in the Glass Blowers' Association, and replaced P. J. McGuire on the AFL executive council.
     John F. Tobin, a socialist, was head of the Shoemakers' Union.

3   Eugene V. Debs (1855-1926) of Terre Haute, Indiana, worked as a locomotive fireman and became involved in local union affairs. In 1878 he became associate editor and, two years later, editor of the *Firemen's Magazine*, organ of the Brotherhood of Locomotive Firemen. Debs also served as secretary and treasurer of BLF. Resigning in 1892, he launched the American Railway Union in 1893, which was organized as an all-inclu-sive union for railroad workers. His leadership of the ARU resulted in his imprisonment during the famous 1893 Pullman strike. Debs became a socialist shortly thereafter and played an important role in the form-ation of the Social Democratic Party in 1897. In 1905 he helped found the Industrial Workers of the World, but resigned over an ideological dispute. During World War I, he was convicted for violating the Espionage Act and began a ten-year sentence in 1918, but President Harding pardoned him in 1921. Debs served one year in the Indiana state legislature dur-ing the 1880s, and ran as presidential candidate on the Socialist ticket in 1900, 1904, 1912, and 1920.

4   H. W. Sherman served as third president of the International Brother-hood of Electrical Workers, 1894-97.

5   For the New Orleans General Strike, see pp. 14-24.

6   For the Louisville convention, see pp. 5-6.

7   The article referred to probably was "The Best Free Labor in the World," *Southern Estates Farm Magazine* (January 1898): 496-98.

8   Booker Taliaferro Washington (1856-1915) was born a slave in Virginia. His mother moved to West Virginia, near Charleston, after freedom came, where Washington worked in a mine. With but little formal education, he set out across the Allegheny Mountains to attend Hampton Institute,

an industrial education institution. Washington became a prize pupil,
and after graduating in 1875, he continued to teach at the school until
1881. In that year he was chosen to organize Tuskegee Institute in
Alabama, which he fashioned after Hampton. From Tuskegee Washington
built a political power base that led him to become the most prominent
Afro-American of his day. Washington was catapulted to fame by his
Atlanta Exposition address of 1895, which articulated a race relations
policy of acquiescence to segregation, and abdication of political rights
for economic self-development. White southerners, who were putting the
final touches on the "Jim Crow" system just then, were instantly captured
by Washington's message. This posture won Washington extraordinary gifts
from philanthropists, and even grants from southern state legislatures
to erect and operate vocational schools for blacks. Washington became
the chief power broker for the race between 1895 and 1915 when he died.
Of his numerous books, *Up From Slavery,* his autobiography, is the most
popular.

8   The Alabama State Federation of Labor, formed in 1900, included delegates from black unions and central labor councils during the first five
years of its existence, and each year two or three Negroes were among the
five vice-presidents elected. That attitude did not persist, however,
and the Federation was soon controlled by racist elements in the labor
movement.

9   See pp. 9-11.

10   Christopher Evans, President of District One Ohio Miners Amalgamated
Association during the Hocking strike of 1884-1885 (see note 47), was one
of the leading figures in the fledgling American labor movement. Born in
England in 1841, he immigrated to America in 1869, and settled in the
coal mining town of Straitsville, Ohio, in 1877. One of the founders of
the United Mine Workers of America, during the 1890s Evans served as
national secretary of the union under John McBride (see note 17). He
also had been prominent in the Federation of Organized Trades and Labor
Unions (1881-86). After that organization became the American Federation
of Labor, Evans became its secretary from 1889 to 1895. Well known to
all trade unionists, Evans was genuinely popular in the coal fields
throughout his career. He became the official historian of the UMW, and
wrote a two-volume *History of the United Mine Workers of America,* (n.p.,
1920).

11   For James E. Porter, see also pp. 47, 48.
         For John M. Callaghan, see also pp. 42-49. Some authors have used the
"Callahan" for Callaghan, the English spelling. The editors have retained
the name as it appeared in the documents.

12   The Noble Order of the Knights of Labor (K. of L.) is examined in
Vol. III of this series.

13   Central labor unions were organized in many American cities during
the 1880s. Established by the Socialist Labor Party, these city labor
bodies attempted to affiliate local labor unions and to stir public
interest in issues of concern to working people.

14   Peter James McGuire (1852-1906) of New York City worked as an apprentice wood joiner as a youth, became involved in local union politics, and
served as an organizer for the Social Democratic party during the 1870s.
After moving to Missouri, McGuire was instrumental in the establishment of
the Missouri Bureau of Labor Statistics. McGuire organized the carpenters
of St. Louis, and in 1881, inspired the meeting of twelve carpenters'
unions in Chicago, where they formed the United Brotherhood of Carpenters
and Joiners. McGuire was elected to head the new union, and also edited
The Carpenter, its official organ. Through his efforts, legislation was
passed in 1894 making Labor Day a national holiday. Also one of the
founders of the AFL, McGuire became its first secretary, and later a
vice president.

15   Augustine McCraith, secretary of the AFL in 1895, did not run for
reelection in 1896. The probable reason for his decision was his apparent personality conflict with Samuel Gompers (see note 1), president
of the organization. At the 1896 convention, McCraith charged Gompers
with violating the nonpartisan policy of the AFL by endorsing Democratic
party candidates during the general elections, but the convention supported Gompers. McCraith was replaced by Frank Morrison who served in
that office for the next forty years (see note 33). In 1901 Gompers
described McCraith as "difficult personally [but] so far as financial
honesty is concerned, cannot be questioned. He was also a competent
official. He did seek to impose his theories upon the movement, regardless of the attitude of the organization. It was this which caused
friction between him and me. He seemed to suspect everyone of wrong-
doing who did not agree entirely with him in his theories of philosophical anarchy. This, with an additional failing of overweening con-
ceit which prompted him to imagine that he 'knew it all and that there
was no depth' to any one whose studies and convictions of the social
problem did not coincide absolutely with his, was his gravest fault.
This fault made it exceedingly difficult for any one to get along with
him, and which brought upon his retirement." Gompers to James E. Bell,
January 31, 1901, cited in Philip Taft, *The A.F. of L. in the Time of
Gompers* (New York, 1957), p. 131.

16   "Talking label" refers to the attempt by organized labor to label
goods produced by union workers. In this way union men could increase
their ability to mount a successful boycott of non-union companies.

17   I.M.U. refers to the International Machinists' Union. See pp. 49-57.
        John McBride (1854-1917), born in Wayne County, Ohio, went to work
in the coal mines when he was still a child. Active in the Ohio Miners'
Amalgamated Association, he was elected president of that organization
in 1883. That same year he won a seat in the Ohio legislature, and was
reelected to another term in 1885. In 1883 he also organized the Amalgamated Association of Miners of the United States, and after its quick
destruction by a long strike, in 1885 he helped found and became president of the National Federation of Miners and Mine Laborers. McBride
was instrumental in uniting the major mine unions into the United Mine
Workers of America in 1890. He was elected president in 1892, and
served in that post until 1895 when he resigned to be president of the
AFL for one year. He lost his bid for reelection to Samuel Gompers by
only eighteen votes. In 1896 he purchased the *Columbus Record,* which
he edited until 1917 when he moved to Arizona for reasons of health.

18   See also pp. 21-22, 47-48.

19   D. Douglas Wilson (d. 1915) was editor of the *Machinists' Monthly
Journal* from 1895 until his death in 1915. As editor, he turned the
Journal into one of the best trades publications of the time.

20   James P. O'Connell (1858-1936) became a machinist's apprentice at age
sixteen in Oil City, Pennsylvania, where he subsequently organized a local
of the International Association of Machinists, Knights of Labor Lodge
113. In 1893 he was elected to the chief administrative post in the
IAM, a position he held until 1911. O'Connell served on the AFL executive
council from 1895 to 1918, and as president of the AFL metal trades
department from 1911 to 1934. A close associate of Samuel Gompers, he
was a conservative, "pure and simple" unionist.

21   James Duncan (1857-1928) was born in Scotland, but immigrated to the
United States in 1880. Active in the Granite Cutters' National Union in
Baltimore, Maryland, Duncan was elected president of the GCNU in 1885,
and later became second and then first vice-president of the AFL in
1894 and 1900 respectively. He also served as a labor representative
with the American delegation at the Paris Conference in 1919.

22   Thomas J. Morgan (1847-1912) was born in England and immigrated to
Chicago Illinois. Between 1875 and 1895 he worked as a machinist in
the shops of the Illinois Central Railroad, and eventually graduated
from Chicago Law College. During the 1870s Morgan was one of the
founders of the Chicago Trade and Labor Assembly, from which he and
other radicals split in 1884 to form the Chicago Central Labor Union.
He was instrumental in the movement which ended in the creation of the
Illinois Bureau of Labor Statistics in 1879. Morgan advocated public
ownership of all means of production and distribution, and was active
in the Social Democratic Party (Socialist) making several unsuccessful
bids for public office on that ticket.

23   William J. Bowen (1868-1948) of Albany, New York, became a bricklayer's apprentice and eventually became president of Local 6 of the
Bricklayers' Masons' and Plasterers' International Union in 1895. Rising through the ranks, Bowen was elected president of the BMPIU in 1904,
a position he held until 1928, and was responsible for its affiliation
with the AFL in 1916.

24   The Colored Screwmen's Association No. 2, of Galveston, Texas, grew
out of the Cotton Jammers' Association. Founded in 1879, the Jammers
consisted of Negro longshoremen who were prevented from entering the
screwmen's trade by the all-white Screwmen's Benevolent Association.
The Jammers unsuccessfully attempted to gain contracts on some of the
company wharves. No. 2 was organized by a local black leader, Norris
Wright Cuney, in March 1883, and gained its first contract the following
month. The new contract precipitated a strike by white screwmen, the
immediate outcome of which was an agreement between the black and white
screwmen to share the work available.

25   The Pullman Palace Car Company was founded in 1867 by George M. Pullman. The company built sleeping cars for long-distance railroad passengers, offering them the finest luxury and personal service possible.
Working for George Pullman had its drawbacks, however, for employees
found the feudal paternalism he exercised over them an intolerable burden.
Employees were forced to live in overcrowded tenements in the company
town of Pullman, Illinois (which excluded blacks), compelled to pay
exorbitant rents, even more exorbitant utility rates, and were subjected
to innumerable shop abuses. When the Panic of 1893 (see note 55) brought
wholesale dismissals and wage cuts, while rents and other living costs
remained high, workers became restive. The 1894 strike against Pullman
was organized by the American Railway Union, led by Eugene V. Debs (see
note 3), and was one of the most serious of the decade.

26   The American Railway Union, founded by Eugene Debs (see note 3) in
1893, attempted to organize all railroad workers, skilled and unskilled,
into one industrial organization. Except for blacks (Debs opposed this
exclusion on the floor of the convention but was overruled), all railroad workers were accepted as members, and the dues were set low enough
($1 per year) so that anyone could afford to join. The ARU grew to about
150,000 within six months. A depression year, 1894 was the year in which
the ARU saw glorious victory on the one hand, and devastating defeat on
the other. In April 1894, James J. Hill slashed wages on the Great
Northern Railroad, and Debs led his union out on strike. The strike was
submitted to arbitration and the workmen won most of their demands. After
the Pullman Company (see note 25) followed Hill's example and cut wages,
without lowering other costs in its company town of Pullman, Illinois,
Pullman workers went on strike and urged Debs to help. This request
raised a serious question for the ARU leadership. There was little sympathy for losing the recently won gains from Hill, but the union would
also lose face among the workers if it did not come to their assistance.
The quandary was settled when the railroad companies began to dismiss
switchmen who refused to handle Pullman cars, and the stoppage was
called. Eventually, the strike was defeated by the opposition of the
Railway Brotherhoods, the AFL, the General Managers Association, and the

federal government. The other railroad unions naturally resented the
burgeoning presence of the ARU, and Gompers opposed the ARU as "dual
unionism." The Managers Association, composed of representatives of
twenty-four railroads, orchestrated the firing of participating workers,
and the federal government under orders of President Grover Cleveland
and Attorney General Richard Olney (see notes 27, 28) ordered federal
troops into Chicago to maintain order, although it had never been
threatened.

27   John Peter Altgeld (1847-1902) was born in Nassau and came to the
United States with his parents while still an infant. He grew to
maturity in Richmond County, Ohio, with scant education. Altgeld drifted west in 1869, working variously as a laborer, school teacher, and
law student. He was quick to learn, however, and after serving in minor
political posts, he was elected to the superior court of Cook County
(Chicago), Illinois. By the time he resigned in 1891, he was chief
justice of the court. Altgeld came to have great influence among
Illinois Democrats, and in 1892 he was their successful candidate for
governor. Altgeld's political reputation in American history is fixed
to his pardon of the three Haymarket anarchists (see note 94) who had
been convicted of murder in 1886; four of their colleagues already had
been executed. Altgeld came to believe that the jury had been packed,
the judge prejudiced, and that the conviction of the anarchists was
miscarriage of justice. Historians have sided with Altgeld, but his
pardon created a furor. He was renominated for governor in 1896, but
lost to the Republican candidate, John R. Tanner (see note 95).
      For biographical background on President Grover Cleveland, see Vol.
III, note 61.

28   Richard Olney (1835-1917), a native of Massachusetts, graduated from
Brown University and Harvard Law School before he began to practice law
in Boston in 1859. He remained aloof from politics until 1893, when
Grover Cleveland selected him for attorney-general. When the American
Railway Union went on strike in 1894, he charged the union with obstruction of the mails, and ordered deputy marshals to protect the trains.
Moreover, he obtained restraining orders from federal judges in Chicago
prohibiting the activities of the strikers. Federal troops were sent to
Chicago as well, and Eugene V. Debs was arrested. During the appeals
which ensued Olney learned something about the basic grievances involved,
became more sensitive to them, and afterwards supported the rights of
organized labor. When Walter Q. Gresham died, Cleveland chose Olney to
fill the office of secretary of state in 1895. Olney retired from public
life in 1897, and returned to his private practice.

29   "Mr. Jeff Davis & Co." is an obvious reference to Jefferson Davis and
the Confederate States of America, of which he was president. For biographical background on Davis, see Vol. I, note 53.

30   Frank P. Sargent (d. 1908) was born in Vermont, but moved to Arizona
for reasons of poor health. After serving in the United States Cavalry,
he went to work for the Southern Pacific Railroad. Active in the Brotherhood of Locomotive Firemen and Enginemen, he was elected vice-grand
master in 1883, and then grand master from 1885 to 1902. Sargent served
on the United States Industrial Commission, before being appointed United
States Commissioner General of Immigration in 1902. He also was a member
of the National Civic Federation.

31   S. E. Wilkinson was president of the Brotherhood of Railway Trainmen
from 1885 to 1895.
      F. S. Sweeney was one of the early leaders of the Switchmen's Union
of North America. Its chief rival was the Railway Trainmen, which was
recognized by the AFL as the only spokesman for yard workers within the
organized labor movement. After years of considerable friction, the
Switchmen were absorbed into the Trainmen Brotherhood in 1922.

32   William D. Mahon (1861-1949), born in Athens County, Ohio, worked
in the Hocking Valley coal mines before moving to Columbus in 1888.
There he found employment with the city streetcar company, and assisted
in organizing the local transit union. In addition to holding the
presidency of his local union, Mahon served two terms as president of
the Columbus Trades and Labor Council, and after helping found the
Amalgamated Association of Street, Electric Railway and Motor Coach
Employees of America, he became its president in 1893. Mahon affiliated
AASERMCE with the American Federation of Labor that same year. During
his long career, Mahon served in numerous industrial relations capacities
as a representative of organized labor, and served in the administrations
of Woodrow Wilson and Franklin Roosevelt. Few labor leaders can match
Mahon's longevity of fifty-two years at the head of a national union.

33   Frank Morrison (1859-1949), born in Canada, immigrated to the United
States in 1873. A printer, he worked for various newspapers as a compositor and was active in the International Typographical Union, Chicago
Local 16. He attended Lake Forest University Law School in 1893 and
1894. In 1896 Morrison was an ITU delegate to the AFL Convention, and
the following year was elected secretary of the AFL. He served in that
office for the next forty years with distinction as an administrator.

34   Peter M. Arthur (1831-1903) immigrated to the United States from
Scotland in 1842, and settled in Schenectady, New York. Beginning as an
engine wiper in 1894, Arthur quickly rose to become a locomotive engineer
on the New York Central Railroad. A member of the Brotherhood of Locomotive Engineers, he was elected grand chief engineer (president) in 1874
and held that post until his death in 1903. A very conservative trade
unionist, he refused to affiliate with either the Knights of Labor or the
American Federation of Labor.
        The B.L.E. refers to the Brotherhood of Locomotive Engineers, O.R.C.
to the Organization of Railway Companies, B.L.F. to the Brotherhood of
Locomotive Firemen, B.R.T. to the Brotherhood of Railway Trainmen, O.R.T.
to the Organization of Railway Trainmen.

35   William Samuel Carter (1859-1923) was born in Austin, Texas, attended
the Agricultural and Mechanical College of Texas for two years, and then
went to work as a fireman on the railroad in 1879. For the next fourteen
years he worked as fireman and engineer on several railroads in the
Southwest. Active in the Brotherhood of Locomotive Firemen and Enginemen, he became the editor of the union's official organ in 1894, was
elected secretary-treasurer of the BLFE in 1904, and served as president
from 1909 to 1922.

36   The AFL prohibited an affiliated union to have constitutional restrictions on race. Unions could avoid the restriction, however by
placing it in the ritual for membership. Thus they could affiliate with
the AFL and still bar black members.

37   For the Industrial Commission, see the Introduction to Part VI.

38   David Hume (1711-1776) was born in Edinburgh, Scotland. His father
was an attorney, and his mother was the daughter of the president of the
College of Justice. Hume entered Edinburgh University in 1723, but left
in 1726 to read law. Privately, Hume continued to study philosophy, and
published his first work in 1739. After several years of financial strain,
and disappointment as a writer, Hume's reputation as an historian and
philosopher began its ascent in 1748 with the publication of his numerous
books. A moral philosopher, he is known for his skepticism, empiricism,
and the application of inferential method to the study of human nature.

39   Communism as an ideology and social movement holds to the belief
that property ownership should rest with the community rather than individuals, and that the benefits of the economic system ought to be

distributed in such a way as to promote the common good. The modern
ideology is largely the work of Karl Marx. Although revised or elab-
orated upon by his followers, Marx argued that human society moves
through historical stages, which are distinguished by the mode of
economic production: 1) primitive communal society, 2) slavery, 3)
feudalism, 4) capitalism, 5) socialism.

Anarchism as a social philosophy was confined primarily to the
nineteenth century. According to the theory of social relations,
society should be controlled entirely by voluntary organizations without
coercive power, not by the state. Without coercion each individual will
achieve his greatest potential. The economic system under anarchism
would be one in which goods would be distributed without profit, and
all members of society have equal access to the means of production.
Some anarchists believed in nonviolence as a tactic, while others believed
in the efficacy of terror as a political tool.

Nihilism comes from the Latin noun *nihil*, meaning "nothing." More
particularly, it usually refers to a phase of the Russian revolutionary
agitation against Czar Alexander II of the last half of the nineteenth
century. It was used as a perjorative term to describe those who articulated an ideal of personal independence as opposed to the archaic
tyranny of the state and its stifling of human behavior. Eventually,
they became apostles of self-sacrifice for the benefit of the poor.
Persecution pushed them further toward anarchism, but they usually shrunk
from violence as a tool for toppling governments, and adhered to insistence upon an elected representative assembly.

Agrarianism probably refers to the political movement and ideology
espoused by spokesmen of the farmers' Alliances and the Populist Party
(see Vol. III, note 47).

40   See Jerome Dowd, "Cheap Labor in the South," *Gunton's Magazine*, 18
(February 1900): 113-21. The editor refutes Dowd's thesis on pages
121-30 in the same issue. Dowd was a professor in the department of
economics and sociology, Trinity College, North Carolina.

41   "Black marbles" is a reference to the practice of blackballing
applicants for membership in an organization.

42   R. L. Smith (b. 1861) left his native South Carolina and moved to
Texas in the late 1870s or early 1880s. A graduate of Atlanta University, Smith became the principal of Oakland Normal School (Colorado
County), in 1885. He also became an associate of Booker T. Washington,
and an ardent champion of black self-help. In 1889 he founded the
Farmers' Improvement Society, a self-help organization with a program
which called for: abolition of the crop mortgage credit system; improved
methods of farming; the formation of cooperatives; creation of insurance
funds; encouragement of home and land ownership. Serving in the Twenty-
third and Twenty-fourth legislatures, Smith was one of the last two blacks
who sat in that body during the social Reconstruction era.

43   The correct name is Edwin Markham, author of the poem, "The Man With
a Hoe."

44   The senator from South Carolina who admitted keeping Negroes from the
polls probably was Benjamin Tillman. For biographical background on
Tillman, see Vol. III, note 60.

45   There was a strike in 1898 where operatives threatened violence because of the hiring of black mill hands. Violence had occurred at Atlanta
cotton mills specifically, and southern mills generally when Negroes were
brought in as mill hands. When they worked in these mills it was usually
off the shop floor, or as clean-up men. See also, note 103.

46   For the most thorough study of Richard L. Davis to date, see Herbert
G. Gutman, "The Negro and the United Mine Workers of America: The Career
and Letters of Richard L. Davis, and Something of Their Meaning: 1890-

1900," in Julius Jacobson (ed.), *The Negro and the American Labor Movement* (Garden City, 1968), pp. 49-127.

47   Davis was referring to the Hocking Valley coal strike of 1884-1885, which erupted after years of hostility between miners and the mine owners. The strike was precipitated when the operators imposed sharp wage reductions from 80 cents to 60 cents per ton. On June 23, 1884, the long and bitter strike began involving 4,000 miners and helpers, forty-six mines, and lasted over nine months. Immigrants and a few blacks were imported to work some of the mines under protection of heavily armed guards. In the end, the miners inflicted considerable property damage, but nevertheless lost in a crushing defeat which destroyed the Ohio Miners' Amalgated Association. For a short study of this strike, see George B. Cotkin, "Strikebreakers, Evictions and Violence: Industrial Conflict in the Hocking Valley, 1884-1885," *Ohio History* 87 (Spring 1978): 140-50. For a study of an earlier strike in the valley, see Herbert G. Gutman, "Reconstruction in Ohio: Negroes in the Hocking Valley Coal Mines in 1873 and 1874," *Labor History*, 3 (Fall 1962): 243-64.

"Blacklegs" was a perjorative term for strikebreakers.

48   "Edmunds" was a misspelling of "Edmonds."

49   District 17 of the UMW included the state of West Virginia.

50   For "Brother Riley" see pp. 177-83.

51   In January, 1890, several rival miners' organizations met in Columbus, Ohio, and founded the United Mine Workers of America. During its formative years, the UMW competed with the dying Knights of Labor, which had organized a large number of coal miners into its National Trades Assembly 135. Despite the rivalry at official levels, rank-and-file workers themselves often made little distinction between the two groups. Some miners even maintained dual membership, although national union officials vigorously denounced this practice as "dual unionism." Riley apparently recognized that he would be addressing himself to "exclusive" as well as "dual" unionists, and in fact, possibly held dual membership himself.

52   In June 1882, 3,800 workers of the Carnegie steel mills at Homestead, Pennsylvania, went on strike over wages and working conditions. Henry Clay Frick, chairman of the board, hired 300 Pinkerton detectives to protect the strikebreakers he had hired to break the strike. As the detectives were being towed up the Monongahela River aboard barges, strikers fired on them, precipitating one of the gravest labor conflicts in American history. During the battle which ensued, three Pinkertons and ten strikers died, and a large but unknown number of men were wounded. When the tug pulled away stranding the Pinkertons, they surrendered to the strikers. The militia was sent in to restore order, but the strikers held out for several months. The ultimate failure of the strike devastated the 24,000 member Amalgamated Association of Iron and Steel Workers, and destroyed union organization in the steel industry until the 1930s.

53   John Nugent, president of UMW District 17 (West Virginia), was elected to the West Virginia state legislature during the 1906 election.

54   "Stanley's works" is a reference to the explorations and publications of Sir Henry Morton Stanley (1841-1904). Born in England, John Rowlands (his original name) immigrated to the United States in 1859. After the Civil War he became a reporter for the *New York Herald*. His most spectacular assignment was a search of central Africa for the lost missionary-explorer, Dr. David Livingstone, whom he found in 1871. He continued the explorations of Livingstone, and worked toward the creation of the Congo Free State. In 1895 he resumed his English citizenship, and was knighted in 1899. Among his most popular writings are *How I Found Livingstone*

(1872), *Through the Dark Continent* (1878), and *In Darkest Africa* (1890).
An "iron-clad" oath was one in which a worker signed his name,
agreeing as a condition of employment that he would not join a union.

55   The Panic of 1893 began in February when the Philadelphia & Reading
Railroad collapsed into bankruptcy. The financial panic accelerated
before the year ended, and became one of the most severe depressions of
the nineteenth century. There were several major causes of the depression: an overexpansion of railroads and other industries; banking
reserves had been used too freely for speculation; the agricultural
depression, which had already been chronic for several years, further
reduced purchasing power; the withdrawal of foreign capital reduced
capital at precisely the time it was needed most.

56   The Pocahontas coal field is located in the southernmost tip of
West Virginia, particularly in Mercer and McDowell counties, near the
western border of Virginia. Traditionally, black coal miners were
relatively numerous in this district.

57   "The great coal miners' strike" probably refers to the Great Strike
of 1894 in Alabama.

58   Uriah Smith Stevens (1821-1882), a tailor, organized the Garment
Cutters' Association of Philadelphia in 1862. In 1869 he organized the
Noble Order of the Knights of Labor, and became its first Grand Master
Workman, serving until 1879, when Terrence V. Powderly succeeded Stevens.
For biographical background on Stevens, see Vol. III, note 20. James
R. Sovereign, in turn, supplanted Powderly as Grand Master Workman of
the Knights of Labor in 1894.

59   The Spanish-American War (1898) had its origins in American expan-
sionism which coveted the annexation of Cuba. But there were other more
immediate causes of the war, some noble, others not. American sympathy
for Cubans rose dramatically after the Revolution of 1895, which the
Spanish brutally suppressed. Also, by the late 1890s, American investment in the sugar industry had grown to major proportions, and the
economic depression in Cuba threatened those interests. Then too,
America contracted the imperialist fever for foreign possessions elsewhere in the world to which Europeans had succumbed decades earlier.
The rising spread-eagle chauvinism was fanned into hysterical proportions by sensationalist journalism.
    President Cleveland (see note 17) did his best to enforce neutrality,
but the U.S. was deeply involved in the Revolution of 1895 from the
beginning. In 1896 William McKinley (see Vol. III, note 37) was elected
to the presidency on a platform which included a demand for Cuban
independence. On February 15, 1898, the U.S. battleship *Maine* suffered
an explosion which sent it to the bottom of Havana harbor with 260
Americans aboard. McKinley succumbed to the clamors for war which re-
verberated throughout the nation, and on April 20, 1898, Congress adopted
a resolution of war, which McKinley quickly signed.
    The war lasted only ten weeks, but the United States acquired status
as a world power, with possessions or client states in the Caribbean,
the Pacific, and Asia. In the Philippine Islands, rebels against Spanish
rule rejoiced at the news that the U.S. had acquired power over the
Islands by the Treaty of Paris (1898), which ended the Spanish-American
War. When it became apparent that the U.S. did not intend to bring
immediate independence to them, however, the Filipinos continued their
insurrection against outside rule until they were defeated in 1902. In
that year the islands became an unincorporated territory of the U.S.
The Philippines finally gained their independence on July 4, 1946.

60   Michael D. Ratchford (1860-1927) immigrated to the United States
from Ireland in 1872, and settled in Stark County, Ohio. Almost immediately he went to work in the coal mines, and became active in the
Union movement. In 1890 he was elected president of the United Mine

Workers of America local in Massillon, Ohio. His ascent in the organization was rapid, serving successively as general organizer (1893-1894), and president of District 6 (1895-1898). Due to high unemployment and other grievances which grew out of the depression of 1894, UMW membership had plummeted dangerously prior to his presidency, but Ratchford was able to reverse this downward spiral. He served as a labor representative on the Industrial Commission from 1898 to 1900, and as Ohio's Commissioner of Labor Statistics from 1900 to 1908. Switching sides at the bargaining table, Ratchford became commissioner of the Ohio Coal Operators (1909-1912), and the Illinois Coal Operators' Association in 1914.

61   For the eight-hour day movement, see Vol. I, note 69.

62   Coal-cutting machines increasingly replaced pick-and-shovel mining after the Civil War. Driven by steam, water, or compressed air, the "iron miner" dramatically increased coal production, reduced costs, and freed humans from the tedious and difficult task of winning coal from the seam by means of the pick.

63   Riley referred to the annual convention of UMW District 6 which met in January 1892 in Columbus, Ohio. *United Mine Workers' Journal*, January 28, 1892.

Prior to the use of machine loaders in underground mines, coal was handloaded into cars by individual miners who identified their cars with special chips. A company "weighmaster" then weighed each car and the miners were paid according to the tonnage they produced. The system was laden with abuses, such as understating the tonnage, which worked to the detriment of the miners. Therefore, one of the early changes sought by the UMW was company acceptance of a "checkweighman" who weighed the coal along with the company's employee in order to prevent cheating. The checkweighman was elected and paid by the miners themselves to insure his loyalty. He was, therefore, usually a strong labor man of tested conviction and known influence in the community. How race affected the chances of a black being elected to that post depended on local race relations. Prejudiced whites usually objected to dependency on a black checkweighman.

"Master Workman" referred to a local assembly leader of the Knights of Labor, a semi-secret labor organization founded in 1869 on the "one big union" concept.

64   Mine Number 3 was located in Rendville, Ohio, where Richard L. Davis, the black UMW official was employed. Number 3 employed a sizable black work force. The mines in the Rendville sub-district had all gone out on strike under an agreement that none of them would work until all had agreed on new terms. The other mines resumed to full operation, however, when the miners at Number 3 were still out, thus placing them in a vulnerable position (*U.M.W.J.*, July 21, 1892). Apparently, this caused considerable friction among blacks at Number 3, and since Davis was black *and* a union official, he fell under suspicion. Davis wrote that he was considered "dangerous" by some of the black miners at Number 3 who vowed to replace him as checkweighman. While many of these men were "true as steel," Davis believed that most of the black workers were more race conscious than class conscious, and therefore constituted a danger to union recognition in the district. In fact, he wrote, they believed that capital had a "right to its supremacy and that labor should bow submissively to the demands of capital." Moreover, they did not like "being led by white men" (*U.M.W.J.*, August 11, 1892).

In response to Riley's letter, Davis wrote that he was delighted to see that there were others besides himself who had "the pluck and the energy" to express their thoughts in print. He hoped that "our people" would reconsider their position. While Riley might have a majority of "good men" in Tennessee, at Number 3 they were in the distinct minority. At the last meeting, for example, one of these black anti-union men took the floor and asserted that if there had been no union, pay and conditions

would not have been any different than they were then. Davis admonished
them for being "blind in every sense of the word" (*U.M.W.J.*, September
1, 1892). Another black union activist, F. H. Jackson, also of Rendville, Ohio, in a subsequent issue of the *U.M.W.J.*, encouraged Riley
and Davis to continue their valuable efforts. He thought Riley's
letters were "grand" for he had "written my sentiments all the way
through" (*U.M.W.J.*, September 15, 1892).

   "Brother Willing Hands" was a pseudonym for a black UMW organizer
whose given name remains unknown. He generally applauded the letters
of Riley, and other black unionists, published in the *U.M.W.J.*

65   The Coal Creek "war," "rebellion," or "trouble," took its name from
the creek along which many of the mines were located in northeastern
Tennessee. The village of Coal Creek was renamed Lake City in 1936.
The struggle itself occurred between miners, operators, and the State
of Tennessee, over the use of convict labor in the coal mines. This
practice earned the state revenues and saved the expense of another
prison, but cost miners a means of livelihood.

   The uprising against the system began in the spring of 1891 when
the miners struck the Tennessee Coal and Mining Company and were subsequently replaced by convicts. What followed over the next two years
was a series of incidents which followed the same scenario: Miner
"armies" captured the mines, sent the convicts to Knoxville or Nashville
by train, whereupon the Governor returned them under military escort.
By the spring of 1893 the state government determined to bring an end
to the orderly but defiant activities of the coal miners. Trainloads
of troops were sent to the coal field with artillery and Gatling guns
which they used to disperse the miners.

   Although the miners lost the battles, they won the war. Public opinion was so aroused that by 1896 the State found it inexpedient to renew
the convict lease system. See Pete Daniel, "The Tennessee Convict War,"
in *Tennessee Historical Quarterly*, (Fall 1975): 273-93; Philip S. Foner,
History of the Labor Movement in the United States, Vol. II (New York),
pp. 219-29.

   William C. Webb was president of UMW District 19 (Jellico, Tennessee)
during the Coal Creek troubles, and was a leading spokesman for Tennessee
miners. Apparently Webb did not practice racial prejudice in his union
activities, and evidence exists that he possessed a strong social conscience: "The miners of the South for several years have been but little
better treated in the convict camps than the colored man before the
late war. Emancipation must come legally or the people will take the law
in their own hands. And why not?" See *U.M.W.J.*, July 30, 1891.

66   "Show" referred to a job, or to an opportunity to earn a living.
"Kicking" was a popular term for complaining.

67   This letter was signed in Brazil, Indiana, and appeared in the
U.M.W.J., March 24, 1892. A black organizer himself, "Willing Hands"
experienced similar difficulties with white racial hostility when con-
ducting union work in Kentucky.

68   Referred to William C. Webb and William R. Riley himself.

69   The Chattanooga Southern Railroad ran between Chattanooga, Tennessee,
and Gadsden, Alabama. The line was later renamed the Tennessee, Alabama,
& Georgia Railway Company. The reasons for the strike are unknown.

70   The "paper question" referred to a mild debate among readers of the
U.M.W.J. over the paper's format.

71   By "mites" Riley meant small sums of money which the miners had saved
from their meager wages.

72   Blacks probably went to work at Indian Mountain in 1893 as strikebreakers and stayed on after the strike ended. This was a common pattern of

entry for blacks into employment which previously had been closed to them. This pattern existed in many American industries until recognition of the unions as collective bargaining agents was mandated by the federal government during the 1830s.

73   Apparently, "Little Rhody" referred to the state of Rhode Island.

74   James G. Blaine (1830-1893) graduated from Washington College in Pennsylvania, and after several years of teaching, settled in Maine to become a newspaper editor. Blaine was one of the founders of the Republican party, and over the years became the party's chief power broker in Maine. Subsequently, he served in the state legislature for three terms, sat in the United States Congress from 1863 to 1876, and became speaker of the house from 1869 to 1875. In 1876 he began his service in the United States Senate. Blaine was a liberal during Reconstruction, and became associated with the reform wing of the Republican party during the internecine struggles of the Grant administration. In 1876 his chances for the nomination were thwarted by charges of corruption, and he again lost his bid for the nomination in 1880. Finally in 1884, Blaine was nominated for the presidency, but he lost the election to Grover Cleveland (see note 17). From 1889 to 1892 he served as Benjamin Harrison's (see Vol. III, note 63) secretary of state, and surprised friends and enemies alike by rising above partisan politics to become genuinely interested in foreign affairs.

75   "Cahoba" is properly spelled Cahaba.

76   George R. Gliddon, an Englishman who came to the U.S. in 1837, was an Egyptologist with a special interest in mummies. He provided data on crania sizes used by pro-slavery apologists to "prove" that Negroes had smaller brains than caucasians. Originally he had no interest in such uses of his data; however, he realized the significance such materials had for selling books in the South.
        Gliddon and Josiah C. Nott, of Mobile, Alabama, published *Types of Mankind* . . . in 1854, in which they argued that applied anthropology had an immense importance for Americans, because proper race management (i.e., control of blacks) required an understanding of their intrinsic racial character. The most ardent apostle of this creed was Nott, who became a leading figure in the defense of slavery school by using pseudo-scientific arguments to make his case. He published a considerable body of writings "proving" the innate inferiority of blacks.

77   T.C.I. & R.R. Co. refers to the Tennessee Coal, Iron, and Railroad Company which was the largest corporation of its kind in the South by the 1890s.
        Henry Fairchild DeBardeleben was one of the leading figures in the development of the Alabama coal industry. The son of a widowed mother, he came under the guardianship of Daniel Pratt, one of the pioneer coal mine operators in the South. Pratt placed DeBardeleben in positions of responsibility in his businesses at a very early age. After marrying Pratt's daughter, DeBardeleben entered a business partnership with his father-in-law. In 1878, he and two other mine operators formed a partnership to found the Pratt Coal and Coke Company. DeBardeleben also founded or purchased several other major coal mine enterprises in the state. By 1891, the Tennessee Coal, Iron, and Railroad Company had purchased or otherwise acquired control over most of the major coal mines in Alabama, including those of DeBardeleben. DeBardeleben became the Vice-president of the Tennessee Company, and was responsible for protecting the company's interests during the miners' strike of 1894. The career of DeBardeleben is treated extensively in Ethel Armes, *The Story of Coal and Iron in Alabama* (Birmingham, 1910).

78   W. J. Kelso was a major figure in the Alabama UMW, and a regular correspondent to the *United Mine Workers' Journal*. Kelso played a major role in the Alabama miners' strike of 1894. As chairman of the committee which decided to attack a group of strikebreakers, an assault in which

several men died, the court sentenced Kelso to one year at hard labor
in the mines. For a study of the strike, see Robert David Ward and
William Warren Rogers, *Labor Revolt in Alabama: The Great Strike of
1894* (University, Ala., 1965).

79   The "Mary Lee Disaster" probably refers to the difficulties which
beset the miners at these Alabama pits in 1894. In January the men had
not received their pay for two months, and the company refused to allow
the men to have their own "checkweighman" (see note 63). When seven
men left the mines in protest, the company announced a wage reduction
from .425 to .35 cents per ton, and the miners voted to strike.

80   The reference to national UMW officers, "like McBride" who "are
willing to leave their old parties and try others" is a reference to the
fact that John McBride (see note 17) organized a convention of Ohio
union leaders which endorsed the 1890 Omaha platform of the People's
Party (see Vol. III, notes 47 and 52). They also ran a Populist-Labor
slate in Ohio, although it garnered only five percent of the vote.

81   James Buchanan (1791-1868) became the fifteenth President of the
United States. Following graduation from Dickinson College in 1809, he
turned to law and Pennsylvania politics and was elected to Congress
from 1821-1831. Buchanan served as minister to Russia from 1832 to
1833, and then in the Senate from 1835 to 1845 before his appointment as
Secretary of State under President Polk. From 1853 to 1856 Buchanan
served as minister to England, a position which removed him from the
acrimonious debate over slavery, and enabled him to emerge in 1856 as a
compromise Democratic candidate for the Presidency. Southerners gained
his support for the proslavery Kansas Lecompton Constitution, but Congress refused to sanction the document. Buchanan desperately sought to
mediate the slavery dispute, which had reached critical dimensions
during his presidency, but to no avail.
         The Supreme Court's decision in *Dred Scott v. John F. A. Sanford,*
issued March 6, 1857, was two-fold: 1. a Negro whose ancestors were
slaves cannot himself become a citizen of the United States; 2. the
Missouri Compromise, which prohibited slavery in the territories, is
unconstitutional. Dred Scott, the plaintiff in the case, was a slave
born in Virginia, c. 1795, and then taken to Missouri with his master
in 1827. In 1833 he was purchased by Dr. Emerson and accompanied him
into federal territory north of 36°30', established in the Missouri
Compromise of 1820 as the dividing line between slave and free soil.
Emerson and Scott returned to Missouri in 1838, and after the doctor's
death in 1846, Scott sued the widow for his freedom, arguing that he was
legally free because of his residence in the North. The case eventually
reached the U.S. Supreme Court, having won an initially favorable judgment which was overturned by the Missouri Supreme Court. Expected to
settle the broader issue of slavery, the Supreme Court's decision, that
black slaves "had no rights which the white man was bound to respect,"
only heightened the sectional conflict and drew the nation closer to war.
Two months after the historic decision, Scott was purchased by a white
man who emancipated him. The following year, on September 17, 1858,
Dred Scott died of tuberculosis.
         Sponsored by Henry Clay, the Missouri Compromise was passed by Con-
gress in 1820, and quieted the slavery extension issue for nearly thirty
years. The act admitted Missouri as a slave state and Maine as a free
state, while prohibiting slavery above latitude 36°3o' in the Louisiana
Territory. The issue of slavery's extension into the western territories
was opened again during the 1850s.
         Fugitive slave laws, acts passed by Congress in 1793 and 1850, re-
quired that fugitive slaves be returned to their owners. Because northern
states either ignored or haphazardly enforced the 1793 act, Congress
passed the much strengthened 1850 law to appease southern demands that
northerners cease harboring runaways.

82   "Patrick Henry the Great" is a reference to Patrick Henry (1736-1799).

A famous Virginia lawyer and orator, he took an uncompromising stand against British control in the American colonies. He is known to every American child as the patriot who delivered the impassioned speech in which he announced: "Give me liberty or give me death." Henry was elected first governor of Virginia, serving during the Revolution from 1776-1779, but he steadfastly refused all offers of high office in the new republic.

83   The "check-off" system was fundamental to a union's security, for unions did not have the ability to collect dues and keep accurate rosters of those who were members in good standing and those who were not. Thus, the company agreed to check-off dues, assessments, fines, and provide the union with accurate monthly statements of dues collected.

84   Congressional Radicals adopted the Fourteenth Amendment and sent it to the states for approval in the early summer of 1866. Section 1 declared that all persons born or naturalized in this country were citizens of the United States and their states of residence, establishing the first national definition of citizenship. Moreover, it proclaimed that no state could deprive a citizen of life, liberty, or property without due process of law, nor deny any citizen equal protection of the law. There is no doubt that the framers intended to protect the citizenship rights of Negroes. It was the Fourteenth Amendment to which civil rights advocates of the 1950s and 1960s appealed.

85   O. H. Underwood was a black miner from Mystic, Iowa.

86   F. A. Bannister was a Negro elected to the vice-presidency of UMW District 17 in West Virginia during the 1890s.

87   For the Pana-Virden Strike, see pp. 207-47.

88   W. R. Fairley (b. 1845) was born in England. A coal miner, he became active in the Miners' Association of Durham, and served on its executive board for seven years. Fairley was also a member of the Miners' National Association of Great Britain. Fairley immigrated to the United States in 1880, living in Ohio for two years before settling in Alabama. He became one of the leading figures in the labor movement in that state.

89   John Swinton (1829-1901) was managing editor of the *New York Times* during the Civil War. He became interested in the labor movement, and in 1874 was nominated for mayor of New York City by the Industrial Political Party. From 1883 to 1887 he published a weekly labor periodical, *John Swinton's Paper*, and remained an ardent supporter of the union movement until his death.

90   For the "Hocking Valley troubles," see note 47.

Unions vehemently opposed the importation of contract labor by American companies for several reasons. Aliens provided with passage to the United States in exchange for their labor were frequently viciously exploited by employers. Moreover, the practice purposely created a surplus of labor in order to drive down wages, and provided a ready pool of potential strikebreakers.

Coal companies usually operated in relatively isolated areas, and because employees found it difficult to purchase supplies at distant points, they had to rely on stores operated by the companies. As payment for their labor, miners often received "script," which was redeemable only at the company store. In either case, miners became dependents, and forced to pay exorbitant prices for the necessities of life. Hence miners called this system of exploitation the "pluck me" system.

Joseph Emerson Brown (1821-1894) was reared in the mountains of Georgia, and for most of his youth, worked as a farm laborer. After attending school for a few years, he returned to northern Georgia, where he read law and was admitted to the bar in 1845. In 1846 he graduated

from Yale Law School, and began his practice at home. He was elected
to the state senate in 1849, and then to the bench. The Democrats
successfully ran Brown for governor in 1857, and he was reelected to
that office for three consecutive terms thereafter. As governor he was
in constant conflict with legislators because of his independent will
and his advocacy of institutional reforms. Following the Civil War,
Brown practically stood alone among Georgia's leaders in urging compliance with the Fourteenth Amendment, which would qualify the state
for readmission to the Union. Switching to the Republican Party, Brown
assisted in the implementation of the Radical plan for Reconstruction.
He resigned from the Supreme Court of Georgia in 1870, where he had
been appointed as Chief Justice in 1868, and became president of the
Western & Atlantic Company, which ran the state-owned railroads. Brown
also was highly successful in the coal and iron mining business. Governor Colquitt appointed him to an unexpired term in the United States
Senate in 1880, and he was subsequently reelected to that office twice.

92   For T. Thomas Fortune, see note 119, and Vol. III, note 10.

93   Thomas Carlyle (1795-1881), *The French Revolution: A History* (New
York, 1837).

94   The Haymarket anarchists were labor martyrs of the riot which
occurred in Haymarket Square, Chicago, Illinois, on May 4, 1886. The
riot grew out of the famous strikes for the eight-hour day. On May 3,
the police precipitated a confrontation in which several people were
killed or wounded. A meeting was called to protest the incident on
May 4, and an unidentified person threw a bomb into the midst of the
police. Seven policemen died in the ensuing panic. Seven of the
rioters were sentenced to death, two of whom had their sentences com-
muted to life imprisonment. In 1893, John P. Altgeld became governor
of Illinois, and he pardoned the remaining three anarchists. For a
discussion of anarchism, see note 39.

95   John R. Tanner (1844-1901) was elected Sheriff of Clay County,
Illinois, and subsequently served as clerk of the circuit court, as a
state senator from 1880 to 1883, and then as United States Marshal for
southern Illinois. In 1886 he was elected state treasurer, and served
in various other posts until 1897, when he defeated the Democratic
incumbent John P. Altgeld (see note 27) for the governorship. His
decision not to send troops to the coal fields to protect strikebreakers
from violence during the Pana-Virden Strike, was very unpopular, and in
large measure accounted for his failure to be reelected.

96   John Mitchell (1870-1919) was born into a mining family in Braidwood,
Illinois, entered the mines himself, and worked in several states before
resettling in Illinois. In 1885 he joined the Knights of Labor, National Assembly 135, and was one of the founders of the United Mine Workers
of America in 1890. Mitchell served as president of the UMW from 1898
to 1909, during which time the union's membership rose dramatically from
34,000 to about 300,000. An extremely popular labor leader, he also
served as fourth vice-president of the American Federation of Labor from
1900 to 1914. Mitchell was a member of the National Civic Federation,
and was chairman of the New York State Industrial Commission from 1915
until his death in 1919.

97   For a brief discussion of the "Filipino rebels", see note 59.

98   For biographical background on President Benjamin Harrison, see Vol.
III, note 63.

99   Richard R. Wright, Sr. (1855-1945) founded Savannah State College
for Negroes in 1891, and served as its first president.

100   For biographical background on Bishop Henry M. Turner, see Vol. II,
note 2.

101   For the war with Spain, see note 59.

102   For the Paris Commune, see Vol. II, pp. 151-52, 281.

103   The Fulton Bag and Cotton Mills employed 1,400 operatives, and constituted the largest industrial enterprise in Atlanta in the 1890s. On
August 4, 1897, the company hired twenty black women to work in the
folding department. White women immediately quit work, and the men
followed them out of the plant in a protest strike. The strike immediately degenerated into a riot when the police attempted to arrest
several agitators. One of them, John O'Connor, was arrested, but upon
being released that same night, formed the Textile Workers' Protective
Union. The company's president refused to deal with the new union, but
moved to undercut the strike by discharging the black workers, and the
strike ended on August 5.

104   The exact number of lynchings from 1890-1899 are as follows:

1890 - 176	1893 - 200	1896 - 131
1891 - 192	1894 - 190	1897 - 156
1892 - 241	1895 - 171	1898 - 127
		1899 - 107

See Ida B. Wells-Barnett, *On Lynching* (New York, 1969), pp. 46-47.

105   The best known member of the anti-lynching committee was George W.
Cable. For biographical background on this prominent white southern
liberal, see Vol. III, note 13.

106   William Saunders Scarborough (1852-1926) was born a slave in Macon,
Georgia. He graduated from Oberlin College with a BA in 1875, and an
MA in 1878, whereupon he returned to Macon and taught Latin, Greek, and
mathematics at Lewis High School. In 1881 Scarborough published a Greek
textbook. The following year he traveled to Africa, where he attended
Liberia College and received an LL.D. degree. Proficient in several
classical languages, Scarborough eventually joined the faculty of
Wilberforce University, and served as its president from 1908 to 1920
when he retired.

107   For biographical background on Senator George F. Hoar, see Vol. II,
note 54.
        For biographical background on Senator William E. Chandler, see Vol.
III, note 31.

108   Tuskegee Institute was founded on July 4, 1881, when the Alabama
legislature authorized $2,000 annually for the operation of the school.
It began as a normal and agricultural institution for Afro-Americans,
and since the addition of a college department in 1927, the Institute
has grown dramatically in size and mission. It was assumed by the
legislators that Tuskegee would provide trained teachers, businessmen,
and farmers who would lead their black communities in a segregated
society. Much of the success of Tuskegee must be credited to its first
principal, Booker T. Washington, who put the school on a strong foundation during his tenure from 1881 to 1915 (see note 7). The work of
George Washington Carver, director of agricultural research for most of
his long professional career, revolutionized southern agriculture and
brought international attention to Tuskegee.

109   Vol. I in this series provides abundant materials on slaves in industry and in the crafts.

110   James Falconer Wilson (1828-1895) was born in Scotland, and immigrated
to America in 1851, settling on a farm in Iowa. After attending Iowa
College, he devoted his life to the advancement of agriculture. He
served in the Iowa legislature from 1867 to 1872, and then was elected to
the United States Congress as a Republican for three terms. Upon returning to private life, he devoted much of his time writing for farm
journals. Wilson was appointed professor of agriculture at Iowa State

College in 1891. Subsequently, Presidents William McKinley, Theodore
Roosevelt, and William Howard Taft appointed him to their cabinets as
Secretary of Agriculture.

111   John Wesley (1703-1791), the founder of Methodism, was born in
Lincolnshire England. One of ten children, John went to Oxford in 1720
and remained for fifteen years, earning an MA in 1727. In 1735 he
volunteered for service in Georgia as a missionary to the Indians under
the auspices of the Society for the Propagation of the Gospel in Foreign
Parts. Instead, George Oglethorpe, the Governor of Georgia, appointed
him minister of the English colonists living there. Wesley returned to
England in 1738 more frustrated than ever with the rigid structure of
the Church of England. That same year he had a religious experience
which shaped the rest of his life. Excluded from many high church pulpits, he began to preach in the open air to ever larger throngs of poor
people, and utilized laymen as preachers. Wesley organized his followers
into Methodist societies, which, after his death, took on the shape of
the Methodist Episcopal Church.
         The comparison was being drawn between Wesley and Booker T. Washing-
ton, the "Master of Tuskegee" (see note 7).

112   Joseph A. Tillinghast published *The Negro in Africa and America*
(1902), a book which influenced an entire generation of scholars. Applying "social darwinism" to Africans and their American descendents,
he argued that the Negro's character had been formed in Africa, and that
this racial heredity could be altered only over the indefinite period
of time required for the process of natural selection. The "inferior"
qualities of African life, such as "sexual licentiousness" and "inefficiency," would be weeded out only by nature. African peoples, he
argued, simply had not evolved as far along the human chain as members
of other races, especially caucasians. Because the forces of nature
controlled the state of their social life, it was a foolish waste of
time to artificially try to uplift them. See "The Negro in Africa and
America," *Publications of the American Economic Association,* 3d Ser.,
3 (May 1902).

113   Fanny M. Jackson Coppin (1835-1912) was born a slave in Washington,
D.C. An orphan, her aunt purchased her freedom and sent her to school
in Rhode Island. From 1860 to 1865 she attended Oberlin College. After
the Civil War Fanny Coppin organized schools to help educate freedmen
who migrated to Ohio. In 1869 she became the principal of the Institute
for Colored Youth in Philadelphia. Subsequently, she became a leader
in the black women's club movement, lecturing on racial and sexual
equality. Through her efforts Fanny became a well-known personality in
America. Her autobiography, *Reminiscences of School Life* (1913), is a
classic of its genre.

114   For biographical background on Robert Toombs, see Vol. III, note 57.

115   Matthew Arnold (1822-1888) was educated at Oxford University, and
then became professor of poetry at that university from 1857 to 1867.
Arnold was a prolific author, writing numerous volumes of poetry,
literary criticism, lectures, and treatises on education. A leader in
the movement to improve secondary education in England, he served as
inspector of schools from 1851 to 1883.

116   Henry Clay Frick (1849-1919), a Pennsylvania capitalist, acquired extensive holdings in the manufacture of coke. In the 1880s he took over
management of Andrew Carnegie's steel mills in Pittsburgh. His violently
anti-labor posture precipitated the infamous Homestead Strike of 1892
(see note 52). He was at various times a business associate of many of
the leading entrepreneurs of the day, including Carnegie, Mellon, and
Rockefeller, and in the process accumulated one of the largest fortunes
in America.

117   John Burns (b. 1858) was born in London. Following a grammar
school education he worked variously in a candle factory, an engine
works, as a pageboy, and finally as an apprentice engineer for seven
years. Burns continued his education at night schools, and through
extensive reading. A socialist with a gift for speaking, he was arrested several times for political agitation. In 1884 the Social
Democratic Federation unsuccessfully forwarded Burns as a candidate
for Parliament. He was an active member of the Amalgamated Engineers'
Union, and was still plying his trade when the workmen elected him as
a Progressive to London County Council. That same year, 1889, he was
one of the organizers of the London dock strike. In 1892, he began
what would be the first of four terms as a member of Parliament from
Battersea, and became a famous independent Radical.

118   The Rev. Alexander Walters (b. 1858) was born in Kentucky, and
attended school in Lexington. After moving to Indianapolis, Indiana,
he began his study of theology and was licensed to preach in the African Methodist Episcopal Zion Church in 1877. Walters served as a pastor
and teacher in Kentucky for two years, and then moved to St. Louis,
Missouri, in 1879 where he was ordained deacon. He returned to Kentucky
for several years until called to a pulpit in San Francisco, California,
in 1883, where he built the largest church in the Zion connection. He
had risen to considerable influence as a black spokesman by 1884, for
on a trip to New York City that year, he was granted conferences with
President Chester A. Arthur, and the Governor of Pennsylvania. In
1887 Walters moved to Knoxville, Tennessee, rose to national prominence
as a race leader, and became a bishop. Walters was interested in African
missionary work, and in 1900 he and W. E. B. DuBois (see 136) attended
a London conference of African and American Negro intellectuals. He was
appointed chairman of the conference. Walters articulated a militant
stance on racial uplift and European imperialism in Africa. See his
autobiography, *My Life and Work* (New York, 1917).

119   The Afro-American League was conceived and organized primarily by
T. Thomas Fortune (see Vol. III, note 10). In 1887 Fortune argued that
blacks must organize and fight for civil rights themselves. Finally,
in 1889 he was able to organize local protective leagues in scores of
cities from coast to coast. At the first national organizing convention
in 1890, the strategy of the League took shape. Addressing the convention, Fortune advocated a range of self-help programs, such as political
agitation and the confrontation of injustice, an emphasis on racial
solidarity, an Afro-American bank, the creation of bureaus of industrial
education, and co-operative business development. The League's constitution also called for a non-partisan agency to protest against racial
discrimination in all forms. All the militant fervor notwithstanding,
the League's membership declined until by 1893 it was, for all practical
purposes, defunct. In 1898 it was revived as the Afro-American Council,
but came under the control of Booker T. Washington, and finally ended
its days in 1908. See August Meier, *Negro Thought in America, 1880-
1915: Racial Ideologies in the Age of Booker T. Washington* (Ann Arbor,
1963), Chapters 8 and 10, and Emma Lou Thornbrough, *T. Thomas Fortune:
Militant Journalist* (Chicago: The University of Chicago Press, 1972),
Chapter 4.

120   District 49, Knights of Labor, commonly known as the "Home Club,"
was located in New York. During the convention of 1886 in Richmond,
Virginia, they created an uproar in the South by insisting on equal
treatment for one of their black members, Frank J. Ferrell. See Vol.
III, Part 4.

121   Edward McHugh came to the United States in 1896 to organize a dock
workers' union. That same year, the Dockers' Union of England contributed $1,500 to launch a plan to organize longshoremen and waterfront
workers throughout the world. Since an estimated 70,000 men were at work
on American docks, they believed the chances of success were good. Thus,
they sent McHugh to undertake the task. In New York he found thousands

of men who recognized the need for organization. McHugh instantly won
their trust, and launched a new union in October, 1896, known as the
American Longshoremen's Union. The men called it the "McHugh organization," and he became president. The union grew rapidly, until by
early 1898 it had twenty-one branches, mostly in Brooklyn, with about
15,000 members. The prospects for the union were bright until it was
discovered that the general secretary, Frank J. Devlin, had absconded
with the treasury. No serious doubt existed regarding McHugh's integrity, but support for the organization evaporated. McHugh could not
save the union, and in late 1898 he returned to England. However, a
new organization arose out of the old, which became known as the Longshoremen's Union Protective Association of Greater New York.

122   Albion Winegar Tourgee (1838-1905) was born near Williamsfield,
Ohio, and attended the University of Rochester for two years before
joining the Union Army during the Civil War. Following the secession
of hostilities in 1865, Tourgee settled in North Carolina. By 1866 he
became increasingly concerned that the political climate in the state
would frustrate the establishment of racial equality. He became involved in local Radical politics for this reason, and by the late 1860s
had made himself obnoxious to ex-Confederates for advocating that the
franchise be extended to blacks. He was elected superior court judge,
and despite his record as a fearless man of principle, conservative
whites vehemently denounced Tourgee. In 1879 he gave up his efforts to
make North Carolina a bi-racial democracy and returned to the North,
settled in New York, and became a famous novelist. In his most famous
novel, *A Fool's Errand* (New York, 1879), which became a best-seller,
Tourgee wrote about his experiences in Reconstruction North Carolina,
addressing himself to the question of how to achieve Negro equality. In
his career as a novelist and journalist, much of Tourgee's attention
focused on the seemingly inexorable downward spiral of southern blacks
into ever deeper poverty and segregation. In addition to the significant role he played in the court struggles to oppose segregation through
the National Citizens Rights Association, Tourgee also denounced the
accommodationist strategy of Booker T. Washington, arguing for militant
protest to achieve civil rights. See Otto H. Olsen, *Carpetbagger's
Crusade: The Life of Albion Winegar Tourgee* (Baltimore, 1965).

123   Chile was in a state of political instability and social turmoil in
1891. Following eight months of Civil War, Jose Manuel Balmaceda was
defeated by the forces of Jorge Montt for control of the government. The
American government had supported Balmaceda, and consequently was on
unfavorable terms with the people. American sailors on shore leave in
Valparaiso from the *U.S.S. Baltimore* got involved in a street brawl. As
the police looked on, two Americans were killed and several others
wounded. In response, Secretary of State James G. Blaine issued an
ultimatum for a public demonstration of apology. Montt refused, and the
Chileans demanded war with the United States. The incident was officially
closed when the Montt government paid $75,000 to the families of the
dead men.

124   The *Interocean* was a black-owned newspaper published in Chicago,
Illinois.
         The Citizens Equal Rights Association was formed in February 1890
when several hundred Afro-American leaders met in Chicago to devise a
strategy to counter the growing trend of racial discrimination. The
Association stressed the widespread belief that increased education,
wealth, and "respectable" behavior would end racial discrimination.
Blacks had formed the Equal Rights Association in 1865 at Syracuse, New
York, to advance civil rights, and a similar organization was proposed
in 1879 which never came to fruition. But they should not be confused
with the 1890 Association. Many of the same delegates had been in Chicago
one month earlier to found the Afro-American League (see note 119).
         For biographical background on Ida B. Wells, see Vol. III, note 40.

125   Born in Philadelphia, Ignatius Donnelly (1831-1901) moved to Minnesota where he practiced law and entered upon a political career. From
1859 to 1863 he served as lieutenant governor, as representative to
Congress for three terms from 1863 to 1869, and for many years thereafter as a Minnesota state legislator. A reformer, Donnelly edited two
periodicals, the weekly *Anti-Monopolist* (1874-1879), and the *Representative* (1894-1901), an organ of the Populist Party. A leading organizer
of the Granger movement, he also became one of the founders of the
Populist Party, running as its presidential candidate at the time of his
death. A colorful reformer, Donnelly expressed his utopian visions in
numerous novels. At least two of them were very popular, although his
Doctor Huguet was not among them. The leading biography of Donnelly is
Martin Ridge, *Ignatius Donnelly: The Portrait of a Politician* (Chicago,
1962). See also Vol. III, note 47.

126   Daniel Webster (1782-1852) was born in New Hampshire, graduated from
Dartmouth College in 1801, and served in the United States House from
1813-1817. He achieved fame as a constitutional lawyer by winning several of the most significant cases in constitutional history, such as the
Dartmouth College Case (1819), McCulloch v. Maryland (1819), and Gibbons
v. Ogden (1824). After moving to Massachusetts, Webster was elected to
the United States Senate where he served from 1827 to 1841. In that
body, he rose to preeminent political leadership. From 1841 to 1843 he
was Secretary of State, but returned to the Senate in 1845. Webster was
the supreme speaker, and his name became synonomous with spellbinding
oration.
     William Ewart Gladstone (1809-1898) was one of the greatest British
politicians of the nineteenth century. A graduate of Oxford University,
he was elected to Parliament in 1832 as a Conservative, but gradually
converted to the Liberal party, and served in cabinets as Chancellor of
the Exchequer. He became famous for lowering taxes, and later for
broadening the franchise in the Reform Bill of 1867. Gladstone served
as Prime Minister from 1868 to 1874, during which time he was responsible for important liberal reforms in the governance of Ireland. Benjamin Disraeli returned the Conservatives to power, and Gladstone retired.
When the belligerent foreign policy of Disraeli outraged his sense of
propriety, however, Gladstone returned to politics and regained his position as Prime Minister from 1880 to 1885. In 1892 he once again became
Prime Minister, but retired from office in 1894.

127   George W. Perkins (d. 1934) was closely associated with Samuel Gompers in craft as well as philosophy. Like Gompers (see note 1), Perkins
was a leading figure in the Cigarmakers' Union, and also like Gompers,
opposed industrial unionism. In 1891 he was elected president of the
Cigarmakers' International Union of America, and held that office until
1926. His early origins remain unknown.

128   The *Constitution* and the *Journal* were two newspapers of Atlanta,
Georgia.

129   William E. Gregg (1800-1867) was four years old when his mother died
and his uncle Jacob became the boy's guardian. After serving an apprenticeship as a watchmaker, William Gregg settled in Columbia, South
Carolina, where his business earned him a comfortable fortune. Upon his
early retirement, he moved to Edgefield and purchased the Vaucluse cotton
factory, quickly turning it into a prosperous enterprise. Convinced that
reliance on a single staple crop was economically unwise, Gregg conceived
of industrial villages in the southern countryside where home markets
would be created, and where poor whites would labor in the manufacture
of products which would diversify the region's economy. In 1846, he began erecting a cotton mill near Aiken, called the Graniteville Manufacturing Company. The mill was to be a model industrial village. At
Graniteville, Gregg took care to institute schools, a library, and otherwise administered to the health, housing, and recreation of the community.
More than any other single man, he was the leading pioneer in southern
cotton manufacture.

130   Rufus Brown Bullock (1834-1907) was born in New York, and moved
to Augusta, Georgia, just before the Civil War, where he organized the
Southern Express Company. An expert in telegraphy, he assisted in the
establishment of a telegraph and railroad network throughout the Con-
federacy. By the war's end, he had achieved the rank of assistant
quartermaster-general. Returning to his home in Augusta, Georgia, in
1867 Bullock became president of the Macon & Augusta Railroad. Bullock
favored the Radical Reconstruction plan, and became the leading Republican delegate at the state constitutional convention of 1868. Nominated for governor, Bullock defeated his Democratic opponent in the
November election, and served in that office from 1868 to 1871. Charged
with corruption by the Democratic "Redeemers," he resigned on October
23, 1871, and fled the state. He was finally captured in 1876 and
tried for embezzlement, but was acquitted for lack of evidence. After
the trial, Bullock remained in Atlanta, and eventually became president
of the Atlanta Cotton Mills, and held other influential positions in
business.

131   James Henderson Kyle (1854-1901) attended the University of Illinois
from 1871 to 1873, before transferring to Oberlin College where he
graduated in 1878 with a degree in the classics. After studying law
for a time, he turned to theology, and in 1882 graduated from the
Western Theological Seminary, in Allegheny, Pennsylvania. Kyle served
in several clerical posts before entering politics as a Populist. In
1890 South Dakota Democrats and Populists nominated Kyle for the state
senate. He was elected to the legislature, and became a successful
compromise candidate for the United States Senate in the following session. Kyle was reelected to the Senate in 1897, and became chairman of
the U.S. Industrial Commission.

132   Allen D. Chandler (1834-1910) was born in Auraria, Georgia, and
graduated from Mercer University in 1859. He taught school for several
years, interrupted by service in the Confederate Army. He began his
political career when he was elected to the Georgia General Assembly
from 1873 to 1880. This was followed by four terms in the United States
Congress. Chandler also served four terms as Georgia's secretary of
state. A staunch conservative noted for his honesty, he won the guber-
natorial election in 1898, and again in 1900. From 1903 to 1910 Chandler served as the state historian.

133   Joseph Arch (b. 1826) was born in Warwickshire, England. Because he
could not accept the class perquisites demanded by his "betters," he
was soon branded a troublemaker. Although poor, Arch educated himself,
and acquired oratical skills as a Methodist minister. In 1872 he founded
and became president of the National Agricultural Labourers' Union. Arch
was elected to Parliament in 1885, and with the exception of one term,
held his seat until 1900. Arch was highly respected in the House of
Commons.

134   For the New Orleans General Strike of 1892, see pp. 15-24.

135   For William H. Councill, see Vol. III, introduction to Part 2.

136   For nearly three-quarters of a century, W. E. B. DuBois was a prominent black educator, historian, and spokesman for his people. Born
February 23, 1868, in Great Barrington, Massachusetts, he won a scholarship which enabled him to attend Fisk University; he later earned graduate degrees from Harvard University. DuBois also studied at the University of Berlin and traveled widely in Europe, before coming back to
America to begin a teaching career which included positions at Wilberforce University, the University of Pennsylvania, and Atlanta University.
        DuBois wrote over twenty books, more than one hundred scholarly
articles, and edited numerous volumes. His first major historical contribution was *The Suppression of the African Slave Trade to the United
States of America, 1638-1870* (1896). His *Black Reconstruction in America*

(1935) is one of the standard works on that topic, and *The Philadelphia Negro* (1899) and Atlanta University research studies were pioneer sociological explorations into Afro-American life. Overshadowing DuBois' scholarship at this time, however, was his debate with Booker T. Washington concerning the type of education necessary for Afro-Americans; DuBois favored training in the liberal arts and humanities while Washington stressed vocational skills.

With the hope of bringing an end to racial discrimination and segregation, DuBois launched the Niagara Movement in 1905. This organization was the forerunner of the National Association for the Advancement of Colored People which came into existence four years later. *Crisis,* the official organ of the NAACP, was founded and edited by DuBois from 1910 until 1934. In 1919 he initiated the Pan-African Conference in Paris, in order to mobilize public opinion against the oppression of black peoples throughout the world. However, his leadership of the Peace Information Center brought an indictment as an "unregistered foreign agent" during the Communist witch-hunts of the early 1950s. Although the case was eventually dismissed, DuBois became a pariah in many quarters of the black community, where they feared to associate with a reputed Communist. In 1961 he immigrated to Ghana, became a member of the Communist party, and began work on a monumental study of African culture. He died on August 27, 1963. There are numerous biographical studies of DuBois and his thought. See for example, Elliott M. Rudwick, *W. E. B. DuBois: Propagandist of the Negro Protest* (Philadelphia, 1960); Rayford W. Logan (ed.), *W. E. B. DuBois: A Profile* (New York, 1971).

137   George Henry Evans (1805-1856) was born in England and immigrated to the United States. By 1829 he had become the editor of the *New York Working Man's Advocate,* and then editor of the *Man,* also published in New York. In 1841 he began to espouse land reform in *The Radical* and *Young America,* and organized a campaign for a homestead act through his National Reform Association.

138   For race riots in Philadelphia during the ante-bellum period, see Vol. I, Part 3.

139   For Tammany Hall, see Vol. II, note 72.
        Horace Greeley (1811-1872) began publication of the *New York Tribune* in 1841. An advocate of Fourierism, he also was an ardent Republican and an opponent of slavery. He served as president of the New York Printers' Union, and in 1872 ran for president of the United States as a candidate for the Liberal Republican Party.

140   For the National Labor Union, see Vol. II, Parts 1-3.

141   See George E. McNeill (ed.), *The Labor Movement. The Problem of To-day. Comprising a History of Capital and Labor, and its Present Status* (New York, 1888). An advocate of the eight-hour philosophy of Ira Steward (see Vol. I, note 69(, McNeill (1837-1906) worked in the woolen mills of Amesbury, Massachusetts, before becoming an officer in the Grand Eight-Hour League during the 1860s and 1870s. After serving as deputy director of the Massachusetts Bureau of Labor Statistics, he became president of the International Labor Union in 1878. He bought and edited the *Boston Leader* in 1868. Then turning to a writing career, he published several books dealing with labor.

142   Henry O. Tanner (1859-1937) was born in Pittsburgh, Pennsylvania, and attended the Pennsylvania Academy of Fine Arts, and the Academie Julian in Paris. In 1888 he moved to the South, where some of his most famous American paintings were finished, particularly *The Banjo Lesson* (1890). Tanner then moved to Europe where the color bar was not so strict against blacks, and there he spent the remainder of his life. His *Daniel and the*

Lion's Den (1896) received an enthusiastic reception, and the following year, *The Resurrection of Lazarus,* his most famous work, was completed.

INDEX